complete structure chart or stepwi   eck
program flow and each algorithm.

CODE

Use the stepwise chart (or the structure chart and the pseudocode ~~ ... ~~ ms)
and the I/O sketch as *blueprints* for writing code. Start by loading program template
file template.pas from the *Examples* or *Utilities Library*. Immediately save this file, using
your program's name as the file name. Insert other needed procedure templates
(template.pro) and function templates (template.fun) by using the editor's **Ctrl-K R**
command. Enter code and *desk check* the listing for correct syntax and consistency
with design algorithms. Don't reinvent the wheel! Insert any appropriate prewritten code
from the Examples and Utilities Libraries (see listings and page references below). *Save*
the program as you go! Don't wait until the end. *Back up* the program!

TEST

Repeatedly compile and run the program to eliminate compile-time, run-time, and logic
errors. *Desk check* as needed. Try using the IDE's *debugging tools* (see Module A).
For long, elaborate programs consider *top-down development* by developing one module at a time. *Save* the program as you go! Don't wait until the end. *Back up* the program!

EXAMPLES LIBRARY

• • • • • • • • • • • • • •

The following sample programs are in the Examples Library on disk, under the given
name. Identical root names with an attached digit or letter indicate different versions of
the same application. Most exercises marked with the symbol Ⓛ are revisions of these
sample applications. Use these files either to solve review exercises or to cut and paste
code into new programs described by the additional exercises.

* All names are source files with .PAS extensions; some have associated object files with .EXE extensions and data files with .DAT or .BIN extensions, as described in the program's documentation.
† Unit that includes both a source (.PAS) file and an object (.TPU) file.

UTILITIES LIBRARY

· · · · · · · · · · · ·

The following utility modules are in the Utilities Library on disk, under the given name. Utilities in color are also included in unit source file OurUnit.PAS and unit object file OurUnit.TPU within the Examples Library. Identical root names with an attached digit or letter indicate different versions of the same utility. Many exercises marked with the symbol Ⓛ require or revise these utilities. Use these files to solve review exercises or incorporate them in new programs described by additional exercises.

* All names are source files, with extensions .PAS for programs, .PRO for procedures, and .FUN for functions. Name prefixes longer than eight characters are truncated at eight characters by Turbo Pascal, for consistency with the maximum length allowed by DOS. Names in color reside in OurUnit as well.

EXERCISES

. . . .

The following exercises are described in the book. Multiple references indicate design changes through revisits. Use this table to look up exercises by name and chapter/module, and to observe the evolution of exercises having multiple references.

To HC,

where'er you are, for inspiration...

TURBO PASCAL

Richard Mojena
The University of Rhode Island

PWS Publishing Company
Boston

Computer Science Editor: Frank Ruggirello
Editorial Assistant: Rhonda Gray
Production: Janelle Rohr, Bookman Productions
Designer: Vargas/Williams/Design
Print Buyer: Karen Hunt
Copy Editor: Elizabeth Judd
Cover Design: Image House Inc.
Cover Photo: Comstock Inc.
Signing Representative: Maria Tarantino
Compositor: Beacon Graphics
Printer: R. R. Donnelley & Sons

PWS Publishing Company is a division of Wadsworth, Inc.

TURBO Pascal is a registered trademark of Borland International, Inc.

3 4 5 6 7 8 9 10 — 96 95 94 93

Library of Congress Cataloging-in-Publication Data

Mojena, Richard.
   Turbo Pascal / Richard Mojena.
      p.   cm.
   Includes index.
   ISBN 0-534-13050-X
   1. Pascal (Computer program language)   2. Turbo Pascal (Computer
program)   I. Title.
QA76.73.P2M64   1992
005.265 — dc20   91-36344
                                                                        CIP

Brief Contents

Detailed Contents

• • • • • • • • • • • • • • • • • •

X

---

‡Optional, more advanced material. Skip without loss of continuity, study at this point, or wait until later.

PREFACE

• • • • • • • • • • • • • • • • • • • •

This textbook is designed for a first course in Pascal programming. No prerequisites are required, other than a willingness to develop problem-solving skills coupled with patience, endurance, and hard work.

The combination of features described below distinguishes this book from others in the field.

TURBO PASCAL IMPLEMENTATION

The basis of the Pascal material is Borland's Turbo Pascal Version 6.0, as described in the *Turbo Pascal Programmer's Guide, Library Reference, User's Guide,* and *Turbo Vision Guide.* The emphasis on realistic implementations of Pascal favors the treatment of Turbo Pascal over Standard Pascal. Key chapter-by-chapter differences between Turbo and Standard Pascal are summarized in Appendix H.

Syntax is introduced in *syntax boxes* with pseudocode-like syntax, examples, and explanations. These are more descriptive and less intimidating than the traditional *syntax diagrams.*

SOFTWARE DEVELOPMENT CYCLE (SDC)

A four-stage software development cycle (Requirements, Design, Code, Test) is first described and illustrated in Chapter 1. Subsequently it's used in all major applications programs throughout the text. Problem solving and program design are especially emphasized. The use of *desk-check scripts* is encouraged throughout the SDC. Students are asked to develop each end-of-chapter assignment using the SDC. An SDC Guide on the inside front cover summarizes elements in this process.

TOP-DOWN DESIGN AND PROGRAMMING

Top-down design principles and stepwise refinement are introduced and motivated in Chapter 1 within the design stage in the SDC. Top-down programming, including its modular and structured programming implementations, is consolidated early in the book (Chapter 3). A new design tool called a **stepwise chart** is introduced at the end of Chapter 3 and is used where appropriate in the remainder of the book.

MODULAR PROGRAMMING

Modular programs with *procedures* and *functions* are introduced early (in Chapter 3) as a natural implementation of top-down programming. *Include files* and *units* are delayed until Chapter 8.

STRUCTURED PROGRAMMING

Structured programming concepts are adhered to throughout the book. All programs strictly use defined control structures: sequence, selection, and repetition. Structured programming is introduced early (Chapter 3), just after elementary Pascal material in Chapter 2.

SOFTWARE ENGINEERING

Software engineering principles are emphasized throughout in keeping with the current (and future) emphases on both reducing software development/maintenance costs and improving the user interface. Software engineering principles are summarized at the end of each chapter in the "Programming Tips" section, which includes two subsections: "Design and Style" and "Common Errors."

INTERACTIVE AND PC-STYLE PROGRAMMING

Design issues regarding the user interface in interactive applications are discussed throughout. Menus, screen design, error trapping, sound, and screen-control effects such as screen clears, reverse video, and color are treated where appropriate. This material is consolidated in Chapter 8.

CHARACTER AND STRING PROCESSING

Character and string processing is introduced in Chapter 2 and used throughout the text, which reflects the enormous extent of information processing applications in practice. Certain specialized and more difficult character and string processing applications are delayed until and consolidated in Chapter 10.

FILE PROCESSING

Data files are introduced early (Chapter 4) as input text files and are used where appropriate throughout the text. The early introduction of data files is important because interactive input is inappropriate in many realistic problems. As a formal topic, however, file processing includes detailed, specialized material that's delayed until and consolidated in Chapter 12, just after the record type is covered in Chapter 11.

OBJECT-ORIENTED PROGRAMMING (OOP) AND TURBO VISION (TV)

OOP principles and examples are introduced in Chapter 14. By this time, the reader is well grounded in top-down principles, modular and structured programming, and the record type and is ready for an introduction to this newer bottom-up programming variant. Module E follows through with TV, Turbo Pascal's OOP applications framework and object library.

TOPICAL ORGANIZATION

The organization of the book is based on three guiding design principles: (1) *Introduce top-down design principles from the beginning,* (2) *keep topical fragmentation to a minimum,* and (3) *give the instructor flexibility in assigning optional and advanced topics.*

Core design and development topics are introduced early and expanded as the reader moves along. These include the software development cycle (Chapter 1), top-down programming (Chapter 3), modular programming (Chapter 3), and structured programming (Chapter 3). Structured programming is completed in Chapters 4 to 6; modular programming is concluded in Chapter 8, with emphases on user-defined units and Turbo Pascal's crt and graph units.

Unlike most texts, this one introduces repetition (Chapters 4 and 5) before selection (Chapter 6). This allows early illustrations of realistic programs that show the power of repetitive processing, which, after all, is the *raison d'être* for computing. Again unlike traditional books, this text introduces repetition using the for-do loop (Chapter 4) instead of the while-do loop (Chapter 5). This postpones Boolean expressions, which would add considerable detail to the introduction of the repetition structure. Classroom experience shows that this approach provides an early and painless mastery of programs with "counter loops." It also opens the door to a meaningful and early introduction of text files for input. Repetition is concluded in Chapter 5 with while-do and repeat-until implementations. Chapter 5 also includes two other loop implementations: while-do eof file processing and error routines.

All selection structures are consolidated in Chapter 6: if-then-else, if-then, else-if, and case structures. Input and range error handling is also covered at the end of this chapter.

The organization of repetitions, selections, and error handling gives a cohesive treatment to a topic that's often difficult for beginning students and that's fragmented in most textbooks.

Data typing is also consolidated to reduce fragmentation. Standard and string types are introduced in Chapter 2. Subrange, enumerated, and set types are covered in Chapter 7. ADTs are introduced in Chapter 7 and revisited as units in Chapter 8. The other data types are presented in their own chapters: array types in Chapter 9, revisits to character and string types in Chapter 10, record types in Chapter 11, file types in Chapter 12, pointer types in Chapter 13, and object types in Chapter 14.

Optional, more advanced material is placed in sections marked with the † symbol. These sections give the instructor added flexibility in assigning certain topics. For example, text data files are optionally covered in Sections 4.3 and 5.4 but can be assigned later if desired. The placement of advanced topics in isolated chapters in the second half of the book also promotes flexibility. For instance, advanced character and string processing (Chapter 10), files (Chapter 12), and dynamic data structures (Chapter 13) can be assigned in any order. OOP (Chapter 14) could be assigned after records (Chapter 11), provided that the section on dynamic objects is skipped (which presupposes Chapter 13).

Utility modules are used not only to promote code reusability but also to add flexibility through procedural abstraction. For example, opening a data file to store a linked list in Chapter 13 does not require knowledge of files in Chapter 12, because the programmer simply calls utility procedure OpenNewFile

Flexibility is also enhanced by...

Optional Chapterlike Modules

Selected optional, more advanced material is placed in modules following appropriate chapters. A module serves the purpose of presenting certain material as a major topic in its own right. A module is like a minichapter; it has the same structure as a chapter. Unlike a chapter, its topic is not part of the book's common core of knowledge, in the sense that the modular topic is not a prerequisite to the topics in succeeding chapters. These topics include the IDE's debugger (Module A), recursion (Module B), simulation (Module C), sorting and searching (Module D), and Turbo Vision (Module E).

Modules A through D can be omitted without loss of continuity, assigned based on their physical placement, or delayed until a later time. Module E concludes the text. Modules and other optional material are marked with the † symbol.

Diversity of Applications

Meaningful applications of the computer are emphasized in our choice of sample programs and programming assignments. They are described in a wide variety of contexts, including areas in engineering, the sciences, business, economics, mathematics, and statistics, as well as public-sector areas like health-care delivery and governmental administration. Diversity of easily understood applications in a variety of disciplines has obvious advantages. This diversity benefits heterogeneous classes having students from several disciplines. It also exposes specialized students — such as engineering students — to interesting applications in other disciplines, which broadens their educational experience and fosters an appreciation for the problem-solving similarities across disparate disciplines.

All sample programs are described on the inside front cover. We also include an index of all programming exercises inside the front cover.

EXERCISES

The book has a carefully designed and extensive set of exercises, many with multiple parts. Each chapter and module includes two kinds of exercises: review exercises and additional exercises.

Review exercises reinforce, integrate, and extend syntax and examples. These exercises are ordered according to the chronological presentation of material and examples in the chapter or module. Multiple parts such as part **a, b, c,** and so on are arranged from least to most difficult. Exercises marked with Ⓛ make use of programs and utilities in the Examples and Utilities Libraries on disk. All review exercises are consolidated at the end of the chapter, for easier lookup and reduced, less intimidating length.

Review exercises without answers are marked with an asterisk (*). These exercises are more difficult or comprehensive than unstarred exercises. Answers to starred exercises are in the *Instructor's Manual.* Answers to unstarred review exercises are included at the end of the text. All review exercises are graded according to three difficulty levels.

Review exercises can be worked either after the chapter is completed or while the chapter is read. Selected sections include **Self-Review Exercises boxes** with references to unstarred review exercises at the end of the chapter, for readers who wish to self-check their understanding before continuing with the material in the next section.

Review exercises are an excellent basis for planning many classroom lectures. Moreover, starred review exercises form a pool of potential open book exam or quiz questions. Finally, many review exercises include programming projects as extensions to the examples.

Additional exercises focus on new programming projects that are not directly related to the sample scenarios that are used in examples. They also include revisits to earlier additional exercises from other chapters or modules. These are generally arranged in ascending order of difficulty, as are their multiple parts. They are graded according to difficulty, and their answers are included in the *Instructor's Manual.* Many of the tougher (and some normal) additional exercises are ideally suited to team projects.

PROGRAMMING EVOLUTION

We often return to preceding examples and exercises as we introduce new programming concepts and syntax. This can be seen from the inside front cover, since multiple page references there for a programming exercise show that this exercise is revisited. Program names like Temp2 and Engine3 on the inside front cover suggest that applications programs evolve over time. This evolutionary approach to programming problems has several advantages: It mimics program maintenance over time; it emphasizes the software development cycle as a cyclical process; and it shows alternative means to solving the same problem, with attendant advantages and disadvantages.

APPEARANCE OF PROGRAMS

All complete programs and their input/output are reproduced by camera rather than typeset. This increases the realism of the programming material and ensures the reliability of programs. Moreover, most programs include color, screens , and arrowed notes to enhance student understanding. Reserved words and standard identifiers are shown in **boldfaced** characters throughout, to emphasize their use and syntax. Programs use a standardized style and documentation format that clearly decomposes sections for declarations, functions, procedures, and main body. The program template that we use throughout the text is available to students.

EXAMPLES, UTILITIES, AND SOLUTIONS DISK LIBRARIES

Adopting instructors receive three libraries of programs on diskettes: the Examples Library, Utilities Library, and Solutions Library.

The **Examples Library** contains all programming examples in the text, including program (.PAS) files, data (.DAT, .TXT, .BIN) files, units (.PAS and .TPU files), and a program template that standardizes the appearance of programs. Students can use the given template as a basis or starting point for every program they write. Or they can customize the template according to their own (or their instructor's) wishes.

The **Utilities Library** includes utility function (.FUN) files, utility procedure (.PRO) files, and utility program (.PAS) files. The book and this library emphasize code reusability through utilities that serve as tools in toolkits.

The **Solutions Library** contains program and data files as solutions to programming assignments in starred review exercises and additional exercises.

The inside front cover includes a listing, chapter/module references, and page references to the files in these three libraries. Students should have access to the Examples and Utilities Libraries when solving exercises marked with the (L) symbol. Students are also encouraged to develop their own libraries.

USE OF COLOR, SCREENS, ARROWED NOTES, BOLDFACE, AND ITALICS

Special effects are used to facilitate the understanding of selected material, as follows: Color type, for user input in the computer runs, user-defined identifiers in syntax boxes, arrowed notes, and highlighted code in programs; color screens , to highlight and draw attention to block code; arrowed notes, to explain tricky syntax or programming concepts; **boldface**, for reserved and standard identifiers and newly defined important terms; *italics*, for emphasis, reinforcement of important terms, and newly defined not-so-important terms.

NOTE BOXES

Important concepts, explanations, and pitfalls are set off from the rest of the text by specially marked **Note boxes**. For example, we utilize notes in Chapter 2 for name and case selection, use of the semicolon, and other items we wish to emphasize.

INSIDE COVERS

The inside covers of the text are used as quick references for the SDC Guide; Examples Library, Utilities Library, and exercise indexes; program composition; reserved words and selected standard identifiers; and selected hot keys in the IDE.

APPENDIXES

For flexibility and convenience, the following topics are in appendixes: references for selected DOS commands and conventions, the IDE, and the editor; a classification of Turbo Pascal's data types; selected predeclared procedures and functions; selected compiler directives; chapter-by-chapter key differences between Turbo Pascal and Standard Pascal; and the extended ASCII character set.

TEXT SUPPLEMENTS

The text is supplemented by transparency masters and an *Instructor's Manual* with teaching hints, answers not given in the text to review exercises, solutions to end-of-chapter programming assignments, lecture supplements, and test questions with answers. Adopting instructors also receive diskettes with the Examples Library, Utilities Library, Solutions Library, and test questions with answers.

COURSE COVERAGE

This book emphasizes topics for courses that cover the ACM's recommended curriculum for *CS1*. Advanced topics in the *CS2* curriculum — such as recursion, sorting and searching, files, and dynamic data structures — are covered either in optionally assigned modules and sections or as chapters in the second half of the book.

This book is appropriate for (1) a course that includes an introduction to Pascal as one of several programming languages, (2) an introductory course that strictly focuses on Pascal as a vehicle to teach CS1 and selected CS2 topics, and (3) a more advanced CS1/CS2 course. It may also be appropriate for a two-term CS1/CS2 sequence of courses, especially in those schools on the quarter system.

ACKNOWLEDGMENTS

I wish to express my deep appreciation to many who have contributed to this project: to Frank Ruggirello, my main man and editor, for long-standing support, encouragement, humor, and market intelligence; to Rhonda Gray, who keeps Frank's wheels well greased; to Hal Humphrey, for taking over from Frank and delivering outstanding production services; to Janelle Rohr, for magic and hard work in managing the production and editorial tasks of a complex book; to Elizabeth Judd, for the best copy editing in the business; to Juan Vargas for superb book design; to Stuart Paterson for superior cover design; to Holly Allen and Karen Culver for the best marketing and ads east (and west) of Belmont; to the rest of the Wadsworth team for all the help in getting the book "out the door"; to Marco Urbano from the University of Rhode Island, for manuscript corrections and tireless, outstanding programming of solutions to additional exercises; to Phillip Kinnamon for helpful, thoughtful reviews and corrections to answers; to my reviewers

David Akins
El Camino College

David Boddy
Oakland University

John Buck
Indiana University

Greg Chamberlain
Bakersfield Community College

W. S. Curran
Southeastern Louisiana University.

Edmund Deaton
San Diego State University

Alice Galuppo
North Hennepin Community College

Bruce Kelley
Missouri Southern State College

Phillip Kinnamon
Tarrant County Junior College

Thomas Lyon
Mississippi County Community College

Diane Morris
Tyler Junior College

Theresa Phinney
Texas A&M University

Ali Salehnia
South Dakota State University

Charlene Wagstaff
San Jacinto College

Steve Wampler
Northern Arizona University

Richard Weinand
Wayne State University

who provided invaluable suggestions and corrections for manuscript revisions; to my students, who always teach me something about teaching; to Rick Jardon and John Dunn, my entertaining running buddies, for getting me away from the computer; and to Cynthia Mello, for patiently being there.

Kingston, Rhode Island   **Richard Mojena**

THE BIG PICTURE

This book teaches programming *principles* that focus on program design, development, and problem-solving concepts that are fundamentally relevant to any programming language. Pascal in general and Turbo Pascal in particular are uniquely suited for *teaching* these principles. Moreover, Pascal is widely used in practice as well.

This chapter gives the big picture: It reviews some preliminary computer concepts and terminology for a course in programming and presents a step-by-step framework for developing Turbo Pascal programs.

There are two major prerequisites for doing well in this course: a curiosity about computers and a desire to learn more about computer programming. By the time this course is over we hope that the book and your instructor will have helped you translate that curiosity and desire into a productive, rewarding, and continuing experience.

1.1 PRELIMINARIES

Let's start by describing some concepts and terms. Many of these are important to an understanding of the material in the rest of the text; others are important in rounding out your knowledge of computers and programming; a select few are there just to entertain you with computer trivia.

HARDWARE

Hardware includes the physical machinery and media that make up a computer system. Examples are the computer itself, printers, keyboards, monitors, and storage media like magnetic disks. The **computer system** is a collection of related hardware and software. **Software** denotes the **programs** or sets of symbolic instructions that are acted on by the computer. An **instruction** is a programmer-specified task for the computer to accomplish. For example, we might want the computer to process the following three instructions in sequence:

- Input and store a student's name and grades.
- Calculate and store the grade-point average.
- Display the name and grade-point average.

Note that instructions are different from data. By **data** we mean values that the computer inputs, manipulates, and outputs. In our grading example, the student's name, grades, and grade-point average are all examples of data.

We can simply say that a **computer** is a device that executes programs. By **execute** or **run** we mean that the computer carries out the instructions in the program. One way of describing a computer is to consider a classification of its hardware as the following five functional components.

1. Input units
2. Output units
3. Primary memory unit
4. Secondary memory units
5. Central processing unit (CPU)

Let's take a quick tour of each of these components.

Input Units

The input unit brings data and programs from the "outside world" to the computer's primary memory. For most of us, this is accomplished by a *keyboard*. Entries at the keyboard are displayed on the screen of a *monitor*. Another common input unit is a mouse, for moving a screen pointer and implementing actions with clicks of its buttons.

Output Units

The function of an output unit is exactly opposite that of an input unit: It receives data from the computer in the form of electronic signals and converts them into a form that's usable by either humans or computers. The most common output units are *monitors* for output on a screen and *printers* for output on paper.

Primary Memory Unit

This unit stores programs and data during input, output, and processing operations. The most common primary memory unit is actually a set of fingernail-sized *memory chips* made of silicon. Primary memory is often called **random-access memory (RAM).**

Computers store a character like the letter R, the digit 8, or the symbol $ as a packet or series of bits called a **byte.** A **bit** is a *binary digit* that assumes one of two possible values: 0 or 1 from a mathematical point of view; off or on from a mechanical perspective; and low voltage or high voltage from an electronic viewpoint. A common coding scheme abbreviated as **ASCII** (American Standard Code for Information Interchange) uses seven bits to represent a byte or character. For example, the letter R is coded and stored as 1010010 and the digit 8 is coded and stored as 0111000. Most computers extend the ASCII code to eight bits, which allows additional characters like graphics and foreign-language symbols. As a result, the usual assumption is that *a byte is eight bits.*

The amount of primary memory is usually expressed in multiples of bytes. For instance, 640 **kilobytes** (or 640**KB**) is 655,360 bytes and 4 **megabytes** (or 4**MB**) is 4,194,304 bytes.[1]

Data and programs in RAM are temporary in the sense that they reside in RAM as long as the power is on, or they are not replaced by other data and programs; otherwise, they are lost. This is one reason we need . . .

Secondary Memory Units

Secondary memory units "permanently" (is anything physical permanent?) store data and instructions for later recall into primary memory. Common secondary memory units are magnetic *disk drives* and *tape drives.* As in stereo systems, these drives are devices that rotate, read from, and write to *disk* and *tape media.*

Secondary memory is often called *external memory* or *external storage* because its contents are read into *internal* (primary) *memory.* Compared with internal memory, external memory has greater storage capacity at much less cost per byte, but the amount of time it takes to access data is greater.

The term *file* is used frequently in computing, so let's define it while we're on the subject of disk media. Data and programs are stored as **files** on a disk; that is, a file holds the contents of a particular program or a particular set of data. A file that stores a program is called a **program file**; one that stores a set of data is called a **data file.** Files are identified by name. For example, ENGINE1.PAS is the name of a Turbo Pascal program file that we discuss later in this chapter; CYNTHIA.DAT might be the name of a data file that stores a love letter (not to be discussed).

Central Processing Unit (CPU)

The CPU, or simply the **processor,** repetitively performs the following three steps:

1. Fetching or obtaining the next instruction from the program
2. Interpreting the instruction
3. Executing the instruction by transmitting directions to the appropriate computer component

A *logic chip* or **microprocessor** is a processor on a chip. These seem to be everywhere: in our stereos, cars, telephones, kitchen appliances, and so on. The pace of technology is such that the microprocessor we can balance on

---

[1]Computers use base 2 arithmetic instead of base 10 (decimal) arithmetic. Two raised to the tenth power gives the number 1024, which is the computer's equivalent of kilo or "one thousand." The expression 640KB thus represents 655,360 bytes, given by the product 640 × 1024. Similarly, a million is a thousand thousands, so the computer equivalent of mega or "one million" is 1024 × 1024, or 1,048,576. In other words, 4MB is 4,194,304 (4 × 1,048,576) bytes.

the tip of our finger is more powerful than the CPUs of room-sized computers from the 1970s.[2]

A **microcomputer** is a computer whose processor is a logic chip. Other common terms for "micros" are *home computers* for low-end models, *personal computers (PCs)* for mainstream models, *workstations* for high-end models, and *portable computers* for computing on the go.[3]

SOFTWARE

As defined earlier, **software** is just another term for **program,** a set of instructions that solves a specific problem. Software has two useful classifications: systems software and applications software.

Systems Software

Systems software is designed for tasks that facilitate the use of hardware. The **operating system (OS)** is the most important piece of systems software. It supervises system resources and directly interfaces with the user at the command prompt (such as the prompt C:\> on many microcomputers). A popular OS is the **disk operating system (DOS),** which was developed and licensed by Microsoft Corporation. An **operating environment** is a *shell* over the OS that enhances the user interface. Typical operating environments use the *desktop metaphor,* where the screen is meant to resemble a desktop. The most popular operating environment for DOS-based computers is Microsoft **Windows.**

Applications Software

Applications software solves problems called *applications.* Examples of applications are: processing a payroll, forecasting population patterns, maintaining a grade roster, and matching couples in a dating service. All of the programs in this book, and the programs you will write, are examples of applications programs. The inside front cover of the book identifies applications programs in the examples and exercises.

On Languages

We communicate among ourselves in our **natural language,** a combination of oral, written, and nonverbal languages. We distinguish a particular written language from any other written language by its **syntax,** or rules for arrang-

---

[2]The *ENIAC* computer was completed in 1946. It covered 1500 square feet of floor space (bigger than many two-bedroom apartments), tipped the scales at 60,000 pounds (equivalent to the combined weight of about 20 compact cars), sported some 18,000 vacuum tubes, and failed about every 7 minutes.

[3]The Boston Computer Museum has a two-story working model of a PC called the *WalkThrough Computer.* It includes a 108-square-foot monitor, a 25-foot keyboard with keys that are activated by stepping on them, a 6-foot disk, and a 9-by-6-foot trackball (a moving mouse would have been dangerous). No kidding! Actually, it looks and acts like a computer, but its movements are controlled by a Macintosh computer.

ing symbols like letters and punctuation into recognizable patterns like words and sentences. Computers communicate in a language that's compatible with electronic circuitry, called **machine language.** We communicate with a computer by writing instructions in a **computer language.**

Pascal

Pascal made its debut in 1971. This computer language was designed by Nicklaus Wirth, a Swiss computer scientist, and named for Blaise Pascal, the seventeenth-century philosopher and mathematician who is credited with inventing the first mechanical calculator. Two principal aims dominated the design of Pascal. It was intended to be a suitable language for teaching programming and a reliable and efficient language for implementation on existing computers.

In the 1980s, Pascal's popularity really picked up steam. In the educational arena, it was selected by the Educational Testing Service for its advanced placement course, and its features closely conform to the programming course topics proposed by the Curriculum Committee of the Association for Computing Machinery (ACM), a prominent computer science society. In the commercial arena, its popularity as a language for systems and applications programs exploded with the advent of the microcomputer. Its commercial success and portability were further enhanced by its standardization. We will use the term **Standard Pascal** when we need to distinguish the standardized version from the version in this book, **Turbo Pascal.**[4]

Turbo Pascal

Turbo Pascal, from a company called Borland International, arrived on the scene in 1983. It included significant enhancements to Standard Pascal; it had a very fast compiler; it was the first to provide an integrated development environment for programmers to write, compile, and execute their programs within a single software system; and it was inexpensively priced to boot. It took the PC Pascal market by storm, and has not let up since. Turbo Pascal is the focus of this text.

Compilers

We program in a computer language and the computer communicates only in machine language. How does the computer "understand" our programs? This is where the compiler makes its entrance. The **compiler** is a systems program that translates the instructions in a computer language into machine-language instructions. The original program, the one written in a language such as Pascal, is called the **source program** or **source file;** the compiled program, the one in machine language, is called the **object program** or **object file.**

---

[4]Standard Pascal is treated in detail in the publication cited in Appendix H. You might want to refer to this appendix after each chapter, to be aware of differences between Turbo and Standard Pascal.

The computer thus directly executes the object program, not the source program.

1.2   SOFTWARE DEVELOPMENT CYCLE

• • • • • • • • • • • • • • •

The *systems life cycle* is a stage-by-stage story of the understanding, design, acquisition and development, installation and testing, implementation, maintenance, and eventual demise of a *computer system*. What we will be doing in this course is a very simplified version of this process.

If we just consider the first four stages and narrow the focus to software, we have the **software development cycle.**

1. Specify the *requirements.*
2. *Design* the program.
3. *Code* the program.
4. *Test* the program.

All major programs in this book, and the programs you will write as end-of-chapter assignments, will use the software development cycle as a framework.

SPECIFY THE REQUIREMENTS

We start by understanding the problem environment and the requirements of the user. In an academic course, the problem is stated for you and the requirements primarily center around the *data requirements*. As you read the statement of a problem, try to identify the following:

Data requirements...

> *Output data*, or variable data written to output units
> *Input data*, or variable data entered from input units
> *Constant data*, or fixed data
> *Computational data*, or data computed from formulas and other logical steps

Let's get down to specifics. Suppose that Harvey CORE, the chief executive officer (CEO) of HC ENGINE Corporation, wishes a program that displays a sales report for any one of the firm's automotive engines, as described in Table 1.1. As you can see, Harvey likes to build *big* engines. (He's also a principal stockholder in an oil drilling company.) The *Two, Four,* and *Six* refer to the number of valves per cylinder. (All of Harvey's engines have eight cylinders.) Each engine size is expressed in cubic centimeters (cc).

Table 1.1   HC ENGINE Data

Engine Name	Size (cc)	Price per Unit	Units Sold
Baby Two	7000	$3,000	1,500
Momma Four	8500	4,000	2,000
Poppa Six	10000	5,500	1,000

The name, size, price, and units for a selected engine are to be entered at the keyboard, and the displayed (screen) report is to include the engine's name, size in both cubic centimeters and cubic inches (the old-timers don't think metric), price, units sold, and sales revenue. An engine size in cubic centimeters (cc) is multiplied by the metric conversion value 0.06102 to express its cubic-inch (ci) equivalent. Sales or revenue is the product of price and units sold.

That's the statement of the problem. Now, it's up to us to identify the following data requirements.

Output data: Engine name, Engine size (cc), Engine size (ci), Engine price ($/unit), Engines sold (units), Sales ($)

Input data: Engine name, Engine size (cc), Engine price ($/unit), Engines sold (units)

Constant data: Metric conversion (0.06102 ci/cc)

Note: The Size in ci and the Sales are not input or constant data; these data are part of the output and are computed by the program from the input and constant data, as seen next.

Computational data: We need to make sure that we understand the problem's environment by doing the required computations ourselves. In this case we have:

$$\text{Size in ci} = \text{Metric conversion} * \text{Size cc}$$
$$= 0.06102 \text{ ci/cc} * 7000 \text{ cc} \quad \text{(for Baby Two)}$$
$$= 427.14 \text{ ci}$$

$$\text{Sales} = \text{Price} * \text{Units}$$
$$= \$3,000/\text{unit} * 1500 \text{ units} \quad \text{(for Baby Two)}$$
$$= \$4,500,000$$

DESIGN THE PROGRAM

The design of a program includes how data will be represented and provided, the *user interface* or visual look of input and output, a breakdown of the problem into meaningful subproblems, and a list of steps (an algorithm) that shows the problem solution to each subproblem. At this time we will not break up

> # NOTE
>
> **1. What input and constant data?** In specifying the required input and constant data we need to ask ourselves: "Do the input and constant data provide the necessary values to generate the required output?" Keep in mind that these data do not include values that the program calculates itself. In our example, Sales is not a value that's input or fixed; it's calculated by the program through the given formula.
>
> **2. What required output?** Make sure that you identify each output value by name, as we did in our example.
>
> **3. Units of measure.** Be careful to specify units of measure (like cc, ci, $) for data values, to ensure clarity in the requirements and computations.
>
> **4. Desk check.** Our computations above are examples of desk checks. Make sure you understand the problem by desk checking any required calculations. *If you don't understand the computational and logical steps in a problem, then you won't be able to correctly design and code the program.* As we will see, desk checking also applies in the design, code, and test stages.

this rather simple problem into subproblems. We treat this important issue starting in Chapter 3, as problems get more complex.

Algorithm

The solution of a programming problem requires an **algorithm,** a set of rules or steps that prescribes how to solve the problem. To illustrate, consider the following first version of our algorithm for the HC ENGINE problem.

Program Engine1

Read input data
Calculate Size in ci and Sales
Write report

◄— ⌐ Algorithm

As you can see, the algorithm uses English-like phrases to describe step-by-step instructions for the computer to execute. This plain-English description of an algorithm is sometimes called **program design language** or **pseudocode.** Using this natural language in our design algorithm frees us from concern over the exact syntax of the programming language, thereby allowing us to focus on the design itself.

Take a look at the algorithm again and note the following characteristics.

1. Steps specify actions to be taken, and their order.

2. Algorithms are unambiguous in the sense that no steps are omitted that would require intelligent assumptions on the part of the *doer* (person or computer). The doer follows the algorithm blindly, neither omitting nor adding steps. Otherwise, the algorithm is incomplete.

3. Algorithms that describe programs commonly specify input actions first, then processing actions as in computing values, and finally output actions.

Stepwise Refinement

Our current algorithm has all the necessary steps for solving our defined problem, but it's not very detailed from the point of view of the doer. We can add more detail by *refining* individual steps, as follows.

Stepwise refinements...

Step 1: Read input data
Read Name
Read Size in cc
Read Price
Read Units sold

Step 2: Calculate Size in ci and Sales
Size in ci = Metric conversion * Size in cc
Sales = Price * Units

Step 3: Write report
Write blank line
Write title
Write solid line
Write blank line
Write name
Write Size in cc
Write Size in ci
Write Price
Write Units
Write Sales
Write solid line

Just what steps we select to refine and how much refinement detail we include depend on the complexity of the step and the preferences of the designer/ programmer.

Note from the refinement in step 1 that the metric conversion value is not read in from input units like the keyboard or a disk drive; it's directly included within the program in the step 2 refinement. Metric conversion is a *constant.* So there's no sense in making the user input the constant each time the program is run. However, the engine name, size in cc, price, and units sold can change from run to run. Thus, we designate these items as *variables* whose values are provided by user input.

We have just demonstrated what's called **stepwise refinement,** a process that implements *top-down design.* In **top-down design,** we start with a general look at the problem from the "top," where the level of detail is minimal. Subsequently, we refine the problem further by working "down" through successive levels of greater detail. The idea is consistent with the fact that humans solve problems more effectively by first understanding the "big picture," then refining elements of the big picture as needed.

User-Interface Design

Specifics on how the program looks to and interacts with the user are a further refinement of the input and output steps in the algorithm. Let's try the following user-interface design, including the look of keyboard entry—called **interactive input**—and the output report.

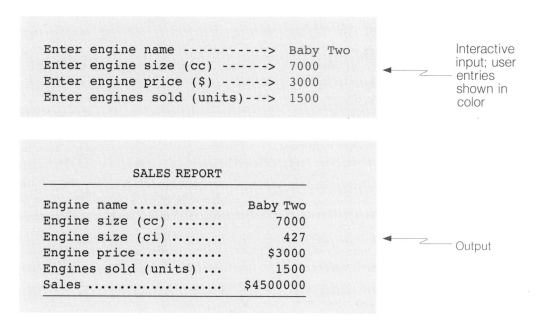

```
Enter engine name ----------->  Baby Two
Enter engine size (cc) ------>  7000
Enter engine price ($) ------>  3000
Enter engines sold (units)--->  1500
```
Interactive input; user entries shown in color

```
              SALES REPORT
    _____

    Engine name .............  Baby Two
    Engine size (cc) ........      7000
    Engine size (ci) ........       427
    Engine price ............     $3000
    Engines sold (units) ...      1500
    Sales ...................  $4500000
```
Output

Note that the sales report includes the output specified earlier in the requirements stage of the software development cycle. The input likewise includes the specified input data.

The application of program design and style principles is called **software engineering.** In practice, good software engineering plays an enormously important role in reducing the high cost of software throughout its life cycle. Studies indicate that software costs are three times higher than hardware costs during the systems life cycle.

NOTE

5. On pseudocode syntax. Don't worry about the exact way an algorithm in pseudocode is expressed. The idea is to focus on the actions to be taken, not on the syntax. We worry about syntax when we convert the pseudocode to Pascal. The pseudocode syntax in this book is influenced by the syntax and style in our Pascal programs, but only by preference, not by necessity. Theoretically, pseudocode design applies to any computer language.

6. Desk check the algorithm. Make sure your algorithm is correct by "executing" each step yourself. Have you provided all required data through input variables and constants? Are the calculations correct? Have you accounted for all required output?

CODE THE PROGRAM

Coding is the act of writing a program in a computer language. In our case, we will use Turbo Pascal. Figure 1.1 shows a listing of the Turbo Pascal program for our sample problem.

At this point you don't have to worry about specifics in the program. We will discuss these in (excruciating) detail in the next chapter. However, the program should make sense given our discussion up to this point. In particular, note the following.

1. Any text within braces { } documents the program for a human reader. *Documentation* improves the style of programs by increasing their clarity or readability. We come back to this in the next chapter.

2. The declarations in the program relate to the issues we mentioned earlier regarding constants and variables. Again, we look at this in the next chapter.

3. The main body shows the program algorithm, which is based on the design algorithm (pseudocode) that we developed earlier. Note how it follows the refined pseudocode.

4. We use boldfacing to highlight certain words of interest, as explained in the next chapter. You will not use boldfacing in your own programs (the compiler wouldn't like it).

TEST THE PROGRAM

The next step is to enter, compile, and run the program on the computer. The program is tested to eliminate three kinds of programming errors.

FIGURE 1.1   Listing for Program Engine1

```
program Engine1;

   {* * * * * * * * * * * * * * * * * * * * * * * * * * * * * * * * *
    *                                                               *
    *          Harvey CORE ENGINE Corporation:  Version 1.0         *
    *                                                               *
    *            Inputs engine name, size (cc), price, units sold   *
    *            Calculates engine size (ci) and sales revenue      *
    *            Outputs engine name, sizes, price, units, sales revenue *
    *                                                               *
    * * * * * * * * * * * * * * * * * * * * * * * * * * * * * * * * *}

   {=========================== Declarations ===========================}
const
   MetricConversion = 0.06102;                {cc = 0.06102 ci}
   Title = '              SALES REPORT';      {Output report title}
   Line  = '_____';  {Output report line}

var
   Name     : string;               {Name of engine}
   Price    : real;                 {Price of engine in $ per unit}
   Sales    : real;                 {Sales revenue in $}
   Size_cc  : real;                 {Engine size in cubic centimeters, cc}
   Size_ci  : real;                 {Engine size in cubic inches, ci}
   Units    : integer;              {Number of engines sold in units}

   {========================== Main Body ==========================}
begin   {Engine1}

   write   ('Enter engine name ------------> ');   readln (Name);
   write   ('Enter engine size (cc) -------> ');   readln (Size_cc);
   write   ('Enter engine price ($) -------> ');   readln (Price);
   write   ('Enter engines sold (units) ---> ');   readln (Units);

   Size_ci := MetricConversion * Size_cc;
   Sales   := Price * Units;

   writeln;
   writeln (Title);
   writeln (Line);
   writeln;
   writeln ('Engine name............',        Name    :10);
   writeln ('Engine size (cc).......',        Size_cc :10:0);
   writeln ('Engine size (ci).......',        Size_ci :10:0);
   writeln ('Engine price..........',   $', Price   :4:0);
   writeln ('Engines sold (units)...',        Units   :10);
   writeln ('Sales................. $',       Sales   :7:0);
   writeln (Line);

end.   {Engine1}
```

◄⁓ Algorithm

Compile-Time Errors.   An error that violates the syntactic rules of the language is called a **syntax error.** It's also called a **compile-time error** because it's detected by the compiler during compilation of the source program. An example might be incorrect punctuation within an instruction. The compiler fails to translate this instruction because it doesn't "understand" its structure. Any syntax errors within a program are thus flagged with appropriate error messages. Once we correct all compile-time errors, compilation of the source program generates the object program. The object program is then executed, and we might have to look forward to . . .

Run-Time Errors.   These are errors that take place while the program is running. A **run-time error** or **execution error** occurs when the system can't take an appropriate action in executing an instruction. An example would be attempted division by zero, which is mathematically undefined. We can classify run-time errors as fatal or nonfatal. A *fatal* run-time error halts program execution, and an appropriate error message is displayed; a *nonfatal* run-time error causes the system to take a corrective action, and execution continues. Attempted division by zero is a fatal run-time error; the calculation of a numeric value that's too small for the system to handle is a nonfatal run-time error. In the latter case, the system sets the value to zero and execution continues. If we escape run-time errors, we might still run into . . .

Logic Errors.   If our program runs but gives us unexpected, unwanted, or erroneous output, then we have one or more **logic errors.** For example, we might have incorrectly programmed a formula, or misunderstood the way a particular output feature works, or misplaced a particular instruction. These can be the most difficult errors to uncover because they're often subtle.

The process of locating and correcting errors is called **debugging.**[5] In practice, a high proportion of a programmer's time is spent on debugging. We will point out common errors throughout the book in the "Programming Tips" sections toward the end of chapters. We will also demonstrate a number of debugging techniques.

Debugging is one aspect of what's called program **verification,** or proving the correctness of a program. We will return to this topic as we develop new material over the next several chapters.

Turbo Pascal provides the **Integrated Development Environment (IDE)** for integrating common tasks in a programming environment: creating a new source program or accessing a previously stored source program, editing the source program, printing a paper listing of the source program, saving the source program on disk, compiling the source program into an object program, and running the object program.

---

[5]According to computer lore, the term **bug** was born when the Mark I computer at Harvard University stopped working one day in 1945. It seems that a moth got crushed between a set of relay contacts, thereby causing the malfunction. The computer was *debugged* by removing the moth with tweezers. A number of computer scientists believe that we should replace the word *bug* with the word *error.* They basically argue that all anthropomorphic words (those that give humanlike qualities to objects like computers, cars, ships, airplanes, and so on) are misleading to beginners. We disagree with this antiseptic viewpoint. Besides, a bug is not a human anyway . . . (If you're interested in exploring this and other controversial issues, see "A Debate on Teaching Computing Science," *Communications of the ACM,* vol. 32, no. 12, Dec. 1989, pp. 1397–1414.)

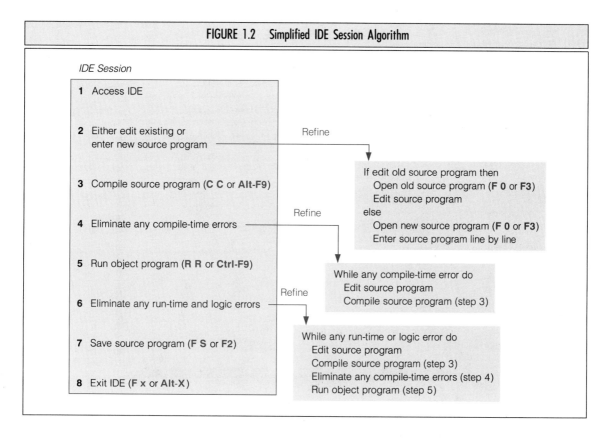

FIGURE 1.2   Simplified IDE Session Algorithm

You're going to spend a lot of time editing, saving, compiling, running, and debugging programs. A simplified IDE session implements the algorithm in Figure 1.2. Note the following points.

- Your instructor will give you the specifics on how to access the IDE in your course. Typically, we type turbo at the DOS prompt, unless the IDE is selected from a menu system.
- Appendix B summarizes IDE details. Appendix C highlights the most commonly used editing functions. The *Turbo Pascal User's Guide* is your best source for the most detail.

Let's describe an IDE session mostly in general terms. Don't worry about too many specifics just yet. We're taking a "top-down" look at this right now (we try to practice what we preach). We guide you through refined actual sessions in the exercises at the end of this chapter.

Step 1: Access IDE. When we access the IDE we're faced with a **menu bar** of ten main menu choices or commands, as seen in screen 1 of Figure 1.3.

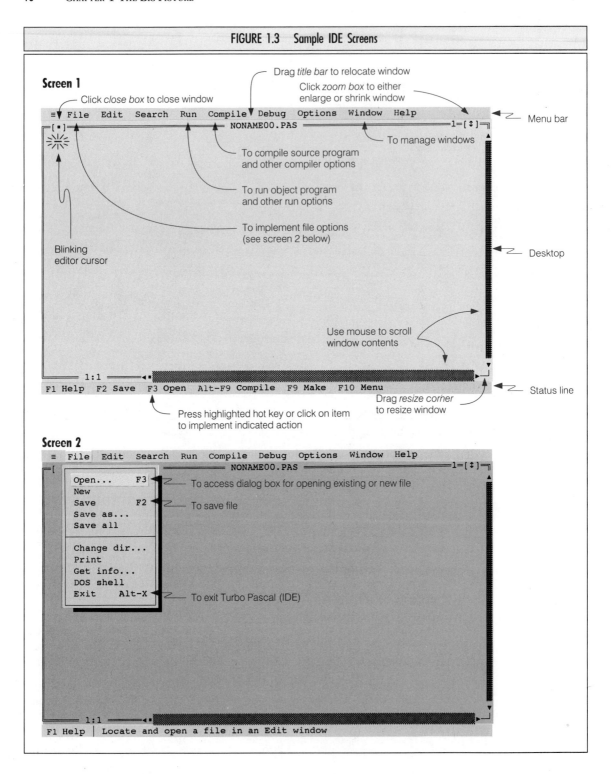

FIGURE 1.3   Sample IDE Screens

Screen 1

Click *close box* to close window

Drag *title bar* to relocate window

Click *zoom box* to either enlarge or shrink window

Menu bar

To manage windows

To compile source program and other compiler options

To run object program and other run options

To implement file options (see screen 2 below)

Blinking editor cursor

Desktop

Use mouse to scroll window contents

Status line

F1 Help   F2 Save   F3 Open   Alt-F9 Compile   F9 Make   F10 Menu

Drag *resize corner* to resize window

Press highlighted hot key or click on item to implement indicated action

Screen 2

≡   File   Edit   Search   Run   Compile   Debug   Options   Window   Help

NONAME00.PAS

Open...   F3 — To access dialog box for opening existing or new file
New
Save   F2 — To save file
Save as...
Save all

Change dir...
Print
Get info...
DOS shell
Exit   Alt-X — To exit Turbo Pascal (IDE)

1:1

F1 Help   Locate and open a file in an Edit window

FIGURE 1.3   (*continued*)

Screen 3

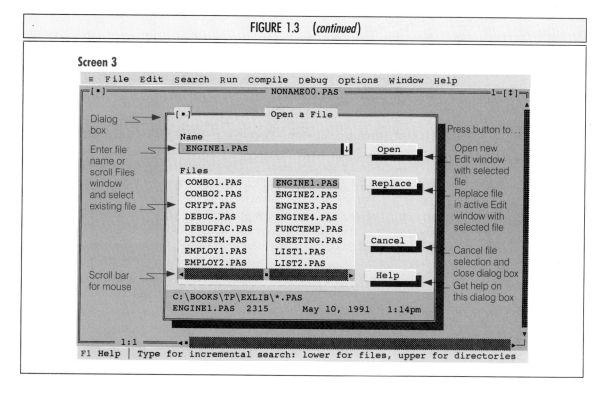

Take a few moments to orient yourself to the first screen. We select a main menu command by (1) clicking on it with the left *mouse* button, or (2) holding down the Alt key and pressing the letter key that corresponds to the highlighted first letter in the command, or (3) pressing function key **F10** and then either (a) pressing the highlighted first letter displayed in the command or (b) moving the *menu cursor* using a Cursor key to the command and pressing the Enter key. For example, to get from screen 1 to screen 2 in Figure 1.3, we selected File. This gave the *pull-down menu* seen in screen 2.

Take a moment to study this menu. A command in a pull-down menu is selected by a mouse click on the command, or by pressing the letter key that corresponds to the highlighted letter in the command, or by moving the pull-down menu cursor to the command and pressing the Enter key, or by pressing any indicated key that's displayed to the right of the command. For example, we got to screen 3 in Figure 1.3 by selecting Open.

Alternatively, we can use a *hot key* to shortcut the menu system, as seen by the keys or key combinations in pull-down menus and in the **status line** at the bottom of the screen. For example, right from screen 1 we could have jumped to screen 3 by pressing the hot key **F3**, or by clicking on it with the mouse. See inside the back cover of the book for a summary of selected hot keys.

The pop-up box in screen 3 is called a *dialog box,* since its purpose is to communicate with us. The selection of any pull-down menu command with an attached ellipsis (...) is followed by a displayed dialog box. We got a little bit ahead of ourselves in order to explain the menu system, so let's get back to our algorithm in Figure 1.2.

Step 2: Either Edit Existing or Enter New Source Program. Typically, we need to either edit an old source program or enter a new source program. This step is refined in Figure 1.2 as follows.

a. Edit Old Source Program. If we wish to work with a program that we previously saved, we open its file by selecting either the command sequence File Open or the hot key **F3**. This gives the *Open a File* dialog box seen in screen 3 of Figure 1.3. We can enter Engine1 in the *Name box* and then press the Enter key to open the file. In this case, the Enter key selects the default *Open button*. The IDE now loads the program, displays as many lines as will fit in the **Edit window** on the **desktop,** and starts the **editor.** We may now edit the program if needed. Alternatively, we can select program file Engine1 by scrolling the *Files window* within the dialog box using either the mouse on the scroll bar or the horizontal cursor keys. As usual, a selection is made either by a mouse click or by pressing the Enter key when the selection is highlighted, as seen in screen 3.

b. Enter New Source Program. We open a file as described earlier, type the name of a new file within the Name box in the dialog box, and press the Enter key. The next screen shows an empty Edit window, with a blinking *Editor cursor* in the upper-left corner. Now type the program line by line, ending each line with the Enter key.

Step 3: Compile Source Program. We now compile the source program by selecting either the command sequence Compile Compile starting at the main menu or the hot key **Alt-F9** from anywhere. Note that the hot-key sequence given by holding down the **Alt** key and pressing the **F9** key is expressed in writing with a connecting dash, as in **Alt-F9.**

Step 4: Eliminate Any Compile-Time Errors. The compiler will stop when it detects a syntax error and display an error message, with the cursor on or near the offending line. Presumably, we see the error, use the editor to correct it, and compile once more. Note that *the tasks edit and compile are repeated while we have compile-time errors,* as seen in the refinement for step 4 in Figure 1.2.

Step 5: Run Object Program. Having eliminated all compile-time errors, we now run the object program by selecting either the command sequence Run Run starting at the main menu or the hot key **Ctrl-F9** from anywhere. Actually, as a shortcut, we can compile and run just by pressing **Ctrl-F9**; the IDE automatically compiles the source program if any changes have been made since the last run command, and returns to the editor should there be a compile-time error. When we eliminate all compile-time errors and get a program to run, the IDE immediately switches from the Edit window to the

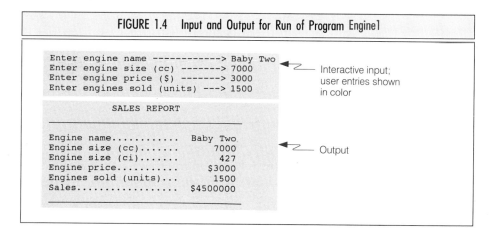

FIGURE 1.4   Input and Output for Run of Program Engine1

```
Enter engine name ------------> Baby Two          Interactive input;
Enter engine size (cc) -------> 7000              user entries shown
Enter engine price ($) -------> 3000              in color
Enter engines sold (units) ---> 1500

            SALES REPORT


Engine name............  Baby Two                 Output
Engine size (cc).......      7000
Engine size (ci).......       427
Engine price..........    $3000
Engines sold (units)...      1500
Sales.................  $4500000
```

User screen, which looks like the DOS screen. For our sample problem, the User screen would appear as in Figure 1.4. Unfortunately, we really don't get to see the output report at this time. It gets displayed very rapidly, and then the IDE immediately switches back to the Edit window. To view the User screen at leisure, select either **Window User screen** from the main menu or the hot key **Alt-F5**. Press any key to return to the Edit window. We can also view the input and output in what's called the **Output window.** To display this window, select **Window Output**. The Output window appears below the Edit window on the same screen, which is convenient while we test the program.

Step 6: Eliminate Any Run-Time and Logic Errors.   As seen in the refinement for step 6 in Figure 1.2, while we have run-time or logic errors we repeat the tasks edit and compile, eliminate any new compile-time errors we may have introduced, and run. As soon as the IDE detects a fatal run-time error, it stops the run, displays an error message, and places the cursor in the editor at the line that provoked the error. *These steps are repeated while we have fatal run-time errors.* If we have a nonfatal run-time error or logic error, then the IDE continues the run; *it's up to us to root out the causes of nonfatal and logic errors.*

Step 7: Save Source Program.   Next, we save the source program by selecting either the menu sequence **File Save** or the hot key **F2**. During long sessions, we suggest frequent savings of the program file while eliminating compile-time, run-time, and logic errors. This reduces the likelihood of lost edits if we should have a power loss, system "hang" (no response when we press keys), or some other predicament.

Step 8: Exit IDE.   When we're ready to call it a day (or night), we quit the IDE by selecting either the menu sequence **File Exit** or the hot key **Alt-X**. If we had not saved our latest edits, the IDE prompts us to save the source file, which we can choose to do or reject.

Let's assume that the program in Figure 1.1 has been opened, compiled, and executed. Input and output for this run are shown in Figure 1.4. Note that the input follows the design, as does the output report. Moreover, the output values are correct; that is, 427 cubic inches (the whole-number part of 427.14) is equivalent to 7000 cubic centimeters, and $4,500,000 is the product of price ($3000 per unit) and engines sold (1500 units).

NOTE

7. On program lines. A program line is equivalent to a physical line on the screen. We terminate a program line by pressing the *Enter key* when editing the program. Turbo Pascal has a maximum line length of 126 characters.

8. On PAS and EXE files. When we save a source file to disk, the IDE automatically gives our file name a **.PAS** extension (provided we didn't give an extension ourselves). When we press **Alt-F9** to compile, the object program is in RAM if *Memory* is active in the menu choices Compile Destination. If we toggle Destination to *Disk,* then the object program gets stored on disk in an *object file* under the same name as the source file, but with a **.EXE** extension. *We can execute object files on disk directly from the DOS prompt.* For this reason, EXE files are often called *executable files.* We ask you to check this out in Exercise 4.

9. Desk check, again. Just because your program runs (that is, you get output) doesn't mean your program is correct. Logic errors may be present. Always validate your program under varying conditions using a set of *test data* that you previously desk checked in the requirements and design stages.

10. Help facility. The IDE has an excellent context-sensitive help facility that explains elements of the IDE, editor, and Turbo Pascal language. Press the **F1** key anywhere within the IDE and up pops the help facility. We have more on this in Appendixes B and C, and ask you to check it out in Exercise 2.

11. IDE tutorial. There is an interactive tutorial that introduces the IDE. Try it out in Exercise 1.

1.3   PROGRAMMING TIPS

. . . .

Each chapter and module in the book ends with programming tips that summarize and reinforce program design and style considerations and highlight common errors.

DESIGN AND STYLE

1. Importance of. We can't overemphasize the importance of good software engineering in actual computer environments (and perhaps in the grade you get for this course). Careful attention to design techniques like stepwise refinement, together with stylistic considerations like indentation within programs, have major "bottom-line" payoffs in reducing the high cost of program development, implementation, and maintenance. Moreover, good software engineering increases the reliability and performance of programs. This has implications that go far beyond monetary considerations, because it can improve the quality of life or save lives in medical, defense, air travel, space, and countless other applications.

2. On Science and Art. Good programming requires the type of scientific methodology outlined in the software development cycle, with its attention to detail and organization; art and creativity elevate what might have been good or merely average programs into great programs—those that solve previously "unsolvable" problems, define new user interfaces, or implement elegant algorithms compared to their predecessors. Approach your programs as you might a written composition and let your creative energies loose. You just might surprise yourself.

COMMON ERRORS

1. On Feedback. Interactive computing is a great medium for feedback—be cheered by the positive feedback and challenged by the negative. Don't be afraid to experiment. Try new things.

2. The Doomed Discipline? Edsger Dijkstra, one of the pioneers in software engineering, claims that "as economics is known as 'The Miserable Science,' software engineering should be known as 'The Doomed Discipline.' "[6] He argues that the absence of formal mathematical proofs within software engineering means that "program testing may convincingly demonstrate the presence of bugs but can never demonstrate their absence." While this is true, we need not strictly compare software engineering principles to mathematical principles. A more apt comparison is that of software engineering and *effective writing.*[7]

This view leads to a style of programming called **literate programming,** where the program is considered a work of literature.[8] In this view, the programmer is an essayist, with main concerns focused on exposition and style. The goal of a literate program is a clear explanation to a reader of what the program does, with subsequent reductions in software costs over the life cycle of the program, particularly in the test and maintenance cycles.

---

[6]Edsger W. Dijkstra in "On the Cruelty of Really Teaching Computing Science," *Communications of the ACM,* vol. 32, no. 12, Dec. 1989, p. 1400.

[7]R.W. Hamming, *Communications of the ACM,* vol. 32, no. 12, Dec. 1989, p. 1410.

[8]D. Knuth, "Literate Programming," *Computer Journal,* vol. 27, no. 2, 1984, pp. 97–111.

ON REVIEW EXERCISES

- Reinforce, integrate, extend examples in chapter
- Appear in same order as examples
- Starred (*) exercises have no answers in back of text
  These are usually more difficult than unstarred exercises
- Exercises with (**L**) use Examples or Utilities Library on disk
- Exercise parts (**a**, **b**, **c**, . . .) are in increasing order of difficulty

EASIER   For the busy. . .
          1 2

NORMAL   For the thinkers . . .
          3 4

TOUGHER   For the hard CORE . . .

NOTE

12. DOS appendix. See Appendix A if you need to review some DOS fundamentals.

13. IDE appendix. Our coverage of the IDE in this chapter, together with Exercises 3 and 5 below, is enough to give you a good working knowledge of the IDE. Appendix B is a reference for the IDE.

14. Editor appendix. If you have already used editors or wordprocessors on PCs, you should have no problems with the simple editing in the exercises below. If not, then read over Appendix C before starting these exercises. In particular, check out document navigation with *cursor, Page Up, Page Down, Home, End, Ctrl-Page Up,* and *Ctrl-Page Down* keys; use of the *Insert* key as a toggle between insertions and overwrites, and as a means to insert blank lines; differences between the *Delete* key and the *Backspace* key; and the use of *Ctrl-Y* to delete program lines. These are the basic keys and key combinations for straightforward editing. In fact, you can get by with these keys for all of your editing needs. But then you would miss out on some powerful, time-saving functions, like block copies and moves.

15. Examples library. We provide to instructors a library on diskette of all sample programs in the book. We often ask you to start with one of these sample programs in an exercise marked (**L**). Your instructor will describe how you can access these source files.

1. **IDE tutorial.** Turbo Pascal has a nice, interactive tutorial for the IDE. It's an object file called *TPTOUR.EXE.* From the DOS prompt type tptour, assuming you're in the directory that contains the object file. Try the tutorial if it's available to you.

2. **IDE Help facility.** Try the following to familiarize yourself with the excellent help facility within the IDE.
   a. Find out how to access the IDE on your system. When Turbo Pascal loads you will see the *menu bar* at the top of the screen, an empty *desktop* in the middle, and the *status line* at the bottom.
   b. If you're using a mouse or other pointing device, click on **F1** in the status line. If you're using the keyboard, press the **F1** key. Scroll the contents of the *Help dialog box.* Select highlighted terms for more help on that term. Select **F1** again for help on help. Explore!
   c. Click on **H**elp in the menu bar, or press **Alt-H**, or press **F10 H**. Check out the offered **H**elp pull-down menu choices.

(L) 3. **HC ENGINE.** This exercise assumes that you have access to the Engine1 program in Figure 1.1. You need to know where this program is (floppy disk or particular directory on a hard disk). Use the IDE session algorithm in Figure 1.2 as a framework for this exercise.

   Note: For keyboard users, remember that pressing **F10** activates the menu bar.
   We use the term *select* to mean either "press one or more keys" or "click the mouse."

   a. Access the IDE, select **F**ile, select **C**hange dir . . ., and change the directory to the path that contains **Engine1** on your system. It's not actually necessary to change the directory, since we could enter the entire *file specification* (like C:\examples\engine1) when entering a file name (see step **b** below). If you plan to work with multiple files within the same directory in one session, then retrieving and storing files is easier if you change the current directory accordingly.
   b. Load Engine1 by pressing or clicking hot key **F3** (or selecting **F O** from the main menu) and either typing or selecting ENGINE1.
   c. Compile Engine1 by selecting **C**ompile **C**ompile from the main menu. Alternatively, press hot key **Alt-F9**. Note the "stats" given in the *Compiling dialog box.*
   d. Run the program by selecting **R**un **R**un from the main menu or hot key **Ctrl-F9**. Reproduce our run in Figure 1.4.
   e. Did you get a (quick!) look at the output report? View the *User screen* by pressing hot key **Alt-F5**. Press **Alt-F5** several times and see what happens.
   f. Move the cursor within the Edit window by using the arrow keys. Play around with **Page Up**, **Page Down**, **Home**, and **End** keys. Try **Ctrl-Page Up** and **Ctrl-Page Down**. Note the *Line* and *Col indicators* at the bottom left corner of the Edit window as you navigate. Check out the menu commands under **W**indow in the menu. Try these. Press **F1** to get help on any highlighted pull-down menu command. For you "mousiers," use the *scroll bars*

at the bottom and right borders of the Edit window. Click on the arrowheads at the ends of the scroll bars and see what happens. Hold down the left mouse button on one of these arrowheads. Click on either side of a tiny *scroll box* within one of the scroll bars. Drag a scroll box along its scroll bar by pressing the mouse button with the pointer on the scroll box and moving the mouse at the same time. Drag the *resize corner* at the bottom right of the Edit window. Drag the *title bar* at the top of the Edit window.

g. Compile-time errors. Let's introduce some deliberate compile-time errors. Try the following changes in the Edit window. The line indicator at the bottom left of the screen locates the line number for each part below.

(1) Delete the **semicolon** at the end of the first line.

(2) As you watch the line indicator, move the cursor down to line 13 and delete } at the end of the line.

(3) At line 38 delete : in the Sales calculation.

(4) At line 41 replace **i** with **o**, giving the misspelled word **wroteln**.

(5) At line 44 delete the second **apostrophe** (single quotation mark).

(6) At line 52 delete the **period** after **end**.

Now go through six repetitions of the procedure described in the refinement for step 4 in Figure 1.2 by correcting these compile-time errors one at a time. You will see some common syntax error messages.

h. Run-time error. Assuming you have eliminated all compile-time errors, run the program again and enter the number of units using a decimal point (as in 1500). Is this run-time error *fatal*? Press the **Esc** key to get rid of the error message (actually, any key will do).

i. Logic error. Delete the program line that reads in Name by moving the cursor to line 32 and pressing **Ctrl-Y**. Run the program again. What happens? The program runs, but a "blank" name is output.

j. Type in line 32 as it was, and then replace the underscore characters with = characters in line 18. Compile and run this version of the program. Let's store this version on your floppy disk in drive A. Access the main menu and select **S**ave as . . . from the **F**ile pull-down menu. Enter the new name a:engine1a. You now have a new source file named ENGINE1A.PAS on a floppy disk.

k. Get back to the main menu and confirm the existence of ENGINE1A.PAS by selecting **D**OS shell from the **F**ile pull-down menu. If you're actually in a DOS shell, exit to the command prompt. Display the directory of the drive that has your floppy disk (type **dir a:** at the DOS command prompt). You should see ENGINE1A.PAS listed as a file name. Get back to the IDE by typing **exit** at the command prompt.

l. Quit the IDE by selecting either hot key **Alt-X** or E**x**it from the **F**ile pull-down menu.

That's a fairly complete tour of IDE essentials, and pretty much what you will be doing.

4. **Object files.** Reread Note 8 regarding EXE files.

    a. Access the IDE and select Compile from the main menu. Look at Destination in the pull-down menu. Does it show *Disk* or *Memory*? Normally, we want it to show *Memory,* which means the source file is compiled to an object file in RAM. This allows faster compilations, because slower secondary storage media don't have to be used. This is fine for program development, but what about the working version of a program? We would want to execute its object file from a copy on disk, outside the IDE. The **D** key acts as a toggle switch between the *Memory* and *Disk* options. Press this key and note what happens. Select Compile again from the main menu to view the change. Make sure that the destination is set to *Disk*.

    b. Let's store the object file on a floppy disk in drive A. Open Engine1. Change the EXE directory to drive A by selecting Options Directories . . . from the main menu and typing A:. Compile Engine1. The object file ENGINE1.EXE should be on your floppy. Let's confirm its existence.

    c. Exit to DOS (see Exercise 3k). Display the directory in drive A by typing dir a:. Is ENGINE1.EXE listed? If not, rework parts **a** and **b** above. If you see it, then . . .

    d. Execute the program by typing a:engine1. What do you think? This is the way commercial programs are implemented.

    e. Type exit to return to the IDE.

ADDITIONAL EXERCISES

ON ADDITIONAL EXERCISES

- Programming projects for new problems, or revisits of new problems from earlier chapters
- Arranged in ascending order of difficulty
- No answers for these in back of text
- Exercise parts (**a**, **b**, **c**, . . .) add increasingly difficult features to programs
- Make use of Examples and Utilities Libraries to improve productivity, when warranted

EASIER	For the busy . . .
NORMAL	For the thinkers . . .
	5 6 7
TOUGHER	For the hard CORE . . .
	8

FIGURE 1.5   Listing of Program **Learn**

```
program Learn;

   { This is file LEARN.PAS

       Inputs whole number and outputs its cube }
var
  Number : integer;

begin  {Learn}

  writeln;
  write ('Enter whole number... ');  readln (Number);

  writeln;
  writeln ('  The cube of ', Number, ' is ', Number * Number * Number);

end.   {Learn }
```

---

5. **Learn program.** Consider the program in Figure 1.5. Let's work through the IDE session described in Figure 1.2. This is similar to the session in Exercise 3, except that we're going to enter a new source file and store it in the root directory on a floppy disk in drive A.

  a. Access the IDE, select **F**ile, and select **C**hange dir... Does the display show the drive that has your floppy? If not, type **a:** (or **a:***DirectoryName* if you plan to store in a directory other than the root directory, or **b:** if your floppy is in drive B). Alternatively, we could enter the *file specification* (like **a:\learn** or **a:***DirectoryName*\learn) when entering a file name (see step **b** below). If you plan to work with multiple files within the same directory in one session, retrieving and storing files is easier if you change the current directory accordingly.

  b. Select **F**ile **O**pen and name the file **learn**. Enter the program in Figure 1.5 just as you see it (unless you like to live dangerously). Carefully proofread it. Save it directly from the editor by selecting hot key **F2**. (Alternatively, you could exit the editor with **F10** and save it with **F S**.

  c. Compile program Learn by selecting hot key **Alt-F9**. (You could select **C**ompile **C**ompile from the main menu.) Alternatively, we recommend pressing **Ctrl-F9**, which not only runs the program but compiles it if it had not been previously compiled or if editing changes had been made since the last compilation. If you have compile-time errors, then you made one or more mistakes in typing the program. Correct any errors and press **Ctrl-F9** again. Repeat this process while you have compile-time errors (this is the refinement in step 4 of Figure 1.2).

  d. In your run, input a whole number like **5** (without a decimal point). Are you back to the *Edit window*? View the *User screen* by pressing the hot key **Alt-F5**. Correct results? Press **Alt-F5** several times and see what happens.

e. Output window. Display the *Output window* by selecting **W**indow **O**utput from the main menu. The **F6** key toggles the active window between the Edit window and the Output window. The *active window* is the window that responds to our actions, and it is identified by a highlighted double border. To nail this down, press **F6** several times and watch what happens. Make sure the Output window is active, and move around this window with navigation keys or the mouse. Zoom and unzoom the active window with the **F5** key, or by clicking the *zoom box* in the upper-right corner. You can also access these and other window management features from the **W**indow pull-down menu. Select **T**ile to keep the Output window visible. Get help by pressing **F1**. Try more runs with input data of your choice.

f. Compile-time errors. Let's introduce some deliberate compile-time errors. (You didn't have any compile-time errors in step **c**, right?) Try the following changes in the Edit window.

(1) Misspell program as progran in line 1.

(2) Delete { at the beginning of line 3.

(3) Delete the semicolon at the end of line 8.

(4) At line 13 delete both quotes.

Now go through four repetitions of the process described in the refinement for step 4 in Figure 1.2 by correcting these compile-time errors one at a time. You will see some common syntax error messages.

g. Run-time error. Assuming you have eliminated all compile-time errors, run the program again and input a lowercase L (old-time typists often use this for the digit 1). Is this run-time error *fatal*?

h. Logic error. Delete the instruction in program line 13 that reads in Number, readln (Number);. Run the program again. What happens? Zero is output for Number and its cube.

i. Type in line 13 as it was originally, and then change line 16 to write the square instead of the cube. Compile and run this version of the program. Let's store this revised program on your floppy disk. Access the main menu and select **S**ave as . . . from the **F**ile pull-down menu. Enter the new name learn2. You now have a new source file on a floppy disk named LEARN2.PAS.

j. Confirm the existence of this new source file by selecting **D**OS shell from the **F**ile pull-down menu and displaying the directory of the drive that has your floppy disk (type dir). You should see LEARN2.PAS as a file name. Get back to the IDE by typing exit at the DOS prompt.

k. Object file. Create a user version of Learn as described in Exercise 4.

l. Quit the IDE by selecting hot key **Alt-X** (or E**x**it from the **F**ile pull-down menu).

6. **Temperatures.** Consider the formula that calculates degrees Celsius from degrees Fahrenheit.

$$\text{Celsius} = \frac{5}{9}(\text{Fahrenheit} - 32)$$

A user at the Weather Channel for station WROC recently got a PC and wishes to convert degrees Fahrenheit to degrees Celsius rounded to the nearest whole degree.

   a. Specify the data requirements for this problem. Desk check the following Fahrenheit temperatures: −10.5, 0, 32, 70, and 212.

   b. Design exactly how you want the input to look. Do the same for the output. Make it look nice—no clutter and no confusion about what the values represent.

   c. Design the algorithm in pseudocode.

7. **Disk areas.** The formula for the area A of a circle with radius r is

$$A = \pi r^2$$

where π is the irrational number 3.14159265... A user who orders magnetic materials for computer disks wants to type a single-letter disk-type code, the *diameter* of the disk type, and the daily production quantity of these disks. The screen is to show the input data, the surface area (area of top surface plus area of bottom surface) per disk, and the total surface area for all disks produced of this type.

   a. Specify the data requirements for this problem. Desk check the following data.

Data for Three Disk Types

Disk Code	Diameter (Inches)	Quantity (Disks)
X	2.00	50,000
Y	3.50	100,000
Z	5.25	5,000

   b. Design exactly how you want the input to look. Do the same for the output. Make it look nice—no clutter and no confusion about what the values represent.

   c. Design the algorithm in pseudocode.

8. **ATM withdrawal algorithm.** Design an algorithm in pseudocode that dispenses cash in an Automated Teller Machine. The ATM dispenses bills in $10 and $20 denominations provided the requested withdrawal is legitimate. Legitimate requests are withdrawals of $10 to $100 in increments of $10. Assume this algorithm is a subsystem within the overall ATM system.

SIMPLE PROGRAMS

This chapter introduces elements of the Turbo Pascal language. By the end of it, you will be writing and running complete programs like those in Chapter 1.

We will use the HC ENGINE problem as a key example throughout this chapter. For convenience, we reproduce its listing and I/O in Figure 2.1. *Suggestion: Save yourself some grief by marking this page with a paper clip or some other marker;* we return to this program time and again throughout the chapter. By the end you'll know this program in your sleep (and you can trash the paper clip by then).

2.1 RESERVED WORDS AND IDENTIFIERS

· · · · · · · · · · · · ·

Look at the program in Figure 2.1. What do you see? At the simplest level, the elements in the program are **characters** like v and 2. Turbo Pascal programs use lowercase and uppercase alphabetic characters, numeric characters, symbol characters such as a plus sign or an asterisk, the space (blank) character, and ASCII control characters for actions like beeping the speaker or issuing a carriage return.

RESERVED WORDS

Languages like Pascal have words with special meaning. These are called **reserved words** or **reserved identifiers** because they cannot be *redefined* by the programmer. For example, the reserved word **program** tells the compiler that Engine1 is the name of the program shown in Figure 2.1. We cannot redefine the reserved word **program** to mean anything else in our programs.

The program in Figure 2.1 uses the following reserved words: **program, const, var, string, begin,** and **end.** Their use is explained later in this chapter. The *inside back cover* shows a complete list of reserved words in Turbo Pascal.

IDENTIFIERS

Reserved words are sometimes called reserved identifiers because the term **identifier** suggests a *name* or *identity.* Pascal includes two other kinds of identifiers.

A **standard identifier** also has a predefined meaning to the compiler, but its name is not "reserved"; that is, the compiler lets us redefine its meaning

---

FIGURE 2.1   Listing and I/O for Program Engine1

(a) Listing in Edit Window

```pascal
program Engine1;

    {* * * * * * * * * * * * * * * * * * * * * * * * * * * * * * * *
     *                                                             *
     *           Harvey CORE ENGINE Corporation:   Version 1.0     *
     *                                                             *
     *              Inputs engine name, size (cc), price, units sold    *
     *              Calculates engine size (ci) and sales revenue  *
     *              Outputs engine name, sizes, price, units, sales revenue  *
     *                                                             *
     * * * * * * * * * * * * * * * * * * * * * * * * * * * * * * * *}

    {============================== Declarations ==========================}

const
    MetricConversion = 0.06102;                    {cc = 0.06102 ci}
    Title = '          SALES REPORT';              {Output report title}
    Line  = '_____';  {Output report line}

var
    Name    : string;        {Name of engine}
    Price   : real;          {Price of engine in $ per unit}
    Sales   : real;          {Sales revenue in $}
    Size_cc : real;          {Engine size in cubic centimeters, cc}
    Size_ci : real;          {Engine size in cubic inches, ci}
    Units   : integer;       {Number of engines sold in units}

    {============================= Main Body ============================}

begin  {Engine1}

    write   ('Enter engine name ------------> ');   readln (Name);
    write   ('Enter engine size (cc) -------> ');   readln (Size_cc);
    write   ('Enter engine price ($) -------> ');   readln (Price);
    write   ('Enter engines sold (units) ---> ');   readln (Units);

    Size_ci := MetricConversion * Size_cc;
    Sales   := Price * Units;

    writeln;
    writeln (Title);
    writeln (Line);
    writeln;
    writeln ('Engine name............',         Name    :10);
    writeln ('Engine size (cc).......',         Size_cc :10:0);
    writeln ('Engine size (ci).......',         Size_ci :10:0);
    writeln ('Engine price...........    $',    Price   :4:0);
    writeln ('Engines sold (units)...',         Units   :10);
    writeln ('Sales................. $',        Sales   :7:0);
    writeln (Line);

end.    {Engine1}
```

within the program. The standard identifiers in Figure 2.1 are **real, integer, write, readln,** and **writeln.**

For example, **integer** is used in Figure 2.1 to declare the use of integer or whole-number numeric values. Each of these standard identifiers is explained shortly. *The inside back cover also shows the standard identifiers in Turbo Pascal that we use in this book.*

```
                        FIGURE 2.1    (continued)
```

(b) Input/Output in Output Window

```
    Enter engine name ------------> Baby Two
    Enter engine size (cc) -------> 7000
    Enter engine price ($) -------> 3000
    Enter engines sold (units) ---> 1500

              SALES REPORT


    Engine name............   Baby Two
    Engine size (cc).......       7000
    Engine size (ci)......··       427
    Engine price..........     $3000
    Engines sold (units)...       1500
    Sales.................     $4500000
```

User-defined identifiers are names that programmers select; they have meaning to us but no *predefined* meaning to the compiler. The user-defined identifiers in Figure 2.1 are Engine1, Line, MetricConversion, Name, Price, Sales, Size_cc, Size_ci, Title, and Units. For example, Price represents the price of an engine.

To summarize, we have three types of identifiers in Pascal programs.

1. **Reserved identifier...Reserved word** is an alternative term. It has predefined meaning and cannot be redefined by the programmer.

2. **Standard identifier**...It has predefined meaning, but can be redefined by the programmer. We suggest not redefining these, because it increases the likelihood that programs will be misunderstood by readers when standard identifiers don't behave as expected. Moreover, we would lose the intended benefits. For example, if we were to redefine the standard identifier **write,** then we could not use it for standard output (Turbo Pascal's intended benefit). *For these reasons, we make no distinction between reserved and standard identifiers in this book.*

3. **User-defined identifier**...It has *no* predefined meaning. Its creation and use are entirely at the programmer's discretion.

Rules for Naming Identifiers

We have to observe the following rules when naming user-defined identifiers in Turbo-Pascal.

1. Number of Characters.   An identifier can have *up to the maximum line length of 126 characters,* but only the first 63 are meaningful or significant to the compiler.

2. First Character.   The first character must be alphabetic (uppercase or lowercase letter) or an underscore.

Table 2.1   Sample User-Defined Identifiers

Identifier	Acceptable?
1 Velocity	Yes ....
2 velocity	Yes .... These are identical to the compiler
3 VELOCITY	Yes ....
4 Price1$	No ..... Has symbol $
5 1Price	No ..... Can't begin with digit
6 Price1	Yes
7 Rock Group Nineties	No ..... Has blanks
8 Rock-Group-Nineties	No ..... Has hyphens
9 Rock_Group_Nineties	Yes .... Underscore gives illusion of blank
10 RockGroupNineties	Yes .... Cap R, G, and N make easier reading
11 rockgroupnineties	Yes .... But not as easy to read as preceding

3. Remaining Characters. The remaining characters can be any of the alphabetic or numeric characters or underscore. *No other characters are permitted.* The alphabetic characters are *case-insensitive;* for example, there's no distinction between A and a.

Table 2.1 shows examples of both acceptable and unacceptable names for user-defined identifiers.

NOTE

1. On selecting identifiers...It's best to select names for identifiers that have descriptive meaning within the context of the application. For example, if we need to represent velocity, then Velocity is better than V. Check out the user-defined identifiers in the Engine1 program. They all have descriptive meaning.

2. On selecting uppercase or lowercase...Identifiers are case-insensitive; however, be alert to using case for improved readability. For instance, compare examples 10 and 11 in Table 2.1. We prefer the approaches in examples 9 and 10 to that in example 11.

3. On our use of case, boldface, and color in programs...Our programs will follow these conventions (see Figure 2.1):

a. All lowercase for reserved words. This is conventional practice in the field. It's common in some journals, however, to use all uppercase letters for reserved words, to better distinguish them from other identifiers. We use boldfacing for this purpose.

b. All lowercase for standard identifiers. Many programmers mix case here, as in **Writeln.** We mostly use lowercase because we're not

continued

making a distinction between reserved words and standard identifiers. At times we use mixed case for certain standard identifiers, to improve clarity.

c. Mixed case for user-defined identifiers. For example, we capitalize the first letter, as in Price, and first letters in compound names, as in RockGroupNineties. This improves their readability and better distinguishes them from the reserved and standard identifiers.

d. Boldface for reserved identifiers and standard identifiers. This further improves the readability of the programs. *You will not use boldface in the programs you type;* it's not allowed in an actual program.

e. Color. We use color in programs to draw your attention to specific items or sections. In Figure 2.1, color distinguishes user-defined identifiers from other identifiers (shown in boldface) and other punctuation and text.

SELF-REVIEW EXERCISE

This exercise at the end of the chapter has answers at the back of the book. Try it out now to self-test your understanding of the material in this section.

1

2.2 DATA TYPES

• • • • • • • • • • • • • • •

Computers manipulate data, so it's useful to first understand the notion of a data type. A **data type** defines both the *type* or kind of data represented by that data type and the *operations* or kinds of manipulations that can be performed. For example, the data type *integer* represents whole-number numeric values like 7 and 10. Moreover, we can perform certain arithmetic operations, such as the addition of integers (7 + 10).

OVERVIEW

Turbo Pascal has six *basic* data types:

1. **Integer** . . . . Whole numbers like 7 10 −50
2. **Real** . . . . Fractional numbers like 3.14 and −0.516

3. **Character** .... Single characters like A c . – $
4. **String** .... Strings of characters like Harvey CORE and 023-66-9872
5. **Boolean** ...... The logical values **true** or **false**
6. **Pointer** .... Addresses of memory locations

We discuss integer, real, character, and string next; we leave Boolean and pointer for other chapters.

INTEGER

An **integer** is an unsigned or signed whole number. Sample integers include −50 0 + 123 123. The last two are taken to be the same integer. Program Enginel uses the integer data type for the number of engines sold. At appropriate points in the book we will have a need for other integer types. We can perform input/output, arithmetic, and assignment operations on integers, which we show shortly.

REAL

The **real** data type identifies the storage of real numbers, such as 0.06102, 0.0, and −8000.319. The real value 0.06102 is expressed in standard notation; the alternative form 6.102×10^{-2} is expressed in scientific notation, where the −2 is the *exponent* (power of 10). In Pascal, scientific notation for this example would be written as 6.102E-2, where E-2 represents $\times 10^{-2}$. Program Enginel uses the real data type for the metric conversion constant, price, sales, and engine sizes.

Note that real numbers in Pascal require at least one digit to the left of the decimal point. For example, the number .06102 would give a compile-time error. ☹

Real type is often called **floating-point type** because the placement of the decimal "floats" depending on the choice of exponent. In our example, we could just as well have represented 0.06102 as 6102E-5. Scientific notation is useful for stating very small or very large real numeric values. You will often see this type of notation when viewing the output of real values. We might note that the computer stores all real values in its *floating-point representation,* a special binary version of scientific notation.

CHARACTER

Data type **char** defines character values consisting of exactly *one* character and taking up *one* byte of storage. Any single character in the extended ASCII character set shown in Appendix I is a legitimate value in the char data type.

STRING

Data type **string** defines a *string* or sequence of characters. In the I/O in Figure 2.1, the string Baby Two is a string data value that describes the name of the engine. In general, string data can include any set of characters supported by the computer system. Turbo Pascal allows maximum string sizes of 255 characters.

OTHER DATA TYPES

The rich variety of data types sharply distinguishes Pascal from many other computer languages. Appendix D shows the data types supported by Turbo Pascal. Note that types integer and real include variations with respect to range, precision (for the real types), and memory requirements. Turn to these tables as a reference to the BIG PICTURE, as a means to get your bearings when we use data types. (You might want to "paper clip" this appendix.)

NOTE

4. Integer Overflow and Underflow. We need to be very aware of the *range* of values for numeric data types. For example, if we are working with type **integer** and a computation exceeds the upper range limit of 32767 (see Appendix D), then we have an error condition called **overflow**; a value below the lower range limit is an **underflow** error. These are particularly insidious *run-time errors* because many systems don't detect them. *Turbo Pascal does not flag integer underflow and overflow conditions, giving "junk" values to resulting calculations.*

5. Real overflow and underflow. Computed floating-point values outside the range limits given in Appendix D cause overflow (value above range) or underflow (value below range). Turbo Pascal flags a floating-point overflow as a *fatal run-time error*. A floating-point underflow returns a value of zero.

6. Precision. You might be surprised to learn that not all real values are "created equally." A real value given by $\frac{1}{2}$ to an integer power (like $\frac{1}{2}, \frac{1}{4}$, and so on) or sums of these (like $\frac{1}{2} + \frac{1}{4}$) has an *exact representation,* and so is perfectly accurate or precise. Any other real value, like 0.2, has an *approximate representation* in that its value is approximated. This type of *roundoff error* can cause intolerable inaccuracies in certain applications that rely on precision, such as space-trajectory estimates and certain financial calculations. Increasing the number of significant digits by using double, extended, or comp types is a simple way of postponing roundoff errors.

SELF-REVIEW EXERCISES

These exercises at the end of the chapter have answers at the back of the book. Try these out now to self-test your understanding of the material in this section.

2 3

2.3 PROGRAM COMPOSITION

• • • • • • • • • • • • • • •

A Turbo Pascal program has three distinct sections: (1) **program heading,** (2) **program declarations,** and (3) **program main body.** Figure 2.1 identifies these three sections as shaded blocks. A detailed composition of Turbo Pascal programs is shown *inside the back cover* of the book.

HEADING

The **program heading** is at the top of Turbo Pascal programs. It identifies the name of the program according to the syntax in the accompanying syntax box.

SYNTAX BOX

In these **syntax boxes** we use **boldface** for reserved words and standard identifiers and color for user-defined identifiers and other user-selected options

Program heading ... Identifies name of program

Syntax .... **program** ProgramName;

Examples ..... **program** Engine1;

Explanation ... **program** is a reserved word and ProgramName is a user-defined identifier for the name of the program. The semicolon separates the program heading from what follows next in the program. The program heading is optional in Turbo Pascal; it's required and has a standard form in Standard Pascal, as seen in Appendix H.

The program heading is optional in Turbo Pascal, but we strongly recommend its use to document the name of the program and identify its file. In the example, Engine1 is both the name of the program and the name of the file that stores the program. The listing inside the front cover shows the program files you have access to.

DECLARATION OF CONSTANTS

A **constant** is a value that explicitly appears within a program. The most common constants by data-type classification are *integer constants* like 2001 and −56; *real constants* like −99.99 and 6.789E12; *character constants* like '$', 'A', and '7'; and *string constants* or *character strings* like 'Computer Aided Decisions'. Note that character and string constants must be enclosed within single quotation marks (apostrophes).

A **declared constant** is a user-defined identifier that's associated with a constant and its data type. For example, look at the const declaration section of the Engine1 program in Fig. 2.1. MetricConversion is the *real* constant 0.06102. The other declared constants are the string constants Line and Title, which are used in writing the output report. The accompanying syntax box describes the declaration of constants.

SYNTAX BOX

Declaration of constants . . . . Associates declared constant identifiers with corresponding constants in const section

```
Syntax ........ const
                ConstantName1 = ConstantExpression1;
                ConstantName2 = ConstantExpression2;
                ...

Examples ....... const
                IntegerConstant = 2001;
                RealConstant1   = -99.99;
                RealConstant2   = 6.789E12;
                RealConstant3   = RealConstant1 * RealConstant2;
                CharConstant    = '$';
                StringConstant  = 'Computer Aided Decisions';
```

Explanation . . . . **const** is a reserved word, ConstantName is a user-defined identifier, and ConstantExpression is the constant. The operator = means "is the same as." For example, "IntegerConstant is the same as 2001." Each constant declaration ends with a semicolon, to separate it from the next declaration.

NOTE

7. Constant violations. Commas and other special symbols are not permissible within *numeric* constants. For example, the representations 7,845,000 and $67.99 would provoke compile-time errors. *Character* and *string* constants must be enclosed in single quotation marks. Note that '123' is a string constant, but 123 is an integer constant.

8. When should we declare constants? Declare constants when they have descriptive meaning, since this improves *program clarity.* For example, we declared MetricConversion as the constant 0.06102 because this constant is used to convert volume in cubic centimeters to volume in cubic inches. Similarly, we declared constants Title and Line in Figure 2.1.

DECLARATION OF VARIABLES

A **variable** is a *user-defined identifier* that references a storage location having a *value* of a particular *data type*. For instance, in the Engine1 program in Figure 2.1, Units is a variable that stores an integer value that represents "number of engines sold." In the sample run, 1500 is entered and stored in this variable. Unlike declared constants, the *values associated with variables can change* as the program executes, or from one program run to another, without changes in the program itself. For example, a second run of Engine1 might include an entry like 2200 for Units. In this sense, variables in Pascal are similar to algebraic variables.

A variable thus has a name (the user-defined identifier that we select ourselves), a referenced value, and an associated data type. The program in Figure 2.1 has six variables. The var declaration section declares variable names and their associated data types. Take a look at this section now, noting that:

- Name is a *string variable* that holds up to 255 characters.
- Price, Sales, Size_cc, and Size_ci are *real variables* that store real values.
- Units is an *integer variable* that stores an integer value.

Since variables have names and reference storage locations that contain values, it's constructive to visualize a variable as the following *memory* cell.

VariableName

For example, following execution of the program in Figure 2.1, we can describe the six variables as follows.

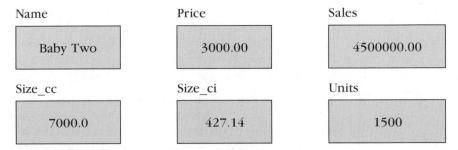

Name | Price | Sales
Baby Two | 3000.00 | 4500000.00

Size_cc | Size_ci | Units
7000.0 | 427.14 | 1500

During compilation the compiler identifies these variables and their data types; it's only during execution that these variables reference defined values.

Before we design and code a program, we need to clearly specify the variable requirements in stage 1 of the software development cycle. This means that we need to identify and describe each variable in the program. These variables are then used in the pseudocode version of the program (stage 2) to describe the algorithmic or execution logic. In stage 3, we code the program itself and declare these variables by specifying their names and data types. The accompanying syntax box describes the details for these declarations.

SYNTAX BOX

Declaration of variables ... Identifies variables and their data types in var section

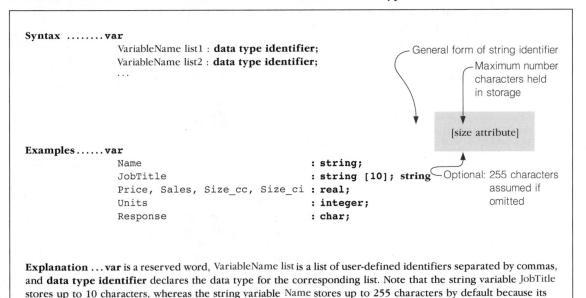

Syntax .... **var**
VariableName list1 : **data type identifier;**
VariableName list2 : **data type identifier;**
...

General form of string identifier
Maximum number characters held in storage

[size attribute]

Examples ...... **var**
Name   : **string;**
JobTitle   : **string [10]; string**
Price, Sales, Size_cc, Size_ci : **real;**
Units   : **integer;**
Response   : **char;**

Optional: 255 characters assumed if omitted

Explanation ... **var** is a reserved word, VariableName list is a list of user-defined identifiers separated by commas, and **data type identifier** declares the data type for the corresponding list. Note that the string variable JobTitle stores up to 10 characters, whereas the string variable Name stores up to 255 characters by default because its size attribute is omitted. Each variable declaration is separated from the next with a semicolon.

> ## NOTE
>
> **9. Variables: Compilation versus execution.** The compiler uses var declarations to identify the *names* and *data types* of all variables. It also reserves memory cells for their use. *Values* for these variables are processed only during execution.

OTHER DECLARATIONS

Up to this point, we have covered the following optional declarations within the program declarations section:

- **const** declarations
- **var** declarations

We have yet to cover the following three optional declarations:

- **type** declarations
- **procedure** declarations
- **function** declarations

The **type** declarations are used to construct new data types different from the standard data types discussed thus far. We introduce these in Chapter 7.

The **procedure** and **function** declarations enable us to break down programs into smaller, more manageable segments called *procedures* and *functions,* a practice that's consistent with good program design. These declarations are extremely important. We take a detailed look in the next chapter.

The **label** declaration is a sixth kind of declaration that's used to unconditionally move execution from one section of the program to another. We will not cover this declaration, since its use is inconsistent with good program design.

MAIN BODY

The third major section of a Pascal program is the **main body**, also called the **program body**. As seen in Figure 2.1, this section is bracketed by the reserved words **begin** and **end**. *Note that the entire program ends with the period following* **end**.

The main body contains *statements* that correspond to the algorithmic design or pseudocode in the design stage. A **statement** is an instruction that describes algorithmic action, *executable* tasks like "Read name" and "Calculate and store sales." Elements of the program in the program heading, const section, and var section *declare* certain information needed by the compiler. They do not, however, cause *executable* actions while the program is running. *It's the statements that cause executable action.*

In Figure 2.1 we have 21 statements in the main body, *each separated from the other by a semicolon.* The first eight statements carry out a keyboard input dialog with the user, the next two compute and store values, and the remaining statements output the required report.

NOTE

10. On semicolons. A semicolon is used to *separate* (a) the program heading from what follows, (b) consecutive declarations in the declarations section, and (c) consecutive statements in the main body. Take a look at program Engine1 in Figure 2.1. Ignore for now the text between each pair of braces { }. We have a semicolon at the end of the program heading to separate it from the first declaration, a semicolon at the end of each constant declaration, a semicolon at the end of each variable declaration, and a semicolon after each statement in the main body. The last semicolon just before **end** is optional. So how come we don't have semicolons just after **const**, **var**, and **begin**? Because these define the beginning of a declaration or statement, not the end. Strictly speaking, the semicolon is not a part of the program heading, constant declaration, variable declaration, or statement. It is a *separator* between these successive elements.

2.4 PROGRAM COMMENTS

• • • • • • • • • • • • • •

Comments are explanatory remarks within a program that aid reader understanding. In Figure 2.1,

```
{Name of engine}
```

is a comment that describes the declared variable *Name.*

SYNTAX

The syntax box on page 43 describes the comment.

DOCUMENTATION

Documentation is the use of comments within a program to aid human understanding. The "bottom-line" objective in program documentation is the reduction of software costs associated with program maintenance. Programs have a useful life cycle that includes costly maintenance for adding, deleting,

SYNTAX BOX

Comment...Documents programs

Syntax ....{ Comment }
          or
          (*Comment*)

Examples......{This is a comment}
           (*This is another comment*)

Explanation...The left *brace* { or left (* signals the compiler that what follows is a Comment, or text. All text to the right brace } or right *) is ignored by the compiler. If the first character of text is $, however, the comment is taken as a *compiler directive,* as described in Appendix G. We can place comments anywhere in a program that accepts a blank, although generally we place comments at the beginning or end of program lines. Comments may also extend across multiple lines.

and revising requirements, not to mention fixing bugs. Actual programs are long, complex creations that are full of pitfalls for either the now-rusty developers or the newly assigned programmers.

Complicating the picture is the fact that programmers like to program ... even live to program! And many of these same programmers don't view documentation as programming. So, the tendency is to give documentation short shrift, adding it as a hurried afterthought, if at all. The result is programs that are more difficult to understand and change—in short, programs that are more costly to maintain.

You may not like documenting your programs. Just take the perspective that it's useful, that it's the correct thing to do, that it can include creative writing, that the program possibly lives for others to nurture... *and that you will get a better grade!*

With this in mind, consider the following documentation for your programs, using the documentation in Figure 2.1 as a guide.

- Include a title, brief description, your name, date, and other "title page" information that's useful (or required by your instructor) following the program heading.
- Describe each variable on the same line as its declaration.
- Segment major sections of the program with "dividing" lines for better visual and functional focus.
- Include the name of the program following **begin** and **end** in the main body. This is useful in distinguishing other **begin** and **end** words that we will have in programs starting in the next chapter.
- Later, as algorithmic logic gets more complicated, additional explanatory comments help to clarify logic.

Don't restrict yourself to the preceding ideas or format. There is room to express your creativity. Try not to be too brief, or too elaborate. The right balance depends on the program, and comes with experience.

2.5 INPUT/OUTPUT STATEMENTS

An **input statement** transfers data from an external device like the keyboard to memory cells. An **output statement** copies data from memory cells to an external device such as a monitor or printer. Pascal implements I/O statements as procedure calls. A **procedure** is a piece of code that performs a specific task, like input or output. The Turbo Pascal compiler provides a set of built-in procedures called **standard** or **predeclared procedures** for common tasks. A **procedure call** is a statement that implements the action associated with a procedure. Input and output statements are procedure calls.[1]

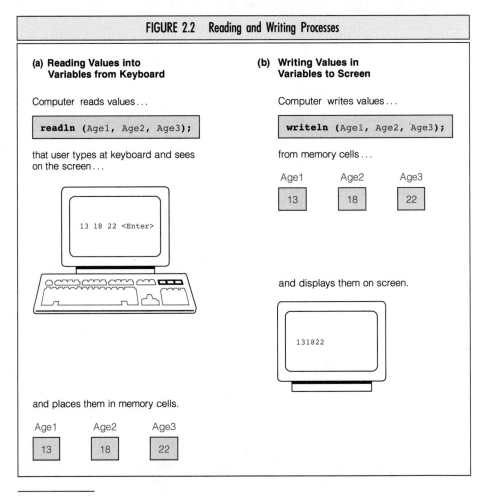

FIGURE 2.2   Reading and Writing Processes

(a) Reading Values into Variables from Keyboard

Computer reads values...

readln (Age1, Age2, Age3);

that user types at keyboard and sees on the screen...

```
13 18 22 <Enter>
```

and places them in memory cells.

Age1   Age2   Age3

13   18   22

(b) Writing Values in Variables to Screen

Computer writes values...

writeln (Age1, Age2, Age3);

from memory cells...

Age1   Age2   Age3

13   18   22

and displays them on screen.

```
131822
```

---

[1]Appendix E describes selected standard procedures in Turbo Pascal.

Calls to Predeclared I/O Procedures

The following syntax boxes describe calls to three standard I/O procedures. For now, assume that the input device is the keyboard and the output device is the monitor. Study these together with the examples in Figure 2.2. The sample programs that follow further illustrate their use.

SYNTAX BOX

Call to procedure readln ... Read values from the keyboard into memory cells

---

Syntax .... **readln** (InputVariable list);

	Sample keyboard entry:	*Resulting storage:*
Examples....... **readln** (Name);	Baby Two <Enter key>	Baby Two in Name
readln (Age1, Age2, Age3);	13 18 22 <Enter key>	13 in Age1, 18 in Age2, 22 in Age3

Explanation ..... **readln** is a standard identifier. InputVariable list is a list of variables separated by commas. Only variables of type integer, real, character, and string are permitted. Enter a value for each variable in the list. Press the *Enter key* after entering the last value. Order the values according to the order of variables in the list. Match variables and values with respect to type: integer value with integer variable, string value with string variable, and so on. The input rules for entering multiple values are complicated. For now, follow these guidelines to avoid errors.
 (1) Avoid mixing types in the same list.
 (2) Separate the input of successive numeric values with a space or the Enter key.
 (3) Input successive character values without intervening spaces, or press the
     Enter key after each character value.
 (4) Terminate the input of a string value with the Enter key.

SYNTAX BOX

Call to procedure writeln or write ... Display values

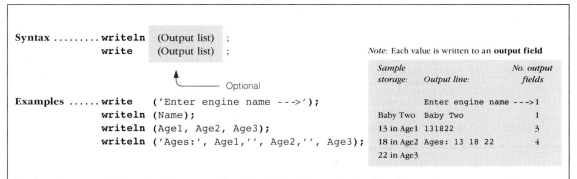

Syntax .... **writeln**   (Output list) ;
             write   (Output list) ;

              ———— Optional

Note: Each value is written to an **output field**

	Sample storage:	*Output line:*	*No. output fields*
Examples ...... **write** ('Enter engine name --->');		Enter engine name --->1	
writeln (Name);	Baby Two	Baby Two	1
writeln (Age1, Age2, Age3);	13 in Age1	131822	3
writeln ('Ages:', Age1,'', Age2,'', Age3);	18 in Age2	Ages: 13 18 22	4
	22 in Age3		

Explanation ... **writeln** and **write** are standard identifiers. Output list is a list of output items separated by commas. For now, assume each item is either a constant or a variable. An expression (Section 2.6) is also a valid item. Only items of type integer, real, character, string, or Boolean are permitted. After values in the output list are written, the **writeln** procedure advances the cursor to the beginning of the next line; the **write** procedure does not advance the cursor. If the parenthetic output list is omitted in the call to **writeln**, the cursor moves to the beginning of the next line from its current position.

EXAMPLE 2.1   INPUT AND OUTPUT MEDLEY

Study the program and its I/O in Figure 2.3 along with the following related points.

1. The first four lines in the program illustrate **conversational** or **interactive input.** This means that any value that's to be entered at the keyboard is preceded by a *prompt* that conversationally requests the value. See the I/O lines labeled 1–4 in the Output Window. Paired write and readln statements are the best way to accomplish this. If we were to use **writeln** instead of **write**, then we would enter data values immediately below the prompt at the left margin.

FIGURE 2.3   Listing and I/O for Program Medley1 (Example 2.1)

(a) Listing in Edit Window

```
program Medley1;

   {* * * * * * * * * * * * * * * * * * * * * * * * * * * * * * * * * * *
    *                                                                   *
    *            Input and Output Medley                                *
    *                                                                   *
    *            Inputs integer, real, character, and string values     *
    *            Outputs entered values                                 *
    *                                                                   *
    * * * * * * * * * * * * * * * * * * * * * * * * * * * * * * * * * * *}

   {============================ Declarations ============================}

const
   Blanks = '     ';                    {Five-blank constant}

var
   IntVar1,  IntVar2   : integer;       {Integer variables}
   RealVar1, RealVar2  : real;          {Real variables}
   CharVar             : char;          {Character variable}
   StringVar           : string;        {String variable}

   {============================ Main Body ============================}

begin   {Medley1}

   write (' 1: Enter two integer values---> ');   readln (IntVar1, IntVar2);
   write (' 2: Enter two real values------> ');   readln (RealVar1, RealVar2);
   write (' 3: Enter character value------> ');   readln (CharVar);
   write (' 4: Enter string value--------> ');    readln (StringVar);
   writeln;
   writeln (' 5: Two integers............', IntVar1, IntVar2);
   writeln (' 6: Two integers w/Blanks...', IntVar1, Blanks, IntVar2);
   writeln (' 7: First real..............', RealVar1);
   writeln (' 8: Second real.............', RealVar2);
   writeln (' 9: Two reals...............', RealVar1, RealVar2);
   writeln ('10: Character...............', CharVar);
   writeln ('11: Two characters..........', CharVar, CharVar);
   writeln ('12: String..................', StringVar);
   writeln ('13: Two strings w/Blanks....', StringVar, Blanks, StringVar);
   writeln ('14: Constants...............', ' $', 123, 9.99, '   123', '%');
   writeln ('15: Embedded apostrophe.....', 'Don''t do it!  Well... OK');

end.    {Medley1}
```

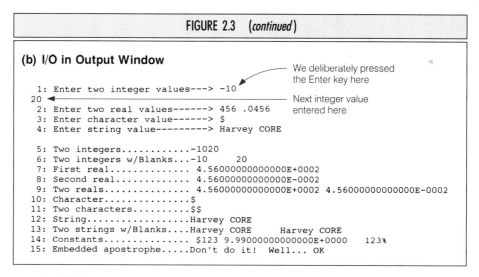

FIGURE 2.3 *(continued)*

(b) I/O in Output Window

```
                                              We deliberately pressed
                                              the Enter key here
 1: Enter two integer values---> -10
20                                            Next integer value
 2: Enter two real values------> 456 .0456    entered here
 3: Enter character value------> $
 4: Enter string value--------> Harvey CORE

 5: Two integers............-1020
 6: Two integers w/Blanks...-10     20
 7: First real............. 4.56000000000000E+0002
 8: Second real............ 4.56000000000000E-0002
 9: Two reals.............. 4.56000000000000E+0002 4.56000000000000E-0002
10: Character..............$
11: Two characters.........$$
12: String.................Harvey CORE
13: Two strings w/Blanks...Harvey CORE     Harvey CORE
14: Constants.............. $123 9.99000000000000E+0000    123%
15: Embedded apostrophe.....Don't do it!  Well... OK
```

---

2. In I/O line 1, we deliberately followed the first integer value with a press of the Enter key to show you that the readln procedure waits for the second value to be entered, which we did on the next line at the left margin.

3. Line 2 in the Output window shows the entry of two real values. Note that we *separated these values by a space*. The system terminates input of the first value when it encounters the space. Also note that we didn't use a decimal point for the first one; the system converts it internally to its floating-point representation. If the input variable is type integer, however, we may not place a period at the end of the integer value. This would give a run-time error.

4. Character values and string values are entered without surrounding single quotations, as in lines 3 and 4. Quotation marks are used only for character constants and string constants within the program itself, as seen in each write statement.

5. The writeln statement without an output list in the fifth line of the program is used for vertical spacing in the Output window; it visually separates the input portion from the output portion, thereby improving the readability of the screen.

6. Compare lines 5 and 6 in the Output window. Integers are written without leading or trailing spaces. To separate two output values, we can output a blank string constant between them.

7. Lines 7–9 show the output of real values in scientific form. We show conventional fractional output in our next example.

8. Lines 10–13 show that character and string output are written as stored, with no surrounding blanks. To separate character or string output fields, we can include a blank constant between each pair of output variables, as seen in the statement that writes line 13.

9. Line 14 shows the output of various string, integer, real, and character constants.

10. Line 15 illustrates the need to embed a double apostrophe to represent the single apostrophe within a string constant.

11. Finally, we called **writeln**, not **write**, to output lines 5–15; otherwise, we would not get a separate line of output for each output statement.

The term **formatted output** or output with **formats** means that the programmer uses language features that allow more precise control of output, rather than letting the compiler use its default formats. Output is formatted by applying the field-width option described in the next syntax box.

All output in Example 2.1 is **unformatted output** because compiler defaults determine the width of output fields and the form of real values (scientific). The next example illustrates formatted output.

SYNTAX BOX

Call to procedure writeln or write...Display formatted values

Syntax........	**writeln** (List of OutputItem :FieldWidth : DecimalPlaces);		
	write (List of OutputItem :FieldWidth : Decimal Places);		

	Sample storage:	*Output line:*	*No. output fields*
Examples......**writeln** ('X =', X :6:2);	3.1 in X	X = 3.10	2
writeln (Age1 :2, Age2 :3, Age3 :4);	13 in Age1	13 18 22	3
	18 in Age2		
	22 in Age3		

Explanation...These calls are similar to those in the preceding syntax box, except output items are optionally formatted by specifying output field widths and decimal places. FieldWidth is an integer expression and :Fieldwidth specifies the minimum number of character positions in the output field. DecimalPlaces is an integer expression and : DecimalPlaces specifies the number of decimal places displayed in the fixed-point form of a real value. Values are written *right-justified* (at the extreme right) in the output field.

EXAMPLE 2.2   INPUT AND OUTPUT MEDLEY... WITH FORMATTED OUTPUT

Now take a look at the program in Figure 2.4 and consider the following points regarding formatted output.

1. Line 1 shows the output of integer value 123 in a field width of three. The field width and number of characters in the value are identical. Line 2 shows what

---

FIGURE 2.4   Listing and I/O for Program Medley2 (Example 2.2)

(a) Listing in Edit Window

```
program Medley2;

    {* * * * * * * * * * * * * * * * * * * * * * * * * * * * * * * * * *
     *                                                                 *
     *         Input and Output Medley... With Formatted Output        *
     *                                                                 *
     *           Inputs integer, real, and string values              *
     *           Outputs entered values using field widths            *
     *                                                                 *
     * * * * * * * * * * * * * * * * * * * * * * * * * * * * * * * * * *}

    {============================ Declarations ============================}
var
    IntVar    : integer;      {Integer variable}
    RealVar   : real;         {Real variable}
    StringVar : string;       {String variable}

    {============================ Main Body ============================}
begin   {Medley2}

    write ('Enter integer value---> ');  readln (IntVar);
    write ('Enter real value------> ');  readln (RealVar);
    write ('Enter string value----> ');  readln (StringVar);
    writeln;
    writeln (' 1: Integer.................', IntVar :3);
    writeln (' 2: Integer.................', IntVar :5);
    writeln (' 3: Integer.................', IntVar :1);
    writeln (' 4: Two integers...........', IntVar :10, IntVar :5);
    writeln (' 5: Integer with %.........', IntVar :6, '%');
    writeln (' 6: Real...................', RealVar :10:3);
    writeln (' 7: Real...................', RealVar :10:2);
    writeln (' 8: String.................', StringVar :6);
    writeln (' 9: String.................', StringVar :3);
    writeln ('10: String.................', StringVar :10);

end.    {Medley2}
```

(b) I/O in Output Window

```
Enter integer value---> 123
Enter real value------> -3.176
Enter string value----> Pascal

 1: Integer.................123
 2: Integer...............  123
 3: Integer.................123
 4: Two integers...........       123   123
 5: Integer with %.........   123%
 6: Real...................    -3.176
 7: Real...................     -3.18
 8: String.................Pascal
 9: String.................Pascal
10: String.................    Pascal
```

happens when the field width is greater than the number of positions needed to output the value. In this case the field width is five and the value takes up three positions. The system thus prints the value *right-justified* within the output field; that is, the leftmost unused positions (two in this case) are padded with blanks by the system. Line 3 shows the third possibility: The field width is not large enough to accommodate the value. In this case the value is written as in line 1; any other fields that might be written on the same line are simply pushed to the right. Generally, we would want to select a field width that's somewhat larger than the number of positions needed to output the value (including any negative sign). This allows precise control of horizontal spacing and vertical alignment in columns, as seen in Figure 2.1.

2. Line 4 shows the use of field widths to write multiple integer values on one line with appropriate spaces as visual separators.

3. The example in line 5 demonstrates how we can attach certain common symbols to numeric output, in this instance the percent sign. Figure 2.1 shows the same idea for the dollar sign.

4. Line 6 shows the output of a real value in the conventional decimal form rather than the scientific form. To avoid output in scientific form (which is generally unappealing but sometimes necessary), we have to specify *both* field width and decimal places.

5. Line 7 shows that the system *rounds* real values when the specified number of decimal places is smaller than the stored number of decimal places. In this case, the value -3.176 was rounded to -3.18.

6. Lines 8–10 show the output of string values with field widths that are equal to, less than, and greater than the number of characters stored in the string. As with integer output, unused leftmost positions in the output field are padded with blanks (the string is right-justified), as seen in line 10. If the programmer provides insufficient space to output the string, the system grabs it anyway, as seen in line 9.

NOTE

11. Multistatement lines. The use of the semicolon as a statement separator means that the placement of more than one statement on a program line is permissible. The conventional wisdom has it that multistatement lines should not be used because they degrade program readability. In general this is true. As with all rules, however, it's the exceptions that are interesting. Our guiding wisdom should be *do what improves program readability.* In our view, pairing readln statements with their corresponding write statements—as in Figures 2.1, 2.4, and 2.5—improves program clarity.

12. On good output design. Good program design includes good output design. Take care in designing output that clearly communicates. Avoid clutter, unlabeled output, and otherwise *ugly* output. The latter, of course, is in the "eye of the beholder" (probably your instructor). The output design in Figure 2.1 looks good (in our opinion); that in Figures 2.3 and 2.4 is unavoidably messy, but presumably serves the intended purpose of describing output features.

13. On good input design. In designing and writing your programs, take the perspective that others will be using your programs. When you write interactive programs, always use conversational input, because this clearly communicates to the user the values that are requested by the program. *Generally, it's best to request a single input value per line.* Multiple input values with mixed types on one line promote input errors, as in entering values out of proper sequence and mismatching type. As usual, we have exceptions to rules. *There are circumstances when more than one input value per line is okay.* For example, we are inclined to use multiple inputs of *related numeric values,* as in the three ages entered in the syntax box example for the readln statement.

Keyboard Versus Data-File Input

Input from a file on a disk is a common alternative to input from the keyboard. This form of input is especially suitable for processing large amounts of data, such as payroll applications and bank statement mailings.

A **data file** is a file that gets processed by a program. From a functional standpoint, we now have two types of files: the **program file** that contains the Pascal program and the data file that contains the input data.

Data-file processing is an enormously important task in practice. Its meaningful implementation, however, requires more sophisticated programming than the programming in this chapter. Chapter 4 introduces data files.

Screen Versus Printer Output

As you know, Turbo Pascal assumes the *monitor* as the default output device. Other common output devices include printers and disk drives. We describe output to the printer next, and save output to disk files until later in the book.

First some preliminaries. A Turbo Pascal **unit** is a related collection of constants, data types, variables, procedures, and functions. It's similar to a precompiled program for a specific purpose like printer output, graphics, or screen control with colors and other special effects. Turbo Pascal has six **standard units** that we can use in our programming. We describe and use some of these later in the book. For now, our interest is in the standard unit named **printer**.

To use the printer for output, we first need to include the following stipulation or *clause* between the program heading and the first set of program declarations:

    uses printer;

The reserved word **uses** indicates that we wish to use a unit, and the standard identifier **printer** specifies that we wish to specifically use the printer unit. The printer unit itself declares a variable named **Lst** that is associated with the printer. All we need to do is place **Lst** as the first variable in the output list of a write or writeln statement. For example, the statements

    writeln (Lst, Title);
    writeln (Lst, Line);
    writeln (Lst);

are a rewrite of three output statements in Figure 2.1. The title, line, and a line skip would be printed by the printer. We let you try this out in Exercise 8.

SELF-REVIEW EXERCISES

These exercises at the end of the chapter have answers at the back of the book. Try these out now to self-test your understanding of the material in this section.

4 8

2.6 ASSIGNMENT STATEMENTS

• • • • • • • • • • • • • • •

There are two common approaches to placing values in variables: Use an input statement to copy a value from an external device to a variable in primary memory; use an **assignment statement** to copy a value into a variable when the value is either computed, stored in another variable, or a constant.

SYNTAX

The assignment statement is described by the syntax box on the facing page. An **expression** is a combination of one or more constants, variables, operators, function calls, and special symbols like parentheses. Sample *operators* include + and * in arithmetic expressions. We describe these below. *Function calls* are used for specialized manipulations like taking square roots and editing strings. We cover these in the next chapter.

SYNTAX BOX

Assignment statement... Evaluates expression and places resulting value in variable

Syntax ....Variable := Expression;

Examples......
```
Sum   := 0;
Best  := Last;
Grade := 'A';
Month := 'March';
Count := Count + 1;
Sales := Price * Units;
```

Results:
0 placed in integer variable Sum
3.25 placed in real variable Best if 3.25 is in real variable Last
A placed in character variable Grade
March placed in string variable Month
10 placed in integer variable Count if Count previously stored 9
4500000.0 placed in real variable Sales if 3000.0 is in real variable Price and 1500 is in integer variable Units

Explanation...Variable is any legitimate program variable, := is the *assignment operator,* and Expression is a constant, a variable, or one of the forms defined on page 52. Expression and Variable must be *assignment compatible* (see below). Any previous value in Variable is replaced. The assignment operator is two adjacent symbols (: and =) with no intervening space. It's treated as a single entity in Pascal. Its meaning is not the same as the equal sign in algebra; rather it means "is assigned" as in "Variable is assigned the value of the expression" or "is replaced by" as in "The value in Variable is replaced by the value of Expression." The fifth example clearly shows this distinction.

Components in an expression have associated types, and the expression itself evaluates to a particular type. We need to pay attention to type because components within an expression must be *type compatible.* For example, we can't add an integer variable and a string variable (obvious), but we can multiply an integer variable and a real variable (not so obvious). Moreover, the value of the expression itself must be *assignment compatible* with the variable to the left of the assignment operator. For instance, we can assign an integer value to a real variable, but not a real value to an integer variable. We mention this here to provide perspective. We look at the details next.

INTEGER AND REAL EXPRESSIONS

An **integer expression** evaluates to an integer value; a **real expression** evaluates to a real value. More generally, these are **arithmetic expressions,** which commonly include arithmetic operations like addition and multiplication. For example, the multiplication

is an integer expression that evaluates to 10. The asterisk is an *arithmetic operator* for multiplication; the 5 and 2 are *operands,* the elements on each side of the operator.

Table 2.2   Arithmetic Operators

Arithmetic Operator	Operation	Operand Types	Type of Result	Sample Operation	Resulting Value
+	Addition	Integer and integer	Integer	5 + 2	7
		Real and real	Real	5.0 + 2.0	7.0
		Integer and real	Real	5 + 2.0	7.0
−	Subtraction	Integer and integer	Integer	5 − 2	3
		Real and real	Real	5.0 − 2.0	3.0
		Integer and real	Real	5 − 2.0	3.0
*	Multiplication	Integer and integer	Integer	5 * 2	10
		Real and real	Real	5.0 * 2.0	10.0
		Integer and real	Real	5 * 2.0	10.0
/	Real division	Integer and integer	Real	5 / 2	2.5
		Real and real	Real	5.0 / 2.0	2.5
		Integer and real	Real	5 / 2.0	2.5
div	Integer division quotient	Integer and integer	Integer	5 div 2	2
mod	Integer division remainder	Integer and integer	Integer	5 mod 2	1

Table 2.2 describes the **arithmetic operators** *for binary operations* where each operation is an arithmetic operator sandwiched between two operands. A *unary operation* is defined by a single *operand,* as in negation.

The arithmetic operators + and − are both binary and unary arithmetic operators. The other arithmetic operators are strictly binary.

Type Compatibility

Pay attention to the allowable operands in Table 2.2, and the resulting value of the completed arithmetic operation. In particular, note the following arithmetic **type-compatibility** rules.

1. Addition, subtraction, and multiplication allow both *same-type operands* (both integer or both real) and *mixed-type operands* (one integer and the other real). Addition, subtraction, and multiplication with same-type operands give the expected corresponding results (real operands give real results and integer operands give integer results), but *mixed-type operands always give real results.* For example, in Table 2.2 the operation 5 * 2 gives *integer* 10, but the operations 5 * 2.0 gives *real* 10.0.

2. Real division allows any combination of operands, but *the result is always real.* In Table 2.2, for example, the real division 5/2 has *integer* operands, but the result is *real* 2.5.

3. Integer division with the operators **div** and **mod** strictly requires integer operands. Any real operand provokes a compile-time error. In Table 2.2, note that 2 goes into 5 twice (5 **div** 2 evaluates to 2) with a remainder of one (5 **mod** 2 gives 1).

Assignment Compatibility

When an assignment statement is executed, the expression is evaluated and its value is assigned to the variable. For example, in the Engine1 program from Figure 2.1, we might describe execution of the second assignment statement as follows.

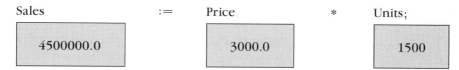

Sales   :=   Price   *   Units;

| 4500000.0 | 3000.0 | 1500 |

Note that the operation has mixed-type operands real and integer, but that these are type compatible and the resulting value is real according to the first arithmetic type-compatibility rule. The multiplication 3000.0 * 1500 gives the result 4500000.0, which is then stored in Sales. The variable Sales must be typed real (see the var section in the program) to maintain *assignment compatibility* with the resulting real value for the expression Price * Units. If Sales had been typed integer, then we would get a compile-time error for this assignment statement. The upshot? We need to pay attention to the following arithmetic **assignment-compatibility** rules.

1. If both the numeric value of an expression and a numeric variable have the same type, then they are assignment compatible, as in the example Price * Units is real and Sales is real.

2. If the numeric value of the expression and the numeric variable have different type, then. . .

    a. an integer value is assignable to a real variable, as in integer 4 is assignable to real Cost, but. . .

    b. a real value is not assignable to an integer variable (the compiler does not permit the assignment statement).

Precedence Rules

Suppose we were given the expression

        Var1 + Var2 * 2

where Var1 stores 10 and Var2 stores 5. What's the value of this expression? Is it 30, as in evaluating (10 + 5) * 2? Or is it 20 as in 10 + (5 * 2)? In Pascal the correct answer is 20. If we intended the former, then we would be guilty of a *logic error*.

When arithmetic expressions include multiple operations, we need to pay attention to the following rules.

Arithmetic Operator-Precedence Rule. A unary operation is performed first. Multiplication (*) and division (/ **div mod**) are performed before addition (+) and subtraction (−). In our example Var2 * 2 is evaluated first, giving 5 * 2 or 10, since multiplication has a higher precedence than addition. Next, the addition Var1 + 10 is performed, giving 10 + 10 or 20.

Left-to-Right Rule. The order of evaluation when two or more operators have the same precedence is consistent with a *left-to-right* scan of the arithmetic expression. For example, the expression

```
Var1 / Var2 * 2
```

where Var1 stores 10 and Var2 stores 5 evaluates to 4.0 as follows. Division and multiplication have the same precedence, so according to the left-to-right rule the division operation is implemented first, giving 2.0. Next, the operation 2.0 * 2 is executed, giving 4.0.

Parentheses Rule. Expressions within parentheses are called *subexpressions*. All subexpressions are evaluated before expressions. If more than one subexpression is present, then subexpressions are evaluated in a *left-to-right* scan of the subexpressions. If subexpressions are *nested*, as in one set of parentheses inside another, then innermost subexpressions are evaluated first. Example 2.3 illustrates the use of parentheses.

CHARACTER AND STRING EXPRESSIONS

A **character expression** is a character constant, character variable, or function call that evaluates to a single character. For example, 'A' is a character constant that we can assign to the character variable Grade with the assignment statement

```
Grade := 'A';
```

A **string expression** evaluates to a string value; it can include a string constant, string variable, function call, or some combination of string and character constants, variables, function calls, and operators. For example, we can assign the string constant 'March' to the string variable Month as follows:

```
Month := 'March';
```

If we had typed Month in the var section with the declaration

```
Month : string [7];
```

EXAMPLE 2.3   USE OF PARENTHESES

The following assignment statement converts temperatures from Fahrenheit to Celsius.

        Celsius := 5 / 9 * (Fahrenheit - 32);

Suppose both variables are typed real and Fahrenheit stores 212.0. This assignment statement would be evaluated as follows.

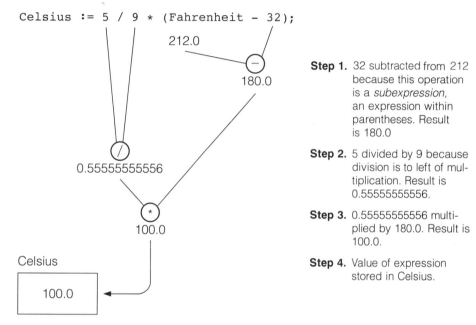

Step 1. 32 subtracted from 212 because this operation is a *subexpression*, an expression within parentheses. Result is 180.0

Step 2. 5 divided by 9 because division is to left of multiplication. Result is 0.55555555556.

Step 3. 0.55555555556 multiplied by 180.0. Result is 100.0.

Step 4. Value of expression stored in Celsius.

Note that the elimination of parentheses in the subexpression (Fahrenheit − 32) would give the following assignment statement.

        Celsius := 5 / 9 * Fahrenheit - 32;

Its evaluation would give 85.777777778, a logic error. (Check it out!)

then Month stores up to seven characters. The assignment statement above would produce the following memory cell allocation.

Month

String value fits in storage

Since the value March is five characters, we have unused or excess storage capacity of two characters. Suppose, however, that the executed assignment statement is

Month := 'September';

Now storage is given by

Month

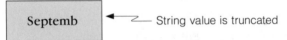

The processor thus *truncated* the last two characters er, since September has nine characters and only seven characters fit in storage. As in input operations, we need to specify large enough size attributes to avoid unintended truncation.

We can use the **concatenation operator +** to join two string operands within a string expression. For example, given the current storage

execution of the assignment statement

```
MaleGreeting := 'Dear Mr.' + LastName;
```

changes storage as follows.

We can use square brackets following a string variable to access individual characters in a string by position, as follows.

StringVariable[character position]

For example, LastName[1] references the first character in LastName, or C given the storage above. LastName[3] would reference R. Given the storage

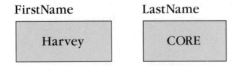

the assignment statement

Initials := FirstName[1] + LastName[1];

would store HC in Initials

Initials

HC

As in arithmetic expressions and assignments, string expressions and assignments live by type- and assignment-compatibility rules. The character-string **type-compatibility** rule simply states that string and character types are type compatible in an expression. The character-string **assignment-compatibility** rule states the following.

1. If both the value of the expression and the variable have the same type, then they are assignment compatible, as in the assignment of the character type value A to the character variable Grade.
2. If the value of the expression and the variable have different type, then . . .

    a. a character value is assignable to a string variable, as in character A is assignable to string Month, but . . .
    b. a string value is not assignable to a character variable (the compiler does not permit the assignment statement).

The manipulation of string expressions is a rather interesting and involved subject in programming. In Chapter 10 we will take up the subject in earnest.

SELF-REVIEW EXERCISES

These exercises at the end of the chapter have answers at the back of the book. Try these out now to self-test your understanding of the material in this section.

9 10 11 12

2.7   PROGRAMMING TIPS

Consider the following tips to improve the design and style of your programs and to avoid some common errors.

DESIGN AND STYLE

Methods for improving the design and style of programs are important in commercial applications for two reasons: First, good design and style improve the readability or clarity of programs. This increases the reliability and facilitates the development, testing, and subsequent maintenance of programs—all of which reduce software costs. Second, programs that are easier to use because of good I/O design are more effective (and sell better!) than programs that pay scant attention to this so-called *user interface*. In your program writing for this course, you should take this commercial perspective to appreciate what's happening in practice.

The following suggestions should improve the design and style (and the grades!) of your programs.

1. On Providing Data. Before designing and writing programs, think carefully about the treatment of provided data. There are four choices:

   a. As *constants*
   b. As *declared constants* in the const section
   c. As *assigned variables* in the left member of assignment statements
   d. As *input variables* in the input lists of an input statement.

The first key decision is whether to treat a data item as a constant or a variable. If the data item has little or no likelihood of changing over time, then it's a good candidate for a constant; otherwise, declare it as a variable. For example, the metric conversion value 0.06102 in the HC ENGINE application is fixed forever, and we treated it as a constant. The price of an engine, however, is likely to change every time the program is run, so we declared the variable Price in the var section. If price were a constant rather than a variable, then we would have to edit the program before each run to change the price, a clearly costly strategy. Between these two extremes we have a gray area. Constants that change often (such as tax rates!) require costly program maintenance; variables that change infrequently require higher input costs. The high cost of program maintenance relative to the cost of input (programmers get paid more than data entry clerks) favors the selection of variables over constants.

If we decide on a constant, then we have a secondary decision. Should we *declare* this constant in the const section? Constants with descriptive meaning, like MetricConversion, should be declared. This improves program clarity and simplifies maintenance in case we have to change the constant in the future.

If we decide on a variable, we need to consider whether we will provide its value via an assignment statement or an input statement. If the value is computed, the choice is obvious: Use an assignment statement. If the value is provided by a user, the choice is equally obvious: Use a readln statement.

2. On Selecting Data Type. Variables need to be explicitly typed in the var section. If the variable is numeric, then our fundamental choices are *type integer* versus *type real*. Use type integer for variables that strictly store whole-number values, unless they're too big; otherwise, use type real.

Use type char for variables that store single characters and type string for those that store strings of characters. If you use a *size attribute* for a string variable, make sure that it's large enough to accommodate the largest string that it would store.

3. On Naming Identifiers. Select names that have descriptive meaning for declared constants, variables, and other user-defined identifiers. For example, the identifier Price suggests a price. Be aware that we can't select a name that's identical to a *reserved word* and we don't suggest that you redefine *standard identifiers*. See the inside back cover of the book if you're unsure whether a name you're considering would conflict with reserved or standard identifiers.

4. On Spacing. Use the *blank space character* where it's required to separate identifiers from surrounding material. For example, **program** must be separated from the name of the program by at least one blank space. Otherwise use blank spaces to improve readability, as in surrounding operators like + with spaces or following a comma with a space (it's not all that different from spacing rules in typing papers).

Also use spaces to *indent* program lines for greater readability. For example, look at the indentation in Figure 2.1. We place the reserved words that define major sections of the program (**program, const, var, begin,** and **end**) flush against the left margin. All other program lines are indented (how much is a matter of personal preference). A scan of the left margin thus easily identifies major program sections, and indentation within a section clearly implies membership in that section.

Use *blank lines* to further improve clarity. Just where we place blank lines and to what extent is a matter of preference. Notice our choices in the program shown in Figure 2.1. A good rule is to precede the major sections like **const, var,** and **begin** with a blank line. Keep on spacing...

5. Document, Document. Don't forget to document your programs. See the discussion in Section 2.4 on documentation.

6. On Input Design. In using interactive input, make sure it's *conversational*. It's usually best to request only *one data item per input line*. This reduces the likelihood of input errors. There are exceptions, however, as described in Note 13.

7. On Output Design. Pay attention to output design. Facilitate its readability and understanding by well-chosen labels, alignment, and spacing. Avoid clutter and unlabeled output. Use *natural capitalization* (upper- and lowercase letters as we're accustomed to in written English). Before actually writing your write or writeln statements, you should *map out* your output design on a sheet of paper.

8. On Saving and Backing Up Files.   Most of us who have been around computers for a while are paranoid about losing program files. Disk-head "crashes" that render program files unusable are common occurrences. Make sure you *save* a program file that you finish editing before you turn off the machine. In a long session at the keyboard, it's best to periodically save the file (say, every half hour).

Also, *back up* your program file by having a duplicate under another name. For example, if your program file is called PROG1, back it up under the name PROG1.BAK. So, if you had a bad night and the next morning you inadvertently delete a large section of your program (or, worse yet, the entire program), you can fall back on the "cloned" backup. You can back up your program file from within the IDE by the commands File and Save as. . . Within the DOS environment, you can use the **COPY** command.

Paper is another backup medium. You should always have a *paper copy* of your latest program file. Print the file from within the IDE by the command sequence File Print. If this turns out to be your only backup medium, then at the very worst you've lost typing time instead of the very demoralizing "refiguring" time.

All of this might seem like a nuisance and a bit exaggerated. You will change your mind the first time you lose an important file that you have to recreate from scratch. Over the years our students have fried diskettes on sunny car dashboards, scrambled them in front of 15-inch woofers, and spilled all kinds of concoctions on their surfaces. *There are only two kinds of computer users: Those who have lost files and those who will lose files.*

COMMON ERRORS

1. Typing Errors.   Watch the spelling of reserved words and standard identifiers. Many typos will get flagged as the compile-time error *Unknown identifier*. A more subtle problem: Mistyped variable names appearing in more than one place. For example, if the declared variable is Units and elsewhere we use Unit (forgetting the s), then it's an unknown identifier.

2. Incorrect Names.   Take care with the naming rules for user-defined identifiers, as described in Section 2.1. Remember that spaces are not allowed in names, nor any other special symbol except underscore. A syntax violation here will earn you a compile-time error message for each program line that contains the variable.

3. Not Declaring Identifiers.   Don't forget to declare variables and their data types before using them. This also gives the compile-time error *Unknown identifier*.

4. On Spacing Out (On Syntax Rules).   Inattention to the syntax rules described in the syntax boxes is common. Take care with the proper use of the semicolon (see Note 10). If you forget to place one where it's needed you get the compile-time error *";" expected.* Don't use commas or other special symbols within constants. And remember to enclose comments with a pair of braces. Forgetting the right brace is very common. If the program has no other right brace, then the entire program is taken as a comment, giving an *Unexpected end-of-file* error message! Don't forget that the IDE's Help facility includes syntax help. For example, place the cursor on an identifier like **writeln**, and press **Ctrl-F1** for an explanation of its use, syntax, and examples.

5. Incorrect Assignment Statements.   Remember that the assignment operator is the coupled symbols := without a space. The = symbol is not an assignment operator in Pascal (like it is in many other languages). Instead it's used in constant declarations (we will see other uses for it later as well).

Try not to violate the *type-* and *assignment-compatibility rules* discussed in Section 2.6. A common error here is trying to assign a real value to an integer variable, which gives the error message *Type mismatch.*

Pay close attention to precedence, left-to-right, and parentheses rules when forming arithmetic expressions. Two especially common syntax errors are unmatched parentheses and missing arithmetic operators.

6. Incorrect Output Statements.   Don't forget to include the surrounding single quotation marks for character and string constants in output lists. This error is very common, giving the likely message *String constant exceeds line.* Also, make sure successive items in the output list are separated by a comma. If not, you will most likely get the error message *")" expected,* which you may not find that illuminating.

7. Input Errors.   Make sure to enter the exact number of values required by the variable list in the readln statement, and that they *match by type* (especially numeric values paired with numeric variables, and string values paired with string variables). A common run-time error message is *Invalid numeric format;* the system expects a numeric digit and finds an illegal numeric character like a letter.

8. Logic Errors.   Most beginning programmers breathe a *big* sigh of relief once their program compiles without errors and executes without run-time errors. But it's not over yet. . . *Always validate your program by checking your output data against results that you know are correct.* Common logic errors include not paying attention to units of measure (like mixing meters and yards), missing or incomplete output statements, incorrect data input, misunderstanding how arithmetic expressions are evaluated ("*What* precedence rules?"), initialization errors, and statements out of logical sequence (like a writeln statement before a needed readln statement).

9. I Have an Error!   So what happens when we have errors? The system places us back in the editor when it detects compile-time and fatal run-time errors, and an error message appears at the top of the editor. Basically, we're on our own in figuring out the error. A press of the help (F1) key gives additional information on the error, and a press of **Ctrl-F1** gives syntax help at the cursor's position. We then correct the error and recompile/run (**Ctrl-F9**). If we have a logic error, the system is no help; it's up to us to detect this error by comparing test output to results that we know are correct. A good way to detect run-time and logic errors is to develop a ...

10. Desk-Check Script. A classic way of reducing the likelihood of compile-time, run-time, and logic errors is to **desk check** (also called **desk test** and **roleplay**) the program. We do this by mentally going over each line in a listing of the program. One pass of the program could be a syntax check, where we carefully confirm the syntax of each line. For example, do we have necessary commas and apostrophes in output lists? Does each statement end with a semicolon?

Another desk-check pass would be a statement by statement roleplay of computer execution; that is, we "execute" each statement as if we were the computer, keeping track of memory contents of variables as we go along. This is an extremely effective technique for uncovering run-time and logic errors in our *program algorithm*.

A good way to document a desk check is to develop a **desk-check script**, a written statement of the desk check as we "execute" each line in the pseudocode or program. To illustrate, let's develop a desk-check script for program Engine1 in Figure 2.1.

Line 1. Prompt and enter engine name ...
Baby two stored in Name.

2. Prompt and enter engine size in cc ...
7000.0 stored in Size_cc.

3. Prompt and enter engine price ...
3000.0 stored in Price.

4. Prompt and enter units sold ...
1500 stored in Units.

5. Assign engine size in ci ...
0.06102 * 7000.0 or 427.14 stored in Size_ci.

6. Assign sales revenue ...
3000.0 * 1500 or 4500000 stored in Sales.

7. Space down one row on screen.

8. Write Title or SALES REPORT and space down one row.

... and so on.

Get the idea? Note that the format of a desk-check script is based on personal preference. Just make sure it follows the pseudocode or program algorithm line by line, and keep track of I/O, stored values, and other actions. *Get in the habit of desk checking your design and program algorithms before you compile/run, and afterward should you encounter errors.*

REVIEW EXERCISES

ON REVIEW EXERCISES

- Reinforce, integrate, extend examples in chapter
- Appear in same order as examples
- Starred (*) exercises have no answers in back of text
  These are usually more difficult than unstarred exercises
- Exercises with Ⓛ use Examples or Utiities Library on disk
- Exercise parts (**a**, **b**, **c**, . . .) are in increasing order of difficulty

EASIER   For the busy. . .
           1 2 9 10a–d

NORMAL   For the thinkers. . .
           3 4 5 6 7 8 10e 11 12

TOUGHER For the hard CORE. . .
           13

NOTE

14. Examples library reminder. The sample programs in each chapter are available on disk. The names of program and data files are consistent with program names, and are also displayed inside the front cover. Your instructor will describe how you can access these files. Use this library of sample programs as a starting point for solving exercises that reference examples. Simply load and edit the existing program according to the exercise, save it under a new name, and compile/execute it. The exercises that explicitly make use of the library are marked with the symbol Ⓛ.

---

1. Which of the following are legal identifiers? If a name is unacceptable, indicate why.
   a. X
   b. x
   c. 3Item
   d. Item3
   e. $Rate

      f. String
      g. Musical Score
      h. Musical-Score
      i. Musical_Score
      j. MusicalScore

2. Identify the data type of each acceptable constant below. Identify and correct any unacceptable constants.

    a. 5,000
    b. 5000
    c. −5000.0
    d. +5000
    e. 5.0E03
    f. '5000'
    g. '5'
    h. 'you're OK, I'm OK'
    i. 'Dick Tracy
    j. $

(L) **3.** **Overflow.** Consider program Engine1 in Figure 2.1.
    a. Desk check the effect of declaring Sales and Price as *integer* variables.
    b. Load, edit, and run Engine1 with Sales and Price as integer variables. What happens? Fix the problem and try two separate runs: (1) Input **Test** for name, **7000** for size, **3** for price, and **1500** for units; (2) as in the first run, but input **3000** for price. Comment on your results.
    c. Declare Sales and Price as *long integer* variables (see Appendix D), and reword part **b**. Comment on your results.

4. Roleplay I/O for the following statements. Assume that the input is 70, 80, and 90.
    a. **write ('Enter three grades . . .'); readln (Grade1, Grade2, Grade3);**
    b. Same as part **a** except use **writeln** in place of **write**.
    c. Same as part **a** except place the readln statement on the line below the write statement.
    d. **write ('Enter three grades . . .');**
       readln (Grade1);
       readln (Grade2);
       readln (Grade3);

(L) ***5.** Load program Medley1 from Example 2.1 and Figure 2.3. Play around with different input. For example, try two spaces between successive numeric input, enter a letter when a numeric value is expected, try different string values, change the number of blanks in constant **Blanks**, and so on. Observe results and output. This is a great medium for learning by experimentation.

(L) *6. Make the following changes to program Medley2 in Example 2.2 and run the revised program using the input data in Figure 2.4
  a. In lines 1, 4, 5, 6, and 8 output numeric and string values with a field width of 12, and real values to 4 decimal places. Use the declared constants **Fieldwidth** for 12 and **DecimalDigits** for 4.
  b. In lines 2 and 10 use double the declared field width; in line 3 use five less than the declared field width; in line 7 use two less than the declared decimal digits; in line 9 use two more than the declared field width.

(L) *7. How would you change the input statements and prompts for program Engine1 in Figure 2.1 to reproduce the following I/O?
  a. `Enter engine name.............. Momma█Four`
     `Enter size, price, and units... 8500█4000█2000`
  b. `Enter name, size, price, units... Baby█Two██7000█3000█1500`
     This is how we show any necessary blanks ──────◄
  c. In part **b** why do we need to make sure that we type exactly 10 characters in the input field for engine name? Why isn't this a problem in part **a**? Comment on the desirability of these input designs compared to the original design. To confirm your answers, load Engine1, edit according to each part above, and run.

(L) 8. **Printed output.** Specify the changes needed in program Engine1 in Figure 2.1 to reroute the output report from the screen to the printer. Load, edit, and run Engine1 to confirm your changes.

9. Desk check the following program lines for syntax errors by identifying what is wrong (if anything). *Note:* Type is consistent with descriptive names.
  a. `5.65 := RealVar;`
  b. `IntVar := RealVar1 + RealVar2;`
  c. `RealVar = 2 * IntVar;`
  d. `const Constant1 := Constant2 := 10;`
  e. `IntVar1 := 4 * - IntVar2;`
  f. `CharVar := StringVar;`
  g. `CharVar := StringVar[3];`

10. Write arithmetic expressions for each of the following algebraic expressions. Assume all variables are type real.
  a. x^3
  b. $\dfrac{(x - a)^2}{s + 4}$
  c. $(7 - x)^{1/2}$
  d. x^{k+1}
  e. $\dfrac{x - y}{100} \cdot \dfrac{1}{a + b} + y - \dfrac{5}{x \cdot t}$

11. Consider the following sequence of statements

```
IntVar  := IntVar + 3 * IntVar;
IntVar  := IntVar div 3 + IntVar mod 3;
RealVar := IntVar / 3 - 2;
```

and the current contents in memory described below.

IntVar

| 10 |

RealVar

| 1.23 |

Develop a desk-check script as these statements get executed.

12. **City, state, zip.** Consider the three string variables **City**, **State**, and **Zip**.

a. Write program lines that declare these string variables. Assume the following maximum number of stored characters for each: 10, 2, 5.

b. Write assignment statements that store **Incline Village** for City, **NV** for State, and **89450** for Zip. Any problem here? If so, fix it.

c. Write statements that would reproduce the following interactive input.

```
Enter city............   Incline Village
                                          ← Blank line
Enter state initials...   NV
                                          ← Blank line
Enter zip code.........   89450

                                          ← Three blank lines
```

d. Design a writeln statement that writes the following using the concatenation operator.

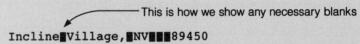
This is how we show any necessary blanks

Incline█Village,█NV███89450

e. How would you get the computer to display the following code consisting of the state abbreviation and the last two digits in the zip code?

```
Code: NV50
```

(L) *13. **Debugging problem.** Consider the buggy program in Figure 2.5. Load this program from the Examples Library and compile/execute it exactly as is.

a. Systematically let the compiler identify syntax errors, and correct these one by one.

b. Let the system identify any run-time errors and correct these if possible. Finish with an error-free run. Try the following values for the two integers: 5 and 3; 5 and 0.

c. Check out the IDE's interactive syntax help by placing the cursor on **var** and pressing **Ctrl-F1**. Also check out **program**, **begin**, **write**, **readln**, **writeln**, and **end**.

FIGURE 2.5   Listing for Program Buggy (Exercise 13)

```
program Buggy;

   {* * * * * * * * * * * * * * * * * * * * * * * * * * * * * * *
    *                                                           *
    *         This is file BUGGY.PAS                            *
    *                                                           *
    * * * * * * * * * * * * * * * * * * * * * * * * * * * * * * *

var
   Diff, Div, Mult, Sum, Int1, Int2  :   integer

begin

   write ('Enter two values);   readln (Int1, Int2);

   Sim    := Int1 + Int2;
   Diff   = Int1 - Int2;
   Int1 * Int2 := Mult;
   Div    := Int1 div Int2;

   writeln ('Sum            = ', Sum,  ' Difference = '  Diff);
   writeln ('Multiplication = ', Mult, ' Division   = ', Div ;

end
```

ADDITIONAL EXERCISES

ON ADDITIONAL EXERCISES

- Programming projects for new problems, or revisits of new problems from earlier chapters
- Arranged in ascending order of difficulty
- No answers for these in back of text
- Exercise parts (**a**, **b**, **c**, ...) add increasingly difficult features to programs
- Make use of Examples and Utilities Libraries to improve productivity, when warranted

EASIER   For the busy...
                14

NORMAL   For the thinkers...
                15 16 17 18

TOUGHER   For the hard CORE...
                19

NOTE

15. Programming assignments. Additional exercises are usually given as programming assignments that are turned in for grades. Your instructor will describe the program's documentation requirements and what you need to hand in. You can print program listings from within the IDE by the command sequence File **P**rint. The easiest way to print I/O is to "dump" the User Screen by pressing the Print Screen key. A second alternative is to press Ctrl-Print Screen while the program runs. This key combination acts as a toggle switch that turns printer output on and off as characters are written to the screen. A third alternative is to route output to the printer, as described in Section 2.5. Use the test data given in the exercise to debug your program. The I/O that you hand in should include the test data and any other I/O required by your instructor. Parts of exercises like part **a**, part **b**, and so on usually don't imply separate programs; rather they reflect either alternative or different features within the same program. There's a lot of room for new ideas and creativity in programming. Try including other features in the program that you think might improve it. The Examples Library also includes a file called template.pas. This file is a template for programs...kind of like an outline that you fill in. We use this for our examples to save effort and ensure consistency. Load file TEMPLATE.PAS to start a program from scratch. Then type your program using this template and save it under a different name using the Save as... option in the File menu. You might want to revise the template itself to suit your own needs and tastes (or your instructor's).

16. Software development cycle. Make sure you follow the four stages in the software development cycle when developing your programs. You might want to review Section 1.2 now. It's especially important that you *design the algorithm using pseudocode before you write actual program code.* Also, don't forget to *desk check your algorithm and program.*

17. On capitalization in actual programs. We use the following convention in our program listings and fragments: Reserved words and standard identifiers are boldfaced, and user-defined identifiers are given uppercase first letters. This convention improves the readability of coding by making a visual distinction between identifiers that we can't or shouldn't redefine and identifiers that we ourselves name. As you know, however, we can't boldface identifiers in our actual programs. This means that all programs in our Examples Library have the same look as the equivalent programs in our camera listings, but without boldfacing. An alternative style that's favored by some journal publications and books is to upcase all reserved words, down-case all standard identifiers, and first-letter upcase all user-defined identifiers. For example, the major elements in program Engine1 might appear as follows.

```
PROGRAM Engine1;

CONST
  MetricConversion = 0.06102;
  ...

VAR                                    ——— Reserved word
  Name    : STRING;
  Price   : real;
  ...                                  ——— User-defined identifier
  Units   : integer;

BEGIN  {Engine1}                       ——— Standard identifier

  write ('Enter engine name ------------> '); readln (Name);

  ...

  Sales := Price * Units;

  ...

END. {Engine1}
```

Note that STRING is a reserved word, but real and integer are standard identifiers (see the list inside the back cover of the book). This alternative not only makes distinctions among the different kinds of identifiers but also is acceptable to Pascal compilers. You might want to consider this approach in your own programming (or some other variation favored by your instructor).

18. On the right perspective. You might find it useful to take the perspective that applications programs you develop are to be actually used by others. This will increase your awareness and appreciation of the issues that face the developers of applications software (and should improve your grade ...).

14. **Mailing address.** Develop a program that inputs and then outputs a person's complete mailing address: full name, street number and street, and city, state, and zip. Design your own I/O and test data.

15. **Revisit: Temperatures.** Code the program that was designed in Exercise 6 of Chapter 1. Use the given test data to debug the program.
    a. Write output to the screen.
    b. Also write output to the printer.

16. **Revisit: Disk areas.** Code the program that was designed in Exercise 7 of Chapter 1. Use the given test data to debug the program.
    a. Write output to the screen.
    b. Also write output to the printer.

17. **Metric conversion.** Write an interactive program that inputs the volume and weight of a container in U.S. units (gallons and ounces) and outputs the corresponding volume and weight in metric units (liters and kilograms). A gallon is 3.7853 liters and an ounce is 0.0283495 kilogram. For test data use a 6-gallon container weighing 150 ounces.
    a. Write output to the screen.
    b. Also write output to the printer.

18. **Grade report.** Write a program that inputs a student's name (up to 19 characters), social security number (11 characters), semester grade (1 character), and a remark (up to 50 characters). It then prints a report on paper that summarizes the input. Use exactly 10 lines of output for the report, including blank lines. The report includes a title for the class. The instructor plans to print these reports at the end of the semester for distribution to the students. Do a nice design job on the report. Try the test data below.

Class Title: TurboPascal 101!

Name	SSN	Grade	Remark
Dunn, John K.	023-66-9871	C	You tried!
Mello, C.	123-45-6789	B	Not bad . . .
Morfella, Yarta	001-99-9999	F	Too many parties!

19. **Drag races.** Consider the following formulas for the speed and distance of an object undergoing constant acceleration in a straight line.

$$\text{Speed} = v_0 + at$$

$$\text{Distance} = v_0 t + 0.5at^2$$

where v_0 is the initial velocity, a is the constant acceleration, and t is the elapsed time. For example, a drag racer starting from rest and constantly accelerating at 25 miles per hour per second (mi/h/s) will achieve in 10 seconds a speed of 250 miles per hour and a distance of just over one third of a mile. Take care with units of measure here, as the following calculation illustrates:

$$\text{Distance} = \frac{(0 \text{ mi/h})(10 \text{ s})}{(3600 \text{ s/h})} + \frac{0.5(25 \text{ mi/h/s})(10 \text{ s})^2}{(3600 \text{ s/h})}$$

$$= 0 \text{ mi} \quad + \quad 0.347222 \text{ mi}$$

$$= 0.35 \text{ mi}$$

That is, we need to account for mixed units of measure (hours and seconds) by converting hours to seconds. Write a program that inputs initial velocity, acceleration, and elapsed time, and outputs speed and distance. Use the same units of measure as the example. Who wins a 10-second race? A dragster starting from rest but accelerating at 25 mi/h/s or a dragster getting a running start at a speed of 30 mi/h but with the slower acceleration of 20 mi/h/s? What would be a fair initial velocity for the slower dragster? (Find the initial velocity that puts both dragsters even at the 10-second finish.)

TOP-DOWN PROGRAMMING

We introduced *top-down design* and its implementation as *stepwise refinement* of algorithms in Section 1.2. In this chapter we take a detailed look at the use of top-down design principles in program development.

3.1   Top-Down Design Revisited

• • • • • • • • • • • • • • • •

Behavioral research shows that we best solve problems by a "divide-and-conquer" strategy starting at the "top." By *top* we mean the least level of detail, where we first divide or *refine* a problem into its major subproblems or tasks. Then we separately move *down* to and refine each subproblem, generally solving one subproblem before going on to the next. Finally, when all subproblems are completely solved, we have a solution to the overall problem.

For example, suppose the problem is to write a book. What's the least level of action or algorithmic detail (and the greatest level of abstraction)? It's to write a book on subject such and such. What's the next level of detail or refinement? Write each chapter. What's the next refinement? Write the major sections within each chapter. These refinements continue step by step until the final level of detail: Write actual words, punctuation, and so on.

We have just described a **stepwise refinement** strategy using *top-down principles* that always starts at the *top* (least refinement or level of detail) and works *down* to the bottom (greatest refinement or level of detail). Its use at the design stage in the software development cycle is called **top-down design.** By now (we hope) you have used stepwise refinement in designing a program from the first two chapters.

Top-Down Programming

The use of top-down principles at the coding stage is called **top-down programming;** it includes two fundamental approaches to programming that implement top-down principles: *modular programming* and *structured programming.* Let's consider modular programming next and delay structured programming until later in this chapter.

Modular Programming

Modular programming breaks down a program into *blocks.* Up to now, we have worked with just one *main block* that includes the entire program from just below the program heading. It's also possible to nest other blocks within the main block. We can think of a block as one of the subproblems that we identified at the design stage. In our book example, the main block is the book itself and the other blocks are the chapters and other major segments like appendixes.

In Pascal programs, we have two kinds of additional blocks: *procedure blocks* and *function blocks.* The breaking down of a program into a main block with internal procedure and function blocks is called **modular programming.**

A **modular program** is a program with the block structure seen in Figure 3.1:

- A **main program** defined by a *program heading* followed by the *main block,* and optionally...

- One or more **procedures,** each defined by a *procedure heading* followed by a *procedure block*

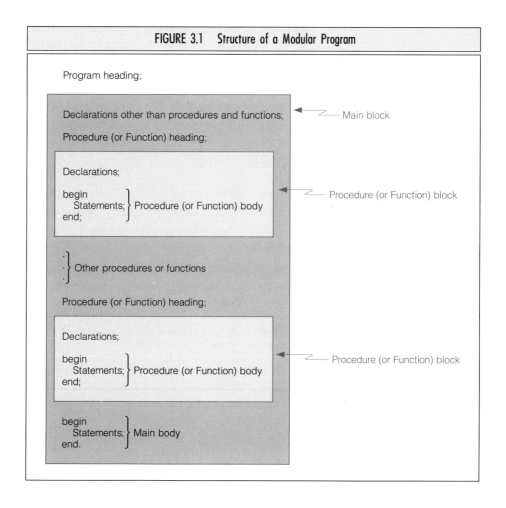

FIGURE 3.1   Structure of a Modular Program

- One or more **functions,** each defined by a *function heading* followed by a *function block*

The main program, procedures, and functions are examples of **modules,** blocks of code identified by a heading.

Let's look at the big picture and leave the details for later. Note the following in Figure 3.1.

1. The main program is the entire program; it optionally includes procedures and functions.

2. A procedure or function is like a "miniprogram" within the main program. It includes its own *heading, declarations* (including other procedures or functions within it), and *algorithm* flanked by a begin-end pair. In the main program, the algorithm is the *main body.* Similarly, the algorithm in a procedure is called a *procedure body;* the algorithm in a function is the *function body.*

3. As before, a modular program is executed starting at the main body. Now, however, the main body includes statements that *call* the procedures or functions. For example, suppose a particular procedure has the task of implementing all input for the program. A *call statement* is placed where the input procedure is needed in the main body. When this call statement is executed, the input described by that procedure is carried out, after which processing continues as usual in the main body.

EXAMPLE 3.1   HC ENGINE, VERSION 2.0

Let's get more specific by returning to a familar problem and making another pass at the software development cycle, noting changes as we go.

Requirements
We only make one change in the requirements: the output of a program introduction at the beginning of the run that states "Start of program Engine, Version 2.0."

Design
The top level of detail is simply "satisfy the requirements using program Engine2." The following first pass of the design algorithm is the next level of detail.

Program Engine2

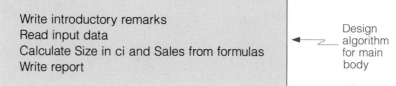

Write introductory remarks
Read input data
Calculate Size in ci and Sales from formulas
Write report

Design algorithm for main body

These steps are the major subproblems or tasks in the algorithm. *The main body will use this design.*

Now, let's refine each step in turn.

Stepwise Refinements...

Step 1: Write introductory remarks
Procedure WriteIntro

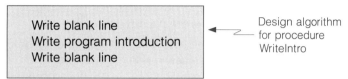

Write blank line
Write program introduction
Write blank line

← Design algorithm for procedure WriteIntro

Step 2: Read input data
Procedure ReadInput

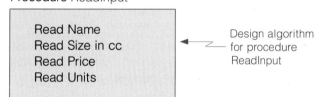

Read Name
Read Size in cc
Read Price
Read Units

← Design algorithm for procedure ReadInput

Step 3: Calculate Size in ci and Sales
Procedure Calculate

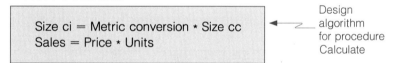

Size ci = Metric conversion * Size cc
Sales = Price * Units

← Design algorithm for procedure Calculate

Step 4: Write report
Procedure WriteReport

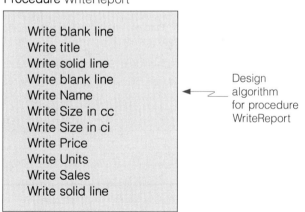

Write blank line
Write title
Write solid line
Write blank line
Write Name
Write Size in cc
Write Size in ci
Write Price
Write Units
Write Sales
Write solid line

← Design algorithm for procedure WriteReport

The major difference in the pseudocode from our previous version in Chapter 1 is the conceptualization and identification of each refinement as a *procedure body*.[1]

---

[1] In our design, we're selecting procedures rather than functions for reasons that will become clear in Section 3.3.

The relationships and data flows among the main body and procedures (or functions) are often described at the design stage using a **structure chart,** as seen in Figure 3.2. We read the chart from top to bottom and left to right, as follows.

1. The main program *calls* procedure WriteIntro, which writes the required introductory remarks. Note that WriteIntro neither *receives* values from nor sends values to the main program Engine2.

2. Next, the main program *calls* procedure ReadInput, which reads all required input. Values in Name, Price, Size in cc, and Units are sent to the main program. Note that ReadInput does not *receive* values from the main program, but it does send the four indicated values.

3. Next, the main program *calls* procedure Calculate. This procedure *receives* values in Size in cc, Price, and Units; calculates Size in ci and Sales; and sends values in Size in ci and Sales to the main program.

4. Finally, the main program *calls* procedure WriteReport. This procedure *receives* values for the indicated six variables, writes the report, and sends no values back to the main program.

5. The top level of the structure chart is often designated as *Level 0. Level 1* is a refinement of *Level 0,* and so on. As our algorithms get larger and more complex, we will have additional levels of refinement in our structure charts.

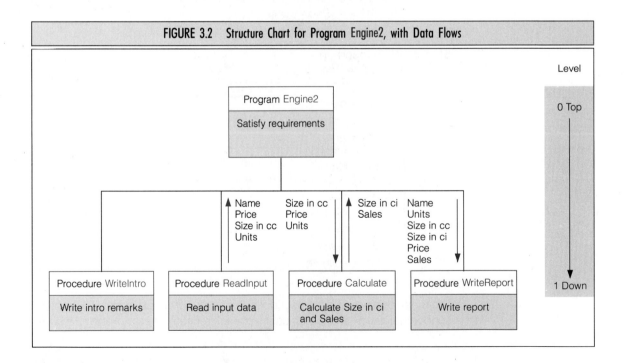

FIGURE 3.2   Structure Chart for Program Engine2, with Data Flows

The terms *receives* and *sends* are used figuratively to describe the data flows, or how data are *passed* between modules. In practice, it's not quite so literal. For now, don't worry about the actual mechanics of calls and data flows. We cover these soon enough. Instead, focus on the fact that these procedures directly reflect the top-down philosophy of refinement.

Code and Test

Figure 3.3 shows the listing and I/O for this program. Don't worry about the syntactic details (just yet), but do notice the following.

1. The modular structure of this program is the same as that shown in Figure 3.1. These procedures are declarations within the main program. Each procedure is like a "miniprogram." It has a heading, documentation, optional declarations of its own, and a body of its own defined by its begin-end pair. Unlike the main body, *procedure (and function) bodies end with a semicolon.*

2. The heading for a procedure defines its name. For example, the first procedure is called WriteIntro and the next procedure is called ReadInput.

3. Now, look at the main body at the bottom of the program. As usual, this is where the executable action takes place when a program runs. The first statement is the procedure name WriteIntro. This is an example of a *call statement*. At this point, the processor executes the statements that were declared in the body of procedure WriteIntro. The next statement in the main body calls procedure ReadInput. The arguments inside the parentheses indicate the input values that the main program will receive once procedure ReadInput accomplishes its task (see the data flows in Figure 3.2). Next, procedure Calculate is called. It receives values in Size_cc, Price, and Units; calculates Size_ci and Sales (see the procedure itself); and sends values in Size_ci and Sales back to the main body. Finally, procedure WriteReport is called; it receives the indicated six values and writes the report.

The execution of a main body with procedure calls is summarized by the following *call process*.

- The main program calls a procedure from its main body and passes values (if any).
- The procedure receives values (if any), executes the statements in its procedure body, and sends values (if any) back to the main program.
- The main program receives values (if any) and continues execution at the next statement following the procedure call.

As we will see later, it's also possible for a procedure or function to call other procedures or functions (or even call itself!).

That's all there is to it! Actually, there are some tricky mechanics in the data-flow process, plenty of syntax, and pitfalls we haven't dealt with yet.

FIGURE 3.3   Listing and I/O for program Engine2

(a) Listing in Edit Window

```
program Engine2;

  {* * * * * * * * * * * * * * * * * * * * * * * * * * * * * * * * *
   *                                                               *
   *          Harvey CORE ENGINE Corporation:  Version 2.0         *
   *                                                               *
   *          Inputs engine name, size (cc), price, units sold     *
   *          Calculates engine size (ci) and sales revenue        *
   *          Outputs engine name, sizes, price, units, sales revenue *
   *                                                               *
   *          Modular structure                                    *
   *            Main program                                       *
   *            |___ Procedure WriteIntro                          *
   *            |___ Procedure ReadInput          Structure chart, *        Main block
   *            |___ Procedure Calculate          sort of          *
   *            |___ Procedure WriteReport                         *
   *                                                               *
   * * * * * * * * * * * * * * * * * * * * * * * * * * * * * * * * *}

  {============================= Declarations =============================}

  var
    Name    : string;                   {Name of engine}
    Price   : real;                     {Price of engine in $ per unit}
    Sales   : real;                     {Sales revenue in $}
    Size_cc : real;                     {Engine size in cubic centimeters, cc}
    Size_ci : real;                     {Engine size in cubic inches, ci}
    Units   : integer;                  {Number of engines sold in units}

  {===================== Procedure Declarations =====================}

procedure WriteIntro;

  { Writes introductory remarks
    Receives nothing                                                      Procedure
    Sends nothing }                                                       WriteIntro
                                                                          block
begin  {WriteIntro}

  writeln;
  writeln ('Start of program Engine, Version 2.0');
  writeln;

end;   {WriteIntro}
{-----------------------------------------------------------------------}
procedure ReadInput (var Name  : string;
                     var Price, Size_cc : real;
                     var Units : integer);

  { Reads input data
    Receives nothing
    Sends Name, Price, Size_cc, Units }

begin  {ReadInput}

  write   ('Enter engine name ------------> ');   readln (Name);
  write   ('Enter engine size (cc) -------> ');   readln (Size_cc);        Procedure
  write   ('Enter engine price ($) -------> ');   readln (Price);          ReadInput
  write   ('Enter engines sold (units) ---> ');   readln (Units);          block

end;   {ReadInput}
```

FIGURE 3.3 *(continued)*

```
{------------------------------------------------------------------}
procedure Calculate (Size_cc, Price : real;  Units : integer;
                       var Size_ci, Sales : real);

  { Calculates Size_ci and Sales
    Receives Size_cc, Price, Units
    Sends Size_ci, Sales }

const
  MetricConversion = 0.06102;                      {cc = 0.06102 ci}

begin  {Calculate}

  Size_ci := MetricConversion * Size_cc;
  Sales   := Price * Units;

end;  {Calculate}
{------------------------------------------------------------------}
procedure WriteReport (Name : string;  Units : integer;
                        Size_cc, Size_ci, Price, Sales : real);

  { Writes report
    Receives Name, Units, Size_cc, Size_ci, Price, Sales
    Sends nothing }

const
  Title = '            SALES REPORT';          {Output report title}
  Line  = '_____';  {Output report line}

begin  {WriteReport}

  writeln;
  writeln (Title);
  writeln (Line);
  writeln;
  writeln ('Engine name............',      Name    :10);
  writeln ('Engine size (cc).......',      Size_cc :10:0);
  writeln ('Engine size (ci).......',      Size_ci :10:0);
  writeln ('Engine price..........  $', Price    :4:0);
  writeln ('Engines sold (units)...',      Units   :10);
  writeln ('Sales.................. $',  Sales   :7:0);
  writeln (Line);

end;  {WriteReport}

{============================= Main Body =============================}

begin  {Engine2}

  WriteIntro;
  ReadInput    (Name, Price, Size_cc, Units);
  Calculate    (Size_cc, Price, Units, Size_ci, Sales);
  WriteReport  (Name, Units, Size_cc, Size_ci, Price, Sales);

end.   {Engine2}
```

Procedure
Calculate
block

Main
block

Procedure
WriteReport
block

Procedure
calls

continued

FIGURE 3.3   (*continued*)

(b) I/O in Output Window

```
Start of program Engine, Version 2.0

Enter engine name ------------> Baby Two
Enter engine size (cc) -------> 7000
Enter engine price ($) -------> 3000
Enter engines sold (units) ---> 1500

              SALES REPORT
      _____

Engine name............ Baby Two
Engine size (cc)....... 7000
Engine size (ci)....... 427
Engine price........... $3000
Engines sold (units)... 1500
Sales.................. $4500000
```

NOTE

1. Procedural abstraction. Think of a procedure as a "specialist" that takes care of certain algorithmic needs without our having to worry about the details of how it's done. This idea is known as *procedural abstraction*.

2. Modular motivation. Did you notice that Engine2 is about twice as long as its unmodularized version Engine1? Are you thinking "Do I need to do all of this extra typing when a shorter version of the program does the same thing?" "Is this really worth it?!" We can't answer for *you*. We can say that modular programming reflects good software engineering practice, which in the "real world" reduces costs in the software life cycle. Long, complex programs are considerably easier to understand, write, debug, and modify than unmodularized programs. For now, take our word for it.

3.2   PROCEDURES

• • • • • • • • • • • • • •

A **procedure** is a group of code defined by a *procedure heading* followed by a *procedure block,* as illustrated in Figure 3.1. The "look" of a procedure is very similar to that of a main program, and its purpose in life is the accomplishment of some specified task or set of tasks.

PREDECLARED PROCEDURES

We have used procedures all along for reading and writing. The readln and writeln statements are examples of calls to predeclared procedures. A **standard** or **predeclared procedure** is a procedure that's provided by the compiler. We never see the procedure itself; we just *call* it.

A *procedure call statement* executes a procedure. For example, the procedure call

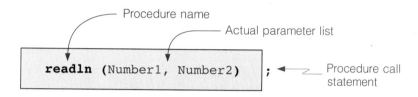

executes a keyboard read operation for entering two numbers. These two numbers are *sent* to the calling module as the contents in the Number1 and Number2 memory cells, and are available to other statements in the module body.

The *procedure name* for a standard procedure is a standard identifier. The part following the name is an *actual parameter list* enclosed in parentheses. In the example, it's Number1, Number2. The actual parameter list describes the data flows in the call process.

Appendix E summarizes the predeclared procedures used in this book.

PROCEDURE DECLARATION

Before we can call our own procedure, we must first *declare* it in the declarations section of the program. The accompanying syntax box describes procedure declarations.

Note the following in the procedure declaration syntax box.

1. The **procedure heading** defines the beginning of the procedure, identifies the procedure by name, and provides an optional *formal parameter list* for handling data flows. The **procedure block** runs from just below the procedure heading to the end of the **procedure body** defined by the begin-end pair. The **procedure** itself comprises the procedure heading and procedure block taken together.

2. The example shows the declaration of Adjust, a procedure that receives two values and returns an adjusted sum of these two values. The three *parameters* in the formal parameter list define data flows between the procedure and calling module. One and Two are examples of **value parameters** because their declaration in the formal parameter list is not preceded by the reserved word **var**. AdjSum is a **variable parameter**;

SYNTAX BOX

Procedure declaration . . . Declares procedure within declarations section of calling module

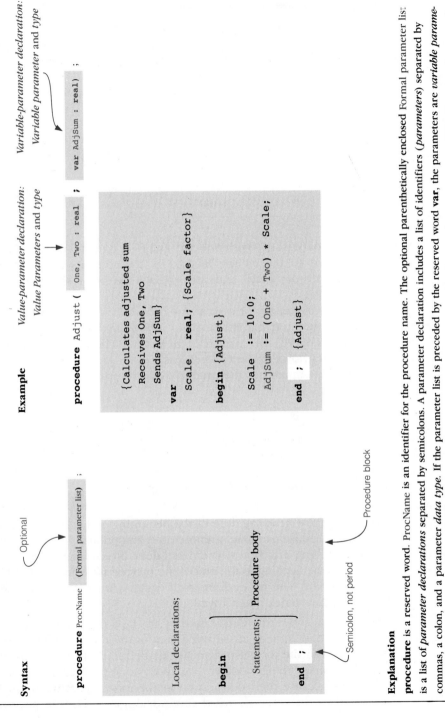

Syntax

Optional

procedure ProcName (Formal parameter list) ;

Local declarations;

begin

Statements; } Procedure body

end ;

Semicolon, not period

Procedure block

Example

Value-parameter declaration:
Value Parameters and type

Variable-parameter declaration:
Variable parameter and type

procedure Adjust (One, Two : real ; var AdjSum : real) ;

```
{Calculates adjusted sum
 Receives One, Two
 Sends AdjSum}
var
    Scale : real; {Scale factor}

begin {Adjust}

    Scale := 10.0;
    AdjSum := (One + Two) * Scale;

end ; {Adjust}
```

Explanation

procedure is a reserved word. ProcName is an identifier for the procedure name. The optional parenthetically enclosed Formal parameter list is a list of *parameter declarations* separated by semicolons. A parameter declaration includes a list of identifiers (*parameters*) separated by commas, a colon, and a parameter *data type*. If the parameter list is preceded by the reserved word **var**, the parameters are *variable parameters*; otherwise, the parameters are *value parameters*. A size attribute is not allowed with a string parameter type (255 characters is assumed). The syntax of local declarations is the same as that in main programs. These declarations are *local* to the procedure in that the declared identifiers are not available to other modules, unless the modules are themselves declared within this procedure. An identifier within the formal parameter list cannot be declared as a local identifier. The *procedure body* is defined by a begin-end pair and terminates with a semicolon. Statements in the procedure body describe the procedure's algorithm.

its declaration is preceded by **var.** Typically, value parameters identify the data received and variable parameters identify the data sent by the procedure. The procedure "receives" One and Two and "sends" AdjSum. For example, if Adjust receives *50* and *100*, it returns *1500.0*. The compiler establishes different mechanisms for passing data, depending on whether it's a value or variable parameter. Before we can explain this further, we need to consider the procedure call.

Procedure Call

A **call statement** in the body of the calling module executes a procedure's algorithm. The next syntax box provides the details.

Note the following in the syntax box for the call statement.

1. The procedure call WriteIntro illustrates a call without an actual parameter list. This call is used in the main algorithm of program Engine2 in

SYNTAX BOX

Call statement ... Calls a procedure from within the body of the calling module

Syntax .... ProcName   (Actual parameter list)   ;

— Optional

Examples ...... WriteIntro;
Adjust (2*Var1, Var2, SumScaled);

Explanation ... ProcName is an identifier that's identical to the procedure name in the declared procedure. The optional parenthetically enclosed Actual parameter list is a list of expressions separated by commas. The actual parameter list is coupled with the formal parameter list to manage the data flows in the call process. These parameter lists must correspond with respect to *number* of parameters, their *order*, and their *type*. The number of actual parameters must be the same as the number of formal parameters. The first actual parameter is matched to the first formal parameter, the second to the second, and so on. An actual parameter that corresponds to a variable parameter must have the same type; otherwise, it must be assignment compatible. Use a variable as the actual parameter if the corresponding formal parameter is a variable parameter.

Figure 3.3. Note that the declaration of WriteIntro does not include a formal parameter list. Its call, therefore, cannot include an actual parameter list. Moreover, the absence of parameter lists is consistent with the absence of data flows to or from WriteIntro in the structure chart of Figure 3.2.

2. The actual parameters in the call to Adjust correspond to the formal parameters in the earlier declaration of this procedure. Each parameter list has three parameters.

3. We need to be careful how we type actual and formal parameters, to ensure the following *parameter-compatibility* rules:

   - An actual parameter must have the *same type* as its corresponding formal parameter if the latter is a *variable* parameter.
   - An actual parameter must be *assignment compatible* with its corresponding formal parameter if the latter is a *value* parameter.

To illustrate, let's restate Adjust's procedure heading and call.

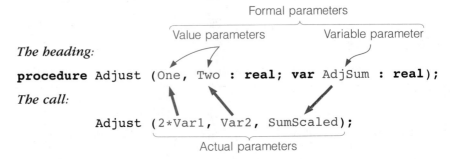

One and Two are *value* parameters with type *real,* so their corresponding actual parameters must be assignment compatible: 2*Var1 and Var2 can be *real* or *integer* to be assignment compatible with One and Two. AdjSum is a *variable* parameter, also typed *real.* This means that its corresponding actual parameter SumScaled must have the same type: *Real.*[2]

4. The third actual parameter SumScaled is a variable; it can't be an expression because its corresponding formal parameter is a variable parameter. The reason for this will be clear in the next section.

OTHER CONSIDERATIONS

Let's take a look at the details of how data flows and storage are handled. We also consider a related issue called *scope.*

---

[2]See the assignment compatibility rules in Section 2.6 if you're rusty.

Pass-by-Value and Pass-by-Reference

A *value* parameter receives a *value* that gets stored in the procedure's data storage area, within a memory cell identified by the value parameter's name. Its corresponding actual parameter passes that *value*. This one-way data flow is known as a *pass-by-value*. A *variable* parameter is passed a *reference* to the actual memory cell of its corresponding actual parameter. What gets passed is a reference to (address of) the actual *variable*, not the value itself. This is a *pass-by-reference*. Let's nail this down with an example.

EXAMPLE 3.2   DATA FLOWS AND DATA-STORAGE AREAS

Consider the following sample program and its data-storage areas depicted in Figure 3.4.

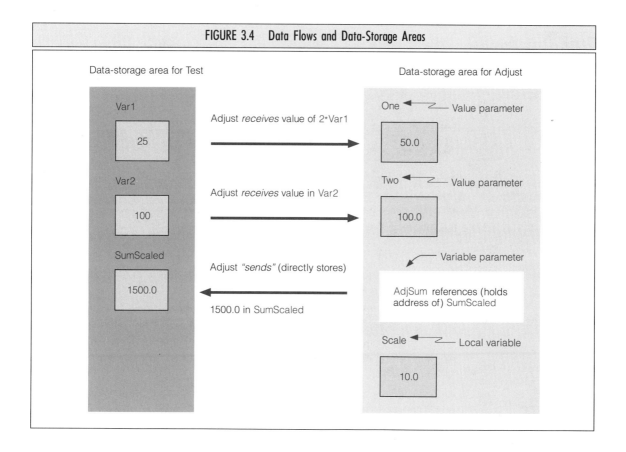

FIGURE 3.4   Data Flows and Data-Storage Areas

Data-storage area for Test

Data-storage area for Adjust

Var1

25

Adjust *receives* value of 2*Var1

One ◄ ╱ Value parameter

50.0

Var2

100

Adjust *receives* value in Var2

Two ◄ ╱ Value parameter

100.0

SumScaled

1500.0

Adjust *"sends"* (directly stores)

1500.0 in SumScaled

Variable parameter

AdjSum references (holds address of) SumScaled

Scale ◄ ╱ Local variable

10.0

```
program Test;

var
   SumScaled  : real;
   Var1, Var2 : integer;


   procedure Adjust (One, Two : real; var AdjSum : real);

   var
      Scale : real;

   begin {Adjust}
      Scale  := 10.0;
      AdjSum := (One + Two) * Scale;
   end;    {Adjust}


begin   {Test}

   Var1 := 25;
   Var2 := 100;

   Adjust (2*Var1, Var2, SumScaled);

   writeln ('Scaled sum = ', SumScaled :10:1);

end.    {Test}
```

Note the following points.

1. Variables Var1, Var2, and SumScaled have memory cells in the data-storage area allocated to program Test. The *actual parameters* in the call to procedure Adjust are 2*Var1, Var2, and SumScaled.

2. Formal parameters One and Two are *value parameters*, and AdjSum is a *variable parameter*. In the data-storage area for Adjust, the value parameters have memory cells like those for Test, but not the variable parameter. Instead, AdjSum references or holds the address of its corresponding actual parameter SumScaled.

3. When Adjust is called, *pass-by-value* is used for value parameters: The values 50 and 100 are passed (received by or assigned) to One and Two. This is why an actual parameter has to be assignment compatible with its corresponding value parameter. When we say a procedure "receives" a value, we

generally mean that its value parameter is initialized to the value of its corresponding actual parameter.

4. *Pass-by-reference* is used to "pass" the value to SumScaled. When Adjust is called, the system allocates memory space for variable parameter AdjSum to reference SumScaled. In the procedure, the assignment to AdjSum is actually a direct access to the memory cell of SumScaled. Think of AdjSum as SumScaled in disguise. This is why an actual parameter and its corresponding variable parameter must have the same type. When we say a procedure "sends" a value, we really mean that the evaluation of its variable parameter results in a direct change in the memory cell of its corresponding actual parameter. This is also why an actual parameter can't be an expression when it's coupled with a variable parameter.

5. Variable Scale in procedure Adjust is a *local variable;* hence, it has a memory cell in Adjust's data-storage area. Its use is restricted to procedure Adjust, and it may not appear as a formal parameter. If Adjust were to call some other procedure, however, Scale could be an actual parameter in the call statement.

Scope Rules

The block structure of Pascal programs seen in Figure 3.1 raises an important question: How are identifiers "visible" to the different blocks? For example, if an identifier is declared in one block, can it be referenced in another? The following *scope rules* address this question.

Fundamental Scope Rule.   The **scope** of an identifier runs from its declaration to the end of its declaring block. For instance, in the program of Example 3.2, the scope of Var1 includes the procedure block and the main body; the scope of Scale includes just the procedure body. This means that Var1 could be referenced within procedure Adjust, but we would not want to for reasons outlined shortly; it also means that any references to Scale are restricted to Adjust's body. Scale is said to be *local* to procedure Adjust. Similarly, the scope of a formal parameter in the procedure's heading is the procedure's block. Thus, One, Two, and AdjSum are visible to Adjust, but not to the main body in Test. The compiler gives an *Unknown identifier* error if an identifier is used but not visible within a block.

Redeclaration Rule.   Suppose block Outer encloses block Inner. If Outer and Inner both declare an identifier with the same name (say, I), then Inner's I is visible only to Inner and Outer's I is visible to Outer but not Inner. In Example 3.2, suppose we replace the name Scale with the name SumScaled. This identifier is now redeclared within the inner block defined by procedure Adjust. The results from running the program would be the same as before. Within Adjust's block, SumScaled is the scale factor that stores 10.0; elsewhere within Test's block, SumScaled is the scaled sum that ends up storing 1500.0.

In Example 3.2, we could have entirely eliminated the actual and formal parameter lists, and referenced variables Var1, Var2, and SumScaled within Adjust by using the following assignment statement:

```
SumScaled := (Var1 + Var2) * Scale;
```

These references are permissible because the first scope rule states that Adjust's block is within the scope of these variables. This is called a **side effect:** Identifiers Var1, Var2, and SumScaled are used "on the side," in a module other than their declaring module.

Using side effects is a poor programming practice, for several reasons: Programs are harder to follow because data flows are unclear when they're not shown in missing or incomplete parameter lists; interdependence among modules is promoted, thereby discouraging the development of modules that are reusable by other programs; and the door is opened to some subtle logic errors (as we show in Exercise 18).

Take a look at program Engine2 in Figure 3.3. This program has six variables, and their scope includes every procedure. This means that we could have eliminated all parameter lists in the program. The program would compile and run without error. Since we use the same variable names in all blocks (arbitrarily changing them would be confusing), it would actually be simpler to eliminate all parameter lists. We did not as a matter of good programming style, to avoid side effects.

NOTE

3. Value or variable parameter? The following is a good rule of thumb for deciding whether to make a formal parameter a value or variable parameter:

> Use a value parameter if a parameter needs to receive but not send a value; use a variable parameter if a parameter must send a value.

Look at the data flows in the structure chart in Figure 3.2 and confirm in Figure 3.3 that we selected value and variable parameters according to this rule.

4. Procedural abstraction, again. Local identifiers promote independence of procedures and functions, since we need not worry about unintended side effects should the same identifier name be used in different modules for different purposes. This is consistent with the concept of procedural abstraction first mentioned in Note 1, and very relevant to the use of general-purpose utility modules in programming libraries, as we will see.

5. Preconditions and postconditions. The list of receiving parameters implies that their corresponding actual parameters are correctly evaluated before the procedure is called. This is called a **precondition** to using the procedure. The precondition must be true for correct use of the procedure. Similarly, there is a **postcondition** that must be true in using the procedure: The sending parameters must have been assigned values by the time the procedure ends. In our documentation, the list of received identifiers implies the precondition and the list of returned identifiers implies the postcondition.

SELF-REVIEW EXERCISES

1 4 5 6

3.3 FUNCTIONS

• • • • • • • • • • • • • •

A **function** is a group of code defined by a *function heading* followed by a *function block*, as illustrated in Figure 3.1. The composition of a function is very similar to that of a procedure. The key difference is that a function is designed to return a single value. Function calls are especially useful within expressions.

PREDECLARED FUNCTIONS

A **standard** or **predeclared function** is a function that's built in to the compiler. As with standard procedures, we don't declare standard functions (the compiler does this for us). We simply *call* them when needed in a statement. Appendix F briefly describes the predeclared functions used in this book.

A standard *function call* is implemented by using a *standard function name* and an *actual parameter list* (if required) in an expression. For example, consider the following call to the square root function:

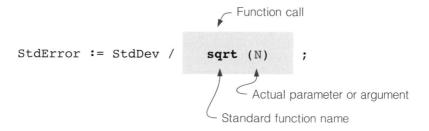

If StdDev stores 10.0 and N stores 25, then the square root function *returns* the single value 5.0, the expression is evaluated as 2.0, and StdError stores 2.0.

FUNCTION DECLARATION

As with procedures, our focus here is on writing our own functions. The syntax box on page 93 shows how we declare functions. Note the following:

1. The **function heading** defines the beginning of the function, identifies the function by name, provides an optional *formal parameter list* for handling data flows, and declares the type of the value returned by the function. The **function block** runs from just after the function heading to the end of the **function body** defined by the begin-end pair. The **function** itself consists of the function heading and function block taken together.

2. In the example, SqDiff is the name of the function, and this identifier is assigned a value in the function's algorithm.

3. The function returns a single value, through its name. That's why we don't use variable parameters in a function's formal parameter list: It would imply that more than one value is returned. Use a procedure to return multiple values.

FUNCTION CALL

Just as with standard functions, we execute a user-defined function by including a **function call** in an expression, as seen in the syntax box on page 94. Note the following.

1. The actual parameters in the calls to SqDiff are assignment compatible with the integer value parameters in the earlier syntax box that declares SqDiff. For example, 5 and 3 are integer constants that match up with integer First and Second.

2. Let's roleplay the assignment statement

        Result := 100 * SqDiff (5, 3);

    The call to SqDiff sends 5 and 3 to First and Second, respectively. The procedure evaluates the difference (5 − 3) as 2, calls predeclared function **sqr**, which returns 4 as the square of 2, and assigns 4 to SqDiff. Back in the calling module, 100 and 4 are multiplied and 400 is stored in Result.

OTHER CONSIDERATIONS

Scope and the mechanics of data flows and storage operate the same way in functions that they do in procedures. As mentioned earlier, however, we avoid

SYNTAX BOX

Function declaration . . . Declares function within declarations section of calling module

Syntax

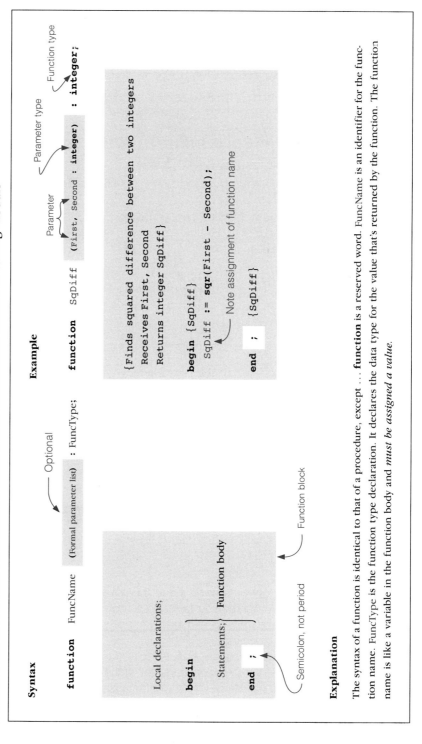

```
function  FuncName  (Formal parameter list)  : FuncType;
```
Optional

```
Local declarations;

begin

  Statements;

end ;
```
Function body
Function block
Semicolon, not period

Example

```
function  SqDiff  (First, Second : integer)  : integer;
```
Parameter type
Parameter
Function type

```
{Finds squared difference between two integers
Receives First, Second
Returns integer SqDiff}

begin {SqDiff}
  SqDiff := sqr(First - Second);
                 Note assignment of function name
end ;   {SqDiff}
```

Explanation

The syntax of a function is identical to that of a procedure, except . . . **function** is a reserved word. FuncName is an identifier for the function name. FuncType is the function type declaration. It declares the data type for the value that's returned by the function. The function name is like a variable in the function body and *must be assigned a value.*

SYNTAX BOX

Function call... Calls a function from an expression within the body of the calling module; the function returns a value to this point in the expression

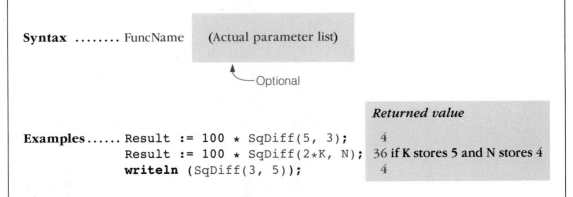

Syntax .... FuncName   (Actual parameter list)

└─Optional

Returned value

Examples...... `Result := 100 * SqDiff(5, 3);`   4
`Result := 100 * SqDiff(2*K, N);`   36 if K stores 5 and N stores 4
`writeln` `(SqDiff(3, 5));`   4

Explanation ... FuncName is an identifier that's identical to the function name in the declared function. The Actual parameter list is as described for procedure calls in the call statement syntax box.

the use of variable parameters when working with functions. Variable parameters are meant to send values back to the calling module. Since functions are designed to return a single value through the function name itself, we usually have no need for variable parameters in the formal parameter list of functions.

EXAMPLE 3.3   **POWER FUNCTION, VERSION 1.0**

Consider the problem of evaluating the power function

$$y = x^p$$

where both the base x and the power term p are general algebraic expressions. Many programming languages have an exponentiation operator and would program the right-hand-member expression as `X ^ P`, where `^` is a sample exponentiation operator.

Unfortunately, Pascal lacks an exponentiation operator. So how do we program this expression in Pascal? If the power term p is a small integer constant, say 3, then we could simply use the assignment statement

`Y := X * X * X;`

If the power term is a large integer constant, say 30, then our initial approach still applies, but at a tedious, inelegant price. And what if the power term is a real value, as in $x^{3.2}$, or an expression, as originally stated?

The solution to our problem first requires some creative algebra. The problem is to evaluate the following power function.

$$y = x^p$$

If we take the natural log of both sides, we have

$$\ln(y) = p \cdot \ln(x)$$

FIGURE 3.5   Listing and I/O for Program CkPower1

(a) Listing in Edit Window

```
program CkPower1;

    {* * * * * * * * * * * * * * * * * * * * * * * * * * * * * * * *
     *                                                            *
     *        Driver checks Power1 function by raising real X to real P   *
     *                                                            *
     *            Inputs X and P                                  *
     *            Calls function Power1                           *
     *            Outputs X, P, and X raised to P                 *
     *                                                            *
     * * * * * * * * * * * * * * * * * * * * * * * * * * * * * * * *}

    {=========================== Declarations ===========================}

    var                                                   Function
       X, P : real;                                       Power1

    {========================= Function Declarations ===============}

    function Power1 (Base, Power : real) : real;

       { Utility raises real base to real power          Note: Same identifier
         Receives Base, Power
         Returns  real Power1 }

    begin   {Power1}

       Power1 := exp( Power * ln( Base ) );

    end;    {Power1}

    {=========================== Main Body ===========================}

    begin   {CkPower1}

       writeln;
       writeln ('Evaluates x raised to the p power...');
       writeln;
       write ('Enter x... ');   readln (X);
       write ('Enter p... ');   readln (P);
       writeln;
       writeln (X  :12:2, ' raised to the...');
       writeln (P  :12:2, ' power is...');
       writeln (Power1( X, P ) :12:2);

    end.    {CkPower1}                — Function call
```

continued

FIGURE 3.5   *(continued)*

(b) I/O in Output Window

```
Evaluates x raised to the p power...

Enter x... 2
Enter p... 3

        2.00 raised to the...
        3.00 power is...
        8.00

Evaluates x raised to the p power...

Enter x... 2.1
Enter p... 3.2

        2.10 raised to the...
        3.20 power is...
        10.74
```

By the definition of a logarithm[3], we have

$$e^{p \cdot \ln(x)} = y$$

Now we're cookin'... In Pascal we have the exponential function **exp** for powers of *e*, and we have the natural logarithm function **ln.** The Pascal equivalent of our last equation is the assignment statement

```
Y := exp (P * ln(X));
```

Messy, but it works, assuming that *X* stores a positive value.

Figure 3.5 illustrates a function Power1, which is equivalent to the right member in the preceding assignment statement. The program itself is a *driver* whose purpose is to test the function. Study this figure and note the following.

1. The formal parameters Base and Power are *value* parameters, so corresponding actual parameters can be any legitimate expression (not just variables, like X and P in the sample program).

2. The formal parameters are typed real. This means that corresponding actual parameters must be expressions that are *assignment compatible* with type real; that is, X and P must be typed either real or integer. Also, the function itself is typed real, and so returns a real value. This particular function must be typed real, because its evaluation uses the standard functions *exp* and *ln*, which themselves return real values (according to Appendix F).

3. The assignment statement in the function body necessarily uses the name of the function Power1 as its left member. *All functions must assign a value to the function name by the end of the function body.*

---

[3]If you're rusty, remember that ln $a = b$ is defined as $e^b = a$.

4. A *function call* can appear at any point that allows an expression. The function call itself can define the entire expression, or it can be a part of some other expression. In Figure 3.5, the function call Power1(X, P) is an expression within the output list of a writeln statement.

NOTE

6. Function or procedure? If we decide to modularize a subproblem or task, we need to decide whether to make it a function or a procedure. Try the following guidelines.

- Use a procedure to send none or more than one value to the calling module, or if I/O tasks are required.
- Use a function to return just one value within an expression in an assignment statement or output list.

7. Utility functions and procedures. Actual programming environments include libraries of functions and procedures as tools that are available to different programs. In this book we include a set of these **utility modules** within the *Utilities Library* on disk. The Power1 function in our last example is one of the utility functions provided. We name utility function files as the name of the function followed by a .FUN extension, as in POWER1.FUN. Utility procedures have a .PRO extension. See the utility modules list inside the front cover. We can import one of these utility modules directly into a program as follows.

- Place the cursor at the beginning of the program line where you want the utility module to begin.
- Press **Ctrl-K R** and enter the name of the file (including a drive and directory path, if needed).

That's it! The library also includes a procedure template template.pro and a function template template.fun that you can insert into your programs using the same technique.

SELF-REVIEW EXERCISES

9 10 11

3.4   STRUCTURED PROGRAMMING

• • • • • • • • • • • • • • •

Let's reconsider top-down design and programming. In *top-down design* we first state the major steps or subproblems that would give a solution to the overall problem, listing these in plain English (pseudocode). If these major steps require additional refinements, we start thinking in terms of a *modular program* and construct a *structure chart* to show subproblems (modules), their relationships, and data flows.

If we need to break down (refine) any of the subproblems, we have another level in the structure chart and additional modules in our program. This process of *modularizing* the top-down design continues until we do not need to refine any remaining modules. We can think of the modules in the structure chart as *blocks* that are used to construct or put together a program. In *top-down programming* we implement these modules as a main program, procedures, and functions.

The structure chart actually takes form as we develop the pseudocode algorithm for the main body. Each procedure and function also requires its own algorithm. As we list steps in an algorithm, we can start thinking of additional building blocks that are more elemental than modules. In fact, we can think of using these *elemental blocks* to construct the algorithm for a particular module. (Were you into "Legos" as a kid?)

These elemental blocks are technically called **control structures:** They precisely *control* the flow of action within blocks that serve as *structures* in "building" an algorithm. In a classic and now famous paper,[4] two Italian computer scientists mathematically proved that we can construct any algorithm using just three fundamental control structures: *sequence, repetition,* and *selection.*[5] A **structured program** is a program that strictly uses these three control structures (and their variations), as defined below.

SEQUENCE STRUCTURE

As we consider the control structures, it's useful to roleplay or desk check execution, as if we were processing statements ourselves (which we are indeed at the design stage). It's also best to think of a control structure as a *control block* that precisely defines execution action *within* the block.

The **sequence structure** defines sequential execution, as described by the block design shown in Figure 3.6. Within the sequence block, the flow of

---

[4]C. Bohm and G. Jacopini, "Flow Diagrams, Turing Machines, and Languages with Only Two Formation Rules," *Communications of the ACM,* vol. 9, no. 5 (May 1966), pp. 366–371.

[5]Actually, and even more impressively, it was just two, not three, as the title of the paper implies. We can show that the selection structure is a convoluted special case of the repetition structure. We'll skip this. It would just muddy the waters, for our purposes.

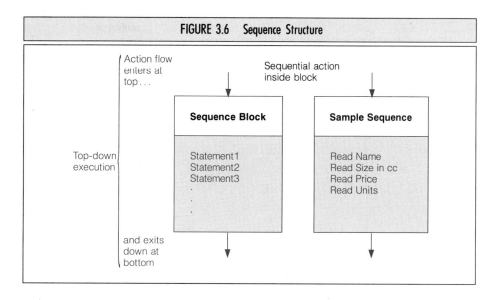

FIGURE 3.6   Sequence Structure

execution is *sequential;* that is, we execute the first statement, followed by the second statement, followed by the third statement, and so on.

We have already implemented the sequence structure in our programming. Every program we have written up to now uses a single sequence structure as the main body, procedure body, or function body.

Figure 3.6 also describes the concept of **top-down execution:** The flow of execution enters at the *top* of the block, behaves in a manner dictated by that block (in this case, sequential behavior), and exits *down* at the bottom of the block (and into the next control block or structure).

REPETITION STRUCTURE

The **repetition** or **iteration structure** specifies the *repeated* execution or *iteration* of a set of statements. This structure defines a **loop**, which has two distinct components.

- **Loop body,** the set of statements that gets repeatedly executed
- **Loop control,** the test condition that determines when to exit the loop

The **while-do** structure is the fundamental repetition structure, as seen in Figure 3.7. The first action in this structure is the loop control test. When the test result is *true* (the condition is satisfied), the loop body is executed; otherwise, the body is bypassed and the execution flow exits the structure. Whenever the body is executed, the execution flow loops back to the test condition, and the process is repeated. Thus, the while-do structure continues looping *while* the test condition is *true.*

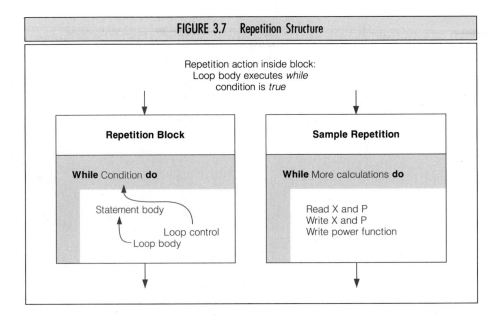

FIGURE 3.7   Repetition Structure

The example in Figure 3.7 shows a repetition structure for the power function application in Example 3.3. In this design, *we continue making power function calculations while we have more calculations.* The advantage of looping should be obvious here: Assuming we need to make more than one calculation, the loop design saves us from having to rerun the program for each additional calculation.

The while-do structure defines what's called a *pretest loop,* where the loop control precedes the loop body. A common variation in loop design is the *posttest loop,* where the loop control follows the loop body. The structure of a posttest loop is called a *repeat-until structure:* Looping continues *until* the test condition is true.

Keep in mind that the concept of a control structure in general and a repetition structure in particular is a *design* concept. Control structures just describe algorithmic design. Our particular descriptions are in pseudocode. Traditional flow diagrams or flowcharts also describe these. Just how a particular computer language *implements* these control structures is another matter altogether. The syntax varies from language to language. The design does not. We're going to spare you the details of Pascal implementations of all repetition structures until the next two chapters.

SELECTION STRUCTURE

The **selection structure** describes the *selection* of a flow branch based on a *condition* such as "Is the gender female?" The fundamental selection structure

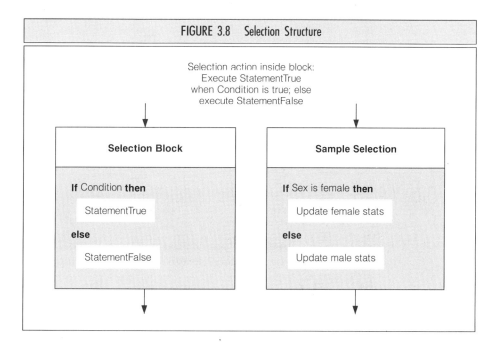

FIGURE 3.8   Selection Structure

Selection action inside block:
Execute StatementTrue
when Condition is true; else
execute StatementFalse

Selection Block

If Condition **then**

StatementTrue

else

StatementFalse

Sample Selection

If Sex is female **then**

Update female stats

else

Update male stats

is the **if-then-else structure** shown in Figure 3.8. On entering the selection block, a condition is evaluated, and the result is either true or false. **If** the condition is *true,* **then** a particular group of statements is executed (labeled StatementTrue in the figure), and execution exits the structure: **else** (the condition is *false*) another group of statements is executed (labeled StatementFalse in the figure), and execution exits the structure.

Note that the execution flow immediately exits the structure after either StatementTrue or StatementFalse is executed. *For a given test of the condition, just one group of statements (StatementTrue or StatementFalse) will be executed.*

If we omit the else portion of the if-then-else structure, we have a special case of the if-then-else structure called an **if-then structure.** The following illustrates sample pseudocode for an if-then structure.

If Units sold > 1500 **then** Decrease Price by 5%

It turns out (by mathematical proof) that we can describe all possible selections in algorithms by sequences of nested if-then-else structures. For example, we could place an inner if-then-else structure (block) within StatementTrue. We also have simplifications of nested selection structures called *else-if* and *case structures,* as we will see. We cover all Pascal implementations of selection structures in Chapter 6.

> # NOTE
>
> **8. The power structure.** Loop structures are the most powerful features of programming languages, because they allow automated I/O and computational processing of large amounts of *similar* data. Without looping, computers would not be cost effective, and IBM would be a typewriter company. Looping is introduced in the next chapter.

3.5 FROM THE TOP

• • • • • • • • • • • • •

Let's work with another application to review the software development cycle, and to reinforce top-down design and programming.

REQUIREMENTS

Harvey CORE, the president of METHsea Corporation, wants to locate an off-shore support facility for three of its seaweed methanol processing platforms. METHsea pioneered the manufacture of methanol from seaweed as an environmentally sound replacement for gasoline.[6]

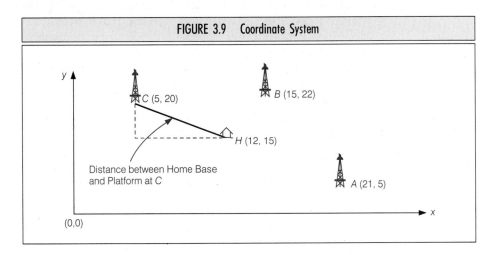

FIGURE 3.9   Coordinate System

---

[6]Yes, this is the very same Harvey CORE who also heads up the HC ENGINE Corporation. (Those BIG engines use up a lot of gas.) Actually, since we're into this little digression, it's Harvey CORE, Jr. Corporate folklore has it that his father, Harvey CORE, Sr., changed his surname from Abacus to CORE after claiming that he invented the computer memory used in early computers. Primary memory used to be called *magnetic core storage;* it was made up of thousands of "doughnut"-shaped magnetic cores strung together like beads on a wire. You heard it here first...

Figure 3.9 shows the coordinates for the three platforms, labeled A, B, and C. A sample Home Base location is shown at H. The coordinates are given in kilometers from the Origin $(0, 0)$ of the system. For example, the coordinate $(21, 5)$ for Platform A means that this platform's relative location from the Origin is 21 km along the x-axis (East) and 5 km along the y-axis (North).

The distance between any two pairs of coordinates (x_1, y_1) and (x_2, y_2) in a rectangular coordinate system is given by the *Euclidean distance formula*

$$d = \sqrt{(x_1 - x_2)^2 + (y_1 - y_2)^2}$$

For example, the distance between coordinates H and C in Figure 3.9 is calculated as

$$d = \sqrt{(5 - 12)^2 + (20 - 15)^2}$$
$$= \sqrt{74}$$
$$= 8.60 \text{ km}$$

HC wants an interactive decision support program that writes a report showing the distance between a proposed Home Base and each existing platform, and the total distance (sum of distances) from the Home Base to all platforms. He also requires the output of coordinate codes (H, A, B, and C), and all relevant coordinates. The user should only have to enter the proposed coordinate for the Home Base: 12 and 15 in the example. We're now ready to formalize the following *data requirements*.

Output data

For each location:

Code (H, A, B, or C)

x-coordinate (km)

y-coordinate (km)

Distance (km) between H and platform

Total distance from H to all platforms (km)

Input data

x-coordinate for Home Base

y-coordinate for Home Base

Constant data

For each platform location

Code = A B or C

x-coordinate (km) = 21.00 15.00 or   5.00

y-coordinate (km) =   5.00 22.00 or 20.00

Computational data

Each distance (using the Euclidean distance formula)

13.45 km between H and A

7.62 km between H and B

8.60 km between H and C

Total distance = 13.45 + 7.62 + 8.60

= 29.67 km

Note that the coordinate data for existing platforms are treated as constants. We would not want to force the user to tediously enter the same platform coordinate data for each proposed Home Base coordinate. In the next chapter we show a better approach to handling this kind of constant data: Place it in a data file and have the program read it in.

DESIGN

Let's start with the *user-interface design,* to better see where we are going. Note the following in Figure 3.10.

1. We show an introductory screen remark, the Home Base coordinate is interactively input, and the output report is in the form of a table, with title, head, body, and foot.
2. The illustrated data satisfy the data requirements at the requirements stage, including the computational data.

A sketch of the I/O design has several benefits: It ties the design to the data requirements; it simplifies the coding of output formats by serving as a blueprint; and it reminds us to desk check the calculations, which we use to confirm correct results in the test stage.

We should also put some thought into our intended treatment of *data types.* For example, single character codes for our coordinates suggest type *char;* distance coordinates and calculations suggest a need for numeric fractions, or type *real.*

FIGURE 3.10   I/O Design for Program MethSea1

```
Program MethSea, Version 1.0 ◄─────── ⎰── Introductory screen remark

Enter Home Base X-coordinate... 12 ◄─⎰── Interactive input
Enter Home Base Y-coordinate... 15
                                                    ┌── Distance report table


 HC METHsea Platform Distances                          ⎱ Table title


 Facility        X-Coordinate   Y-Coordinate      Distance     ⎱ Table head


 Home Base  H       12.00          15.00
 Platform   A       21.00           5.00          13.45
 Platform   B       15.00          22.00           7.62      ⎱ Table body
 Platform   C        5.00          20.00           8.60


                     Total distance...            29.67       ⎱ Table foot
```

The platform codes and coordinates also define a group of related data, which allows us to think of these data as a single structure, called a *data structure*. More on this when we consider data files in the next chapter.

To design the program's code, let's start with a view near the top by specifying the major tasks. We often treat these major tasks as subproblems or modules. These tasks are also actions that are implemented in the main body. In our current example, this idea translates into the algorithm for the main body.

Program Methsea1

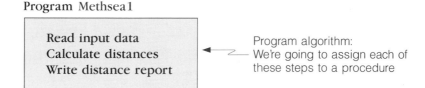

This algorithm is a single-sequence structure, and it's short. A key design goal for the main algorithm is to keep it short, to improve understanding. By "short" we mean from a handful of statements to less than a one-page listing.

Next, let's try some refinements. Consider the chart in Figure 3.11. This diagram combines the modules and data flows of a structure chart with stepwise refinements in pseudocode. Let's call this a **stepwise chart.** A sketch of the stepwise chart is a very natural precursor to coding the various algorithms in a program. It clarifies and identifies the program's blocks (by the boxes), the data flows among modules, and the major tasks as algorithms within the program and its modules. We like this approach better than separate sketches of stepwise refinements and structure charts and will use it often throughout the book.

Note the following in Figure 3.11.

1. We develop the stepwise chart by starting with the program's main algorithm at the left. Each task in this particular main algorithm is then refined into a procedure; that is, each task is a procedure call. This will not always be the case, since some tasks in main algorithms are simple enough not to require refinement.

2. The order of refining each task (module) is a matter of preference. We refined in the following order: ReadInput, CalcDistances, Distance, WriteReport.

3. In CalcDistances we refine the distance calculations with a distance function. Note that we require three separate distance calculations using the distance formula specified in the requirements. The only change from one distance calculation to the other is a change in the platform coordinate. So it makes sense to call a function for each distance calculation. We're using a function instead of a procedure because (a) we only need to return a single value and (b) it's conceptually appealing, since we really are dealing with a (mathematical) function.

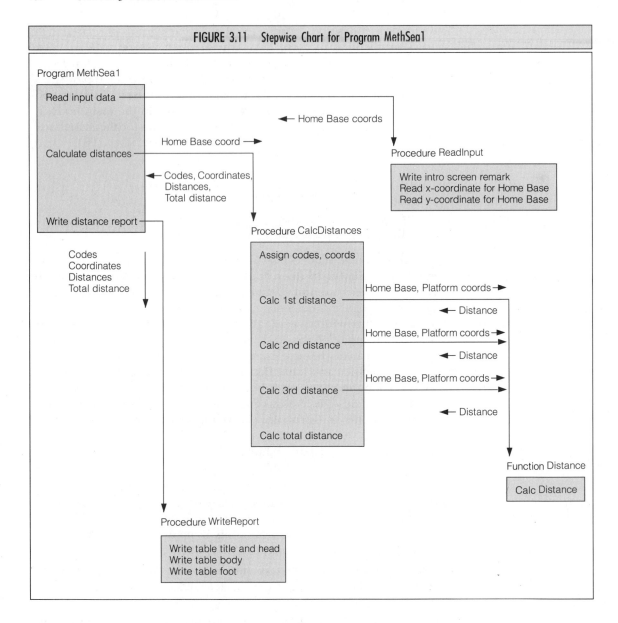

FIGURE 3.11   Stepwise Chart for Program MethSea1

4. This stepwise chart is equivalent to a *three-level structure chart* (levels 0, 1, and 2), where the distance function defines the third level. Note that the function is called by a procedure, not by the main program. Up to now, all calls had been issued from main programs (which always give two-level structure charts).

5. Make sure that you sketch either a stepwise chart or a structure chart before you begin writing code for the program itself. It's especially useful in

constructing the lists of actual and formal parameters from the indicated data flows. Look at the data flows in Figure 3.11. Do they make sense? ReadInput reads the Home Base coordinate and passes it to the main program. The main program then passes the Home Base coordinate to CalcDistances, which uses it to calculate each distance. To calculate a particular distance, CalcDistances uses the services of function Distance. It passes the Home Base coordinate and a Platform coordinate to the function, and gets Distance back. When CalcDistances is through with all distance calculations, it passes all platform Codes, Coordinates, Distances, and the Total distance to the main program. The main program in turn passes these values to WriteReport. Note that the codes and platform coordinates appear to originate within CalcDistances, which we confirm from the assignments in the procedure algorithm for CalcDistances.

Code

Armed with our design blueprints (user-interface sketch and stepwise chart with module algorithms and data flows), we're now ready to access the IDE, enter, and debug the program. Figure 3.12 shows a listing of this program. Study the program, and note the following points.

1. All values that flow through the main program are declared as variables within the main program, as seen in the var declarations. The stepwise chart clearly shows these flow variables.

2. Procedure CalcDistances assigns values to platform codes and coordinates. These values are stored in variables instead of declared as constants; otherwise, we could not pass these to the main program.

3. Function Distance is declared within the declarations section of procedure CalcDistances, to clearly show that the function is used only by the CalcDistances module. Its scope is the body of CalcDistances. Alternatively, we could have declared function Distance as a program declaration, placing it *before* the declaration of procedure CalcDistances. The function must be declared *before* its use by other modules to avoid an *Unknown identifier* compile-time error.

4. The value parameters X1,Y1 and X2,Y2 in the function are not the same identifiers as X1,Y1 and X2,Y2 elsewhere in the program. This illustrates how value parameters promote independence of modules according to the scope rules. In naming value parameters within a module, we only have to focus on identifiers that are meaningful within the module. If these identifiers appear in the formal parameter list, then the calling module just needs to focus on sending the proper values, not on what names these values are stored under within the called module. In fact, function Distance is stored in our utilities library of modules and can be used without any changes by any program that requires a Euclidean distance function.

FIGURE 3.12   Listing for Program MethSea1

```
program MethSea1;

  {* * * * * * * * * * * * * * * * * * * * * * * * * * * * * * * *
   *                                                              *
   *         Harvey CORE  METHsea Corporation:  Version 1.0       *
   *                                                              *
   *         Decision support for Home Base location              *
   *           Inputs Home Base coordinate                        *
   *           Calculates distances of Home Base to methanol platforms *
   *           Outputs distance report                            *
   *                                                              *
   *         Modular structure                                    *
   *           Main program                                       *
   *             |___ Procedure ReadInput                         *
   *             |___ Procedure CalcDistances                     *
   *             |   |___ Function Distance                       *
   *             |___ Procedure WriteReport                       *
   *                                                              *
   * * * * * * * * * * * * * * * * * * * * * * * * * * * * * * * *}

  {============================= Declarations =============================}

var
  Code1, Code2, Code3 : char;                {Coordinate codes}
  Xhome,Yhome,                               {Home Base coordinate}
  X1,Y1, X2,Y2, X3,Y3,                       {Platform coordinates}
  Distance1, Distance2, Distance3,           {Home Base to each platform}
  TotalDistance : real;                      {Home Base to all platforms}

  {======================= Procedure Declarations =======================}
                                             ⟵——— Note: Parameter list correspondence
procedure ReadInput (var Xhome, Yhome: real);      to ReadInput call in main body

  { Writes introduction and reads Home Base coordinates
      Receives  nothing  ⟵————————— No value parameters
      Sends Xhome, Yhome} ⟵————————— Variable parameters

const
  Intro = 'Program MethSea, Version 1.0';   {Introductory remark}

begin   {ReadInput}                                    ⟵—— ReadInput
                                                           algorithm
  writeln;                                                 (body)
  writeln (Intro);
  writeln;
  write ('Enter Home Base X-coordinate... ');  readln (Xhome);
  write ('Enter Home Base Y-coordinate... ');  readln (Yhome);

end;    {ReadInput}
  {----------------------------------------------------------------------}
```

---

5. In procedure WriteReport, note how we consciously aligned the table parts in the const section and declared constants W and D. In our table design, we selected numeric output fields having 15-position widths and 2-place decimals. By declaring the 15 and 2 as constants W and D, respectively, we make it easier to change and experiment with the output design.

6. Finally, note how variables in the parameter lists correspond to the data flows in the stepwise chart. We use the stepwise chart (or a structure

FIGURE 3.12 (*continued*)

```
                                        ┌─ Note: Parameter list correspondence
                                        │   to CalcDistances call in main body
procedure CalcDistances (Xhome, Yhome : real;
                         var Code1, Code2, Code3 : char;
                         var X1,Y1, X2,Y2, X3,Y3 : real;
                         var Distance1, Distance2, Distance3 : real;
                         var TotalDistance : real);

  { Assigns platform data and calculates all distances
    Receives Xhome, Yhome ◄─────────────────────────── Value parameters
    Sends Code1, Code2, Code3, X1,Y1, X2,Y2, X3,Y3, Distance1, Distance2◄
          Distance3, TotalDistance}        Note: Parameter list correspondence  Variable parameters
  {_____ to Distance call in CalcDistances body }
  function Distance (X1,Y1,  X2,Y2 : real) : real;

    { Calculates Euclidian distance between two pairs of coordinates
      Receives two pairs of coordinates ◄───────┐
      Returns  Euclidian distance }              └─ Value parameters

  begin   {Distance}

    Distance := sqrt( sqr( X1 - X2 ) + sqr( Y1 - Y2) );    ◄──┐ Distance
                                                              │ algorithm
  end;    {Distance}                                          (body)
  {_____ }

begin   {CalcDistances}

  Code1 := 'A';   X1 := 21.00; Y1 :=  5.00; {Code, coordinates 1st platform}
  Code2 := 'B';   X2 := 15.00; Y2 := 22.00; {Code, coordinates 2nd platform} ◄──┐ CalcDistances
  Code3 := 'C';   X3 :=  5.00; Y3 := 20.00; {Code, coordinates 3rd platform}    │ algorithm
              {All coordinates in kilometers}                                   (body)
                                     ┌─ Note: Parameter list
  Distance1    := Distance (Xhome, Yhome, X1, Y1);  correspondence to Distance
  Distance2    := Distance (Xhome, Yhome, X2, Y2);  declaration above
  Distance3    := Distance (Xhome, Yhome, X3, Y3);
  TotalDistance := Distance1 + Distance2 + Distance3;

end;    {CalcDistances}
{----------------------------------------------------------------------}
```

chart) as a guide in constructing these parameter lists. All formal parameters that correspond to values that are sent back to the calling module are declared as *variable parameters*. For example, the stepwise chart shows that the Home Base (x, y) coordinate is returned to the main program; thus, parameters Xhome and Yhome are variable parameters in the procedure heading for ReadInput. This procedure does not receive any values; thus, it has no *value parameters*.

TEST

Figure 3.10 also shows our final test run for program MethSea1. After various iterations, we eliminated several compile-time errors. We had no run-time errors. The correct output in Figure 3.10 also suggests the elimination of logic errors. If we notice logic errors, a careful *desk check* of the program often uncovers the cause of these errors.

FIGURE 3.12   (*continued*)

```
procedure WriteReport (Code1, Code2, Code3 : char;          Note: Parameter list correspondence
                       X1,Y1,  X2,Y2,  X3,Y3,  Xhome,Yhome,  to WriteReport call in main body
                       Distance1, Distance2, Distance3,
                       TotalDistance : real);

  { Writes distance report
    Receives all codes, coordinates, and distances          Value parameters
    Sends nothing  }                                         No variable parameters
const
  Title = 'HC METHsea Platform Distances';
  Line  = '_____';
  Head  = 'Facility        X-Coordinate   Y-Coordinate        Distance  ';
  Foot  = '                      Total distance... ';

  W = 15; D = 2;    {Width of output fields and number of Decimal places}

begin   {WriteReport}

  writeln;  writeln;                                         WriteReport
  writeln (Title);                                           algorithm
  writeln (Line);  writeln;                                  (body)
  writeln (Head);
  writeln (Line);  writeln;
  writeln ('Home Base ', 'H',   Xhome :W:D, Yhome :W:D);
  writeln ('Platform  ', Code1, X1    :W:D, Y1    :W:D, Distance1 :W:D);
  writeln ('Platform  ', Code2, X2    :W:D, Y2    :W:D, Distance2 :W:D);
  writeln ('Platform  ', Code3, X3    :W:D, Y3    :W:D, Distance3 :W:D);
  writeln (Line);  writeln;
  writeln (Foot, TotalDistance :W:D);

end;    {WriteReport}

  {============================ Main Body ============================}

begin   {MethSea1}                                           MethSea1
                                                             algorithm
  ReadInput (Xhome, Yhome);                                  (body)

  CalcDistances (Xhome, Yhome, Code1, Code2, Code3, X1,Y1, X2,Y2, X3,Y3,
             Distance1, Distance2, Distance3, TotalDistance);

  WriteReport (Code1, Code2, Code3, X1,Y1, X2,Y2, X3,Y3,  Xhome,Yhome,
             Distance1, Distance2, Distance3, TotalDistance);

end.    {MethSea1}
                                                  Note: Parameter list correspondences
                                                  to declarations above
```

3.6   PROGRAMMING TIPS

• • • • • • • • • • • • •

Consider the following tips to improve the design and style of your programs
and to avoid some common errors.

DESIGN AND STYLE

1. On Using Modular Programming.   Let's review why it makes sense
to use modular programming.

a. It's a direct reflection of *top-down design* principles like "divide and conquer" through *stepwise refinement*. It's also consistent with the idea behind *procedural abstraction*. When coding a particular task that we plan to implement by a procedure or function, we don't have to be concerned at that time about the details within that module. We just have to know (in an abstract way) what that module will do for us, not how it does it.

b. It supports *literate programming* principles that promote program readability by clearly stated algorithms. The main algorithm in a modular program almost reads like pseudocode in its calls. For example, in Figure 3.12, the main algorithm "reads" ReadInput, CalcDistances, and WriteReport. This is about as literate as it gets (other than using still longer names that read like sentences).

c. It facilitates the creation of *utility module* libraries. If certain general tasks have already been programmed, a utility module saves us from "reinventing the wheel." All we really need to know about a utility module is how to incorporate it in our program (see Note 7) and what actual parameters we need to use. We don't have to know how it works; just what it does. This is the ultimate expression of *procedural abstraction*, and it is the idea behind standard procedures like readln.

d. It saves or simplifies coding when tasks are repeated at different points in a program. For example, distance is calculated three times in Figure 3.12 within procedure CalcDistances, so we wrote a distance function for this purpose. Our function doesn't save or simplify coding in this small example. However, if the task is elaborate, taking many lines of code, then this advantage is easier to visualize. Later in the book we show several examples where this benefit is apparent.

e. It promotes *specialization* and *division of labor,* where specific modules are assigned to specific programmers. This project management approach is typical in the development of large programs that are written by teams of many programmers.

f. It facilitates coding and testing, since tasks are more clearly defined and bugs are better isolated. The process called **top-down development** or **top-down testing** is a direct reflection of this idea. In this approach we code and test one module at a time. Modules not yet tested are included in the program as stubs, with nothing more than the proper heading and a body that prints a message to the effect that the module was activated but is not yet ready. After a module is successfully coded and tested, we go on to the next stub. We illustrate this approach later in the book. In a variation called **bottom-up testing,** a stub or new module is coded and tested independently of the program. A simple main program called a driver or driver program is written to test the module. The program CkPower1 in Example 3.3 is an example of a driver that tested function Power1. The finished module is then placed in its intended program or library. Bottom-up testing is common when adding modules to utilities libraries or to large existing programs.

2. On Selecting Modules.   Beginning programmers are often at a loss as to how to select modules or what tasks to assign as modules. Pascal in general and Turbo Pascal in particular are especially adept at implementing and promoting these top-down principles. These are good reasons why Pascal is the language of choice for teaching programming. There is no one, simple answer to this. And different programmers have different opinions. But we offer the following guidelines.

a. The initial design algorithm, the one for the main body, often suggests modules one level down from the top (level 1 in the structure chart). The major tasks of "Reading data," "Processing data," and "Writing data" are good candidates for modules, as seen in Figure 3.11.

b. Any major refinements in the stepwise refinement process may suggest a module.

c. Tasks that need to be repeated at different points suggest a module. See item 1d above.

d. A task that's already programmed as a utility module is an obvious module. Be aware of available utility modules in your programming environment, and see inside the front cover of this book. Also see Note 7.

e. Function or procedure? See Note 6.

f. Modules should be neither too long nor too short. An industry rule of thumb says that "modules should not exceed 100 lines of code"; otherwise, the programmer may lose "intimacy" with the task. A program with a few, very long modules is *undermodularized.* Very short modules promote *overmodularization,* or too much refinement. This might impair readability and degrade performance. Textbook programs like those in this chapter tend to be overmodularized, since the focus is on teaching principles rather than demonstrating realistically long programs. For example, procedures WriteIntro and Calculate in program Engine2 are not "worthy" modules from this viewpoint. The introductory remark is easily folded into either the main body or procedure ReadInput (as we did in program MethSea1); the two calculations are best placed in the main body.

3. Documentation.   Good documentation is another key component of *literate programming.* Look at our documentation in Figure 3.12 as we stress the following points.

a. Include a description of the modular structure. We use a diagram that kind of looks like a sideways structure chart.

b. In each module, include a brief description of its purpose, the values it *receives,* and the values it *returns.*

c. Visually separate modules from one another by spacing and ruled comment lines.

4. Side Effects.   Avoid side effects by ensuring that all variables in a procedure (or function) are declared through either the formal parameter list or the procedure's (or function's) declarations section. You might want to review the discussion on scope in Section 3.2.

5. Optimization Note.   An overmodularized program degrades processor time over a less modularized version. This is because modules increase *overhead*, or processor time that's devoted to housekeeping chores. For example, the compiler has to generate extra code to keep track of module calls and returns.

6. SDC Guide.   A *Software Development Cycle Guide* is listed inside the front cover. Take a look now... As seen, it's a step-by-step summary description of how we might go about developing programs. It's just a reminder. You might find it useful in developing your own programs.

Common Errors

1. Incorrect Module Placement.   Don't forget to declare the procedure or function before it's used in a body. Otherwise the call is outside the *scope* of the procedure or function and the compiler gives an *Unknown identifier* error message.

2. Noncorresponding Parameter Lists.   Be careful that corresponding actual and formal parameters in parameter lists agree in number, order, and type. A compile-time error like " *,*" *expected* or "*)*" *expected* may mean that the number of items don't agree between the two lists. To avoid *Type mismatch* compile-time errors, make sure that actual parameters that correspond to formal *value* parameters are *assignment compatible;* actual parameters that correspond to formal *variable* parameters are *typed identically.*

3. Missing var.   Don't forget that any formal parameters that "send" values must be *variable parameters,* thereby requiring the reserved word **var** in the parameter declaration. Otherwise, a value is not "sent" and the calling module uses whatever value it formerly had for that variable, giving a logic error. Also, the actual parameters that correspond to formal variable parameters must be variables themselves. Otherwise, it's a *Variable identifier expected* compile-time error.

4. Violated Precondition or Postcondition.   Make sure that the calling program satisfies the *precondition* of assigning values that it passes to other modules. For example, if

we had forgotten to call ReadInput in Figure 3.12

values in Xhome and Yhome would be incorrect (initialized to zero by Turbo Pascal's compiler) when CalcDistances is called. The program runs without compile-time or run-time errors, but gives incorrect distances based on a Home Base location at the origin $(0,0)$ of the coordinate system.

Similarly, make sure a module satisfies its *postcondition* by assigning returning values to all of its variable parameters. If

we had forgotten to read Yhome in the ReadInput procedure

we would have a postcondition error. The wrong value (zero) for Yhome would be "returned" to the main program, and the output report would show incorrect distances from a Home Base location at $(12, 0)$.

5. Side-Effect Error.   We have a side-effect error by using a variable whose scope includes a module, coupled with not having declared that variable in the formal parameter list or in that module's declaration section. To illustrate, consider function Distance in Figure 3.12. In the assignment statement for Distance, let's

mistakenly replace X2 with X3 and Y2 with Y3.   ☹

X2 and Y2 are value parameters in this function (they are in the formal parameter list without a qualifying **var**). X3 and Y3 are visible to this module (they were declared in the program's var section) *and* they neither appear in the formal parameter list nor are declared locally within the function. We have a *side-effect error*. These errors can be particularly subtle. The output would show that all distances were calculated from the Home Base to platform C, since (X3,Y3) is the coordinate for platform C.

SELF-REVIEW EXERCISES
16 17 18

REVIEW EXERCISES

EASIER	For the busy... 16 17 18
NORMAL	For the thinkers... 1 2 5 6 7 8 9 10 11 12 13 14
TOUGHER	For the hard CORE... 3 4 15

(L)   **1.**   **HC ENGINE.** Reduce modularization in Engine2 in Example 3.1 by eliminating procedures WriteIntro and Calculate. Of course, we still want the introductory comment and the necessary calculations. Test the revised program.

(L) *2.   HC ENGINE. Add a new procedure to program Engine2 in Example 3.1. This procedure displays the following company logo at the start of the program.

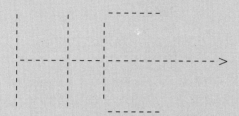

Use a series of writeln statements to display the logo. Consider storing the logo under declared constants within the procedure. Test the revised program.

*3.   HC ENGINE. The company plans to display the logo in the preceding exercise at the start of all programs used by its employees. Write a utility procedure that displays this logo when called. Name it Logo and test it by writing a simple driver program. (HC himself might be impressed if you improve the logo design. How's your artistic flair?)

4. Answer the following regarding Figure 3.4 in Example 3.2.

a. Suppose we were to insert the following statements in the main body just after the first call.

```
Var1 := 5;
Var2 := 15;
Proc (Var1, Var2, SumScaled);
```

Indicate the contents for all memory cells following the second call.

b. Modify the original program by using the following two statements.

```
SumScaled := Var1 + Var2;    ←── Insert just before
                                  call to Adjust
AdjSum := AdjSum * Scale;    ←── Replace original
                                  in Adjust
```

Indicate the contents for all memory cells following the call. What can you say about variable parameter AdjSum regarding precondition and postcondition values?

c. Rewrite procedure Adjust as function SumScaled. Accordingly revise program Test. Which approach do you prefer and why?

5. Let's check your understanding of value and variable parameters. Assume the following procedure body.

```
begin  {Test}
  E := 2*E;
  F := D + E;
end;   {Test}
```

Fill in the memory cells after each call, where *A*, *B*, and *C* store 5, 10, and 15, respectively, just before each call.

The Call	The Procedure Heading	..Memory Cells..
		A B C D E F
		5 10 15
a. Test (A, B, C);	**procedure** Test (D, E : **integer; var F : integer);**	
b. Test (C, B, A);	**procedure** Test (D, E : **integer; var F : integer);**	
c. Test (A, B, C);	**procedure** Test (D, E, F : **integer);**	
d. Test (A, B, C);	**procedure** Test (**var** D, E, F : **integer);**	

6. Let's check your understanding of scope. In the parts below, assume the following nested procedures.

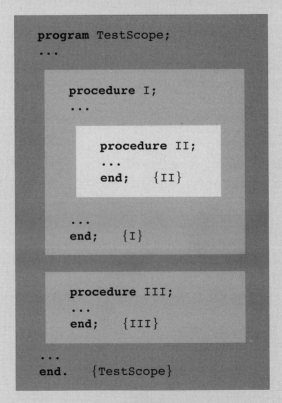

```
program TestScope;
...

    procedure I;
    ...

        procedure II;
        ...
        end;    {II}


    ...
    end;    {I}


    procedure III;
    ...
    end;    {III}

...
end.    {TestScope}
```

a. Is I callable from TestScope? Explain.
b. Is I callable from III? Explain.
c. Is II callable from I? Explain.
d. Is II callable from III? Explain.

   e. Is II callable from TestScope? Explain.
   f. Is III callable from TestScope? Explain.
   g. Is III callable from I? Explain.

*7. Write a driver that tests function SqDiff in the function declaration syntax box. The driver inputs two values and outputs their squared difference.

(L) ***8.** **Storing a utility module.** If you worked the preceding exercise, try storing function SqDiff in a utilities library as follows: Place the cursor at the beginning of the function; mark the function by pressing the **Shift** key while pressing a **cursor** key to move the cursor to the end of the function; write the marked block to a file by pressing **Ctrl-K W** and entering the file specification (give function files **fun** extensions). This is the basic technique for creating your own utilities library.

(L) **9.** **Function Power1.** Use program CkPower1 in Example 3.3 to check out the following.
   a. Run the program to evaluate $(-2)^3$. Problem?
   b. Run the program to evaluate 2^{-1}. Problem?
   c. Run the program to evaluate 2^0. Problem?
   d. Run the program to evaluate 20^{30}. Problem?
   e. Correct the problem in part **d** by creating utility function **power1a.fun**, which uses **double** real type (see Appendix D). Accordingly change CkPower1 and come up with an answer to the calculation in part **d**.

(L) **10.** **Function Power1.** Make changes in the main body of program CkPower1 in Example 3.3 to evaluate $(1 + x)^{p-1}$. Test the revision by using the same inputs for x and p as the original example. *Note:* Don't change the function itself.

(L) **11.** **Function Power1.** In Example 3.3 . . .
   a. Can we type X and P integer and still call function Power1? Explain why or why not.
   b. Revise the driver and run the program to confirm your answer in the preceding part. Input 2 for X and 3 for P. What happens if you input 2.1 for X? *Hint:* You also need to change the driver's output formats to eliminate fractional output.

(L) ***12.** Reread Note 7 and try the following: Load the template **template.pas**; place the cursor in the function section and insert function **power1.fun** from the Utilities Library. What do you think? Check out two other templates that we have in the program library: Insert a procedure template named **template.pro**; insert a function template named **template.fun**. You might want to use these as you add new procedures or functions to your programs.

(L) ***13.** **HC METHsea.** Use program MethSea1 from Section 3.5 to find the location (to the nearest kilometer) that minimizes total distance. The winner receives a gift certificate for free lifetime fillups of METHsea brand methanol. Send your entry and optimal coordinate to

Professor Harvey CORE
Computer Aided Decisions
57 Wandsworth Street
Narragansett, RI 02882

Good luck! There's no consolation prize...

(L) *14.   **HC METHsea.**   Revise program Methsea1 in Section 3.5 to include a fourth platform at location D (5, 30). Test the program using the original Home Base location at (12, 15). Then repeatedly use the program to find the best location for the Home Base.

(L) *15.   **HC METHsea.**   An alternative distance criterion to that used in Section 3.5 is distance-squared. This criterion penalizes long distances more then short distances. Revise program MethSea1 to give an output report that includes a new column and total for squared distances. Test the program using the same Home Base coordinate at (12, 15). Repeatedly use the program to find the best location based on distance. Then use it again to find the best location based on distance-squared. Plot your proposed Home Base locations in Figure 3.9. Do their locations make sense?

(L) 16.   **Precondition error.** Confirm the precondition error discussed in item 4 under "Common Errors." Load program MethSea1, place comment braces around the call to ReadInput, execute, and see what happens.

(L) 17.   **Postcondition error.** Confirm the postcondition error discussed in item 4 under "Common Errors." Load program MethSea1, place comment braces around the readln statement that reads Yhome, execute, and see what happens.

(L) 18.   **Side-effect error.** Confirm the side-effect error discussed in item 5 under "Common Errors." Load program MethSea1, make the indicated changes, execute, and see what happens.

ADDITIONAL EXERCISES

EASIER	For the busy...
	19 20 21
NORMAL	For the thinkers...
	22 23
TOUGHER	For the hard CORE...
	24

19. **Revisit: Temperatures.** Redesign the problem in Exercise 6 of Chapter 1 to modularize the program in Exercise 15 of Chapter 2. Create function Celsius in this revision.

20. **Revisit: Disk areas.** Redesign the problem in Exercise 7 of Chapter 1 to modularize the program in Exercise 16 of Chapter 2. Creat function AreaCir in this revision.

21. **Revisits.** Modularize one of the following programs from the "Additional Exercises" in Chapter 2.
    a. **Mailing address**
    b. **Metric conversion**
    c. **Grade report**
    d. **Drag races**

22. **Hypotenuse.** Consider the right triangle

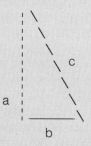

and the Pythagorean theorem

$$c^2 = a^2 + b^2$$

Write a modular program that inputs values for *a* and *b*, uses a function that returns *c*, and writes the results using a facsimile of the accompanying triangle drawing, except use actual values in place of letters. Test your program using the following set of test data for *a* and *b*: 5 and 5; 0.5 and 10; 50 and 100. Assume that *a* or *b* never exceeds 999.99, and output numeric values to one decimal place.

23. **Initials function.** Write a string function that receives a person's first and last name, extracts the first letter in each, combines them into the identifier Initials, and returns the initials. The function also ensures that these initials are uppercase. (*Hint:* See standard function **upcase**.) Test the function by writing a driver that inputs first name and last name, calls function Initials, and writes the person's first name, last name, and initials. Use the following test data: Harvey CORE, yarta Morfella, rick jones.

24. **Bank savings.** A monetary compounding formula is

$$Future = Starting \cdot (1 + Rate/100/Times)^{Years \cdot Times}$$

where

$Future$ = Future accumulation of money at end of time horizon

$Starting$ = Starting amount of money

$Rate$ = Percent interest on annual rate of return

$Times$ = Number of times per year account is compounded
(for example, 12 if interest is added monthly)

$Years$ = Number of years in time horizon

For example, if we start with $10,000 and gain 10 percent per year compounded just once a year, then after 30 years we end up with

$$Future = \$10,000 \cdot (1 + 10/100/1)^{30 \cdot 1}$$
$$= \$10,000 \cdot 17.449402$$
$$= \$174,494.02$$

Albert Einstein said it best: "The greatest innovation of mankind is compound interest."

a. Develop a modular program that inputs starting amount, annual interest rate, times compounded per year, and years; computes future amount; and displays a report that shows all input data and future amount. Use the test data given above.

b. Try the following test data: $10,000 starting amount, 10-year horizon, 10 percent interest rate, and one compounding per year. Does quarterly compounding make much of a difference in the future amount? How about monthly compounding? Weekly compounding? Daily? Hourly?

c. The ultimate account compounds continuously according to the formula

$$Future = Starting \cdot e^{Years \cdot Rate/100}$$

where e is the base of natural logarithms (see **exp** in Appendix F). Wouldn't you want to earn money even as you read this? Add the continuously compounded future amount to the report in part **a**.

d. Manhattan Island purchase. In 1626 Peter Minuit, the first Director General of the Dutch Province of New Netherlands, bought Manhattan Island from the Native Americans for a dollar equivalent of about $22. If the Native Americans had invested this amount at 7 percent per year compounded annually and let it ride, how much would it be worth today? (You might be surprised by the answer...it's conceded that this amount exceeds today's real estate valuation for Manhattan.)

REPETITION: *FOR-DO* LOOP

‡Optional, more advanced material. Skip without loss of continuity, study at this point, or wait until later.

This chapter introduces the first of our repetition-structure implementations, the *for-do loop*. We also show how the for-do loop is convenient for data-file input.

4.1   FOR Statement

• • • • • • • • • • • • • •

We use the for statement to implement the for-do loop, as described next.

Implementation of For-Do Loop

From our work in Section 3.4, we know that the *repetition structure* iteratively executes a *loop body* based on a *loop control* test. The fundamental repetition structure is the *while-do structure,* which says that the loop body is executed *while* the loop control tests *true.* We postpone the direct implementation of the while-do structure until the next chapter. Here we consider a special implementation of the while-do structure, called the for-do loop.

The **for-do loop** executes the loop body *while* a variable called the *control variable* changes values from an initial value to a final value. The control variable always starts at an *initial value*, and either increments by one up to its final value or decrements by one down to its final value. The for-do loop is often called a *counter loop*, because the control variable is like a *counter* that changes by one as it moves from its initial to its final value. The pseudocode in Figure 4.1 illustrates this design, and the syntax box shows its implementation in Pascal as a **for statement.**

Before going on to the next section, study the design in Figure 4.1, relate it to the syntax in the syntax box, make sure you follow the examples and their I/O, and note the following.

1. The integer control variable Counter in the first example within the syntax box simply varies from 3 to 5 in *increments* of one. Thus, this loop repeats or *iterates three times,* which is to say that the loop body is executed three times. The sample output confirms these iterations.

2. The second example is like the first, except the reserved word **to** is replaced by the reserved word **downto**, the initial value is now High instead of Low, and the final value is now Low instead of High. In other words,

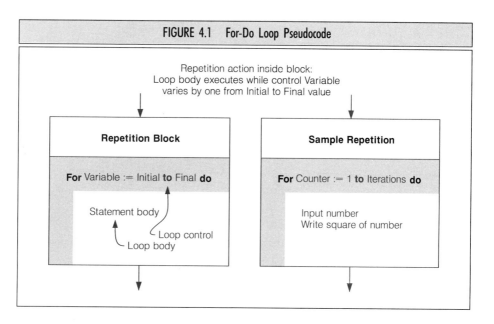

FIGURE 4.1   For-Do Loop Pseudocode

Repetition action inside block:
Loop body executes while control Variable
varies by one from Initial to Final value

Repetition Block

For Variable := Initial **to** Final **do**

Statement body

Loop control
Loop body

Sample Repetition

For Counter := 1 **to** Iterations **do**

Input number
Write square of number

Counter now starts at 5 and *decrements* down to 3, as confirmed by the output.

3. The third example simply emphasizes that the initial and final values are evaluated as expressions. In this case, the initial value is evaluated as the constant 1 and the final value is evaluated as 2 based on the expression High **div** 2, where High stores 5. Now the loop *iterates twice,* as Counter changes from 1 to 2.

4. The fourth example shows how it's possible to bypass the execution of a loop body altogether. In this case Counter is supposed to increment from its low value to its high value, but the low value 8 is initially greater than the high value 5. Thus, it's not possible for Counter to change from 8 to 5, and the loop *iterates zero times;* that is, the loop body does not get executed at all. This emphasizes that *the for-do loop executes the loop body while the control variable varies within its range of defined values.* If we had used **downto** in this example, the loop would iterate three times as Counter varies from 8 down to 5.

5. The fifth example emphasizes that the control variable can be any of the ordinal types described in Appendix D. Remember that the values defined by an *ordinal type* are listable. In this example, the listable values are characters based on the ordinal type **char**. Here the control variable Character varies over the range of values a to c, giving the *three iterations* confirmed by the output.

SYNTAX BOX

For-do loop (for statement)... Repeat body while control variable ranges by one
from initial to (or downto) final value

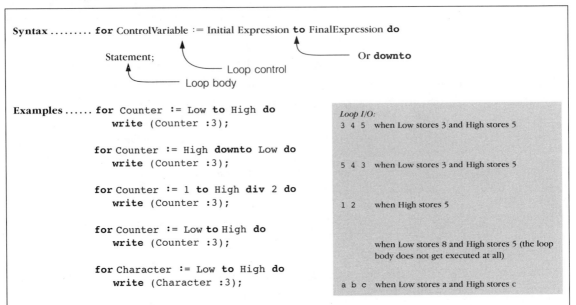

Explanation... ControlVariable is a variable identifier, Initial Expression is an expression whose value is the initial
value in ControlVariable, and FinalExpression is an expression whose value is the final value taken on by
ControlVariable. The control variable is one of the *ordinal types* (Appendix D), and the initial and final expressions
must be *assignment compatible* with the control variable. **for, to, downto,** and **do** are reserved words. If the
initial value is greater than the final value in the **to** case, the loop body is not executed. Similarly, if the initial value
is less than the final value in the **downto** case, the loop body is not entered. The change in the control variable is
always one position in the ordered list of values, as in 3 to 4 to 5 for integers and a to b to c for characters. This
one-position change is called the *increment* in the **to** case and the *decrement* in the **downto** case. Statement is a
simple or compound statement and is executed for each repetition of the loop. If a loop body requires multiple
simple statements, these must be enclosed by a **begin-end** pair, giving a *compound statement* as the body.

EXAMPLE 4.1   LOOP BODY AS COMPOUND STATEMENT

Each example in the syntax box illustrates a loop body having a simple statement.
A **simple statement** is a single statement as defined in Chapter 2: an instruction
that describes algorithmic action, like assigning or writing a value. *The syntax of
the for statement dictates a single-statement loop body.* So what do we do if we
want the loop body to include multiple simple statements as seen in Figure 4.1? We
wrap them in a **begin** and **end** pair, which Pascal defines as a **compound statement**. By definition, a compound statement is a single statement, which satisfies
the syntactic needs of the for statement.

For example, the code fragment

```
write ('Iterations?'); readln (Iterations);
for Counter := 1 to Iterations do
```

This compound statement is a *single* statement containing three simple statements

```
   begin
     write   ('Enter number ');
     readln (Number);
     writeln ('    Square = ', sqr(Number));
   end; {for}
```

shows a compound statement as the body of a for-do loop. A sample run with two loop iterations would look like this.

```
Iterations? 2
Enter number 5
       Square = 25
Enter number 3
       Square = 9
```

NOTE

1. On compound statements. Don't forget that multiple simple statements in a for-do body must be enclosed in a begin-end pair; otherwise, the compiler takes the body to be the first simple statement, giving a logic error. We need not place a semicolon following the last statement, just before **end**.

2. On indentation. It's good form to indent a loop body, since it more clearly highlights the body and visually separates it from any statements that might follow the for-do loop.

OUTPUT TABLES

Loops are ideally suited to tablelike processing, as in the input of a table of data, the output of a report table, or the manipulation of related data in a table format.

The familiar structure of an output table with columns of data is a *title* at the top, followed by column *headings*, followed by the rows of data or *body* of the table, and finally followed by an optional *foot*, as in column sums or footnotes. Typically, the table components are separated by ruled or blank lines.

We considered this type of output table structure in program MethSea1 in the last chapter (see Figure 3.10). Unlike that example, the next example shows the generation of a table body from within the body of a for-do loop.

EXAMPLE 4.2   ASCII TABLE GENERATOR

We mentioned the ASCII method of coding individual characters in Section 1.1 and used it in describing elements of the Pascal language in Chapter 2. Appendix I

FIGURE 4.2   Listing and I/O for Program Ascii

(a) Listing in Edit Window

```
program Ascii;

   {* * * * * * * * * * * * * * * * * * * * * * * * * * * * * * * * * *
    *                                                                 *
    *            ASCII Table Generator                                *
    *                                                                 *
    *            Inputs low and high ASCII values                     *
    *            Outputs corresponding range of ASCII characters as table  *
    *                                                                 *
    * * * * * * * * * * * * * * * * * * * * * * * * * * * * * * * * * *}

   {============================ Declarations ============================}

const
  Intro = 'ASCII Table Generator...';
  Title = 'ASCII Table';
  Line  = '                                                    ';
  Head  = '*Decimal      Character';
  Foot  = '*Decimal position or ASCII value';

var
  Position,                          {Decimal position or ASCII value}
  LoASCII, HiASCII : integer;        {Low, high ASCII values that define range
                                      for Position}

   {============================ Main Body ============================}

begin   {Ascii}

  writeln;
  writeln (Intro);
  writeln;
  write (' Enter low  ASCII value... ');   readln (LoASCII);
  write (' Enter high ASCII value... ');   readln (HiASCII);
  writeln;   writeln;
  writeln (Title);
  writeln (Line);   writeln;
  writeln (Head);
  writeln (Line);   writeln;

  for Position := LoASCII to HiASCII do
     writeln (Position :5, '          ', chr( Position ));

  writeln (Line);   writeln;
  writeln (Foot);
end.    {Ascii}
```

Simplifies visual alignment of table parts

Table parts that precede table body

For-do loop

Table body written within loop

Table parts that follow table body

FIGURE 4.2   (*continued*)

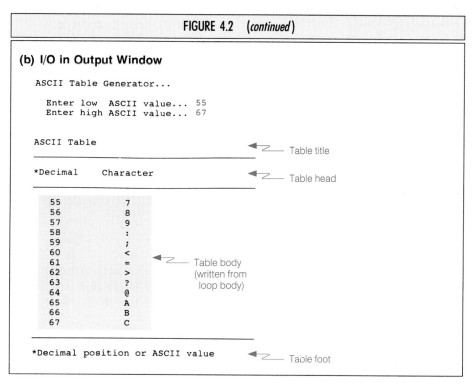

(b) I/O in Output Window

```
ASCII Table Generator...

  Enter low  ASCII value... 55
  Enter high ASCII value... 67


ASCII Table                                    Table title


*Decimal      Character                        Table head


    55           7
    56           8
    57           9
    58           :
    59           ;
    60           <                              Table body
    61           =                              (written from
    62           >                              loop body)
    63           ?
    64           @
    65           A
    66           B
    67           C


*Decimal position or ASCII value               Table foot
```

shows the extended ASCII character set that's used in Turbo Pascal. The column labeled *Decimal or ASCII value* is the position of the corresponding ASCII character in an ordered sequence. For example, we can say that the character A (with ASCII value 65) is "less than" the character C (with ASCII value 67).

The program in Figure 4.2 shows an ASCII table generator. Note the following.

1. The output table has the standard table structure of title, head, body, and foot. All elements but the body are declared as constants in one place. This improves the readability of writeln statements and facilitates the visual alignment of these components.

2. The for-do loop generates the table body. A call to the standard function **chr** is used to return the appropriate ASCII character based on the provided decimal position. For the given ASCII-value range 55 to 67, the control variable Position iterates through the *13* values 55, 56, 57, ... , 67, as seen in the output table. Thus the loop *iterates 13 times*. This means that the single writeln statement gets executed 13 times, giving the 13 rows in the table.

3. Don't be insulted. We need to say this: The table title and head are written before the loop, and the foot is written after the loop. This may seem obvious, but for some reason we've seen more than a few beginning programmers place the title and head within the body of the loop. This means, of course, that our sample run would generate 13 titles and heads as part of the table body!

SELF-REVIEW EXERCISES

1 2 3 4 6a 7 8

4.2   SELECTED IMPLEMENTATIONS

The for-do loop is ideally suited for implementing a number of tasks. Let's take a look at some of these.

SUMS

The repetition structure is a natural for accumulating a series of values into a *sum*. In this case, we initialize the variable that stores the sum to zero before the loop, accumulate it within the loop body, and when the loop is finished we have the required sum.

EXAMPLE 4.3   SUMMING ALGORITHM

Let's read in successive values for an integer variable named Score (as in scores for your programming assignments) and accumulate these values in another integer variable called SumScores. The number of scores is stored in integer variable NumberScores. The following algorithm does the job.

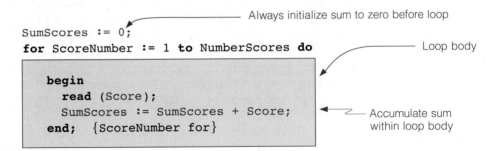

For example, if NumberScores stores 3, then the loop iterates three times. If we successively input the scores 95, 90, and 100, then SumScores successively stores the values 0 (at initialization), 95 (after the first iteration), 185 (after the second iteration), and 285 (after the third and final iteration).

FACTORIAL FUNCTION

The *factorial* of a number x (written $x!$, or x *factorial*) is a necessary calculation in many problems in mathematics and statistics. By definition, $x!$ is the product

$$1 \cdot 2 \cdot 3 \cdot \ldots \cdot (x - 2) \cdot (x - 1) \cdot (x)$$

For example, if the value of x is 5, then

$$5! = 1 \cdot 2 \cdot 3 \cdot 4 \cdot 5$$
$$= 120.$$

The factorial of zero $(0!)$ is defined as 1; the factorial is undefined if x is negative $(x < 0)$.

EXAMPLE 4.4   FUNCTION FAC

Figure 4.3 shows *Fac*, our utility factorial function, and the driver that we used to test it. Study this figure and note the following.

1. The function receives an *integer* value for X. Factorials apply only to whole-number values.

2. The function returns a real value with type **extended** (as defined in Appendix D). Obviously, the factorial of an integer number is necessarily an integer itself. So the natural inclination is to type the function as one of the integer types given in Appendix D. From this table, the largest integer that the function could return is *2,147,483,647* (just over *2 billion*), for type **longint**. This number looks and sounds big, but it's small fry as far as factorials are concerned. For example, 13! exceeds this number, thereby causing *integer overflow*. To make this function more useful, we selected the real type with the biggest range, **extended**. This type handles values with exponents up to *4932*, which means that our function will calculate factorials of numbers up to the 1700s (as we ask you to confirm in Exercise 12b). The use of type real to represent a theoretical integer introduces some approximation errors for very large values. But this is a small price to pay for the benefit of a greater range, in most but not all applications.

3. The use of real types with ranges greater than **real** requires certain floating-point calculations that use the 8087 and 80287 numeric coprocessors. This means that we have to enable the *numeric processing compiler directive* {**$N+**} within either the program or the IDE menu system (as described in the function's note in Figure 4.3). If the computer is not equipped with one of those pricey numeric coprocessors, we need to emulate with the directive {**$E+**}. In Exercise 12c we ask you to "play" with this compiler directive.[1]

---

[1]We explain selected Turbo Pascal compiler directives in Appendix G. Use this appendix as a reference throughout the book whenever we mention or illustrate compiler directives.

FIGURE 4.3   Listing and I/O for Program CkFac

(a) Listing in Edit Window

```
program CkFac;

   {* * * * * * * * * * * * * * * * * * * * * * * * * * * * * * * * * *
    *                                                                 *
    *          Driver checks Factorial function                      *
    *                                                                 *
    *             Inputs Number of Xs and each X                      *
    *             Calls function Fac                                  *
    *             Outputs X and its factorial                         *
    *                                                                 *
    * * * * * * * * * * * * * * * * * * * * * * * * * * * * * * * * * *}

   {=========================== Declarations ===========================}

var
  Number,                    {Number of factorials desired}
  X,                         {The number whose factorial is to be calculated}
  Item   : integer;          {Control variable in for-do loop}

   {======================= Function Declarations =======================}

function Fac (X : integer) : extended;

   { Utility determines factorial of X, or X!
     Receives integer X
     Returns  extended Fac }

   { NOTE:  Use num. processing compiler directive $N+ or IDE menu sequence
            Options --> Compiler --> 8087/80287

            Use emulation compiler directive $E+ or IDE menu sequence
            Options --> Compiler --> Emulation  }
var
  K          : integer;   {Control variable in for-do loop}
  Factorial : extended;   {Stores factorial calculations}

begin  {Fac}                ── Initialize product

  Factorial := 1;
  for K := 2 to abs(X) do
    Factorial := Factorial * K;          ── For-do loop that calculates
                                            running product
  Fac := Factorial;          ── Update product

end;  {Fac}

   {============================= Main Body =============================}

begin  {CkFac}

  writeln;  writeln ('Evaluates x!');  writeln;
  write ('Enter number of factorials to evaluate... ');  readln (Number);

  for Item := 1 to Number do
    begin
      writeln;  writeln;
      write ('Enter x... ');  readln (X);          ── For-do loop for
      writeln;                                         multiple factorials
      writeln (X :5, '! is... ', Fac(X));            in one run
    end;  {for}

end.    {CkFac}
```

FIGURE 4.3   *(continued)*

(b) I/O in Output Window

```
Evaluates x!

Enter number of factorials to evaluate... 3

Enter x... 5

    5! is...   1.20000000000000E+0002

Enter x... 100

  100! is...   9.33262154439442E+0157

Enter x... 1000

 1000! is...   4.02387260077094E+2567
```

---

4. We call the standard function **abs** in the for statement to ensure the use of absolute (nonnegative) values when calculating factorials. In Chapter 6, we let you redesign the function to trap the possible error of receiving a negative value for X.

5. The for-do loop in the function calculates the necessary factorial. Note that the calculation of a *running product* is very similar to the calculation of a *running sum*, as in Example 4.3. The running product (factorial in this case) is initialized just before the loop and iteratively calculated within the body of the loop. We ask you to roleplay this *product algorithm* in Exercise 12a.

6. The driver's main body uses a for-do loop to process multiple factorials in one run. In Figure 4.3 this loop iterated three times.

---

‡Increments Other Than One

Suppose we wish to systematically vary the values for a *numeric* variable over a range. For example, we might want to vary an *integer* weight from a low value of 15 to a high value of 25. The first inclination is to use weight as a control variable in the for statement, letting it vary from 15 to 25. This works, but it restricts the increment to one. Suppose we want an increment of 5? Now we can't use weight as a control variable because the for statement assumes an increment of one. As a second example, suppose an increment of one is acceptable, but weights are typed *real*. Again we can't use weight as a control variable because type real is not an ordinal type.

---

‡Optional, more advanced material. Skip without loss of continuity, study at this point, or wait until later.

The solution to our little dilemma is to calculate the number of iterations based on the low, high, and incremental values for weight; use iterations as the final value for an integer control variable; and assign values to weight within the body of the loop. Let's show the particulars by example.

EXAMPLE 4.5   WEIGHT CONTROL

Suppose *integer* variable Weight is to vary from Lo to Hi in increments of Increment, and we wish to output the progression of weights over this range. Assume Lo stores 15, Hi stores 25, and Increment stores 5. The following code segment does the trick, where Iterations is typed integer.

```
Weight     := Lo;
Iterations := (Hi - Lo + Increment) div Increment;

for Counter := 1 to Iterations do
  begin
    write (Weight :4);
    Weight := Weight + Increment;
  end; {for}
```

Weight is initialized to 15 and Iterations is assigned 3, or the whole-number part of $(25 - 15 + 5)$ divided by 5. The for-do loop thus iterates three times, giving the output

     15   20   25

If Weight, Lo, High, and Increment were typed *real*, then the proper formula for Iterations is

```
Iterations := round( (Hi - Lo + Increment) / Increment);
```

where the standard rounding function evaluates a real expression and returns its rounded integer value.

NESTED FOR-DO LOOPS

The act of placing one control structure within another is called *nesting*. Up to now the body of each for-do loop has included a single sequence structure—that is, a sequence structure nested within a repetition structure. In general, the body of a loop can include any number of control structures, unnested and nested. Here we consider another for-do loop entirely within the body of the original for-do loop. The inner for-do loop is said to be *nested* within the outer for-do loop.

EXAMPLE 4.6   NESTED FOR-DO LOOPS

The key to understanding nested for-do loops is careful attention to iterations and the values stored within the control variables of each. To illustrate, consider the following nested for-do loops.

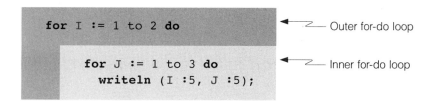

```
for I := 1 to 2 do                          ◄— Outer for-do loop

    for J := 1 to 3 do                      ◄— Inner for-do loop
        writeln (I :5, J :5);
```

The output would look like this:

```
1       1
1       2
1       3
2       1
2       2
2       3
```

Changes in inner control variable, J
Changes in outer control variable, I

As seen, for every iteration of the outside loop, the inside loop iterates through its complete cycle.

We can also have additional levels of for-do nesting, as in an *outer* for-do loop, an *inner* for-do loop, and an *innermost* for-do loop. We ask you to consider this variation in Exercise 16a.

EXAMPLE 4.7   AVERAGE SCORES

Let's further illustrate nested for-do loops and summing by developing an interactive program that calculates an average exam score for each student in a class.

Requirements

The *output data* for each student are name and average score. The *input data* are number of students, number of scores per student, and (for each student) name and a set of scores. We have no *constant data,* and the *computational data* item is the average score for each student given by the sum of scores divided by the number of scores.

FIGURE 4.4   I/O Design for Program AveScore

```
AVERAGE SCORE CALCULATOR

Enter number of students... 2
Enter number of scores..... 3


Enter student name... Joshua Clay
Enter 3 scores....... 95 90 100

    Name...... Joshua Clay
    Average...  95.0


Enter student name... J. K. Dunn
Enter 3 scores....... 50 90 68

    Name...... J. K. Dunn
    Average...  69.3
```

Design

Figure 4.4 illustrates the I/O design. In our sample run, we process three scores for each of two students. This implies that we have a nested loop design: an outer "student" loop and an inner "score" loop. The student loop iterated twice, and the score loop iterated three times for each student.

Figure 4.5 shows a stepwise chart with four refinements: Two of these are procedures Preliminaries and WriteReport, and the other two are nonmodular refinements in the main algorithm. In Exercise 17 we ask you to convert these nonmodular refinements into procedures.

Preliminaries takes care of reading the number of students and the number of scores and sends these to the main algorithm, as seen by the data flows. These are used to specify the iterations in the student and score loops, respectively. The main algorithm uses the student loop to "process students." In processing a student we need to initialize the sum, read a name, "process the scores," calculate an average, and write the report with a call to WriteReport. This call sends a student's name and average, which are written by the procedure. Scores are processed by another loop, as seen in the refinement that iteratively reads and sums scores for a student.

Code and Test

Figure 4.6 on page 136 shows the program listing and Figure 4.4 shows an actual run. Study these figures and note the following.

1. The outer for-do loop processes students and the inner for-do loop processes the different scores for a particular student. Thus, scores must be summed within the inner loop.

2. The sum must be reinitialized to zero each time a new student is processed; otherwise, we have a logic error and incorrect averages for all but the first stu-

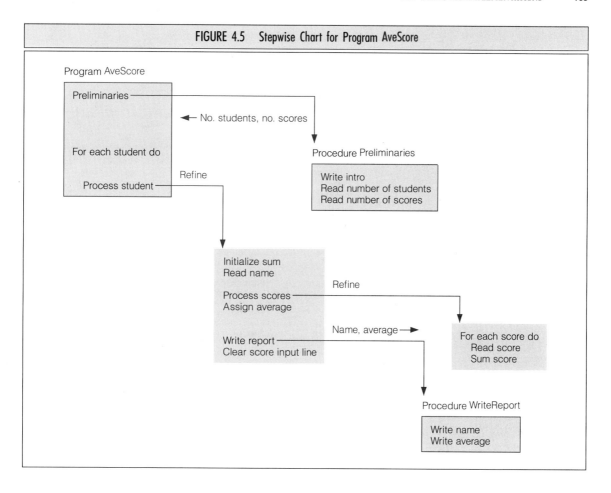

FIGURE 4.5   Stepwise Chart for Program AveScore

Program AveScore

Preliminaries

◄— No. students, no. scores

For each student do

Process student —— Refine

Procedure Preliminaries

Write intro
Read number of students
Read number of scores

Initialize sum
Read name

Process scores —— Refine
Assign average

Name, average —►

Write report ——
Clear score input line

For each score do
Read score
Sum score

Procedure WriteReport

Write name
Write average

dent. This reinitialization must be within the outer loop and must precede the inner loop. Try out this error in Exercise 17a.

3. The average is calculated and written *following* the inner loop, once the sum is determined. We often see beginning programmers place the assignment of average just after the assignment of sum within the body of the inner loop. This does calculate the proper average at the last iteration of the inner loop, but inefficiently includes the calculation of incorrect intermediate averages.

4. Did you notice that we called predeclared procedure **read** instead of **readln** to input the score for each student? This allows the entry of all scores for a particular student on one line because **read** does not issue a line feed at the end of the input operation. Normally we counsel one value per input line but make exceptions whenever input data are related and identically typed. In these cases, multiple data entries on a line are visually appealing and efficient. And we need not fret over the rules for entering mixed-type data on a

---

FIGURE 4.6   Listing for Program AveScore

```
program AveScore;

 {* * * * * * * * * * * * * * * * * * * * * * * * * * * * * * * * *
  *                                                               *
  *             Average Score Calculator                         *
  *                                                               *
  *             Inputs students' names and scores                *
  *             Calculates their averages                        *
  *             Outputs students' names and averages             *
  *                                                               *
  *             Modular structure                                *
  *                  ___  Preliminaries                          *
  *                  ___  WriteReport                            *
  *                                                               *
  * * * * * * * * * * * * * * * * * * * * * * * * * * * * * * * * *}

 {============================= Declarations =============================}
var
  Average         : real;         {Average score for a student}
  Name            : string;       {Name of student}
  NumberScores,                   {Number of scores per student}
  NumberStudents,                 {Number of students}
  Score,                          {Student's score}
  ScoreNumber,                    {For-do control variable in score loop}
  StudentNumber,                  {For-do control variable in student loop}
  SumScores       : integer;      {Sum of scores for a student}

 {===================== Procedure Declarations =====================}

procedure Preliminaries (var NumberStudents, NumberScores : integer);

  { Writes Intro and reads number of students and number of scores
    Receives nothing
    Sends NumberStudents, NumberScores }

const
  Intro = 'AVERAGE SCORE CALCULATOR';

begin   {Preliminaries}

  writeln;
  writeln (Intro);
  writeln;
  write ('Enter number of students... ');  readln (NumberStudents);
  write ('Enter number of scores..... ');  readln (NumberScores);
  writeln;

end;    {Preliminaries}
 {----------------------------------------------------------------------}
```

single input line. Note that the last statement in the outer loop's body (the **readln**) clears the score input line; otherwise, the next input operation (the next student's name) will continue reading from that line.

5. The sample run includes two students and three scores per student. These values were input and stored in the variables NumberStudents and NumberScores, which serve as the upper limits for the control variables in the

FIGURE 4.6 *(continued)*

```
procedure WriteReport (Name : string;  Average : real);

  { Writes student report
    Receives Name, Average
    Sends nothing }

begin  {WriteReport}

  writeln;
  writeln ('  Name...... ', Name);
  writeln ('  Average... ', Average :5:1);

end;   {WriteReport}

  {=========================== Main Body ============================}
```

Outer (student) loop →

```
begin  {AveScore}

  Preliminaries (NumberStudents, NumberScores);

  for StudentNumber := 1 to NumberStudents do
    begin

      SumScores := 0;  ◄─── Logic error if not initialized

      writeln;  writeln;
      write ('Enter student name... ');  readln (Name);
      write ('Enter ', NumberScores, ' scores....... ');

      for ScoreNumber := 1 to NumberScores do
        begin
          read (Score);
          SumScores := SumScores + Score;
        end;   {ScoreNumber for}                        ◄─── Inner
                                                             (score)
                                                             loop
      Average := SumScores / NumberScores;

      WriteReport (Name, Average);

      readln;    {Clears score input line for proper read of next name}

    end; {StudentNumber for}

end.   {AveScore}
```

two for statements. By using a variable as the final value expression for each control variable, we promote the *generality* of this program; that is, the program can process *any* number of students and *any* number of scores.

SELF-REVIEW EXERCISES

11 12 14a–d 16 17a–b

‡4.3 INPUT FROM TEXT FILES

• • • • • • • • • • • • • • • •

This section describes statements for reading input data from a file rather than the keyboard.

DATA, PROGRAM, AND TEXT FILES

A **data file** is any file that contains data. To distinguish these from files that contain programs, we use the term **program file** for the latter. In Turbo Pascal, we create a *source program* using the IDE's editor. The resulting program file is given a .PAS extension in its file name. If we compile this source program to disk as an *object program,* the IDE uses the same file name, but with a .EXE extension. To clearly identify a data file, we will use a .DAT extension in its file name.

Files are also classified by the *data type* in storage. In this section, we're concerned with files of type **text,** or text files. A **text file** strictly contains text characters formatted into lines, where each line ends with a "hidden" *end-of-line* marker (from pressing the Enter key). The one-byte characters in the text file are encoded and decoded according to the processor's coding scheme, or *ASCII* in our case.

We can create, edit, view, and print text files by using the editor. We can also display text files using the DOS TYPE command. A program file created with the IDE's editor and stored as a source program (with a .PAS extension) is an example of a text file. A program file stored as an object file (with a .EXE extension) is not. The latter is an example of a *binary file,* which contains the internal binary coding for that processor.

In this section we create data files using the IDE's editor. Therefore, our data files are also examples of text files. We then use these text files as input data for our programs. In Chapter 12 we extend the use of data files to output and describe different kinds of data files and file types. *Between now and Chapter 12 all of our data files are text files.* So we pretty much use the terms *data file* and *text file* interchangeably.

TEXT-FILE CREATION

Figure 4.7 shows a text file for the HC ENGINE data introduced earlier in Table 1.1. We created this data file just as you see it, using the same IDE editor that we use to create program files. Note that the input data are identical to input data that we would enter interactively at the keyboard. The only difference is the method for providing the data. In *online data* or *interactive*

---

‡Optional, more advanced material. Skip without loss of continuity, study at this point, or wait until later.

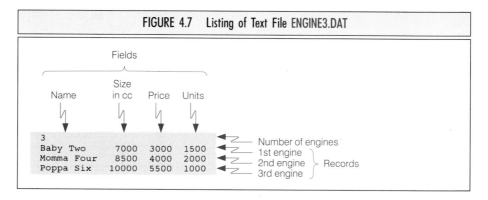

FIGURE 4.7   Listing of Text File ENGINE3.DAT

input we enter the data at the keyboard based on program prompts *during* execution of the program; in *offline data* or *noninteractive input* we place the data in the text file *before* we execute the program that processes the text file.

Let's define some useful terminology when working with data files. Look at Figure 4.7. A **field** is an attribute that describes some entity, like an engine. In our example we have the four fields Name, Size in cc, Price, and Units. A **record** is the group of fields that describe the entity, or engine in our example. Figure 4.7 shows three records, one for each engine. The **data file** is the collection of related records, as seen in Figure 4.7. This kind of file structure is called a *flat file*, where each line in the file is a record and each column is a field. Later in the book we will see how Pascal's *record type* simplifies the processing of records.

The first data item in the file, the 3, is the number of records that follow. We need this data item to process the file using a for-do loop. In the next chapter we show another loop design that won't require this item. Accordingly, we don't conceptually consider the line with 3 a "record."

We created the data file just like we create a program file. We selected File Open . . . , named the file ENGINE3.DAT, typed the data just as you see it in Figure 4.7, and saved it with File Save. That's it! Nothing to it.[2]

NOTE

3. On naming the data file. We can give the data file any legitimate DOS name, but we suggest the following as a convention that we will use throughout the book. We relate the program file and data file by using the same name with a different extension. In our example we used the name ENGINE3, becuase the program is the next version of ENGINE2. Turbo Pascal automatically gives files the extension .PAS,

continued

---

[2]Actually, there is a little more to it: We need to decide just how we will space the data in each line of the file. We'll come back to this shortly.

which is fine for our program files but not for our data files. We will use the .DAT extension for data files. This gives the name ENGINE3.DAT for the data file in Figure 4.7. *Where should we place the data file?* We suggest using the same drive and directory that store program files. This simplifies our programming, as described in the next section.

4. What's a data structure? A **data structure** is a collection of *related* data that are arranged in some meaningful pattern or structure. We can view a text file as a data structure of characters arranged into lines. In our example, ENGINE3.DAT contains a data structure in a tablelike pattern, where the rows (records) represent different engines and the columns (fields) describe the characteristics of a particular engine. As we will see in later chapters, we can read a record in the file into RAM as a *record data structure;* we can also read all records in the file into an *array-of-records data structure.* Variables that directly reflect data structures by their typing are called *structured variables,* as opposed to the *simple variables* we have been using. For now, we will process our data structures using simple variables; later we will use structured variables. We got ahead of ourselves, but we just wanted to make you aware that data-structure considerations are important in the first three stages of the software development cycle.

TEXT-FILE PROCESSING

We're now ready to describe statements that process a text file for entering input data. We start with a familiar example.

EXAMPLE 4.8   HC ENGINE, VERSION 3.0

Let's recycle through the software development cycle from where we left off in Example 3.1, which itself is a rework of the SDC description from Section 1.2.

Requirements

We have two changes in the requirements. First, the users wish to include all three engines in the output report, together with a total for all sales. The company may add new engines in the future, so the number of engines should be part of the input data. Total sales as the sum of individual engine sales is added to the output data. Second, the users don't want to type in data interactively—they would rather see all data in a disk file and keyed by the (lower-paid) members of the company's typing pool.

FIGURE 4.8   Output for Program Engine3

```
               Start of program Engine, Version 3.0


                         SALES REPORT
         ─────────────────────────────────────────

         Engine name............Baby Two
         Engine size (cc).......        7000
         Engine size (ci).......         427
         Engine price...........      $3000
         Engines sold (units)...        1500
         Sales..................  $4500000
         ─────────────────────────────────────────



         ─────────────────────────────────────────
         Engine name............Momma Four
         Engine size (cc).......        8500
         Engine size (ci).......         519
         Engine price...........      $4000
         Engines sold (units)...        2000
         Sales..................  $8000000
         ─────────────────────────────────────────



         ─────────────────────────────────────────
         Engine name............Poppa Six
         Engine size (cc).......       10000
         Engine size (ci).......         610
         Engine price...........      $5500
         Engines sold (units)...        1000
         Sales..................  $5500000
         ─────────────────────────────────────────


         Total sales........... $18000000
```

Design

The new requirements foster two key changes in the design. First, we must include a repetition structure that processes all engines in one run. Second, we change the user interface by placing all input data in a text file (Figure 4.7), which requires design changes in the algorithm. The design of the original output report is satisfactory. Figure 4.8 shows the revised output report and Figure 4.9 shows the new design algorithms.

In Figure 4.9 note the following.

1. The program algorithm shows a very common design for programs with a major processing loop: an opening-tasks procedure, a processing loop, and a closing-tasks procedure. Keep this design in mind for your own programming.

2. One of the opening tasks is the preparation of a text file for processing. One of the closing tasks is the closing of this text file. Design algorithms that process data files should include these tasks. We describe these when explaining the program's code.

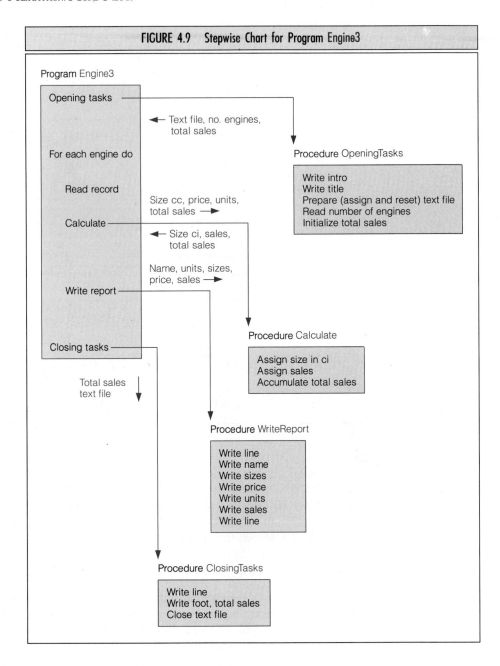

FIGURE 4.9   Stepwise Chart for Program Engine3

Code and Test

Figure 4.10 lists the code for program Engine3. Sections of the program with color screens indicate text-file processing material. We created program file Engine3 by editing the previous version, file Engine2.[3]

```
┌─────────────────────────────────────────────────────────────────────────┐
│                   FIGURE 4.10    Listing for Program Engine3              │
├─────────────────────────────────────────────────────────────────────────┤
│                                                                           │
│  program Engine3;                                                         │
│                                                                           │
│     {* * * * * * * * * * * * * * * * * * * * * * * * * * * * * * * * *     │
│      *                                                          *          │
│      *        Harvey CORE ENGINE Corporation:   Version 3.0     *          │
│      *                                                          *          │
│      *          Inputs engine name, size (cc), price, units sold *         │
│      *             from text file ENGINE3.DAT                   *          │
│      *          Calculates engine size (ci), sales revenue, total sales * │
│      *          Outputs engine name, sizes, price, units, sales revenue, * │
│      *             total sales                                  *          │
│      *                                                          *          │
│      *          NOTE:  Data for all engines processed in one run *         │
│      *                                                          *          │
│      *          Modular structure                              *          │
│      *            Main program                                 *          │
│      *                    ___  Procedure OpeningTasks          *          │
│      *                   |___  Procedure Calculate             *          │
│      *                   |___  Procedure WriteReport           *          │
│      *                   |___  Procedure ClosingTasks          *          │
│      *                                                          *          │
│      *          Data structure of text file                   *          │
│      *          --------------------------------------------------- *     │
│      *          Number of engines                             *          │
│      *          Name---->| Size_cc  Price  Units  <-- 1st engine *         │
│      *          Name---->| Size_cc  Price  Units  <-- 2nd engine *         │
│      *            ...                                          *          │
│      *                                                          *          │
│      * * * * * * * * * * * * * * * * * * * * * * * * * * * * * * * *}       │
│                                                                           │
│     {=========================== Declarations ===========================} │
│                                                                           │
│  const                                                                    │
│     Size = 10;                         {Size attribute for Name}          │
│                                                                           │
│  var                                                                      │
│     Engine         : integer;      {Engine number, for-do control variable}│
│     Name           : string [Size]; {Name of engine}                     │
│     NumberEngines  : integer;      {Number of engines}                    │
│     Price          : real;         {Price of engine in $ per unit}        │
│     Sales          : real;         {Sales revenue in $}                    │
│     Size_cc        : real;         {Engine size in cubic centimeters, cc} │
│     Size_ci        : real;         {Engine size in cubic inches, ci}      │
│     TextFile       : text;         {Text-file variable}                   │
│     TotalSales     : real;         {Total sales revenue in $}             │
│     Units          : integer;      {Number of engines sold in units}      │
│                                                                           │
│     {====================== Procedure Declarations ======================} │
│                                                                           │
└─────────────────────────────────────────────────────────────────────────┘
```

Note: Screens and color show text-file processing material

continued

[3]In your own work the best way to develop a new version of an old program is to **F**ile **O**pen... the old program, revise it as necessary, and **F**ile **S**ave as... using a new name. In our case, we opened program file Engine2, revised it accordingly, and stored it under the new name Engine3.

FIGURE 4.10   (*continued*)

```pascal
procedure OpeningTasks (var TextFile      : text;
                        var NumberEngines : integer;
                        var TotalSales    : real);

   { Writes intro remark and title, prepares text file, inputs number of
       engines, initializes total sales
     Receives nothing
     Sends TextFile, NumberEngines, TotalSales }

const
   Intro    = 'Start of program Engine, Version 3.0';   {Intro remark}
   FileSpec = 'ENGINE3.DAT';                            {Drive:PathFileName}
   Title    = '          SALES REPORT';                 {Report title}

begin   {OpeningTasks}

   writeln;
   writeln (Intro);
   writeln;   writeln;
   writeln (Title);

   assign (TextFile, FileSpec);        {Assign FileSpec to TextFile}
   reset  (TextFile);                  {Open text file, reset file position}
   readln (TextFile, NumberEngines);   {Read first value in text file}

   TotalSales := 0;

end;   {OpeningTasks}
{-----------------------------------------------------------------------}
procedure Calculate (Size_cc, Price : real;   Units : integer;
                     var Size_ci, Sales, TotalSales : real);

   { Calculates Size_ci, Sales, TotalSales
     Receives Size_cc, Price, Units, TotalSales
     Sends Size_ci, Sales, TotalSales }

const
   MetricConversion = 0.06102;                  {cc = 0.06102 ci}

begin   {Calculate}

   Size_ci    := MetricConversion * Size_cc;
   Sales      := Price * Units;
   TotalSales := TotalSales + Sales;

end;   {Calculate}
{-----------------------------------------------------------------------}
```

First, notice the *documentation* changes. The input description now includes the name of the text file. We also describe the data structure of the text file. Get in the habit now of documenting the data structure of any text files used by a program.

Let's consider the other text-file processing changes one by one.

1. **Text-file variable declaration.** We need to declare a *text-file variable* with data type **text**. The standard identifier **text** is a data type for text files. The text-file variable is used by statements in the program to reference the data

FIGURE 4.10   *(continued)*

```
procedure WriteReport (Name : string; Units : integer;
                       Size_cc, Size_ci, Price, Sales : real);

   { Writes report for single engine
     Receives Name, Units, Size_cc, Size_ci, Price, Sales
     Sends nothing }

const
  Line  = '_____';

  W = 10; D = 0;                {Width of fields, decimals in real output}

begin  {WriteReport}

  writeln (Line);  writeln;
  writeln ('Engine name............',         Name     :W);
  writeln ('Engine size (cc).......',         Size_cc :W:D);
  writeln ('Engine size (ci).......',         Size_ci :W:D);
  writeln ('Engine price...........     $', Price    :W-6:D);
  writeln ('Engines sold (units)...',         Units    :W);
  writeln ('Sales................. $',      Sales    :W-3:D);
  writeln (Line);

end;   {WriteReport}
{-------------------------------------------------------------------------}
procedure ClosingTasks (TotalSales : real;  var TextFile : text);
```
— Declare as variable parameter
```
   { Writes table foot and total sales, closes text file
     Receives TotalSales, TextFile
     Sends nothing }

const
  Line  = '_____';
  Foot  = 'Total sales........... $';

  W = 10; D = 0;                {Width of fields, decimals in real output}

begin  {ClosingTasks}

  writeln (Line);  writeln;
  writeln (Foot, TotalSales :W-2:D);

  close (TextFile);             {Close text file}

end;   {ClosingTasks}

  {============================= Main Body =============================}

begin  {Engine3}

  OpeningTasks (TextFile, NumberEngines, TotalSales);

  for Engine := 1 to NumberEngines do
    begin
      readln (TextFile, Name, Size_cc, Price, Units);
      Calculate   (Size_cc, Price, Units, Size_ci, Sales, TotalSales);
      WriteReport (Name, Units, Size_cc, Size_ci, Price, Sales);
    end; {for}

  ClosingTasks (TotalSales, TextFile);

end.   {Engine3}
```
— Reads single record in data file for each iteration of loop

file. In Figure 4.10 we selected the name TextFile for the text-file variable and declared it in the var section as follows:

```
TextFile : text;
```

We declared this variable *globally* (in the main program) rather than *locally* (in a procedure) because the main program is its "hub." That is, it needs to be passed from procedure OpeningTasks to the main program, it's used in the main program, and it's passed again from the main program to procedure ClosingTasks. By the way, text-file variables must be declared as *variable* parameters in parameter lists, even if only received and not returned (as done in procedure ClosingTasks); otherwise, the compiler flags an error.

2. **Text-file name.** We need to provide the name of the text file, or ENGINE3.DAT in our example.[4] We can provide this name either through a constant or a string variable. If a particular program is to be wedded to a particular data file for life, the name of the data file will never change, which suggests a constant. Programs that are designed to process different data files over time require data-file names that we input and store in string variables. In our current example, we use a constant; in Exercise 20 we ask you to use a string variable.

   Having decided on using a constant for the file specification, the next decision is using either the constant 'ENGINE3.DAT' or a *declared* constant like FileSpec. We prefer the latter as a better design choice because file-specification constants can appear in more than one place in a program. By declaring file-specification constants in one place (the const section), we simplify potential program maintenance. Accordingly, we declared the constant FileSpec as ENGINE3.DAT in the const section of OpeningTasks.

```
FileSpec = 'ENGINE3.DAT';
```

We declared FileSpec *locally* because its only use is within procedure OpeningTasks. By the way, we don't have to use uppercase letters for the name of the data file. We use caps as a matter of programming style: The data-file name stands out better and DOS expresses all file names in caps.

---

[4]More accurately, we need to provide the **file specification** (see the DOS review in Appendix A if you're fuzzy here), which includes the drive, directory path, and file name. If we omit the drive and directory path, then the default drive and directory path are assumed when Turbo Pascal looks for the data file. To check and change (if necessary) your default directory, select **C**hange dir from the **F**ile pull-down menu. For example, if you use a diskette in drive B and the root directory for all your program and data files, your default should be B:. If you have the right default directory, you need only specify the name of the data file, which simplifies things; otherwise, you need to provide the entire file specification, as in B:ENGINE3.DAT.

3. **assign statement.** This predeclared procedure call associates or couples the text-file variable and the file specification. In Figure 4.10 we used the following assign statement.

These two now coupled; subsequent file-processing statements use TextFile instead of FileSpec

```
assign (TextFile, FileSpec);
```

4. **reset statement.** This predeclared procedure call "opens" the file for processing and resets the file position to the beginning of the file. The *file position* indicates the next character position that's to be processed. Execution of the reset statement is analogous to inserting a cassette tape and *rewinding* it to the beginning, or inserting a musical CD and selecting the first cut. In Figure 4.10 we used the following reset statement.

Note use of text-file variable, not the file specification.

```
reset (TextFile);
```

Note that the text-file variable TextFile is used to identify the file that's to be reset. The actual file is ENGINE3.DAT, as the declared constant FileSpec. Turbo Pascal "knows" it's ENGINE3.DAT because we coupled TextFile and FileSpec through the earlier execution of the assign statement. *The **assign** statement thus needs to precede the **reset** statement that resets that file.*

5. **readln statement.** This statement is the same as that described earlier in Section 2.5. To indicate that input is from a text file we simply include the text-file variable as the *first* variable in the variable list of the readln statement. In Figure 4.10 we used the following readln statements:

```
readln (TextFile, NumberEngines);
```

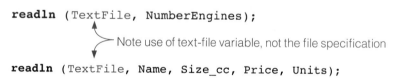

Note use of text-file variable, not the file specification

```
readln (TextFile, Name, Size_cc, Price, Units);
```

The first call reads a single value from the text file (the 3 in Figure 4.7), stores it in variable NumberEngines, and sets the file position to the beginning of the next line in the file (the file position would stay just after the 3 if we had used a *read* statement instead of a *readln* statement).

The second call reads the next four values from the text file; stores them respectively in variables Name, Size_cc, Price, and Units; and sets the file position to the beginning of the next line in the file. Note that this readln statement is within the body of a for-do loop that iterates three times (NumberEngines stores 3). Each execution of this readln statement processes an entire record in the file, since the variable list contains the four variables that define a record.

6. **close statement.** This predeclared procedure call "closes" the file, as follows:

Note use of text-file variable, not the file specification

```
close (TextFile);
```

We need not use this statement when processing a file just once during a given run. But it is needed when we have to reuse the file or write to a file (as we show in Chapter 12). We use it here as a matter of good programming style.

7. **Data placement and readln correspondence.** Note the correspondence illustrated in Figure 4.11. For each record line, we allocated positions 1–10 for engine name, spaced two positions to separate names and sizes, allocated positions 13–17 for engine size, spaced two positions, allocated positions 20–23 for price, spaced two positions, and allocated positions 26–29 for units. Basically, we needed to allocate ten positions for engine names and align the rest of the numeric data in columns for easy visuals. We could have just as easily separated fields with one blank position, although the data would look more cluttered.

FIGURE 4.11   Correspondence Between Records in Figure 4.7 and Executions of readln Procedure in For-Do Loop of Figure 4.10

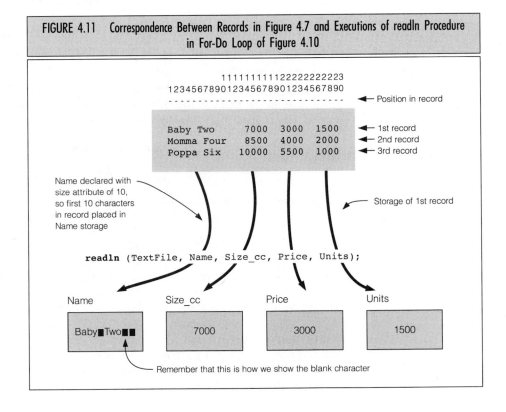

In program Engine3, we declared Name with a *size attribute* of 10, assuming any new engine names that might be added in the future will never exceed 10 characters. When the readln statement reads a value for Name, it picks off the first 10 characters in the record and stores these in Name. Looking at the first record, it stored Baby Two■■ in Name. Next, the processor ignores the blanks in positions 11–13 of the first record, picks up 7000 in positions 14–17, terminates this input with the blank in position 18, and stores the 7000 in Size_cc. Next, the processor ignores the blank in position 19, picks up the 3000 in positions 20–23, terminates this input with the blank in position 24, and stores the 3000 in Price. Finally, the processor ignores the blank in position 25, picks up the 1500 in positions 26–29, terminates this input as the end of the line, and stores the 1500 in Units.

We used mixed-type input lines to be consistent with our conceptualization of a record as a line in the text file. We discourage mixed-type input lines for interactive input to avoid potential errors in separating the different input values. For example, it's easy enough to use field widths of 10 for engine name when placing data in a data file (the editor shows column numbers); it's not so easy in interactive input. In Exercise 19 we ask you to consider the unmixed-type alternative for placing data in the file.

NOTE

5. Correspondence between loop iterations and records. Use a for-do loop (in this chapter) to read records in a file. The number of records is the final value for the control variable; that is, the number of loop iterations is identical to the number of records in the text file. Sometime before the for-do loop, read in the number of records from the text file itself and store this in the variable that represents the final value in the for statement. Use a single readln statement in the body of the loop to read a single record. Ensure this by making the variable list in the readln statement the same as the list of fields in the record.

6. Data placement in text file. In placing mixed-type data in a text file we need to pay special attention to the separation of data. Records that strictly contain numeric fields pose no problem: Simply separate each field from its preceding field by one or more blank characters. Records that mix field types have minefields. In Figure 4.7, the record layout shows a string value followed by three numeric values. In these designs, we must match the placement of string data to the size attribute of corresponding string variables. Nail this down by reviewing Figure 4.11 and working Exercises 18b and 19.

4.4   PROGRAMMING TIPS

• • • • • • • • • • • • • • •

· Consider the following tips to improve the design and style of your programs and to avoid some common errors.

DESIGN AND STYLE

1. Design of Main Algorithm.   Remember the following design when designing your main algorithm.

> Opening tasks procedure
> Processing loop
> Closing tasks procedure

This design is particularly common when a program has a major processing loop for implementing repetitive input, repetitive calculations, or repetitive output. For example, see Engine3 in Figures 4.9 and 4.10.

2. Literacy.   Indent the body of the for-do loop, to visually isolate it. If the body is a compound statement, indent and align the begin-end pair and further indent the set of statements that make up the body. Further improve literacy by documenting the end, as in

```
end; {for}
```

or

```
end; {ScoreNumber for}
```

Pascal programs have many **ends**. Their alignment and documentation reduces potential confusion.

3. Generalized For-Values.   Generalize initial value and final value expressions that are likely to change. For example, in program CkFac we used

```
    for Item := 1 to Number  ☺
```

instead of

```
    for Item := 1 to 3       ☹
```

where Number is an input variable that stores 3. This means that we can process any desired number of factorials, *without changing the program itself.* This reduces potential software maintenance costs, an important consideration in practice.

In cases where for-values remain fixed for life, it's best to use constants instead of variables, since the input of for-values would be an unnecessary operation.

4. Data Files. In practice, large amounts of input data are entered from data files rather than interactively. For example, picture the entry of payroll data like name, social security number, rate of pay, hours worked, and so on for a company with 5000 employees. We would not want to enter these data interactively! The program's run would take forever, and most of these data don't change from run to run. Instead, our design would call for a data file with 5000 records. In practice, data would be entered and maintained using a *database* program (which could be written in Pascal, as we show in Chapter 12). In many cases, data are captured *online*, as in "punching" an automated clock for hours worked, or updating inventory using point-of-sale terminals in a restaurant or grocery store.

Don't forget to document the text file's data structure, as seen in program Engine3.

5. Optimization Notes. We have two common computational efficiencies regarding for-do loops.

a. Nesting Efficiency. Nest long for-do loops (those with more iterations) within short for-do loops, if feasible. Each time an outer for-do loop iterates, the inner for-value expressions and control variable get reinitialized, which takes time. If the outer for-do loop is the short loop, we have fewer reinitializations.

b. Calculating Efficiency. Avoid unnecessary calculations within loop bodies to improve execution efficiency. For example, many beginning programmers place the calculation of an average just after the summing operation within the loop body, rather than following the loop itself.

COMMON ERRORS

1. Nonordinal Control Variable. Don't forget that control variables must be ordinal types: integer or character in our work up to now. If you forget and declare a control variable as type real, for example, the compiler reminds you with an *Invalid FOR control variable* error.

2. Improper for Values.   Avoid the following pitfalls in using initial- and final-value expressions.

for Counter := 1 to Iterations **do** 🙁 ◄── Inactive
loop (body not
entered) if Iterations
not initialized in main
algorithm (compiler
assigns zero to Itera-
tions); unpredictable
if for statement is in
procedure or function
("junk" number used
for iterations)

for Counter := High to Low **do**   🙁 ◄── Inactive loop if High
stores greater value
than Low; Use
downto instead of **to**

3. Incorrect Loop Body.   Consider the following for-do loop.

```
for ScoreNumber := 1 to NumberScores do
   read (Score);
   SumScores := SumScores + Score;  🙁
```

Do you see anything wrong with this? The compiler wouldn't. The apparent intent here (based on indentation and purpose) is a body with two simple statements. Since the for-do loop just has a single statement in its body syntax, the compiler would take the body as the read procedure. The summing operation would follow the loop, giving a logic error! Don't forget to enclose bodies with multiple simple statements in a begin-end pair, giving a single compound statement as the body of the for-do loop. While we're at it, we get this error message by forgetting to include the **do**: *DO expected.* The compiler needs the **do** to identify the beginning of the statement body.

4. Initialization Errors.   As a matter of good programming style, all variables that are used in expressions should have been explicitly assigned a value earlier. For example, the summing statement

```
SumScores := SumScores + Score;
```

should have been preceded by the initialization

```
SumScores := 0;
```

Do this explicitly as shown, or you'll have a logic error in Turbo Pascal. If you forget to initialize a numeric variable that needs initialization, one of two values will be used in Turbo Pascal: a value of zero if the variable is global or a "junk" value if the variable is local to a procedure or function (whatever was in that local data cell is used). For example, if we had forgotten to initialize SumScores in program AveScore (Figure 4.6), the first student's average would be correct, but not the second student's (J. K. Dunn would be delighted: Try Exercise 17a).

5. Text-File Errors.   Text files provide some nice opportunities for errors.

a. Make sure that the placement of data in the file and the corresponding readln procedures are consistent. Review the example in Figure 4.11, reread Note 6, and check out Exercise 19.

b. A common error when using a text data file is placing fewer values in a text-file line than variables in the input list of a readln statement. This error is subtle and treacherous because Turbo Pascal doesn't flag it with a message. Instead it assigns zero values to numeric variables and nulls to string variables (try Exercise 18a). Make sure data values in the text file are properly delimited and that the number of values in the data file matches the number of variables read through the input variable lists.

c. Don't forget that the textfile variable must be declared a *variable* parameter in parameter lists, as done in procedure ClosingTasks in program Engine3; otherwise, the compiler gives a *Files must be var parameters* error message.

d. If we forget the assign procedure, we get a *File not assigned* error message. If we forget the reset procedure (or really "space" and forget both the assign and reset procedures), we get a *File not open for input* error message.

e. We have a real "head scratcher" if we forget the text-file variable at the beginning of the variable list in the read or readln procedure. The system assumes online input (and we don't have the usual program prompt that identifies interactive input!). So the processor waits for us to enter data, while we scratch our heads wondering why nothing's happening.

6. Tracing.   Sometimes we get incorrect output values, but we're not sure just how we got these. In many cases, these values are based on values for other variables that are not part of the output. In other cases, the values are the end result of repetitive calculations, as in a sum. **Tracing** is the act of following the execution sequence in a program. It's equivalent to desk checking a program's algorithm. One way of tracing actual execution is to use temporary output statements, called **trace statements**, that track the evolution of key calculations. These output statements provide intermediate results that may be helpful in tracing what, where, and when something went wrong. When the error is corrected, these statements are removed. To illustrate, suppose we had forgotten to initialize SumScores in program AveScore (see item 4 above). The trace statement

```
{Trace} writeln ('***Trace*** SumScores = ', SumScores);
```

just after the summing operation in the for-do loop would clearly show that we failed to reinitialize the value in SumScores for each new student (see Exercise 17a). Note that it's a good idea to clearly identify these temporary trace statements by documentation like {Trace}. It makes them easier to locate (using the editor's search facility) and delete when we have many in a program.

Tracing is a partial alternative or supplement to *desk checking* when the latter is tedious or includes difficult calculations by hand. This debugging technique is so common that Turbo Pascal's IDE provides special tools for tracing, which we illustrate in Module A following this chapter.

NOTE

7. On disappearing output. Output that takes up more than one screen partially disappears off the top of the screen as it scrolls. Loops give us an opportunity to really express ourselves with lots of output, as in long tables. In fact, many examples and programming exercises from now forward will write output that covers more than one screen. So how do we view this output? The simplest way is to print the output on paper by either toggling Ctrl-Print Screen or directly writing to the printer using unit *printer*. Another alternative is output to a text file. Here we have two approaches: DOS *redirection* (see Appendix A and Exercise 26 below) and methods using the writeln procedure (which we don't take up until Chapter 12). A final alternative is screen output that gets paused. We show this approach in Chapter 6.

REVIEW EXERCISES

EASIER	For the busy...	
	1 2 3 4 6 7 8 12 17a–b 18	
NORMAL	For the thinkers...	
	5 9 10 11 13 14 15 16 17c–e 19 20 26	
TOUGHER	For the hard CORE...	
	21 22 23 24 25	

1. What values get written for each of the following for-do loops? (Assume Lo stores 10 and Hi stores 15.) How many times does each loop iterate?

   a. ```
   for IntVar := Lo to 2 * Hi do
      writeln (IntVar);
   ```
   b. ```
   for IntVar := 2 * Lo to Hi do
      writeln (IntVar);
   ```
   c. ```
   for IntVar := 2 * Lo downto Hi do
      writeln (IntVar);
   ```

2. Code a loop that always writes the uppercase letters of the alphabet from
   a. A to Z, on one line with no spaces in between each character.
   b. Z to A, each character on a separate line.

3. Code a loop that always writes the Boolean values false and true, on separate lines.

4. **Functions length and upcase.** Check out these function calls in Appendix F and roleplay output for the following (or write a test program and see what actually happens).

   ```
   StringVar := 'Turbo';
   for Position := 1 to length (StringVar) do
      writeln (upcase (StringVar[Position]));
   ```

*5. **Blank-lines procedure.** Write and debug a utility procedure named WriteBlk that receives an integer value for Lines and writes the requested number of blank lines. For example, the procedure call WriteBlk (10) would write 10 blank lines.

6. Revise Example 4.1...
   a. To eliminate **begin** and **end**. How would the I/O change?
   *b. As a program that reads real values and displays their squares and square roots to two decimal places. Use 9.0 and 13.3 as test data.

(L) 7. **ASCII table generator.** Test drive program Ascii in Example 4.2. Output all 256 ASCII characters (ASCII values 0 to 255).

(L) 8. **ASCII table generator.** Modify program Ascii in Example 4.2 to ring a bell at the beginning of the intro and again after the table is written. Check out ASCII 7 in Appendix I.

(L) *9. **ASCII table generator.** Modify program Ascii in Example 4.2 to print (on paper) as many identical tables as the user desires. Use an outer for-do loop to process tables. The number of desired tables is input interactively.

(L) *10. **ASCII table generator.** Rework the preceding exercise, except that each table printed is different, based on the low and high ASCII values entered by the user for each table desired.
   ```

11. **Summing algorithm.** In Example 4.3...

   a. Fill in the following desk-check table at the end of each iteration for the five input scores 70, 60, 90, 100, 90.

NumberScores	ScoreNumber	Score	SumScores	
5			0	} Before loop
				⎫ Snapshot after each ⎬ iteration ⎭

   b. Revise the code to replace the assignment statement that accumulates SumScores with a call to predeclared procedure **inc.**

Ⓛ 12. **Function Fac.** In Example 4.4...

   a. Develop a desk-check script for a run that processes 0!, 1!, and 3!. Confirm your desk check by running program CkFac for these factorials.

   b. Use the program to find the precise value for *x* that causes an overflow error.

   c. **Numeric processing and emulation compiler directives.** Disable *numeric processing* through the IDE command sequence **O**ptions **C**ompiler **8**087/80287. Similarly, disable *emulation* with **O**ptions **C**ompiler **E**mulation. Now recompile the program and run it. *Don't forget to recompile before running, because the presence or absence of compiler directive code is associated with the object file.* What happens? Enable numeric processing, recompile, and run. What happens? If you don't have a numeric processor on your machine, enable emulation, recompile, and run. Is the run okay?

Ⓛ *13. **Function Fac.** In Example 4.4, revise program CkFac to generate factorials that range from initial value Initial to final value Final in increments of one. The user now enters Initial and Final, and the program outputs a table of factorials over the indicated range. Try the following test values for Initial and Final: 1, 10; 35, 50.

14. **Weight control.** Assume Weight is typed integer in Example 4.5.

   a. By formula, calculate the number of iterations if Weight is to vary from −15 to 20 in increments of 5. Describe output.

   b. What happens if Lo, Hi, and Increment respectively store 40, 20, and 5?

   c. Rework part **b**, but with an increment of −5.

   d. Assert what must be true about values in Lo, Hi, and Increment for correct loop iterations.

   *e. Implement a program that includes the sample loop. Interactively input values for Lo, Hi, and Increment. Use test data in the original example and in parts **a**–**c** above.

*15. **Weight control.** Rework part **e** in the preceding exercise, except that Weight, Lo, Hi, and Increment are typed real. Use a weight range of 1.1 to 1.5 in increments of 0.1. Output weights to two decimal places in fields of width eight.

16. **Nested for-do loops.** In Example 4.6, roleplay the following variations.

```
a. for I := 1 to 2 do
     for J := 1 to 3 do
       for K := 1 to 2 do
         writeln (I :5, J :5, K :5);
b. for I := 1 to 2 do
     for J := 1 to 3 do
       K := I + J;
   writeln (I :5, J :5, K :5);
c. for I := 1 to 2 do
     for J := 1 to 3 do
       begin
         K := I + J;
         writeln (I :5, J :5, K :5);
       end; {fors}
d. for I := 1 to 2 do
     begin
       for J := 1 to 3 do
         K := I + J;
       writeln (I :5, J :5, K :5);
     end; {I for}
e. for I := 1 to 2 do
     for J := 1 to 3 do
       write (J :5);
```

(L) 17. **Average scores.** In Example 4.7, revise AveScore to...

a. Delete the initialization for SumScores and trace the values in SumScores within the loop. What happens?

b. Delete the readln statement at the end of the student loop. What happens?

*c. Create new procedure ProcessStudent (see Figure 4.5) and reproduce the run in Figure 4.4.

*d. Create new procedure ProcessScores (see Figure 4.5) and reproduce the run in Figure 4.4.

*e. Add procedure Farewell that beeps the speaker at the end of the run by writing **chr** (7) and writes the farewell message

```
End of run...
    Students processed............. 2
    Number of scores per student... 3
    Overall average score.......... 82.2
```

(L) **18.**   **HC ENGINE.** In Example 4.8...
   a. Change the first item in the data file from 3 to 4. Run the program. What happens?
   b. Change the size attribute for Name to 9. Run the program. What happens? What happens if the size attribute is 15?
   c. Output average sales just after total sales.

(L) **19.**   **HC ENGINE.** In Example 4.8, create the following new data file ENGINE3A.DAT.

```
        3
       Baby Two
         7000 3000 1500
       Momma Four
         8500 4000 2000
       Poppa Six
         10000 5500 1000
```

Do we need to make any changes in the program to process this file? Process this file. Any advantages and disadvantages to this text-file data structure?

(L) ***20.**   **HC ENGINE.** In Example 4.8...
   a. Declare FileSpec as a 50-character string variable instead of a constant. Interactively input its value.
   b. Instead of input for the value in FileSpec, input the following variables:

   Character variable **Drive**
   String variable **Path** with up to 37 characters
   String variable **FileName** with up to 12 characters

   Variable **FileSpec** is now given its value through an assignment statement, where the expression is the concatenated string

   Drive:PathFileName

   Accordingly revise and debug Engine3. Enter the proper drive and path for your system. Process the original file ENGINE3.DAT.

(L) ***21.**   **HC ENGINE.** In Example 4.8, rework program Engine3 to write the report as a standard columnlike table with title, head, body, and foot.

(L) ***22.**   **HC ENGINE.** In Example 4.8, rework program Engine3 to keep track of two separate sales regions in the country, East and West. The original data are for the East. The names and sizes of engines are the same in both regions, but prices and units sold in the Western region differ as follows. (Our West Coast neighbors like *big* engines, and so are willing to pay more...and buy more.)

Name	Price	Units
Baby Two	$3,500	2200
Momma Four	4,700	3000
Poppa Six	6,500	4000

Process both sets of data in one computer run. Also, input the number of regions (HC might expand in the future) and the name of each region. Write the name of each region as part of the report title above each region's report. Include total sales for each region and overall total sales for all regions combined. Clearly define the revised text-file data structure. Output to paper.

(L) *23.   **Average scores.** In Example 4.7, use input from a text file instead of interactive input. Use the student data below. Allow 20 characters for name.

Joshua Clay	95	90	100
J. K. Dunn	50	90	68
Rick Jardon	88	72	87
Cynthia Mello	85	92	95

(L) *24.   **Average scores.** Rework the preceding exercise, except allow the processing of a different number of scores for each student. Modify the data by deleting the third score for the third student (the 87). Take care in redefining the text-file data structure.

(L) *25.   **Revisit: HC METHsea.** Revise the program in Section 3.5 as follows.
   a. Store all platform data (codes and coordinates) in a text file. The only interactive input is the Home Base coordinate.
   b. Use nested loops to systematically vary integer (x, y) coordinates for the proposed Home Base location. Interactively input the range (low and high values) for each coordinate. Use increments of 1 km. In your test run, try a range of 10 to 15 km for x and 15 to 22 km for y. Redesign the output to write a table with the following headings: X-Home, Y-Home, and Total distance. Use this version of the program to answer the question posed in Exercise 13 of Chapter 3.
   c. Use an innermost loop to process the text file in part **a**. Now we don't need separate variables for the coordinates of and distances to each platform. Note that the text file gets processed anew for each proposed Home Base coordinate. So make sure that the file position pointer gets reset each time the file is reprocessed.
   d. Use this program to solve Exercise 14 in Chapter 3. If you designed it properly, you should only need to change the data file, not the program.

(L) *26.   **Alternative output media.** We have three alternative output media in this book: screen, paper, and disk. The screen, of course, is our default and most common medium. But, as described in Note 7, our output might require more than one screen. In these cases, we need to resort to the other alternative media.
   a. Screen output. Run program Engine3. What happens? In Chapter 6 we show how to pause output to the screen.
   b. Paper output. Revise Engine3 so all output is to the printer (see Section 2.5 if you're rusty).

c. Disk output. Try redirection of output (see Appendix A) as follows.
- Compile program Engine3 to disk, giving the object file ENGINE3.EXE.
- Get into DOS and execute/redirect by typing the following at the DOS prompt:

```
engine3 > engine3.out
```

- All output is now in the output file ENGINE3.OUT. Display this file by typing the following at the DOS prompt:

```
type engine3.out 1 ¦ more
```

Or...
- Load file ENGINE3.OUT using the IDE and browse at your leisure. Print this file.

ADDITIONAL EXERCISES

EASIER	For the busy... **27 28**
NORMAL	For the thinkers... **29 30 33 34 35**
TOUGHER	For the hard CORE... **31 32 36**

27. **Revisits.** Revise one of your earlier programs by using a loop to process multiple sets of input data in one run.

28. **Revisits.** Same as the preceding exercise, except input all data from a text file.

29. **Revisit: Temperatures.** Revise Exercise 19 in Chapter 3 as follows:
    a. Write a table that displays degrees Fahrenheit and their Celsius equivalents. Round Celsius temperatures to the nearest degree. Assume integer values for degrees Fahrenheit, and input their table range from a low value to a high value (in increments of one degree). Use the range 65 to 80 degrees Fahrenheit as test data.
    b. Same as part **a**, except input an increment for the range. Use the range 0 to 100 in increments of 10.

    c. Have the program print multiple copies of the *same* table in one run. Input the value for the number of copies desired. Print two copies in your test run.

    d. Same as part **c**, except print *different* tables in one run, based on different ranges for degrees Fahrenheit. Print two tables in your test run.

30. **Revisit: Disk areas.** Revise Exercise 20 in Chapter 3 as follows:

    a. Use an outer loop that processes different disks. Input disk code, diameter, and quantity for each disk. Use the test data originally given in Exercise 7 from Chapter 1.

    b. Instead of the ouput from part **a** try the following. Use an inner loop that varies quantity and writes for each disk a 10-row table having two columns: quantity and corresponding area. Use the quantity input from part **a** as the center of the range for quantity. Calculate the increment in quantity as quantity divided by 5. For example, if the input quantity is 50,000, then the increment is 10,000 and the table varies quantity from 10,000 to 100,000 in increments of 10,000. Precede the output of each table with the disk code and diameter for that disk.

    c. Input all data from a text file.

31. **Revisit: Drag races.** Revise Exercise 21d in Chapter 3 as follows.

    a. Interactively input a range of times that runs from 10 to 20 seconds in increments of 1 second. Use a loop to write a table of times, speeds, and distances.

    b. Interactively input a range of accelerations that runs from 20 to 40 mi/h/s in increments of 5 mi/h/s. Use a second loop to process separate tables from part **a**. For the given acceleration range, five separate tables will be written. Give each table a title that includes the specific acceleration for that table.

    c. Interactively input a range of initial velocities that runs from 20 to 30 mi/h in increments of 5 mi/h. Use a third loop to process separate tables from part **a**. For the given data we now have 15 separate tables. Include the initial velocity in the title of each table, along with the acceleration.

32. **Revisit: Bank savings.** Revise Exercise 24 in Chapter 3 as follows.

    a. Use a loop to process different sets of data in one run.

    b. Include an inner loop that varies years from 1 to the number of years input, in increments of 1.

    c. Instead of the increment in part **b**, let the user input the increment. Try a 5-year increment in your test run.

33. **Multiplication Tables.** Consider the following multiplication table:

Multiplication Table for the Number 9

       0 times 9 =   0
       1 times 9 =   9

          ⋮

    12 times 9 = 108

a. Develop a program that writes a multiplication table. The user enters the number used for the multiplication. The table always ranges from 0 to 12.

b. Have your program automatically generate multiplication tables for any range of numbers entered by the user. For example, if the user enters the range 2 to 11, then the program automatically generates ten multiplication tables.

34. **Individual Retirement Account (IRA).** IRAs are an excellent means by which to build up tax-deferred retirement accounts. Essentially, under certain conditions, a taxpayer can deduct from earned income an annual contribution to an IRA, thus reducing the federal taxes owed. The contribution is invested in stocks, bonds, money market account, savings account, or other approved investment vehicles. Over time, this amount increases in value (for the astute investor), with taxes still deferred. At retirement, the person can begin withdrawals, which are then taxed as if ordinary income were being earned. Develop a program that reproduces the sample run below.

```
Enter current year............................................ ? 1992
Enter retirement year ........................................ ? 1995
Enter annual IRA contribution................................. ? 2000
Enter assumed annual % return................................. ? 10
```

Projected IRA Accumulations

Year	Contribution	Return	Accumulation
1992	2000	200	2200
1993	2000	420	4620
1994	2000	662	7282
1995	2000	928	10210

For simplicity, assume that all contributions are made at the beginning of the year. Thus the $2000 investment at the beginning of 1992 accumulates to $2200 by the end of 1992. In 1993 the investor contributes an additional $2000, which gives an account with $4200 at the beginning of 1993. This also earns a return of 10 percent for the year, or $420, which gives an accumulation of $4620 by the end of 1993..., and so on. After 1995, the taxpayer can withdraw all or part of the accumulated $10,210. Of course, federal income taxes have to be paid at that time on any amount withdrawn. Debug your program with the above test run. Then try a second test run that changes the retirement year to 2026. Finally, try a third test run that generates a table from 1992 to 2026, but use an annual contribution of $1000. What's the effect of a change in the annual return to 15 percent?

35. **Bates Motel.** The motel owner wants to prepare a bill for each customer at check-out time. The desk clerk is to enter the following data:

Customer name
Room number
Room charge
Restaurant charges
Bar charges
The program computes the following:
Service charge . . . . 5% of room and restaurant charges
Sales tax . . . . 6% of room, restaurant, and bar charges
Total bill . . . . Sum of room, restaurant, bar, service,
                                            and sales tax charges.

a. Develop a program that prepares a bill for each customer. Take some time
to plan the I/O design. Use the following test data to process two bills in
one run.

	First Customer	Second Customer
Customer name	Ms. Lovelace	Mr. Hollerith
Room number	80	82
Room charge	$110.00	$160.00
Restaurant charges	45.15	83.50
Bar charges	0.00	15.00

b. Have the program print the following block letters across the top of the bill:

```
* * * *           *          * * * * *     * * * * *     * * * * *
*     *       *      *            *            *            *
* * * * *     * * * * *          *          * * * *      * * * * *
*     *       *      *            *            *                 *
* * * *           *      *        *          * * * * *     * * * * *
```

c. Use a text file for the input data.

36. **Econometric model.** *Econometrics* is a field of study that applies mathematical models to describe the behavior of economic systems. To illustrate a simple
econometric model, suppose that the cost per credit charged by a college directly affects student enrollment according to the following *demand curve.*

$$s = d_1 - d_2 c$$

where s = student enrollment (students)
      c = cost per credit ($/credit)
      d_1 = first parameter in demand curve (students)
      d_2 = second parameter in demand curve (students/$/credit)

For example, if the tuition charge is $80 per credit and the demand curve pa-
rameters are 14,000 and 100, then enrollment is estimated by

$$s = 14{,}000 \text{ students} - (100 \text{ students/\$/credit})(80 \text{ \$/credit})$$
$$= 6000 \text{ students}$$

If the cost per credit is increased to $90, then estimated enrollment drops to 5000 students. The average balance due the college is given by the *price function*

$$b = ac + f$$

where b = average balance due the college ($/student)
a = average number of credit hours (credits/student)
f = fee ($/student)

and c is defined as before. For example, if the average number of credit hours taken by students is 14, the cost per credit is $80, and fees are $250, then the average bill is

$$b = (14 \text{ credits/student})(80 \text{ \$/credit}) + 250 \text{ \$/student}$$
$$= \$1370 \text{ per student}$$

The *revenue function* is given by

$$r = bs$$

where

$$r = \text{projected revenue (\$)}$$

and b and s are defined as before. Continuing our example, we have a projected revenue for the college of

$$r = (1370 \text{ \$/student})(6000 \text{ students})$$
$$= \$8,220,000$$

a. Develop a program for this econometric model. Use a loop that varies c over a range. Process the following input data.

d_1	d_2	a	f	.......c-range.......	
14000	100	14	250	50	80

Write an output table headed by four columns: Cost per Credit, Average Bill, Expected Enrollment, and Expected Revenue. What cost per credit maximizes expected revenue for the college?

b. Add an outer loop that processes all colleges in a statewide system. Use the following test data.

College name	d_1	d_2	a	f	.. c-range...	
OK State U	14000	100	14	250	50	80
AOK State U	14000	25	14	250	200	300
NotOK State U	30000	250	13.5	500	10	60

Use the same output design as in part **a**, except just before each table print the name of the college. What tuition (cost per credit) should be charged at each college to maximize revenue? Would you say there's a flaw in the econometric model if students freely change colleges within the state system on the basis of tuition?

c. Input the *c*-range interactively, and all other data through a text file.

d. Solve this problem by calculus. Do your analytic and computer results agree?

Integrated Debugger

‡Optional, more advanced material. Skip without loss of continuity, study at this point, or wait until later.

Turbo Pascal includes a suite of debugging tools within its Integrated Development Environment (IDE). These tools are implemented through the IDE's menu commands and hot keys. Taken together, the set of debugging tools is a **debugger.** A debugger that's implemented through a separate program is called a **standalone debugger;** one that's integrated within an environment that includes editing and compiling tasks (as in the IDE) is called an **integrated debugger.** This optional module illustrates Turbo Pascal's integrated debugger.[1]

A.1 PRELIMINARIES

• • • • • • • • • • • • • • •

Let's cover some preliminaries to debugging. Remember that **tracing** is the act of following the execution sequence in a program, noting what happens as each line is executed. This process is comparable to desk checking a program's execution, except that it's computerized when using a debugger.

MOTIVATION

Wouldn't it be nice to *trace* the execution of a program one line at a time, while *watching* the changing values of key expressions and variables (kind of like automated desk checking)? Or to trace the program's line-by-line output or other actions, starting either at the position of the cursor or at predetermined *breakpoints* within the program? Or to change the values of key variables while debugging, to *evaluate* the effects of certain values? Wouldn't it be great to do all of this without leaving the *integrated* functions of the IDE? And even better, to accomplish these tasks *on the fly,* or *interactively* as we debug, without making changes in the program itself and recompiling? Well, look no further. Turbo Pascal's integrated debugger does all of this, and more, as we will see.

DEBUGGER COMMANDS

Debugging techniques within the IDE are implemented through certain hot keys and main menu commands, especially Run and Debug. Table A.1 lists these techniques. Look this table over to get an idea of what the debugger can

---

[1]Turbo Pascal also supports Borland's *Turbo Debugger,* a standalone debugger for Turbo Pascal and other languages from Borland.

Table A.1 Debugger Hot Keys and Menu Commands

Hot Key	Command Sequence	Description
	Search → Find procedure	Displays *Find Procedure dialog box* for finding procedures or functions; places cursor on first statement of desired module. Use to locate modules in long programs. Available only during debugging session.
Ctrl-F9	**Run** → **Run**	Runs program in Edit window, compiling first if necessary.
Ctrl-F2	**Run** → **Program reset**	Ends debugging session and resets (reinitializes) debugger.
F4 *	**Run** → **Go to cursor**	Runs program up to (stopping at) line having cursor. Use to skip debugging up to line with cursor. At this point we can start tracing.
F7 *	**Run** → **Trace into**	Executes current line (line with *execution bar*). Traces into any called module (procedure, function, unit, or object). Use for single-step or line-by-line tracing.
F8 *	**Run** → **Step over**	Executes current line (like **F7**), but without tracing into called module. Use to skip tracing within (step over) a module.
Ctrl-F4	**Debug** → **Evaluate/Modify**	Pops up *Evaluate and Modify dialog box*. Use to evaluate an expression by viewing its result (value). Also use to assign new values to selected variable.
	Debug → **Watches** →	Displays pull-down menu with the following commands for controlling watchpoints...
Ctrl-F7	Add watch	Adds expression to *Watch window*.
	Delete watch	Deletes *current* (highlighted or bulleted) watch expression from *Watch window*.
	Edit watch	Displays *Edit watch dialog box* to edit the watch expression that's current in the *Watch window*.
	Remove all watches	Clears all watch expressions from *Watch window*.
Ctrl-F8	**Debug** → **Toggle breakpoint**	Sets or clears breakpoint at line given by current cursor position.
	Debug → **Breakpoints** →	Displays *Breakpoints dialog box* with list of breakpoints and the following buttons for managing breakpoints...
	Edit	Displays *Edit breakpoint dialog box* to add a new breakpoint to list.
	Delete	Removes breakpoint from list.
	View	Displays (moves cursor to) breakpoint in Edit window that's selected in breakpoint list.

Table A.1   Debugger Hot Keys and Menu Commands

Hot Key	Command Sequence	Description
	Clear all	Clears all breakpoints in list.
	Options → Compiler →	Displays *Compiler Options dialog box* that includes the following *Debugging check boxes...*
	Debug information	Enables or disables the generation of information that's useful in debugging, as in setting breakpoints and single stepping. Check this box to enable debugging. (Equivalent to **$D** compiler directive in Appendix G.)
	Local symbols	Enables or disables the generation of information that's useful in debugging, as in evaluating and modifying local variables and examining the Call stack window. Check this box if the program has procedures or functions. (Equivalent to **$L** compiler directive in Appendix G.)
	Options → **Debugger** →	Displays *Debugger dialog box* that includes the following two *Debugging check boxes* and three *Display swapping radio buttons...*
	Integrated debugging	Check this box to enable (and use) the integrated debugger; disable if more memory is needed to compile and run program. Check as default setting.
	Standalone debugging	Check this box to enable standalone debugging; disable otherwise. Adds debug information to object program (.EXE) files that will use standalone debugger. Disable as default setting.
	None display swapping	Press this button to keep IDE screen visible at all times during debugging. Gets messy when I/O overwrites the screen. Don't press this button.
	Smart display swapping	Press this button to swap from IDE screen to User screen when program line accesses the video unit during debugging. Press this radio button as default setting.
	Always display swapping	Press this button to swap the IDE and User screens as each statement executes during debugging. This button is useful if the program is overwriting the IDE screen with the smart setting.
Ctrl-F3	Window → Call stack	Shows current call stack as pop-up *Call stack window.* Use to trace back through module calls up to current line during debugging. The window shows each module call by name, including list of passed parameter values.

*Use any one of these hot keys to initiate the debugging session.

do. But don't worry about the details just yet. This table is our debugger reference table. We will return to it time and again throughout this module. You might want to attach a paper clip to this page. Table A.1 is handy not only for our examples below, but also for your own debugging sessions.

Screen Displays and Window Management

As you know, the **IDE screen** displays a menu bar, desktop, and status line. Up to now we have displayed an Edit window and possibly an Output window on the desktop. The **Edit window** displays our source code and includes special visual effects during our debugging session (as we will see shortly). The **Output window** displays a copy of the User screen; we display it with the menu command sequence Window Output. The **User screen** is the normal DOS screen. It's the screen that displays our I/O during program execution; it's also the screen that the IDE swaps to (based on the particular display-swapping radio button that's pressed) when interactive input and output statements are executed during debugging. As usual, we can view this screen by pressing the hot key **Alt-F5**.

The **Watch window** is an important debugging window; it displays expressions (usually variables) that we select, together with their current values. This window is useful for viewing the values of important expressions as we trace execution. We can open this window by selecting the menu command sequence Window Watch.

A debugging session requires some window management, particularly when we wish to view, use, and manipulate multiple windows on the desktop. All window management commands are available through the main menu command Window, which we describe in Appendix B. In the discussion that follows we focus on the use of hot keys and the mouse.

The *active window* on the desktop is the window with the highlighted double border; it's the window that responds to keyboard or mouse activity, like cursor movements, scrolls, or edits. We can change the active window to the *next* window on the desktop by pressing the hot key **F6**; we can activate the *previous* window on the desktop by pressing **Shift-F6**. Repeated presses of the **F6** or **Shift-F6** keys cycle the active window among the existing windows on the desktop. Alternatively, we can activate a window by pressing the **Alt** key and a window number, or by pressing **Alt-0** to get a complete list of all open windows, from which we can activate any listed window.

If we press the hot key **F5** the active window *zooms* to full size; press **F5** again and the window returns to its former size. We can close the active window by pressing **Alt-F3**. Finally, we can move and resize the active window by pressing **Ctrl-F5** and then pressing either *unshifted* Arrow keys to move the window or *shifted* Arrow keys to resize the window, followed by a press of the Enter key when the desired effect is achieved.

Table A.2   Hot Keys and Mouse actions for Window Management

Hot Key	Mouse Action	Description
Alt-0		Displays list of open windows within *Window List dialog box*; selection from this list activates selected window.
Alt-NumKey		Displays window whose number is NumKey
Alt-F3	Click on close box	Closes active window.
F5	Click on zoom box	Zooms and unzooms active window.
Alt-F5		Cycles between IDE screen and User screen.
Ctrl-F5	Drag title bar to move Drag resize corner to resize	Moves (with unshifted arrow keys) and resizes (with shifted arrow keys) active window.
F6	Click on visible window	Activates next window on desktop; repeated presses cycle forward through active windows.
Shift-F6	Click on visible window	Activates previous window on desktop; repeated presses cycle backward through active windows.

With a mouse we can activate any visible window by clicking on it with the left mouse button. We can also zoom and unzoom the active window by clicking on the *zoom box* in its upper-right corner; close the window by clicking on its *close box* in the upper-left corner; move the window by dragging the *title bar* at the top; and resize the window by dragging the *resize corner* at the bottom right.

Table A.2 summarizes the hot keys and mouse actions that invoke window display activity.

STARTING DEBUGGING SESSION

Before starting a session with the debugger, make sure that...

- Integrated debugging is enabled (box checked) with the command sequence Options Debugger Integrated (see Table A.1).
- Source-level debugging is enabled (box checked) with the command sequence Options Compiler Debug (see Table A.1).
- Local symbols evaluation is enabled (box checked) with the command sequence Options Compiler Local (see Table A.1).
- Display swapping is set to *Smart* (button pressed) with the command sequence Options Debugger Smart (see Table A.1).

- The Edit window is active (see Table A.2) and contains a loaded program for debugging.

We're now ready to begin the debugging session, usually by pressing one of the hot keys **F7**, **F8**, or **F4** (the hot keys with * in Table A.1), as described next.

A.2 DEBUGGING TECHNIQUES

The basic debugging techniques in the Turbo Pascal integrated debugger are tracing, setting breakpoints that halt execution at predetermined lines, watching values for selected expressions, evaluating and changing values for a selected expression, reviewing module calls, and finding modules. We discuss each of these techniques in this section.

Our examples use the program listed in Figure A.1. This program is a revision of program CkFac from Figure 4.3, as follows: We eliminated most of the documentation to better focus on the execution sequence and shorten the program; we added line numbers to the main body and function body, as reference points in following the execution sequence; and we introduced a bug. Do you see it?

We often refer to specific debugging commands in our discussions and examples. You might want to reference these commands in Table A.1 as they are mentioned.

TRACING

Tracing is the central debugging technique, because it allows us to follow the execution sequence as it evolves. In fact, the other techniques essentially support and enhance tracing. We have three commands that implement tracing.

Single-Step Tracing (F7 Key)

The execution of a single line is the simplest debugging technique. Take a look at Figure A.1. If the current line is line 3, pressing the **F7** key (command sequence **Run Trace into**) executes the statement in line 3, the current line then becomes line 4, and execution pauses indefinitely (the debugger awaits our next command). Press **F7** again, and line 4 gets executed. Press **F7** again, and line 5 gets executed. And so on.

How do we know a line is the *current line,* that is, the line that would be executed next? The debugger identifies the current line by enclosing it in a highlighted bar called the *execution bar.* The **F7** key executes just the line having the execution bar.

Be aware that the basic unit of execution by the debugger is a *minimum* of one line. Typically, we have a single statement taking up a single line. If this

---

FIGURE A.1   Listing for Program DebugFac

```
program DebugFac;

  {* * * * * * * * * * * * * * * * * * * * * * * * * * * * * * *
   *                                                           *
   *         Debugger session program for function Factorial   *
   *                                                           *
   * * * * * * * * * * * * * * * * * * * * * * * * * * * * * * *}

  {$N+  Enables num processing compiler directive; needed for extended type}

  var
    Number,                 {Number of factorials desired}
    X,                      {The number whose factorial is to be calculated}
    Item   : integer;       {Control variable in for-do loop}


  function Fac (X : integer) : extended;

  var
    K           : integer;   {Control variable in for-do loop}
    Factorial : extended;    {Stores factorial calculations}

  {10a} begin  {Fac}

  {10b     Factorial := 1; }
  {10c}    for K := 2 to abs(X) do
  {10d}       Factorial := Factorial * K;

  {10e}    Fac := Factorial;

  {10f} end;     {Fac}
```

In single-step tracing, execution bar moves among screened lines, in sequence indicated by line numbers

```
  {1} begin   {DebugFac}

  {2}  writeln;
  {3}  writeln ('Evaluates x!');
  {4}  writeln;
  {5}  write ('Enter number of factorials to evaluate... ');  readln (Number);

  {6}  for Item := 1 to Number do
          begin
  {7}        writeln; writeln;
  {8}        write ('Enter x... ');  readln (X);
  {9}        writeln;
  {10}       writeln (X  :5, '! is... ', Fac(X));
  {11}    end;   {for}

  {12} end.    {DebugFac}
```

is the current line, a single execution step executes a single statement, as in line 4 of our example. But how about line 5, which has two statements? In this case, a single press of the **F7** key executes both statements, pausing next at line 6. In other words, the debugger executes the entire line 5 before pausing. If a single statement covers more than one line, the debugger executes the entire statement with a single press of the **F7** key. Okay?

Tracing by Stepping Over (F8 Key)

Suppose the execution bar is at line 10 in our sample program, which includes the call to function Fac. If we press **F7**, execution traces into the function, moving the execution bar to line 10a. Repeated presses of **F7** would single-step through the function's algorithm, eventually getting us back to the next line in the main algorithm (line 11). Suppose, however, that we don't want to trace into the function at line 10. In this case, we *step over* the function by pressing the **F8** key (command sequence **Run Step over**). Now, line 10 gets executed without tracing into function Fac, and the execution bar moves on to line 11. If we want to single-step a line containing a module call (and don't need to trace through this module), we should press **F8** instead of **F7**.

As a reminder, *module* usually means a procedure or function. However, modules also include units (Chapter 8) and objects (Chapter 14).

Tracing to Cursor (F4 Key)

If we start a debugging session by pressing **F7**, tracing starts at **begin** in the main body. Suppose we want to start tracing at a specific line somewhere in the main body? In this case, we move the cursor to the line where we want to begin tracing, and press the **F4** key (command sequence **Run Go to cursor**). The debugger now executes the program full-tilt from the beginning. When it gets to the line with the cursor, it halts execution and marks the line with the execution bar. At this point, we can issue any debugging command (usually tracing with **F7** or **F8**).

EXAMPLE A.1   TRACING PROGRAM DEBUGFAC

Let's try some tracing for the program shown in Figure A.1. We assume it's already loaded in the Edit window. As suggested in Exercise 1, it would be a good idea if you were to try this yourself while you read our sample sessions. *The series of Examples A.1–A.6 are linked together as a tutorial on using the debugger.*

1. Let's practice single-step tracing. Press **F7**. The program compiles (if necessary) and the execution bar is placed at **begin** in line 1. Repeatedly press **F7**, while watching the execution bar. Enter 1 at line 5 and 5 at line 8. Note how the IDE screen and User screen swap at these I/O operations. Keep pressing **F7** and watching the screen. Note how we traced into the function at line 10, and how execution seems to "stall" at line 10d as the debugger repeatedly executes the single statement in the loop body. Eventually we end up at line 12 and the execution bar disappears, giving a single-step tracing through the entire program. Note that only *executable* lines get traced (those that we gave line numbers to). It's the algorithms (module bodies) that get traced, not the declarative sections.

2. Let's try a step over. Single-step through line 9, with the execution bar now at line 10. (Input 1 and 5 as before.) At line 10 press **F8**. Note that the execution bar now moves to line 11. Lines 10a–10f got executed, but we stepped over these in our trace. Finish execution by pressing **Ctrl-F9**.

3. Let's start our trace at line 10. Move the cursor to line 10 and press **F4**. The debugger now executes the program up to line 10 and then pauses. (Input 1 and 5 as before.) At the pause in line 10 (or any pause), we can press **F7** to single-step with trace into, **F8** to single-step with a step over, **F4** to execute to a new cursor position, or **Ctrl-F9** to finish execution without tracing. Move the cursor to line 12 and press **F4**. Lines 10 and 11 get executed, and execution now halts at line 12. Press **F4**, **F7**, **F8**, or **Ctrl-F9** to finish execution.

4. View the User screen by pressing **Alt-F5**. Definitely the wrong factorial! So far, we haven't really been debugging our sample program. We're just familiarizing ourselves with tracing methods. In some cases, however, viewing a step-by-step execution sequence can uncover some unexpected turns, especially with our coding in the next two chapters. Get back to the Edit window by pressing any key.

To be continued . . .

SETTING BREAKPOINTS

In some cases we may want to stop execution at predetermined lines. We can mark these lines as **breakpoints.** A program executes normally until it encounters a line with a breakpoint. At this time, the debugger halts execution, places an execution bar at the breakpoint, and awaits our debugging command.

We mark a breakpoint by placing the cursor on the desired *executable* line (it must contain a statement) and pressing **Ctrl-F8** (or command sequence **Debug Toggle breakpoint**). We can have multiple breakpoints in a program. To remove a breakpoint, we move the cursor to the breakpoint and press **Ctrl-F8** again. The command sequence **Debug Breakpoints** opens up the *Breakpoints dialog box.* This includes a breakpoint list and a set of buttons to Edit, Delete, View, and Clear all breakpoints.

A manual breakpoint that works on the fly is **Ctrl-Break**. This has the effect of halting execution in its tracks, as if a breakpoint had been placed at the next line. This is handy whenever we feel a need to stop execution, as in being stuck in an infinite loop.

EXAMPLE A.2   BREAKPOINT IN PROGRAM DEBUGFAC

We now continue our previous example, where we established that the factorial calculation is incorrect.

5. Let's create a breakpoint at line 10d, which iteratively stores incorrect values for the factorial. Move the cursor to this line and press **Ctrl-F8**. Note how the breakpoint is highlighted (it's screened red in our configuration).

6. Issue the standard run command **Ctrl-F9** and input the values 1 and 5 as before. Note how execution stops at the breakpoint. What we want to do now is single-step these loop iterations. But first we need to find out how to watch the successive values stored in Factorial.

To be continued . . .

Watching

Up to now we have learned to follow the execution flow, in line-by-line detail if necessary. But we have not considered an important enhancement to tracing: *watching* the values change at each step for key variables or expressions. The *Watch window* displays expressions that we select, and their current values. We use the term *expression* to mean any legal Pascal expression, including a constant and variable.

To add a variable to the Watch window, we first move the cursor to that variable and press **Ctrl F7** (command sequence Debug Watches Add watch). A pop-up *Add Watch dialog box* now appears, as seen in Figure A.2 when the cursor is on variable Factorial in program DebugFac. To select this variable we press the Enter key (or click on the OK button). The variable would now appear in the Watch window as a *watch expression*, along with its current value. If we don't wish to select the variable in the Add Watch dialog box, we simply press the Esc key (or click the Cancel button). We can also type the variable name directly in the Add Watch dialog box.

We can add other watch expressions by repeating the steps just described. Alternatively, we can activate the Watch window by pressing F6 (see Table A.2), moving the cursor to the point where we want to insert a new variable (using the Arrow, Home, and End keys), pressing the Insert key, typing the variable in the Add Watch dialog box, and pressing the Enter key. Adding expressions other than variables works similarly: Type the expression directly

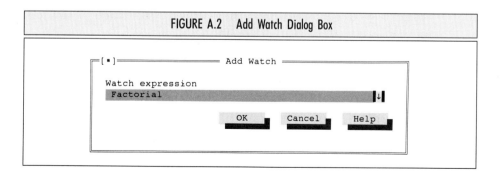

FIGURE A.2   Add Watch Dialog Box

into the Add Watch dialog box; or place the cursor at the first member of the expression in the Edit window, press **Ctrl-F7**, use the Right arrow key to copy characters from the expression, and press the Enter key.

To delete the *current* variable or expression from the Watch window (the one that's highlighted and has a leading bullet ·), use the command sequence **Debug Watches Delete watch.** Or get into the Watch window, select the variable or expression you want to delete by cursor movements, and press the Delete key. To remove all entries from the Watch window, use the command sequence **Debug Watches Remove all watches.**

To edit the highlighted expression in the Watch window, use the command sequence **Debug Watches Edit watch,** edit the expression in the *Edit Watch dialog box,* and press the Enter key when through editing. Or get into the Watch window, select the expression you want to edit by cursor movements, press the Enter key, edit the expression in the Edit Watch dialog box, and press the Enter key when through editing.

As we will see in the examples, the Watch window displays values to the right of corresponding expressions. If a particular expression is outside its *scope* based on the current line, its value will be displayed as *Unknown identifier.*[2]

EXAMPLE A.3   ADDING WATCH VARIABLES FOR PROGRAM DEBUGFAC

In the previous example we established a breakpoint at line 10d.

7. Let's add variable Factorial to the Watch window. Place the cursor anywhere on identifier Factorial (in line 10d, 10e, or 10b). Press **Ctrl F7** and the Enter key. The Watch window displays the following.

Factorial   5.0242241339E-4168

Watch expression   Value

8. Let's also add variable K to the Watch window. Place the cursor anywhere on identifier K (in line 10c or 10d). Press **Ctrl-F7** and the Enter key. If the Watch window disappears, we can get it back by pressing **F6**. Menu command sequence **W**indow **T**ile will keep it on the screen until we close it. The Watch window now contains the following.

---

[2]Other debugger features for watch expressions include the control of value displays through *format identifiers* and the ability to *typecast,* or change the type of displayed values. If you're interested, check out the *Turbo Pascal User's Guide.*

```
Factorial: 5.0242241339E-4168
K: 2
```

— Second watch expression and its value added

9. Single-step through loop iterations by repeatedly pressing **F7**. Keep an eye on how values change in the Watch window at each step. Note how these local variables become *Unknown identifiers* when outside their scope as execution exits the function at line 11. Finish execution with **Ctrl-F9**.

10. At item 7 above it's obvious that we have the wrong initial value in Factorial (it's implicitly initialized at machine zero by the compiler). Fix the bug in line 10b by deleting the right brace and reinserting it just after the 10b.

11. Let's debug once more. Press **Ctrl-F9** and enter the input values 1 and 5. Execution halts at the breakpoint in line 10d. Now watch the values in the Watch window as you single-step through the loop. Now they're correct, right? Finish execution with **Ctrl-F9**.

12. We're through watching, so let's remove all watch variables by pressing **Alt-D W R**. Activate the Watch window (**F6**), close it (**Alt-F3**), and zoom the Edit window (**F5**).

To be continued . . .

EVALUATING AND MODIFYING

The watch feature shows values for watch expressions at every step throughout the execution flow. If we just wish to evaluate a single variable or expression at a particular point in the execution flow and perhaps change its value, we can use the debugger's evaluate feature. This feature is particularly useful if logic or run-time errors seem to surface when a certain variable or expression has a specific value. In these cases, we can set this variable or expression to the indicated value and sit back for the fireworks.

To evaluate a variable or expression, place the cursor at that variable or expression and press **Ctrl-F4** (command sequence Debug Evaluate). For example, if we place the cursor on identifier Factorial in program DebugFac and press **Ctrl-F4**, an *Evaluate and Modify dialog box* pops up with three fields and four buttons, as seen in Figure A.3. Note that Factorial appears in the *Expression input box*. We select the offered expression in the same way that we select an expression in the Add Watch dialog box. For instance, if we press the Enter key or click the Evaluate button, the current value in Factorial would be placed in the *Result box*.

To change the current value, move to the *New value box* with the Tab key, enter the new value, and press the Enter key. This new value is assigned to the expression in the Expression input box, and now appears in both the

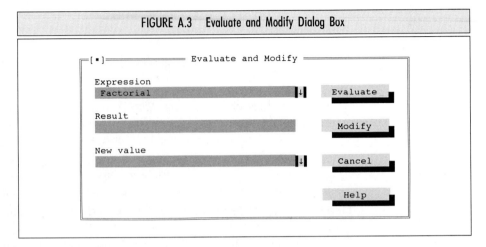

FIGURE A.3   Evaluate and Modify Dialog Box

Result box and the New value box. We can also enter assignment-compatible expressions in the New value box.

We exit the Evaluate and Modify dialog box by pressing the Esc key. If we assigned a new value, this new value is retained when we continue the debugging session.

NOTE

1. Source code changes while debugging. If we change the program while the debugger is *active* (we would see an execution bar), it will ask the following question before implementing our next debugging command:

Source has been modified. Rebuild?

If we answer y, the debugger recompiles the program and resets (reinitializes) itself; otherwise it does not. Answer y to incorporate the change. Note that we made a source code change in Example A.3, but it was done while the debugger was *inactive*. In the next example, we show a source-code change while the debugger is active.

EXAMPLE A.4   EVALUATING AND MODIFYING A VARIABLE IN PROGRAM DEBUGFAC

Continuing our previous example...

13. Let's create a new bug by replacing 1 with 0 in line 10b.
14. Press **Ctrl-F9** and enter 1 and 5 as before. Execution halts at our breakpoint in line 10d.

15. Let's evaluate Factorial. Place the cursor on this identifier, press **Ctrl-F4**, and press the Enter key. The Result field shows 0.0, an incorrect initial value. Let's test the correct value without first modifying the source code. Use the Tab key (or mouse) to move to the New value box, enter 1, and press the Enter key (or click the Modify button). Press the Esc key (or click the close box) to exit the Evaluate and Modify dialog box.

16. Step through loop iterations with **F7**, until the execution bar rests at line 10e. Evaluate Factorial again by placing the cursor on Factorial, pressing **Ctrl-F4**, and pressing the Enter key. The Result box now shows the correct value 120 for the factorial of 5. Press the Esc key.

17. Let's make the initial value in Factorial permanent. Change the 0 in line 10b to 1.

18. Single step with **F7**. The debugger asks the question posed in Note 1 above. Answer y. The debugger recompiles the program, reinitializes itself, and places the execution bar at the beginning of the main body.

19. Let's delete the breakpoint at line 10d. Place the cursor on line 10d and press **Ctrl-F8**. Start execution by pressing **Ctrl-F9**. Enter 1 and 5 again. Confirm the correct factorial *120* once more by checking the User screen (press **Alt-F5**). Press any key to get back to the Edit window.

To be continued . . .

RECALLING AND FINDING MODULES

A long, complex program with many modules makes tracing a bit more difficult. The debugger has two additional features that are specific to modules.

Whenever the debugger makes a module call, it keeps track of this call by recording the module's name, parameter values, and local variables in a group of memory locations named the *call stack*. We can trace back through all module calls that led to the current line by displaying a *Call stack window*. To display the Call stack window we press Ctrl-F3 (command sequence Window Call stack) while the debugger is active. We illustrate this in the next example.

The debugger also includes a module find or search feature. This is handy when we wish to trace or set breakpoints within specific modules in a program with many modules. If we press **Alt-S p** (Search Find procedure), we get a pop-up *Find procedure dialog box,* asking us to enter the name of the module. After entering the name, the debugger places the cursor at the beginning of the module.

Example A.5   Recalling and Finding Modules in Program DebugFac

Continuing our previous example...

20. Let's set a new breakpoint just after the loop. Move the cursor to line 10e and press **Ctrl-F8**.

21. Execute with **Ctrl-F9**, enter 2 for number of factorials to evaluate, and enter 5 for the first *x*. Execution stops at the breakpoint in line 10e.

22. Press **Ctrl-F3** to view the Call stack window, which displays the following contents.

```
FAC(5)
DEBUGFAC
```

Note that the earliest call was the main module DebugFac, followed by the call to function Fac. Moreover, the parameter value *5* was passed during the call to Fac.

23. Continue execution by pressing **Ctrl-F9**. This time enter 10 for *x*. Again, the breakpoint at line 10e halts execution. The revised call stack is...

```
FAC(10)
DEBUGFAC
```

As expected, the only change is in the passed parameter value, which is now 10 instead of 5.

24. Finish the test run by pressing **Ctrl-F9**. Close the Call stack window. Check the User screen, if you're curious about the evaluation of 10!, and then get back to the Edit window.

25. Just for practice, let's find (that difficult to find!) function Fac. Press **Alt-S p**. Enter Fac and press the Enter key. The cursor moves to line 10a.

To be continued...

A.3   Concluding Tasks

• • • • • • • • • • • • • •

We conclude a debugging session by issuing commands that reset the debugger and end the debugging session.

Resetting Debugging Session

To reset the debugger while debugging we press **Ctrl-F2** (command sequence **Run Program reset**). This reinitializes the debugger by closing open files, clearing the call stack, and releasing storage allocated during the debugging session.

Ending Debugging Session

Breakpoints and watch expressions are not cleared when we reset the debugger. If these are present, end the debugging session by also pressing **Alt-D B C** (command sequence Debug Breakpoints Clear all) and **Alt-D W R** (command sequence Debug Watches Remove all watches).

Example A.6   Ending Debugging Session for Program DebugFac

Concluding our debugging session . . .

26. Press **Ctrl-F2** to reset the debugger and **Alt-D B C** to clear our only breakpoint (we need not press **Alt-D W R** to remove watch expressions because we removed them earlier).

NOTE

2. Out of memory. If you run out of memory while debugging, reset the debugger by pressing **Ctrl-F2**.

3. No implicit ends to debugging. The act of loading a new program into the Edit window does not end the debugging session (from the IDE's point of view). Explicitly end the debugging session by pressing **Ctrl-F2**, **Alt-D W R** (if you have watch expressions), and **Alt-D B C** (if you have breakpoints).

SELF-REVIEW EXERCISES

1 2 3

A.4　Programming Tips

Consider the following tips to improve the design and style of your programs and to avoid some common errors.

Design and Style

1. Classic Tracing Techniques.　In *B.D.* (*Before Debugger*) days we used classic tracing techniques within programs by strategically inserted *trace* or *diagnostic statements* (as described in Section 4.4) that traced key calculations, entries into modules, and the values of parameters both before and after calls. As seen in Examples A.1–A.6, we need not use these in time *A.D.* (at least when working within Turbo Pascal's IDE).

2. Care with Multistatement Lines.　Remember that the minimal unit of execution by the debugger is the line. As seen in Example A.1, the two statements in line 5 of the program were executed as one step by the debugger. This is fine for simple uses of multistatement lines (as in our example), but not so if we were to bunch statements on a line, as in

```
Factorial := 1; for K := 2 to abs(X) do Factorial := Factorial * K; Fac := Factorial;
```

This is perfectly legal in Pascal, and does produce fewer lines in a program, but it's not a good idea for two reasons: It degrades program readability and eliminates key executable steps when using the debugger.

3. The Best Cure Is Preventive Debugging.　As in preventive health and defensive football, the best approach to debugging is to take steps that reduce the likelihood of having bugs in the first place. As discussed in the first four chapters, write *literate, top-down, modular,* and *structured* programs. In general, pay attention to the *software engineering* issues and *common errors* that we raise in the "Programming Tips" section at the end of each chapter and module. And develop your programs using the *software development cycle* guidelines summarized inside the front cover. In particular, *desk check* computations in the requirements stage and the algorithms in the design and coding stages. In practice, this kind of roleplaying is carried out by small groups of programmers and is called the **group** or **structured walkthrough.** In our years of programming, we've seen tremendous reductions in debugging efforts by those who practice these programming principles.

Common Errors

1. Forgetting to End Debugging Session.　If we load a new program to execute or debug and don't explicitly end the previous debugging session, the IDE assumes a continuation of the previous debugging session. This can wreak havoc with memory requirements, watch expressions, and breakpoints. Explicitly end all debugging sessions (see Note 3 earlier and Exercise 3).

2. Not Rebuilding the Source Program When Needed. Reread Note 1.

3. Lack of Experience and the Wrong Attitude. Learn by your mistakes. Experience is *the* classic teacher. Time and again we have seen students get frustrated and upset during the debugging process. If you get stuck and find yourself getting upset, take a break, walk, jog, meditate, scream, take a shower (great thoughts come in showers), or do anything else that relaxes you and (temporarily at least) takes your mind off debugging.[3] Actually, debugging can be fun, in a perverse sort of way. Finding and correcting errors (ideally not your own) can be a challenging and very satisfying experience. Many people get well paid for this too.

REVIEW EXERCISES

EASIER	For the busy...	
NORMAL	For the thinkers...	
	1 2 3	
TOUGHER	For the hard CORE...	

(L) **1.** **Debugger tutorial.** Load program DebugFac from the Examples Library and reproduce our sample debugger session in Examples A.1–A.6. (First make sure that you enable the options settings suggested at the end of Section A.1.) Along the way, try pressing **F1** or clicking **Help** to get explanations on objects like the Watch window, Add Watch dialog box, and Evaluate and Modify dialog box.

(L) **2.** **Function Fac.** Include the expression Factorial * K in...

    a. The Watch window (in addition to Factorial and K) and rework Example A.3.

    b. The Evaluate and Modify dialog box (in place of Factorial in Example A.4).

---

[3]We might call this *Zen and the Art of Debugging*. Inform yourself that we have a problem to solve. Then, let it go (practice detachment), take up some other activity, and the solution will likely come within a few days (while you're doing something else).

(L) 3.   **Function Fac and program AveScore.** Load DebugFac, establish a break-point at line 10, and add Item and X to the Watch window. Execute the program and try a little single stepping. Then, load in program AveScore (Example 4.7) without explicitly ending the previous debugging session. Place a breakpoint at the line that accumulates SumScores, and add ScoreNumber and SumScores to the Watch window. Execute the program and try some single stepping. Any problems?

ADDITIONAL EXERCISES

EASIER	For the busy...
NORMAL	For the thinkers... **4 5 6**
TOUGHER	For the hard CORE...

(L) 4.   **Revisit: Average scores.** Load program AveScore from the Examples Library (Example 4.7). Introduce a bug by deleting the line that initializes SumScores. Set a breakpoint at the line that accumulates SumScores. Add variables StudentNumber, Name, ScoreNumber, Score, and SumScores to the Watch window. Execute the program, using the same input data as the original example. Single-step through inner loop iterations, while watching the changing values. Correct the bug and repeat the debugging session.

5.   **Revisit.** Revisit one of your own programs. Add key variables to the Watch window. Set some breakpoints. Try some tracing variations with **Ctrl-F9**, **F4**, **F7**, and **F8**. Try some evaluations. Check out several call stacks. Find some modules. Explicitly end the debugging session.

(L) 6.   **Debug program.** Consider the program in Figure A.4. This program supposedly computes and writes the sum of squared differences between pairs of entered numbers. Confirm by desk checking that the three pairs of numbers

        10   5
         5   10
         5   2

have 59 as the sum of squared differences. Load program Debug into the Edit window. Add variables Pair, First, Second, and SumSqDiff to the Watch win-

---

FIGURE A.4   Listing for Program Debug

```
program Debug;

  {* * * * * * * * * * * * * * * * * * * * * * * * * * * * * * * * *
   *                                                               *
   *          Module A   Exercise 6                                *
   *                                                               *
   * * * * * * * * * * * * * * * * * * * * * * * * * * * * * * * * *}
var
  First, Second, Pair, Pairs, SumSqDiff : integer;

begin  {Debug}

  write ('Enter number of pairs ');  readln (Pairs);
  writeln;

  SumSqDiff := 0;

  for Pair := 1 to Pairs do
    write ('Enter pair ', Pair :2, ': ');  readln (First, Second);
    SumSqDiff := SumSqDiff + sqr( First - Second );

  writeln;
  writeln ('Sum of squared differences = ', SumSqDiff :5);

end.   {Debug}
```

---

dow. Set a breakpoint at the line that accumulates the sum. Execute the program and single-step the loop iterations. What do the I/O and Watch window tell you about the bug? Correct the bug and try an error-free debugging run. Explicitly end the debugging session.

Repetition: While-Do and Repeat-Until Structures

---

‡Optional material. Skip without loss of continuity, study at this point, or wait until later.

We defined the repetition structure in Section 3.4 and introduced a popular implementation called the *for-do loop* in Chapter 4. This chapter completes the treatment of loops by covering the standard Pascal implementations of the *while-do* and *repeat-until structures.*

We also cover operations on the *Boolean data type*, which are necessary for these loop implementations; introduce a style of programming called *PC-style programming,* which pays careful attention to the user interface; and revisit input from *text files.*

5.1   OPERATIONS ON BOOLEAN DATA TYPE

- - - - - - - - - - - - - - -

One of the predefined data types in Pascal is the **Boolean data type,** which represents the *logical values true* and *false.* We need to cover this data type at this time because the loop controls in this chapter use Boolean expressions.[1]

BOOLEAN CONSTANTS, VARIABLES, AND EXPRESSIONS

Let's start by defining certain elements when working with operations on the Boolean data type: constants, variables, and expressions.

Boolean Constants
Up to this point we have worked with *integer, real, character,* and *string constants.* A **Boolean constant** is one of the standard identifiers **true** or **false.** We can use a Boolean constant directly, or we can give it contextual meaning by *declaring* it in the usual way, as in

```
const
    Trace = false;
```

where Trace is a *declared Boolean constant* having the value false.

Boolean Variables
A **Boolean variable** (sometimes called a **logical variable**) is declared with the **Boolean** *data type identifier* in the var section of the program. For example,

```
var
    CorrectReply, MoreTemperatures : Boolean;
```

---

[1]This data type is named after the nineteenth-century English mathematician George Boole, who established the foundation for this type of symbolic logic.

declares the Boolean variables CorrectReply and MoreTemperatures. These variables can only store the Boolean value *true* or *false*.

A Boolean variable is often called a program **flag** or **switch** when it denotes either an existing (*flagged* or *switch on*) or a nonexistent (*unflagged* or *switch off*) condition. Flags are usually associated with the presence or absence of error conditions, as in CorrectReply above; switches usually denote one of two descriptive states, as in true we want MoreTemperatures or false we don't. We show both of these uses shortly.

Boolean Expressions

A **Boolean expression** is an expression that evaluates to a Boolean value. As usual, its members include constants, variables, operators, and special symbols such as parentheses. The simplest Boolean expression is a Boolean constant or Boolean variable.

A **relational expression** is a Boolean expression that compares two *type-compatible* expressions to one another using one of the **relational operators** in Table 5.1. Relational expressions have the following form.

Expression   **Relational operator**   Expression

(Left operand — points to first Expression; Right operand — points to second Expression)

The relational operator relates the expressions by comparing their values and arriving at either a true or a false conclusion. Look at each of the examples in Table 5.1, verbalize it in your head (or out loud), and confirm the resulting Boolean value.

Boolean Expressions as Conditions

Boolean expressions describe *conditions* that have contextual meaning. For example, the first Boolean expression in Table 5.1 might ask "Is the reply no?" In the example, the answer is "No it's not (false)." The second Boolean expression asks "Is the Fahrenheit temperature unequal to -999?" The answer is "Yes (true)."

Relational expressions like those in Table 5.1 are used to describe conditions that serve as loop controls (as we will see in this chapter) and selection alternatives (as we will see in the next chapter). For example, we might use the relational expression Fahrenheit $<> -999$ to loop while Fahrenheit temperatures are unequal to -999.

Type Compatibility

Operands in relational expressions must be *type compatible,* or we get a compile-time error. This means that we can compare

- arithmetic type (integer or real) to arithmetic type, as in integer to integer, real to real, or integer to real
- Boolean type to Boolean type
- character or string type to character or string type, as in character to character, string to string, or character to string

Table 5.1 Relational Operators and Expressions*

Relational Operator	Operation	Sample Relational Expression	Sample Operand Types	Resulting Value
=	Equal to	`Reply = 'N'`	Character and character	False if Reply stores Y
<>	Not equal to	`Fahrenheit <> -999`	Integer and integer	True if Fahrenheit stores 32
<	Less than	`Switch1 < Switch2`	Boolean and Boolean	True if Switch1 stores false and Switch2 stores true
>	Greater than	`Name1 > Name2`	String and string	True if Name1 stores SD and Name2 stores SC
<=	Less than or equal to	`Counter <= Iterations`	Integer and integer	True if Counter stores 2 and Iterations stores 4
>=	Greater than or equal to	`Result >= 2.5 * Original`	Integer and real	False if Result stores 5 and Original stores 3

*Operand types in this table include real, integer, Boolean, character, and string. Other types are covered later in the book. Operands in relational expressions must be type compatible. The resulting value for the relational expression is always type Boolean.

The comparison of arithmetic operands is straightforward, as in

```
2 <- 4       evaluates to true
5 >= 7.5     evaluates to false
32 <> -999   evaluates to true
```

In comparing Boolean operands, the value false is "less than" the value true, so

```
false < true     evaluates to true
false > true     evaluates to false
false = false    evaluates to true
```

In comparing character and string operands, corresponding characters are compared one by one from left to right according to the ASCII values seen in Appendix I. When comparing a character to a string, the character is treated as if it were a string of length 1. This comparison ends in one of three ways: (1) The character in one operand has an ASCII value less than that of the corresponding character in the other operand; (2) the end of one string is reached but not the end of the other, in which case the shorter string has a lesser value; or (3) the end of each string is reached, in which case the two strings have equal value. For example,

```
'three' < 'four'    evaluates to false (t is after f)
'Three' < 'four'    evaluates to true (T is before f)
'bit' < 'bits'      evaluates to true (bit is shorter than bits)
'Yes' = 'Yes'       evaluates to true (end of each string reached)
'SD' > 'SC'         evaluates to true (D is after C)
```

NOTE

1. On comparing real values. Take care in comparing real operands using the = or <> relational operators. The two operands may have equal values (in theory) but *precision* or *roundoff error* may yield a false rather than true comparison. It's best to avoid this kind of comparison; in cases where we must compare the equality between two real values, we should use the *error tolerance* fixup described under common errors at the end of this chapter.

2. On comparing character or string values. Don't forget that uppercase and lowercase letters are distinct. Look at the ASCII table in Appendix I, and note that all capital letters precede all lowercase letters. Also note that numeric digits precede all letters.

BOOLEAN EXPRESSIONS WITH BOOLEAN OPERATORS

Boolean expressions can also include one or more of the **Boolean operators** described in Table 5.2. A *truth table,* as in Table 5.3, is an alternative way of defining Boolean operators by showing all possible combinations of true and false values for the Boolean expressions operated on by the Boolean operators. Make sure that you understand each example in Table 5.2, noting that these examples are consistent with earlier examples in Table 5.1.

PRECEDENCE

The rules first discussed in Section 2.6 for arithmetic operator precedence, left-to-right scans, and use of parentheses also apply to the evaluation of Boolean expressions. When writing Boolean expressions, we also need to be aware of how the relational and Boolean operators fit in to the **operator-precedence rule,** as described in Table 5.4. As before, all *subexpressions* (expressions within parentheses) are evaluated first, and operations with the same precedence are evaluated in a left-to-right scan of the expression.

EXAMPLE 5.1   PRECEDENCE, LEFT-TO-RIGHT, AND PARENTHESES RULES FOR BOOLEAN EXPRESSIONS

Consider a complete evaluation of the following Boolean expression from Table 5.2.

Evaluation	Remark
`(Result >= 2.5 * Original) and (Name1 > Name2)`	
↓	
`( 5    >= 2.5 *   3   ) and ('SD' > 'SC')`	
↓	
`( 5    >=   7.5    ) and ('SD' > 'SC')`	Left subexpression evaluated first according to parentheses rule. Multiplication operation (2nd priority) performed before relational operation (4th priority), giving 7.5.
`false        and ('SD' > 'SC')`	Relational operation >= performed last within subexpression, giving false.
`false        and    true`	Right subexpression evaluated next, giving true.
`false`	Resulting value for Boolean expression is false.

Table 5.2 Boolean Operators and Expressions*

Boolean Operator	Boolean Expression	Operation	Sample Boolean Expression	Resulting Value
not	not B	Boolean negation: true if B is false; false if B is true	`not (Fahrenheit = -999)`	True if Fahrenheit stores 32 (relational expression is false; not changes value to true)
and	B1 and B2	Boolean conjunction: true if both B1 and B2 are true; false otherwise	`(Result >= 2.5 * Original) and (Name1 > Name2)`	False if Result stores 5, Original stores 3 (giving false for left operand), Name1 stores SD and Name2 stores SC (giving true for right operand)
or	B1 or B2	Boolean disjunction: true if either B1, or B2, or both are true; false otherwise	`(Reply = 'Y') or (Reply = 'N')`	True if Reply stores Y (the left operand is true and the right operand is false)
xor	B1 xor B2	Boolean nonequivalence: true if B1 and B2 have unlike Boolean values; false otherwise	`Switch1 xor Switch2`	True if Switch1 stores false and Switch2 stores true

*The Boolean operators are reserved words. B, B1, and B2 represent any Boolean expression. Operand types are strictly Boolean. The resulting value for the Boolean expression is always Boolean.

Table 5.3   Truth Table for Boolean Operators*

B	not B	B1	B2	B1 **and** B2	B1 **or** B2	B1 **xor** B2
true	false	true	true	true	true	false
false	true	true	false	false	true	true
		false	true	false	true	true
		false	false	false	false	false

*B, B1, and B2 represent any Boolean expression.

Table 5.4   Operator-Precedence Rule

Operator	Precedence
not	Highest or 1st priority, evaluated first
and * / div mod	2nd priority, evaluated after highest priority
or xor + –	3rd priority, evaluated after 2nd priority
= <> < > <= >=	Lowest or 4th priority, evaluated last

Look at the precedence rule in Table 5.4 and think for a moment (before reading on) what would happen if we were to omit the right set of parentheses ... As before, we might figure that the left subexpression gets evaluated to false. We now have the following remaining expression.

```
false and 'SD' > 'SC'
```

The **and** operator has a higher precedence than the ≥ operator, so we might think that the processer next evaluates

```
false and 'SD' ☹
```
— Type Boolean
— Type string

We have a problem here. As footnoted in Table 5.2, each operand in the Boolean operation must be type Boolean. In our present case, the left operand is type Boolean, but the right operand is type string.

In reality, we would not get past the compiler if we were to omit parentheses as indicated. This would be flagged as a compile-time error with the message *Type mismatch*. If Name1 and Name2 were type Boolean, however, we would have a logic error rather than a compile-time error!

NOTE

3. On using parentheses in Boolean expressions. To avoid the error noted in Example 5.1, surround relational expressions with parentheses when they act as operands to a Boolean operator. This also improves the literacy of the Boolean expression.

4. Short-circuit evaluation. Example 5.1 illustrated the *complete evaluation* of all operands in a Boolean expression. In *short-circuit evaluation* the evaluation stops as soon as the overall result is evident. In Example 5.1 a short-circuit evaluation would evaluate the left subexpression as false, and conclude that the value of the Boolean expression is also false; that is, once any operand in an **and** operation is false, then the result is false, regardless of the value for the other operand. Similarly, if any operand in an **or** operation is true, then the resulting Boolean expression would be true. By default, Turbo Pascal uses short-circuit evaluation, to speed up execution.

BOOLEAN ASSIGNMENT STATEMENTS

As with arithmetic, character, and string variables, we can use an *assignment statement* to assign a value to a Boolean variable. We primarily use assignment statements to define *flags* and *switches,* which improve program literacy.

EXAMPLE 5.2   DEFINING AN ERROR FLAG WITH AN ASSIGNMENT STATEMENT

Suppose we plan to interactively input a user reply of Y or y (for yes), and N or n (for no). These are the only legitimate replies. Let's store the user's reply in the character variable Reply. Now, suppose we wish to denote legitimate replies using the Boolean variable CorrectReply. We can do this as follows.

```
CorrectReply :=
(Reply = 'Y') or (Reply = 'y') or (Reply = 'N') or (Reply = 'n');
```

For example, if Reply stores N, then the assignment statement completely evaluates as follows.

```
CorrectReply :=
(Reply = 'Y') or (Reply = 'y') or (Reply = 'N') or (Reply = 'n');
    false      or    false     or     true    or    false
                            true
```

That is, the reply is correct.

However, if Reply stores s, then the assignment statement completely evaluates as follows.

```
CorrectReply :=
(Reply = 'Y') or (Reply = 'y') or (Reply = 'N') or (Reply = 'n');
    false      or    false     or    false     or    false
                            false
```

This means that the reply is incorrect.

We can simplify this Boolean expression by using the predeclared **upcase** function.

```
CorrectReply :=
(upcase( Reply ) = 'Y') or (upcase( Reply ) = 'N');
```

For example, if Reply stores y, then **upcase** (Reply) returns the value Y, which is a legitimate response.

The Boolean variable CorrectReply is an example of a program flag that detects errors. In this case, the reply is in error if CorrectReply stores false; otherwise, the reply is correct. Program literacy is improved because CorrectReply has more contextual meaning than the original Boolean expression. Elsewhere in the program we would use the Boolean variable in place of the Boolean expression.

SELF-REVIEW EXERCISES

1 2 3

5.2   WHILE STATEMENT

• • • • • • • • • • • • • • •

The fundamental repetition structure is the **while-do structure,** which repeats the loop body *while* a loop control condition is met (tests *true*). The *for-do loop* from Chapter 4 is an example of a while-do structure. The for-do loop is particularly well suited for *counter-controlled looping,* where a control variable systematically steps by one from an initial value to a final value. This loop control is inflexible, however, because we can't change the condition that prescribes the systematic behavior of the control variable. For example, we might want to control loop iterations on the fly, letting the user decide at any moment when to terminate iterations.

Boolean expressions give us the means to model very flexible *conditions* as loop controls, as seen in the pseudocode for the while-do structure in Figure 5.1. In the example, the loop iterates while the value in Counter ≤ High value. In this case, the condition that describes the loop control is easily coded as the Boolen expression Counter <= High.

IMPLEMENTATION OF WHILE-DO STRUCTURE

Figure 5.1 shows the while-do design in pseudocode, and the next syntax box shows its implementation in Pascal as a **while statement.** Review the design

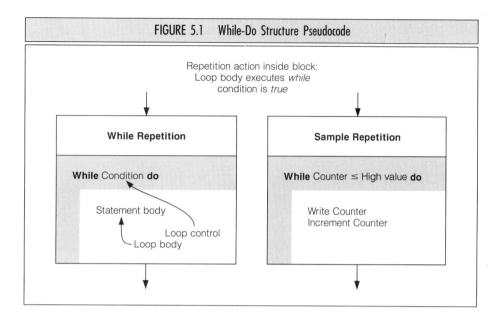

FIGURE 5.1   While-Do Structure Pseudocode

Repetition action inside block:
Loop body executes *while*
condition is *true*

While Repetition

While Condition **do**

Statement body

Loop control

Loop body

Sample Repetition

While Counter ≤ High value **do**

Write Counter
Increment Counter

in Figure 5.1 and relate it to the example in the syntax box. The syntax of the while-do structure is straightforward, now that we have covered Boolean expressions and the for-do loop.

What we need to spend some time on are the two general methods of designing loop termination: based on a computed condition and based on input.

LOOP TERMINATION BASED ON COMPUTED CONDITION

The Boolean expression in the while statement is used as the loop control. In designing a while-do loop we need to think about just how to terminate the loop, because we have several options. The example in the while statement syntax box shows termination based on a *computed condition*. The control variable Counter started with a value of 3, then 4, and finally 5. At the third iteration of the loop, Counter actually incremented to 6, giving a false value for the Boolean expression and an immediate loop exit. The effective values (those of interest) for Counter thus ranged from 3 to 5 in increments of 1. This is called a counter loop. The for-do loop lives as a counter loop, and so it's a better choice than the while-do loop for this purpose. (Convince yourself by comparing the first examples in the present syntax box and the one on page 124.)

Our next example shows that the while-do approach is better than the for-do approach either whenever the control variable varies by an increment other than one or its type is real.

SYNTAX BOX

While-do structure (while statement)...Repeat body while Boolean expression evaluates as true

Syntax.........`while` BooleanExpression **do**
          Statement;

                  ── Loop control
              ── Loop body

Examples......`Counter := Low;`
          while `Counter <= High` **do**
            begin
               write `(Counter :3);`
               `Counter := Counter + 1;`
            end;   `{while}`

Results:

3 4 5   when Low stores 3
and High stores 5

Explanation ... **while** and **do** are reserved words, and BooleanExpression is any legitimate Boolean expression. Statement is a single or compound statement. The first action on entering the while-do structure is a test of the condition expressed by the Boolean expression. If false, the body is bypassed and the first statement following the while-do structure is executed. If true, the body is executed, control loops back to the beginning of the while statement, and the Boolean expression is reevaluated. This cycle is repeated *while* the Boolean expression evaluates as *true*.

EXAMPLE 5.3   LOOP TERMINATION BASED ON COMPUTED CONDITION

Suppose we have a numeric variable Weight that we wish to vary from an initial value to a final value by a certain increment. The initial, final, and incremental values are interactively input, and respectively stored in the variables Initial, Final, and Increment. The following code segment satisfies these requirements (we assume type integer for all variables, but it could be type real just as well).

```
write ('Enter initial, final, and incremental weights... ');
readln (Initial, Final, Increment);
writeln;  write ('Weights: ');
Weight := Initial;                         ──Initialize control variable
                                             before loop

while Weight <= Final do
  begin
    write (Weight :4);                     ──Test control variable
    Weight := Weight + Increment;          ──Increment control variable
  end;   {while}                             at end of body

writeln;  writeln ('  End of looping...');
```

A sample run might look like this.

```
Enter initial, final, and incremental weights... 15 25 5
Weights:   15   20   25

    End of looping...
```

Note that this implementation calls for initialization of the control variable before the loop, a test of the control variable just after the **while** identifier, and incrementation of the control variable at the end of the loop body. A roleplay of the execution beginning with initialization would give the following desk-check script.

1. Weight stores 15
2. Boolean expression is true (15 is less than or equal to 25)
3. Write 15 ⎫
4. Weight stores 20 ⎭ 1st iteration
5. Boolean expression is true (20 is less than or equal to 25)
6. Write 20 ⎫
7. Weight stores 25 ⎭ 2nd iteration
8. Boolean expression is true (25 is less than or equal to 25)
9. Write 25 ⎫
10. Weight stores 30 ⎭ 3rd iteration
11. Boolean expression is false (30 is *not* less than or equal to 25)
12. Write "End of looping..."

Compare this loop implementation to the for-do implementation in Example 4.5. Note that the loop bodies are identical, but the while-do approach is more literate because it directly uses the variable of interest (Weight) in the loop control. Moreover, unlike the while-do implementation, the for-do approach requires the calculation of loop iterations as a precondition to the loop.

LOOP TERMINATION BASED ON INPUT

We can also terminate a while-do loop based on input. Here we have three common approaches.

- Termination based on a unique input value called a *sentinel*
- Termination based on a *yes/no reply* in response to a program query
- Termination based on an *end-of-file (eof)* condition

We illustrate the first two approaches next, and delay the third approach until Section 5.4.

Example 5.4   Loop Termination Based on Sentinel

Consider the following code fragment and its sample execution.

Reads 1st code ──────────┐
                         ▼

```
write ('Enter code (end with X)... '); readln (Code);

while Code <> 'X' do
  begin
    writeln ('  Code ::::::::::::::::::::::> ', Code);
    writeln;
    write    ('Enter code (end with X)... ');  readln (Code);
  end;  {while}
```

Reads all other codes ───┘

```
      Enter code (end with X)... A
         Code ::::::::::::::::::::::> A
      Enter code (end with X)... B
         Code ::::::::::::::::::::::> B
      Enter code (end with X)... C
         Code ::::::::::::::::::::::> C
      Enter code (end with X)... X ◄──────┐
```

Loop terminates when sentinel *X* is entered ──┘

A **sentinel** is a unique input value that serves the purpose of terminating loop iterations. In the example, the value X is a sentinel. The loop iterates while the value in the character variable Code is not equal to X. The loop control directly tests for the sentinel value, as seen in the Boolean expression

```
Code <> 'X'
```

An alternative Boolean expression for sentinel testing uses the **not** logical operator, as in

```
not (Code = 'X')
```

We believe the first approach reads more easily in this case.

In selecting a sentinel, we first have to pick an input variable, and then we have to pick the sentinel itself. In general, we must select a sentinel that would never be part of regular input for that variable.

EXAMPLE 5.5   LOOP TERMINATION BASED ON Y/N OR y/n REPLY

We can also terminate loop iterations by directly asking the user if the loop should continue with the next iteration. We then input the reply and use it as a basis for loop control. We usually design this style of termination by requesting a yes/no reply. For convenience, this is usually shortened to a Y/N or y/n reply. The reply itself is stored in a character variable.

Check out the following program segment.

```
                                                              Reads first reply
write ('Do you want to feel better? (Y/N) ');  readln (Reply);

while upcase(Reply) = 'Y' do
  begin                               Loop control based on reply
    writeln;
    writeln ('  YOU are my FAVORITE programmer!');
    writeln;
    write ('Feel better again? (Y/N) ');  readln (Reply);
  end;   {while}
                                              Reads subsequent
writeln; writeln ('  All better...');         replies
```

Our little dialogue might go something like this.

```
Do you want to feel better? (Y/N) y          Lowercase acceptable
   YOU are my FAVORITE programmer!
Feel better again? (Y/N) Y
   YOU are my FAVORITE programmer!
Feel better again? (Y/N) n
   All better...
```

Note that this loop design calls for a reply before loop entry, a test of the reply just after the **while** identifier, and all subsequent replies at the end of the loop body. We ask you to develop a desk-check script for this example in Exercise 7.

PC-STYLE PROGRAMMING

The term **PC-style programming** is often used to describe a collection of programming approaches and features that were popularized by applications specifically written for use on personal computers. The underlying, unifying philosophy in PC-style programming is "Let's make programs easier to use." This basically translates into user-interface improvements that include careful screen design, menu selection, reactions to incorrect user responses, and the effective use of windows, graphics, color, sound, and other special screen effects. The bottom line? An increased likelihood of attracting new users, more productive current users, and more profits for the software industry.

Turbo Pascal has outstanding features for PC-style programming. The while statement is well suited for implementing some of these features, with the help of the **crt** *unit* for designing and controlling screens.

EXAMPLE 5.6   TEMPERATURES, VERSION 1.0

Let's work with some temperatures...

Requirements

Harvey CORE, the boss at Computer Aided Decisions (a PC software firm), wants an interactive program that inputs degrees Fahrenheit and outputs degrees Fahrenheit and its corresponding Celsius equivalent. From our earlier work in Example 2.3, we have the following formula.

Celsius = $5/9 \cdot$ (Fahrenheit $- 32$)

Sample computations include 0 Celsius for 32 Fahrenheit and 27 Celsius (to the nearest degree) for 80 Fahrenheit.

We also require output for the number of temperature calculations processed in one run. This gives us three output values (the two temperatures and the number of temperature comparisons processed), one input value (degrees Fahrenheit), and three constants.

This program will be used by TV weather personalities who are not meteorologists. Translation: They fear computers and want friendly programs. This means that we pay particular attention to screen design at the user interface. (It's rumored that HC is consulting a lot with Ms. MeteoRITE, the weather star at cable station WROC, which gives the project added importance.)

Design

The I/O design is shown in Figure 5.2. Note that we now have a distinct *screen orientation*. This includes the specification of each screen design, as follows.

- *Opening screen* (screen 1). It includes a title, sentinel message, and input of the first temperature.

- *Output screen* (screens 2 and 4). This screen includes a title, labeled output, and a pause message. Note that this screen pauses (remains in place) until the user presses a key.

- *Input screen* (screens 3 and 5). This screen has a title and an input prompt for Fahrenheit temperature. This screen is used for all temperature inputs but the first.

- *Farewell screen* (screen 6). It has a title, outputs the number of temperatures processed, and writes a farewell message. This screen also pauses.

FIGURE 5.2   Screen Designs (I/O) for Program Temp1

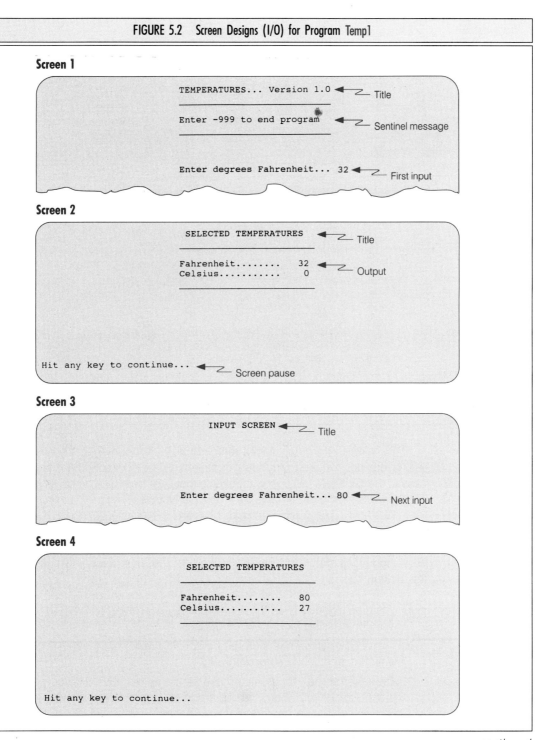

Screen 1

```
            TEMPERATURES... Version 1.0 ◄       Title
            ─────────────────────────
            Enter -999 to end program ◄         Sentinel message
            ─────────────────────────


            Enter degrees Fahrenheit... 32 ◄    First input
```

Screen 2

```
            SELECTED TEMPERATURES ◄             Title
            ─────────────────────
            Fahrenheit........    32 ◄          Output
            Celsius..........     0
            ─────────────────────




Hit any key to continue... ◄                    Screen pause
```

Screen 3

```
            INPUT SCREEN ◄                      Title




            Enter degrees Fahrenheit... 80 ◄    Next input
```

Screen 4

```
            SELECTED TEMPERATURES
            ─────────────────────
            Fahrenheit........    80
            Celsius..........    27
            ─────────────────────




Hit any key to continue...
```

continued

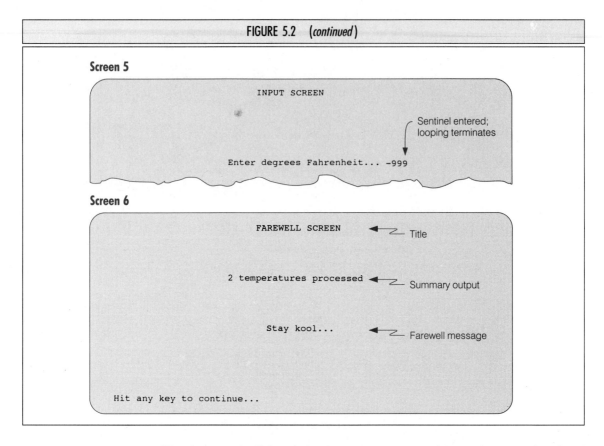

FIGURE 5.2 *(continued)*

We plan to treat Fahrenheit temperature as type integer, because fractional values are not required. As seen in screen 5, the Fahrenheit variable also processes the sentinel −999. Arithmetic sentinels are best typed integer, to avoid the problem with real comparisons described in Note 1.

We must type Celsius as real, because the division 5/9 in the formula is a floating-point operation. By proper format control we can write Celsius temperatures to the nearest degree, as seen in screens 2 and 4.

Figure 5.3 shows our stepwise chart for the algorithm. Note the following in this design.

1. The mail algorithm has the usual design that proceeds from opening tasks, to main processing loop, to closing tasks.

2. The opening screen is the primary opening task in procedure OpeningTasks, which makes sense chronologically.

3. The other screen types also make sense as modules: The output screen in procedure WriteScreen, the input screen in procedure ReadTemp, and the Farewell screen in procedure ClosingTasks.

4. The screen-pause task is used twice in the program, by two different modules. Several steps are needed to pause a screen: Write a message to inform

FIGURE 5.3   Stepwise Chart for Program Temp1

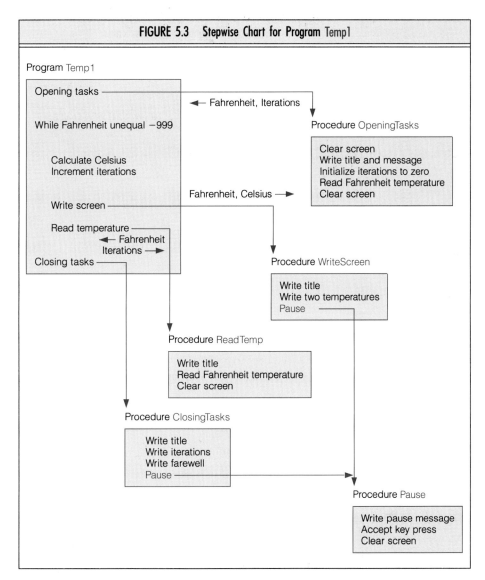

the user what to do (as in "Hit any key to continue..."), accept a key press, and clear the screen. To avoid duplicate code and ensure consistency, it makes sense to refine the pause task as a separate module. In fact, the screen pause is so common in practice, that we made Pause a utility module.

5. It's also important to clear (refresh) screens and position the cursor at any desired point on the screen. Notice in Figure 5.3 how each procedure that writes to the screen either clears the screen at the beginning (so it doesn't overwrite previous screen material), or clears it at the end (so the next screen is not superimposed on the current screen), or both. Tasks like screen clears and cursor positioning are implemented by standard procedures in Turbo Pascal's *standard unit* **crt**.

FIGURE 5.4   Listing of Program Temp1

```
program Temp1;

    {* * * * * * * * * * * * * * * * * * * * * * * * * * * * * *
     *                                                         *
     *          Temperatures... Version 1.0                    *
     *                         w/ while-do structure, sentinel termination, *
     *                         PC-style programming            *
     *                                                         *
     *          Inputs degrees Fahrenheit while desired        *
     *          Calculates degrees Celsius                     *
     *          Outputs degrees Fahrenheit and Celsius         *
     *                                                         *
     *          Modular structure                              *
     *              |___ Opening tasks                         *
     *              |___ WriteScreen                           *
     *              |    |_____                     *
     *              |___ ReadTemp        |                     *
     *              |___ ClosingTasks    |                     *
     *                   |_____|__ Pause             *
     *                                                         *
     * * * * * * * * * * * * * * * * * * * * * * * * * * * * *}

    {============================ Declarations ============================}

uses crt;                     {Needed for PC-style programming}

var
  Celsius     : real;         {Degrees Celsius}
  Fahrenheit,                 {Degrees Fahrenheit}
  Iterations : integer;       {Loop iterations, or temperatures processed}

    {======================= Procedure Declarations =======================}

procedure Pause;

  { Utility writes pause message, pauses for any key press, clears screen
    Receives nothing
    Sends nothing }

  { NOTE:  Requires uses clause for crt unit in host program          ◄─── New
           Writes message on line 25 of screen }                            utility
                                                                            procedure
var
  Dummy : char;                         {Single-character dummy input}

begin  {Pause} ────── Moves cursor to column 1 and line 25

  gotoxy (1,25);  write ('Hit any key to continue...');

  Dummy := readkey;   {readkey is standard function in crt unit}

  clrscr; ◄── Clears screen; moves cursor to position (1, 1)
end;  {Pause}
    {---------------------------------------------------------------------}
```

FIGURE 5.4   *(continued)*

```
procedure OpeningTasks (var Fahrenheit, Iterations : integer);

   { Clears screen, writes title and sentinel message, initializes
       iterations counter, reads first Fahrenheit temperature,
       clears screen again
     Receives nothing
     Sends Fahrenheit, Iterations }

const
   Title   = 'TEMPERATURES... Version 1.0';
   Line    = '_____';
   Message = 'Enter -999 to end program  ';

begin   {OpeningTasks}

   clrscr;
   gotoxy (25, 5);   write (Title);
   gotoxy (25, 6);   write (Line);
   gotoxy (25, 8);   write (Message);
   gotoxy (25, 9);   write (Line);

   Iterations := 0;
                                                    ┌──── Reads 1st temperature
   gotoxy (25,13);
   write ('Enter degrees Fahrenheit... ');   readln (Fahrenheit);
   clrscr;

end;   {OpeningTasks}
{----------------------------------------------------------------------}
procedure WriteScreen (Fahrenheit :integer;   Celsius : real);

   { Writes title and both temperatures, calls pause
     Receives Fahrenheit, Celsius
     Sends nothing }

const
   Title = ' SELECTED TEMPERATURES  ';
   Line  = '_____';

begin   {WriteScreen}

   gotoxy (25,10);   write (Title);
   gotoxy (25,11);   write (Line);
   gotoxy (25,13);   write ('Fahrenheit........', Fahrenheit :5  );
   gotoxy (25,14);   write ('Celsius...........', Celsius    :5:0);
   gotoxy (25,15);   write (Line);

   Pause;  ◄───── Pause until any key is pressed

end;   {WriteScreen}
{----------------------------------------------------------------------}
```

continued

Code and Test

Figure 5.4 shows Pascal coding, and Figure 5.2 shows an actual run. Study the program, relate it to the design shown earlier, and note the following points.

1. Crt Unit. Turbo Pascal includes unit crt for handling specialized I/O tasks. In this program we use it to clear screens, control cursor movement within a screen, and accept single key presses from the keyboard. These tasks are implemented as calls to certain standard procedures and functions in **crt,** as

FIGURE 5.4   (*continued*)

```pascal
procedure ReadTemp (var Fahrenheit : integer);

   { Writes title, reads Fahrenheit temperature, clears screen
     Receives nothing
     Sends Fahrenheit }

const
  Title = 'INPUT SCREEN';

begin   {ReadTemp}

  gotoxy (30, 5);  write (Title);
  gotoxy (25,13);
  write ('Enter degrees Fahrenheit... ');  readln (Fahrenheit);
  clrscr;

end;   {ReadTemp}
{-------------------------------------------------------------------------}
procedure ClosingTasks (Iterations : integer);

   { Writes title, iterations and farewell message, calls pause
     Receives Iterations
     Sends nothing }

const
  Title    = 'FAREWELL SCREEN';
  Farewell = 'Stay kool...';

begin   {ClosingTasks}

  gotoxy (30, 5);  write (Title);
  gotoxy (25,10);  write (Iterations, ' temperatures processed');
  gotoxy (32,15);  write (Farewell);

  Pause;

end;   {ClosingTasks}

  {============================== Main Body ==============================}

begin   {Temp1}

  OpeningTasks (Fahrenheit, Iterations);                        ──── While-do structure

  while Fahrenheit <> -999 do
    begin                                                       ──── Sentinel
      Celsius := 5 / 9 * (Fahrenheit - 32);
      inc (Iterations);                                         ──── Standard procedure
      WriteScreen (Fahrenheit, Celsius);                             for incrementing
      ReadTemp (Fahrenheit);
    end;   {while}

  ClosingTasks (Iterations);                            ──── Reads all temperatures but first

end.    {Temp1}
```

described in the next item. To use the crt unit we insert the clause **uses crt** just after the program heading, as we did earlier when using the printer unit.

2. **Procedure Pause.** This procedure pauses (holds) the current screen until a user presses any key, and then clears the screen. It also uses screen cursor control to write its message. We accomplish these tasks by calling the following standard procedures and function in the **crt** unit.

- Procedure **gotoxy.**
  This procedure moves the cursor to the specified column and row coordinate. By row we mean a line on the screen. The column is the position of the cursor on that line. All of our examples use full screens with 25 lines (rows) and 80 character positions (columns). We call this procedure as follows.

  ```
  gotoxy (Column, Row);
  gotoxy (1,25);
  ```
  Moves cursor to 1st position
  in 25th line

- Procedure **clrscr**
  This procedure clears the screen and places the cursor at the *home coordinate*, or upper-left-hand corner at coordinate (1,1). We call this procedure as follows.

  ```
  clrscr
  ```

- Function **readkey**
  This function reads and returns a single character from the keyboard and does not echo the pressed key. It processes any key press, including the Enter key. We call this function as follows.

  ```
  readkey
  ```

  Note that we assign the returned character from **readkey** to a character variable named Dummy. This dummy variable has no function other than to invoke the **readkey** function. We don't do anything with the returned character.

  Procedure Pause is declared before other procedures that use it (WriteScreen and ClosingTasks). We wrote Pause as a utility procedure, and added it to our Utilities Library on diskette (see the listing inside the front cover of the book).

3. **Procedure OpeningTasks.** This procedure makes extensive use of the **gotoxy** procedure. Note how simple it is to control the cursor.

4. **Procedure WriteScreen.** This procedure also makes good use of the **gotoxy** procedure. Note how we need to pause the screen at the end of this procedure; otherwise, the output screen would be immediately overwritten by the input screen that follows. At any pause, the user can read the screen at leisure, take a break, or whatever. Pressing any key continues with program execution.

5. **Procedure ReadTemp.** Note how we clear the screen at the end of this procedure; otherwise, procedure WriteScreen would next overwrite the input screen.

6. **Procedure ClosingTasks.** We need to pause at the end of this procedure; otherwise, the farewell screen would be replaced immediately by the IDE screen (the screen is faster than the eye!).

7. **Main Body.** Note our use of the Turbo Pascal standard procedure **inc** to increment the value in Iterations by one.

```
inc (Iterations);
```

We could just as well have used the classic approach:

```
Iterations := Iterations + 1;
```

As with many other nonstandard procedures in Turbo Pascal, we have alternative means (classic approaches) for accomplishing the same end. Using the provided procedures is generally easier, more readable, and optimizes compiler code for faster execution.

SELF-REVIEW EXERCISES

4 5a–d 6 8a–c

5.3 REPEAT STATEMENT

• • • • • • • • • • • • • • •

The while-do structure describes a *pretest loop,* meaning that the loop control precedes the loop body. The **repeat-until structure** in Figure 5.5 is a repetition structure that describes a *posttest loop,* where the loop control follows the loop body. It is like a *mirror image* of the while-do structure. Compare Figures 5.1 and 5.5, noting the following.

- The loop controls and loop bodies are sequentially reversed.
- The conditions are complements of one another (Counter ≤ High value versus Counter > High value).
- The repeat-until design achieves loop exit when the condition tests *true,* whereas the while-do design exits when the condition is *false.*
- The repeat-until design requires at least one loop repetition (because the loop body is entered before the first loop control test), a provision not imposed by the while-do design.

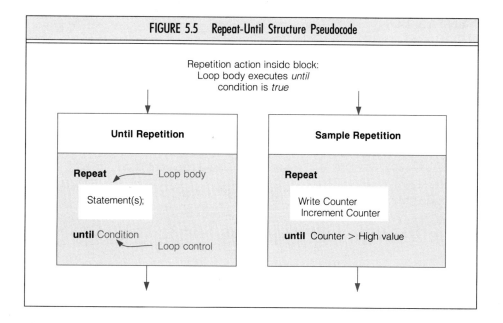

FIGURE 5.5   Repeat-Until Structure Pseudocode

Repetition action inside block:
Loop body executes *until*
condition is *true*

Until Repetition

Repeat —— Loop body

Statement(s);

until Condition —— Loop control

Sample Repetition

Repeat

Write Counter
Increment Counter

until Counter > High value

IMPLEMENTATION OF REPEAT-UNTIL STRUCTURE

We use the **repeat statement** to implement the repeat-until structure in Pascal, as shown in the next syntax box. The example is the same as that given in the syntax box for the while statement. Make sure you understand the example and compare the differences to its while-do counterpart. In particular, note that we don't need to create a compound statement (with a **begin-end** pair) for the sequence of simple statements in the loop body. The **repeat** and **until** identifiers serve the purpose of defining the loop body as the sequence of statements in between **repeat** and **until.**

LOOP TERMINATION BASED ON COMPUTED CONDITION

As in the while-do structure we can terminate the repeat-until structure according to a computed condition. The only differences between while-do and repeat-until versions are the mirror-image differences described earlier, as seen in the examples within the repeat-until and while-do syntax boxes. In Exercise 9 we ask you to consider the repeat-until version of Example 5.3.

LOOP TERMINATION BASED ON INPUT

The input-termination methods described earlier for the while-do structure also apply to the repeat-until structure. Again, the key implementation differences are the mirror-image descriptions discussed earlier. We leave the repeat-until versions to Exercise 9.

SYNTAX BOX

Repeat-until structure (repeat statement)...Repeat body until Boolean
expression evaluates as true

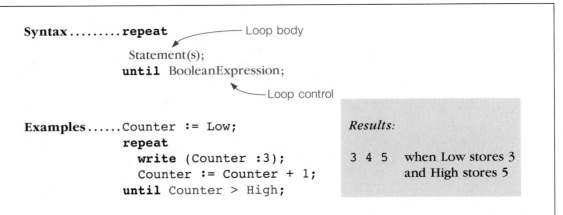

Explanation...**repeat** and **until** are reserved words, and BooleanExpression is any
legitimate Boolean expression. The loop body is one or more statements. The first
action on entering the repeat-until structure is execution of the body. Next, the
Boolean expression is evaluated. If false, the body is executed again, and the
Boolean expression is reevaluated. This cycle is repeated *until* the Boolean expression evaluates as *true,* at which time loop exit is achieved, and the statement immediately following **until** is executed.

PC-STYLE PROGRAMMING

The choice of a loop design has minor effects on PC-style programming. We
like using a repeat-until design when controlling a loop with the Y/N reply;
however, the repeat-until approach is inappropriate when trapping certain
user-input errors. We illustrate both of these considerations next.

EXAMPLE 5.7   TEMPERATURES, VERSION 2.0

Let's say we implemented program Temp1 from Example 5.6, but after some use,
HC informs us that our TV personalities dislike terminating the loop with (in their
words) "This fake temperature of -999." So, it's back to the drawing board.

We asked if they wouldn't mind entering a Y/N reply to the query "Continue?"
for continuing with a new set of temperatures. *This* they like! It's more like human
dialogue (which after all *is* their business).

They also plan to calculate at least one temperature whenever they use the
program, so we decide to use a *repeat-until* design for this Y/N controlled loop. A

while-do design would require either input or initialization of the reply variable to Y just before the loop. This is an unnecessary task that we can avoid altogether with the repeat-until design.

We also realize (without telling them) that they're not too great at pounding the keyboard. In fact, chances are pretty good that they would occasionally hit the T, 6, 7, U, H, or G key when intending the Y key. If we were to use the Y/N approach from Example 5.6, execution would bomb out of the loop (check it out!). If this were to happen, they would probably take our TVs away.

So, we also decide to include an **error routine** that traps incorrect Y/N replies. Specifically, this error routine requests reinput of the Y/N response *while* the reply is incorrect, according to the following design.

Y/N error routine:

```
Assign correct reply flag (true if reply is Y, y, N, or n;
                           false otherwise)
While not correct reply do
    Beep the speaker (politely)
    Write "Please enter Y or y for Yes, N or n for No"
    Clear screen line with previous input prompt and incorrect reply
    Read reply
    Assign correct reply flag
```

Note that the while-do structure is uniquely suited to trapping incorrect replies. First, if the reply is initially correct, execution never enters the loop body (this would not be true if we were to use the repeat-until structure). Second, if the initial reply is incorrect, then we do enter the loop body, *and remain there by iterating while the reply is incorrect.* Thus, the while-do loop has the desirable characteristics of never getting executed if the initial reply is correct, and otherwise forcing a correct reply eventually (to get out of the loop).

The revised screens and a sample run are shown in Figure 5.6. Note the following.

1. The opening screen (screen 1) doesn't input a temperature.

2. The input screen (screen 2), output screen (screen 3), and farewell screen (not shown) are identical to the earlier designs in Figure 5.2.

3. The reply screen (screen 4) is a new screen. In screen 4 we first entered an incorrect reply of ok. In line with our design, the error routine caught this error, beeped the speaker, displayed the error message at the bottom of the screen, cleared the input reply line, and reinput the correct y. If we were to enter nope, "no" would be interpreted. This is because our reply variable is typed character, thereby just storing the first character n. Note that a rogue reply like nag would be interpreted as a "no." We leave this type of error trapping to Exercise 10.

FIGURE 5.6   Screen Designs (I/O) for Program Temp2

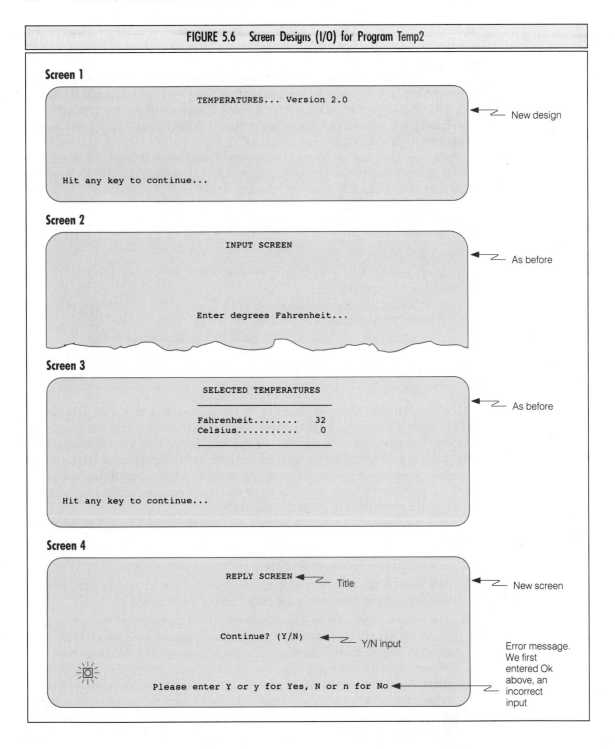

Screen 1

```
                    TEMPERATURES... Version 2.0
```
New design
```
Hit any key to continue...
```

Screen 2

```
                         INPUT SCREEN
```
As before
```
                   Enter degrees Fahrenheit...
```

Screen 3

```
                    SELECTED TEMPERATURES
                    _____

                    Fahrenheit........   32
                    Celsius...........    0
                    _____
```
As before
```
Hit any key to continue...
```

Screen 4

```
                    REPLY SCREEN
```
Title

New screen
```
                    Continue? (Y/N)
```
Y/N input

Error message. We first entered Ok above, an incorrect input
```
        Please enter Y or y for Yes, N or n for No
```

The two key changes in the overall program design are (1) the replacement of the sentinel-controlled while-do loop with the Y/N-controlled repeat-until loop and (2) a ReadReply procedure that includes the error routine. We leave the stepwise chart to Exercise 10, and directly move to the code in Figure 5.7.

Program Temp2 is an edited version of program Temp1, with the following significant changes.

1. The main body algorithm uses a repeat-until structure. All temperatures are now read at the top of the loop body, which reads more naturally than the while-do design of reading the first temperature before the loop and the remaining temperatures at the end of the loop body. The loop control is now based on the Y/N reply. Specifically, we process temperatures until the reply is no. As expected, the reply is read at the end of the loop body, just before the loop control test.

2. Procedure ReadReply is a new module. It clears the screen, inputs the reply, and applies the error routine. Within the error routine we beep the speaker by "writing" the bell (ASCII 7) with

    ```
    write ( chr(7) );
    ```

    The error routine also calls a new procedure from the **crt** unit as follows.

    ```
    clreol;
    ```

This procedure clears a line from its current position to the end of the line, without moving the cursor itself. In the program,

```
gotoxy (29,13);  clreol;
```

first moves the cursor to column 29 and row 13 (placing the cursor over the C in Continue, as in screen 4 in Figure 5.6), and then erases line 13 from column 29 to column 80. This clears the previously incorrect reply, in preparation for the new input prompt issued by the next program line.

Note that CorrectReply is a Boolean variable that acts as an error flag. Its use considerably improves the literacy of the loop control as

not CorrectReply ☺

More literate loop control

instead of

Less literate loop control

not (upcase(Reply) = 'Y')
or (upcase(Reply) = 'N') ☹

We wrote procedure ReadReply as a utility procedure, and added it to the Utilities Library.

FIGURE 5.7   Listing for Program **Temp2**

```
program Temp2;

  {* * * * * * * * * * * * * * * * * * * * * * * * * * * * * * * * * *
   *                                                                 *
   *         Temperatures... Version 2.0                             *
   *                         w/ repeat-until structure, Y/N termination, *
   *                         PC-style programming                    *
   *                                                                 *
   *           Inputs degrees Fahrenheit until reply is no           *
   *           Calculates degrees Celsius                            *
   *           Outputs degrees Fahrenheit and Celsius                *
   *                                                                 *
   *           Modular structure                                     *
   *                 |___ Opening tasks                              *
   *                 |_____                               *
   *                 |___ ReadTemp     |                             *
   *                 |___ WriteScreen  |                             *
   *                 |_____  |                             *
   *                 |___ ReadReply     |                            *
   *                 |___ ClosingTasks  |                            *
   *                 |_____|___ Pause                      *
   *                                                                 *
   * * * * * * * * * * * * * * * * * * * * * * * * * * * * * * * * * *}

     {============================= Declarations =============================}

  uses crt;                      {Needed for PC-style programming}

  var
    Celsius     : real;          {Degrees Celsius}
    Fahrenheit,                  {Degrees Fahrenheit}
    Iterations : integer;        {Loop iterations, or temperatures processed}
    Reply       : char;          {Y/N reply for loop control}  ◄──⌐── New variable

     {======================= Procedure Declarations =======================}

         Procedures Pause, WriteScreen, ReadTemp, and ClosingTasks are
         identical to those in Temp1, Figure 5.4.

  {------------------------------------------------------------------------}
  procedure OpeningTasks (var Iterations : integer);

    { Clears screen, writes title, initializes iterations, calls Pause
      Receives nothing
      Sends Iterations }

  const
    Title   = 'TEMPERATURES... Version 2.0';

  begin  {OpeningTasks}                                      ◄──⌐── Minor
                                                                    changes
    clrscr;                                                         from
    gotoxy (25, 5);  write (Title);                                Temp1
    Iterations := 0;
    Pause;

  end;   {OpeningTasks}
  {------------------------------------------------------------------------}
```

continued

FIGURE 5.7   (continued)

```
procedure ReadReply (var Reply : char);

  { Utility clears screen, reads Y/N reply while incorrect reply with
    error message, clears screen at end
    Receives nothing
    Sends Reply }

  { NOTE:  Requires uses clause for crt unit in host program }

const
  Title = 'REPLY SCREEN';

var
  CorrectReply : Boolean;    {Flag or switch for correct replies Y, y, N, n}

begin  {ReadReply}

  clrscr;
  gotoxy (30, 5);  write (Title);
  gotoxy (29,13);  write ('Continue? (Y/N) ');  readln (Reply);
  CorrectReply := (upcase( Reply ) = 'Y') or (upcase( Reply ) = 'N');

  while not CorrectReply do
    begin
      write (chr(7));                        {Beep speaker}

      gotoxy (17,24); write ('Please enter Y or y for Yes, N or n for No');

      gotoxy (29,13); clreol; {Clears to end of line without moving cursor}

      write ('Continue? (Y/N) ');  readln (Reply);

      CorrectReply := (upcase( Reply ) = 'Y') or (upcase( Reply ) = 'N');
    end;  {while}

  clrscr;

end;  {ReadReply}
```

New utility procedure

Note use below

True when Reply stores Y, y, N, or n

Error routine: Repeats while not correct reply

```
{============================= Main Body =============================}

begin  {Temp2}

  OpeningTasks (Iterations);

  repeat
    ReadTemp (Fahrenheit);
    Celsius := 5 / 9 * (Fahrenheit - 32);
    inc (Iterations);
    WriteScreen (Fahrenheit, Celsius);
    ReadReply (Reply);
  until upcase( Reply ) = 'N';

  ClosingTasks (Iterations);

end.    {Temp2}
```

Repeat-until structure

All temperatures now read at beginning of loop body; compare this design to that in Temp1

Reads reply, ensuring correct reply

Looping terminates when reply is no

NOTE

5. On revising a modular program. The task of changing the design and coding of a program is considerably easier if the program is modular. It allows us to compartmentalize in our minds the program blocks that need minor changes, those that need no changes, those that get deleted, and those that get added. For example, in planning and implementing the changes from program Temp1 to program Temp2, we had no changes in procedures Pause, WriteScreen, ReadTemp, and ClosingTasks; minor changes in procedure OpeningTasks; added variable Reply to the declaration of variables in the main program; changed the main body algorithm; and added the new module ReadReply. It's also interesting to note that a fairly minor change in design can cause significant revisions to a program. For example, initial changes in the 1986 federal tax law required financial institutions to withhold taxes from interest and dividend income. By some estimates the cost of software changes nationwide amounted to about $1 billion! This provision of the tax was rescinded before it took effect (but not before some institutions had already started the anticipated software maintenance.)

SELF-REVIEW EXERCISES

10a–b

---

‡5.4   INPUT FROM TEXT FILES REVISITED

• • • • • • • • • • • • • • •

All of our input so far in this chapter has been interactive. Let's now consider input from text files.

REVIEW

In Section 4.3 we defined *data file, text file, field, record, type* **text,** and *file specification.* We also introduced the file-related procedures **assign, reset,** and **close.** Finally, we noted that the *text-file variable* must be the first variable in the variable list of the readln procedure. Review this section now if you're hazy on these terms and procedures.

---

‡Optional material. Skip without loss of continuity, study at this point, or wait until later.

LOOP IMPLEMENTATIONS

We have three methods for reading records from a file.

- Place the number of records at the beginning of the file and process the file using the for-do loop.
- Place a sentinel at the end of the file and process the file using a while-do loop.
- Don't place number of records or a sentinel and process the file using a while-do loop that detects an *end-of-file* (*eof*) condition.

We used the for-do loop approach in Chapter 4, leave the sentinel approach to Exercise 12, and consider the third method here.

The following general loop design shows how we read records from a file by an eof-controlled while-do loop.

While not eof (Text file) do

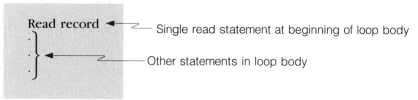

This approach to input termination of a loop calls the standard function **eof,** as follows.

    eof (TextFile)

As before, TextFile is the text-file variable that corresponds to the data file. The function returns *true* if the next character in the file is the *eof character,* a special nondata character that the system places at the end of a file; otherwise, it returns *false*. Here's how it works. When the eof condition is tested and the eof function is called, the system "looks ahead" in the file to see if the next character is an unprintable *end-of-file character* that defines the end of a file. If not, the eof function returns false, **not** changes the Boolean value to true (yes it's true, we don't have an eof condition), and the body of the loop is entered. Iterations continue while the end of the file is not encountered.

EXAMPLE 5.8   HC ENGINE, VERSION 4.0

Let's modify the design in Example 4.8 by changing the file's data structure. We now eliminate the number of engines from the top of the file shown in Figure 4.7, giving us Figure 5.8.

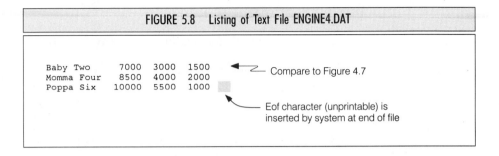

FIGURE 5.8   Listing of Text File ENGINE4.DAT

```
Baby Two      7000   3000   1500          Compare to Figure 4.7
Momma Four    8500   4000   2000
Poppa Six    10000   5500   1000

                                          Eof character (unprintable) is
                                          inserted by system at end of file
```

FIGURE 5.9   Listing of Main Body in Program Engine4

```
begin   {Engine4}                          NumberEngines deleted

   OpeningTasks (TextFile, TotalSales);

   while not eof( TextFile ) do             For statement replaced by while statement
      begin
         readln (TextFile, Name, Size_cc, Price, Units);
         Calculate   (Size_cc, Price, Units, Size_ci, Sales, TotalSales);
         WriteReport (Name, Units, Size_cc, Size_ci, Price, Sales);
      end;   {while eof}

   ClosingTasks (TotalSales, TextFile);

end.    {Engine4}
```

As usual, a change in either requirements or design has a domino effect on the program itself, although the revisions in this case are minor. Figure 5.9 shows the main body in program Engine4, a revision of Engine3 from Chapter 4. The key changes are the elimination of variable NumberEngines and the replacement of the for statement with the while statement. The output is unchanged from that shown earlier in Figure 4.8.

NOTE

6. The method of choice. In commercial applications the eof-controlled while-do loop is used over the other approaches because it simply requires normal records in the file, that is, we don't need to place the number of records at the beginning of the file or a sentinel record at the end of the file. This simplifies file maintenance. If we need to know the number of records, we simply use a counter in the loop (see Exercise 12). Thus, we say goodbye to the for-do loop as a file processing loop (it did its job when we needed it).

┌───┐
│   SELF-REVIEW EXERCISES   │
│   12a–b   │
└───┘

5.5 Programming Tips

Consider the following tips to improve the design and style of your programs and to avoid some common errors.

Design and Style

1. Literacy. Indent the bodies of while-do and repeat-until structures. For while-do loops it's a good idea to document the **end** identifier for any compound statement that defines the body, as in

```
end;   {while}
```

to clearly show the end of the loop structure.

Use *switches* and *flags* when appropriate, to improve the meaning of Boolean conditions. For example, the flag CorrectReply in program Temp2 clearly gives contextual meaning to its corresponding Boolean expression.

2. On Selecting a Loop Design. If the loop processes a data file, select an eof-controlled while-do design, for the reasons described in Note 6. Otherwise, the choice depends on several considerations.

    a. Select the For-Do Loop If... we need to systematically vary an ordinal control variable over a range from an initial value to a final value in single-unit *increments*. The for-do loop is specifically designed as this kind of *counter loop;* otherwise, the loop designs in this chapter are more direct.

    b. Select the While-Do Loop If... the loop is controlled by a sentinel, or there are times when we don't wish to enter the loop body. The repeat-until loop processes the sentinel as a legitimate value, which is undesirable. Also, remember that the repeat-until design guarantees at least one iteration of the body. So, if the loop is controlled by Y/N input, and there's a chance that the user may not wish to enter the body, then use a while-do design as well. Error routines that loop also use a while-do design, so we don't enter the body if an error is not committed in the first place.

    c. Select the Repeat-Until Loop If... we have a Y/N controlled loop and assume that the user wishes at least one iteration (which is why the program was run in the first place). Program Temp2 in Example 5.7 illustrates this use of the repeat-until loop. We can use a while-do loop here (see

Exercise 10), but it's not as straight forward as the repeat-until approach. In other cases, the choice of while-do versus repeat-until is irrelevant, and depends on the preferences of the programmer. This is particularly true for loops that depend on a computational result for their termination.

3. Input Statements in While-Do Loops.   If a while-do loop includes input processing, take care where to place the input statement(s). For example, if the loop processes a sentinel or Y/N response, then we need an input statement just before the loop (to input the first value or set of values) *and* another (identical) input statement at the end of the loop body (to input all other values). For instance, see Example 5.5. If the loop is eof-controlled, then place a single input statement at the beginning of the body, as in Example 5.8.

4. Sentinel Versus Y/N Termination.   As described in Example 5.7, the Y/N approach is friendlier and appeals to nontraditional computer users. The sentinel approach is efficient (we don't need to work with another variable that stores a reply), and often appeals to the technically inclined. The approach to take simply depends on the kind of users that will use the program and on the requirements.

By the way, the termination option in a menu is an example of a sentinel. For example, to exit the IDE (which is exiting a loop!) we either press **Alt -X** or select the menu sequence **F x**. These are sample *menu sentinels,* which we can look forward to in the next chapter.

5. Screen Designs.   The I/O design of interactive programs takes special care. Input prompts (requests) should be stated concisely and clearly, without clutter. Likewise, output should be designed to enhance readability. It's also best to segregate screen functions by design, as in making distinctions among opening, output, input, reply, and farewell screens. Identify screens by title, clear screens to avoid overwrites, and pause screens when needed. Include both audio and visual features to enhance communication, as in beeping an error. Our work in Examples 5.6 and 5.7 gave us a push in this direction. We reinforce these ideas in later chapters by adding color and other special effects. Pay attention to other programs that you use for ideas. A great place to start is the IDE environment! It's excellent at implementing PC-style programming.

6. Defensive Programming.   The *error routine* illustrated in Example 5.7 is an example of **defensive programming,** a collection of techniques that seek to avoid, capture, or recover from potential execution errors. Think defensively from now on, looking for opportunities to apply this principle. As we develop new material, we will point out common defensive programming techniques.

7. On Portability.   Standard-conforming Pascal programs are those whose syntax and features strictly adhere to the officially approved version of Pascal. As mentioned in Chapter 1, we call this *Standard Pascal.* As you're aware,

Turbo Pascal includes a number of differences from (mostly enhancements to) Standard Pascal, which we summarize in Appendix H. These differences are particularly obvious when using the crt unit for PC-style programming. These procedures and functions are very much wedded to both the software environment and hardware configuration.

There are many advantages to nonstandard enhancements, including the PC-style programming features that we've mentioned, more readable coding, and faster execution. That's the upside. The downside? Programs that use nonstandard features are not *portable* from one kind of computer system to another. Theoretically, a standard-conforming program can be ported or moved from one system to another, and executed without changes to the program, provided standard-conforming compilers are used.

Programmers need to keep portability in mind if their programs are to be used in different computer systems; otherwise, the expense of porting the program may be prohibitive. Most commercial Pascal programs are not portable, because strict conformance with Standard Pascal would be catering to the lowest common denominator of features, and their look and performance would show it.

In this book we sacrifice portability to take advantage of the Turbo Pascal environment. So you're aware of this issue, we do note key chapter-by-chapter differences in Appendix H. We ask you to think about this portability issue in Exercise 17.

8. Optimization Notes.   The calculating efficiency mentioned in item 5b on page 151 also applies here. Also, standard procedures and functions generate optimized (more compact and faster) object program code compared to alternatives that don't use these. Incrementation with the **inc** procedure is an example, as seen in Example 5.6.

Common Errors

1. Boolean Expression Lapses.   Boolean expressions are great for trying out our debugging skills. Watch out for mental lapses like forgetting single quotations around character and string constants, not paying attention to precedence rules, and missing parentheses surrounding relational expressions that serve as operands in a Boolean expression.

2. Incomplete Boolean Expressions.   We can't tell you how often we've seen the following kind of error.

```
Value > 1 and < 5;  ☹
```

Do you see the problem? The right operand is incomplete, and ignores the precedence rule. Compilation would give an *Error in expression* message. The Boolean expression should read as follows.

```
(Value > 1) and (Value < 5);  ☺
```

We tend to make this error because of our algebraic training with expressions like

$$1 < \text{Value} < 5$$

and verbalizations like "Value greater than 1 and less than 5."

3. Incorrect Loop Body.   As in the for statement, make sure that you have the right body in the while statement. Use a compound statement if the body includes multiple statements.

4. Infinite Loop.   In designing the loop control, take care that the loop control test satisfies the exit condition (*true* for the repeat-until loop and *false* for the while-do loop) at least once during execution of the loop structure. Otherwise, we have an **infinite loop,** where looping continues indefinitely, or until we press the **Ctrl**-**Break** key.

5. Incorrect Number of Repetitions.   This is a common mistake in loop designs that call for termination based on a computed condition. One common cause of this error is forgetting to initialize operands in the condition of a while-do loop. For example, we might forget to initialize `Weight` in Example 5.3, thereby giving us a loop that iterates six times (the weights are $0, 5, \ldots, 25$), instead of the intended three for the sample run.

Another common error is an incorrect boundary description in the Boolean expression. In particular, pay attention to $>$ versus $>=$ and $<$ versus $<=$ relational operators. To illustrate, suppose we had mistakenly used the operator $<$ instead of $<=$ in Example 5.3. This would give us two iterations in the sample run, instead of the intended three. Another cause of incorrect repetitions is . . .

[‡]**6. Error Tolerance Fixup.**   Reread Note 1. Suppose we have to use a real variable to control a loop. For example, let's say that real variable Speed is computed within the loop, and we wish to terminate the loop when the value in Speed hits the real value in Target. We might write the following.

```
repeat
   . . .
until Speed = Target;  ☹
```

In this case, the speed may never exactly hit the target speed, for one of two reasons: The particular application may not theoretically ensure this event (as in overshooting the target), and precision or roundoff errors may apply (as described in Note 6 in Chapter 2). The potential result is an *infinite loop,* because the Boolean expression may never test true during a particular run.

A simple fixup might be to use the relational operator $>=$ in place of $=$. In this case, the nature of the condition changes from "Speed hits the target" to "Speed achieves the target."

[‡]Optional material. Skip without loss of continuity, study at this point, or wait until later.

Suppose we can guarantee that the speed will theoretically hit the target, it's just a question of when. With this provision, we can modify the loop as follows.

```
repeat
  ...
until abs(Speed/Target - 1) < 1.0E-9;  ☺
```

When speed hits the target, the left member should theoretically equal zero. If the precision or roundoff error is off by less than nine decimal places, we still get the expected *true* evaluation for loop exit. The term *1.0E−9* is called an *error tolerance*. As long as precision is within the error tolerance, we get the expected "equality." Appendix D gives an idea of how to set the error tolerance, depending on real typing. For example, the above error tolerance is within the number of significant digits for all real types but **single**. For this type, we would have to increase the error tolerance to, say, 1.0×10^{-6}.

[‡]**7. Text-File Errors.**   The text-file errors described in Chapter 4 also apply here. Exercise 12 in this chapter show what happens when we short data in the file.

[#]**8. Verification.**   The issues discussed in items 4–6 above all relate to loop verification: Does the loop behave as intended? For example, can we guarantee termination in all circumstances? Is the number of iterations always correct? Are evaluations within the loop correct? Are they correct after the loop? Careful attention to our earier discussion helps to ensure correct loops. More formally, we can verify loops specifically and programs generally, both empirically and logically.

Verification is the process of proving that a program is correct. We have two general approaches to verification: empirical and logical (inductive).

Empirical verification uses test data and results that are known to be correct by other means, as in having been desk checked. We've been doing empirical verification all along in the stages of the software development cycle. First, we desk checked design and program algorithms in the design and coding stages. Then we ran test data through the programs in the test stage. Another common technique during the test stage is using a *debugger* to trace program execution while watching changing values for selected variables. We illustrated this technique in Module A preceding this chapter. In specifically debugging loops, make sure that the test data include variations that are likely to occur in practice for the data elements that make up the loop control.

Logical or *inductive verification* uses logical reasoning during the design and testing stages to "prove" correctness. Logical verification is an advanced (and controversial) topic in programming. For example, it includes formal

---

[‡#]Optional material. Skip without loss of continuity, study at this point, or wait until later.

mathematical proofs called *correctness proofs,* and addresses philosophical questions like "Is it possible to absolutely prove correctness in programming?"

Simple techniques for logical verification include specifying preconditions and postconditions as assertions, and loop behavior as invariants. An **assertion** asserts what should be true about some condition at that point in the execution sequence. In loop design, *preconditions* and *postconditions* respectively assert what must be true before and after the loop is executed. An **invariant** is a special kind of assertion that applies to loops. Invariants assert behavior that remain true before the loop, at the beginning or end of each iteration, and after the loop. To illustrate, consider the following documented preconditions, invariants, and postconditions for the loop in Example 5.3.

```
{Precondition assertion... Increment is
    positive integer whenever Initial <= Final}

write ('Enter initial, final, and incremental weights... ');
readln (Initial, Final, Increment);
writeln;  write ('Weights: ');

{Precondition assertion... Weight is Initial}

Weight := Initial;

while Weight <= Final do

{Invariants... Weight >= Initial; At any iteration:
    Increment is fixed, Weight increases by Increment}

begin
 write(Weight :4);
 Weight := Weight + Increment;
end;   {while}

{Postcondition assertion... Weight >= Initial}

writeln;  writeln ('  End of looping...');
```

Note that the precondition of a positive (nonzero and nonnegative) increment is necessary whenever the initial weight does not exceed the final weight; otherwise, either weight would not change within the loop (if the increment were zero) or weight would never exceed its final value (if the increment were negative). In these cases, the result would be an *infinite loop,* because the test condition would always be true. This would be a good error to trap (see Exercise 5).

Our conclusion about the legitimate range of values for the increment demonstrates the value of assertions in verification. We drew this correctness conclusion without using test data. An actual program that would use this loop should trap the potential error that would be provoked by a nonpositive increment. Also, the variables and expressions that we single out in our assertions make good candidates for watching when we trace execution.

The documentation of assertions and invariants in simple loops is overkill, but useful in long programs with complex computations and loop tests.

For the most part, we will omit this type of documentation in our programs, primarily to simplify the look of programs and reduce their length. In your own programming, at a minimum, you need to start using logical verification (primarily in the design and code stages), in addition to empirical verification (primarily in the test stage).

REVIEW EXERCISES

> **EASIER**   For the busy...
> **2 3 4 7 8a–b 10a 12a**
>
> **NORMAL**   For the thinkers...
> **1 5 6 8c–d 9 10b–e 11 12b–c 13 14 16 17 19**
>
> **TOUGHER**   For the hard CORE...
> **12d 15 18**

1. Given the following assignments

```
B := true;
C := 'C';
S := 'Sure';
K := 0;  L := 1;  M := 2;  N := 3;
```

indicate true or false Boolean values for the following Boolean expressions.

a. K + N >= L - M

b. not (K + N >= L - M)

c. L **div** M <> 1 + L * M - N

d. B **and** (K = N)

e. B **and not** (K = N)

f. B **and** (K = N) **or not** B

g. C <> S

h. (C < S) **or** (C < '2')

i. (C < S) **or** (C < **chr** (50))

j. (C < S) **xor** (C < **chr** (50))

k. Indicate in parts **a–j**, when appropriate, the operands that don't get evaluated in short-circuit evaluation.

2. In Example 5.1, evaluate the Boolean expression for each of the following changes.

a. As in the original, except place **not** in front of the entire expression.

b. As in the original, except replace **and** by **or**.

c. As in the original, except remove the left set of parentheses.

3. In Example 5.2, state an assignment statement for the flag **WrongReply**.

4. In Example 5.3, indicate output and number of iterations if the input is . . .
   a. 15 20 1.
   b. 20 15 1.

5. In Example 5.3, indicate output and number of iterations if the input is . . .
   a. 15 20 0.
   b. 15 20 −1.
   c. 20 15 −1.
   d. What can we assert about values in Initial, Final, and Increment to guarantee correct loop execution?
   *e. Modify the loop control code to handle the data-input relationship seen in part **c**.
   *f. Write an error routine that traps any input data that's inconsistent with the assertions in part **d**.
   *g. Suppose all variables are real instead of integer. Do we have any problems or do we need any code changes?

6. In Example 5.4 . . .
   a. Change the code to accept either X or x as sentinels.
   b. Roleplay I/O if we were to delete the **write/readln** pair just before the loop and we were to move the other from the end of the body to the beginning.

*7. In Example 5.5 . . .
   a. Write the desk-check script for the sample run.
   b. Roleplay inputs of Yep and ok.
   c. Delete the **write/readln** pair just before the loop and move the other input pair from the end to the beginning of the loop body. How would the I/O look?

Ⓛ **8.** **Temperatures.** In Example 5.6 . . .
   a. Test drive program Temp1. We have a definite improvement in our user interface, right?
   b. Revise the loop control to use the **not** operator. State why you like or don't like this approach.
   c. Revise the loop control to use the switch **MoreTemperatures**. State why you like or don't like this approach.
   *d. Make changes in Temp1 if the requirements called for real Fahrenheit temperatures.

*9. For each of the following, rewrite the while-do structure as a repeat-until structure. Comment on the pros and cons of each approach.
   a. Example 5.3
   b. Example 5.4
   c. Example 5.5

(L) **10.**   **Temperatures.** In Example 5.7 . . .
   a. Test drive program **Temp2**. What do you think?
   b. Revise the repeat statement's loop control to use the switch **Stop**. State why you like or don't like this approach.
   *c. Draw the stepwise chart for this application.
   *d. Replace the repeat-until structure with the while-do structure. State why you like or don't like this approach.
   *e. Revise the program and error routine to accept the following correct replies: Y, y, N, n, yes, no, YES, NO, yep, nope, YEP, NOPE.

(L) ***11.**   **Pause alternatives.** Rewrite the Pause procedure in Temp2 by replacing the line having **readkey** with the following.
   a. readln;
   b. readkey; (*see the extended syntax directive* **$X** in Appendix G)
   c. repeat until keypressed;

   Do we need variable Dummy now? Write a driver to test each alternative by pressing each of the following keys: Enter key, space bar, a letter key. What happens? State pros and cons of each approach versus the original approach.

(L) **12.**   **HC Engine.** In Example 5.8 . . .
   a. Run program Engine4.
   b. Delete the last item (the 1000) in data file ENGINE4.DAT, and rerun program Engine4. What happens?
   *c. Revise the loop design to terminate using a sentinel. Assume the file has the sentinel **X** as the last record.
   *d. Write a procedure that displays file ENGINE4.DAT. Display the entire file *before* the output report. Include screen clears and pauses. Use the following format.

```
File ENGINE4.DAT

-----------------------------------------------------
Name            Size cc          Price          Units
-----------------------------------------------------

 . . .           . . .           . . .          . . .

-----------------------------------------------------
Number of engines = 3
```

*13.   What values get written for the following repetition structure?
```
a. Threshold := 3.0;  Variable := 4.0;
   while  10 * Variable  >  Threshold do
     begin
       writeln (Variable :5:2, 10*Variable :7:2);
       Variable := Variable / 2;
     end;  {while}
```

   b. Same as part **a** except Variable is initialized to 0.1.

   c. Same as part **a** except Threshold is initialized to −3.0.

   d. What must we assert about the value in Threshold and the initial value in Variable to avoid the problem in part **c**?

   e. Confirm your assertions in part **d** by running test data through a program that includes this code fragment.

*14. Rewrite the code fragment in the preceding exercise as a repeat-until structure. Answer the same questions.

*15. **Error tolerance fixup.** In Example 5.3, suppose all variables were real instead of integer.

   a. Develop a program that includes the given code fragment, and use 10.0 10.5 0.1 as test input. Look at the output. Is it correct? Do you see the problem?

   b. Modify the program to include an error tolerance that ensures *boundary* weights (where value in Weight equals value in Final) are output. Use the constant ErrorTol, and give it the value 1.0×10^{-9}. *Hint:* See item 6 on page 226, but keep the while-do structure and think about the applicability of a call to the abs function.

(L) ***16.** **Revisit: Average scores.** Revise program AveScore in Example 4.7 to input names and scores from a text file. Store the sample input data in a file. The revised program interactively inputs the name of this data file, and terminates data file input using an eof condition. Appropriately use screen clears and pauses.

(L) ***17.** **Portability.** Reread item 7 under "Design and Style" and try coding the following tasks as Standard Pascal alternatives. (Eliminate the uses clause.)

   a. **Screen clear.** Instead of using **clrscr**, develop procedure ClearScreen to write 25 blank lines to the screen (use the proper loop design). Accordingly revise program Temp2, and run the revised program.

   b. **Pause.** Revise Pause as PauseSP by using **readln** instead of **readkey** to pause the screen. Also eliminate **gotoxy**. Run the revised program Temp2.

*18. **Assertions and invariants.** Write documented loop assertions for preconditions, postconditions, and the loop invariant for the following programs.

   a. Temp1 in Example 5.6

   b. Temp2 in Example 5.7

   c. Engine4 in Example 5.8

(L) ***19.** **Revisit: HC METHsea.** Revise Exercise 25c in Chapter 4 as follows.

   a. Terminate input of the text file using an eof condition.

   b. Apply PC-style programming.

ADDITIONAL EXERCISES

EASIER	For the busy... **20 22 23**
NORMAL	For the thinkers... **21 24 25 26**
TOUGHER	For the hard CORE... **27 28 29 30**

20. **Revisits.** Revise one of the following exercises from Chapter 4 by using a while-do or repeat-until structure (your choice) that terminates with a control-variable condition.
   a. **Temperatures.**
   b. **Disk areas.**
   c. **Drag races.**
   d. **Bank savings.**

21. **Revisits.** Revise one of the following exercises from Chapter 4 by including ideas from this chapter. For example, design a loop using one of the input data termination methods, include error routines, and apply PC-style programming.
   a. **Bates motel.**
   b. **Econometric model.**

22. **Average weights, interactive version.** Develop an interactive program that inputs a character code and associated real weight (in kilograms) and calculates the average weight. *Echo* (immediately write) the input data. After loop termination, display the number of entered codes and the average weight. All uppercase and lowercase letters are legitimate codes. Use the following test data.

Code	Weight (kilos)
A	10.2
B	15.1
C	12.5
d	3.3
e	1.5
X	50.0
Y	75.2
Z	61.5

23. **Average weights, noninteractive version.** Store the codes and weights in the preceding exercise in a text file. Use the following title as the first record in

the text file: **Test run: January 1**. Input the name of the text file. Display the text file using a tablelike format, including its title. Display number of codes and average weight in the table foot.

24. **Harmonic series function.** Develop and test a function that returns the sum of the first *n* terms in the harmonic series

$$1 + 1/2 + 1/3 + \ldots + 1/n.$$

The function receives *n*. Design a driver that inputs values for *n* while *n* is *positive. Display n* and the sum. Try the following test values of *n*: 5, 10, 25, 50, 100, 1000, 0.

25. **Text-file viewer.** Develop a program that "dumps" text files. For each file, the program interactively inputs the text file specification (drive, path, and name), and then uses a while-do, eof-controlled loop to repeatedly read and write single characters. Write the following files in one test run: ENGINE4.DAT and ENGINE4.PAS. At the end, write the number of characters processed. We have two versions of the program.
    a. **Display version.** Display the file on the screen.
    b. **Print version.** Print the file on paper.

    Hint: Use the read and write procedures; the end of the line is processed as a nondata *end-of-line character.*

26. **Economies of scale.** The manufacturing industry often exhibits the phenomenon known as *economies of scale.* As the number of units manufactured increases, the per unit cost decreases. If at some point the unit cost starts increasing, the system exhibits *diseconomies of scale.* Reasons for economies include lower costs of material for bulk purchases, and the operation of a *learning curve* as workers gain more experience over time. The main reason for diseconomies beyond a certain point is loss of control due to large size.

    Let's look at a specific scenario. HC Enterprises is bankrolling a startup firm that will manufacture the ManzanaX computer model. A similar (and successful) past venture exhibited the unit cost function

    $$C = 80,000,000/U + U + 500$$

    where *C* is the average cost per computer ($/unit) and *U* is the number of units manufactured. Management believes that the ManzanaX will have about the same unit cost function.

    Develop a program that inputs an initial value and increment for *U*, and writes a table that displays units and unit cost (to the nearest dollar). Terminate the table when unit cost begins to rise. Trap input that might lead to incorrect loop behavior. In your test run, start at 1000 units in increments of 1000 units. Use the program to answer the following question posed by HC: At how many units do we minimize the unit cost?

27. **Break even analysis.** Let's return to the preceding manufacturing problem for ManzanaX computers. HC is interested in unit cost, but he's even more inter-

ested in the bottom line given by projected profits. Let's define the following relationships from economics.

$$TR = P \cdot U$$
$$TC = U \cdot C + SC$$
$$TP = TR - TC$$

where

P = Price (wholesale) of each computer ($/unit)
U = Units manufactured (units)
C = Average cost, given in preceding exercise ($/unit)
SC = Startup cost for the new company ($)
TR = Total revenue ($)
TC = Total cost ($)
TP = Total profit ($)

The *break-even point* is the number of units that must be sold to break even (where profits are zero). We assume an anticipated terrific demand, where all units manufactured can be sold (a *seller's market*). Typically, as the number of units sold approaches the break-even point, losses get smaller and smaller. Beyond the break-even point, profits are generated. If the unit cost function describes diseconomies of scale (begins rising again), then a second break-even point is approached, beyond which losses are incurred once more. HC currently figures on charging resellers a price of $30,000 per copy. The projected startup cost is $75 million.

Develop an interactive program that inputs P, SC, and a range of values for U. The program displays a table with column headings for U, C, TC, TR, and TP. All monetary data are to the nearest dollar. In the table's title include P and SC. Trap input that might lead to incorrect functioning of the program. In your test run, use the given values for P and SC, and try a range of 5000 to 25000 in increments of 1000 for U. Use the program to answer the following questions posed by HC: What's the break-even point for a price of $30,000? At how many units do we maximize profits? What if we were to drop the price to $25,000? What if the startup cost is 10 percent more than we expected?

28. **Mutual Funds.** Investors who do not wish to buy individual stocks and bonds can invest in mutual funds, which offer a portfolio of professionally managed stocks or bonds. In so-called load funds, a sales charge is levied on the amount invested. Some funds also have a redemption fee, which levies a charge on the amount withdrawn from the fund. For example, if $10,000 is invested and the sales charge is 2 percent, then the amount actually invested is 10,000 × 0.98, or $9,800. If this amount grows at an annual return of 10 percent per year, then after, say, five years the investment is worth $(9800) \times (1.1)^5$, or $15,783. However, if the fund charges a 1 percent redemption fee, then the investor can withdraw 15,783 × 0.99, or about $15,625. The amount that can be withdrawn is computed from the formula

$$W = A(1 - s)(1 + r)^t(1 - f)$$

where W = amount that can be withdrawn after t years

$\quad\quad A$ = amount originally invested

$\quad\quad s$ = sales charge as a proportion

$\quad\quad r$ = annual return as a proportion

$\quad\quad t$ = time in years

$\quad\quad f$ = redemption fee as a proportion

For our example, we have

$$W = 10000(1 - 0.02)(1 + 0.1)^5(1 - 0.01)$$
$$= 15625$$

a. Develop a program that inputs A, s, r, t, and f and displays W. Use the following test data:

	A	s	r	t	f
Test 1	10000	0.020	0.10	5	0.01
Test 2	10000	0.085	0.10	5	0.00
Test 3	10000	0.020	0.10	25	0.01
Test 4	10000	0.020	0.15	25	0.01

Tests 1 and 2 represent two typical types of mutual funds: one with a low front load charge with a redemption fee and one with a high front load charge and no redemption fee. Which is best for our hypothetical investor?

b. Also output the fees (sales and redemption) that are retained by the mutual fund.

29. **Forecasting population growth.** In recent years, the prediction of world population levels into the next century has been a concern of many political, environmental, and agricultural planners. The following equation can be used to predict future levels of world population:

$$p = c \cdot [1 + (b - d)]^n$$

where p = predicted level of future population

$\quad\quad b$ = birth rate

$\quad\quad c$ = current level of population

$\quad\quad d$ = death rate

$\quad\quad n$ = number of years into the future

For example, estimated data for the year 1989 show $c = 5.234$ (billions), $b = 0.025$ (2.5 percent), and $d = 0.006$ (0.6 percent). If b and d essentially remain constant over a 10-year period ($n = 10$), then we can predict the world population in 1999 as

$$p = 5.234[1 + (0.025 - 0.006)]^{10}$$
$$= 5.234(1.019)^{10}$$
$$= 5.234(1.2071)$$
$$= 6.318 \text{ billions}$$

a. Develop an interactive program that processes input data for c, b, d, and n. Calculate and display the predicted level of future population. Use the following test data:

c	b	d	n
5.234	0.025	0.006	10
5.234	0.025	0.006	20
5.234	0.025	0.006	30
5.234	0.020	0.006	30

Does a drop in the birthrate to 0.020 make much difference?
Repeatedly change the value of n to determine the number of years it would take for the population to double. Try different values for n and observe the output values for p. Answer this question for both the 0.025 and the 0.020 birthrates.

b. Let N be a counter for "years into future" in an "inner" loop that lies entirely within the outer loop in part **a**. This inner loop increments N by 1, calculates predicted population, and prints N, corresponding year, and predicted population. Exit from the loop when the ratio of predicted population to current population exceeds a desired ratio (R). Run the program for the following three sets of input values.

Current Population	Base Year	b	d	Initial N	R
5.234	1989	0.025	0.006	10	2
5.234	1989	0.025	0.006	25	3
5.234	1989	0.020	0.006	30	3

For example, your output for the first run might look like this:

Years into Future	Corresponding Year	Predicted Population
10	1999	6.318
11	2000	6.438
.	.	.
.	.	.
.	.	.

◄— Exit when predicted population exceeds 10.468

Comment on the number of years it takes the current world population to double and triple relative to changes in the birthrate.

30. Police car replacement. Captain Josephine Friday, the police administrator in Gotham City, would like to estimate the mileage at which a police cruiser should be replaced. Data analyses show that the *cost of operation* (gasoline, maintenance, and so on) is approximated by

$$c = f + v \cdot m + s \cdot m^2$$

where f, v, and s are coefficients, and m is the mileage reading (in thousands) on the odometer. For example, a cruiser that is driven for 30,000 miles and is characterized by $f = 1000$, $v = 200$, and $s = 2$ incurs an operating cost of approximately

$$c = 1000 + (200) \cdot (30) + (2) \cdot (30)^2$$
$$= \$8800 .$$

The police department has an arrangement with Generous Motors (GM) for trade-ins of used police cruisers. The automaker has agreed to reduce the price of a new cruiser by the following amount

$$r = pd^m$$

where r is the trade-in (salvage) value of a used cruiser, p is the original (new) car price, d is some depreciation factor, and m is defined as before. For example, if $p = \$10,000$, $d = 0.95$, and $m = 30$, then

$$r = (10,000) \cdot (0.95)^{30}$$
$$= \$2146 .$$

This means that the police department pays $10,000 for a new cruiser, drives it for 30,000 miles, and gets $2146 on a trade-in. The *depreciation cost* in this case is $7854, or the difference between the new car price and the salvage price.

Thus, a cruiser driven for 30,000 miles costs $8800 to operate and $7854 in depreciation cost, for a total cost of $16,654. If this type of cruiser is replaced by a new cruiser of the same type at 30,000-mile intervals, then the total cost per 1000-miles (K-miles) is approximately $555 (that is, $16,654 ÷ 30).

a. Design, write, and run a program that determines the mileage (to the nearest thousand) at which cruisers should be replaced. Input for each cruiser should include the following.

1. Cruiser name
2. f, v, s, p, d

Output for each cruiser might appear as follows:

Analysis for Cruiser...   Write cruiser name here

Replacement Mileage (1000)	Operating Cost	Operating Cost per K-Miles	Depreciation Cost	Dept. Cost per K-Miles	Total Cost per K-Miles
1					
2					
3					
.					
.					
.					
100					

Thus the best mileage at which to replace a cruiser is that which gives the smallest value in the last column. Note that 100,000 miles is the maximum replacement mileage that Captain Friday is willing to consider. She is evaluating several types of cruisers, one of which must be selected. The following characteristics are provided courtesy of GM.

Cruiser Name	f	v	s	p	d
Buster	1000	200	2.0	10,000	0.95
Truster	800	300	2.5	8,000	0.93
Terminator	1200	225	1.6	13,000	0.98

At what mileage should each type be replaced and what is the total cost per K-miles? Which cruiser is the cheapest on the basis of total cost per K-miles?

b. As you go down the last column in this type of table, costs typically begin high, decrease to a minimum, and begin increasing again. Design your program to exit from the table loop either once total cost begins to increase or when mileage exceeds 100K.

SELECTION

The **selection structure** is a control structure that prescribes the *selection* of a flow branch based on a *condition*. This chapter defines and implements various selection structures based on one or more conditions. It also introduces the use of menus and techniques for handling errors during program execution.

6.1   IF-THEN-ELSE STRUCTURE

• • • • • • • • • • • • • • •

The basic selection structure is the **if-then-else structure**, as described earlier in Figure 3.8 and here in Figure 6.1. On entering the selection block, a condition is tested and the result is either true or false. **If** the condition is *true*, **then** a particular group of statements is executed (labeled StatementTrue in the figure), and execution exits the structure; **else** (the condition is *false*) another group of statements is executed (labeled StatementFalse in the figure), and execution exits the structure. Note that the execution flow immediately exits

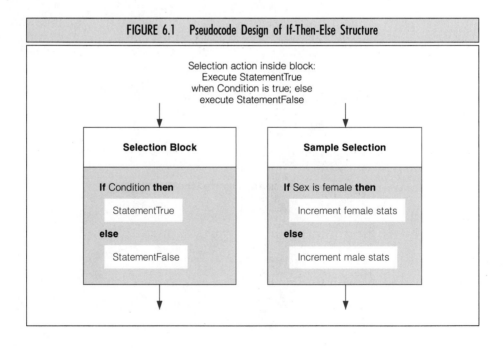

FIGURE 6.1   Pseudocode Design of If-Then-Else Structure

the structure after either StatementTrue or StatementFalse is executed. Also note that Figure 6.1 describes the *design* of the if-then-else structure, not its *implementation.* The design is identical regardless of the computer language.

IF STATEMENT

We implement the if-then-else structure by using an **if statement,** as seen in the accompanying syntax box. Study the examples and note the following.

1. We have wide latitude in indentation and line placement of if-statement components (**if, then, else,** StatementTrue, StatementFalse). At one extreme, we can place the entire structure on one line, as done in the first example. At the other extreme, we can place each component on a separate line, which we didn't do. All of the examples show "good form," although we only recommend the form in the first example for simple conditions and statements. As usual, the objective is program literacy.

2. Take care with the use of semicolons. As usual, the semicolon is a statement separator. Each of our examples includes a semicolon to separate the if statement from any statement that might follow. Within the if statement itself, the semicolon is used to separate simple statements within a compound statement, as seen in the last example.

Let's look at another example that we will use throughout the chapter.

EXAMPLE 6.1   IF-THEN-ELSE-STRUCTURE

Electra Appliances has a runaway best-seller in its TurboElectraCombo (TEC for short), a combination cooler, freezer, microwave oven, and alarm clock. Each TEC has a price of $300 for order sizes below 100 units, and a price of $275 for orders of 100 units or more. A program that quotes order costs based on order sizes might include the following if-then-else design.

If order size < 100

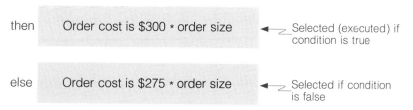

SYNTAX BOX

If statement (if-then-else structure) . . . If condition is true, then executes StatementTrue; else executes StatementFalse

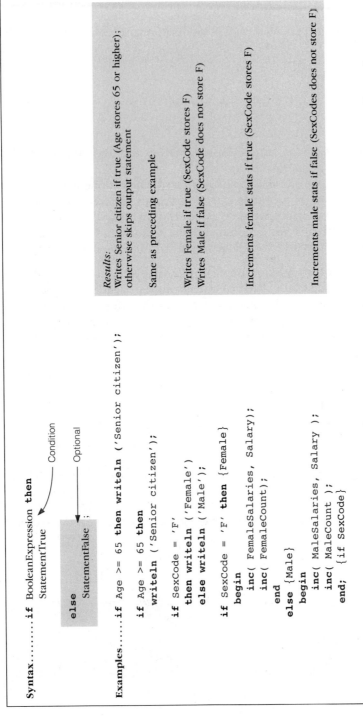

Syntax . . . . **if** BooleanExpression **then**
StatementTrue   *Condition*

     else   *Optional*
     StatementFalse
     ;

Examples . . . . . **if** Age >= 65 **then** **writeln** ('Senior citizen');

```
if Age >= 65 then
   writeln ('Senior citizen');
```

```
if SexCode = 'F'
   then writeln ('Female')
   else writeln ('Male');
```

```
if SexCode = 'F' then  {Female}
   begin
      inc( FemaleSalaries, Salary);
      inc( FemaleCount);
   end
else {Male}
   begin
      inc( MaleSalaries, Salary );
      inc( MaleCount );
   end; {if SexCode}
```

Results:
Writes Senior citizen if true (Age stores 65 or higher);
otherwise skips output statement

Same as preceding example

Writes Female if true (SexCode stores F)
Writes Male if false (SexCode does not store F)

Increments female stats if true (SexCode stores F)

Increments male stats if false (SexCodes does not store F)

Explanation . . . **if**, **then**, and **else** are reserved words. BooleanExpression is any legitimate Boolean expression. StatementTrue and StatementFalse are any simple or compound statement. If the Boolean expression is true, then StatementTrue is executed, after which execution exits the if-then-else structure; else StatementFalse is executed, and the execution flow exits the structure. When **else** and StatementFalse are omitted, execution immediately exits the structure if the Boolean expression is false. Indentation and line placement of reserved words and statements are stylistic (not syntactic) issues.

In Pascal, we might implement this design as follows.

If `OrderSize < BreakPoint`

then   `OrderCost := Price1 * OrderSize`

else   `OrderCost := Price2 * OrderSize`   `;`

where BreakPoint, Price1, and Price2 are the declared constants 100, 300, and 275, respectively.

Suppose we also wish to count the number of quotes within each price category. Now we might rewrite the pseudocode as

If order size < 100 then

| Order cost is $300 * order size |
| Increment first counter | ← Selected if condition is true

else

| Order cost is $275 * order size |
| Increment second counter | ← Selected if condition is false

and the Pascal code as

```
If OrderSize < BreakPoint then {Higher price}
  begin

    OrderCost := Price1 * OrderSize;
    inc( Count1 );

  end
else {Lower price}
  begin

    OrderCost := Price2 * OrderSize;
    inc( Count2 );

  end;   {if OrderSize}
```

Note how comments are useful in describing the two selection branches and the end of the if statement.

IF-THEN STRUCTURE

If we omit the **else** and StatementFalse components of the if statement, we have a special case of the if-then-else structure called the **if-then structure.** In this variation, the statement following **then** is executed if the condition given by the Boolean expression is true; otherwise, the statement following **then** is bypassed, and execution continues with the next statement following the if statement. The first two examples in the preceeding syntax box demonstrate this structure.

EXAMPLE 6.2   MINIMUM VALUE

The determinations of minimum and maximum values are very common tasks in programming. Here we illustrate how to find a *minimum value*. The *maximum value* is a simple variation that we leave to Exercise 5.

Let's continue with the Electra Appliances example. Suppose we wish to determine the minimum order size from all entered order sizes. The pseudocode algorithm that processes cost quotations and find this minimum reads as follows.

Read first order size
Initialize minimum order size ◄──── Needed for 1st test in if-then structure below
While order size > 0
    Determine order cost ◄──── See refinement in Example 6.1
    Write order cost

    If order size < minimum order size then ◄──── If-then structure
      Minimum order size is order size ◄──── New minimum found

    Read next order size
Write minimum order size

Let's consider only the code segments (those in color) that relate to the determination of minimum order size (we leave the complete Pascal version to Exercise 6). Before the loop, we need to initialize the minimum order size, because this minimum is used within the loop as part of the condition in the if-then structure that tests for a new minimum. The most common approach is to initialize the minimum to the first item under consideration. In our case, just after the input of the first order size (and before the loop), we would write

```
MinOrderSize := OrderSize:
```

Within the loop, we use an if-then structure to check for a new minimum, and assign its value if found. The following code does the trick.

```
If OrderSize < MinOrderSize then
   MinOrderSize := OrderSize:
```

Note that a true condition means that a new minimum is assigned. After the loop we can display the minimum order size by a statement like

writeln ('Smallest order size is ', MinOrderSize);

We can best see how these code fragments work by desk checking. Consider the following sample run.

```
Enter order size (End with zero)... 50
                                     Order cost = $15000
Enter order size (End with zero)... 100
                                     Order cost = $27500
Enter order size (End with zero)... 25
                                     Order cost = $7500
Enter order size (End with zero)... 300
                                     Order cost = $82500
Enter order size (End with zero)... 0
              Smallest order size is 25
```

Let's watch how values for OrderSize, the Boolean expression for the minimum condition, and MinOrderSize vary for each iteration of the loop. Table 6.1 shows these "watch" values, as if a "snapshot" of memory cells is taken at each repetition *just after* the if-then structure. Make sure you understand the execution steps in this table.

What would happen if we had forgotten to initialize MinOrderSize? If the algorithm is in a procedure (or function), Turbo Pascal would use a "junk" number in MinOrderSize (whatever value currently resides in that local memory cell). Thus, we can't say what the Boolean expression would evaluate to. If the algorithm is in the main program, then the processor uses a compiler-initialized zero for MinOrder-Size, thus giving a false value for the first and all subsequent evaluations of the Boolean expression. Subsequently, a minimum value of zero would be output, giving a logic error.

Table 6.1   Watch Values for Minimum-Value Problem (Example 6.2)

Repetition	OrderSize	MinOrderSize	OrderSize < MinOrderSize	Remark
1	50	50	false	No new minimum...false because MinOrderSize was initialized to OrderSize
2	100	50	false	No new minimum...100 is greater than 50
3	25	25	true	New minimum...25 is less than 50
4	300	25	false	No new minimum...300 is greater than 25

NOTE

1. Watch out for semicolons! This is the single most common source of logic and compile-time errors in programming the if statement. For example, the following would produce a compile-time error because the first semicolon "ends" the if statement, giving a "dangling" else clause.

```
if SexCode = 'F'
   then writeln ('Female')  ;   ☹
   else writeln ('Male');
```

Nail this down now! Reread item 2 on page 243 and look over our examples once more.

2. Be literate. If statements are great for practicing literacy (or illiteracy, depending on your point of view). Pay careful attention to your indentation and line placement of elements within the if statement. Study our examples in this respect. Use our goal of program literacy as your guide; otherwise, it's very easy to code a confusing (and perhaps incorrect) if statement.

SELF-REVIEW EXERCISES

1 2a 3 4

6.2 MULTIPLE SELECTIONS

• • • • • • • • • • • • • • •

In this section we illustrate selections based on *multiple conditions,* which usually means the existence of *multiple selections,* or more than two selections. By a *selection* or *branch* we mean the code fragment that's executed based on the evaluated condition. For example, the if-then structure has one condition and one selection, labeled StatementTrue earlier; the if-then-else structure has one condition and the two selections StatementTrue and StatementFalse.

We can model multiple selections by either *sequencing* or *nesting* (layering) if-then-else structures. This is why the if-then-else structure is the *fun-*

damental selection structure: We can use it to represent any possible set of selections in programming!

We start this section by showing *nested selection structure*. Next, we describe a simpler arrangement of nested if-then-else structures called the *else-if structure*. Finally, we introduce a specialized multiple selection structure called the *case structure*.

NESTED SELECTION STRUCTURES

As in repetition structures, a **nested selection structure** is one or more selection structures within an outer selection structure. The typical nested selection structure is a set of layered if-then-else structures, although the term is perfectly general. For example, we can nest an if-then structure within an if-then-else structure.

Nested selection structures are useful in implementing the following selection problems.

- Multiple conditions using more than one variable, leading to two or more selections

- Multiple conditions using one variable, leading to multiple selections

We illustrate both of these implementations in the next two examples.

EXAMPLE 6.3   NESTED SELECTION STRUCTURES: MULTIPLE CONDITIONS USING TWO VARIABLES, LEADING TO TWO SELECTIONS

Consider the following pseudocode

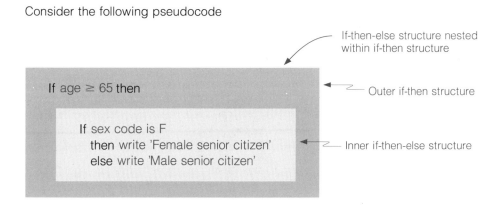

and its Pascal implementation

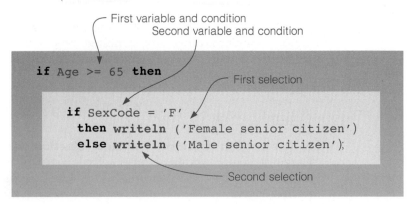

First variable and condition
Second variable and condition

```
if Age >= 65 then

    if SexCode = 'F'
        then writeln ('Female senior citizen')
        else writeln ('Male senior citizen');
```

First selection

Second selection

Note the following.

1. We have two conditions based on two variables: Age and SexCode

2. Then if-then-else structure (second if statement) is nested within the if-then structure (first if statement). *The compiler assumes that the **else** is paired with the closest unpaired **then**.* Our choice of indentation and alignment makes this clear to the reader. Yes?

3. The first selection is the statement that writes the female message; the second selection writes the male message. See Exercise 7 for a variation with more than two selections.

We can also rewrite our design and code as a *sequence* of two-if-then structures, where each condition includes both variables. The following does the trick in Pascal.

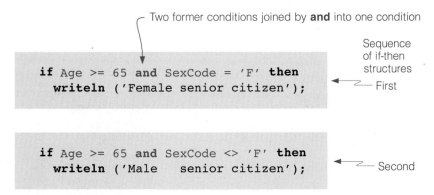

Two former conditions joined by **and** into one condition

Sequence
of if-then
structures

```
if Age >= 65 and SexCode = 'F' then
    writeln ('Female senior citizen');
```
First

```
if Age >= 65 and SexCode <> 'F' then
    writeln ('Male   senior citizen');
```
Second

Compared to the nested approach, this approach simplifies the structure (nesting is avoided), but at the expense of a more complex condition and possibly greater computational *inefficiency.* A sequence of if-then structures is computationally nonoptimal if *complete evaluation* is used in Boolean expressions. In our example, complete evaluation always forces the evaluation of two conditions (which takes time), whereas the nested approach does not evaluate the second condition (on the sex code) unless the first condition (on the age) is true. This computational inefficiency becomes more meaningful in selection structures having many more branches, especially when nested within a repetition structure. For these reasons, most programmers opt for the nested approach over the sequential approach.[1]

EXAMPLE 6.4   NESTED SELECTION STRUCTURES: MULTIPLE CONDITIONS USING ONE VARIABLE, LEADING TO MULTIPLE SELECTIONS

Let's revisit Electra Appliances, which by the way is headed by Ms. Electra, a close confidant of you know who.[2] Suppose that, instead of the single break point at an order size of 100 units, we have the price-break schedule given in Table 6.2. For example, an order for 400 TECs would cost $118,000 (400 units × $295 per unit).

This is called a **table lookup** in programming. We need to look up the proper size category in the first column and use the corresponding price in the second column. For example, given an order size of 400, we first ask "Is 400 less than 100?" The answer is no (false), so we go down one row in the table and ask "Is 400 less than 500?" The answer is now yes (true), so we look to the right and find the corresponding price of $295.

A nested if-then-else structure is one way of coding a table-lookup task; we show other approaches later in the book.

Table 6.2   Price-Break Schedule for the TEC (Example 6.4)

Order Size (Break Point)	Price per TEC
Less than 100	$300
100 but less than 500	295
500 but less than 1000	285
1000 or more	275

---

[1]As mentioned in Note 4 of the last chapter, Turbo Pascal uses *short-circuit evaluation* for Boolean expressions, which makes the nested and sequential approaches equally efficient. In the nested approach, efficiency is imposed by algorithmic design; in the sequential approach, efficiency is imposed by an enabled Boolean evaluation compiler directive (Appendix G). The former approach guarantees efficiency, without regard to compiler directives.
[2]One Harvey CORE, in case you haven't been following snatches of our computational sciences hero (check out the index at the back of the book).

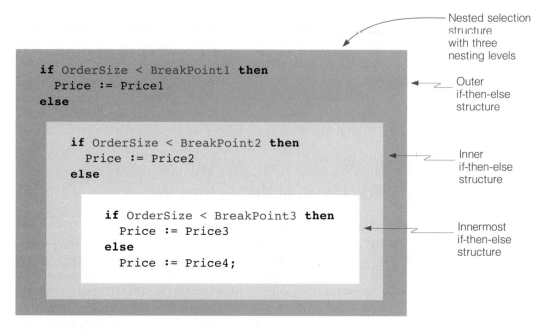

Nested selection structure with three nesting levels

```
if OrderSize < BreakPoint1 then
   Price := Price1
else

      if OrderSize < BreakPoint2 then
         Price := Price2
      else

            if OrderSize < BreakPoint3 then
               Price := Price3
            else
               Price := Price4;
```

Outer if-then-else structure

Inner if-then-else structure

Innermost if-then-else structure

```
OrderCost := Price * OrderSize;
```

Note the following.

1. BreakPoint1, BreakPoint2, and BreakPoint3 respectively are declared constants 100, 500, and 1000; Price1, Price2, Price3, and Price4 are 300, 295, 285, and 275.

2. We simplified coding (and increased its efficiency) by just setting the proper price within the selection structure, leaving the assignment of OrderCost after the selection structure. We also could have taken this tack in Example 6.1 (the payoff was too small to bother).

3. Note (again!) how proper indentation and alignment clarify the nesting logic. This nested selection structure has three conditions (one for each break-point test) and four selections (one for each price).

4. Let's roleplay an order size of 400 units.

    a. First test is false (400 is not less than 100); the second condition is evaluated next.

    b. Second test is true (400 is less than 500). Price is assigned Price2 (295) in the second selection, and execution exits the nested selection structure.

    c. Order cost is assigned 295 * 400, or 118000.

Note that the third condition was never evaluated in our sample desk check.

> ## NOTE
>
> **3. Marriage made in heaven.** When using nested selection struc-
> tures, don't forget that each **else** is married to its closest unmarried
> **then**. This is how the compiler determines the nesting arrangement.
> We can make this clear to ourselves and any reader by the conscious
> alignment of **then-else** pairings (as in Example 6.3) or **if-else** pair-
> ings (as in Example 6.4).

ELSE-IF STRUCTURE

The form of nesting described in Example 6.4 is so common in practice that
it's often called the **else-if structure.** Some languages include a specific else-if
statement in their syntax. We don't need this statement in Pascal because the if
statement's flexibility handles the job, as seen in the next syntax box.

Study the examples in this syntax box, and note the following.

1. The syntax in the first example is identical to that in Example 6.4. The
    else-if syntax is simply a visual rearrangement of the nested if-then-else
    syntax. Convince yourself that the else-if approach is more literate than
    the nested if-then-else approach by picturing 10 or more branches, which
    is common in practice. Moreover, as we keep indenting in the Ex-
    ample 6.4 version, we eventually run out of room at the right.

2. The second example shows the common use of an *error routine* in the
    last else branch. In the event that all conditions test false, the error rou-
    tine would alert the user to this problem. Why don't we have an error
    routine in the first example? The else branch captures all other possible
    order sizes, correctly reflecting the lowest price.

3. Note the use of documentation in the second example. Generally, it's
    best to briefly describe **end**s and error routines.

> ## NOTE
>
> **4. Ordering of conditions.** Take care with the ordering of condi-
> tions in else-if structures. For example, ordering is immaterial in the
> second example of the preceding syntax box in the sense that the
> structure executes correctly whether or not Red (or any other color) is
> tested first. This is not the case with our price-break example. For in-
> stance, if we were to reverse the ordering of conditions, our sample
> order size of 400 would be incorrectly assigned Price3 (285), since
> 400 is less than BreakPoint3 (1000).

SYNTAX BOX

Else-if structure . . . Select the branch associated with the first true (Boolean expression) condition

Syntax . . . . .if BooleanExpression **then**
　　Statement1
　　else if BooleanExpression2 **then**
　　　Statement2
　　else if BooleanExpression3 **then**
　　　Statement3
　　. . . ⎤ Other else-if and statement lines

　　else   ⎦ Usually error routine (optional)
　　　StatementLast
　　;

Examples . . . . . .if OrderSize < BreakPoint1 **then**
　　Price := Price1
　　else if OrderSize < BreakPoint2 **then**
　　　Price := Price2
　　else if OrderSize < BreakPoint3 **then**
　　　Price := Price3
　　else
　　　Price := Price4;

　　if Color = 'Red' **then**
　　　inc (CountRed)
　　else if Color = 'White' **then**
　　　inc (CountWhite)
　　else if Color = 'Blue' **then**
　　　inc (CountBlue)
　　else {Error in color} ⟵ Error routine
　　　begin
　　　　writeln (chr(7)); {Beep}
　　　　writeln (Color, ' is incorrect');
　　　end; {else-if}

Results:

Price assigned Price2 if OrderSize is 400 and BreakPoint1, BreakPoint2, and BreakPoint3 respectively represent the constants 100, 500, and 1000. Exit from structure immediately follows assignment of Price.

If Color stores Redd, the error routine is executed (all three conditions tested false to get to the error routine).

Explanation . . . Each if statement has the syntax described in the if statement syntax box on page 244. The executed selection is that corresponding to the first true condition. Execution then exits the structure. The else-if structure is the artful arrangement of a nested if-then-else structure, achieved by placing an **if-then** pair on the same line as the preceding **else.**

CASE STRUCTURE

The **case structure** is a multiple selection structure with *ordinal lists* as conditions, and selections as *cases*. First, we need some definitions. A **list** is an ordered (ascending) group of values, as in the integer list 1, 2, 3, 4, 5 or the character list A, B, C. A value having an **ordinal type** is an item from a list. Each value has an associated *ordinality*, an integer value that denotes its position in the list. For example, the ordinality of integer 1 is 1 (naturally), and the ordinality of character B is 66 (its decimal position or ASCII value). The ordinal types (from Appendix D) are *integer, Boolean, character, enumerated,* and *subrange*. We know all about the first three ordinal types; we consider the last two in the next chapter.

The accompanying syntax box describes the syntax of the case statement and illustrates its use. Study the examples and note the following.

1. The conditions (the lists of constants in front of each case) and the corresponding selectors are *ordinal*. For now, we work with *integer* and *character* values. We don't use *Boolean* selectors and conditions because it would limit us to two cases, which is better modeled by the if-then-else structure. If conditions include *real* or *string* values, we have to use nested or else-if structures.

2. The example is an alternative to the third example in the if-statement syntax box on page 244.

3. Use an else clause to trap out-of-range errors, unless earlier code fragments in the program ensure that the selector's value is within range. Our example, unlike earlier versions, traps sex codes other than F or M. In Exercise 8 we ask you to revise an earlier example to trap inadmissible sex codes.

4. Note how we use documentation to describe cases, error routines, and **end**s.

EXAMPLE 6.5   CASE STRUCTURE WITH INTEGER SELECTOR

Consider the following case statement.

```
                      ┌─ Integer selector
                     ↙
    case OrderSize of
       {1}     0 ..  99  : Price := Price1;
       {2}   100 .. 499  : Price := Price2;
       {3}   500 .. 999  : Price := Price3;
    else
       {4}                 Price := Price4;
    end;  {case}
```

SYNTAX BOX

Case statement (structure)... Select case whose list of case constants includes the value of selector

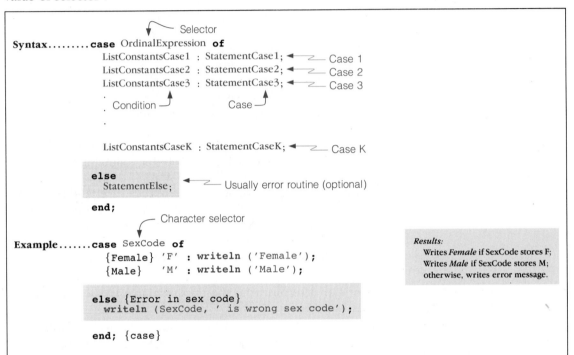

Explanation...case, of, else, and **end** are reserved words. OrdinalExpression is any expression of *ordinal type (integer, Boolean, character, enumerated,* and *subrange).* We cover enumerated and subrange types in the next chapter. All integer types except longint are permitted (see Appendix D). The ordinal expression is sometimes called the *selector.* ListConstantsCase is a *list* (ordered group) of unique ordinal constants that prefixes a *case* and is type-compatible with the selector. Any two individual constants in a list are separated by a *comma;* a range is specified by using the ellipsis $..$, as in $0..99$. No two lists may "intersect" (have any common constants). StatementCase and StatementElse are statements. Turbo Pascal includes an optional *else clause.* The flow of execution works as follows: The selector is evaluated; the case statement whose list of constants includes the evaluated selector is executed; execution exits the structure. If the evaluated selector is not within one of the lists of constants, the statement in the else clause is executed (if present); otherwise, execution immediately exits the case structure, without any statement being executed.

OrderSize is an integer selector that's used to select the first case if its value is anywhere in the range 0 to 99, inclusive; the second case if its value is 100 to 499; the third case if its value is 500 to 999; and the fourth (or last case) if its value is outside the range 0 to 999. For example, if OrderSize stores 300, the second case is selected (the value in Price2 gets copied to Price), and execution exits out the case structure to the next statement that follows **end**.

Note that the *ellipsis* $..$ is a legitimate symbol in Pascal. As in literature (which uses the ellipsis $...$), it represents missing elements. For example, $1..5$ means the list of integers $1,2,3,4,5$.

Also note that the else clause is handy not only for error routines but also for open-ended ranges with no explicit upper bounds, as seen in this example. Assuming nonnegative values in OrderSize, the else clause handles the fourth case of order sizes in excess of 999.

Finally, this sample case structure is an alternative to the sample else-if structure in the syntax box on page 254. The case approach is often "cleaner" looking than the else-if approach, although as usual "beauty is in the eye of the beholder."

SELF-REVIEW EXERCISES

7a–b 8a–b 11a

6.3 MENU APPLICATION

Interactive software is frequently designed as **menu-driven programs.** These programs present the user with a **menu,** a list of entries (not entrees!), and then take appropriate action based on the user's selection. Menu-driven programs are very common in commercial software like wordprocessors and spreadsheets, since they are less intimidating than *command-driven programs* (like DOS!), facilitate the training of users, and reduce the likelihood of user-initiated errors.

As we might imagine, the *design* of a menu, its "look and feel," is an important consideration at the requirements and design stages. The IDE's menu bar is an example of design excellence. This is a typically designed **menu system** or **menu structure,** a set of interrelated menus not unlike a structure chart. At the top we have a *Main menu* with selections described by one-word phrases like File and Run. The selection of a main menu entry spawns a related menu called a *submenu, popup menu,* or *pull-down menu.* The method of selecting menu entries is also part of the design, the more versatile and easier the better. As you know, the IDE excels here as well by allowing first-letter entries, mouse clicks, highlighted cursor movements followed by a press of the Enter key, and hot-key presses. Other design elements include the use of figures, shading, help screens, and color.

In this section we consider a simple menu system of one main menu... with no frills like pull-down menus, color, or hot keys. In Chapter 8 we add colors, and in Module E we go all the way by developing a menu application that exactly reproduces the "look and feel" of the IDE.

REQUIREMENTS

Let's develop a simple statistical program that offers the calculation of factorials and combinations. The *factorial* of a number x is defined as

$$x! = 1 \cdot 2 \cdot 3 \cdot \cdots \cdot (x - 1) \cdot x$$

For example, 5 factorial is

$$5! = 1 \cdot 2 \cdot 3 \cdot 4 \cdot 5$$
$$= 120$$

Combinations describe the number of different sets or groups of k items when we have n items to choose from. For example, combinations of 5 taken 2 at a time mean that we're asking "How many possible groups do we have, each having two different items from among the five available?" To answer, if we have the items A, B, C, D, and E we can enumerate the answer 10 by listing the following sets:

AB   AC   AD   AE   BC   BD   BE   CD   CE   DE

Thus, we have 10 possible groups, where each group consists of two different items from among the available five items, and where order within the group is immaterial.

Combinations are an important calculation in many diverse applications, including statistical probabilities, business, engineering, and the sciences. In practice, combinations of n taken k at a time is calculated from the formula

$$_nC_k = \frac{n!}{(n - k)!\,k!}$$

In our example, we have

$$_5C_2 = \frac{5!}{(5 - 2)! \cdot 2!} = \frac{5!}{3! \cdot 2!} = \frac{120}{6 \cdot 2} = \frac{120}{12}$$
$$= 10$$

Let's assume that users want a friendly, menu-driven program. Input includes the menu selection, a value for x (when a factorial is selected), and values for n and k (when combinations is selected). They also want a help facility that briefly describes each menu entry. Output, depending on the selection, includes x and $x!$; n, k, and $_nC_k$; and the help descriptions. The computations were described above, and they include no constants.

DESIGN

The I/O design is seen in Figure 6.2. As in programs Temp1 and Temp2 from the last chapter, the I/O design has a screen orientation, with task-dedicated screens, screen pauses, and screen clears. As usual, we have an *opening*

FIGURE 6.2   Screen Designs (I/O) for Program Combo1

Screen 1

```
                    FACTORIALS & COMBINATIONS... Version 1.0




Hit any key to continue...
```

Screen 2

```
                          MAIN MENU

                   ┌─────────────────────┐
                   │  F  Factorial       │
                   │  C  Combinations    │
                   │  H  Help            │
                   │  Q  Quit            │
                   └─────────────────────┘

          Enter selection... h  ◄───┐
                                    └─ Lowercase OK
```

Screen 3

```
HELP Facility... Main Menu Selections

   F  Factorial...... Inputs number
                      Displays its factorial

   C  Combinations... Inputs n & k
                      Displays combos of n taken k at a time

   H  Help.......... This help facility!

   Q  Quit.......... Quit this program



Hit any key to continue...
```

Screen 4

```
                          MAIN MENU

                   ┌─────────────────────┐
                   │  F  Factorial       │
                   │  C  Combinations    │
                   │  H  Help            │
                   │  Q  Quit            │
                   └─────────────────────┘

          Enter selection... g ◄───┐
                                   └─ Incorrect selection
```

continued

FIGURE 6.2   (*continued*)

Screen 5

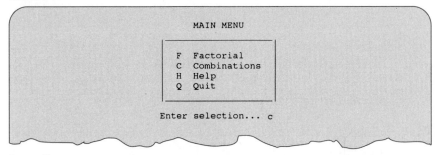

```
                    Please enter menu selection again...

            Beep

        -O-
    Hit any key to continue...
```

Screen 6

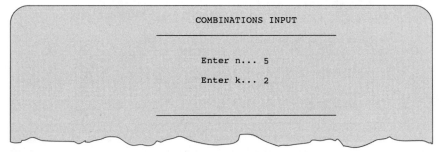

```
                        MAIN MENU

                    F   Factorial
                    C   Combinations
                    H   Help
                    Q   Quit

                Enter selection... c
```

Screen 7

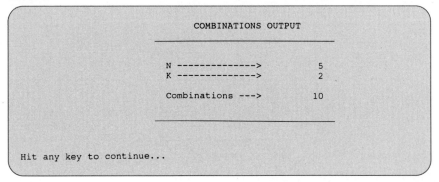

```
                    COMBINATIONS INPUT


                    Enter n... 5

                    Enter k... 2
```

Screen 8

```
                    COMBINATIONS OUTPUT


        N -------------->        5
        K -------------->        2

        Combinations --->       10


    Hit any key to continue...
```

FIGURE 6.2   (*continued*)

Screen 9

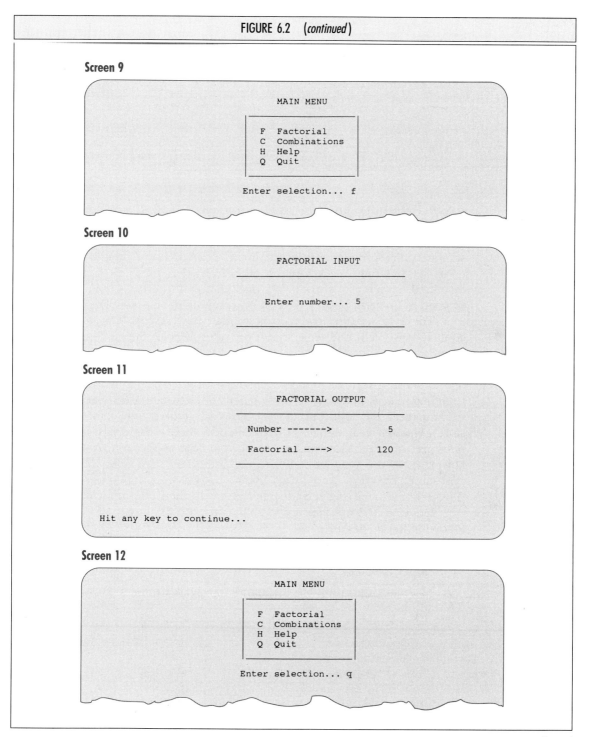

```
                    MAIN MENU

              ┌─────────────────────┐
              │  F  Factorial       │
              │  C  Combinations    │
              │  H  Help            │
              │  Q  Quit            │
              └─────────────────────┘

              Enter selection... f
```

Screen 10

```
                 FACTORIAL INPUT
        ───────────────────────────────

              Enter number... 5

        ───────────────────────────────
```

Screen 11

```
                 FACTORIAL OUTPUT
        ───────────────────────────────

        Number ------->        5

        Factorial ---->       120

        ───────────────────────────────




   Hit any key to continue...
```

Screen 12

```
                    MAIN MENU

              ┌─────────────────────┐
              │  F  Factorial       │
              │  C  Combinations    │
              │  H  Help            │
              │  Q  Quit            │
              └─────────────────────┘

              Enter selection... q
```

continued

FIGURE 6.2 *(continued)*

Screen 13

```
                    We make a great COMBO... 'til we meet again...




Hit any key to continue...
```

---

screen (screen 1), an *input screen* (screens 7 and 10), an *output screen* (screens 8 and 11), and a *farewell screen* (screen 13).

The *menu screen* is a new feature in the present example. As seen in screen 2, this screen identifies the menu as the main menu and lists four entries. The input act is a key press followed by the enter key. As usual, lowercase and uppercase entries are acceptable. Incorrect menu entries are trapped by an error routine (screen 4), resulting in an *error screen* (screen 5).

The *help screen* (screen 3) is another new screen. The help facility is context sensitive in the sense that it provides help for the current screen (the menu screen in this case).

We plan to treat the menu selection input as character input, which makes sense given the indicated menu entries. The input variables corresponding to x, n, and k will store integer values, which is consistent with their mathematical use. The output variables for factorial and combinations will store *extended* real values. In mathematical theory, factorials and combinations are integers. As mentioned in our factorial application from Chapter 4, however, we use type extended to accommodate very large values, thereby postponing overflow. And, as we've seen before, we can output real values as "integers" by specifying zero decimal places in their output formats.

Figure 6.3 shows the stepwise chart for the design algorithms. Note the following in our design.

1. We don't show procedures **Pause** and **Fac**, since these were covered in earlier chapters.

2. The main algorithm has a common design for menu-driven algorithms:

```
Opening tasks
Repeat
    Offer menu
    Case structure to route menu selection
until menu selection is quit
```

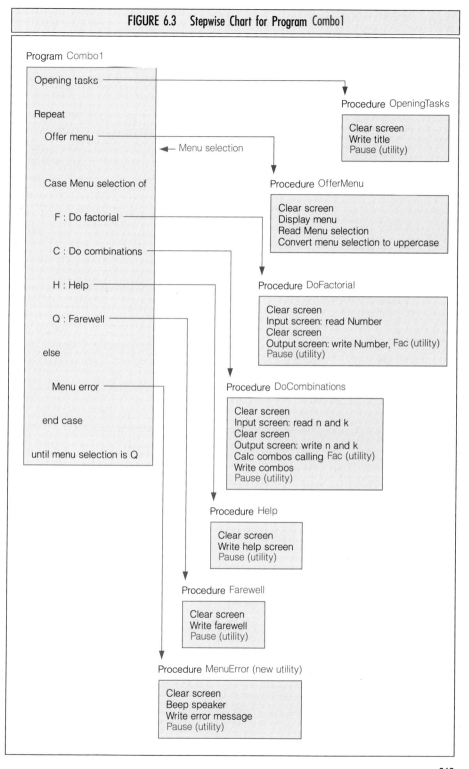

FIGURE 6.3   Stepwise Chart for Program Combo1

Program Combo1

Opening tasks

Repeat

   Offer menu

← Menu selection

   Case Menu selection of

      F : Do factorial

      C : Do combinations

      H : Help

      Q : Farewell

   else

      Menu error

   end case

until menu selection is Q

Procedure OpeningTasks

Clear screen
Write title
Pause (utility)

Procedure OfferMenu

Clear screen
Display menu
Read Menu selection
Convert menu selection to uppercase

Procedure DoFactorial

Clear screen
Input screen: read Number
Clear screen
Output screen: write Number, Fac (utility)
Pause (utility)

Procedure DoCombinations

Clear screen
Input screen: read n and k
Clear screen
Output screen: write n and k
Calc combos calling Fac (utility)
Write combos
Pause (utility)

Procedure Help

Clear screen
Write help screen
Pause (utility)

Procedure Farewell

Clear screen
Write farewell
Pause (utility)

Procedure MenuError (new utility)

Clear screen
Beep speaker
Write error message
Pause (utility)

Alternatives include using a while-do structure in place of the repeat-until structure, and using an else-if structure instead of a case structure. We believe our choices are more literate, but we ask you to consider other alternatives in the exercises.

3. This type of modular design facilitates menu maintenance when adding, changing, or deleting menu entries. Note that each selection in the case structure is a procedure call (a module). Thus, adding a new menu entry means adding a new procedure and doing some housekeeping in the case structure and menu module; deleting a menu entry means deleting the procedure that implements that entry, along with some housekeeping in the case structure and menu module. We ask you to add a new entry in the exercises.

CODE

Figure 6.4 shows the program. Relate the program to our design, and note the following.

1. Procedure Pause (from Chapter 5) and function Fac (from Chapter 4) were inserted directly from the Utilities Library. Note that each utility is used by more than one module, which considerably simplifies and optimizes coding over nonmodular designs.

2. The selector in the case structure (MenuSelection) is typed *character*. This is the most versatile typing for menu-choice input, since it can handle characters as either letters or digits.

3. The menu selection Q is a *sentinel* for the repeat-until structure.

4. We generalized the coding for procedure MenuError to decouple it from the specific menu used in this application. This means that we can use MenuError with any menu, so we've added this procedure to the Utilities Library.

TEST

Figure 6.2 shows an actual run of program Combo1. Note that our sample test data include the calculations made earlier in the requirements stage. In testing menu-driven programs, be sure that all entries are selected, including wrong entries. To make sure you understand the execution logic, you might want to develop a desk-check script of the sample run (see Exercise 12b).

SELF-REVIEW EXERCISES

12a

```
┌──────────────────────────────────────────────────────────────────────┐
│                FIGURE 6.4    Listing for Program Combo1                │
├──────────────────────────────────────────────────────────────────────┤
│                                                                        │
│    program Combo1;                                                     │
│                                                                        │
│      {* * * * * * * * * * * * * * * * * * * * * * * * * * * * * * *     │
│       *                                                        *       │
│       *      Menu Application:  Factorials & Combinations, Version 1.0  *│
│       *                                                        *       │
│       *         Inputs menu selection, formula values for x, n and k   *│
│       *         Calculates x factorial, combinations of n taken k at a time *│
│       *         Outputs factorial, combination, or help         *      │
│       *                                                        *       │
│       *         Modular structure                               *      │
│       *             ┬───  OpeningTasks                           *      │
│       *             │                                           *      │
│       *             ┼───  OfferMenu                             *      │
│       *             │                                           *      │
│       *             ┼───  MenuError                             *      │
│       *             │                                           *      │
│       *             ┼───  Help                                 *      │
│       *             │                                           *      │
│       *             ┼───  Farewell                             *      │
│       *             │                                           *      │
│       *             ┼───  DoFactorial                          *      │
│       *             │                                           *      │
│       *             └───  DoCombinations                        *      │
│       *                   │                            ──── Pause  *   │
│       *                   └──────────                 │           *   │
│       *                                        ──────  Fac         *   │
│       *                                                        *       │
│        * * * * * * * * * * * * * * * * * * * * * * * * * * * * * *}    │
│                                                                        │
│      {=========================== Declarations ===========================}│
│                                                                        │
│    uses crt;                 {Needed by Pause, and for clrscr and gotoxy}│
│                                                                        │
│    var                                                                 │
│      MenuSelection : char;                    {F Factorial             │
│                                                C Combinations          │
│               ↖                                H Help                  │
│                 ─── Character selector in      Q Quit}                 │
│                     case statement                                     │
│                                                                        │
│                Function Fac and procedure Pause not shown; they are    │
│                identical to those in Figures 4.3 and 5.4.              │
│                                                                        │
│      {======================= Procedure Declarations =======================}│
│                                                                        │
│    procedure OpeningTasks;                                             │
│                                                                        │
│      { Clears screen, writes title, calls Pause                       │
│        Receives nothing                                               │
│        Sends nothing }                                                │
│                                                                        │
│    const                                                              │
│      Title = 'FACTORIALS & COMBINATIONS... Version 1.0';              │
│                                                                        │
│    begin   {OpeningTasks}                                             │
│                                                                        │
│      clrscr;                                                          │
│      gotoxy (20,10);  write (Title);                                 │
│      Pause;                                                          │
│                                                                        │
│    end;    {OpeningTasks}                                             │
│    {----------------------------------------------------------------------}│
│                                                                        │
└──────────────────────────────────────────────────────────────────────┘
```

continued

FIGURE 6.4   (continued)

```
procedure OfferMenu (var MenuSelection : char);

  { Clears screen, offers menu, inputs selection
    Receives nothing
    Sends MenuSelection }

begin   {OfferMenu}

  clrscr;  gotoxy (1,5);

  writeln ('                              MAIN MENU       ');
  writeln ('                         _____  ');
  writeln ('                        |                   | ');
  writeln ('                        |  F  Factorial     | ');
  writeln ('                        |  C  Combinations  | ');
  writeln ('                        |  H  Help          | ');
  writeln ('                        |  Q  Quit          | ');
  writeln ('                        |_____| ');
  writeln;
  write   ('                         Enter selection... ');
  readln (MenuSelection);

  MenuSelection := upcase( MenuSelection );
```
◄ ╱ Converts any lowercase
input character to uppercase
```
end;    {OfferMenu}
{--------------------------------------------------------------------}
procedure MenuError;

  { Utility clears screen, beeps, displays menu selection error message,
      calls Pause
    Receives nothing
    Sends nothing }

  { NOTE:  Requires: uses clause for crt unit in host program
                     Pause from utility library }

const
  Beep    = chr(7);
  Message = 'Please enter menu selection again...';

begin   {MenuError}

  clrscr;
  write (Beep);                         {Audio alert}
  gotoxy (23,12);  write (Message);     {Video alert}
  Pause;

end;    {MenuError}
{--------------------------------------------------------------------}
```

6.4 ERROR HANDLING

• • • • • • • • • • • • • •

Error handling is the act of trapping potential execution or logic errors and taking corrective action. *Error-handling routines,* or simply *error routines,* implement error handling. We have already illustrated several error routines: an else clause in the case structure that detects inadmissible sex codes, as seen

```
┌──────────────────────────────────────────────────────────────────────┐
│                    FIGURE 6.4   (continued)                            │
└──────────────────────────────────────────────────────────────────────┘

  procedure DoFactorial;

    { Clears screen, inputs number, clears screen, displays number and its
        factorial by calling utility function Fac, calls Pause
      Receives nothing
      Sends nothing }

  const
    Title1 = '        FACTORIAL INPUT        ';
    Title2 = '        FACTORIAL OUTPUT       ';
    Line   = '_____ ';

  var
    Number : integer;                  {Number whose factorial is evaluated}

  begin   {DoFactorial}

   {Display input screen}
    clrscr;
    gotoxy (25, 9);   write (Title1);
    gotoxy (25,10);   write (Line);
    gotoxy (25,15);   write (Line);
    gotoxy (30,13);   write ('Enter number... '); readln (Number);

   {Display output screen}
    clrscr;                   ──── Nonsequential output
    gotoxy (25, 9);   write (Title2);
    gotoxy (25,10);   write (Line);
    gotoxy (25,15);   write (Line);
    gotoxy (27,12);   write ('Number -------> ', Number :10);
    gotoxy (27,14);   write ('Factorial ----> ', Fac( Number ) :10:0);
    Pause;                              ──── Function call

  end;    {DoFactorial}
  {-----------------------------------------------------------------------}
```

continued

in our case statement syntax box in Section 6.2; procedure ReadReply for trapping incorrect Y/N input replies, as displayed in Figure 5.7; and procedure MenuError for alerting the user to a menu input error previously trapped by the calling module, as seen in Figure 6.4.

Turbo Pascal provides some compiler directives and language features that are useful in trapping I/O, range, and other run-time errors.

I/O ERRORS

I/O errors occur during input and output operations. Our Y/N input and menu input procedures are sample error routines that trap *logical input errors*. For instance, a user might type an inadmissible character that can lead to a logical error in the program. We can also trap potential *fatal input errors,* as when a user mistakenly types a character or real value instead of the intended integer value. Without an error-handling routine, execution would terminate, assuming Turbo Pascal's *Input/Output checking* compiler directive is enabled.[3]

---

[3]Remember that we summarize compiler directives in Appendix G.

FIGURE 6.4 *(continued)*

```
procedure DoCombinations;

  { Clears screen; inputs n and k; clears screen; calls Fac for n!,
      (n-k)!, and k!; displays n, k, and combinations of n taken k at a
      time; calls Pause
    Receives nothing
    Sends nothing }

const
  Title1 = '        COMBINATIONS INPUT        ';
  Title2 = '        COMBINATIONS OUTPUT       ';
  Line   = '_____';

var
  N, K          : integer;
  Combinations : extended;         { Combinations = n!/(n-k)!k! }

begin   {DoCombinations}          ── To handle large combos
                                        (as done in function Fac
  {Display input screen}                 for large factorials)
  clrscr;
  gotoxy (25, 8);   write (Title1);
  gotoxy (25, 9);   write (Line);
  gotoxy (25,17);   write (Line);
  gotoxy (33,12);   write ('Enter n... ');  readln (N);
  gotoxy (33,14);   write ('Enter k... ');  readln (K);

  {Display output screen}
  clrscr;
  gotoxy (25, 8);   write (Title2);
  gotoxy (25, 9);   write (Line);
  gotoxy (25,17);   write (Line);
  gotoxy (27,12);   write ('N -------------> ', N :10);    Round to nearest
  gotoxy (27,13);   write ('K -------------> ', K :10);     whole number

  Combinations := Fac(N) / Fac(N-K) / Fac(K);
                                                              │
  gotoxy (27,15);   write ('Combinations ---> ', Combinations :10:0);
  Pause;

end;    {DoCombinations}
{-------------------------------------------------------------------------}
```

In the next two examples we illustrate error routines that handle noninteger input and file-specification errors.

EXAMPLE 6.6   INTEGER-INPUT ERROR-HANDLING PROCEDURE ReadLnInt

Take a look at procedure ReadLnInt in Figure 6.5 on page 271. Its purpose is to input an integer value. If the value is noninteger, it beeps and displays an error message. It traps this error while input is inadmissible.

Before we explain the coding, consider the following I/O script based on test runs of the driver CkRdInt

---

FIGURE 6.4 (*continued*)

```
procedure Help;

   { Clears screen, displays help for main menu selections, calls Pause
     Receives nothing
     Sends nothing }

const
   Title = 'HELP Facility... Main Menu Selections';

begin   {Help}

   clrscr; gotoxy (1,5);
   writeln (Title);
   writeln;
   writeln ('  F  Factorial...... Inputs number');
   writeln ('                     Displays its factorial');
   writeln;
   writeln ('  C  Combinations... Inputs n & k');
   writeln ('                     Displays combos of n taken k at a time');
   writeln;
   writeln ('  H  Help.......... This help facility!');
   writeln;
   writeln ('  Q  Quit.......... Quit this program');
   Pause;

end;    {Help}
{------------------------------------------------------------------------}
procedure Farewell;

   { Clears screen, displays farewell screen, calls Pause
     Receives nothing
     Sends nothing }

const
   Farewell = 'We make a great COMBO... ''til we meet again...';

begin  {Farewell}

   clrscr;
   gotoxy (20,10);  write (Farewell);
   Pause;

end;    {Farewell}
```

continued

1. We have a clean run in the first test run.

   Enter integer... 3 ◄───z── Integer value admissible
   Echo............ 3

2. In the second test run we try the following inadmissible input, where at this point we have not yet pressed the Enter key.

   Enter integer... 3.3 ◄───z── Real value not admissible

3. When we press the Enter key, the error routine traps this input error by sounding the speaker, clearing the input field, displaying a message to the right of the input field, and positioning the cursor at the beginning of the input field for reentry of the input value. At this point the input line would appear as follows.

   Enter integer... ▮   <---Please reenter
                    └─Cursor position └─Error message

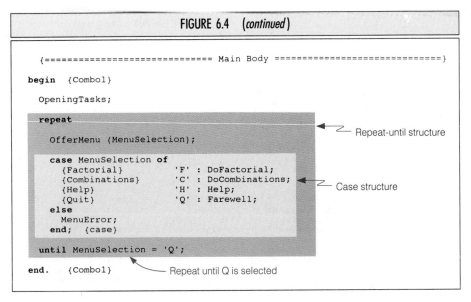

```
                          FIGURE 6.4   (continued)
```

```
   {============================= Main Body ============================}

begin   {Combo1}

   OpeningTasks;

   repeat                                              ◄───── Repeat-until structure

      OfferMenu (MenuSelection);

      case MenuSelection of
         {Factorial}         'F' : DoFactorial;
         {Combinations}      'C' : DoCombinations;    ◄───── Case structure
         {Help}              'H' : Help;
         {Quit}              'Q' : Farewell;
      else
         MenuError;
      end;  {case}

   until MenuSelection = 'Q';

end.     {Combo1}  ◄─────── Repeat until Q is selected
```

4. Let's goof again by missing the 3-key and pressing the nearby e-key. Just before pressing the Enter key we have the following.

   Enter integer... e   <---Please reenter

5. After pressing the Enter key, the error routine clears the error message, issues a line feed, and repeats the sequence in step 3 above. Note that this sequence of events is repeated while the input is inadmissible. The error routine insists on a legitimate integer value.

6. If we now input an integer value, the error routine clears the error message, issues a line feed (as does the predefined procedure readln), and sends the integer value to the calling module.

In effect, we have developed a utility procedure that is considerably more specialized than the readln procedure. It forces the user to enter an integer value, trapping any noninteger input, and issuing audiovisual error messaging while the input is incorrect.

Note the following regarding our coding in Figure 6.5.

1. Calls to the predefined functions **wherex** and **wherey** in the *crt unit* respectivey return the *x*- and *y*-coordinates of the current cursor position. Note that *x* is the column position and *y* is the row. In our example, the cursor is at position 18 in row 1 of the screen—or coordinate (18, 1)—when ReadLnInt is called. In other words, the cursor is just to the right of the input prompt

   Enter integer... ▮

   Cursor at coordinate (18, 1)

FIGURE 6.5   Listing for Procedure ReadLnInt and Its Driver CkRdInt

```
program CkRdInt;

  {* * * * * * * * * * * * * * * * * * * * * * * * * * * * * * * * * *
   *                                                                 *
   *          Driver checks error-handling procedure ReadLnInt       *
   *                                                                 *
   *             Inputs integer value                                *
   *             Calls ReadLnInt                                      *
   *             Outputs value                                        *
   *                                                                 *
   * * * * * * * * * * * * * * * * * * * * * * * * * * * * * * * * * *}

  {============================= Declarations =============================}

uses crt;

var
  TestVar : integer;                                     New utility procedure

  {======================= Procedure Declarations =======================}


procedure ReadLnInt (var Variable : integer);

  { Utility reads integer value with line feed while handling input error
    Receives nothing
    Sends Variable }

  { NOTE:  Requires uses clause for crt unit in host program
           Displays error message immediately to right of input value }

const
  Beep = chr(7);

var
  X, Y : integer;                    {Current coordinates of cursor
                                     ... at beginning of input field}
begin  {ReadLnInt}

  X := wherex;  Y := wherey;      {Predefined functions in crt unit}

  {$I-  Turn off automatic I/O error checking}

    readln (Variable);                    {Predefined function ioresult}
    while ioresult <> 0 do                {returns zero if no I/O error}
      begin
        write (Beep);                         {Beep speaker}
        gotoxy (X,Y);  clreol;                {Clear input field}
        gotoxy (X+10,Y);                      {Cursor to right of input field}
        write ('<-- Please reenter');         {Write error message}
        gotoxy (X,Y);                         {Cursor to input field}
        readln (Variable);                    {Reenter value}
        gotoxy (X+10,Y);  clreol;             {Clear error message}
        writeln;                              {Issue line feed}
      end;   {while}

  {$I+  Turn on automatic I/O error checking}

end;    {ReadLnInt}
```

continued

FIGURE 6.5   (continued)

```
{============================== Main Body ==============================}

begin   {CkRdInt}
                                              ——— Procedure call
   clrscr;
   write   ('Enter integer... ');   ReadLnInt (TestVar);
   writeln ('Echo........... ',    TestVar);

end.    {CkRdInt}
```

where we should note that the screen was cleared just before input, putting the cursor in the home position at (1,1), and a space follows the last dot in the input prompt. Thus, in our example, X stores 18 and Y stores 1.

2. The compiler directive {$I-} turns off automatic I/O error checking. If we were not to issue this directive, execution would terminate the moment we entered an inadmissible value (assuming I/O error checking is active in the IDE or calling module). Note that we turn this directive back on just before the end of the error procedure.

3. The predefined function **ioresult** returns an integer value that represents the status of the most recent I/O operation. Specific values identify specific I/O errors, which are summarized in the *Turbo Pascal Reference Manual*. For our purposes we only need to know that the returned value is *zero* if no I/O error is detected. Accordingly, our Boolean expression in the while statement tests for nonzero values. While the test is true, the input error is trapped and the error routine does its job.

4. We explained the predefined procedures **gotoxy** and **clreol** in the *crt unit* earlier in Example 5.7. Their use here ensures that the cursor is positioned at the beginning of an empty input field, after having written a message immediately to the right of the input field that also subsequently gets cleared. The procedure's documentation explains this logic.

We added procedure ReadLnInt to the Utilities Library as file READLNIN.PRO. Try a test drive of CkRdInt in Exercise 17. In Exercise 18 we ask you to consider input error trapping for types real, character, and string.

Example 6.7   File-Specification Error-Handling Procedure PrepFile[4]

Procedure PrepFile in Figure 6.6 inputs a file specification, assigns the text-file variable, and resets the pointer. As in Example 6.6, it turns off automatic I/O error checking, in this case to trap the entry of an incorrect file specification. For ex-

---

[4]This example requires previous study of Sections 4.3 and 5.4.

FIGURE 6.6   Listing for Procedure PrepFile

```pascal
procedure PrepFile (var TextFile : text);

  { Utility reads file specification with line feed while handling
      input error, prepares file with assign and reset
    Receives nothing
    Sends TextFile }

  { NOTE:  Requires uses clause for crt unit in host program
            Displays error message immediately to right of input value }

const
  Beep = chr(7);

var
  FileSpec : string;      {File specification as \path\file name}
  X, Y     : integer;     {Current coordinates of cursor
                              ... at beginning of input field}
begin  {PrepFile}

  {$I-  Turn off automatic I/O error checking}

  {Input file spec and prep file}
    write ('Enter data file (like A:\GRADES\HC101.DAT)... ');

    X := wherex;  Y := wherey;               {Predefined functs in crt unit}

    readln (FileSpec);
    assign (TextFile, FileSpec);
    reset  (TextFile);

                                             {Predefined function ioresult}
  while ioresult <> 0 do                     {returns zero if no I/O error}
    begin
      write (Beep);                          {Beep speaker}
      gotoxy (X,Y);  clreol;                 {Clear input field}
      gotoxy (X+20,Y);                       {Cursor to right of input field}
      write ('<-- Reenter');                 {Write error message}
      gotoxy (X,Y);                          {Cursor to input field}
      readln (FileSpec);                     {Reenter value}
      assign (TextFile, FileSpec);           {Reprep file}
      reset  (TextFile);
      gotoxy (X+20,Y);  clreol;              {Clear error message}
      writeln;                               {Issue line feed}
    end;  {while}

  {$I+  Turn on automatic I/O error checking}

end;  {PrepFile}
{-----------------------------------------------------------------------}
```

ample, suppose we were to mispecify a file, as in mistyping its name, drive, or directory. PrepFile would sound the speaker, clear the input field, display a message to the right of the input field, and position the cursor at the beginning of the input field for reentry of the file specification. This input error would be trapped while the file-specification input is inadmissible.

Other than text-file-related statements, this error-handling routine is the same as that in Example 6.6. We placed it in the Utilities Library under the name PREPFILE.PRO. In Exercises 20 and 21, we ask you to try it out.

RANGE ERRORS

Range errors are run-time errors that occur when an attempt is made to store a value that's outside its allowable range of values. These are usually called *out-of-range* or *out-of-bounds values*. We will show error handling for range-check errors starting in the next chapter.

OTHER RUN-TIME ERRORS

Turbo Pascal includes other procedures for trapping a gaggle of run-time errors, including memory, graphics, and DOS errors. These error-trapping routines are not illustrated in this text.

NOTE

5. On setting compiler directives in the IDE. The code that's generated by compiler directives is part of the object program. If we include compiler directives in the source code by using the comment form within braces, then compilation of the source program generates the compiler directives' code in the object program. If we don't include compiler directives in the source code, then the IDE's settings apply (as accessed through Options Compiler). If we have already compiled a program not having source-code compiler directives, make no further changes in the source program, and then change compiler directives through the IDE, a run of the program would not reflect the revised settings. The source program is not recompiled because we did not change it! Thus, the object program with the previous compiler directive settings is executed. (Remember that it's the object program that gets executed, not the source program.) *To incorporate the new directives in the object program, we must recompile before running.*

SELF-REVIEW EXERCISES

17

6.5   PROGRAMMING TIPS

• • • • • • • • • • • • • • •

Consider the following tips to improve the design and style of your programs and to avoid some common errors.

DESIGN AND STYLE

1. Literacy.   Keep on spacing. Indent statements that represent selections (see Note 2). Align corresponding then-else pairs and if-else pairs (see Note 3). Use comments to document **ends** and error routines. When helpful, also document then clauses, else clauses, and cases.

2. On Selecting the Selection Structure.   The number and variations of selection structures often confuse the beginning student when the time comes to decide "Which selection structure should I use?" The following case structure may be helpful in selecting the right selection structure.

{Selection-structure selection is based on number of selections, number of variables in conditions, and ordinality}

case Number of selections of
    One: Use **if-then structure**
                  {See Example 6.2}

    Two: If *one-variable condition*
                  then Use **if-then-else structure**
                      {See Example 6.1}
                  else Use **nested if-then-else structure**
                      {See Example 6.3}

    Multiple: If *ordinal conditions*
                  then Use **case structure**
                      {See Combo1, Figure 6.4}
                  else Use **else-if structure**
                      {See else-if syntax box}

Nested if-then-else structures and else-if structures are the most versatile selection structures, because they can handle multiple variables within multiple conditions (like sex code and age) and nonordinal variables (like string and real variables) in addition to ordinal variables. If you have a choice, the case structure is often more readable than the else-if structure, and the else-if structure is more readable than nested if-then-else structures.

3. Defensive Programming.   Use error routines to capture an *out-of-range condition* in multiple selection structures. This means that we should include an else clause in else-if and case structures when out-of-range conditions are possible. Error routines are also used to trap I/O, range, and other run-time errors, as described in Section 6.4.

4. Optimization Notes.   A poorly designed algorithm is an important factor that contributes to excessive computer time. This factor is so important in certain applications that professionals in statistics, computer science, and other applied mathematical sciences like operations research have devoted extensive research efforts to improving the time efficiency of many algorithms. Consider the following regarding computational times.

a. An else-if or case structure is more efficient than a sequence of if-then structures, because the former exits the structure as soon as the first true condition is encountered, whereas the latter tests all conditions.

b. In ordering multiple conditions, if possible, place these in the order of decreasing likelihood of a true result. For instance, in the color example on page 254, we have an optimal ordering if red is more frequent than white and white is more common than blue. Do you see why? Over time, the processor will test fewer conditions (will exit the structure faster) if the most frequent colors are first in the list of conditions.

COMMON ERRORS

1. Incorrect Boolean Expressions. The same kinds of Boolean-expression errors singled out in Chapter 5 apply here as well.

2. Error-Tolerance Fixup. In situations where we need to test the equality (or inequality) of two real expressions, we should use the error-tolerance fixup first described in Section 5.5. For example, we should use

abs(RealExpression1/RealExpression2-1) < ErrorTolerance ☺

instead of

RealExpression1 = RealExpression2 ☹

where ErrorTolerance is a constant like *1.0E-9*. This ensures our accounting for the storage of *approximate* rather than *exact* real values. Check out Exercise 24.

3. Using the Wrong Structure. Make sure that you apply the proper control structure to the task at hand. All too often, we have seen students try to use a repetition structure instead of a selection structure, or vice versa. The confusion seems to lie in the fact that both types of structures use Boolean expressions as conditions. We need to focus on the overall task first: Do we need to repeat a body? Or do we need to select one or more alternatives? A yes answer to the first means we have a repetition structure; a yes answer to the second means we have a selection structure; a yes answer to both means we have a selection structure nested within a repetition structure, or vice versa. For example, in our menu-driven program Combo1, we had a primary task of repetitively offering a menu, entering the selection, and routing execution based on the selection. We handled this primary task by a repetition (repeat-until) structure. The routing task within the body of the repetition structure was solved by a selection (case) structure.

4. Logic Errors in Nesting.   Take care with the ordering sequence of conditions in else-if structures (see Note 4). Another common error in nesting is an inconsistency between our interpretation (what we intended) and the computer's (what it actually does). For example, suppose we state the following pseudocode.

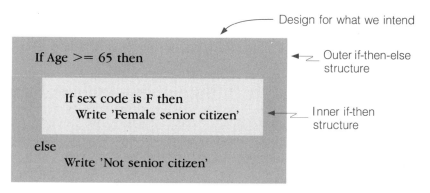

Design for what we intend

If Age >= 65 then
    If sex code is F then
        Write 'Female senior citizen'
else
    Write 'Not senior citizen'

Outer if-then-else structure

Inner if-then structure

Our intention is clear from our indentation and alignment. If the person is at least 65, then we wish to write the message 'Female senior citizen' when the person is female; else (if the person is under 65) we wish to write the message 'Not senior citizen.' Note that no action is taken (there is no corresponding selection) if we have a male senior citizen. Now, suppose we were to code this as follows.

Code for what we intend

```
if Age >= 65 then

    if SexCode = 'F' then
        writeln ('Female senior citizen')

else
    writeln ('Not senior citizen');
```

☹

Do you see the problem? Desk check a male who is 70 years of age. What happens? The message 'Not senior citizen' gets written. The first condition tests true, so the second condition is evaluated next. The second condition tests false, so the else clause is executed. The following alignment shows the computer's interpretation more clearly.

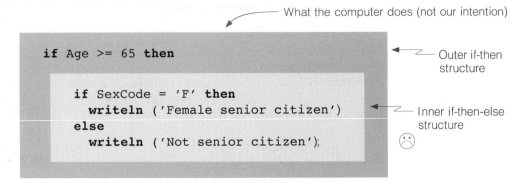

What the computer does (not our intention)

Outer if-then structure

Inner if-then-else structure

```
if Age >= 65 then

    if SexCode = 'F' then
       writeln ('Female senior citizen')
    else
       writeln ('Not senior citizen');
```

Our intent was to not write anything for males, regardless of age. The compiler pairs the **else** with the nearest preceding unpaired **then** (remember Note 3?), meaning that the processor "sees" an if-then-else structure nested within an outer if-then structure. We intended an if-then structure nested within the then clause of an outer if-then-else structure. Right? The following code fragment correctly codes our design.

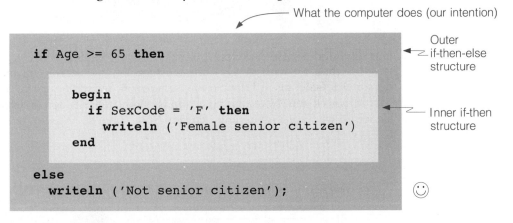

What the computer does (our intention)

Outer if-then-else structure

Inner if-then structure

```
if Age >= 65 then

    begin
       if SexCode = 'F' then
          writeln ('Female senior citizen')
    end

else
    writeln ('Not senior citizen');
```

The begin-end pair effectively isolates the inner if statement, so the **else** is now paired with the first **if**.

5. Misplaced Semicolon.   Remember that the semicolon is not part of an if statement. It's used to separate the if statement from any following statements (see Note 1).

6. Wrong Type in Case Statement.   Remember that the tested conditions in the case structure (the selector and case constants) must be ordinal (*integer, character,* or *Boolean* in our work up to now). If we were to use data type real or string, we would get the compile-time *Type mismatch* error message.

7. Verification.   The verification issues discussed in Section 5.5 apply to selection structures as well. In *empirical verification* make sure that the selected test data flow through all selections. For example, in our sample run of Combo1 in Figure 6.2, we deliberately entered menu selections that would take execution to each case, including the error routine in the else clause. Empirical verification for modular programs in facilitated by *top-down testing*, as first mentioned in Section 3.6. The process of adding and debugging a new module in Combo1 reflects the top-down testing philosophy (see Exercise 12g).

Logical verification might include *assertions* that relate to particular selection structures. For example, we might include the following documented assertion just before the case structure in program Combo1.

{Character variable MenuSelection stores F, C, H, or Q for proper routing; else MenuSelection stores incorrect character}

This assertion clearly shows four legitimate values for variable MenuSelection, four corresponding selections or routings, and an error routine for incorrect values. If testing shows incorrect case-structure behavior, variable MenuSelection should be watched when we trace execution.

REVIEW EXERCISES

EASIER	For the busy . . .
	1 2 12a
NORMAL	For the thinkers . . .
	3 4 5 6 7 8 9 10 11 12b–f 13 14 15 16 17 18 19 20 21 22
TOUGHER	For the hard CORE . . .
	12g 23 24

1. Write code fragments for each of the pseudocode-like descriptions below.
   a. If LastName is not CORE, then write "Where's Harvey?"; otherwise continue execution.
   b. If LastName is CORE, then write 'Harvey is my kind of guy'; else update Counter.
   c. If Credits are 12 or more, then Tuition is $1200, update FullTimeTuitionSum, and update FullTimeStudentCount; else Tuition is $100 per credit, update PartTimeTuitionSum, and update PartTimeStudentCount.

2. Write a *desk-check script* for each of the following.
   a. LegalAge is the integer constant 21, Count stores 50, and Age stores 18. What if Age stores 21?

```
AgeOk := Age >= LegalAge;
if AgeOk
   then writeln ('Entry permitted')
   else writeln (chr(7), 'Entry denied!');
inc (Count);
```

*b. Adjust is the real constant 1.5, RegularHoursMax is the integer constant 40, HoursWorked stores 50, and Rate stores 10.0. What if HoursWorked stores 40?

```
ExcessHours := HoursWorked - RegularHoursMax;
if ExcessHours > 0 then
    begin {Overtime pay}
        RegularPay  := Rate * RegularHoursMax;
        OvertimePay := Rate * Adjust * ExcessHours;
    end {Overtime pay}
else
    begin {Regular pay}
        RegularPay  := Rate * HoursWorked;
        OvertimePay := 0;
    end; {Regular pay and if}
GrossPay := RegularPay + OvertimePay;
```

3. In Example 6.1, modify the first code fragment so that the lower price is given only if the order size is 100 or more *and* character variable Code is D or P.

4. **Minimum value.** In Example 6.2, answer the following.
   a. Suppose a string value for CustomerAccount is read in along with Order-Size. Modify the if-then structure to also assign MinCustomerAccount as that customer account number that corresponds to the minimum order size.
   b. Write a new code fragment that also initializes and assigns MinOrderCost.

*5. **Maximum value.** Modify the code in Example 6.2 as follows.
   a. Initialize, assign, and output the maximum order size instead of the minimum order size.
   b. Same as part **a** in the preceding exercise, except work with the maximum order size.
   c. Same as part **b** in the preceding exercise, except work with the maximum order cost.

*6. Write and debug a program that...
   a. **Minimum value.** Implements the pseudocode shown in Example 6.2. Duplicate our desk-check run.
   b. **Maximum value.** Implements Exercise 5a. Use the test data given in Example 6.2.

7. In Example 6.3, revise the nested if-then-else structure to...
   a. Update CountFemale and CountMale.
   b. Update CountAtLeast65 (regardless of gender).
   *c. Update CountAtLeast 65 and CountUnder65.

8. Code or revise the following code fragments.

   a. If $b^2 - 4ac$ is positive, then write 'Two real roots exist'; if zero, then write 'One repeated real root exists'; if negative, then write 'No real roots exist'.

   b. If **ClassCode** is integer 1 then update **FreshmanCount**; if 2 then update **SophomoreCount**; if 3 then update **JuniorCount**; if 4 then update **SeniorCount**; otherwise write the message 'Class code *x* is incorrect'.

                                                  └ Ring bell   └ Value in ClassCode

   *c. In Example 6.4, rewrite the nested selection structure as a sequence of if-then structures. Any advantages to this approach over the original? Disadvantages?

   *d. Trap an inadmissible sex-code value in the last example within the if statement syntax box. Write the error message "Unrecognized sex code." Use an else-if structure.

   *e. Rework the preceding part using a case structure. Which approach do you like best? Why?

*9. **Table lookup: Prices.** Rewrite the first else-if structure in the else-if syntax box by including a count of the number of entries in each selection (as done in the second code fragment in Example 6.1).

*10. **Table lookup: Prices.** Rewrite the case structure in Example 6.5 to use declared constants **BreakPoint1**, **BreakPoint2**, and **BreakPoint3**, as done in Example 6.4.

11. Answer the following

   a. Can we rewrite the second example in the else-if syntax box as a case structure? Why or why not?

   *b. **Standard Pascal case structure.** Standard Pascal does not support an else clause in the case structure. Rewrite the code in the case-structure syntax box to conform to Standard Pascal. *Hint:* Nest the case structure within an if-then-else structure.

(L) **12.** **Menu application.** Answer the following regarding program Combo1 in Figure 6.4.

   a. Test drive Combo1 by duplicating the run in Figure 6.2

   *b. Develop a desk-check script for the sample run in Figure 6.2.

   *c. Revise the main body to use

```
until Quit;
```

   where **Quit** is a Boolean variable. Rerun the revised Combo1.

   *d. Revise procedure OfferMenu to use

```
MenuSelection := upcase(readkey);
```

   Rerun the revised Combo1. How does the user's entry differ from the earlier approach?

*e. Implement a while-do structure instead of the repeat-until structure. Which do you like best, and why?

*f. Implement an else-if structure instead of the case structure. Which do you like best, and why?

*g. Revise the program to include the following help submenu when Help is selected from the Main menu. This menu is reoffered until the user enters Q. Implement this version. Include new modules that get called when items 2 and 3 are selected.

    1   Description of main menu items
    2   Factorial example
    3   Combinations example
    Q   Quit this menu

(L) ***13.** **Tracing.** Duplicate the run in Figure 6.2 while using the IDE's debugger (Module A) to single-step trace execution and watch MenuSelection, Number, the factorial, N, K, and Combinations.

(L) ***14.** **Function Fac.** Revise function Fac within driver CkFac as follows.

a. Trap values in X less than zero by displaying an error message that says 'The factorial of negative values is undefined; absolute value used for' . . .

b. By trial and error, determine the maximum value in X that does not cause overflow for the factorial. Then trap values above this maximum by setting the value to the maximum and displaying the error message 'x is too large . . . The maximum value ? has been used instead . . . '

                  — Value you found   Value in X

*15. **Table line pause.** You might recall our discussion from Chapter 4 (page 154) regarding the problem of displaying long tables that scroll off the top of the screen. We now have a solution for you that's more elegant than those described earlier. The idea is to pause line output every, say, 20 lines. For example, given the test loop

```
for Line := 1 to Lines do
    writeln (Line);
```

we need to insert an if-then-else structure in the body that writes Line only if **ScreenLineCount** is 20 or less; else **ScreenLineCount** is reset and the screen is paused. **ScreenLineCount** needs to be updated within the then clause as well. Write and implement a test program that uses the above loop, suitably revised for a table pause every 20 lines. Input **65** for Lines in your test run.

*16. **Table lookup: Grade.** Consider the following table for a table lookup of character grades based on integer scores. Assume that 90, 80, 70, and 60 are the respectively declared constants BoundA, BoundB, BoundC, and BoundD.

Score	Grade
90 or above	A
80 but less than 90	B
70 but less than 80	C
60 but less than 70	D
below 60	F

    a. Code a nested if-then-else structure that assigns a letter grade to **Grade** based on **Score**.

    b. Same as part **a** except use an else-if structure. Do you like this better? Why or why not?

    c. Same as part **a** except use a case structure. Do you like this even better? Why or why not?

    d. Describe changes in parts **a–c** if Score were typed real. Any advantages or disadvantages here?

(L) 17.   **Error handling.** Test drive program CkRdInt in Figure 6.5.

    a. Use the test data described in Example 6.5. Also try your own test data.

    b. Make sure range checking is on by selecting the command sequence **O**ptions **C**ompiler **R**ange checking. What happens if you input the value **7654321**? Turn off range checking, recompile, and reenter this value. Now what happens?

(L) *18.   **Error handling.** Revise procedure ReadLnInt and its driver in Figure 6.5 as follows.

    a. Procedure ReadLnReal. Input and trap real values. Use **e**, **3.3**, and **3** as test input. How is **3** stored? As an integer or real value?

    b. Procedure ReadLnChar. Input and trap character values. Use **e**, **3.3**, and **3** as test input. Any conclusions?

    c. Procedure ReadLnStr. Input and trap string values. Use **CORE**, **e**, **3.3**, and **3** as test input. Any conclusions?

(L) *19.   **Revisit: Temperatures, Version 2.0.** Revise program Temp2 in Chapter 5 to trap noninteger input for Fahrenheit temperatures by calling procedure ReadLnInt. Input the following temperatures in your test run: **85.5**, **3w**, and **32**.

(L) *20.   **Revisit: HC ENGINE.** Revise Engine4 in Chapter 5 to...

    a. Drop engine size in cc as an input requirement. Let the program select engine size based on engine name.

    b. Call procedure PrepFile in Figure 6.6.

(L) *21.   **Revisit: HC METHsea.** Revise Exercise 19 in Chapter 5 to...

    a. Write a report describing the Home Base coordinate that minimizes total distance. Don't include nonoptimal coordinates in this report. HC just wants one report...the optimal one.

    b. Call procedure PrepFile in Figure 6.6.

(L) *22.   **Revisit: Function Power1.** Revise function Power1 from Example 3.3 by trapping inadmissible base values. If the base is zero or less, set the power function to zero and write an appropriate error message. Run CKPower1 using the
test data in Figure 3.5, as well as −2 for x and 3 for p.

(L) *23.   **Function Power2.** Revise function Power1 from Example 3.3 as follows.

    a. Change the typing on the power to integer. Use a for-do loop that varies
from 1 to the absolute value in the power. The for-do loop computes the
function value as a running product (as in the calculation of factorials). If the
power is zero or more, then the function value is equivalent to the final value
in the running product; else the function value is the inverse of the final
value in the running product.

    b. Write a driver to debug this function, and add the function to your utility
library. Evaluate the folllowing in your test runs: 2.0^3, 2.1^3, 2.0^{-3}, 2.0^0,
$(-2.03)^3$.

*24.   **Error-tolerance fixup.** Check out the problem with comparing the equality of
real values in Boolean expressions by implementing a program with the following design.

    Read three real values————— No fixup
    If **Real1/Real2 = Real3**
        then write 'No Fixup: Equal'
        else write 'No Fixup: Not equal'   Fixup

    If **abs(Real1/Real2/Real3 - 1) < Error tolerance**
        then write 'Fixup: Equal'
        else write 'Fixup: Not Equal'

If real approximations were not a problem, then the first if-then structure would
always evaluate to true for equal real expressions. The second if-then structure
always evaluates to true if the two real expressions are equal. Use an error tolerance of 10^{-9} and try the folllowing three sets of input: **0.25   0.25   1.0;
9.31   9.31   1.0; 1.0   2.0   3.0**. Comment on your results.

ADDITIONAL EXERCISES

EASIER	For the busy. . .
	25 26 27 30 32
NORMAL	For the thinkers. . .
	28 29 31 33 34
TOUGHER	For the hard CORE. . .
	35 36 37

25. **Revisit: Disk areas.** Revise Exercise 20b in Chapter 5 by dropping disk diameter as an input variable. Have the program look up the diameter based on the disk code.

26. **Revisit: Bank savings.** Revise Exercise 20d in Chapter 5 as follows.

   a. Offer a menu with three entries: the first compounding formula, the second, and quit.

   b. Use function Power2 in Exercise 23 above.

27. **Revisit: Econometric model.** Revise Exercise 21b in Chapter 5 to omit output tables. Instead, write a summary table that gives the name of each college, its maximum revenue, and the corresponding enrollment. In the table foot, display total maximum revenue and enrollment for the entire state system.

28. **Revisit: Text-file viewer.** Revise Exercise 25 in Chapter 5 as follows.

   a. Offer the user the option of either screen output or paper output. For screen output, pause every 20 lines (see Exercise 15 in this chapter). For paper output, print 50 lines per page. If you can, check out your printer's manual for a *page eject* control character; otherwise, end a page by printing a sufficient number of blank lines following the 50th printed line.

   b. Count the number of lines processed, and display its value at the very end. *Hint:* Check out the **eoln** function in Appendix F, or the *line feed character* (ASCII 10 in Appendix I) as the argument in the **chr** function.

29. **Revisit: Police car replacement.** Revise Exercise 30a in Chapter 5 by displaying in the table foot the best replacement mileage and its cost per K-miles.

30. **Revisit.** Revise one of your earlier programs using ideas from this chapter.

31. **Table lookup: Electra Appliances.** Develop a program for the pricing table in Example 6.4. Assume this program will be used by a person with minimal computer experience. (Translation: Pay careful attention to PC-style programming issues). This person sits at the keyboard, with a telephone headset, giving order-cost quotes over the telephone. (Rumor has it that FM station WROC plays a role in this operation.) At the end of the day, the main processing loop is terminated and a summary report is displayed. Items in the report include number of quotations (totals for the day and within each price category) and the sum of all order costs. Try the following test input for order size: **60, 120, 600,** and **1200.**

32. **Procedure RangeStat.** Develop a procedure that receives three real values and returns the minimum value, maximum value, and range (maximum value less minimum value). Test this procedure by writing a driver that outputs the three range statistics based on the following test input data: **6 7 8, 6.1 0.5 4.75, 15.13 10.78 0.0, −1 1 1**. Add this procedure to your utilities library.

33. **PIN confirmation.** Develop a program that interactively enters a PIN (Personal Identification Number, as in entering a password to access cash from a machine) and displays either the message 'Valid' or the message 'NOT valid'. Assume PINs are strings of four characters. Only digits or uppercase letters can be input, as in a telephone's push-button set. Valid PINs are stored in the following text file.

File of valid PINs

1942
6666
MOMA
RM77
HC42
CM52
61DR

Use the following test input: HC42 CM52 CN52 −. Note that the main processing loop terminates with a minus sign.

34.   **Quadratic roots.** A quadratic equation is defined by

$$y = ax^2 + bx + c$$

where *a*, *b*, and *c* are its coefficients. Many mathematical applications require the "roots" of this equation. By definition, a root is a value of *x* that when substituted into the equation yields a value of zero for *y*. The following familiar *quadratic formula* determines the appropriate roots.

$$x = \frac{-b \pm (b^2 - 4ac)^{1/2}}{2a}$$

Develop a program that calculates and displays quadratic roots for the following input values of *a*, *b*, and *c*.

a	b	c
5.00	6.00	1.35
1.00	10.00	−1.00
1.00	2.00	1.00
7.00	4.00	2.00

Your program should have three separate selections within a loop, depending on the value of the expression $b^2 - 4ac$. If this expression is negative, have the computer write "No real roots"; if the expression equals zero exactly, evaluate the single root using $x = -b/(2a)$; if the expression is positive, use the above quadratic formula to calculate the two roots.

35.   **SAT report.** Develop a program that
    a. Uses the data file shown below to generate the described SAT report.

Data File

Name	Class Code*	Math SAT	Verbal SAT
Test 1	2	550	630
Test 2	1	500	590
Test 3	1	620	750
Test 4	3	575	520
Test 5	2	620	530
Test 6	1	750	710
Test 7	4	470	420
Test 8	4	450	490
Test 9	2	520	550
Test 10	3	540	520
Test 11	2	560	600
Test 12	3	490	510
Test 13	2	685	670
Test 14	3	560	580

*1 = Freshman   2 = Sophomore   3 = Junior   4 = Senior

SAT Report

Class	Students	............Mean SAT............		
		Math	Verbal	Combined
Freshman	xxxx	xxx	xxx	xxxx
Sophomore				
Junior		↓	↓	↓
Senior	↓			↓
All Classes	xxxxx	xxx	xxx	xxxx

b. In the report table's foot, identify the class for each of the following: least students, most students, lowest combined score, and highest combined score. Trap any class-code errors by displaying an appropriate error message that includes the incorrect code and its associated name. Test this error routine by changing the code for test 7 from 4 to 5.

36. **Fibonacci numbers.** In 1202 Leonardo of Pisa (nicknamed Fibonacci, or Son of Bonacci) solved the following theoretical problem. Consider a starting pair of rabbits (male and female, of course) that produces a new pair at the end of one month. Allowing one month for maturation, each mature pair begets another pair of rabbits each month. How many pairs of rabbits will we have after one month, two months, and so on? Starting at time zero, there are no pairs of rabbits. Just after time zero, however, we have a newborn pair, which gives us

one (mature) pair at the end of the first month. At the end of the second month, we still only have one pair. This pair did its thing, however, and we have a newly arrived pair at the beginning of the third month, giving us two pairs at the end of the third month. At the end of the fourth month, we have three pairs—the original, their firstborns, and their secondborns. In the fifth month, we have two newly arrived pairs, one pair from the original pair (the still-at-it grandparents), and the other pair from the firstborns. This gives us five pairs at the end of five months. The story continues, giving us the sequence of Fibonacci numbers 0, 1, 1, 2, 3, 5, 8, 13, 21, ... Do you see a pattern? Each number (starting with the third) is the sum of the immediately preceding two numbers. Interestingly, it turns out that these numbers have uses other than animal husbandry, particularly in algorithms that search for optimal solutions in applied mathematics and in stock market cycles called Elliot Waves. We will not get that esoteric, so try your hand at a program that inputs the starting and ending positions in the sequence and writes the corresponding Fibonacci numbers. For example, if we input positions 6 through 8, we display the following output.

Position	Fibonacci Number
6	5
7	8
8	13

Try a run for each of the following position ranges: 1 to 20; 6 to 8; 1 to 2; 2 to 5.

37.   **Epidemiological forecasting.** Epidemiology is a branch of medicine that specializes in the causes, prediction, and control of epidemics. Epidemics due to communicable diseases, if left unchecked, can grow in ways that are often predictable by one or more mathematical models in statistics, biology, and diffusion models with differential equations (systems of equations having derivatives or instantaneous rates of change that describe the behavior of diffusion or spreading processes). Write and debug a program that offers a menu of growth formulas, as follows.

    1   Simple compound growth
    2   Simple exponential growth
    3   Limited exponential growth
    9   Quit

Simple compound growth is given by

$$F = S(1 + r)^t$$

simple exponential growth by

$$F = Se^{rt}$$

and limited exponential growth by the logistic equation

$$F = \frac{ke^{rt}}{k/S - 1 + e^{rt}}$$

where F = Forecast of number infected at time t
S = Starting number infected (at $t = 0$)
r = Rate of growth in the infected population
t = Time units from starting time, where starting time is $t = 0$
k = Carrying capacity, or upper limit (asymptote) on size of infected population as $t \rightarrow \infty$

Develop a program that offers the menu, inputs appropriate data based on the menu selection, and writes the forecast table shown below, where T is an upper limit on time (as input by the user).

Forecast Table

Time	Number Infected
0	xxxxxxxx
1	
2	
.	
.	
.	
T	

Use the following test data: $S = 35,000$; $r = 1.15$ (115 percent per year); $k = 200,000,000$; $T = 20$ years.[5]

---

[5]The data for S and r are Center for Disease Control estimates of the number of current (at the end of 1987) diagnosed AIDS cases in the United States. You might want to compare these predictions to those based on Public Health Service data: $S = 63,726$, $r = 0.418$. By the way, don't take the predictions seriously here; our models are far too simplistic for predicting the diffusion of AIDS.

Recursion

‡Optional, more advanced material. Skip without loss of continuity, study at this point, or wait until later.

Up to now, procedures and functions have called other procedures and functions, but not themselves. This module covers the self-calling and mutually calling capabilities of Pascal.

B.1   RECURSIVE CALLS

• • • • • • • • • • • • •

Let's start by surveying some concepts and terminology.

OVERVIEW

A procedure that calls itself is a **recursive procedure;** a function that calls itself is a **recursive function.** The call is a **recursive call,** and **recursion** is the act of executing recursive procedures or functions. If procedures or functions make calls to each other, as in procedure A calling procedure B and procedure B calling procedure A, then these are **mutually recursive calls.**

Recursive and mutually recursive calls have appealing uses in programming, as we will see. To illustrate, let's consider a function that calls itself, the most common form of recursion.

RECURSIVE POWER FUNCTION

In Example 3.3 we developed utility function Power1 to evaluate the power function having the algebraic form $y = x^p$, where x and p are real values and x is nonnegative. In Exercise 23 of Chapter 6 we suggested a version that assumes any real x and any integer p. Let's consider the evaluation of this latter version, where for now we assume p is nonnegative.

First, let's look at pseudocode for an *iterative* (loop) version of this power function.

> Initialize Product to x
> For 2 to p do
>   Product is Product $\cdot$ x
> Assign Product to y

For example, given that x is 2 and p is 3, we would evaluate the power function 2^3 as follows:

> Product is 2
>   Product is 2 · 2, or 4
>   Product is 4 · 2, or 8
> y is 8

Recursion offers an alternative approach to iteration, based on the following reasoning. The original function is given by

$$y = x^p$$

We can redefine and evaluate this original function by using (calling) the recursive function

$$y = x \cdot x^{p-1}$$

That is, the expression $x \cdot x^{p-1}$ is algebraically equivalent to x^p.

We can issue a series of recursive calls to the recursive function, with a successively lower power term at each call, until the power term reaches a *terminating condition* that defines a value for the recursive function. In this case the terminating condition is a power term of zero and the recursive function has a value of 1, called the *terminating* or *stopping case*. Then we can return our way back to the original function by returning successive values for the earlier calls.

Let's get concrete by *recursively* evaluating 2^3.

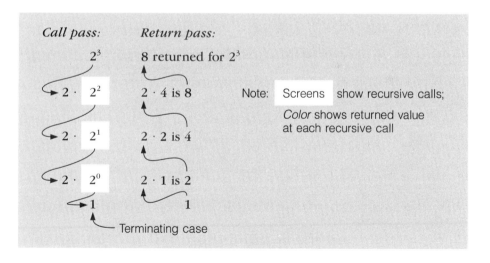

Note that the *call pass* works its way backward with successive calls to the recursive function, until it finds a value at its terminating case. At this point we begin a *return pass* that works its way forward to the original function, by successively returning a value for each call.

In pseudocode we might program this as follows.

> If p is zero
> > then y is 1   {Terminating case}
> > else y is x times y evaluated for x^{p-1} {Recursive case}

Here, the *recursive function* is the algorithm defined by the if-then-else structure. In the call pass, it recursively calls itself in the *recursive case* within the else clause, until it reaches the *terminating case* in the then clause. At this point, it implements the return pass by returning values to each of its recursive calls, until it reaches the original call.

That's the concept and design behind a recursive function. We let you program the recursive power function in Exercise 7. In the next example, we show a recursive function coded in Pascal for another familiar problem.

RECURSIVE FACTORIAL FUNCTION

In Example 4.4 we developed the utility function **Fac** for returning the factorial in integer X. As seen in Figure 4.3, the factorial is calculated iteratively. Figure B.1 shows utility function **FacR**, a function that recursively calculates the factorial for nonnegative integer values in X. Note that the *terminating condition* is X = 0 and the *terminating case* is a factorial of 1, or

FacR := 1

FIGURE B.1   Listing for Recursive Function FacR

```
function FacR (X : integer) : extended;

   { Utility determines factorial of X, or X! using recursive calls
     Receives nonnegative integer X
     Returns  extended FacR }

   { NOTE:  Use num. processing compiler directive $N+ or IDE menu sequence
               Options --> Compiler --> 8087/80287

               Use emulation compiler directive $E+ or IDE menu sequence
               Options --> Compiler --> Emulation  }

begin   {FacR}

   if X = 0
      then FacR := 1                    {Terminating case}
      else FacR := X * FacR (X-1);      {Recursive case}

end;    {FacR}
{------------------------------------------------------------------}
```

That is, the factorial of zero is one ($x! = 1$ when $x = 0$).

When the *recursive condition* values in X greater than zero is satisfied, the following *recursive case* is executed.

Function calls itself

FacR := X * FacR (X − 1)

That is, algebraically we have $x! = x \cdot (x − 1)!$ when $x > 0$. Note that the function identifier FacR appears as the left member of the assignment statement without its argument (as usual). Unlike the iterative version, however, the function calls itself in the expression that makes up the right member.

We have added function FacR to the Utilities Library.

Figure B.2 shows a trace of the call/return passes for the call FacR(3), which returns 6 as the factorial of 3. Note the following.

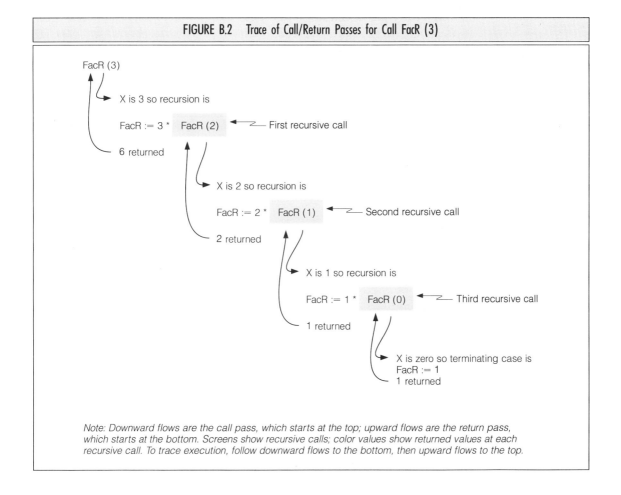

FIGURE B.2   Trace of Call/Return Passes for Call FacR (3)

FacR (3)

X is 3 so recursion is

FacR := 3 * FacR (2)   ← First recursive call

6 returned

X is 2 so recursion is

FacR := 2 * FacR (1)   ← Second recursive call

2 returned

X is 1 so recursion is

FacR := 1 * FacR (0)   ← Third recursive call

1 returned

X is zero so terminating case is
FacR := 1
1 returned

Note: Downward flows are the call pass, which starts at the top; upward flows are the return pass, which starts at the bottom. Screens show recursive calls; color values show returned values at each recursive call. To trace execution, follow downward flows to the bottom, then upward flows to the top.

1. At each recursive call, the problem is reduced to a simpler problem. Eventually, we get to the simplest problem, the terminating case.

2. Each recursive call is *nested* within the previous call. When the computer encounters a recursive call, it suspends its evaluation of the expression in the current call, because it can't complete the evaluation until it evaluates the next call. This nesting process continues until the last recursive call is evaluated at the terminating case. This completes the call pass. In the return pass the computer returns a value to its innermost recursive call. In the example, 1 is returned to the third recursive call. The expression containing the third recursive call is now evaluated, and it also returns 1. The expression containing the second recursive call is evaluated next, and it returns 2. The expression containing the outermost recursive call is now evaluated, and it returns 6 as the value in the original call to the recursive function.

3. At each recursive call the computer needs to keep track of parameters and local variables and to order these in a manner that's consistent with the sequence of recursive calls in the call pass. In the return pass, it needs to reaccess these data to complete the evaluations. It accomplishes this by reserving and using a portion of memory for a *data structure* called a **stack.** A useful analogy in describing the characteristics of a stack is to consider a stack of chips. We add to the top of the stack by placing or *pushing* a single chip. We remove from the top of the stack by taking or *popping* a single chip. These are the only operations allowed on the stack. These are the only defined operations that change the stack. Each recursive call pushes a "chip" onto the stack, and that chip is encoded with the current parameter and local values. As the return pass unwinds, successive "chips" are popped from the top of the stack.[1]

4. Try Exercise 3 to really understand recursive traces.

NOTE

1. Recursion versus iteration. Iteration and recursion are alternative approaches to solving the same problem. Iteration uses a repetition structure and recursion uses a selection structure. Iteration is usually faster and more memory efficient than recursion, because the need to keep track of a stack consumes resources. Recursion is usually more elegant, meaning that its coding is simpler and more intuitive.

---

[1]We take up stacks as a topic in Chapter 13.

SELF-REVIEW EXERCISES

1 2

B.2 MUTUALLY RECURSIVE CALLS

• • • • • • • • • • • • • •

Earlier we defined *mutually recursive calls* as module A calling module B and module B calling module A.

OVERVIEW

Mutual recursion has advantages that we will demonstrate shortly, but one problem immediately comes to mind regarding their declarations. If module A is declared before module B, and module B is called within module A, the compiler issues a compile-time error, since it can't check the validity of the call to module B. If we reverse the placement of the modules, we run into the same problem, since module B calls module A, and now module A follows module B. The solution? Assuming that the module B block follows the declaration of module A, we place the complete procedure heading for module B followed by the predefined directive **forward** just before the declaration for module A, as seen in Figure B.3.

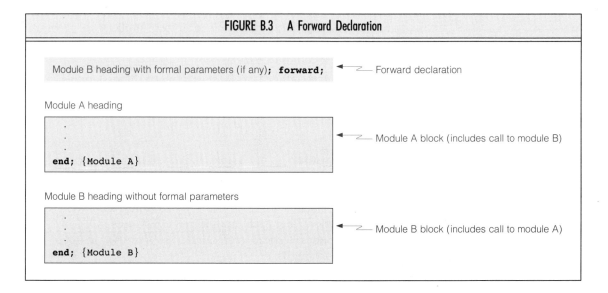

FIGURE B.3   A Forward Declaration

Module B heading with formal parameters (if any); **forward;**   ← Forward declaration

Module A heading

```
        .
        .
        .
  end; {Module A}
```
← Module A block (includes call to module B)

Module B heading without formal parameters

```
        .
        .
        .
  end; {Module B}
```
← Module B block (includes call to module A)

The first module B heading, together with the reserved word **forward,** is called a *forward declaration* for module B. It simply enables the compiler to check the correctness of a call to module B from within module A. Let's get specific.

TEMPERATURES REVISITED

Let's return to the temperature application described in Example 5.7. Figure B.4 shows a revised listing of the program listed earlier in Figure 5.7. We made the following changes to implement mutual recursion.

1. We replaced utility procedure ReadReply with two mutually recursive procedures.

   a. Procedure ReadRep is like the original ReadReply, except we replaced the while structure that traps incorrect replies with an if-then structure that calls procedure RepErr whenever the reply is incorrect.

   b. Procedure RepErr has the same statements as the original loop body in ReadReply, except (i) we replaced the reentry of Reply and the evaluation of the Boolean variable CorrectReply with a call to ReadRep and (ii) we issued a call to the predeclared procedure **delay** to hold the error message on the screen before the recursive call to ReadRep clears the screen.

2. We improved functionality by letting ReadRep strictly handle the input of Reply and its test for correctness, and letting RepErr just handle the error message. In doing so, however, we introduced mutual recursion. Thus, a forward declaration for procedure RepErr precedes the declaration for procedure ReadRep.

3. At the user interface, program Temp2B operates similarly to program Temp2. We ask you to test drive it in Exercise 4. To really understand Temp2B, trace its execution in Exercise 5.

4. We added procedures ReadRep and RepErr to the Utilities Library.

NOTE

2. Why mutual recursion? As in comparing iteration and recursion, mutual recursion has an intuitive appeal rooted in elegance. In our example, we replaced a while structure with a simpler if-then structure. We also better isolated tasks in the two modules. Finally, it's likely in some applications that each module has utility uses in its own right. The price? Greater overhead (computer resource use) in keeping track of modules and calls.

continued

FIGURE B.4   Listing for Program Temp2B

```
program Temp2B;

    {* * * * * * * * * * * * * * * * * * * * * * * * * * * * * * * * * *
     *                                                                 *
     *         Temperatures... Version 2.0B                            *
     *                       Same as Version 2.0 (Temp2) except uses...*
     *                       Mutually recursive procs ReadRep, RepErr  *
     *                                                                 *
     *         Inputs degrees Fahrenheit until reply is no             *
     *         Calculates degrees Celsius                              *
     *         Outputs degrees Fahrenheit and Celsius                  *
     *                                                                 *
     *         Modular structure                                       *
     *             |___ OpeningTasks                                   *
     *             |  |_____ Pause         *
     *             |___ ReadTemp                                       *
     *             |___ WriteScreen                                    *
     *             |___ ReadRep <---------> RepErr                     *
     *             |___ ClosingTasks                                   *
     *             |  |_____ Pause         *
     *                                                                 *
     * * * * * * * * * * * * * * * * * * * * * * * * * * * * * * * * *}

    {=========================== Declarations ===========================}

uses crt,                        {Needed for PC-style programming}
     OurUnit;                    {Needed for call to Pause}

    Variable declarations and procedures Pause, OpeningTasks,
    WriteScreen, ReadTemp, and ClosingTasks are not shown; they are
    the same as those in Figure 5.7.

{-------------------------------------------------------------------------}
procedure RepErr (var Reply : char);  forward;          {Forward declaration}
{-------------------------------------------------------------------------}
procedure ReadRep (var Reply : char);

    { Utility clears screen, reads Y/N reply, mutually calls RepErr if
      reply is incorrect, clears screen at end
      Receives nothing
      Sends Reply }

    { NOTE:  Requires uses clause for crt unit in host program
             Requires mutually called procedure RepErr
             Requires forward declaration before RepErr if placed
               after RepErr }
const
  Title = 'REPLY SCREEN';

var
  CorrectReply : Boolean;    {Flag or switch for correct replies Y, y, N, n}

begin  {ReadRep}

  clrscr;
  gotoxy (30, 5);  write (Title);
  gotoxy (29,13);  write ('Continue? (Y/N) ');  readln (Reply);
  CorrectReply := (upcase( Reply ) = 'Y') or (upcase( Reply ) = 'N');

  if not CorrectReply then RepErr (Reply);    {Mutually recursive call}

  clrscr;

end; {ReadRep}
{-------------------------------------------------------------------------}
```

If-then structure
replaces while-do
structure in
ReadReply

FIGURE B.4   (*continued*)

```
procedure RepErr;                              {Formal parameter list deleted here}

  { Utility beeps, writes error message, clears reply input field,
      mutually calls ReadRep
    Receives Reply
    Sends nothing }

  { NOTE:  Requires uses clause for crt unit in host program
           Requires mutually called procedure ReadRep
           Requires forward declaration before ReadRep if placed
              after ReadRep }

begin {RepErr}

  gotoxy (17,24); write ('Please enter Y or y for Yes, N or n for No');

  write (chr(7));           {Beeps speaker}
  delay (1000);             {Displays error message for one second}
  gotoxy (29,13); clreol; {Clears to end of line without moving cursor}

  ReadRep (Reply);          {Mutually recursive call}

end;   {RepErr}

  {============================ Main Body ============================}

begin  {Temp2B}

  OpeningTasks (Iterations);

  repeat
    ReadTemp (Fahrenheit);
    Celsius := 5 / 9 * (Fahrenheit - 32);
    inc (Iterations);
    WriteScreen (Fahrenheit, Celsius);
    ReadRep (Reply); ◄─────────── Replaces call to ReadReply in Temp2
  until upcase( Reply ) = 'N';

  ClosingTasks (Iterations);

end.   {Temp2B}
```

3. Why forward declarations? Forward declarations are demonstrably needed in mutual recursions. They also have other uses, however, as in rearranging modules in alphabetic sequence or by order of importance. In other situations, calls among multiple modules may require forward declarations, as in module A calls module B, module C calls module A, and module B calls module C. How would you declare these? Check it out in Exercise 6.

SELF-REVIEW EXERCISES

4

B.3   PROGRAMMING TIPS

• • • • • • • • • • • • • • • •

Consider the following tips to improve the design and style of your programs and to avoid some common errors.

DESIGN AND STYLE

Iteration is usually more time and memory efficient than recursion, as mentioned in Note 1. Keep this in mind if resources are limited on a particular system.

COMMON ERRORS

1. Stack Overflow. Turbo Pascal reserves a certain amount of memory for the stack at installation. A common run-time error message in recursion is *Stack overflow error,* meaning that the computer attempted to push onto the stack and ran out of stack memory. This would happen, for example, when evaluating a large factorial using FacR. A possible solution is to increase the stack size with the *Memory allocation sizes* compiler directive (see Appendix G). Make sure that the *Stack-overflow checking* compiler directive is enabled. Check out Exercise 1.

2. Infinite Recursion and Verification. We also have stack overflow if *infinite recursion* occurs. In *verifying* a recursive function or procedure, we need to ensure that the terminating case is executed at either the initial call or one of the recursive calls; otherwise, a series of unending recursive calls will ensue. The verification issues discussed in Section 5.5 also apply to recursion. For example, a *precondition assertion* for recursive function FacR is that X is a nonnegative integer. The call FacR(−3) would result in an infinite recursion. See Exercise 2 to find out what we can do about this.

REVIEW EXERCISES

EASIER	For the busy...
	1 4
NORMAL	For the thinkers...
	2 3 5 6
TOUGHER	For the hard CORE...

(L) 1.   **Factorial function.** We debugged function FacR in Figure B.1 using the driver CkFacR in the Examples Library. Run this driver and reproduce the run in Figure 4.3 for calculating the factorials of 5, 100, and 1000. How long does it take to evaluate the factorial of 1000 by recursion on your machine? How long does it take by iteration using program CkFac from Chapter 4?

(L) 2.   **Factorial function.** Run driver **CkFacR** and try to calculate the factorial of −3. What happened? Modify and debug function FacR to error-trap any negative value it might receive. If a value is negative, ring the bell, display the error message "Factorials of negative values are undefined...Factorial set to 1.", and set the factorial to 1.

(L) *3.   **Factorial function.** To better understand recursive execution, try single-step tracing the execution of FacR by using the IDE's debugger (assuming you studied Module A). Run CkFacR and calculate the factorial of 3. Watch values in X and view the Call stack. Relate the execution flow to Figure B.2.

(L) 4.   **Temperatures.** Consider the following.
     a. Run program Temp2B on your system. Input some incorrect replies.
     b. Describe changes we would need to make in Temp2B if we wished to place the block for RepErr before the block for ReadRep.

(L) *5.   **Temperatures.** To better understand mutually recursive calls, use the IDE's debugger (assuming you studied module A) to single-step trace the mutually recursive calls that are executed in Temp2B when incorrect replies are entered. Watch Reply and view the Call stack.

    *6.   **Forward declarations.** State how you would declare module headings and blocks for the three modules described in Note 3.

ADDITIONAL EXERCISES

EASIER	For the busy...
	7
NORMAL	For the thinkers...
	8 9
TOUGHER	For the hard CORE...

7.   **Revisit: Function Power2.** Rework Exercise 23 in Chapter 6 to develop the *recursive* power function Power2R, based on ideas in Section B.1. Use a selec-

tion structure to account for the cases $p = 0$, $p > 0$, and $p < 0$. Recall from algebra that the function is evaluated as $1/x^p$ when $p < 0$.

8. **Revisit: Fibonacci numbers.** Rework Exercise 36 in Chapter 6 by developing *recursive* function Fib for returning the pth Fibonacci number. Comment on the efficiency and elegance of the iterative and recursive approaches.

9. **Mirror, mirror...** Develop a *recursive* procedure that receives the number of characters to read, reads each character on one line without intervening spaces, and displays the characters in reverse order just under the input line. For example, the call Mirror(4) might show the following I/O.

    abcd
    dcba

The call Mirror(5) might show the following.

    54321
    12345

MORE TYPES

Take a peek at the program composition of Pascal programs inside the back cover. Up to now we have covered the **program** heading, **uses** clause, **const** declarations, **var** declarations, **procedure** declarations, **function** declarations, and the *main body*.

We omit **label** declarations and their affiliated **goto** statements from this book since they potentially allow the development of *unstructured programs*. This is because label declarations and goto statements are used to *unconditionally* transfer execution from one statement to another; that is, the flow of execution is not controlled by conditions (Boolean expressions) or by the precisely defined *repetition and selection structures* that we have used since Chapter 4. Consequently, it opens the door to writing programs that don't follow the top-down execution and control-structure philosophies that we outlined in Chapter 3.[1]

This chapter introduces **type** declarations to construct *user-defined data types* that are different from the predefined data types discussed thus far: real, integer, character, Boolean, string, and text. We also introduce the idea of an *abstract data type* as a means to practice data abstraction. Finally, we spend some time on the predefined *set type,* a data type that handles the concept of sets in mathematics.

7.1 OTHER ORDINAL TYPES

• • • • • • • • • • • • •

Take a look at the last table in Appendix D. (Did you put a paper clip on it like we suggested?) **Simple types** describe values that exhibit an *order* property, as in numbers and letters. In other words, we can arrange these values in some meaningful order, such as sorting numbers from low to high or alphabetizing a list of names. Simple types break down into the five **real types** as floating-point values and the **ordinal types** as listed values. *Listable values* are values that we can state in an ordered list, as in the list of grades

---

[1]To really see the problem, go to the library and look up an old book on FORTRAN or BASIC programming. Check out programs that use GOTO statements and try to follow the execution flow. Most likely you'll find a "spaghetti-like" flow that's difficult to follow and error prone. The structured programming philosophy was born as a "gotoless" reaction to this style of programming. There are error-handling situations where goto statements are acceptable in Pascal, but these are exotic and are not used in this book.

A, B, C, D, F. The ordinal types include **integer types** (all five of them), **Boolean type**, **character type**, **enumerated type**, and **subrange type**.

Each value in an ordinal type has a unique predecessor (except for the first) and a unique successor (except for the last). For example, the predecessor of integer 9 is 8; the successor of character c is d. The predeclared functions **pred** and **succ** return the predecessor and successor, respectively, of their ordinal arguments. For instance, **pred**(9) returns 8 and **succ**('c') returns d. Check these out in Exercise 8.

The *ordinal number* is the relative position of an ordinal value within its sequence of values. The first value in the sequence has an ordinal number of 0, the second value an ordinal number of 1, and so on. The predeclared function **ord** returns the ordinal number of its ordinal argument. An integer argument would return the integer itself, as in **ord**(9) returns 9; a character argument would return the character's ASCII value, as in **ord**('c') returns 99; a Boolean argument returns either 0 or 1, as in **ord**(false) returns 0. We ask you to explore the ord function in Exercise 8.

Do you see now why type real is not an ordinal type? A real value like 3.1 does not have a unique successor (3.11? 3.101? ...) or predecessor (3.0? 3.09? ...), since by mathematical definition these numbers are infinitely divisible. This also means they can't be assigned ordinal numbers (relative positions).

In our previous work we covered integer, character, and Boolean types; in this section we cover the last two of the ordinal types: subrange and enumerated.

SUBRANGE TYPE

A **subrange type** defines a new data type that is a subrange of values from another *ordinal* type called the *host type* or *parent type*. For example, the host type might be integer and the subrange type might be DayInWeek and defined by the subrange 1..7, where .. is the ellipsis symbol. The *subrange* always represents a list of constants. Remember that a *list* is an ordered set of values, as in the list 1, 2, 3, 4, 5, 6, 7. Put another way, the subrange is an ordered subset from the host type's list. Thus, the subrange 1..7 is an ordered subset from the list of all integers. The accompanying syntax box describes the declaration of subrange types.

The defined operations for a subrange type are the same as those for its host type. For example, if the host type is integer, then an integer subrange type includes the I/O, expression evaluation, and assignment operations common to integer types. Moreover, a subrange type is *type compatible* with its host type and with another subrange type of the same host type. A value of type subrange is *assignment compatible* with its host type and with another subrange type of the same host type, provided that the values of its type fall within the range of possible values for the subrange variable being assigned.

SYNTAX BOX

Declaration of subrange type... Declares subrange types in **type** section

---

Syntax .... **type**
            SubRangeType1 = MinValue1 .. MaxValue1 ;
            SubRangeType2 = MinValue2 .. MaxValue2 ;
            . . .
                    Subrange types   Subranges

Examples ...... **type**
            DayInWeek = 1   ..   7 ;   {Integer subrange type}
            Digit   = '0' .. '9';   {Character subrange type}
            Grade   = 'A' .. 'F';   {Character subrange type}

Explanation ... **type** is a reserved word that declares the type declaration section of the program. SubRangeType is a user-defined identifier that corresponds to the defined subrange type. The subrange type is a *list* of values that form a *subrange* from a *host type,* one of the ordinal types integer, character, Boolean, subrange, or enumerated. MinValue and MaxValue are constants that define the lower and upper bounds of the subrange. These may be *constants, declared constants,* or *constant expressions.* A variable of type subrange can store values only in the range defined by MinValue and MaxValue inclusive.

EXAMPLE 7.1   SUBRANGE VARIABLES

Consider the following declarations.

```
const
  BestGrade  = 'A';
  WorstGrade = 'F';

type
  Grade     = BestGrade .. WorstGrade;
  DayInWeek = 1 .. 7;
                                                Subrange types
var
  QuarterGrade, SemesterGrade : Grade;
  Day                         : DayInWeek;
                                  Subrange variables
```

Subrange variable Day has data type DayInWeek; its range of legitimate values is defined by *1..7*, which is a subrange of the host type *integer*. We know that the host type is integer because the declared minimum and maximum values given by 1 and 7 are integer constants.

Now consider the following case structure.

Subrange selector

```
case Day of
  {Weekday}  1..5 : writeln ('Day ', Day, ' is a weekday');
  {Weekend}  6, 7 : writeln ('Day ', Day, ' is a weekend');
end; {case}
```

The selector Day is a variable whose subrange type DayInWeek is permissible as a selector type (it's one of the ordinal types required for case selectors). Also note that we used subrange variable Day in the output list of the writeln statement. Because the host type for DayInWeek is integer, calls to the predefined I/O procedures permit Day as an actual parameter.

If the *range-checking compiler directive* is enabled, any run-time value for Day outside the subrange 1..7 would provoke a run-time error. This automatic range-checking feature guarantees that the value in Day is in the correct subrange by the time the case structure is executed. This is why we would not need to include an else clause (error routine) in this case statement.[2]

If we also declare an integer variable Number, the following statement is *assignment compatible*

```
Number := Day;  ☺
```

but not the following assignment whenever the value in Number is outside the range 1 to 7.

```
Day := Number;  ☹
```

The latter assignment would provoke a *range-check* run-time error.

Subrange variables QuarterGrade and SemesterGrade have data type Grade, defined over the character subrange *BestGrade..Worstgrade*. Note that *BestGrade* and *WorstGrade* are declared constants, given by the character constants *'A'* and *'F'*, respectively. The host type, therefore, is character. This means that operations, type, and assignment compatibilities that apply to character variables also apply to Grade variables. The legitimate range of values for variables QuarterGrade and SemesterGrade are A, B, C, D, E, and F. Any values outside this range would trip a fatal range-check error message, again assuming that range checking is enabled.

---

[2]Later in this section, we show an error routine that handles range-check errors.

ENUMERATED TYPE

An **enumerated type** defines a specific *list* of values as the data type. For example, we might declare data type Color as the ordered set of values Black, Gray, and Silver. Then we might declare variable StereoColor with data type Color. The following syntax box illustrates the declaration of enumerated types.

SYNTAX BOX

Declaration of enumerated type... Declares enumerated types in **type** section

Syntax ....type
        EnumeratedType1 = (List1 of values);
        EnumeratedType2 = (List2 of values);
    ...
         └── Enumerated types   ── Ordering follows sequence
                                              of values in list

Examples ......type
        Color = (Black, Gray, Silver);
        Grade = (A, B, C, D, F);

Explanation ...type is a reserved word that declares the type declaration section of the program. EnumeratedType is a user-defined identifier that corresponds to the defined enumerated type. List of values is a list of user-defined identifiers separated by commas that defines the ordered set of values associated with this type. The only values that an enumerated variable can store are those declared in the list. These values are treated as *constant identifiers* within their declared block. No constant identifier can appear in more than one list of enumerated values. *Note:* Predefined I/O procedures like **readln** and **writeln** cannot read or write enumerated values.

Note that the enumerated type is an *ordinal type,* which means that the list of enumerated values is ordered, as in Black (with ordinal number 0) is less than Gray (with ordinal number 1).

Relational operations in Boolean expressions and assignment operations in assignment statements are permissible for enumerated types, provided that the operands are the same enumerated type. As stated in the syntax box, Pascal's predefined I/O procedures do not support enumerated types; their I/O is accomplished by writing user-defined procedures, as we will see in the next section.

EXAMPLE 7.2   ENUMERATED VARIABLES

Consider the following program segment.

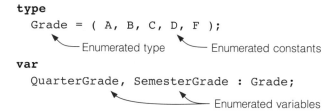

```
type
   Grade = ( A, B, C, D, F );
```
— Enumerated type   — Enumerated constants
```
var
   QuarterGrade, SemesterGrade : Grade;
```
— Enumerated variables

Do you see how variables QuarterGrade and SemesterGrade differ from Example 7.1? By treating these variables as enumerated variables instead of subrange variables, we're able to declare that the legitimate grades are A, B, C, D, and F, thereby eliminating grade E from the declared list of grades.

To illustrate the use of an enumerated type in a relational expression, consider the following.

```
if QuarterGrade <= B then
   writeln ('Dean''s list');
```

Note that QuarterGrade is an enumerated variable and B is an enumerated constant. If QuarterGrade were typed character instead (using **char** in its declaration), we would need to surround the character constant 'B' with the usual single quotation marks. The enumerated version is more literate, since our natural written language would not normally enclose B with apostrophes. The downside? We cannot I/O enumerated variables like QuarterGrade. Its value would have to be assigned by an algorithm, as we will see in Section 7.2.

RANGE CHECKING

As mentioned earlier, an advantage of subrange types is the detection of range-check errors, assuming the range-checking compiler directive is enabled within the IDE (**Options Compiler Range** checking) or within the program with {**$R+**}. Unlike Standard Pascal, Turbo Pascal disables range checking, because doing so optimizes executable object-code sizes and speeds. Disabling range checking, however, opens the door to run-time and logic errors for possibly using inadmissible subrange values. For this reason, Turbo Pascal suggests enabled range checking during debugging but not during implementation. *In our work, we suggest enabled range checking at all times.*

In Section 6.4 we discussed error handling, including the handling of range errors. At that time, however, we lacked a motivating example to show its implementation. Now that we have subrange variables under our belts, we can show how to detect and handle run-time subrange errors.

EXAMPLE 7.3   HANDLING SUBRANGE ERRORS

In Example 7.1 we worked with subrange variable Day, whose type is the declared subrange 1..7. The following code segment shows range-error handling for Day input values.

```
{$R-  Disable range checking}
repeat
  write ('Enter value in range 1..7 : ');  readln (Day);
until (Day >= 1) and (Day <= 7);
{$R+  Enable range checking}
writeln ('...Day is ', Day);
```

Note that we first need to disable range checking; otherwise, an out-of-range input value for Day would cause a fatal run-time error. The repeat-until structure then "insists" on a permissible value for Day, repeating input until an in-range value is entered. Afterward, we reenable range checking (if desired). A sample run might look like this.

```
Enter value in range 1..7 : 9
Enter value in range 1..7 : 0
Enter value in range 1..7 : 1
...Day is 1
```

If a debugged program includes range-error handling for its variables, disabled range checking during its implementation should be "fail-safe," from a range-error standpoint. Still, we suggest enabled range checking to be safe, unless memory and execution time constraints are critical.

GENERIC TYPING

Recall from our previous work that value parameters in procedure and function calls must be assignment compatible and that variable parameters must be the same type. For instance, in Figure 6.5, utility procedure ReadLnInt is designed to input an *integer* value. Thus, its variable parameter Variable is typed *integer*, and the actual parameter TestVar is also typed *integer*. But what if we wanted to input, say, a *real* value? As suggested in Exercise 18 of Chapter 6 we would have to create procedure ReadLnReal by suitably revising ReadLnInt. While this works, the approach is cumbersome and swells the size of utilities libraries.

Now that we have covered the type section, we have an alternative: *Generically type* the formal parameters. For example, we could use the generic type identifier GenType to type the formal parameter Variable. Then the calling module could declare GenType according to its needs. In our example, GenType would be declared as **integer** or **real**. For instance, the declaration

```
type
   GenType = real;
```

in the calling module would permit the input of real values. Let's get specific with...

EXAMPLE 7.4   ERROR-HANDLING PROCEDURES INPUTVAL AND READLNVAL, WITH GENERIC TYPING

In Example 7.3 we showed the following sample input sequence for entering a permissible value for Day.

```
Enter value in range 1..7 : 9
Enter value in range 1..7 : 0
Enter value in range 1..7 : 1
```

As seen, the input routine *handles range errors* by repeating input until the entry of a value is in the range 1..7; however, it does not *handle input errors.* For example, the entry of, say, q in place of 1 would generate a fatal *Invalid numeric format* runtime error. Let's get a bit more sophisticated by also handling input errors, as done earlier in Example 6.6.

Figure 7.1 shows program CkInVal as a revised driver from its predecessor CkRdInt in Figure 6.5. Note the following.

1. We converted our earlier input error-handling procedure ReadLnInt to its generically typed equivalent ReadLnVal. The only editing changes and insertions are shown in color. As seen, we changed the typing on the formal parameter from **integer** to GenType. We also disabled range checking by inserting ,R− within {$I−} and reenabled it at the end of the procedure.

2. The driver declares subrange variable Day and calls procedure InputVal to input its value. The actual parameter list includes Lo and Hi as range bounds for Day. As seen, the declared constants Lo and Hi are the constants 1 and 7, respectively.

3. Procedure InputVal is a new utility procedure that inputs a generically typed value, ensuring error handling for both input and range errors. Its algorithm is similar to that in Example 7.3, except it calls ReadLnVal instead of **readln.**

FIGURE 7.1 Listing for Procedure ReadLnVal, Procedure InputVal, and Driver CkInVal

```pascal
program CkInVal;

  {* * * * * * * * * * * * * * * * * * * * * * * * * * * * * * * *
   *                                                             *
   *          Driver checks error-handling procedure InputVal    *
   *                                                             *
   *             Inputs subrange value                           *
   *             Calls InputVal, which calls ReadLnVal           *
   *             Outputs value                                   *
   *                                                             *
   * * * * * * * * * * * * * * * * * * * * * * * * * * * * * * * *}

  {============================ Declarations ===========================}

uses crt;

const
  Lo = 1;  Hi = 7;               {Declare low and high ends of subrange}

type
  DayInWeek = Lo .. Hi;         {Declare subrange type}
  GenType   = DayInWeek;        {Declare generic type}

var
  Day : DayInWeek;              {Declare I/O variable}

  {======================= Procedure Declarations =======================}

procedure ReadLnVal (var Variable : GenType);

  { Utility reads value with line feed while handling input error
    Receives nothing
    Sends Variable  }

  { NOTE:  Requires uses clause for crt unit in host program
           Displays error message immediately to right of input value
           Generic type GenType must be declared in calling module }
 const
  Beep = chr(7);

var
  X, Y : integer;                       {Current coordinates of cursor
                                         ... at beginning of input field}
begin   {ReadLnVal}

  X := wherex;  Y := wherey;     {Predefined functions in crt unit}

  {$I-,R-  Turn off I/O error and range checking}

  readln (Variable);                      {Predefined function ioresult}
  while ioresult <> 0 do                   {returns zero if no I/O error}
    begin
      write (Beep);                        {Beep speaker}
      gotoxy (X,Y);  clreol;               {Clear input field}
      gotoxy (X+10,Y);                     {Cursor to right of input field}
      write ('<-- Please reenter');        {Write error message}
      gotoxy (X,Y);                        {Cursor to input field}
      readln (Variable);                   {Reenter value}
      gotoxy (X+10,Y);  clreol;            {Clear error message}
      writeln;                             {Issue line feed}
    end;  {while}

  {$I+,R+  Turn on I/O error and range checking}

end;    {ReadLnVal}
```

```
                      FIGURE 7.1    (continued)
```

```
{-----------------------------------------------------------------------}
procedure InputVal (LoBound, HiBound : GenType;  var Variable : GenType);

   { Utility reads value with line feed while handling range and
        input errors
     Receives LoBound and HiBound
     Sends Variable  }

   { NOTE:   Requires uses clause for crt unit in host program
            Calls utility ReadLnVal
            LoBound and HiBound define subrange
            Generic type GenType must be declared in calling module }

begin   {InputVal}

  repeat

    write   ('Enter value in range ', LoBound, '..', HiBound, ' : ');
    ReadLnVal (Variable);      {Utility procedure}

  until (Variable >= LoBound) and (Variable <= HiBound);

end;    {InputVal}

  {============================= Main Body =============================}

begin   {CkInVal}

  clrscr;
  InputVal (Lo, Hi, Day);
  writeln ('Echo..................... ',  Day);

end.    {CkInVal}
```

Also, the range-checking compiler directive is moved to ReadLnVal, because that's the procedure that actually inputs the value. InputVal handles range errors by ensuring that the value received from ReadLnVal is within its proper range; ReadLnVal handles input errors.

We have added ReadLnVal and InputVal to the Utilities Library as files READLNVA.PRO and INPUTVAL.PRO. In Exercise 6 we ask you to play with CkInVal, which is in the Examples Library.

SELF-REVIEW EXERCISES

1a–b   2a–b   3a–c   4a   6a–b

7.2   ABSTRACT DATA TYPES

• • • • • • • • • • • • • • •

In Chapter 3 we discussed the concept of *procedural abstraction* as freedom of thought about how a procedure accomplishes its task. Once a procedure is written and debugged, our only concern is what the procedure does for us and how we call it; we can forget about getting bogged down in the details of how it works. In this section, we apply the same concept to data types.

WHAT'S AN ADT?

Without saying so, we have been practicing abstraction with the predefined data types. Remember from our earlier work that the definition of a *data type* includes not only its legitimate values, but also the operations that we can perform on these values. For example, data type integer defines whole-number values over a specified range, together with operations like reading, writing, addition, and multiplication. We have been practicing *data abstraction* with data type integer by just having to be aware of its defined values and how to implement its set of defined operations. Presumably, we never put a thought into just how Turbo Pascal accomplished these operations.

A powerful feature of Pascal is its ability to let us create our own data types through declarations in the type section. If we also define specific operations that we can perform on a new data type, we have what's called an **abstract data type** (**ADT**). We can create an ADT by first declaring its type and then by developing functions and procedures that define its operations. Finally, we can consolidate its type declaration and all of its associated modules into a program. From this point forward, we can declare and manipulate variables for this data type by practicing the same kind of data abstraction that we practiced with the predefined data types. That's the conceptual part. Now, let's get specific with an application.

ADT GRADE APPLICATION

In Example 7.2 we declared enumerated data type Grade with values (A, B, C, D, F). We also mentioned that I/O operations for this data type are not predefined. Let's treat Grade as an ADT by showing procedures that read and write Grade values.

Before we get into the details, let's practice data abstraction by assuming that we have already created ADT Grade within a program. This program contains the declaration for type Grade as the grades given earlier and defines two legitimate operations for this ADT: a single-value read with a line feed using procedure ReadLnGrade, and a single-value write with a line feed using procedure WriteLnGrade. Program CkADT1 in Fig. 7.2 illustrates these opera-

---

FIGURE 7.2   Listing for Program CkADT1

```
program CkADT1;

   {* * * * * * * * * * * * * * * * * * * * * * * * * * * * * * * * * *
    *                                                                 *
    *   Driver checks ADT Grade procedures ReadLnGrade and WriteLnGrade  *
    *                                                                 *
    *           Inputs grade by calling ReadLnGrade                   *
    *           Outputs grade by calling WriteLnGrade                 *
    *                                                                 *
    * * * * * * * * * * * * * * * * * * * * * * * * * * * * * * * * * *}

   {============================ Declarations ============================}
uses crt;

type
   Grade = (A, B, C, D, F);           {Grade type}

var
   QuarterGrade : Grade;              {QuarterGrade is type Grade variable}

   {======================= Procedure Declarations =======================}
procedure ErrMessage;

   { Utility writes input error message at beginning of last row
     Receives nothing
     Sends nothing }

const
   Beep = chr(7);

begin   {ErrMessage}

   write (Beep);                                    {Beep speaker}
   gotoxy (1,25);                                   {Move to last row}
   write ('Unacceptable value; Please reenter...'); {Display message}
   delay (3000);                                    {Delay 3 seconds}
   gotoxy (1,25);  clreol;                          {Erase message}

end;    {ErrMessage}
{-----------------------------------------------------------------------}
```

continued

tions for Grade variable QuarterGrade. The following script describes sample runs of program CkADT1.

1. The first run gives the following I/O.

       Enter grade for Quarter ... A
       Echo..................... A

2. In the second run we intend an input of B, but incorrectly strike key N.

       Enter grade for Quarter ... N

   When we press the Enter key, we get razzed by the speaker, the error message

       Unacceptable value; Please reenter...

FIGURE 7.2   (continued)

```pascal
procedure ReadLnGrade (var GradeVar : Grade);

  { Reads Grade type value with line feed and error handling
    Receives nothing
    Sends GradeVar }

var
  GradeChar : char;        {Stores character input value for grade}
  Error     : Boolean;     {Stores true if input error; false otherwise}
  X, Y      : integer;     {Stores cursor coordinate}

begin  {ReadLnGrade}

  X := wherex;  Y := wherey;         {Store coordinate at input field}

  repeat
    Error := false;
    readln (GradeChar);
    case GradeChar of
      'A' : GradeVar := A;
      'B' : GradeVar := B;
      'C' : GradeVar := C;
      'D' : GradeVar := D;
      'F' : GradeVar := F;
    else {Error in grade}
        begin
          Error := true;
          ErrMessage;                {Call error message utility}
          gotoxy (X,Y); clreol;      {Clear input field}
        end; {Error routine}
    end; {case}
  until not Error;

end;    {ReadLnGrade}
{-----------------------------------------------------------------------}
procedure WriteLnGrade (GradeVar : Grade);

  { Writes Grade type value with line feed
    Receives GradeVar
    Sends nothing }

begin  {WriteLnGrade}

  case GradeVar of
    A :  writeln ('A');
    B :  writeln ('B');
    C :  writeln ('C');
    D :  writeln ('D');
    F :  writeln ('F');
  end; {case}

end;    {WriteLnGrade}

  {============================ Main Body ============================}

begin  {CkADT1}

  clrscr;
  write ('Enter grade for Quarter... ');  ReadLnGrade  (QuarterGrade);
  write ('Echo..................... ');  WriteLnGrade (QuarterGrade);

end.   {CkADT1}
```

appears for three seconds at the beginning of the last row on the screen, and the cursor is repositioned at the beginning of a cleared input field.

┌── Cursor

Enter grade for Quarter... █

If we now enter an allowable grade, it gets echoed. If we continue entering unacceptable grades, the error-handling response is repeated, until we get it right.

Now that we know the values and operations for ADT Grade, let's temporarily move from abstraction to specifics by studying the listing in Figure 7.2. Note the following.

1. Procedure ReadLnGrade inputs a single value of type Grade and sends it to the calling module. It does this within an error-handling routine that reinputs the value until it's acceptable. GradeVar is the variable parameter typed Grade. GradeChar is a character variable that acts as a surrogate for GradeVar. In other words, we actually enter a grade as a character value by using a readln statement. We then use a case structure to assign the proper allowable grade to the sending variable GradeVar. If the grade is unacceptable, the error routine in the case structure traps the input error by calling ErrMessage and repositioning the cursor in a cleared input field, using ideas from our work in Chapter 6. Note that the input routine is a repeat-until structure that repeats input until the input is acceptable.

2. Procedure ErrMessage is called by ReadLnGrade whenever an unallowable grade is entered. ErrMessage beeps the speaker, displays the error message described earlier, and erases the message after a three-second delay. The delay is implemented by the call **delay** (3000), where **delay** is a predefined procedure in the crt unit that delays execution for the number of *milliseconds* in its argument. We stored this procedure in the Utilities Library as file ERRMESSA.PRO.

3. Procedure WriteLnGrade receives a value of type Grade and uses a case structure to display its character equivalent with a writeln statement. Note that we don't need an error case here, because any value sent to this procedure will have been entered earlier by ReadLnGrade, thereby ensuring its integrity.

Once we develop the type and procedure declarations for ADT Grade, we can *conveniently* forget the algorithmic details of this ADT...we only need to know of its existence, its acceptable values, and its defined operations. In other words, we only need to practice the data abstraction illustrated in the main body of Figure 7.2. Any program that requires ADT Grade just needs to import utility ErrMessage from the Utilities Library, declare type Grade, and import ADT Grade's procedures (ReadLnGrade and WriteLnGrade) into the main block's declarations.[3]

SELF-REVIEW EXERCISES

9a

7.3 SET TYPE

* * * * * * * * * * * * *

In mathematics, the concept of a *set of elements* or a *collection of objects* is fundamental to subjects like geometry and functions. For example, the mathematical set $\{0, 2, 4, 6, 8\}$ represents a collection of the even digits, $\{a, e, i, o, u\}$ is the set of lowercase vowels, and $\{Red, White, Blue\}$ is the set of colors in the American flag. Sets have characteristics, like "Even digits" or "Colors in the American flag." Also, the ordering of elements is immaterial in a set. For instance, $\{a, e, i, o, u\}$ and $\{u, o, a, e, i\}$ are identical sets. Moreover, elements are unique in a set. For example, $\{0, 1, 0\}$ is an improper set since element 0 is repeated. The proper set is $\{0, 1\}$.

In Pascal, we can declare and manipulate sets as well. For instance, the set of even digits in Pascal is $[0, 2, 4, 6, 8]$, the set of vowels is $['a', 'e', 'i', 'o', 'u']$, and the set of colors in the American flag is $[Red, White, Blue]$. A **set** in Pascal differs from its mathematical counterpart as follows.

- Elements in a Pascal set are enclosed in square brackets instead of curly braces.
- The number of elements in the set must be finite (a maximum of 256 in Turbo Pascal).
- All elements in the set belong to the same *ordinal* type, such as integer (our even-digits example), character (our vowels example), or enumerated (our color example).

The **set (data) type** defines permissible set values and a collection of defined operations on those values. In this section, we focus on the declar-

---

[3]We could create a file named ADTGRADE.PAS that declares type Grade, procedure ReadLnGrade, and procedure WriteLnGrade. Then we could import this file into its client program in the usual way that we import our utilities. As we will see in the next chapter, a superior vehicle for defining and using an ADT is a *unit* that declares the ADT. The client program then imports the ADT through its uses clause.

tion of set constants and variables; in the next section, we complete the definition of the set data type by describing predefined operations on sets.

Set Constants

The next syntax box defines set constants and their declaration. Note that a **set constant** is a value defined by [List of elements], as in $[0, 2, 4, 6, 8]$. If we declare this set constant as the name EvenDigitsSet in the const declaration section, we have a **declared set constant.** Note that the set $[0, 2, 4, 6, 8]$ is permissible, but not the set $[0, 2, 4, 6, 8, 300]$. Integer element 300 has an ordinal number of *300*, thereby exceeding the upper limit of 255. Likewise, negative integers are not allowed as set elements, because their ordinal numbers are less than the lower limit 0.

Set Variables

We can declare set types and set variables according to the syntax box on the next page. Note the following.

1. The **base type** is an *ordinal type whose ordinal numbers must be in the range 0 to 255.* This means that base types are restricted to the ordinal types byte, Boolean, character, enumerated, and subrange. Note that type integer can't be a base type (its values include integers less than zero and greater than 255), but a subrange of integers can be (as long as

SYNTAX BOX

Declaration of set constants . . . Associates declared set constants with corresponding names in const section

---

Syntax . . . . const
        SetConstantName = [List of elements];

Examples . . . . . . const

		Ordinal type:
EvenDigitsSet	`= [0, 2, 4, 6, 8];`	integer
LowerVowelsSet	`= ['a', 'e', 'i', 'o', 'u'];`	character
USAflagColorsSet	`= [Red, White, Blue];`	enumerated
DigitsSet	`= [0 .. 9];`	subrange (of integers)
CapsSet	`= ['A' .. 'Z'];`	subrange (of characters)

Explanation . . . SetConstantName is a user-defined identifier and [List of elements] is the *set constant* as a list of elements enclosed in square brackets and separated by commas. Elements must belong to the same *ordinal type* (integer, Boolean, character, enumerated, or subrange). The *ordinal number* of an element must be in the range *0 to 255*. If zero elements are in the set, as in [ ], the set is called an *empty* or *null* set. Enumerated values in a set must be typed in a type section before their declaration in the const section.

SYNTAX BOX

Declaration of set variables... Declares set types in type section and set variables in var section

Syntax........type

    SetType = **set of** base type;

    var

    SetVariable : SetType;

Examples......type

    CapType = **set of** 'A' .. 'Z';

    var

    Codes : CapType;

type

    SetOfChars = **set of** char;

    var

    ScrabbleSet, Sentence : SetOfChars;

type

    Score = **set of** 0 .. 100;

    var

    TestScores : Score;

type

    Colors = (Black, Blue, Green, Red, Brown, Yellow, White);

    FlagColorType = **set of** Colors;

    var

    USflag, PRflag, CanFlag, UniversalColors : FlagColorType;

Comments:

Base type is subrange of characters given by all the uppercase letters; Codes can store any set of uppercase letters.

Base type is char, or all ASCII characters; ScrabbleSet and Sentence can store any set of ASCII characters.

Base type is subrange of integers 0 .. 100; TestScores can store any set of integer scores in the range 0 to 100.

Base type is enumerated set Colors; USflag, PRflag, CanFlag, UniversalColors can store any set of the enumerated colors.

Explanation... SetType is a user-defined identifier, **set of** are reserved words, and base type is an *ordinal type* whose values have *ordinal numbers* in the range *0 to 255*. SetType is the *set data type* whose defined set of ordinal values is in base type. SetVariable is a user-defined identifier of type SetType that stores set values.

the subrange is within the 0 to 255 limitation). Of the integer types, only type **byte** is a legitimate base type. Types Boolean and character are both ordinal and satisfy the ordinal number restriction, so **Boolean** and **char** are permissible base types. In fact, the range of ordinal numbers for characters is precisely the ASCII values 0 to 255. All enumerated and subrange types are allowable base types, as long as the ordinal-number limitation is observed.

2. Set variables can store any number of elements in the base type between the **empty set** or **null set [ ]** that contains no elements and the **universal set** that includes all values in the base type. In the first example, set variable Codes can be empty, or can store any *subset* of capital letters, such as ['S', 'M', 'L', 'X'], or can store all of the capital letters (the universal set).

3. As usual, we store values in variables by executing assignment and input statements. We illustrate these operations for set variables in the next two sections.

NOTE

1. Ordinal versus set values. Each *element* in a set is an *ordinal value* whose ordinal number is in the range 0 to 255. The integers 0, 2, 4, 6, and 8 are sample ordinal values and potential elements in a set. A *set value* or *set* is a set of elements, such as $[0, 2, 4, 6, 8]$. Set variables strictly store set values (not ordinal values).

SELF-REVIEW EXERCISES

10 11 12a–b

7.4 SET OPERATIONS

• • • • • • • • • • • • • •

The definition of a data type also includes an allowable set of operations on that data type. In this section, we take up the predefined operations on the set data type: set expressions, assignments, and Boolean expressions involving set expressions as operands.

SET ASSIGNMENTS

The accompanying syntax box describes set assignments. Note the following.

1. The set constants, types, and variables in the examples are consistent with the examples used in the two preceding syntax boxes.

2. To manipulate and modify the value in a set variable, we first have to *initialize* the set variable through an assignment statement. Typical initializations include the *empty set* and *universal set*, as seen in the initializations for Codes and UniversalColors in the syntax box.

3. As usual, the simplest expressions are constants and variables. We also have set expressions that include set operators, as explained next.

SET OPERATORS

A **set expression** is either a set constant, set variable, or a combination of these as operands for one or more set operators. The **set operators** are defined in Table 7.1. Study the examples and note the following.

1. Take care with the ordering of operands in the difference set operation, because this may affect the result. For instance, if we were to reverse the operands in the third example, the result would be the set [6, 8]. Right? The intersection and union operators are said to have the *commutative property,* meaning that the ordering of their operands does not affect the result. For example, Operand1 * Operand2 always gives the same result as Operand2 * Operand1. To summarize, the set operators * and + are commutative; the set operator − is not.

2. *Operator-precedence* and *left-to-right rules* apply to the evaluation of set expressions as they do to the evaluation of arithmetic expressions. Thus, intersection has a higher precedence than union or difference. Union and difference have the same precedence. For example, try evaluating the following before taking a peek at the answer in the footnote.

$$[0, 2, 4] + [4, 6, 8] * [8]^4$$

3. The union operator is very commonly used to build a set by inserting new elements. For instance, suppose that set variable Codes has uppercase letters as its base type and that character variable Code stores X. As-

---

[4] The result [0, 2, 4, 8] is determined as follows.

$[0, 2, 4] + [4, 6, 8] * [8]$
$[0, 2, 4] + [8]$
$[0, 2, 4, 8]$

You didn't answer [8], did you? We would get this incorrect result if we were to perform the union operation before the intersection operation.

SYNTAX BOX

Set assignment statement... Evaluates set expression and places resulting set value in set variable

Syntax........SetVariable := Set expression;

Examples......Codes := [];

```
ScrabbleSet := ['A' .. 'Z', 'a' .. 'z'];

TestScores := [0, 50, 100];

UniversalColors := [Black .. White];

USflag := USAflagColorsSet;

PRflag := USflag;
```

Results:

Empty set placed in Codes

Set of lowercase and uppercase letters placed in ScrabbleSet

Set value [0, 50, 100] placed in TestScores

Universal set of enumerated colors (see p. 322) placed in UniversalColors

Declared set constant USAflagColorsSet, or [Red, White, Blue] (see p. 321), placed in USflag

Set value in USflag placed in PRflag

Explanation... SetVariable is a set variable, := is the assignment operator, and Set expression is a set constant, set variable, or one or more of the forms shown in Table 7.1. Set expression is *assignment compatible* with SetVariable if (1) their set types are identical or (2) their base types are assignment compatible and all elements in the value of Set expression are within the base type of SetVariable.

Table 7.1   Set Operators[†]

Set Operator	Operand1 . . . . Operation Operand2			Sample Operation	Resulting Value
*	*Intersection of two sets* Set containing elements that are in both Operand1 and Operand2			[0, 2, 4] * [4, 6, 8]	[4]
+	*Union of two sets* Set containing elements that are in Operand1 or Operand2 or both			[0, 2, 4] + [4, 6, 8]	$[0, 2, 4, 6, 8]$
–	*Difference of two sets* Set containing elements that are in Operand1 but not Operand2			[0, 2, 4] – [4, 6, 8]	$[0, 2]$

[†]Operands are sets (set values) based on any legitimate set expression; operands must be *type compatible*—that is, both are set types with type-compatible base types.

suming that Codes currently stores ['S', 'M', 'L'], then execution of the assignment statement

```
Codes := Codes + [Code];
```

changes the value in Codes to ['S', 'M', 'L', 'X']. In other words, we just added a new element to the set in Codes. Note that Code and the elements in Codes have the same type (character) and the element 'X' in Code is within the declared base type for Codes (uppercase letters).

NOTE

2. On a very, very common error. Do you see anything wrong with the following assignment statement, where Codes is a set variable with base-type capital letters?

```
Codes := Codes + 'A';
```

The expression in the right member is type incompatible since 'A' is *type character* and Codes is a *set type*. We have to enclose 'A' in square brackets, giving us the required set constant.

```
Codes := Codes + ['A'];
```

BOOLEAN EXPRESSIONS

In Chapter 5 we covered *relational expressions* having *relational operators* and surrounding integer, Boolean, character, string, or real operands. Table 7.2

Table 7.2 Relational Operators Having Set Operands†

Relational Operator	Relational Expression Operand1 / Operator / Operand2	Sample Relational Expression	Resulting Boolean Value
=	*Equality of two sets* True if both sets have identical elements; false otherwise	[0, 1] = [1, 0] [0, 1] = [0, 2] [0, 1] = [0, 1, 2]	True False False
<>	*Inequality of two sets* True if both sets do not have identical elements; false otherwise	[0, 1] <> [1, 0] [0, 1] <> [0, 2] [0, 1] <> [0, 1, 2]	False True True
<=	*First set subset of second set* True if every element in first set is also an element in second set; false otherwise	[0, 1] <= [1, 0] [0, 1] <= [0, 2] [0, 1] <= [0, 1, 2]	True False True
>=	*First set superset of second set* True if every element in second set is also an element in first set	[0, 1] >= [1, 0] [0, 1] >= [0, 2] [0, 1] >= [0, 1, 2]	True False False
in	*First operand member in set of second operand* True if the ordinal value in Operand1 is a member in the set described by Operand2; false otherwise	1 **in** [0 .. 2] Letter **in** ['a', 'e', 'i', 'o', 'u'] ↳ stores x	True False

†Operations =, <>, <=, and >= have set operands that must be type compatible; the left operand in operator **in** is an ordinal type that's type compatible with the base type of the set represented by the right operand.

describes the relational operators that operate on set operands. Study the examples and note the following.

1. The first four relational operators have arithmetic and character counterparts. In our present work, all operands for these relational operators are set expressions.
2. The reserved word **in** is a nifty little relational operator that's specific to sets. It's often called the *set-membership operator,* because its relational expression tests whether or not the ordinal value on the left is a member of the set on the right. This is a very useful Boolean expression, as we illustrate in the next example.

EXAMPLE 7.5   ERROR ROUTINE FOR CORRECT REPLY

The following code segment shows how we might ensure the input of a correct Y/N reply, where Reply is a character variable and CorrectReply is the declared set constant ['Y', 'y', 'N', 'n'].

```
repeat
   write ('Continue? (Y/N) ');   readln (Reply);
until Reply in CorrectReply;
```

Thus, input is repeatedly requested until the reply is correct. Compare this approach to that in Figure 5.7. This approach is more elegant, don't you think?

SELF-REVIEW EXERCISES

13 14 15 16 17

7.5   SET I/O

• • • • • • • • • • • • • •

Pascal's I/O procedures (**read, readln, write, writeln**) do not process set values. In this section, we show our own procedures for reading and writing set values.

APPROACH

The general approach for reading a set value is as follows.

1. Read an element into an ordinal variable having an appropriate base type (like **byte** or **char**) using a read or readln statement.
2. If this element is a member of the universal set defined by the base type, add this element to the set being read using the union operation.
3. Repeat steps 1 and 2 while more elements need to be input.

Note that the set value is not read in as a whole; rather, we read in individual members in the set one at a time, as base-type values, and build the set as we go.

To write a set value we implement the following general approach: Use a loop to systematically consider each ordinal value in the universal set defined by the base type. In the body of the loop, use a selection structure (like if-then-else or case) to determine if the ordinal value in the universal set is a member in the set being written. If so, use a write or writeln statement to write the ordinal value (which is a confirmed set member). As in the read operation, we don't output the set value as a whole; rather, we output individual members in the set one at a time, as ordinal values.

Let's get specific . . .

APPLICATION

Let's work with an application in the context of the software development cycle.

Requirements

We wish to read a set of codes on the same input line, with no intervening spaces. Each code is a single character, taken from the universal set of upper-case letters. We terminate input with the period (dot) character. The read operation for the set includes a line feed at the end. If one or more input values are not in the base type, let's write an error message to that effect. Let's also write the set of codes that were input, with a line feed at the end of the write operation. Members of the set are written on the same output line, with a space between each. The user interface is "bare bones," with just a simple screen clear, title, input prompt, and output label. To summarize . . .

- Output data are the elements in the set of codes.
- Input data are the candidate elements in the set of codes.
- Constant data are the title, the period sentinel, and the set of universal codes (uppercase letters).
- Computational data include the set of codes that are built up from legitimate input codes.

Design

Based on the requirements, the user interface shown in Figure 7.3 is straight-forward. In the I/O, note that the illegal input lowercase s provokes an error message and does not appear as a member in the written set of codes. Let's work with three modules, based on the design algorithms below.

Program SetIO

> Clear screen
> Write title
> Read codes   (Refined below)
> Write codes   (Refined below)

Procedure ReadCodes

> Initialize codes to empty set ◄──────────────── Set assignment that initializes
> Initialize code error flag to false
> Read character code
> While not last code do
>   If code is legitimate (within universal set) ◄─── Set membership test
>   then add code to code set ◄──────────── Set assignment that builds set with union operation
>   else set code error flag to true
>   Read character code
> If code error then write error message
> Issue line feed

Procedure WriteCodes

> For each ordinal value in universal set do
>   If ordinal value is in code set then write value ── Set membership test
> Issue line feed

FIGURE 7.3   Sample I/O for Program SetIO

```
SET OF CODES I/O

Enter set of codes, ending with . ===> sSMLX.
   Incorrect code(s) in sequence!

Entered legitimate set of codes....... L M S X
```

Note that ReadCodes and WriteCodes are consistent with the general read/write approaches to sets that we described earlier. In ReadCodes, each code is input into a character variable and the set of codes is stored in a set variable. The universal set is the set of legitimate codes, or uppercase letters in this example. ReadCodes sends the set variable to the main algorithm in SetIO. WriteCodes receives the set variable and displays its value.

Code

Figure 7.4 shows the listing for this sample program. Note the following.

1. In the program...

   a. CapLetters is a subrange type (of capital letters from host type char) and SetOfCaps is the set data type with base type CapLetters.

   b. Codes is the set variable whose value we read and write. Its type is SetOfCaps. Codes is the actual parameter in the procedure calls. We also use it as the formal parameter in the headings for procedures ReadCodes and WriteCodes.

2. In procedure ReadCodes...

   a. The declared constant LegitCodes is the universal set of legitimate codes (uppercase letters).

   b. We initialize set variable Codes to the null set, a necessary operation before we can build the set of codes.

   c. Potential elements in the set are read individually into character variable Code.

   d. If a character in Code is in the legitimate set of codes (the universal set), the set stored in Codes is built up (added to) by the assignment statement that uses the union operator.

3. In procedure WriteCodes, the for-do loop repeats for each capital letter. The if-then structure determines if the capital letter is a member in the set of codes. If affirmative, the capital letter is written using a write statement.

Test

Figure 7.3 shows one of the test runs of program SetIO. In Exercise 20a we ask you to try other test data.

NOTE

3. Initialize set variable before building set. Don't forget to initialize a set variable before adding members to its set; otherwise we get a subtle logic error (see Exercise 20b to find out).

FIGURE 7.4   Listing for Program SetIO

```pascal
program SetIO;

   {* * * * * * * * * * * * * * * * * * * * * * * * * * * * * * * * *
    *                                                               *
    *           Set I/O Application                                 *
    *                                                               *
    *              Inputs set of codes from universal code set A .. Z *
    *              Outputs set of codes                             *
    *                                                               *
    *              Modular structure                               *
    *                 |___ ReadCodes                               *
    *                 |___ WriteCodes                              *
    *                                                               *
    * * * * * * * * * * * * * * * * * * * * * * * * * * * * * * * * *}

   {============================ Declarations ===========================}

uses crt;

const
   Title = 'SET OF CODES I/O';

type
   CapLetters = 'A' .. 'Z';          {Type CapLetters is subrange of chars.}
   SetOfCaps  = set of CapLetters;   {Type SetOfCaps is set of cap letters}

var
   Codes : SetOfCaps;                {Set variable Codes has type SetOfCaps}

   {======================= Procedure Declarations =======================}

procedure ReadCodes (var Codes : SetOfCaps);

   { Reads set of codes into set variable Codes having type SetOfCaps;
        writes error message if one or more codes incorrect, and issues
        line feed after all codes are input
     Receives nothing
     Sends Codes }

const
   Quit       = '.';                 {Quit input with sentinel character period}
   LegitCodes = ['A' .. 'Z'];        {Declare constant set of legitimate codes}
   NullSet    = [];                  {Declare empty set}

var
   Code    : char;                   {Character code used in input}
   CodeErr : Boolean;                {False if no error in code input;
                                        otherwise true}

begin   {ReadCodes}

   Codes   := NullSet;               {Initialize Codes to empty set}
   CodeErr := false;                 {Assume no incorrect code input}

   write ('Enter set of codes, ending with ', Quit, ' ===> ' );
   read (Code);
   while Code <> Quit do
     begin
       if Code in LegitCodes
         then Codes := Codes + [Code]    {Build set from legit input codes}
         else CodeErr := true;
       read (Code);
     end;   {while}
```

FIGURE 7.4   *(continued)*

```
    if CodeErr then
      writeln ('  Incorrect code(s) in sequence!');

    writeln;                                      {Issue line feed}

  end;    {ReadCodes}
{----------------------------------------------------------------------}
procedure WriteCodes (Codes : SetOfCaps);

   { Writes set of codes in set variable Codes having type SetOfCaps; places
       blank between each code and issues line feed after all codes are
       written
     Receives Codes
     Sends nothing }

var
   CapLetter : char;

begin  {WriteCodes}

   for CapLetter := 'A' to 'Z' do      {Examine all cap letters}
     if CapLetter in Codes then
       write (CapLetter, ' ');         {Write code in set of codes}

   writeln;                            {Issue line feed}

end;    {WriteCodes}

   {============================ Main Body ============================}

begin  {SetIO}

   clrscr;
   writeln (Title);
   writeln;
   ReadCodes  (Codes);
   write ('Entered legitimate set of codes....... '); WriteCodes (Codes);

end.    {SetIO}
```

SELF-REVIEW EXERCISES

20a–d

7.6   Programming Tips

• • • • • • • • • • • • •

Consider the following tips to improve the design and style of your programs
and to avoid some common errors.

DESIGN AND STYLE

1. Literacy.   Subrange, enumerated, and set types improve program clarity by giving descriptive meaning to subranges (as in DayInWeek), lists (as in Color), and sets (as in SetOfCaps).

2. Defensive Programming.   Trap potential run-time or logic errors with error-handling procedures (Examples 7.3 and 7.4), else clauses in case structures (procedure ReadLnGrade in Figure 7.2), and set membership tests (Example 7.5 and the if statement in procedure ReadCodes in Figure 7.4).

3. Generic Versus Specific Typing.   Consider *generic typing* in the formal parameter lists of utilities that can flexibly handle different data types, as done in procedures ReadLnVal and InputVal in Figure 7.1. These procedures can input a value of any data type that's also supported by the read and readln procedures, without any changes to the procedures themselves. In addition, they handle input and range errors. *Specific typing,* as in ReadLnInt in Figure 6.5, is warranted whenever a calling module requires separate calls with different parameter data types. For example, if a client program or module needs to use our read utility to enter an integer value with one call and a real value with another call, specific utilities like ReadLnInt and ReadLnReal are appropriate.

4. ADTs.   Think abstract data types when working with nonstandard data types that have limited predefined operations, such as enumerated type Grade in Figure 7.2. Our implementation of an ADT in this chapter is cumbersome, requiring the actual incorporation of the ADT's type and module declarations in the client program. The best approach uses a unit to declare the ADT, as we will see in the next chapter.

5. Set Elegance.   The use of sets in certain Boolean expressions is more elegant than the nonset alternatives. Judge for yourself, given the following two equivalent Boolean expressions for testing that an integer value is within a certain range defined by lower and upper limits.

```
(IntVar >= LowerLimit) and (Intvar <= UpperLimit)  ☹
```
versus

```
IntVar in [LowerLimit .. UpperLimit]          ☺
```

Example 7.5 suggests similar elegance.

6. Set Element Sequencing.   To improve readability, we usually list set elements in their ordinal sequence. For example, the following sets are equivalent, but which version is more readable?

['i', 'u', 'a', 'o', 'e'] ☹

versus

['a', 'e', 'i', 'o', 'u'] ☺

7. Structured Data Type. You might recall from Note 4 in Chapter 4 that a **data structure** is a collection of related data that are arranged in a meaningful pattern or structure. We can decompose a data structure into its individual data elements and manipulate these data elements using defined operations. A set is a data structure, where each element is an ordinal data value. If we take a data structure and declare its data type and name, we have a **structured data type.** Thus, the set data type is an example of a structured data type. A variable whose type is a structured data type is called a **structured variable.** Set variables are examples of structured variables.

In the software development cycle, we need to consider the structure of our data. For example, should we treat lowercase vowels as a set or as individual characters? The former is a data structure, the latter is not. If we conceptualize data as a data structure, we have to decide if we need a structured data type. For instance, if we need to build a set, we should declare a structured data type and set variable, as in set variable Codes with set type SetOfCaps in Figure 7.4. The choice we make has implications for how we manipulate the data. We will come back to this issue when we cover other data structures in the book.

COMMON ERRORS

1. Range Errors. Range errors are common when working with subrange types. Make sure that the range-checking compiler directive is active, to detect range errors. Avoid range errors altogether by programming defensively, as done in Examples 7.3 and 7.4.

2. Type Mismatch. An attempt to unite an ordinal value to a set value gives a *Type mismatch* compile-time error. Reread Note 2.

3. Spacing Out on Initialization. Don't forget to initialize set variables before performing any set operations; otherwise we're looking at a cunning logic error. Reread Note 3, and do check out Exercise 20b.

SELF-REVIEW EXERCISES

22

REVIEW EXERCISES

EASIER   For the busy...
1a–b 2a–b 3a–c 6a–b 10 11 12 16 20a 22

NORMAL   For the thinkers...
1c 2c 3d–f 4 5 6c 7 8a–c 9 13 14 15 17 20b–e

TOUGHER   For the hard CORE...
8d 18 19 20f 21

1. Write down type and var declarations for the following:
  a. Variable Code with data type LowLetter consisting of the lowercase letters in the English alphabet.
  b. Variable Day with data type DayName consisting of the days of the week Sun, Mon,..., Sat.
  *c. Modify part **b** to include type Weekday, running from Monday to Friday. Also declare variable Workday having type Weekday.

2. In Example 7.1...
  a. Can we use a subrange type for Grade if the legitimate grades are A, B, C, D, and F (no E)? Explain.
  b. Suppose variables Day and Days are both typed DayInWeek. Indicate output for the following if we enter 3 in Days. What if we enter 9?.

```
write ('Enter days'); readln (Days);
for Day := 1 to Days do
    write (Day :3);
```

  *c. Write a code fragment that displays Excellent for a semester grade of A, Good for B, OK for C, Poor for D, and UhOh! for F.

3. In Example 7.2...
  a. Suppose the legitimate grades are A, B, C, D, F, I, S, and U. State the new declaration for type Grade.
  b. Declare type ItemCode as the enumerated codes F, X, and Y. Is there a problem if this type is declared in the same block as type Grade? Explain.
  c. Is anything wrong with the following assignment?

    QuarterGrade := A;

  What do you think would happen if we replace A with G?
  *d. Suppose passing grades are A, B, and C. Declare type PassingGrade and variable ScholarshipGrade with type PassingGrade.
  *e. Rework the preceding part if S is also a passing grade.

*f. Write a code fragment that assigns 5000 to integer variable Scholarship if ScholarshipGrade is A, 3000 if B, and 1000 if C.

4. Write code fragments for each of the pseudocode-like descriptions below. In doing so, make sure that your coding is as literate as possible. Also, select what you believe to be the best selection structure, but indicate alternative coding (if any). Include type and variable declarations.

a. Month is an integer subrange variable defined over the subrange 1..12. Season is an enumerated variable typed Seasons. If Month is 1, 2, or 12 then Season is Winter; if 3, 4, or 5 then Season is Spring; if 6, 7, or 8 then Season is Summer; if 9, 10, or 11 then Season is Fall. Can we use a writeln statement to write the value in Season? Explain.

*b. If StereoColor is Black, then reduce InventoryBlack by Sales; if Gray, then reduce InventoryGray by Sales; if Silver, then reduce InventorySilver by Sales. Assume that StereoColor is typed Color, where legitimate colors are only Black, Gray, and Silver.

*5. Revise the error routine in Example 7.3 as a while-do structure that rings the bell, displays an error message, and reinputs Day. Which approach do you like best, and why?

(L) 6. In Example 7.4...

a. Test drive program CkInVal by successively entering the values 9, 0, q, and 1.

b. What happens if we forget to deactivate the range-checking compiler directive? Try it and rework part **a**.

*c. Revise the program to declare type LowerLetter as the character subrange 'a'.. 'z', and I/O Letter with type LowerLetter. Input 9, D, and d. What happens for each input? Is an I/O error possible for this type? Why were type changes not required in utility procedures ReadLnVal and InputVal?

(L) *7. Rework Exercise 18 in Chapter 6. Revise CkRdInt to use ReadLnVal in place of ReadLnInt. Explain why generic typing is useful in this exercise.

*8. Functions ord, succ, and pred. Check out the description of these predeclared functions in Appendix F. Write a test program that outputs the ordinal number, successor, and predecessor for the following arguments.

a. The character constants 'A' through 'F'.
b. The integer constants −5 through 5.
c. The Boolean values false and true.
d. The five enumerated grades in Example 7.2.

(L) 9. ADT Grade. In our ADT Grade application...

a. Test drive program CkADT1. Use our sample data on page 317.

*b. Revise CkADT1 as follows. Input two grades, QuarterGrade and LastQuarterGrade. If QuarterGrade is the same or better than LastQuarterGrade, set SemesterGrade to QuarterGrade; display the semester grade with the label "Your semester grade is "; else display the message "You have to take the FINAL EXAM!". Test the revised program over the following runs, where the first grade is this quarter's grade and the second grade is last quarter's grade: B and B; B and A; A and C; A and X.

10. Identify what's wrong (if anything) with the following.
    a. [S, M, L, XL]
    b. ['S', 'M', 'L', 'XL']
    c. [1 . . 7, 'a' . . 'z']
    d. [−10, 0 . . 9, 9, 50 . . 99, 1000 . . 10000]
    e. Letter **not in** ['a' . . 'z', 'A' . . 'Z']

11. Specify code that declares the following set constants.
    a. SexCodes as the set of character values F, f, M, and m.
    b. DaySet as the integers 1 through 7.
    c. DaySet as the enumerated values Sun, Mon, Tue, Wed, Thu, Fri, Sat.
    d. CoinSet as the enumerated values Penny, Nickel, Dime, Quarter, Fifty, Dollar.

12. Specify code that declares the following set types and variables.
    a. DayType as the set of integer values in the range 1 to 7.
    b. Set type DayType as the set of day names declared in Exercise **1b**; set variables WeekDay and WeekEnd having type DayType.
    *c. Enumerated type Months with values Jan, Feb, Mar, Apr, May, Jun, Jul, Aug, Sep, Oct. Nov, Dec; set type MonthType as the set of months; set variables FallSemester, SpringSemester, SummerTerm having type MonthType.

13. Indicate the resulting values for the following set operations, given that SetA stores ['a' . . 'z'] and SetB stores ['a', 'e', 'i', 'o', 'u'].
    a. SetA ∗ SetB
    b. SetA + SetB
    c. SetA − SetB
    d. SetB − SetA
    e. SetA − SetB ∗ SetB
    f. (SetA − SetB) ∗ SetB

14. Indicate the resulting values for the following Boolean expressions, given the same set values as the preceding exercise.
    a. SetA = SetB
    b. SetA <> SetB
    c. SetA <= SetB
    d. SetA >= SetB
    e. SetB <= SetA
    f. **not** ('A' **in** SetB)

15. Rewrite the following Boolean expressions by using sets.
  a. (SexCode = 'F') **or** (SexCode = 'f') **or** (SexCode = 'M') **or** (SexCode = 'm')
  b. (Age <= 18) **or** ((Age >= 65) **and** (Age <= 75))
  c. (Coin = Penny) **or** (Coin = Nickel) **or** (Coin = Dime) **or** (Coin = Quarter) **or** (Coin = Fifty) **or** (Coin = Dollar)

16. **Error routine for correct reply.** In Example 7.5...
  a. Roleplay the input Sure, ok, yep.
  b. Revise the error routine to not use the declared constant CorrectReply. Preference?

17. **Error traps.** Write code that traps incorrect input for MenuSelection, given the following correct choices.
  a. The integer menu choices 1 through 5, and 9.
  b. The character menu choices 'A' through 'F', and 'X'.

(L) *18. **Revisit: Temperatures, Version 2.0.** Revise program Temp2 in Figure 5.7 to use the approach in Example 7.5, based on the following.
  a. Drop the error-messaging feature (sound and text).
  b. Include the error-messaging feature.

(L) *19. **Revisit: Menu application.** Revise program Combo1 in Figure 6.4 to trap menu errors using the approach in Example 7.5, based on the following.
  a. Ignore procedure MenuError.
  b. Utilize procedure MenuError.

(L) 20. **Set I/O.** For the application in Figures 7.3 and 7.4...
  a. What happens if we enter SSMLX.? smlx.? Confirm your answers by running program SetIO.
  b. Delete the initialization for Codes (or set it off in curly braces) and execute the program using the test data in Figure 7.3. What happens?
  c. Delete type CapLetters and revise the program accordingly. Preference?
  d. Change the program to ignore what case is input. The legitimate codes are still the uppercase letters. The program changes all character input to uppercase.
  ***e.** Change the program to reinput any incorrect codes. Input one code per line.
  ***f.** Change the program to also allow lowercase letters as legitimate codes.

(L) *21. **Set I/O.** Revise program SetIO to process the legitimate string codes Small, Medium, Large, XtraLarge. Use Medium, XtraLarge, Tiny, and Small as test data. *Hint:* Input a string value and use an else-if structure to assign enumerated codes. Use a for-do loop and case structure to write appropriate values.

22. Would you say that type string is a structured data type? Explain.

ADDITIONAL EXERCISES

EASIER	For the busy... **23 24a 28**
NORMAL	For the thinkers... **24b 25 26 27 29**
TOUGHER	For the hard CORE... **30**

23. Revisit. Revisit a program that you wrote earlier and assess whether or not it would be useful to include subrange or enumerated types, error handling, and the **in** operator. If useful, revise and test the program accordingly.

24. Revisits. Revise one of the following programs from the end of Chapter 6.
  a. PIN confirmation. Type the input variable as a character subrange type.
  b. SAT report. Type class code as an integer subrange type and class as an enumerated type.

25. Boolean I/O. Pascal supports the output of Boolean values with the write and writeln statements, but not their input with the read and readln statements. Develop and test a procedure that reads string values as surrogate Boolean values. Legitimate input values include t, T, true, and TRUE for the Boolean value **true**; f, F, false, and FALSE for the Boolean value **false**. The driver inputs a surrogate Boolean value and writes the corresponding actual Boolean value.

26. Revisit: Grade report. Revise the grade report application at the end of Chapters 2 and 3 to...
  a. Use ADT Grade.
  b. Store input data in a text file.
  c. Print a frequency distribution that displays the grade and frequency. In the sample data we would have the following.

Frequency Distribution
Turbo Pascal 101!

Grade	Frequency
A	0
B	1
C	1
D	0
F	1
Total.............	3

27. **ADT Day.** Create ADT Day, where type Day is the enumerated type (Sunday, Monday, Tuesday, Wednesday, Thursday, Friday, Saturday). Include the following procedures.

    a. Procedure ReadLnDay receives nothing, reads a value into string variable DayString, assigns the proper value to Day variable AnyDay, and sends AnyDay to the calling module. The following are legitimate input for each day of the week, in either uppercase or lowercase letters: SU SUN SUNDAY; M MO MON MONDAY; TU TUE TUESDAY; W WE WED WEDNESDAY; TH THU THURSDAY; F FR FRI FRIDAY; SA SAT SATURDAY. Make sure that reinput is requested while input is not legitimate. Don't forget to make use of utility procedure ErrMessage. A line feed is issued following a successful read operation.

    b. Procedure WriteLnDay receives Day variable AnyDay, writes the value in AnyDay (not directly!) with a line feed, and sends nothing. Write a driver to debug this ADT. In your test runs, include I/O for each day of the week, and some incorrect input.

28. **Revisit.** Revisit a program that you wrote earlier and assess whether or not it would be useful to include sets. If useful, revise and test the program accordingly.

29. **Menu of set operations.** Develop a program that (1) inputs two sets of integer digits, where the base type is the subrange of digits 0 to 9; (2) offers a menu with choices Intersection, Union, Difference, Quit; and (3) takes appropriate action based on the menu selection. For example, if union is selected, the program writes a set that is the union of the two input sets. Use the examples in Table 7.1 as test data.

30. **Flag colors.** Develop a program that (1) inputs two sets of flag colors, where the base type consists of the enumerated colors Black, Blue, Green, Red, Brown, Yellow, White; (2) offers a menu with choices Intersection, Union, Difference, Quit; and (3) takes appropriate action based on the menu selection. For example, if union is selected, the program writes a set that is the union of the two input sets. Use the following test data for the two input sets: Red White Blue and Black Red Green.

CHAPTER 8

· ·

UNITS

‡Optional, more advanced material. Skip without loss of continuity, study at this point, or wait until later.

This chapter continues the treatment of *modular programming* by extending *PC-style programming,* completing the treatment of *units,* and introducing applications in *graphics.*

8.1 OVERVIEW

• • • • • • • • • • • • • •

In this section we review PC-style programming and survey other approaches to implementing modules.

MORE PC-STYLE PROGRAMMING

We introduced PC-style programming in Chapter 5 as a collection of approaches that facilitate the use of PCs. In Templ and Temp2 in Chapter 5, Combo1 in Chapter 6, and InputVal in Chapter 7, we illustrated the following user-interface features: a screen orientation that included screen-design elements such as screen clears, pauses, and direct cursor addressing; distinct screens for specific functional purposes, as in opening, input, output, menu, and farewell screens; the treatment of user options as yes/no replies and menu selections; and defensive programming techniques like *error routines* that handle input and range errors, including audiovisual error messaging. Predefined procedures and functions in the *crt unit* played an important support role in implementing these features.[1]

In this chapter we extend PC-style programming to include the use of color, time and date displays, and other screen effects such as boldfacing, blinking, and reverse video.

You should be aware that most PC-style programming features, as well as graphics programming, are *hardware and operating system specific.* This means that the implementation of routines like screen clears (**clrscr**) and direct cursor addressing (**gotoxy**) assume the use of specific hardware and operating systems. In our case, the assumption is the use of an IBM-family (or IBM-compatible) PC running under PC-DOS (or MS-DOS). Indeed, the installation of Turbo Pascal itself requires this hardware/OS configuration, or one of its supported variants.

---

[1]Specifically, functions **readkey, wherex,** and **wherey,** and procedures **gotoxy, clrscr, clreol,** and **delay.**

LIBRARIES

A **library** is a collection of prewritten, working, reusable modules. Alternative terms for library include *utilities library* and *toolkit*. Its function is to supply types, constants, variables, and modules for utilitarian tasks, or those tasks that are useful to a wide variety of programs. Its purpose is to reduce software costs by increasing programmer productivity. In short, programmers don't have to "reinvent the wheel" for commonly used programming tasks. Modules in a library are often called *utilities, utility modules, routines, library routines,* or *toolkit routines.*

Since Chapter 3, we have been developing and using our own library of utilities. It's described inside the front cover of the book and supplied as the *Utilities Library* on disk. Your instructor also may have added modules to this library. Have you added any modules based on the exercises? Our utilities library is an example of an *in-house library,* or one that is developed by the using organization's programming staff. These are quite common, particularly in organizations that have large programming staffs or a long history of in-house programming.

An alternative to or a supplement for an in-house library is a *commercial library.* This library is developed by a software vendor and primarily distributed by direct sales, usually by phone or mail order. Commercial libraries have been around for years, particularly libraries of mathematical and statistical routines. More recently, an increasing number of commercial libraries facilitate the implementation of sophisticated user interfaces. These include routines for window management, pull-down menus, mouse support, forms-oriented data entry, context-sensitive help, sophisticated printing capabilities, input error traps, calculators, calendars, phone dialers, and...you name it.[2]

The predefined procedures and functions that we have been calling in the *crt unit* also represent a library that's supplied by Turbo Pascal. We will take a look at other Turbo Pascal units in this chapter.

We also continue the development of our in-house library and show two ways of implementing utility modules without directly incorporating them in our source programs...

- By developing and compiling our own unit
- By including a reference in the source program to a separately stored module that gets compiled into the object program

---

[2]Several commercial libraries specialize in Turbo Pascal. *Turbo Vision* (Module E) also includes a library that supports the same capabilities as the IDE's user interface; it's Turbo Pascal's ultimate approach to PC-style programming. By using it, we can program our user interfaces to have the same "look and feel" as the IDE. Take a quick look at Figure E.1 to see what we mean.

UNITS AND INCLUDE FILES

We have other ways in Turbo Pascal to develop, specify, and manage utilities. In this section, we mention the use of units as one approach and illustrate Include files as a second approach.

The *predefined unit crt* contains a collection of functions and procedures that constitute a library. We use the modules in that library by specifying the unit's name in the *uses clause* and calling the needed modules in our source code. Turbo Pascal also lets us write our own units, called *user-defined units*. We reference these units just like the predefined units. For example, we could place our utility procedures in a unit, declare this unit in the uses clause of a source program, and then call our utility modules just like we call predefined modules. This means, of course, that we don't need to directly include our utility modules in our source programs. A unified treatment of units is presented in the next section.

An **Include file** is a separately stored module that is referenced in the *source program* by the *Include file {$I} compiler directive.* The Include file is compiled and inserted (included) in the *object program.* By treating our utility modules as Include files, we can avoid the direct insertion of utility modules in our source programs, as we have done until now. This shortens our source programs and simplifies access to the Utilities Library.

EXAMPLE 8.1   PROCEDURE READLNINT AS INCLUDE FILE

Let's go back to an earlier program, CkRdInt in Figure 6.5. Take a look at this program now. ReadLnInt is a utility that inputs an integer value with input error handling; CkRdInt is a driver that tests this utility. We placed ReadLnInt in the Utilities Library as file READLNIN.PRO. Figure 8.1 shows a rewritten driver CkRdInt2 that treats procedure ReadLnInt as an Include file. Note the following.

1. Source program CkRdInt2 is an edited version of source program CkRdInt, where we eliminated procedure ReadLnInt and substituted the Include file compiler directive.

2. The Include file compiler directive {$I} identifies the directory path and file name for the Include file. If we were to just use the file name without specifying a directory path, as in

   ```
   {$I READLNIN.PRO}
   ```

   Turbo Pascal searches for the Include file in the current directory and, if it is not found, in the *Include directories* specified by the command sequence **O**ptions **D**irectories **I**nclude directories in the IDE.

```
┌─────────────────────────────────────────────────────────────────────────┐
│            FIGURE 8.1    Listing for Program CkRdInt2                      │
└─────────────────────────────────────────────────────────────────────────┘

  program CkRdInt2;

     {* * * * * * * * * * * * * * * * * * * * * * * * * * * * * * * * * *
      *                                                                  *
      *          Driver checks error-handling procedure ReadLnInt        *
      *             ... as Include file                                  *
      *                                                                  *
      *             Inputs integer value                                *
      *             Calls ReadLnInt                                      *
      *             Outputs value                                        *
      *                                                                  *
      * * * * * * * * * * * * * * * * * * * * * * * * * * * * * * * * * *}

     {============================ Declarations ============================}

  uses crt;

  var
     TestVar : integer;

     {======================= Procedure Declarations =======================}

     {Include utility procedure ReadLnInt}
     {$I \books\tp\utilib\READLNIN.PRO}      {Specify your own directory path}

     {============================= Main Body =============================}

  begin   {CkRdInt2}

     clrscr;
     write   ('Enter integer... ');   ReadLnInt (TestVar);
     writeln ('Echo........... ',  TestVar);

  end.    {CkRdInt2}
```

3. The compiled version of program CkRdInt2 (its object file) is created as though the contents of the Include file appeared at the point where the $I directive is positioned in source program CkRdInt2.

LARGE-SCALE PROGRAMMING

Many commerical PC programs are very large, having thousands of source-code lines, requiring hundreds of thousands of kilobytes for source files and object files, and needing amounts of primary memory that may exceed the 640KB RAM limitation that's associated with early DOS machines. In these cases, special considerations are required to make the programs workable within memory resource constraints. Let's briefly survey approaches to easing this *large-scale programming* problem.

One way of reducing the size of programs is to utilize *user-defined units* or *Include files* (or both) for modules. Units are precompiled and so reduce the sizes of both source and object files for a particular program. Compilation timc for the program is reduced as well, since the modules not included in the source program don't require compilation. The use of Include files reduces the size of the source file but not that of the corresponding object file, since the Include files are compiled each time they're included. This also means, of course, that the compilation-time benefits realized with units are absent with Include files. In short, the use of units can reduce both *secondary memory* on disk and compilation-time requirements. Units don't reduce *primary* or *run-time memory* needs, however, since all object code resides in run-time memory while the program executes.

A major approach to reducing run-time memory requirements is to organize the program into *overlays,* or parts of a program that share a common area of primary memory called the *overlay buffer.* Thus, only parts of an object program reside in memory at any one time, thereby allowing the execution of programs much larger than available primary memory. Unfortunately, this memory benefit comes at a price: Run times increase, since the task of swapping portions of a program in and out of the overlay buffer consumes time. Programming with overlays is an advanced topic that we don't cover in this text. We just wanted you to be aware of this common large-scale programming practice.

Operating systems and memory management utilities within the programming environment also can ease large-scale programming problems. For example, early versions of DOS (before Version 4) could not utilize more than 640KB of run-time memory, even if the machine included more. Later versions of DOS, and operating environments like Microsoft Windows, can access primary memory beyond the 640KB barrier, thus better accommodating the run-time memory needs of large-scale programming.

SELF-REVIEW EXERCISES

1

8.2 USING UNITS

• • • • • • • • • • • • •

We defined a **unit** in Chapter 2 as a related collection of constants, data types, variables, procedures, and functions. Its purpose is usually well defined, as in providing facilities for printing, or screen control, or graphics. Up to now we have used the predefined units *printer* and *crt.* In the preceding section we noted that we can also write our own units, which simplify access to our in-house libraries and reduce secondary memory and compilation-time requirements. In this section we complete the treatment of units by describing Turbo Pascal's predefined units and writing our own unit.

Table 8.1   Predefined (Standard) Units

Unit Identifier*	Description
crt	Exploits PC display and keyboard by managing the screen, providing color, making sound, accepting specific-key input.
dos	Implements DOS tasks, like date and time controls, directory management, and program execution.
graph	Supplies graphics routines for tasks such as displaying and filling lines, circles, bars, and other figures; generating different type styles; supporting different graphics adapters; and creating animation, colors, and palettes.
overlay	Implements overlay manager. See discussion in Section 8.1.
printer	Provides access to printer.
system	Provides run-time library of standard procedures and functions in Standard Pascal (like **write**, **readln**, and **sqrt**), and others not found in other units. This unit is always linked into any program or unit, and so is not specified in a uses clause.

*Except for the *graph* unit, these units are in file TURBO.TPL and are resident in primary memory for use by other programs and units. Selected procedures and functions in these units are described in Appendixes E and F. See the *Turbo Pascal Reference Manual* for complete descriptions of all available standard identifiers within units.

PREDEFINED UNITS

A **predefined** or **standard unit** is a unit that's provided by Turbo Pascal. Table 8.1 describes six predefined units.[3] Each predefined unit is already compiled. All predefined units in the table, except *graph*, reside in primary memory. In the remainder of this chapter, we show additional uses for the *crt* and *system* units and implement for the first time the *dos* and *graph* units.

The syntax box on the next page formalizes the uses clause.

USER-DEFINED UNITS

A **user-defined unit** is a unit that we write — it's not provided by Turbo Pascal. The syntax box on page 351 shows its composition. As seen, it has the four sections *unit heading, interface, implementation,* and the optional *initializa-*

---

[3]There are other units for backward compatibility with earlier versions of Turbo Pascal and new units in Version 6 that support Turbo Vision (Module E).

SYNTAX BOX

Uses clause... Identifies units used by either the "client" program or by other "client" units

---

Syntax........uses ListUnitNames;

Examples......uses crt, dos, OurUnit;

Explanation ... The uses clause, if present, must immediately follow the program heading (in programs) and the reserved words **interface** and **implementation** (in units). The word **uses** is a reserved word and ListUnitNames is a list of identifiers separated by commas. Each identifier is either one of the standard identifiers for a predefined unit (see Table 8.1) or a user-defined identifier for a user-defined unit. The compiler looks for a listed unit as follows. First, it checks the loaded resident units in primary memory (*crt, dos, overlay, printer*). If it's not one of these units, it looks for units on disk, first in the current directory and then in the directories specified in the IDE command sequence Options Directories Unit. If found, the unit's object file is subsequently linked to the program's object file. If not found, a compile-time error aborts compilation.

---

tion. At first glance, the composition of a unit looks quite different from that of a program. Yet, in many ways, a unit is like a program: It includes declarations for constants, variables, data types, procedures, and functions; and the optional *statement* or *initialization section* is the unit's algorithm, as in programs.

Figure 8.2 shows a preliminary "chopped-off" version of OurUnit, a user-defined unit that contains a library of utility modules from this book. The final version of OurUnit includes additional documentation and any utilities and units from chapters following this chapter. OurUnit does not include every utility module in the Utilities Library; it includes only the specifically typed modules (such as ReadLnInt in Figure 6.5) and none of the generically typed modules (such as ReadLnVal in Figure 7.1). If we were to include ReadLnVal in OurUnit, we would also have to declare GenType in OurUnit, to avoid an *Unknown identifier* compile-time error. This is because any client program that uses OurUnit "inherits" or imports the unit's typing in its object file. Since units are already compiled, the client program would import a type like GenType and could not redeclare this type according to its needs.

The listing inside the front cover not only shows the utilities in the Utilities Library but also specifies which of these is in OurUnit. Try Exercise 3 for a look at the final version of OurUnit as file OURUNIT.PAS in the Examples Library.

SYNTAX BOX

User-Defined Unit... Defines a library of declarations and modules

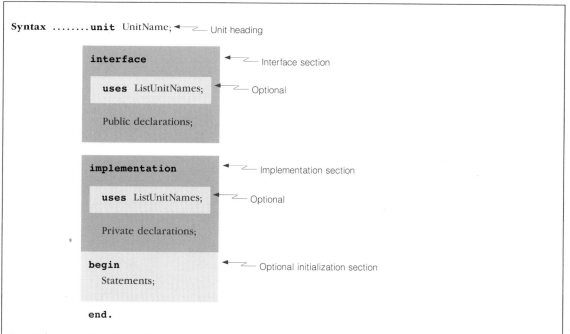

Syntax ....**unit** UnitName; ◄—⌐— Unit heading

      interface   ◄—⌐— Interface section

        uses ListUnitNames; ◄—⌐— Optional

        Public declarations;

      implementation   ◄—⌐— Implementation section

        uses ListUnitNames; ◄—⌐— Optional

        Private declarations;

      begin   ◄—⌐— Optional initialization section
        Statements;

      end.

Examples......See Figure 8.2.

Explanation...The user-defined unit is a source file that must be compiled to disk as an object file with the same name as the source file, but with a .TPU extension added by Turbo Pascal. The word **unit** is a reserved word. UnitName is a user-defined identifier. The word **interface** is a reserved word that defines the beginning of the interface section. The *interface section* defines the unit's public declarations as those declarations that are "visible" to the client programs or units using this unit. By "visible" we mean that the using program or unit has access to these declarations. This section starts with a uses clause, if any, to declare other units available to declarations in this unit and to declarations in other programs and units that use this unit. The interface section also includes public declarations for constants, data types, and variables (not shown in the example), as well as procedure and function *headings* (just the headings, as in the example). The reserved word **implementation** defines the end of the interface section and the beginning of the implementation section. The *implementation section* includes the complete procedures and functions identified by the headings in the interface section. All declarations in the interface section are available to the implementation section. Morever, the implementation section can contain declarations of its own. All declarations in the implementation section are private declarations in the sense that they cannot be used by the client programs and units utilizing this unit. The procedure and function headings in the implementation section that correspond to headings in the interface section can be expressed in a "short form" that eliminates the portion following the module's name. Any units declared in a uses clause within the implementation section are only available to modules within the implementation section. The implementation section ends with either **begin** (if present) or **end** (if **begin** is not present). If **begin** is present, then an *initialization section* is defined. This section can include any legitimate statements in Turbo Pascal. The initialization section, if present, is used to initialize variables, write any messages, and carry out other tasks that are executed before the execution of an algorithm in the client program or unit.

FIGURE 8.2   Partial Listing of Preliminary Version of OurUnit

```pascal
unit OurUnit ;

   {* * * * * * * * * * * * * * * * * * * * * * * * * * * * * * *
    *                                                           *
    *          Preliminary version of OurUnit                   *
    *                                                           *
    *          This example shows what OurUnit would look like with   *
    *        . minimal documentation and the specifically-typed utility   *
    *          modules up to now in this book.  See file OURUNIT.PAS in   *
    *          the Examples Library for the final version.      *
    *                                                           *
    * * * * * * * * * * * * * * * * * * * * * * * * * * * * * * *}

interface

   uses crt;

   function Distance (X1,Y1, X2,Y2 : real) : real;
   function Fac  (X : integer) : extended;
   function FacR (X : integer) : extended;
   function Power1 (Base, Power : real) : real;

   procedure ErrMessage ;
   procedure MenuError ;
   procedure Pause ;
   procedure PrepFile (var TextFile : text);
   procedure ReadLnInt (var Variable : integer);
   procedure ReadRep (var Reply : char);
   procedure ReadReply (var Reply : char);
   procedure RepErr (var Reply : char);


implementation


   function Distance (X1,Y1, X2,Y2 : real) : real;

      { Utility calculates Euclidian distance between two pairs of coordinates
        Receives two pairs of coordinates
        Returns Euclidian distance }

   begin  {Distance}

     Distance := sqrt( sqr( X1 - X2 ) + sqr( Y1 - Y2) );

   end;   {Distance}
{------------------------------------------------------------------------}

             Other function and procedure declarations go here

{------------------------------------------------------------------------}

end.    {OurUnit}
```

— Interface section

— Implementation section

EXAMPLE 8.2   PROCEDURE READLNINT AS MODULE IN UNIT OURUNIT

In Example 6.6 we introduced procedure ReadLnInt and illustrated its use by incorporating it into a driver. In Example 8.1 we took this procedure out of the driver, gave it a separate file name as a utility in our utilities library, and accessed it within the driver as an Include file. In the present example, as seen in Figure 8.3, we access ReadLnInt as a public procedure in unit OurUnit. Note the following.

1. The revised driver CkRdInt3 simply includes unit OurUnit in its uses clause. As before, ReadLnInt is called in the main body.

2. *Unit crt* is needed in the uses clause of program CkRdInt3 because its predefined procedure **clrscr** is called in the main body. If we had no need to clear the screen in the algorithm, we would eliminate the reference to **crt** in the uses clause. This would not be the case in Examples 6.6 and 8.1, because ReadLnInt itself requires unit crt (it calls **wherex, wherey, gotoxy,** and **clreol**). In the present example, ReadLnInt accesses these crt routines through the uses clause in OurUnit, as seen in Figure 8.2.

FIGURE 8.3   Listing for Program CkRdInt3

```
program CkRdInt3;

   {* * * * * * * * * * * * * * * * * * * * * * * * * * * * * * * * *
    *                                                              *
    *        Driver checks error-handling procedure ReadLnInt     *
    *           ... as procedure in OurUnit                        *
    *                                                              *
    *           Inputs integer value                              *
    *           Calls ReadLnInt                                   *
    *           Outputs value                                     *
    *                                                              *
    * * * * * * * * * * * * * * * * * * * * * * * * * * * * * * * * *}

   {============================ Declarations ============================}

uses crt,
     OurUnit;        {OurUnit added here, to import declaration of ReadLnInt}

var
  TestVar : integer;

   {============================ Main Body ============================}

begin   {CkRdInt3}

  clrscr;
  write    ('Enter integer... ');   ReadLnInt (TestVar);
  writeln ('Echo........... ',  TestVar);

end.    {CkRdInt3}
```

A typical commercial programming environment would contain many libraries, each within its own unit. These libraries (unlike our own small library) would be organized into modules that are functionally related, much like Turbo Pascal has organized its own predefined units into a crt library, a DOS library, and so on. For example, we might have unit *OurIO* for specialized I/O routines, unit *OurStats* for a library of statistical routines, and so forth. Also, units are the vehicle of choice for implementing ADTs, as we see next.

NOTE

1. Compile units to disk. Don't forget that user-defined source-file units must be compiled to disk by toggling the command sequence Compile Destination to Disk in the IDE's menu system. Turbo Pascal will automatically name the object file as the name of the source file followed by the extension .TPU, placing it in the current directory.

2. Where should we place unit files? If we always work with a single directory as the current directory, it makes sense to have all unit files in that single directory. If we run different programs from different directories, we should place all of our unit's source and object files in a special directory, say, UNITS. Units in this directory would be accessible by programs in any other directory, if we specify UNITS as the unit directory in the IDE's command sequence Options Directories Unit directories.

3. Your own unit. In exercises throughout the remainder of the book, we ask you to add your own modules to OurUnit. It would be a good idea for you to have your own version of OurUnit for this purpose. Alternatively, you could include the new modules in your own unit, say, MyUnit. Always keep a copy of OurUnit, however, because many of our sample programs use it.

UNITS FOR ADTS

In Section 7.2 we defined an *abstract data type (ADT)* and in program CkADT1 in Figure 7.2 we declared and implemented ADT Grade as the enumerated data type Grade with two operations: reading and writing a Grade value by calling procedures ReadLnGrade and WriteLnGrade.

EXAMPLE 8.3   UNIT ADTGRADE

Unit ADTGrade in Figure 8.4 shows how we placed the ADT Grade declarations in a unit. Note the following.

FIGURE 8.4   Listing for Unit ADTGrade

```
unit ADTGrade;

   {* * * * * * * * * * * * * * * * * * * * * * * * * * * * * * * * *
    *                                                               *
    *          Abstract Data Type Grade Unit                        *
    *                                                               *
    *             ADT Grade exports...                              *
    *                    Enumerated type Grade (A, B, C, D, F)      *
    *                    ReadLn procedure, with error handling      *
    *                    WriteLn procedure                          *
    *                                                               *
    *            Public Procedures                                  *
    *               ReadLnGrade.... Reads Grade type value, with line feed  *
    *               WriteLnGrade... Writes Grade type value, with line feed *
    *                                                               *
    *            Private Procedures                                 *
    *               None...                                         *
    *                                                               *
    *            Uses units crt, OurUnit                            *
    *                                                               *
    * * * * * * * * * * * * * * * * * * * * * * * * * * * * * * * * *}

interface

  uses crt, OurUnit;

  type
    Grade = (A, B, C, D, F);            {Enumerated type Grade declaration}

  {============================= Procedures ============================}

  procedure ReadLnGrade (var GradeVar : Grade);
  procedure WriteLnGrade (GradeVar : Grade);


implementation

  {============================= Procedures ============================}
```

continued

1. The *interface section* declares the use of units **crt** and OurUnit, the public data type Grade, and the public procedures ReadLnGrade and WriteLnGrade. This data type and these procedures are exported to the object files of any unit or program that includes ADTunit in its uses clause.

2. The *implementation section* contains the complete declarations for procedures ReadLnGrade and WriteLnGrade.

3. As before, utility procedure ErrMessage is called by procedure ReadLnGrade whenever an unallowable grade is entered. Now, however, ErrMessage is imported from OurUnit. This is why we included OurUnit in the uses clause of ADTGrade.

Figure 8.5 shows the revised driver CkADT2. Note the following.

1. The uses clause includes ADTGrade.

2. The declarations for type Grade and procedures ReadLnGrade and WriteLnGrade are imported from ADTGrade into CkADT2's object file. Thus,

FIGURE 8.4   (continued)

```
procedure ReadLnGrade (var GradeVar : Grade);

   { Reads Grade type value with line feed and error handling
     Receives nothing
     Sends GradeVar }

var
   GradeChar : char;           {Stores character input value for grade}
   Error     : Boolean;        {Stores true if input error; false otherwise}
   X, Y      : integer;        {Stores cursor coordinate}

begin   {ReadLnGrade}

  X := wherex;  Y := wherey;          {Store coordinate at input field}

  repeat
    Error := false;
    readln (GradeChar);
    case GradeChar of
       'A' : GradeVar := A;
       'B' : GradeVar := B;
       'C' : GradeVar := C;
       'D' : GradeVar := D;
       'F' : GradeVar := F;
    else {Error in grade}
       begin
         Error := true;
         ErrMessage;                 {Call error message utility in OurUnit}
         gotoxy (X,Y); clreol;       {Clear input field}
       end; {Error routine}
    end; {case}
  until not Error;

end;    {ReadLnGrade}
{--------------------------------------------------------------------------}
procedure WriteLnGrade (GradeVar : Grade);

   { Writes Grade type value with line feed
     Receives GradeVar
     Sends nothing }

begin   {WriteLnGrade}

  case GradeVar of
     A :   writeln ('A');
     B :   writeln ('B');
     C :   writeln ('C');
     D :   writeln ('D');
     F :   writeln ('F');
  end; {case}

end;    {WriteLnGrade}
{--------------------------------------------------------------------------}

end.    {ADTGrade}
```

we use Grade to type QuarterGrade, without having to declare Grade in the source program. Similarly, we call ReadLnGrade and WriteLnGrade without declaring them in the source program.

Once we develop unit ADTGrade, we can *selectively* forget how it works...we only need to know of its existence and its declarations. We simply practice data ab-

```
                     FIGURE 8.5    Listing for Program CkADT2

program CkADT2;

    {* * * * * * * * * * * * * * * * * * * * * * * * * * * * * * * * *
     *                                                               *
     *   Driver checks ADT Grade procedures ReadLnGrade and WriteLnGrade *
     *                                                               *
     *       This version imports ADT Grade from unit ADTGrade.      *
     *       Specifically, it imports type Grade and procedures      *
     *       ReadLnGrade and WriteLnGrade.                           *
     *                                                               *
     *         Inputs grade by calling ReadLnGrade                   *
     *         Outputs grade by calling WriteLnGrade                 *
     *                                                               *
     * * * * * * * * * * * * * * * * * * * * * * * * * * * * * * * * *}

    {============================ Declarations ===========================}
uses crt,
     ADTGrade;                        {Imports ADT Grade}

var
   QuarterGrade : Grade;             {QuarterGrade is type Grade variable}

    {============================ Main Body ============================}

begin   {CkADT2}

   clrscr;
   write ('Enter grade for Quarter... ');   ReadLnGrade  (QuarterGrade);
   write ('Echo..................... ');    WriteLnGrade (QuarterGrade);

end.    {CkADT2}
```

straction by including ADTGrade in the uses clause of a client program and referencing its declarations as needed.

SELF-REVIEW EXERCISES

3 4 5 10

‡8.3   CRT AND DOS UNITS

PC-style programming often includes special effects like color screens and
characters, boldfaced text, and special sounds. We implement these and other

‡Optional, more advanced material. Skip without loss of continuity, study at this point, or wait
until later.

crt effects by calling utilities in the *crt unit*. We also illustrate calls to the *dos unit*'s date and time functions.

COLOR

The advantages of using screen colors in our programming are similar to those in using screen colors in our televisions: more realism, enhanced communication, and greater aesthetics (although the latter is often debatable). For example, in our programming, we can use background and foreground colors to individualize screens, as in giving unique colors to the opening screen, the menu screen, and so on; to alert the user to an error condition, as in using red for an error message; and to draw attention to a specific portion of the screen, by changing its colors or reversing the background and foreground colors.

In Turbo Pascal we call procedures **textbackground** and **textcolor** in the crt unit to respectively set background and foreground colors. By *background* we mean the solid screen color that describes an empty screen. The background color is "behind" or "underneath" the superimposed *foreground* color. In a text screen, characters take on the foreground color, as if placed on "top" of the background color. In graphics screens, the foreground includes not only characters but also graphics like circles and lines. Here's how we set background and foreground colors.

- Select the background color using

  textbackground (ColorBackground)

  where ColorBackground is an integer expression whose value is in the range 0..7.

- Select the foreground color using

  textcolor (ColorForeground)

  where ColorForeground is an integer expression whose value is in the range 0..15.

Table 8.2 shows the available colors in Turbo Pascal. These are declared integer constants in the **const** section of the crt unit. Note that background

Table 8.2   Background and Foreground Colors in Turbo Pascal

Where?	*Color Declared Constants*							
Background	Black	= 0;	Blue	= 1;	Green	= 2;	Cyan	= 3;
	Red	= 4;	Magenta	= 5;	Brown	= 6;	LightGray	= 7;
Foreground	Black	= 0;	Blue	= 1;	Green	= 2;	Cyan	= 3;
	Red	= 4;	Magenta	= 5;	Brown	= 6;	LightGray	= 7;
	DarkGray	= 8;	LightBlue	= 9;	LightGreen	= 10;	LightCyan	= 11;
	LightRed	= 12;	LightMagenta	=13;	Yellow	= 14;	White	= 15;

colors are restricted to eight choices; foreground colors include the same eight choices as the background colors, plus eight other choices. Background and foreground colors stay in effect until (1) other calls are issued to **textbackground** and/or **textcolor,** or (2) **normvideo** is called to restore the original colors at program startup, or (3) public variable **TextAttr** is reassigned a value. We show each of these approaches in the coming examples.

EXAMPLE 8.4 · SETTING COLORS

Consider the following program segment and describe what it does before reading on.

We could use *1* here

We could use *4* here

```
Textbackground (Blue);  textcolor (Red);
writeln ('Input error... please reenter');
normvideo;
```

The first line sets the background color to blue and the foreground color to red. Thus, the indicated error message is written in red characters on a blue background. Anything on the screen above this point remains in its original colors. The call to **normvideo** resets the screen colors to those in effect at the *startup* of the program. If the colors just before this program segment are those at startup, the screen effect here is like a blue rectangle containing a red error message.

If we omit the call to **normvideo**, any subsequent text is also written in red on a blue background. If we want to return to colors previously set in the program, in place of **normvideo** we would recall **textbackground** and **textcolor** using the previous colors as parameters. If we clear the screen just after setting the background and foreground colors, the entire screen will have a blue background. Any subsequent text would be in red.

OTHER TEXT EFFECTS

Other special text effects include the ability to display text as *high-intensity (boldfaced)* characters, *low-intensity* characters, and *blinking* characters. A call to procedure **highvideo** displays any subsequently written characters in high intensity. A call to procedure **lowvideo** displays any subsequently written characters in low intensity. If we add the predefined constant **Blink** (=128) to the color integer expressions in **textbackground** and **textcolor**, any subsequently written characters will blink in the specified color. Procedure **normvideo** resets characters to normal.

EXAMPLE 8.5   ADDING SPECIAL TEXT EFFECTS

The following code fragment revises the fragment in Example 8.4.

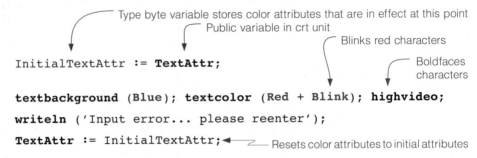

Type byte variable stores color attributes that are in effect at this point
Public variable in crt unit
Blinks red characters
Boldfaces characters

```
InitialTextAttr := TextAttr;

textbackground (Blue); textcolor (Red + Blink); highvideo;

writeln ('Input error... please reenter');

TextAttr := InitialTextAttr;
```

Resets color attributes to initial attributes

The error message is now defined by blinking high-intensity red characters on a blue rectangular background. The screen colors just before and just after this error message are identical, as ensured by the assignment statements for InitialTextAttr and **TextAttr**.

Another special effect is *reverse video*. In this case, we simply reverse the current background and foreground colors, display the reverse-video text portion, and reset the colors that were in effect just before we reversed the video.

SOUND

Up to now we have beeped the speaker by writing the function call **chr**(7). By controlling the sound coming out of the speaker, we can serve many useful purposes, including: alert cues, as in signaling the termination of a long calculation, the completion of a successful task, or the detection of an error condition; game cues, as in signaling specific movements, actions, and outcomes; and music generation, as in musical synthesis, composition, and pure listening pleasure (multimedia-equipped personal computers generate stereophonic sound).

We can spice up our programs with some special sounds by calling procedures **sound, delay,** and **nosound,** which reside in the crt unit.

EXAMPLE 8.6   MAKING SOUND

Consider the following code fragment.

```
sound (Cps);        {Emit tone having frequency Cps}
delay (Duration);   {Delay by Duration milliseconds}
nosound;            {Turn off speaker}
```

If Cps stores 100, the call to **sound** emits a continuous tone having a frequency of 100 Hz (hertz, or cycles per second).[4] If Duration stores 200, execution gets delayed 200 milliseconds, or 0.2 second. The call to **nosound** turns off the speaker. Thus, the sequence of calls **sound** (100), **delay** (200), and **nosound** emits a 100-Hz tone for 0.2 second.

By varying the values in Cps and Duration, particularly within a repetition structure, we can create some distinct sounds. In Exercises 16 and 30 we ask you to get noisy.

DATE AND TIME

The date and time are common displays in many commercial programs. Turbo Pascal's *dos unit* includes two procedures for these purposes.

- The call

    getdate (Year, Month, Day, DayOfWeek)

    receives the current date as type *word* values within the four parameters shown.

- The call

    gettime (Hour, Minute, Second, Second100)

    receives the current time as type *word* values within the four given parameters.

EXAMPLE 8.7   GOT THE DATE AND TIME?

Suppose the current date is Friday, December 25, 1992 and the current time is exactly 50 seconds after 10:30 P.M. The code fragment

```
getdate   (Year, Month, Day, DayOfWeek);
gettime   (Hour, Minute, Second, Second100);

writeln   ('Year.......... ', Year);
writeln   ('Month......... ', Month);
writeln   ('Day........... ', Day);
writeln   ('Day of week... ', DayOfWeek);
writeln;

writeln   ('Time:  ', Hour, ':', Minute, ':', Second, ':',
          Second100);
```

---

[4]The human audible range is roughly 19 to 20,000 Hz, provided our ears haven't been blown out listening to station WROC.

gives the output

```
Year.......... 1992
Month........ 12
Day.......... 25
Day of week... 5

Time:  22:30:50:0
```

Remember that the client program has to include **dos** in its uses clause. In Exercise 17 we ask you for the date and time.

REVISIT: MENU APPLICATION

Let's return to program Combo1 from Section 6.3 to . . .

1. Take advantage of OurUnit to eliminate utility procedures Pause, Fac, and MenuError from the revised program.
2. Call utility procedure ReadLnInt from Example 6.6 to input an integer value whose factorial we wish to display. This procedure is also in OurUnit.
3. Colorize the menu, factorial, and farewell screens.
4. Display the hours and minutes on the menu screen, in a 24-hour format.
5. Use reverse video to highlight menu input and factorial output.

Figure 8.6 shows a partial test run for the revised program Combo2 listed in Figure 8.7. Code fragments in color identify material from this chapter. Study the I/O and listing, and note the following.

1. We need the **dos unit** in the uses clause to get the time with a call to **gettime** within procedure OfferMenu. Screen 2 shows its display.
2. By including OurUnit in the uses clause we completely eliminated the declarations of modules Pause, Fac, MenuError, and ReadLnInt. This shortened the source program considerably. In writing a modular program from scratch, the use of utility modules in units not only reduces program size but also avoids the unproductive act of inserting the actual utility modules in the source code.
3. The statements

   ```
   TextAttr := InitialTextAttr;
   clrscr;
   ```

   at the end of OfferMenu and DoFactorial ensure that exit from these modules is "well behaved" with respect to resetting prior screen attributes; otherwise, the screen attributes for color that were set within

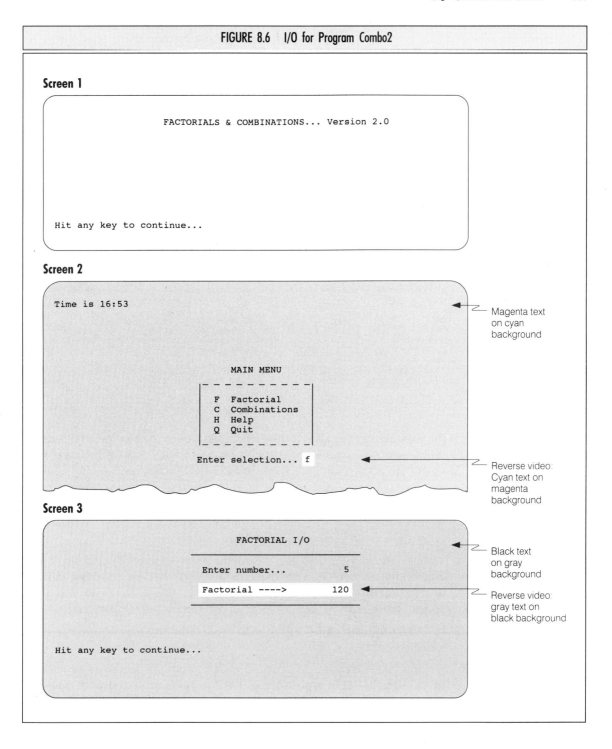

FIGURE 8.6   I/O for Program Combo2

Screen 1

```
              FACTORIALS & COMBINATIONS... Version 2.0




Hit any key to continue...
```

Screen 2

```
 Time is 16:53                                              ◀── Magenta text
                                                                on cyan
                                                                background




                    MAIN MENU
              - - - - - - - - - - - -
              │  F   Factorial      │
              │  C   Combinations   │
              │  H   Help           │
              │  Q   Quit           │
              - - - - - - - - - - - -
              Enter selection...  f                         ◀── Reverse video:
                                                                Cyan text on
                                                                magenta
                                                                background
```

Screen 3

```
                    FACTORIAL I/O                           ◀── Black text
              _____                     on gray
                                                               background
              Enter number...        5
              _____
              Factorial ---->      120   ◀──                ◀── Reverse video:
              _____                     gray text on
                                                               black background

 Hit any key to continue...
```

```
┌─────────────────────────────────────────────────────────────────────┐
│              FIGURE 8.7    Listing for Program Combo2                 │
├─────────────────────────────────────────────────────────────────────┤
│                                                                       │
│  program Combo2;                                                      │
│                                                                       │
│     {* * * * * * * * * * * * * * * * * * * * * * * * * * * * * * * *  │
│      *                                                             *  │
│      *        Menu Application:  Factorials & Combinations, Version 2.0  *
│      *                           w/ time of day, color, use of OurUnit,  *
│      *                           error handling for integer input   *  │
│      *                                                             *  │
│      *        Inputs menu selection, formula values for x, n and k  *  │
│      *        Calculates x factorial, combinations of n taken k at a time *
│      *        Outputs factorial, combination, or help              *  │
│      *                                                             *  │
│      *        Modular structure  ◄──┐                              *  │
│      *              │___ OpeningTasks    ┌ Simplified because we're    *
│      *              │___ OfferMenu         using OurUnit            *  │
│      *              │___ Help                                      *  │
│      *              │___ Farewell                                 *  │
│      *              │___ DoFactorial                              *  │
│      *              │___ DoCombinations                           *  │
│      *                                                             *  │
│     * * * * * * * * * * * * * * * * * * * * * * * * * * * * * * * *}  │
│                                                                       │
│     {=========================== Declarations ===========================}  │
│                                                                       │
│  uses                                                                 │
│     crt,                          {crt needed for clrscr, gotoxy}     │
│     dos,                          {dos needed for gettime}            │
│     OurUnit;                      {OurUnit needed for Pause, Fac, MenuError, │
│                                    ReadLnInt}                         │
│                                                                       │
│     ┌─────────────────────────────────────────────────────────────┐ │
│     │ The var section, procedures OpeningTasks, DoCombinations, Help, and │
│     │ the main body are not shown; they are the same as those in Figure 6.4. │
│     └─────────────────────────────────────────────────────────────┘ │
└─────────────────────────────────────────────────────────────────────┘
```

the module may inadvertently affect subsequent I/O color attributes in other modules. To ensure that the program itself is well behaved with respect to screen attributes, we include the statements

normvideo; clrscr;

in procedure Farewell. This practice ensures that screen attributes at program startup are reestablished just before program exit.

4. We used *reversed video* for the menu entry (screen 2) and the factorial output (screen 3). This effect is accomplished by reissuing calls to **textbackground** and **textcolor** with reversed background and foreground color parameters, as seen in OfferMenu and DoFactorial.

5. In DoFactorial we call ReadLnInt to ensure the input of an integer value for Number.

6. We only made changes in procedure OfferMenu, procedure DoFactorial, procedure Farewell, and in the early documentation and uses clause in program Combo2. No changes were made to any of the other modules, nor to the algorithm in the main body. We leave improvements in the

```
┌─────────────────────────────────────────────────────────────────────┐
│                      FIGURE 8.7   (continued)                         │
└─────────────────────────────────────────────────────────────────────┘
```

```pascal
procedure OfferMenu (var MenuSelection : char);

   { Sets colors, clears screen, gets and writes time, offers menu,
       inputs selection, resets original colors, clears screen, changes
       menu selection to uppercase
     Receives nothing
     Sends MenuSelection }

const
  BackgroundColor = Cyan;
  ForegroundColor = Magenta;          {Set Magenta on Cyan}

var
  Hour, Minute,
  Second, Second100  : word;          {Time parameters for gettime procedure}
  InitialTextAttr    : byte;          {Initial color text attributes}

begin   {OfferMenu}

  InitialTextAttr := TextAttr;        {TextAttr is crt var that stores
                                       current color text attributes}

  textbackground (BackgroundColor);  textcolor (ForegroundColor);

  highvideo;                          {Select high-intensity characters}

  clrscr;

  gettime (Hour, Minute, Second, Second100);      {Get time from DOS}
  write ('Time is ', Hour, ':', Minute);          {Write time}

  gotoxy (1,5);
  writeln ('                          MAIN MENU        ');
  writeln ('                                           ');
  writeln ('                     ┌ ─ ─ ─ ─ ─ ─ ─ ─ ┐   ');
  writeln ('                     │ F  Factorial    │   ');
  writeln ('                     │ C  Combinations │   ');
  writeln ('                     │ H  Help         │   ');
  writeln ('                     │ Q  Quit         │   ');
  writeln ('                     └ ─ ─ ─ ─ ─ ─ ─ ─ ┘   ');
  writeln;
  write   ('                      Enter selection... ');

  {Reverse video for keyboard input}
    textbackground (ForegroundColor);  textcolor (BackgroundColor);

  readln (MenuSelection);

  TextAttr := InitialTextAttr;    {Reset color attributes to originals}
  clrscr;                         {Clear screen, implement reset colors}

  MenuSelection := upcase( MenuSelection );

end;   {OfferMenu}
```

continued

other modules to the exercises. Are you convinced by now that modular programming simplifies maintenance?

7. You need to play around with Combo2 to appreciate its features. First, try some test drives in Exercise 18a. Next, work Exercises 18 and 19 to

FIGURE 8.7   *(continued)*

```
procedure DoFactorial;

   { Sets colors, inputs number by calling utility ReadLnInt, displays
       factorial in reverse video, calls utility Fac, calls utility Pause
     Receives nothing
     Sends nothing }

const
  Title = '          FACTORIAL I/O';
  Line  = '_____';
  BackgroundColor = LightGray;  ForegroundColor = Black;

var
  Number          : integer;      {Number whose factorial is evaluated}
  InitialTextAttr : byte;         {Initial color text attributes}

begin  {DoFactorial}

  InitialTextAttr := TextAttr;    {TextAttr is crt var}

 {Set colors}
  textbackground (BackgroundColor);  textcolor (ForegroundColor);

 {Clear screen, write title and lines, input number}
  clrscr;
  gotoxy (25, 9);  write (Title);
  gotoxy (25,10);  write (Line);
  gotoxy (25,15);  write (Line);
  gotoxy (27,12);  write ('Enter number...       '); ReadLnInt (Number);
```
                                                             ⟵ In OurUnit
```
 {Display output in reverse video}
  gotoxy (27,14);
  textbackground (ForegroundColor); textcolor (BackgroundColor);
  write ('Factorial ----> ', Fac( Number ) :10:0);
```
                                        ⟵ In OurUnit
```
 {Reset this screen's colors and call utility Pause}
  textbackground (BackgroundColor);  textcolor (ForegroundColor);
  Pause;  ⟵  In OurUnit

  TextAttr := InitialTextAttr;  clrscr;  {Reset attributes & clear screen}

end;   {DoFactorial}
{-------------------------------------------------------------------------}
procedure Farewell;

   { Sets colors, clears screen, displays farewell screen, calls utility
       Pause, resets original text attributes and clears screen
     Receives nothing
     Sends nothing }

const
  Farewell = 'We make a great COMBO... ''til we meet again...';
  BackgroundColor = Blue;  ForegroundColor = Yellow;

begin  {Farewell}

  textbackground (BackgroundColor);  textcolor (ForegroundColor);
  clrscr;
  gotoxy (20,10);  write (Farewell);
  Pause;  ⟵————————————————  In OurUnit
  normvideo;  clrscr;  {Reset attributes and implement with clrscr}

end;   {Farewell}
```

reinforce and increase your understanding of these new features. Then go out into the world and make a bundle with your increased skills in state-of-the art user interfaces.[5]

NOTE

4. Menu template utility program. We have added a program to our utilities libary named MenuTemp that provides a skeletal framework for menuing applications. It includes the following: The *main body* implements our usual repetition and case structures for offering and routing menu selections; procedure OpeningTasks offers a colorized opening screen; procedure OfferMenu displays a colorized menu screen, current time, and menu items, and inputs the selection; procedure Farewell writes a colorized farewell screen. This utility is a working program that you can flesh out with your own procedures. Additionally, you can customize it to your liking, as in setting your own screen colors.

SELF-REVIEW EXERCISES

13 14 18 20

---

‡8.4 GRAPH UNIT

• • • • • • • • • • • • • •

Computer *graphics* is the data display of "drawings" or "pictures," as in the display of two-dimensional and three-dimensional bar charts, pie charts, and other statistical graphs; drawings of objects, consumer products, people, structure charts, organization charts, electrical engineering diagrams, and architectural plans; computer-aided design (CAD) applications that scale, rotate, translate (shift), explode, and color drawings for new cars, computers, and other products; text generation for displaying text characters in various styles

---

[5]Well, not quite yet...but take a sneak preview at Module E to see what we can do in Turbo Pascal.

‡Optional, more advanced material. Skip without loss of continuity, study at this point, or wait until later.

(fonts) and sizes; and picture-processing applications like animation in games and movies, photographic recalls in criminal and reference database queries, and training simulations for pilots, astronauts, and other operators.

In recent years, graphics applications have really taken off commercially, primarily because of the increasing use of personal computers, hardware price reductions, the growing availability of sophisticated graphics hardware devices like laser printers and high-resolution color monitors, and the development of more advanced graphics software. To give you a "taste" for these applications, we *introduce* Turbo Pascal's considerable graphics capabilities. We stress the word *introduce* because we're just covering the "tip" of a very extensive and sophisticated (although easy to use) "iceberg."

SCREEN MODES AND OTHER MYSTERIES

Up to now, we have been working in a video mode called **text mode.** In this mode, the character is the smallest unit, and the screen is broken up into character positions that we describe as *columns* (the *horizontal* positions across the screen, or *x-coordinate*) and *rows* (the *vertical* positions up and down the screen, or *y-coordinate*). An entire text screen is described by the grid *80 × 25*, assuming a text mode with *80 columns* and *25 rows.* For example, the coordinate (20, 10) references the character position at column 20 and row 10. Thus, the call **gotoxy** (20, 10) moves the *cursor* to coordinate (20, 10). When using color, settings have a character point of view, as in using procedure **textcolor** to set the colors of individual characters. In short, text mode treats the *character* as the fundamental unit on the screen.

In **graphics mode** the fundamental unit is a *picture element,* or **pixel** for short. The pixel is a screen position. If this screen position is plotted in a color that differs from the background color, it shows up as a "point of light." The graphics screen is divided into columns and rows of pixels, with the same x- and y-coordinate conventions as text screens. In this case, the coordinate (20, 10) references the *pixel* position (address) at column 20 and row 10. The *home coordinate* in a graphics screen is at (0, 0), not (1, 1) as in the text screen.

The text-mode cursor does not show up in a graphics screen, and procedures that move the text cursor (like **gotoxy**) don't apply in graphics mode. Instead, we conceptualize the notion of a **current pointer (CP),** which has a coordinate position on the screen but is not visible. In the next section we show how to move the CP.

The *resolution* of a screen, which depends on the installed video hardware and software, is stated as the number of pixels that fit on a screen. For example, a standard VGA graphics screen has *640 horizontal pixels* by *480 vertical pixels;* its resolution is *640 × 480*, or 307,200 total pixels. The greater the number of pixels, the higher the resolution (the sharper the image). The southeast or bottom-right coordinate in a graphics screen thus depends on its resolution. For example, the southeast coordinate for a standard VGA

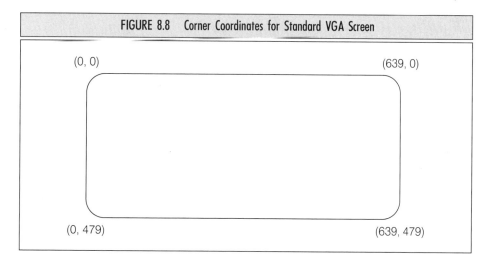

FIGURE 8.8   Corner Coordinates for Standard VGA Screen

(0, 0)   (639, 0)

(0, 479)   (639, 479)

screen is (639,479). Figure 8.8 shows the four corner coordinates for a VGA grahics screen. Note that the x-coordinate 639 is actually the 640th pixel in a row. Similarly, the y-coordinate 479 is the 480th pixel in a column. This is because the Home pixel is at $(0,0)$ rather than $(1,1)$.

Pixels are combined to form drawings of figures like lines, circles, and characters. When characters are drawn, graphics software has the flexibility of displaying characters in different sizes, and in different text styles called *fonts*. Be aware that we can't display text mode characters in graphics mode. Thus, the write and writeln statements don't apply in graphics mode. We use other procedures to display text on a graphics screen, as we will see.

Color is manipulated at the pixel level, as in drawing a line partly or entirely in red. The mix of colors, or color *palette*, varies depending on the installed video hardware. For example, VGA supports 16 colors at one time, from a palette of 256 colors; EGA supports 16 colors, from its palette of 64 colors; and CGA supports 4 colors from four different palettes of 4 colors each.

PREDEFINED GRAPHICS ROUTINES

Turbo Pascal has more than 50 predefined procedures and functions in its set of graphics routines. Additionally, it has even more predefined variables and constants. Let's explain some of these by example.

EXAMPLE 8.8   DEMONSTRATION OF SELECTED GRAPHICS ROUTINES

Figure 8.9 shows the output from program Greeting as listed in Figure 8.10. Note the following.

FIGURE 8.9　Output from Program Greeting

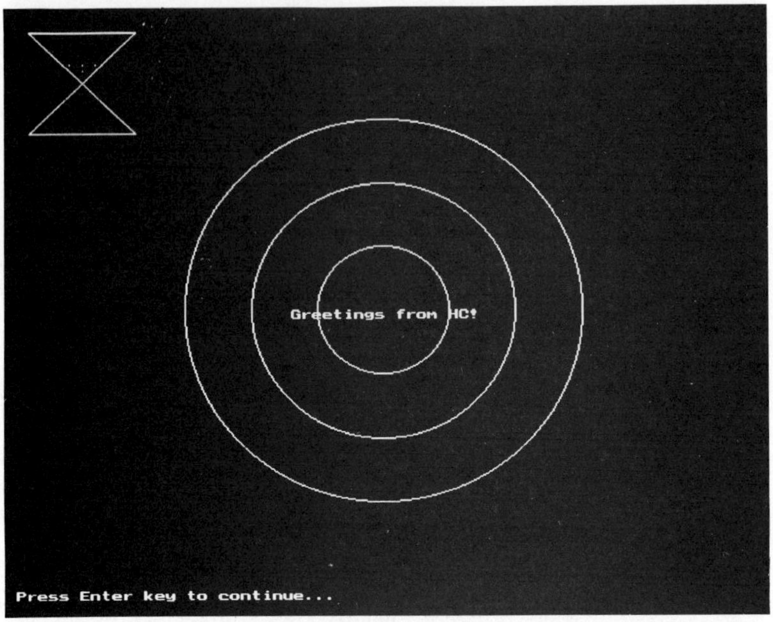

FIGURE 8.10　Listing of Program Greeting

```pascal
program Greeting;

   (* * * * * * * * * * * * * * * * * * * * * * * * * * * * * * * *
    *                                                             *
    *        Demonstrate graphics routines by displaying greeting *
    *                                                             *
    *           Inputs nothing                                    *
    *        Demonstrates graphics routines circle, closegraph, getmaxx, *
    *           getmaxy, initgraph, line, moveto, outtext, outtextxy, *
    *           putpixel, rectangle                               *
    *        Outputs rectangle containing hourglass, sand grains, *
    *           concentric rings, greeting, and pause message     *
    *                                                             *
    * * * * * * * * * * * * * * * * * * * * * * * * * * * * * * * *)

   {============================ Declarations ============================}

uses graph;

const
  DriverPath  = 'C:\TP6\BGI';  {Directory containing graphics driver}
  NumberRings = 3;             {Number of concentric rings}
  RadiusStep  = 50;            {Change in radius from one ring to the next}

var
  Driver, Mode,                {Graphics driver, mode parms. for initgraph}
  MaxX, MaxY,                  {Coordinate for southeast corner of screen}
  Ring        : integer;       {Ring number}
  Radius      : word   ;       {Ring radius}
```

FIGURE 8.10   (*continued*)

```
{============================= Main Body =============================}

begin    {Greeting}

  {Start up graphics system}
    Driver := Detect;                          {Set to autodetect video hardware}
    initgraph (Driver, Mode, DriverPath); {Autodetect driver, mode}

  {Assign southeast screen coordinate in pixels}
    MaxX := getmaxx;
    MaxY := getmaxy;

  {Draw rectangle over entire screen}
    rectangle (0, 0,  MaxX, MaxY);

  {Draw hourglass near northwest boundary}
    line (20, 20,  100, 20);                   {Draw top}
    line (20, 100, 100, 100);                  {Draw bottom}
    line (20, 20,  100, 100);                  {Draw side from upper left}
    line (20, 100, 100, 20);                   {Draw side from lower left}

  {Place two rows of sand grains in upper hourglass}
    putpixel (50,45,White); putpixel (60,45,White); putpixel (70,45,White);
                            putpixel (60,50,White);

  {Draw concentric rings next to center of screen}
    for Ring := 1 to NumberRings do
      begin
        Radius := Ring * RadiusStep;
        circle (MaxX div 2, MaxY div 2, Radius);
      end;

  {Write graphics text greeting centered on screen}
    outtextxy (MaxX div 2 - 70, MaxY div 2, 'Greetings from HC!');

  {Write graphics text pause message near southwest boundary}
    moveto (10, MaxY - 20);
    outtext ('Press Enter key to continue...');
    readln;

  {Close down graphics system}
    closegraph;

end.    {Greeting}
```

1. **Procedures initgraph and closegraph.** We *must* use these procedures to start up and close down the graphics system. The call

$$\textbf{initgraph } (\texttt{Driver, Mode, DriverPath});$$

initializes the graphics system by selecting a graphics driver and mode. Driver is an integer variable or constant that specifies the use of a predefined routine (called a *graphics driver*) for communicating with the system's videoboard (like CGA, EGA, VGA, or others supported by Turbo Pascal). Mode is an integer variable or constant that sets the desired graphics mode (for example, high- or low-resolution EGA). The DriverPath indicates the sub-directory path where Turbo Pascal's drivers are located. If the null ' ' is used for the driver path, then the current directory is assumed. The const section of program Greeting shows the driver path.[6] In our program, we set Driver to the predefined graphics constant **Detect** (= 0) just before the call to **initgraph,**

```
Driver := Detect;
```

which tells Turbo Pascal to select the proper driver and mode based on the automatic detection of the installed video hardware. Thus, we send the constant **Detect** as the value in Driver, and Turbo Pascal does the rest by selecting the proper driver routine and setting the graphics mode that was selected at installation. To exit graphics mode we must issue a call to **closegraph,** as seen at the end of program Greeting. This restores the screen mode to what it was just before the graphics system was initialized.

2. **Functions getmaxx and getmaxy.** We use these functions to return the bottom-right screen coordinate. The call **getmaxx** returns the x-coordinate, or 639 in VGA mode (see Figure 8.8). The call **getmaxy** returns the y-coordinate, or 479 in VGA mode. In program Greeting, we store these in variables MaxX and MaxY. These functions allow us to generalize the locations of drawings and text placement, so that we need not write programs that are video hardware specific.

3. **Procedure rectangle.** The call

```
rectangle (X1, Y1, X2, Y2);
```

draws a rectangle from the upper-left corner (X1, Y1) to the lower-right corner (X2, Y2). Actual parameters (the coordinates) in the call are integer constants, variables, or general expressions. In program Greeting, we specified a rectangle from the Home screen position (0,0) to the bottom-right screen position (MaxX, MaxY), as drawn in Figure 8.9.

4. **Procedure line.** The call

```
line (X1, Y1, X2, Y2);
```

draws a line from position (X1,Y1) to position (X2,Y2). The coordinates in the call are integer constants, variables, or general expressions. In program Greeting, we issued four calls to **line** to draw the hourglass in Figure 8.9.

5. **Procedure putpixel.** The call

```
putpixel (X, Y, Color);
```

plots a pixel at position (X,Y) as a tiny rectangle in the foreground color specified by Color. All parameters are integer constants, variables, or general expressions. See Table 8.2 for Turbo Pascal's colors. In program Greeting, we used **putpixel** to display four "white grains of sand" in the hourglass.

---

[6] It would be a good idea if you find out where the graphics drivers are installed in your system. Ours were installed in C:\TP6\BGI, but yours may be different. Turbo Pascal issues a run-time error if it can't find a graphics driver.

6. Procedure circle. The call

```
circle (X, Y, Radius);
```

draws a circle of Radius centered at position (X,Y). X and Y are integer constants, variables, or general expressions. Radius is type *word*, one of the integer types. In program Greeting, we drew three concentric circles of varying radii centered near the middle of the screen. Note how we used MaxX and MaxY to locate a pixel nearest the center.

7. Procedures outtextxy, outtext, and moveto. The following calls display text.

```
outtextxy (X, Y, TextString);
outtext (TextString);
```

TextString is a string variable or constant. Procedure **outtextxy** outputs the string at position (X,Y) and procedure **outtext** outputs the string at the CP. In program Greeting, we used the former to display the greeting in the middle of the concentric rings and the latter to display the pause message. To move the CP to position (X,Y), we use the call

```
moveto (X, Y);
```

In program Greeting, just before displaying the pause message, we moved the CP to a position near the bottom-left corner (10 pixels from the left border of the screen and 20 pixels above the bottom border). Alternatively, we could have both moved the CP and displayed the pause message in a single call to **outtextxy.**

NOTE

5. Graphics screen pause. Did you notice how we paused the graphics screen in program Greeting? We simply used **readln** without an input list. Our utility procedure Pause is inappropriate here, since it uses procedures that are text mode oriented.

6. Graphics screen dump. To print a graphics screen on paper, hold down a Shift key and press the Print Screen key. First, however, you may have to type the DOS command **GRAPHICS** *before* loading Turbo Pascal.

SELF-REVIEW EXERCISES

21

8.5   PROGRAMMING TIPS

• • • • • • • • • • • • • •

Consider the following tips to improve the design and style of your programs and to avoid some common errors.

DESIGN AND STYLE

1. The User Interface.   The success of a commerical applications program is very much related to the quality of its user interface. PC-style programming addresses many user-interface issues. The computer research literature has taken notice by describing and testing user-interface design principles, including the following.

> **a.** I/O principles like minimize input movements, maximize input channels (as in typing, cursor movement/selection, mouse), and include highly visual and attractive screens
> **b.** Dialog principles like use menus, prompts, and context-sensitive messages
> **c.** General principles like make simple, user-friendly, personalized, and consistent interfaces

As we have encouraged throughout the book, practice these principles in your own programming, as best you can.

2. Defensive Programming.   Issues in defensive programming are also related to commercial success. A program that "crashes" easily is unstable, and one that responds in surprising ways when users make input mistakes is discouraging. Include error-handling routines in your programs that trap I/O, range, and other potentially damaging errors.

3. On Using Units.   Units are the best way to handle modular libraries in practice. In your own programming, make as much use of OurUnit as you can. This reduces the size of your programs, compiles them more quickly, and increases your productivity by not having to "reinvent the wheel" for common tasks. When warranted, add your own routines to your own version of OurUnit.

4. Data and Procedural Abstraction.   In earlier chapters we stressed that procedural abstraction is a big advantage of using modules: We can focus on the essentials of using a module and on what it can do for us and not get burdened with the inessential details of how it accomplishes its tasks. In the last chapter we applied the same concept to data types by developing ADTs. In this chapter we used the unit as a container for an ADT, as we did with ADT Grade in unit ADTGrade. By including the ADT's unit in the uses clause of the client program, we apply the ADT in the abstract, much like we have been using types integer, real, and character. Look for opportunities to use or create ADT units in your own programming.

COMMON ERRORS

1. Unit Pitfalls.   If you get an error message like *Unknown identifier,* and the program line includes a call to a predefined or utility module other than those in the system unit, make sure that you included its unit in the uses clause. Also, don't forget to compile units to disk (see Note 1), and take care where units are stored (see Note 2).

2. Ill-Behavior in Screen Attributes.   If screen attributes are not returning to normal attributes, either after a module executes or when a program terminates, you might need to use the programming techniques discussed on page 362 in item 3 of our menu application.

3. Graphics Pitfalls.   If you get a *BGI error* message (BGI is short for Borland Graphics Interface), you forgot to start up the graphics system with a call to **initgraph.** If string output disappears from a graphics screen, most likely it doesn't fit on the screen. Try reducing the amount of text displayed on a line. Don't forget that text-based procedures calls like **gotoxy** and **writeln** don't have any effects in graphics mode.

4. Compiler Directive Errors.   Don't confuse the compiler directives {$I+} and {$I−} for I/O checking with {$I} for Include files.

NOTE

7. On explorations. In computing, we usually learn new material by exploring on our own. If we have curiosity, motivation, and a sense of excitement and make the time, we have many enjoyable travels ahead. The best guides for these explorations are *Reference Guides,* with the computer as vehicle and us as drivers. Here and there we have exercises that encourage you to go beyond our material (as in Exercise 25 below). But you need not wait for our suggestions. What will you do when this course is over? Happy travels!

REVIEW EXERCISES

EASIER	For the busy... **1 3 5 8 10 13 14 20 21 22a–b**
NORMAL	For the thinkers... **2 4 6 7 9 11 12 15 16 17 18 19a–d 22c**
TOUGHER	For the hard CORE... **19e 22d 23 24 25**

(L) 1. **Include file.** Implement program CkRdInt2 in Figure 8.1 on your system. Make sure you know the proper path for the Include file.

(L) *2. **Revisit: Menu Application.** Revise program Combo1 in Figure 6.4 to use Include files for all utility modules. Reproduce the test run in Figure 6.2.

(L) 3. **OurUnit.** Find out what directory holds OurUnit in your system. Load and view OurUnit. Note its suggestions for inserting your own utilities. Dump the listing to a printer for future reference.

(L) 4. **OurUnit.** Add any utility modules of your own to OurUnit. Save it and compile it to your own disk. Use this version in your future work.

(L) 5. **OurUnit.** Implement program CkRdInt3 in Figure 8.3 on your system.

(L) *6. **OurUnit.** Revise program CkRdInt3 in Figure 8.3 by adding a repetition structure controlled by a Y/N reply. Use utility procedure ReadReply from OurUnit.

(L) *7. **Revisit: Temperatures.** Revise program . . .
   a. Temp2 in Chapter 5 to trap noninteger input for Fahrenheit temperatures using utility procedure RdLnInt. Use OurUnit to import Pause, ReadReply, and ReadLnInt. Input the following temperatures in your test run: 85.5, 3q, 32.
   b. Temp2B in Module B to take advantage of the fact that Pause, ReadLnInt, ReadRep, and RepErr are in OurUnit.

(L) *8. **Revisit: HC METHsea.** Revise program MethSea1 to use utility function Distance in OurUnit. Reproduce the run in Figure 3.10.

(L) *9. **Input error handling.** Revise procedure ReadLnInt to input and trap a real value. Call this procedure ReadLnReal. Test this new utility procedure with the input e, 3.3, and 3, using one of the following approaches.
   a. A driver based on a revision of CkRdInt.
   b. A driver based on a revision of CkRdInt2.
   c. A driver based on a revision of CkRdInt3.

(L) 10. **ADT Grade.** Test drive program CkADT2 in Example 8.3. Reproduce the sample runs described in Section 7.2.

(L) *11. **ADT Grade.** Consider the following changes to unit ADTGrade in Example 8.3. Declare grade type GradeX. The declared grades for this grade type are (A, B, C, D, F, PASS, FAIL). Declare read and write operations that are similar to those for type Grade. Debug this new ADT by suitably revising the driver CkADT2 and processing each of the legitimate values, along with some incorrect values.

(L) *12. **Revisit: Set I/O.** Create unit ADTSet and suitably revise program SetIO from Chapter 7. ADTSet includes declarations for SetOfCaps, ReadCodes, and WriteCodes. Reproduce the sample run in Figure 7.3.

13. Revise the code in Example 8.4 as follows.
   a. Ensure that the screen is entirely blue before the error message is written.

b. Reset the screen to black text on a light gray background after the error message is written.

14. Revise the code in Example 8.5 as follows.
  a. Use a red background and blue characters.
  b. Blink the error message in normal video.

(L) ***15.** **Procedure ReadLnInt.** Revise ReadLnInt as ReadLnXInt to blink the given error message in red on a blue background, starting in column 1 of the last row in the screen. Debug the procedure as follows.
  a. Store the revised procedure in your utilities library and rework Exercise 1.
  b. Store the revised procedure in your version of OurUnit and rework Exercise 5.

*16. **Making sound.** Write a program that...
  a. Implements the sound code in Example 8.6. Input Cps and Duration. Experiment with different input values.
  b. **Procedure Beep.** Develop a procedure that receives Cps and Duration and beeps the speaker. Place it in your version of OurUnit or your own unit.

*17. **Got the date and time?** In Example 8.7...
  a. Write a program that implements the sample code.
  b. Revise the program to display the date in the customary American format, as in: December 25, 1992.

(L) **18.** **Menu application.** In our menu application...
  a. Play around with program Combo2. Reproduce our run in Figure 8.6. Try entering noninteger values for numbers in the factorial option. Now use Combo2 to confirm your answers to the following questions.
  b. What would happen if we were to clear the screen before and not after setting the colors in OfferMenu?
  c. What would happen if we were to forget clearing the screen at the end of Farewell?
  d. What would change in the menu screen if we were to move the write statement for 'Enter selection...' to just before its corresponding readln statement?
  e. Input noninteger values for the combinations input. What happens? Revise the program to trap these input errors.

(L) ***19.** **Menu application.** Revise and test Combo2 as follows.
  a. In procedure Help, display the help screen as yellow text on a green background.
  b. In procedure OpeningTasks, select foreground and background colors of your choice, and delay the screen three seconds instead of pausing it.
  c. In procedure OfferMenu, display the date in the upper-right part of the screen, on the same line as the time.

    d. Spiff up procedure DoCombinations with color and other good stuff.

    e. Revise procedure OfferMenu by confirming the selection Quit with a Y/N reply. For example, if the user selects Q, ask for confirmation at the bottom-left corner of the screen (change the color scheme here). If the user responds yes, continue as before; otherwise, reoffer the menu. Make sure that you trap incorrect Y/N responses (use an approach similar to that in ReadLnInt).

(L) **20.** **Menu template utility program.** Take a look at program MenuTemp in our utilities library. Run it. What do you think? Modify its colors to your liking. Place it in your own utilities library. Use it in one of your programming assignments, if appropriate.

(L) **21.** **Program Greeting.** Run the program in Figure 8.10 on your system. Is your screen the same as that in Figure 8.9?

(L) *22. **Program Greeting.** Revise and run the program in Figure 8.10 based on the following changes.

    a. Draw five concentric circles in radius increments of 30 pixels.

    b. Call procedures **setbkcolor** and **setcolor** (see Appendix E).

    c. Read coordinates for the hourglass. Try runs that place the hourglass: as in Figure 8.9; in the center of the rings.

    d. Add a five-grain row of sand above the three-grain row. Account for the coordinates entered in part **c**.

(L) *23. **Program Greeting.** Scale the rectangular drawing by letting the user input a percent size. For example, 50 percent would mean that the number of columns and rows in the rectangle is 50 percent of the columns and rows available on the graphics screen for that system. Center the rectangular greeting on the screen, and accordingly scale the hourglass and rings.

(L) *24. **Animation.** Animate the sand in Program Greeting as it flows from the top to the bottom of the hourglass. As top grains "disappear," new bottom grains appear. *Hint:* Use Time delays and calls to putpixel.

    *25. **Graphics research.** If you're really getting into graphics, check out and play around with one or more of the following routines: **arc, bar, settextjustify, setviewport, settextstyle, setfillstyle, window,** and any others that strike your fancy. We don't cover these routines, but why limit yourself? This is good stuff...have fun! *Hint:* You need to rely on the *Turbo Pascal Library Reference, User's Guide,* and *Programmer's Guide.*

ADDITIONAL EXERCISES

EASIER	For the busy... **26 27**
NORMAL	For the thinkers... **28 29 30 31**
TOUGHER	For the hard CORE... **32 33**

26. **Revisit.** Revisit one of your earlier programs to include...
   a. Include files.
   b. OurUnit.
   c. Color, text-effect, distinctive sound, or date and time features.
   d. Graphics.

27. **Revisit: Boolean I/O.** Rework Exercise 25 in Chapter 7 by creating unit ADTBool.

28. **Revisit: Grade report.** Rework Exercise 26 in Chapter 7 by using unit ADTGrade.

29. **Revisit: ADT Day.** Rework Exercise 27 in Chapter 7 by creating unit ADTDay.

30. **Procedure Tone.** Create some tones as follows.
   a. Develop a procedure named Tone that emits a number of separate tones having duration and frequency in cps, with a pause between each tone. The procedure receives integer Number, Cps, Duration, and Pause; it sends nothing.
   b. Write a driver to experiment with different tones. The driver has a loop for number of experiments desired. Within the loop, interactively input values for Number, Cps, Duration, and Pause. To get you going, try some combinations using 10 for Number; 20, 100, 500, and 5000 for Cps; 10, 100, and 500 for Duration; and 10, 100, and 500 for Pause.
   c. Add a loop at the end of the driver that varies the frequency of a single tone over the range 1 to Cps. Within this loop use the call

      Tone (1, Range, Duration, Pause).

31. **Time display.** Consider the following time-display alternatives.
   a. Develop utility procedure WriteTime to display time in the format

      Hour : Minute : Second a.m. (or p.m.)

      Hour is an integer from 0 to 12, where 0 is at the midnight crossover and 12 is at the noon crossover. Minute and Second are integers from 0 to 59. The procedure receives Hour24, Minute, and Second. Hour24 is an integer in the range 0..23. Debug the procedure with a driver, and try the following test data sets for receiving values: 15, 16, 51; 0, 10, 5; 12, 5, 59; 0, 0, 0 (midnight is A.M.); 12, 0, 0 (noon is P.M.).

b. Include the debugged procedure in your version of OurUnit. Show its use in program Combo2.

c. Develop utility procedure TimeLive to display the current time in real time, that is, the time components change even as we speak. Make use of procedure WriteTime in part **a**. Terminate the display when the user presses any key. *Hint:* Use an until structure to display time.

32. **Dating service.** The Sure Thing Dating Service has a data file of clients with the following record layout and data file.

Record Layout

Field	Values	Description	Field	Values	Description
Name	···	Last name, first middle	Education	1	Elementary
Sex	1	Female		2	High School
	2	Male		3	College
Age	1	Less than 20		4	Overeducated
	2	20–29		5	Streetwise
	3	30–39	Occupation	1	Professional
	4	Over the hill		2	Skilled
Height	1	Less than 5'0"		3	Student
	2	5'0" but less than 5'7"		4	Surfer
	3	5'7" but less than 6'0"	Income	1	Less than $20K
	4	Tall		2	$20K but less than $30K
Weight	1	Less than 100		3	$30K but less than $50K
	2	100 but less than 120		4	$50K but less than $100K
	3	120 but less than 160		5	Loaded
	4	160 but less than 200			
	5	Big			

Data file

Furcolo, Mark "Copter"	2	2	2	3	4	4	2
Manni, Charlotte "Char"	1	3	2	2	5	2	2
Moxina, Lichade	2	4	2	3	4	1	4
Morfella, Yarta "Yo"	1	1	2	1	2	3	1
Dunn, John "JKD"	2	4	1	5	3	1	5
Mello, Cynthia "Amor"	1	3	3	3	5	2	1
Clay, Joshua "Mapper"	2	1	2	2	1	3	1
Jardon, Rick "Chiro"	2	2	2	3	4	1	4
Carroll, Meg "Bev Francis"	1	2	2	2	4	1	3
CORE, Harvey	2	4	4	4	5	1	5

Harvey CORE, Jr., the Head Date at Sure Thing, wants you to develop a program that services walk-in and telephone clients who request dates. The program inputs the data file and interactively inputs a date request. The date request is a series of interactive inputs of a person's (requestor's) preferences for each of the fields (except name) in the data file. For example, input for the first two preferences might appear as follows:

Enter sex preference . . . 1
Enter age preference . . . 2

A preference of zero indicates "no preference." The program then prints a list of names (possible dates) and their Desirability Index. The desirability index (DI) is the number of matches between preferences in all but the first two fields in the data file. For example, a perfect match between preferences and characteristics is 6. Sex is not used in the DI; rather it is the basis for whether a name is printed or not (unless the requestor enters zero for this preference, in which case all names are printed). Each match adds a point to the DI, unless the preference is zero, in which case we add a half point. Consider the following three date requests.

Request	Sex	Age	Height	Weight	Education	Occupation	Income
First	2	3	3	3	0	4	5
Second	0	1	2	1	2	3	0
Third	1	3	3	3	5	2	1

Output for the first request might appear as follows.

Name	Desirability Index
Mark "Copter" Furcolo	2.5
Lichade Moxina	1.5
John "JKD" Dunn	1.5
Joshua "Mapper" Clay	0.5
Rick "Chiro" Jardon	1.5
Harvey CORE	1.5

Note that only males are output, since the sex preference was 2. Confirm the DI output, and do a desk check for the other two requests.

a. Develop the program described. Use the given data in your test run.

b. Include field descriptions for each person's last six fields in the output report. For example, the output line for "Copter" would include 20–29 for age, 5'0" to 5'7" for height, 120–160 for weight, Overeducated for education, Surfer for Occupation, and $20,000–$30,000 for income.

c. Offer a main menu with the following selections: Make Match, display File, eXit.

Have fun! If you do a good job, HC Jr. might fix you up . . .

33. **Graphics menu.** Develop a program that offers a menu of graphics figures like line, circle, square, rectangle, and so on. When the user selects a menu item, the program then prompts for any needed coordinate(s), color, or other relevant data. Then the program draws the desired figure, and pauses until the user wishes to continue. The option to quit the program is menu selectable.

SIMULATION

---

‡Optional, more advanced material. Skip without loss of continuity, study at this point, or wait until later.

Simulation is a methodology for conducting experiments using models of real or proposed systems. Physical and digital simulations are two common approaches to running simulations. In a *physical simulation* the model is physical, as in simulating airflows over a scaled automobile model in a wind tunnel. In a *digital simulation* the model is an algorithm, and the computer is used to imitate the behavior of the system of interest.

Digital simulations are extensively used in the sciences, engineering, and business. For example, it's been applied to evaluating military war (and business) gaming strategies, studying environmental pollution, assessing air traffic control systems, scheduling jobs in computer and production systems, describing the replication behavior of biological populations, analyzing aircraft metal fatigue, and playing games (mostly for fun) like Microsoft *Flight Simulator*. In this module, we describe Turbo Pascal's facilities for conducting digital simulations and illustrate their use by examples.

C.1 RANDOM NUMBERS

Before we illustrate a digital simulation, let's go over some simulation concepts and definitions.

WHAT'S A RANDOM NUMBER?

Let's consider the process of flipping a balanced coin. Suppose we wish to determine the number of heads that come up out of 100 flips. In the real process, we would simply flip a coin 100 times, while keeping an accurate count of the number of flips and heads. If the experiment called for 1000 flips, the process would be the same but obviously more time consuming.

Now, suppose we're out of coins, but do have two identical gaming chips (from our last trip to Vegas?). We could write a "head" on one side of a chip, and then flip the chip in place of the coin. But suppose we don't trust that the chip is balanced, like our presumed coin. In this case, we can write "tail" on the second chip, place both chips in a paper bag, shake the bag, and blindly draw a single chip. This would be an example of a *physical* simulation. Given our assumptions, the simulation would be a legitimate representation of the real process, because the likelihood of simulating a head (0.5 or 50 percent) is identical to the likelihood of flipping a real coin and getting a head.

Let's take this a step further. Suppose the only prop available to us is a PC outfitted with Turbo Pascal. Moreover, suppose that Turbo Pascal includes a function that returns either the digit 0 or the digit 1, with equal likelihood. We could say that the 0 represents a head and 1 represents a tail. This would be an example of a *digital* simulation. It's also a serviceable representation of reality, again because the likelihood (probability) of getting a head is identical to the probability of getting a tail.

The numbers 0 and 1 in our coin-flipping simulation are examples of *random numbers*—that is, generated equally likely numbers that we can use to replicate the behavior of some probabilistic (chance) process. The following algorithm describes a digital simulation for any number of coin-flip simulations.

> Read NumberSimulations
> For each Simulation do
>   Generate RandomNumber (0 or 1)
>   If RandomNumber = 0
>   then write "Head"
>   else write "Tail"

FUNCTION RANDOM

In Turbo Pascal we generate a random number by calling one of the following versions of the predefined function **random.**

Version 1: Returns integer value in range 0, 1, . . . , UpperBound − 1

random (UpperBound)

Version 2: Returns real value in range 0.0 but less than 1.0

random

In the first version, UpperBound is an integer expression for the upper bound of generated random numbers, and the function returns an *integer* random number within this bound. For example, **random** (2) would return the random number 0 or 1; **random** (6) would return a random number in the range 0 . . 5. *Note that the upper bound is one more than the highest random number returned.*[1]

If we don't use an argument, as in the call **random,** the function returns a *real* random number in the range 0.0 but less than 1.0. This version is useful in reproducing probability distributions that describe chance outcomes. For instance, in our coin-flipping simulation, we could generate a real random

---

[1] Actually, UpperBound and the generated random numbers are integers of type *word*, having a range of 0 to 65535.

number in the interval 0–1, and then assign the outcome "head" if the random number is less than 0.5.

SEEDS

The function that returns a random number uses an algorithm, a *random number generator,* that mathematically generates a random number based on the preceding random number. In other words, to generate its current random number, the random number generator requires the last random number that it generated. This means that the function needs a *seed,* a starting number, to generate its first random number. We have two ways of specifying a seed in Turbo Pascal. First, we can call the predefined procedure **randomize** to initialize the random number generator. In this case, Turbo Pascal uses the system clock to find a seed that gets stored in **RandSeed,** a predeclared longint variable in the public section of the *system unit.* Instead of using **randomize,** we can assign or input a value for **RandSeed** within the program. Separate runs of a program using the same seed generate an identical sequence of random numbers, an important benefit in controlling the chance (random) effect in simulation experiments.

C.2   DICE SIMULATOR

. . . .

The best way to understand digital simulations is to develop a simulation program for a familiar process. Let's simulate throws of a pair of dice.

REQUIREMENTS

For you nongamblers, each die is a cube with six faces. Each face in turn has one to six dots called *spots.* We assume a legitimate operation with perfectly balanced dice. This means that for any one die, the probability of throwing a 1 (the face with one spot facing upward once the die stops rolling) is the same as the probability of throwing 2, 3, 4, 5, or 6. To simulate the throw of a single die, therefore, we need only generate random numbers in the interval $0..5$. By adding one to the generated random number, we have our needed equally likely experimental outcomes of spots in the range $1..6$. By generating two random numbers in one throw, and summing the resulting spots, we have the simulated *score* for throwing a pair of dice. For example, if the first random number is 1 (the first die is 2) and the second random number is 4 (the second die is 5), then the simulated score for this roll is 7 (2 + 5).

In our program, let's input the number of throws and output a table that shows the throw, first die outcome, second die outcome, and score. We want I/O to be repetitive, letting the user decide on the fly when to terminate the run. Also, let's include error handling for noninteger input. Finally, let's limit the number of rows on one screen to 15. If the number of simulated throws is greater than 15, then we wish the program to pause the screen for every 15 rows in the table. The 15 is a constant in the program.

DESIGN

Figure C.1 shows the I/O design for our proposed program. The first screen is a simple input screen and includes input error handling to ensure the entry of an integer value. We're conducting a 25-throw simulation, which means that our output table will take up the next two screens, as seen in the figure.

Figure C.2 shows a stepwise chart for the design algorithms. Note the following.

1. At the beginning of a run, we need to initialize (randomize) the random number generator.

2. The while-do structure repeats separate experiments, where each experiment is a complete simulation table for the number of throws that were input. Before each experiment, we need to initialize the row count (TableRow) to zero for the max-fifteen-row table that fits on one screen.

3. The table body is generated by a counter (for-do) loop that repeats from the first throw to the last throw. The body of this loop simulates the

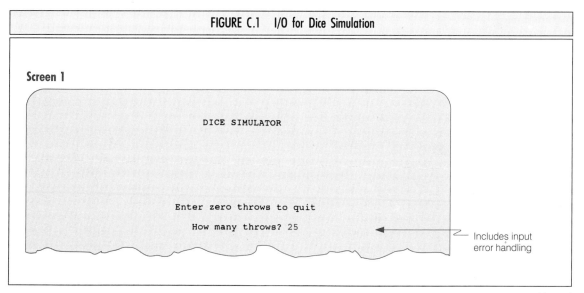

FIGURE C.1   I/O for Dice Simulation

Screen 1

```
                    DICE SIMULATOR




                Enter zero throws to quit

                How many throws? 25          ←────  Includes input
                                                      error handling
```

continued

FIGURE C.1   (*continued*)

Screen 2

```
                Dice Simulations

                First    Second
        Throw   Die      Die      Score

          1      4        4         8
          2      3        4         7
          3      5        3         8
          4      2        2         4
          5      1        2         3
          6      2        5         7
          7      1        4         5
          8      6        1         7
          9      2        6         8
         10      6        2         8
         11      3        2         5
         12      5        1         6
         13      1        6         7
         14      5        5        10
         15      1        6         7


Hit any key to continue...
```

← Pause every 15 rows in table

Screen 3

```
                Dice Simulations

                First    Second
        Throw   Die      Die      Score

         16      4        6        10
         17      3        5         8
         18      1        3         4
         19      4        3         7
         20      6        3         9
         21      6        5        11
         22      3        1         4
         23      6        3         9
         24      1        2         3
         25      1        2         3



Hit any key to continue...
```

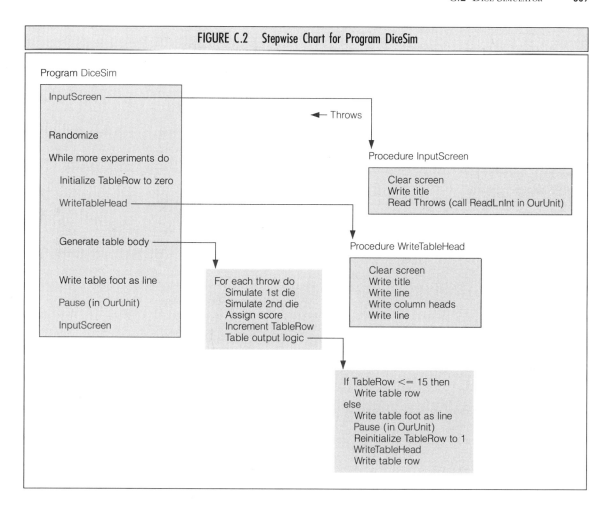

FIGURE C.2   Stepwise Chart for Program DiceSim

Program DiceSim

InputScreen ————————————————┐

                              ◄— Throws

Randomize

While more experiments do   Procedure InputScreen

  Initialize TableRow to zero   Clear screen
                                               Write title
  WriteTableHead ——————————————┐   Read Throws (call ReadLnInt in OurUnit)

  Generate table body ————————┐

                                             Procedure WriteTableHead

  Write table foot as line   Clear screen
                                               Write title
  Pause (in OurUnit)   For each throw do   Write line
                                 Simulate 1st die   Write column heads
  InputScreen   Simulate 2nd die   Write line
                                 Assign score
                                 Increment TableRow
                                 Table output logic ——┐

                                             If TableRow <= 15 then
                                                 Write table row
                                             else
                                                 Write table foot as line
                                                 Pause (in OurUnit)
                                                 Reinitialize TableRow to 1
                                                 WriteTableHead
                                                 Write table row

throw, increments TableRow, and applies an if-then-else structure for the output of the simulated throw. If the current table row is within the 15-row limit, then a row is output; else we need to terminate this table with a line, pause the screen until the user presses a key, and continue the table on the next screen by writing its head and first row.

CODE

Figure C.3 shows the code that corresponds to the design. Note the following.

1. Procedure InputScreen uses our utility procedure ReadLnInt, which is housed in OurUnit.

2. A call to **randomize** is issued before the first experiment; otherwise, each new run would repeat the same random number sequence.

```
┌─────────────────────────────────────────────────────────────────────────┐
│                    FIGURE C.3   Listing for Program DiceSim               │
├─────────────────────────────────────────────────────────────────────────┤
│                                                                           │
│    program DiceSim;                                                        │
│                                                                           │
│       {* * * * * * * * * * * * * * * * * * * * * * * * * * * * * * * * *   │
│        *                                                               *   │
│        *         Dice Simulator                                        *   │
│        *                                                               *   │
│        *            Inputs number of dice throws                       *   │
│        *            Simulates throws of dice                           *   │
│        *            Outputs throw number, spots each die, score        *   │
│        *                                                               *   │
│        *            Modular structure                                  *   │
│        *                 |__  InputScreen                              *   │
│        *                 |__  WriteTableHead                           *   │
│        *                                                               *   │
│        * * * * * * * * * * * * * * * * * * * * * * * * * * * * * * * * *}  │
│                                                                           │
│       {========================== Declarations ===========================}│
│                                                                           │
│    uses crt, OurUnit;                    {Import Pause and ReadLnInt from OurUnit}│
│                                                                           │
│    const                                                                  │
│      Line    = '                                       ';                  │
│                                                                           │
│      MaxRows = 15;                {Maximum rows in sim table on one screen}│
│                                                                           │
│    var                                                                    │
│      Die1, Die2,                  {Face value of or spots on each die}     │
│      Score,                       {Sum of spots on the two dice}           │
│      TableRow,                    {Row number in simulation table}         │
│      Throw,                       {Throw number}                           │
│      Throws      : integer;       {Number of throws of the dice}           │
│                                                                           │
│       {====================== Procedure Declarations ====================}│
│                                                                           │
│    procedure InputScreen (var Throws : integer);                          │
│                                                                           │
│      { Displays title, inputs number of throws                            │
│        Receives nothing                                                    │
│        Sends Throws }                                                      │
│                                                                           │
│    const                                                                  │
│      Title = 'DICE SIMULATOR';                                            │
│                                                                           │
│    begin   {InputScreen}                                                   │
│                                                                           │
│      clrscr;                                                               │
│      gotoxy (30,  5);  write (Title);                                      │
│      gotoxy (25, 12);  write ('Enter zero throws to quit');                │
│      gotoxy (28, 14);  write ('How many throws? ');   ReadLnInt (Throws);  │
│                                                                           │
│    end;   {InputScreen}                                                    │
│       {-----------------------------------------------------------------} │
└─────────────────────────────────────────────────────────────────────────┘
```

3. Each die is simulated by the call **random** (6), which returns a random number in the range 0..5. One is then added to the random number, giving the simulated number of spots for that die.

TEST

Figure C.1 shows the final test run for program DiceSim. Getting the paused tables just right for each screen took a few test runs. Exercises 1–4 motivate other test runs and program improvements.

FIGURE C.3   (*continued*)

```
procedure WriteTableHead;

  { Displays title, column headings, lines for simulation table
    Receives nothing
    Sends nothing }

const
  Title    = '              Dice Simulations';
  Line     = '     _____';
  ColHead1 = '               First    Second';
  ColHead2 = '       Throw    Die      Die     Score';

begin   {WriteTableHead}

  clrscr;
  writeln (Title);
  writeln (Line);  writeln;
  writeln (ColHead1);
  writeln (ColHead2);
  writeln (Line);  writeln;

end;    {WriteTableHead}

  {============================= Main Body =============================}

begin   {DiceSim}

  InputScreen (Throws);
  randomize;                              {Initialize random number generator}

  while Throws > 0 do   {next experiment}
    begin
      TableRow := 0;                      {Initialize table row for new table}
      WriteTableHead;

      for Throw := 1 to Throws do
        begin
          Die1  := random(6) + 1;     {Simulate spots 1st die}
          Die2  := random(6) + 1;     {Simulate spots 2nd die}
          Score := Die1 + Die2;       {Store simulated score this throw}

          inc (TableRow);
          if TableRow <= MaxRows then
            writeln (Throw :9, Die1 :8, Die2 :8, Score :9)
          else
            begin
              writeln (Line);
              Pause;
              TableRow := 1;
              WriteTableHead;
              writeln (Throw :9, Die1 :8, Die2 :8, Score :9);
            end; {if}

        end; {for}

      writeln (Line);
      Pause;
      InputScreen (Throws);
    end; {while}

end.    {DiceSim}
```

— Generates table body

— Row output logic

SELF-REVIEW EXERCISES

1 2

C.3   PROGRAMMING TIPS

• • • • • • • • • • • • • • •

Consider the following tips to improve the design and style of your programs and to avoid some common errors.

DESIGN AND STYLE

Simulation design and style issues primarily revolve around experimental design and other statistical issues that are beyond the scope of this text. In Exercise 3 we ask you to consider the issue of estimating probabilities.

COMMON ERRORS

Common errors in digital simulation programs include the omission or misplacement of the **randomize** procedure and misunderstood upper bounds for function **random.** We ask you to consider the former in Exercise 2.

REVIEW EXERCISES

EASIER	For the busy. . .
	1
NORMAL	For the thinkers . . .
	2
TOUGHER	For the hard CORE . . .
	3 4

(L) **1.** **Dice simulator.** Run program DiceSim to simulate 50 and 100 throws of the dice. From each output table, estimate the probability of rolling a 7. The probability of rolling "snake eyes" (2)?

(L) **2.** **Dice simulator.** Let's explore the effects of the seed as follows.
   a. Temporarily delete **randomize** cr, better yet, enclose it in braces { }. Run the program twice with the following inputs: 5 and 0; 5 and 0. Conclusion?

b. In place of **randomize,** input a value for the predefined variable **RandSeed**. Input the same seed for the runs described in part **a**. Conclusion?

(L) ***3.** **Dice simulator.** Let's estimate the probabilities of rolling different scores.

    a. Revise program DiceSim to count the number of throws scoring 2..12. Display this frequency distribution in the form of a table. Include a third column that displays the probability in percent form. For example, if we simulated 100 throws and scored 15 sevens, we would estimate the probability of throwing a seven as 15 percent. Simulate 100 throws in your test runs. Answer the same probability questions posed in Exercise 1.

    b. Include a user-selectable (Y/N) option of whether or not to display the table of simulated throws. The probability table in part **a** is always written. Simulate 1000 and 5000 throws, but don't display the table of throws. Answer the same probability questions posed earlier. Which probability estimates do you have more confidence in, the ones based on 100, 1000, or 5000 simulations? Why?

(L) ***4.** **Dice simulator.** Let's dress up program DiceSim.

    a. Add color, sound, or whatever else you think will make the dice simulator more appealing.

    b. Instead of displaying integer points for First die and Second die in the simulation table, how about displaying a graphic of the proper die face? For example, the second row in Figure C.1 might look like this:

Hint: Consider using a case structure to draw the proper face (and get hold of a real die for the correct face designs!).

ADDITIONAL EXERCISES

EASIER	For the busy...
	5
NORMAL	For the thinkers...
	6 7
TOUGHER	For the hard CORE...
	8 9

5. **Simulation: State lottery.** Consider a state lottery that generates a three-digit winning number each day. To select a winning number, the state does a nightly TV thing with a machine that has 10 "whirling" balls numbered 0, 1, . . . , 9. These balls are randomly moved by air streams, so that (supposedly) the selection of any one ball is as likely as any other ball. To generate a three-digit random number, three machines are used. The state is going to can the TV show (but not the daily lottery). They plan to trade in the three machines for a PC (the Lottery Commissioner has one at home) outfitted with Turbo Pascal. Develop a program that generates a *n*-digit "drawing." Try six test runs to generate separate three- and five-digit drawings.

6. **Simulation: Starlite, starlite.**[2] Develop a program with the following features.

   a. Plot pixels as "stars" that appear randomly in the "sky" by generating coordinates using the random number generator. Use a repeat-until structure that plots stars until a key is pressed. Input a time delay between plotted stars. Experiment with the time delay to get a good effect.

   b. Use another loop to simulate the disappearance of stars (as dawn approaches?)

7. **Simulation: Coin-flip game.** Sharpie, a long-time resident of Las Vegas, has proposed a game to Harvey CORE on one of his numerous B&P (Business and Pleasure) trips. The conversation, as overheard in the men's room, went something like this:

   SHARPIE: (With a gleam in his eye.) I have a game you can't refuse . . .
   HARVEY: (Skeptical, but definitely interested.) Oh yeah?
   SHARPIE: (Warming up to the occasion.) Yeah. You flip a coin until the difference between the number of heads and the number of tails reaches three.
   HARVEY: (Casually, with a subtle smile.) What kind of bread are we talking . . . ?
   SHARPIE: (Barely containing his excitement.) You pay me $1 for each flip. When the game ends, I pay you $8. Okay . . . ?
   HARVEY: (Feeling the pocket computer in his breast pocket, and figuring his counterproposal will end up paying for this B&P trip . . .) I'll get back to ya in five minutes . . .
   SHARPIE: (Somewhat doubtful). Well, okay . . .

   How sharp is Sharpie? Develop a program that simulates this game. (It will probably take you more than five minutes . . .) Simulate 10, 100, and 1000 games. What's Harvey's expected loss per game? What should Harvey propose in place of the $8 if he wishes to pay for his $5000 B&P trip in 100 games?

   ---
   [2]This exercise assumes you studied Section 8.4.

8. **Simulation: Craps.** A front-line bet in a game of craps works as follows.

   First roll of dice
   1. You win what you bet if on the first toss you roll 7 or 11 (a natural).
   2. You lose what you bet if on the first toss you roll a 2, 3, or 12 (a crap).
   3. If you roll a 4, 5, 6, 8, 9, or 10 on the first toss, then this number becomes your *point* for subsequent rolls.

   Subsequent rolls of dice
   4. To win, you must roll your point again *before* you roll a 7.
   5. If you roll a 7 while trying to get your point, then you lose.
   6. If neither your point nor 7 is rolled, then roll again.

   a. Develop a program that simulates the game of craps. Design a loop that simulates a single game of craps as described in items 1 through 6 above. The outcome of this loop is either "won" or "lost."

   b. Add a second loop that simulates *n* games. Assume $1 is bet on each game. Keep track of wins and losses. Debug your program by simulating five games. In your output for each roll, display the point on the first die, the point on the second die, and the overall score. At the end of a game write "won" or "lost." At the end of the five games write the following summaries: number of games won, number of games lost, your total dollar winnings (or losses), and the percent (of the total amount bet) dollar winnings (or losses).

   c. Provide an option in the program to suppress the output for each roll and the "won" or "lost" output at the end of each game. For each of the following runs just print the summary statistics:
   $$(1) \ n = 100$$
   $$(2) \ n = 500$$
   $$(3) \ n = 1000$$
   $$(4) \ n = 5000$$
   Based on your output, estimate the expected (percent) loss by betting the front line in craps.

9. **Simulation: Stock market.** Adam Smith, Jr., is an up-and-coming investor. (It runs in the family.) For many trading days he has observed the closing price (per share) behavior of a particular stock that he has taken a fancy to, as shown in Table C.1.

   Adam's parents have just given him 100 shares of this very same stock, which currently closed up $1 at $20 a share. This gift, however, is not without a very specific condition: Adam must cash in his shares at the end of 30 days, since the money realized from this sale will become his expense money for his first year in college. Needless to say, Adam is concerned with having a good (extracurricular) time his first year in college, so he has devised an investment strategy that "can't lose," as follows:

   (1) Sell all shares owned at the end of a trading day whenever the price of the stock increases.

Table C.1   Conditional Probabilities for Stock Price Behavior*

Price Change Any Given Day to Nearest $1	Price Change the Following Day			
	Down $1	Same	Up $1	Up $2
Down $1	0.4	0.3	0.2	0.1
Same	0.3	0.3	0.3	0.1
Up $1	0.2	0.4	0.2	0.2
Up $2	0.3	0.4	0.2	0.1

*Each row in the table is a complete probability distribution given (conditional upon) the row event. In the last row, for example, if the price is up $2 today, then chances it's down $1 tomorrow are 3 in 10, the same 4 in 10, up $1 2 in 10, and up $2 1 in 10.

(2) Buy as many shares as cash allows whenever the price of the stock has declined at the end of a trading day.

(3) Do nothing if price remains the same.

a. Simulate Adam's cash position at the end of 30 days given that 1 percent of the price of each share goes to the broker as commission whenever shares are bought or sold. Perform this simulation five times, using the seed 2001 for the first simulation.

b. Would Adam have been better off at the end of 30 days if he had just let the shares "ride" while spending his time at the beach? Why should you use the same seeds as part **a** in this comparison?

c. Can you think of other investment strategies? If so, simulate them and compare.

Arrays

†Optional, more advanced material. Skip without loss of continuity, study at this point, or wait until later.

With few exceptions, our view of variables up to now has been a simple view: A variable stores a single value. We deviated from this view twice: The *text-file variable* stores a collection of characters in an external file medium (Section 4.3) and the *set variable* stores a limited collection of values having the same ordinal type (Section 7.3).

In this chapter we present the *array* or *array variable*, which stores a potentially large collection of values of the same data type. As in mathematics, arrays in Pascal give us the means to store and manipulate *data structures* of sequentially related elements.

9.1 ONE-DIMENSIONAL ARRAYS

Suppose we had to find the average or mean of 500 temperatures. No problem. We would use a repetition structure that repeats 500 times. For each repetition, we would read a temperature and update the sum of temperatures. Following the loop, we would write the mean as the sum divided by 500. Suppose, however, that we wanted to write all temperatures below the mean, or write all differences from the mean. We would have to find the mean after the first loop is completed, and then add a second loop following the first that *rereads* the same temperatures. Within the second loop, we could write temperatures below the mean, or differences of each temperature from the mean. This approach is *I/O inefficient*, since it requires two complete reads of the same data.

Worse yet, suppose we needed to sort temperatures in ascending order. In this case, we could come up with 500 variables to store each temperature in memory, and then develop a tedious algorithm that sorts the data. The input statements alone would have 500 identifiers in their lists! Moreover, program maintenance would be a nightmare, since the need to sort a different number of temperatures, say 600, would require substantial changes to the program itself. This solution would be both *code inefficient* and *maintenance inefficient*.

DATA STRUCTURE

The solution to our temperature problem is to conceptualize the group of temperatures as a *data structure*, a collection of related data that are arranged in a particular pattern or structure. In particular, let's use a data structure called an **array,** which treats data as a group of sequentially indexed and adjacent memory cells that contain values having the same data type. Figure 9.1 shows

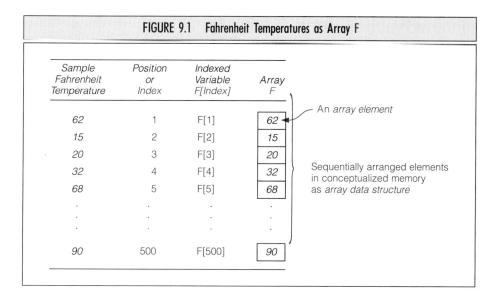

FIGURE 9.1   Fahrenheit Temperatures as Array F

Sample Fahrenheit Temperature	Position or Index	Indexed Variable F[Index]	Array F	
62	1	F[1]	62	← An *array element*
15	2	F[2]	15	
20	3	F[3]	20	
32	4	F[4]	32	Sequentially arranged elements in conceptualized memory as *array data structure*
68	5	F[5]	68	
.	.	.	.	
.	.	.	.	
.	.	.	.	
90	500	F[500]	90	

how we might view the 500-element temperature array F, where each value or *array element* is type integer.[1]

An array identifier like F is termed an **array variable.** An array variable is an example of a *structured variable,* which stores multiple values. Variables that store single values are sometimes called *simple variables.* We can think of an array variable like F as a collection of simple variables, where the simple variables are represented by **indexed variables,** like F[1]..F[500] in Figure 9.1. We can reference an entire array data structure by using its array variable, such as F in Figure 9.1. We can also reference individual array elements, as in the indexed variable F[3] for the third array element (a temperature of *20*) in Figure 9.1.

The **index** is an *ordinal* expression within the brackets in the indexed variable. Its value locates a particular element in the array. For example, the integer index 3 in Figure 9.1 is used to locate the array element addressed as F[3]. Remember that an *ordinal data type* (integer, Boolean, character, enumerated, subrange) describes an ordered list of values. The index is necessarily an ordinal value, because the array data structure positions the elements sequentially, as contiguous memory locations (see Figure 9.1). As we will see, we can also use other ordinal indexes, like character and enumerated values.

---

[1]For those of you that are mathematically inclined, the indexed variable F[Index] is the Pascal counterpart of the algebraic *subscripted variable* F_i. For example, in algebra we might represent the 1st temperature as F_1, the 2nd temperature as F_2, and so on. An *array*, then, is a collection of these subscripted variables. Because of this analogy, many programming authors use the terms **subscript** and **index** interchangeably. Compared to algebra, as we will see, Pascal arrays are richer in their indexing and data-typing capabilities.

The **index range** is the range of allowable values for the index. In Figure 9.1, we show an index range of 1..500, which is a subrange of integers in this example. Note that the system allocates the exact number of memory cells that are needed to cover the index range. For example, the index range 1..500 requires 500 memory cells; the index range $-5..5$ requires 11 memory cells.

The data structure in Figure 9.1 is an example of a **one-dimensional array,** or an array whose elements are located by a single index. It's conceptually useful to think of a one-dimensional array as a column of elements. The index locates the position of the element in the column. For example, an index of 3 in Figure 9.1 locates the 3rd element in the column, a temperature of *20*. A **two-dimensional array** is an array whose conceptualized data structure has rows and columns of elements, like a table. Two-dimensional arrays require two indexes, one to locate the row position and another to locate the column position. In Section 9.3 we take up **multidimensional arrays,** those arrays with two or more dimensions.

Now that we have provided an overview of arrays, let's get down to specifics in their declarations, I/O, and other operations.

NOTE

1. On terminology. Array terminology can be confusing, so let's review some key terms by using the following example.

Array variable, stores multiple values or *array elements*
Index, any legitimate ordinal expression

F[Count - 1]

Indexed variable, stores single value or *array element*

We can think of the *array variable* as the entire collection of array elements (the data structure itself) and the *indexed variable* as the address of the memory cell that contains a single array element. We use the term *array* to mean either the array data structure or the array variable.

Declarations

The accompanying syntax box shows how to declare array types and array variables. Note the following.

1. An **array (data) type** defines an array data structure, where each element has the same data type. Here we assume a *one-dimensional* array type, or one having a single index type. The position of elements in the array is indexed on a value in the index range defined by the index type.

SYNTAX BOX

Array type and variable declarations... Declare array type in type section and array variable in var section

Syntax ....**type**
        ArrayType = **array** [List of IndexType] **of** ElementType;
    var
        ArrayVariable : ArrayType;

Integer elements indexed over
LowerIndexLimit to UpperIndexLimit

Examples......**type**
        ArrayOfInt = **array** [LowerIndexLimit .. UpperIndexLimit] **of integer;**
        ArrayOfReal = **array** [-5 .. 5] **of real;**

Real elements indexed
over −5 to 5

    var
        F : ArrayOfInt;
        ArrayA, ArrayB : ArrayOfReal;

Explanation... ArrayType is a user-defined identifier for an array data type that declares a data structure of elements having type ElementType and an index range defined by IndexType. ElementType is any legitimate data type in Pascal. The identifiers **array** and **of** are reserved words. ArrayVariable is a user-defined identifier for the array variable whose type is ArrayType. IndexType is any of the following ordinal types: **shortint, byte, Boolean, char,** *enumerated,* and *subrange.* The subrange type can be a subrange of any other ordinal type, except type **longint.** Each value in IndexType indexes or identifies the position of an array element. Thus, we have as many array elements as values in IndexType. List of IndexType is a list of index types separated by commas. A list with one index type declares a one-dimensional array; one with two index types declares a two-dimensional array; and so on.

For example, type ArrayOfInt declares a one-dimensional array type indexed over the *integer subrange* LowerIndexLimit..UpperIndexLimit, where each element is type *integer.* If we declare these integer constants (before the type declaration) using

    const
        LowerIndexLimit = 1; UpperIndexLimit = 500;

then type ArrayOfInt has 500 integer elements indexed over the integer subrange 1..500. Type ArrayOfReal defines a one-dimensional array type of 11 *real* elements indexed over the integer subrange −5..5. The array data type is termed a *structured data type,* because it types a data structure.

2. It's best to generalize the index range, index type, and array type as follows.

        const
Index range —⤳ LowerIndexLimit = 1; UpperIndexLimit = 500;
        type
Index type —⤳ IndexType = LowerIndexLimit .. UpperIndexLimit;
Array type —⤳ ArrayOfInt = **array** [IndexType] **of integer;**

First, this simplifies program maintenance for the index range, index type, and array type whenever these are used in other declarations within the program; second, index types and array types are needed when we declare headings in procedures and functions.

I/O AND OTHER OPERATIONS

As mentioned in earlier chapters, a data type defines not only permissible values, but also permissible operations on those values, like read, write, assignment, expression evaluation, and so on. Pascal allows the same set of operations on *indexed variables* as on simple variables having the same data type. Thus, we can perform the same set of operations on integer indexed variables as those we perform on integer simple variables. Similarly, operations allowed on character, Boolean, string, real, subrange, and enumerated simple variables are also allowed on indexed variables that store elements having those data types.

Before illustrating sample operations on indexed variables, let's formalize the reference to an indexed variable with the following syntax box.

SYNTAX BOX

Indexed variable reference... Shows proper syntax for using an indexed variable

---

Syntax ....ArrayVariable [List of Index expression]

Examples......`F[4]`
`F[Index]`
`F[Count-1]`

Explanation... ArrayVariable is the array variable identifier and Index expression is any expression that's *assignment compatible* with the index type in the array's type declaration. The value of the index expression needs to be within the index range declared by the index type; otherwise it's a range error. List of Index expression is a list of index expressions separated by commas. A list with one index expression references a one-dimensional array; one with two expressions references a two-dimensional array; and so on.

EXAMPLE 9.1   WRITE AND ASSIGNMENT OPERATIONS

Consider our earlier example of arrays ArrayA and ArrayB, having data type ArrayOfReal with real elements indexed over the integer subrange −5..5. Suppose these arrays initially store the following.

ArrayA [−5] [−4] [−3] [−2] [−1]   [0]   [1]   [2]   [3]   [4]   [5]

0.1	0.2	0.3	0.4	0.5	0.6	0.7	0.8	0.9	1.0	1.1

ArrayB [−5] [−4] [−3] [−2] [−1]   [0]   [1]   [2]   [3]   [4]   [5]

1.1	1.0	0.9	0.8	0.7	0.6	0.5	0.4	0.3	0.2	0.1

Let's assume that the lower and upper index limits are declared as follows.

```
const
    LowerIndexBound = -5;
    UpperIndexBound =  5;
```

Sample legitimate operations on the *indexed variables* include the following:

Output entire array ArrayA:

```
for Index := LowerIndexBound to UpperIndexBound do
    write (ArrayA[Index] :5:1);
```

Note how values in Index vary from −5 to 5

Displayed output: — Use **write** to display multiple elements on a line and **writeln** to display one element per line

```
0.1   0.2   0.3   0.4   0.5   0.6   0.7   0.8   0.9   1.0   1.1
```

Output of ArrayA[−4]

Output of ArrayA[−5]

Sample assignment statement:

```
ArrayA[5] := ArrayB[-4] / ArrayB[1];
```

Stores 2.0 based on the evaluation of 1.0/0.5

Did you notice that the for-do loop is perfectly suited for sequentially accessing array elements over a defined index range? For-do loops and arrays are a marriage made in heaven...

Allowable operations on *array variables,* however, are not the same as those for indexed variables. For example, we can't simply output all elements in array ArrayA using

```
write (ArrayA);   ☹
```

Instead, we have to use a loop that writes indexed variables, as shown by the for-do loop above. We can, however, copy the contents in one array into the corresponding memory cells of another *identically typed* array, as follows.

```
ArrayB := ArrayA;
```

In this case, assuming one-dimensional arrays indexed over the range −5..5, the value in ArrayB[−5] is replaced by the value in ArrayA[−5], the value in ArrayB[−4] is replaced by the value in ArrayA[−4], and so on for the remaining nine elements.

EXAMPLE 9.2   INTERACTIVE ARRAY INPUT: FOR-DO LOOP VERSION

Let's interactively input the first five elements of temperature array F, using the data structure and elements seen in Figure 9.1. We assume the following declarations.

```
const
   LowerIndexLimit = 1;   UpperIndexLimit = 500;
   MaxElements = UpperIndexLimit - LowerIndexLimit + 1;

type
   IndexType  = LowerIndexLimit .. UpperIndexLimit;
   ArrayOfInt = array [IndexType] of integer;

var
   F          : ArrayOfInt;    {Temperature array}
   Elements   : integer;       {Number of elements filled}
   Index,                      {Array index}
   UpperIndex : IndexType;     {Upper or last index filled}
```

First, we need to realize that we have a task that requires the sequential storage of array elements over a range of integer values for the index. In our example, we wish to fill elements whose indexes (Index) vary from 1 (LowerIndexLimit) to 5 (the value that will be stored in UpperIndex). This means that we have to consider a loop design that varies the index over this range.

Second, we need to ensure that values in Index and UpperIndex are within the index range, or 1..500 in our example. Put another way, we want to avoid range errors for the integer subrange variables Index and UpperIndex.

In our Figure 9.1 example, we wish to fill 5 elements out of a possible maximum of 500 elements. Let's assume that the requirements specify the number of elements as input. In our example, we want to input 5 into Elements. The number of elements is restricted to a maximum that's equivalent to the number of ordinal values in the index type. The index type is an integer subrange, so the maximum number of elements is given by the algebraic relationship

Maximum elements = Upper index limit − Lower index limit + 1.

This is our declared constant MaxElements, which evaluates to 500.

Sample Code:

```
repeat
   write ('Enter number of temperatures (max ', MaxElements,': ');
   readln (Elements);
until (Elements >= 0) and (Elements <= MaxElements);

UpperIndex := Elements + LowerIndexLimit - 1;
writeln;  write ('Enter temperatures... ');

for Index := LowerIndexLimit to UpperIndex do
   read (F[Index]);
```

Sample input:

```
Enter number of temperatures (max 500): 501
Enter number of temperatures (max 500): 5

Enter temperatures... 62 15 20 32 68
```

Let's do some desk checking. The first entry 501 exceeds the maximum, so the number of elements is reinput. The second entry is permissible, so execution exits the repeat-until structure, with 5 in Elements.

Next, the upper index is calculated from the algebraic relationship

Elements = Upper index − Lower index limit + 1

or

Upper index = Elements + Lower index limit − 1

This gives 5 in UpperIndex. Finally, the for-do loop varies Index from 1 to 5, as required. The first repetition is equivalent to the execution of

read (F[*1*]);   ⟋ *1* is in *Index*

The second repetition is equivalent to

read (F[*2*]);   ⟋ *2* is in *Index*

and so on. The call to *read* instead of to *readln* enables the input of multiple array elements in one input line.

EXAMPLE 9.3   INTERACTIVE ARRAY INPUT: WHILE-DO LOOP VERSION

Let's change our input requirements in the last example to terminate input based on a *sentinel*. Now the user does not enter the number of elements.

Sample code:

```
writeln ('Terminate input with ', Sentinel); writeln;
write ('Enter temperatures... ');
Index  := LowerIndexLimit;
{$R- Disable range checking}
read (Temp);

while (Temp <> Sentinel) and (Index <= UpperIndexLimit) do
  begin
    F[Index]  :=  Temp;
    Index     :=  Index + 1;
    read (Temp);
  end; {while}

UpperIndex  :=  Index - 1;
{$R+  Enable range checking}
```

Sample input:

```
Terminate input with -999

Enter temperatures... 62 15 20 32 68 -999
```

Sentinel is declared as −999. As seen, input terminates when −999 is entered for temperature. As before, the index on F varies from 1 to 5 (for our sample input), although Index stores a 6 at the last repetition. If another part of the program requires the index value for the last filled element, then we can assign UpperIndex following the loop. In our sample run, UpperIndex stores 5, the same as the for-do approach.

Do you see why we need to disable range checking for this code? Suppose we were to enter 500 elements. At the last iteration Index would be incremented to 501, which exceeds its declared upper index limit of 500. This would cause a fatal range error if we had not disabled range checking.

Variable Temp is used as a *placeholder* for temporarily holding a temperature. We use it as a means to check for the sentinel, *before* we assign its value to a legitimate temperature cell.

EXAMPLE 9.4   SUM OF ARRAY ELEMENTS

Determining the sum of array elements is a common programming task. For example, suppose we wish to find the mean temperature for the elements entered in Example 9.2 or 9.3. The following code fragment does the trick, where Sum is type integer, Mean is type real, and Elements stores 5.

```
Sum := 0;                                          {Initialize sum}

for Index := LowerIndexLimit to UpperIndex do
  Sum := Sum + F[Index];                           {Accumulate sum}

Mean := Sum / Elements;                            {Use sum}
```

As the for-do loop repeats, the values 62 in F[1], 15 in F[2], 20 in F[3], 32 in F[4], and 68 in F[5] are successively added to the value in Sum, giving the "running" sum 62, 77, 97, 129, and 197. Following the loop, Sum stores 197, and 39.4 is placed in Mean.

EXAMPLE 9.5   NONSEQUENTIAL (RANDOM) ARRAY ACCESS

The sequential access of array elements over a defined range of index values is very common, as all of our preceding examples illustrated. Many applications, however, require nonsequential access to array elements. For example, suppose that we wish to write a routine that retrieves and displays a specific temperature array element, based on the input of an index value in the range LowerIndexLimit to UpperIndex. The following code segment illustrates this approach.

```
{$R-  Disable range checking}
 write ('Enter temperature index (End with 0): '); readln (Index);
 while Index <> 0 do
   begin

     if (Index >= LowerIndexLimit) and (Index <= UpperIndex) then
       writeln ('  Temperature is ', F[Index])
                                                    Random access of array element
     else  {Index out of range}
       writeln (chr(7), '  Enter ',LowerIndexLimit,' to ',UpperIndex);

     writeln;
     write ('Enter temperature index (End with 0): '); readln (Index);
   end;  {while}
 writeln ('  End of run');
{$R+  Enable range checking}
```

The following sample I/O assumes the same temperature elements as those in Examples 9.2 and 9.3.

```
          Enter temperature index (End with 0): 4
             Temperature is 32

          Enter temperature index (End with 0): 8
             Enter 1 to 5

          Enter temperature index (End with 0): 2
             Temperature is 15

          Enter temperature index (End with 0): 0
             End of run
```

Note the following.

1. The indexed variable F[Index] directly accesses the desired array element. This is an example of nonsequential access because the value in Index does not vary systematically; that is, we *randomly* access array elements.[2]

---

[2]The term *random* is not used in a statistical sense here (as in Module C); it's used in a computer sense to mean nonsequential.

2. The *error routine* ensures that the user does not enter an index value that's out of the range of index values used in input. Without this error routine, an entry like 8 would access the *undefined element* in F[8], giving a logic error.[3] An entry like 700 violates the index range of 1..500. By temporarily disabling range checking, we avoid a fatal range error for index input outside the index range.

NONNUMERIC INDEXES

Up to now, we have only worked with integer subrange types as the index type. In Example 9.1, the index type was the integer subrange $-5..5$; in the temperature examples, the index type was the integer subrange $1..500$. Indexes that vary over an integer subrange are the most common, and are consistent with the algebraic treatment of arrays. In most applications, however, integer indexes have no *semantic content* (descriptive meaning), other than 1 is the 1st element, 2 is the 2nd element, and so on. In some cases, integer indexes do have some semantic content. For example, the index range $-5..5$ might represent weeks from the present. Thus, an indexed variable like ArrayA$[-5]$ might store a measurement taken five weeks ago, ArrayA$[0]$ a current measurement, and ArrayA$[3]$ a projected measurement three weeks from now.

For added flexibility, and unlike most other languages, Pascal allows other ordinal types as index types. As we will see in the next example, noninteger indexes can improve readability by suggesting semantic content.

EXAMPLE 9.6   NONUMERIC INDEXES

The declarations below show an array variable Number storing integer elements indexed on the Boolean values **true** and **false**. For example, the indexed variable Number[**false**] might store the number of false responses in a true/false examination.

```
type
   TFcount = array [Boolean] of integer; {Boolean index type}
var
   Number :  TFcount;
```

The next set of declarations shows array type CountArray having integer elements indexed over the subrange of uppercase letters. The elements in array Count

---

[3]The undefined elements of numeric arrays declared in the program's var section (globally declared arrays) are initialized to zero by the Turbo Pascal compiler; the undefined elements of locally declared arrays (those declared in procedures and functions) contain "junk" values.

represent counts of the uppercase letters in, say, a text file. For example, Count['A'] stores the number of As, Count['B'] stores the number of Bs, and so on.

```
type
  UpperLetters = 'A' .. 'Z';
  CountArray = array [UpperLetters] of integer;    {Character subrange
                                                     index type         }
var
  Count : CountArray;
```

Finally, consider the following enumerated index type.

```
type
  CityType = (LosAngeles, Chicago, Toronto, Boston, Miami);
  CityArrayType = array [CityType] of real;    {Enumerated index type}
var
  AveIncome, AveTemp : CityArrayType;
```

Here we have two arrays AveIncome and AveTemp that store real elements indexed over the enumerated cities. Note that an indexed variable like AveIncome[Miami], representing "Average income in Miami," has greater semantic content than the alternative AveIncome[5] or "Average income in city 5."

By the way, we can output the city arrays with the following code fragment.

```
for Index := LosAngeles to Miami do
    writeln (AveIncome[Index], AveTemp[Index]);
```

How we manipulate noninteger ordinal indexes also differs from the classic integer approach. For example, the traditional approach increments and decrements integer indexes as follows.

```
Index := Index + 1;    {Increment integer index}
Index := Index - 1;    {Decrement integer index}
```

For generalized ordinal indexes (including integer), we would call the predefined functions **succ** and **pred**, as follows.

```
Index := succ(Index);    {Increment ordinal index}
Index := pred(Index);    {Decrement ordinal index}
```

For example, if Index stores integer 3, then **succ**(Index) returns 4 and **pred**(Index) returns 2; if Index stores character C, then **succ**(Index) returns D and **pred**(Index) returns B; if Index stores the enumerated value Toronto, then **succ**(Index) returns Boston and **pred**(Index) returns Chicago.

Similarly, the expression for the maximum number of elements changes from the Example 9.2 integer version

MaxElements := UpperIndexLimit − LowerIndexLimit + 1

to the ordinal version

$$\text{MaxElements} := \textbf{ord}(\text{UpperIndexLimit}) - \textbf{ord}(\text{LowerIndexLimit}) + 1$$

where **ord** is the predeclared function that returns the ordinal number of its argument. In the city example we would get

$$\begin{array}{ccccc} \text{MaxElements} := & \textbf{ord}(\text{Miami}) & - & \textbf{ord}(\text{LosAngeles}) & + 1 \\ & 4 & - & 0 & + 1 \end{array}$$

or 5 in MaxElements.

SELF-REVIEW EXERCISES

1 2 3 4a–e 5a–b 6 7a–b 8 9 11a 12

9.2   OTHER ARRAY TOPICS

• • • • • • • • • • • • • •

In this section, we take up a collection of topics that round out our introduction to one-dimensional arrays: more error handling, the use of arrays as parameters, nonnumeric arrays, and the concept of parallel arrays.

MORE ERROR HANDLING

In Examples 9.2, 9.3, and 9.5 we illustrated *error routines* to trap the following errors:

- The indexed variable accesses an *undefined element*, as in F[300] when only the first 200 elements have been filled in an array indexed over 1 . . 500.
- The value of the index expression falls outside the index range, as in F[0] for an array indexed over 1 . . 500.

In Turbo Pascal, access to an undefined numeric element yields either a value of zero (for globally declared arrays) or a "junk" value (for locally declared arrays). In either case, we have a logic error (and possibly a run-time error, as in division by zero).

If the index is outside its range, we have two possibilities: If range checking is enabled, it's a fatal run-time error; otherwise, the array index points to a memory cell that's not part of the array. If this latter error is undetected, we would have one of the following consequences: For access operations like output or expression evaluations, we would access an incorrect value (giving either a logic error or possibly a run-time error); for storage operations like input or assignment, we would replace the contents of some memory cell outside the array with a new value. This could be real bad news, with unpredictable consequences. For example, we might replace the memory cell for some variable in our program. Worse yet, we might replace a memory cell that contains code!

Any "real" program worth its salt must trap these potential errors, as shown by our earlier examples. To facilitate index error handling for the remaining programs in this chapter, consider the utility IndexCk in Figure 9.2, which we have added to our utilities library. Note the following.

1. A call to IndexCk provides the index limits and current index. The index limits can be the index range declared by the index type (like LowerIndexLimit and UpperIndexLimit in the ArrayOfInt declaration) or the index values that correspond to the first and last filled indexes (like LowerIndexLimit and UpperIndex in our earlier examples).

2. The procedure tests the index against its limits. If the limits are violated (IndexError is true), an error message is written and a true value is

---

FIGURE 9.2   Listing for Utility Procedure IndexCk

```
procedure IndexCk (LowerLimit, UpperLimit, Index : IndexType;
                   var IndexError : Boolean);
                                                           ◀———— Generic type
   { Utility checks index for range error; writes message if error
     Receives LowerLimit, UpperLimit, Index
     Sends IndexError }

   { NOTE:   Preconditions assume that LowerLimit and UpperLimit are within
             the index limits imposed by the array type, and
             LowerLimit <= UpperLimit
             Assumes range checking is disabled at time of call}

begin   {IndexCk}

   IndexError := (Index < LowerLimit) or (Index > UpperLimit);
   if IndexError then
     begin
       writeln; writeln (chr(7), '*** Index violates index limits');
       write ('*** Index limits:  ');
       writeln (LowerLimit, ' .. ', UpperLimit);
       writeln ('*** Current value of index is ', Index);
     end;   {if}

end;    {IndexCk}
{----------------------------------------------------------------------}
```

sent; otherwise, the error message is bypassed and a false value is sent. The calling module would then take an appropriate action based on the index test result.

3. The calling module must ensure the *preconditions* that the values sent to LowerLimit and UpperLimit are within the declared index range for the array type, and that the value in LowerLimit does not exceed the value in UpperLimit. If we type indexes with a *generic type* such as IndexType

Values in LowerLimit and UpperLimit must be within these declared index limits

type
    IndexType = *LowerIndexLimit..UpperIndexLimit*;

then active range checking would detect a violation of the first precondition. Note that the index-related formal parameters in IndexCk are generically typed as IndexType.

4. The calling module must disable range checking just before the call to IndexCk, to avoid the possibility of a fatal range error for Index; otherwise, IndexCk would only detect undefined-element errors and not range errors. We want to detect both kinds of errors.

*ARRAYS AS PARAMETERS

Array and indexed variables are perfectly legitimate parameters in procedure/ function calls and headings. Program ArrayIO in Figure 9.3 shows a program that inputs elements into an array from a data file and writes the elements to the screen. During input it implements an index check to ensure that the index is within its limits. Figure 9.4 shows two runs of this program for the sample data file. The first run uses the original index limits 1..500; the second uses the limits 1..3, to trip the error routine into corrective action. Note the following.

1. The call to utility PrepFile enters the file specification and prepares a text data file for input. We explained this utility in Section 6.4.

2. Procedures GetArray and OutArray are *utility* procedures that I/O any array typed generically as ArrayType. GetArray inputs values from a data file while filling the array from its lower index limit to some upper index that's within the upper index limit. OutArray writes elements within the array over any legitimate span of index values. We added these procedures to our utilities library.

---

*This section assumes that you studied Section 5.4.

```
┌─────────────────────────────────────────────────────────────────────┐
│              FIGURE 9.3    Listing for Program ArrayIO                │
└─────────────────────────────────────────────────────────────────────┘

    program ArrayIO;

      {* * * * * * * * * * * * * * * * * * * * * * * * * * * * * * * *
       *                                                             *
       *          Demo of Utility Procedures GetArray and OutArray   *
       *                                                             *
       *            Inputs values from data file into array, w/ index check  *
       *            Outputs all defined array elements               *
       *                                                             *
       *            Modular structure                                *
       *            |___ GetArray                                    *
       *            |    |___ IndexCk                                *
       *            |___ OutArray                                    *
       *                                                             *
       *            Sample data file:  TEMPS.DAT                     *
       *                                                             *
       * * * * * * * * * * * * * * * * * * * * * * * * * * * * * * * *}

      {============================ Declarations ============================}

    uses crt, OurUnit;                {OurUnit needed for PrepFile}

    const
      LowerIndexLimit = 1;  UpperIndexLimit = 500;
      Title = 'DEMO OF ARRAY I/O UTILITIES';

    type
      IndexType  = LowerIndexLimit .. UpperIndexLimit;
      ArrayOfInt = array [IndexType] of integer;
      ArrayType  = ArrayOfInt;

      {IndexType and ArrayType are generic types needed by utilities}

    var
      DemoArray  : ArrayType;                {Array used in I/O demo}
      UpperIndex : IndexType;                {Index of last element entered}
      TextFile   : text;                     {Text file variable for data file}

      {======================= Procedure Declarations =======================}
```

continued

3. Array variable DemoArray is an actual parameter in the calls to procedures GetArray and OutArray. It requires an array type declaration that's identical to the type declaration for the corresponding formal parameter A, the generic type ArrayType. As seen in the program's declarations, DemoArray is typed ArrayOfInt. Thus, we identically type ArrayType as ArrayOfInt in the type section. By redefining ArrayType in the calling module, we can I/O any array type with calls to GetArray and OutArray.

4. Array variable A is necessarily a *variable parameter* in GetArray, because GetArray sends the array to the calling module. A call to GetArray passes the address of the first actual array element in DemoArray, which is then stored in GetArray's data storage area. By knowing the location of the first memory cell, GetArray can directly fill memory cells in DemoArray, since these cells are adjacent and indexed. In OutArray, we made A a *value parameter*, because this procedure simply receives the

---

FIGURE 9.3 (continued)

```
procedure GetArray (var TextFile : text;
                    LowerIndexLimit, UpperIndexLimit : IndexType;
                    var UpperIndex : IndexType;
                    var A : ArrayType);

  { Utility reads array from data file:  While/eof approach w/ Index check
    Receives TextFile, LowerIndexLimit, UpperIndexLimit
    Sends UpperIndex, A }

  { Data structure of text file
    ------------------------------------------------------------
    Value
    Value
    ...
    ------------------------------------------------------------ }

  { NOTE:  Calls utility procedure IndexCk
           UpperIndex is index of last defined element
           Assumes file has already been prepped (utility procedure
             PrepFile can be used for this purpose)
           Preconditions assume that LowerIndexLimit and UpperIndexLimit
             are within the index limits imposed by type ArrayType, and
             LowerIndexLimit <= UpperIndexLimit }

var
  Index          : IndexType;
  RangeViolation : Boolean;     {True if index range violated; else false}

             Procedure IndexCk in Figure 9.2 declared here

begin   {GetArray}

  {$R-  Disable range checking}

  Index := LowerIndexLimit;
  IndexCk (LowerIndexLimit, UpperIndexLimit, Index, RangeViolation);
  while (not eof (TextFile)) and (not RangeViolation) do
    begin
      readln ( TextFile, A[Index] );
      Index := succ(Index);
      IndexCk (LowerIndexLimit, UpperIndexLimit, Index, RangeViolation);
    end; {while}
  UpperIndex := pred(Index);

  close (TextFile);

  {$R+  Enable range checking}

end;    {GetArray}
{------------------------------------------------------------------------}
```

array. A call to OutArray results in an entire copy of DemoArray into the local array A within OutArray's data storage area.[4]

5. Procedure GetArray fills the elements whose indexes span the range from LowerIndexLimit (1) to the assigned value in UpperIndex. In

---

[4]Remember from our work in Chapter 3 that each *value* parameter requires a memory cell for that variable in a procedure's data-storage area; each *variable* parameter specifies the direct manipulation of the actual memory cell of its corresponding actual parameter.

FIGURE 9.3 (*continued*)

```
procedure OutArray (LowerIndex, UpperIndex : IndexType;
                    A : ArrayType);

  { Utility sequentially writes defined array elements
    Receives LowerIndex, UpperIndex, A
    Sends nothing }

  { NOTE:   Preconditions assume that LowerIndex and UpperIndex are within
            the index limits imposed by type ArrayType, and
            LowerIndex <= UpperIndex }

var
  Index : IndexType;

begin   {OutArray}

  for Index := LowerIndex to UpperIndex do
    write ( A[Index], ' ');
  writeln;

end;    {OutArray}

  {============================ Main Body =============================}

begin   {ArrayIO}

  clrscr;
  writeln;  writeln (Title);  writeln;

  PrepFile (TextFile);                    {In OurUnit}

  GetArray (TextFile, LowerIndexLimit, UpperIndexLimit, UpperIndex,
            DemoArray);

  writeln; write ('Entered values... ');
  OutArray (LowerIndexLimit, UpperIndex, DemoArray);

end.    {ArrayIO}
```

Figure 9.4b, UpperIndex stores 5; in Figure 9.4c, in stores 3. In other words, five elements were input in the first run and three elements were input in the second run. Further note that procedure OutArray receives the constant 1 for its local variable LowerIndex and the value in variable UpperIndex as index limits for writing the defined elements.

6. All index limits and indexes in the program are typed IndexType. Assuming range checking is active, this further ensures that the system catches any out-of-range index values in satisfying the index range *precondition* in the procedures. This program guarantees this precondition by its design, declarations, and parameter matches. For example, in procedure GetArray we have the precondition that values passed to the formal parameters LowerIndexLimit and UpperIndexLimit are within the range limit imposed by type ArrayOfInt. The call to GetArray ensures this precondition by using the declared constants LowerIndexLimit and UpperIndexLimit as the corresponding actual parameters. The index range precondition for procedure OutArray is also satisfied by matching

---

FIGURE 9.4   I/O for Program ArrayIO

(a) Data File TEMPS.DAT

```
62
15
20
32
68
```

(b) First Run: Index Range 1..500

```
DEMO OF ARRAY I/O UTILITIES

Enter data file (like A:\GRADES\HC101.DAT)... temps.dat

Entered values... 62  15  20  32  68
```

(c) Second Run: Index Range 1..3

```
DEMO OF ARRAY I/O UTILITIES

Enter data file (like A:\GRADES\HC101.DAT)... temps.dat

*** Index violates index limits
*** Index limits:  1 .. 3
*** Current value of index is 4

Entered values... 62  15  20
```

---

the actual parameters LowerIndexLimit and UpperIndex in the call to the formal parameters LowerIndex and UpperIndex in the heading. The precondition that the lower index limit not exceed the upper index limit is also satisfied.

7. IndexType declares an integer subrange in our example, but our utilities handle any ordinal indexes. This is why we called functions **succ** and **pred** in GetArray. See Exercise 16b for another index type.

8. Procedure GetArray includes an error trap that activates if the value in Index exceeds it allowable limits. It calls utility procedure IndexCk to evaluate the error flag RangeViolation. If IndexCk returns true for the error flag, the index is out of range and the while-do loop terminates. This would happen if we attempt to input more values in the data file than declared total elements in the array. In the run displayed in Figure 9.4c, for example, Index stores 4 at the fourth iteration and 3 is in UpperIndexLimit. Thus, IndexCk places false in RangeViolation, looping terminates, and UpperIndex stores 3 as the index for the last filled ele-

ment. Note that the loop control has two conditions: one for the end of file, and one for a possible range violation of the value in Index. Also note that we temporarily disabled range checking; otherwise, active range checking would terminate execution in reading a file that has more values than total elements in the declared array. Finally, note that the relative placements of the call to IndexCk, the test on RangeViolation, and the indexed variable A[Index] ensure that an out-of-range index is not used in the indexed variable. For example, we would not want to place the read statement just after the index check. Right?

NOTE

2. Array as variable versus value parameter. If the design requires a procedure to send an array, we must treat the array as a *variable* parameter; otherwise, we would normally declare the array variable as a *value* parameter, thereby ensuring the integrity of the actual elements by protecting them from unintended modifications. Unfortunately, applications that use large arrays may require a tradeoff between array integrity and resource use. For example, large arrays used as value parameters require duplicate element storage and time to copy the actual elements into the procedure's data storage area. If memory and processing times are at a premium, we have to consider changing a value parameter to a variable parameter. For instance, each integer element in our temperature array requires two bytes of memory. If we need to process up to 25,000 elements, we would be using about 50KB of memory for the actual array and another 50KB for the local copy. In this case, depending on our available memory, we may need to insert **var** in front of A in the formal parameter list for procedure OutArray in Figure 9.3.

NONNUMERIC ARRAYS

Up to now we have just worked with *numeric* elements having type integer or real. We can also type elements using other data types, as illustrated next.

Boolean Arrays

If we wish an array element to store a Boolean value (**true** or **false**), we would use **Boolean** as the element type. In the sample declarations below, array Flag is a 50-element array that stores Boolean values.

```
type
   FlagTypeArray = array [1 .. 50] of Boolean;
var
   Flag : FlagTypeArray;
```

Character Arrays

If we use **char** as the element type, we have a character array. For example, in the declarations below, array Code is a 105-element array that stores single-character extended ASCII codes.

```
const
   YearAgo = -52;  YearAhead = 52;

type
   WeeksRange    = YearAgo .. YearAhead;
   CodeTypeArray = array [WeeksRange] of char;

var
   Code : CodeTypeArray;
```

In Standard Pascal, character arrays are commonly used to process strings of characters, because data type string is not supported directly. In Turbo Pascal, the string data type considerably reduces the importance of character arrays. For example, the variable declaration

```
var
   Code : string [105];
```

also stores 105 ASCII codes, although any semantic content in the index is sacrificed (as in −13 means "Thirteen weeks ago").

Note that a string variable is essentially a "closet" character array, with an index range that runs from 0 to the length of the string. Element zero stores a value whose ordinal number is the dynamic length of the string, the number of character elements filled in the string.

String Arrays

By using **string** as the element type, we have an array of strings, where each element is a separate string. For example, consider the following declarations.

```
type
   TypeNames    = (Tom, Dick, Harry);
   GuyTypeArray = array [TypeNames] of string [100];

var
   GuyAddress, GuyName : GuyTypeArray;
```

Here we have two three-element arrays, indexed on the names Tom, Dick, and Harry. Each element can store up to 100 characters. For instance, GuyAddress[Harry] might store Harry's address, and GuyName[Harry] might store Harry's full name.[5]

---

[5]Corresponding actual and formal parameters for variable parameters must be typed identically. Turbo Pascal includes a *var-string checking* compiler directive that relaxes this restriction for string types when deactivated with {**$V−**} or Options Compiler strict Var-strings. In this "relaxed" state, corresponding string types of any declared length are allowed as variable parameters.

Enumerated and Subrange Arrays

Check out the following declarations.

```
const
   MinAge = 21;  MaxAge = 67;

type
   TypeNames = (Tom, Dick, Harry);
   TypeAges  = MinAge .. MaxAge;
   NameTypeArray = array [TypeNames] of TypeNames;
   AgeTypeArray  = array [TypeNames] of TypeAges;

var
   GuyName : NameTypeArray;
   GuyAge  : AgeTypeArray;
```

Guyname is an *enumerated* array indexed over (Tom, Dick, Harry), where each element stores one of the *enumerated* values Tom, Dick, or Harry (or a type TypeNames value). GuyAge is a *subrange* array also indexed over (Tom, Dick, Harry), where each element stores an age in the integer *subrange* 21..67 (or a type TypeAges value).

When it comes to data typing and array declarations, the richness of Pascal leaves most other languages in the dust...and 'you ain't seen nothin' yet.

PARALLEL ARRAYS

Consider the sample data structure in Figure 9.5a. This shows a *parallel data structure,* where each row describes attributes for some entity. In the ex-

---

FIGURE 9.5   Parallel Data Structure

(a) As Table

City Name	City Temperature
Los Angeles	62
Chicago	15
Toronto	20
Boston	32
Miami	68
.	.
.	.
.	.

(b) As Parallel Arrays

Index (City Entity)	CityName (Name Attribute)	F (Temp Attribute)
1	Los Angeles	62
2	Chicago	15
3	Toronto	20
4	Boston	32
5	Miami	68
.	.	.
.	.	.
.	.	.

ample, the *entity* is city and the *attributes* are city name and temperature. At this time we're not ready to present a structured data type that would declare this kind of data structure.[6] We do, however, have a rather simple solution for handling parallel data structures, as seen in Figure 9.5b: Use **parallel arrays** as sets of one-dimensional arrays, where each array stores the values for a given attribute and each index represents an entity.

EXAMPLE 9.7   DECLARATION OF PARALLEL ARRAYS

We can handle the parallel data structure shown in Figure 9.5 by declaring two arrays with the same set of indexes, but different types for their elements. Let's assume arrays indexed over the integer subrange 1..500, city names as string elements up to 20 characters in array CityName, and integer temperatures in array F. The following code fragment takes care of the declarations.

```
const
    LowerIndexLimit = 1;   UpperIndexLimit = 500;
    SizeStr = 20;

type
    IndexType  = LowerIndexLimit .. UpperIndexLimit;
    ArrayOfStr = array [IndexType] of string [SizeStr];
    ArrayOfInt = array [IndexType] of integer;

var
    CityName : ArrayOfStr;
    F        : ArrayOfInt;
```

Note how we use the declared constants and IndexType to simplify potential maintenance should we wish to change array attributes or add other array variables in the future.

EXAMPLE 9.8   I/O OF TWO PARALLEL ARRAYS

Figure 9.6 shows the I/O processing of the sample data file by the program in Figure 9.7. Note the following.

1. The driver ArrayIO2 is a reedited version of ArrayIO in Figure 9.3. The primary changes are the declarations of two parallel arrays, their array types, and

---

[6]In Chapter 11 we declare this data structure as an array of records.

FIGURE 9.6   I/O for Program ArrayIO2

(a) Data File CITYTEMP.DAT

```
Los Angeles
62
Chicago
15
Toronto
20
Boston
32
Miami
68
```

(b) Sample Run

```
DEMO OF UTILITIES THAT I/O TWO PARALLEL ARRAYS

Enter data file (like A:\GRADES\HC101.DAT)... citytemp.dat

Two parallel arrays...

        Los Angeles              62
            Chicago              15
            Toronto              20
             Boston              32
              Miami              68
```

calls to two new utilities. Note that IndexType, ArrayType1, and ArrayType2 are *generic types* that we need to declare in the driver. By redeclaring these types, we can process parallel arrays having different types. Our sample run processed the data file that corresponds to the parallel arrays in Figure 9.5. In Exercise 21d we ask you to try other array types.

2. The new utilities GetTwoArrays and OutTwoArrays are reedited versions of our earlier utilities GetArray and OutArray. The key differences are the appearance of two arrays instead of one array in the formal parameter and readln/writeln lists. We added these utilities to our utilities library.

SELF-REVIEW EXERCISES
15 18a–c 19 21a–c

FIGURE 9.7   Listing of Program ArrayIO2

```
program ArrayIO2;

    {* * * * * * * * * * * * * * * * * * * * * * * * * * * * * * * *
     *                                                             *
     *         Demo of Utility Procedures GetTwoArrays and OutTwoArrays  *
     *                                                             *
     *         Inputs values from data file into two parallel arrays,    *
     *            w/ index check                                   *
     *         Outputs two parallel arrays                         *
     *                                                             *
     *         Modular structure                                   *
     *            |___  GetTwoArrays                               *
     *            |    |___ IndexCk                                *
     *            |___  OutTwoArrays                               *
     *                                                             *
     *         Sample data file:  CITYTEMP.DAT                     *
     *                                                             *
     *         See file data structure below                       *
     *                                                             *
     * * * * * * * * * * * * * * * * * * * * * * * * * * * * * * * *}

    {============================ Declarations ============================}

uses crt, OurUnit;                {OurUnit needed for PrepFile}

const
    LowerIndexLimit = 1;  UpperIndexLimit = 500;
    SizeStr = 20;

    Title = 'DEMO OF UTILITIES THAT I/O TWO PARALLEL ARRAYS';

type
    IndexType   = LowerIndexLimit .. UpperIndexLimit;
    ArrayOfInt  = array [IndexType] of integer;
    ArrayOfStr  = array [IndexType] of string [SizeStr];

    ArrayType1  = ArrayOfStr;
    ArrayType2  = ArrayOfInt;

    {IndexType, ArrayType1, and ArrayType2 are generic types needed by
       utilities}

var
    Array1      : ArrayType1;            {First  parallel array}
    Array2      : ArrayType2;            {Second parallel array}
    UpperIndex  : IndexType;            {Index of last element entered}
    TextFile    : text;                {Text file variable for data file}

    {======================== Procedure Declarations ========================}
```

‡9.3   MULTIDIMENSIONAL ARRAYS

• • • • • • • • • • • • •

We can characterize a *one*-dimensional array as a data structure that stores a list of values for an attribute that has *one classification* or *dimension,* like

---

‡Optional, more advanced material. Skip without loss of continuity, study at this point, or wait until later.

FIGURE 9.7   (continued)

```
procedure GetTwoArrays (var TextFile : text;
                        LowerIndexLimit, UpperIndexLimit : IndexType;
                        var UpperIndex : IndexType;
                        var ArrayOne  : ArrayType1;
                        var ArrayTwo  : ArrayType2);

  { Utility reads two parallel arrays from data file:  While/eof
      approach w/ Index check
    Receives TextFile, LowerIndexLimit, UpperIndexLimit
    Sends UpperIndex, ArrayOne, ArrayTwo }

  { Data structure of text file
    --------------------------------------------------------
    ArrayOne 1st element
    ArrayTwo 1st element
    ArrayOne 2nd element
    ArrayTwo 2nd element
    ...
    -------------------------------------------------------- }

  { NOTE:  Calls utility procedure IndexCk
          UpperIndex is index of last defined element
          Assumes file has already been prepped (utility procedure
            PrepFile can be used for this purpose)
          Preconditions assume that LowerIndexLimit and UpperIndexLimit
            are within the index limits imposed by index type, and
            LowerIndexLimit <= UpperIndexLimit }

var
  Index          : IndexType;
  RangeViolation : Boolean;      {True if index range violated; else false}

            Procedure IndexCk in Figure 9.2 declared here

begin  {GetTwoArrays}

  {$R-  Disable range checking}

  Index := LowerIndexLimit;
  IndexCk (LowerIndexLimit, UpperIndexLimit, Index, RangeViolation);
  while (not eof (TextFile)) and (not RangeViolation) do
    begin
      readln ( TextFile, ArrayOne[Index], ArrayTwo[Index] );
      Index := succ(Index);
      IndexCk (LowerIndexLimit, UpperIndexLimit, Index, RangeViolation);
    end; {while}
  UpperIndex := pred(Index);

  close (TextFile);

  {$R+  Enable range checking}

end;  {GetTwoArrays}
{------------------------------------------------------------------------}
```

continued

city. For example, our one-dimensional temperature array F represents temperature readings for different cities, as seen in Figure 9.8. Suppose, however, that we wish to classify temperatures both by city and season, or by city, season, and year. In these cases, we use a **multidimensional array** that stores attribute values across more than one classification (dimension). For example, the **two-dimensional array** in Figure 9.8 shows attribute values classified

---

FIGURE 9.7   *(continued)*

```
procedure OutTwoArrays (LowerIndex, UpperIndex : IndexType;
                        ArrayOne : ArrayType1;
                        ArrayTwo : ArrayType2);

  { Utility writes two parallel arrays
    Receives LowerIndex, UpperIndex, ArrayOne, ArrayTwo
    Sends nothing }

  { NOTE:  Preconditions assume that LowerIndex and UpperIndex are within
           the index limits imposed by type ArrayType, and
           LowerIndex <= UpperIndex }

var
  Index : IndexType;

begin   {OutTwoArrays}

  for Index := LowerIndex to UpperIndex do
    writeln ( ArrayOne[Index] :20, ArrayTwo[Index] :20);

end;    {OutTwoArrays}

  {============================= Main Body =============================}

begin   {ArrayIO2}

  clrscr;
  writeln;  writeln (Title);  writeln;

  PrepFile (TextFile);                       {In OurUnit}

  GetTwoArrays (TextFile, LowerIndexLimit, UpperIndexLimit, UpperIndex,
           Array1, Array2);

  writeln;  writeln ('Two parallel arrays... ');  writeln;

  OutTwoArrays (LowerIndexLimit, UpperIndex, Array1, Array2);

end.    {ArrayIO2}
```

across two-dimensions, city and season; the sample **three-dimensional array** shows values over three dimensions: city, season, and year.

We can view a one-dimensional array as a table with either a single *column* or a single *row,* a two-dimensional array as a *table* with rows and columns, and a three-dimensional array as a *multilayered table* or as *stacked tables.* Because we have forever used tables in our manual work, the *table metaphor* of viewing an array as a table enhances our understanding of arrays. Looking at Figure 9.8, we can identify a row either by number $(1..5)$ or by city (LosAngeles..Miami); a column either by number $(1..4)$ or by season (Winter..Fall); and a table layer either by number $(1..3)$ or by year (Y1990, Y1960, Y1930). More on this shortly.

We can also conceive of *four-dimensional arrays, five-dimensional arrays,* and so on. But we don't have visual metaphors for these hyper-dimensioned arrays, although rumor has it that Albert Einstein did (HC makes the same claim). Still, multidimensional arrays with more than three dimensions are used in classification schemes having more than three categories.

FIGURE 9.8   One-, Two-, and Three-Dimensional Temperature Arrays

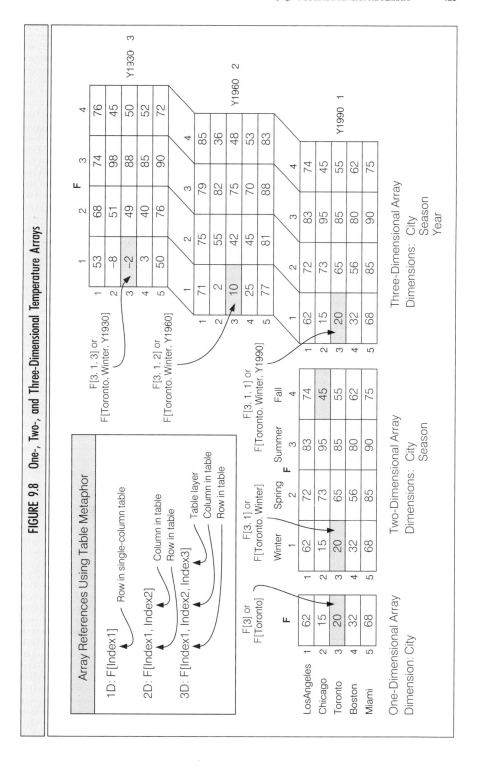

DIFFERENCES FROM ONE-DIMENSIONAL ARRAYS

From the Pascal point of view, we need to learn little that's new in applying multidimensional arrays. We only need to be aware of two key differences.

1. The *declaration* of the multidimensional array type includes a *list of index types,* one index type for each corresponding dimension, as in the two-dimensional array type declaration

   ```
   MultiArrayOfInt = array [RowType, ColType] of integer;
   ```

   Pascal has no restriction on the number of dimensions, although there are practical limitations based on the memory needed for a data structure.[7]

2. The indexed variable *reference* to a multidimensional array uses a *list of index expressions,* one index expression for each corresponding dimension. Figure 9.8 shows our approach to referencing arrays. In our table metaphor, we assume that the first index references a row, the second index a column, and the third index a table layer. Thus, the indexed variable F[3, 1] or F[Toronto Winter] stores 20; the indexed variable F[3, 1, 3] or F[Toronto, Winter, Y1930] stores -2. In any one program, we would use only one of these index types (as in 3 or Toronto for Toronto), depending on their declarations.

EXAMPLE 9.9   TWO-DIMENSIONAL TEMPERATURE ARRAY DECLARATIONS AND REFERENCES

Consider the following declarations.

```
const
   LowerRowLimit = 1;  UpperRowLimit = 500; {Row index limits}
   LowerColLimit = 1;  UpperColLimit =   4; {Col index limits}

type
   RowType = LowerRowLimit .. UpperRowLimit; {1st dim or row index type}
   ColType = LowerColLimit .. UpperColLimit; {2nd dim or col index type}

   MultiArrayOfInt = array [RowType, ColType] of integer;

var
   F          : MultiArrayOfInt;  {2D array}
```

Array type MultiArrayOfInt describes an array type having integer elements arrayed over two dimensions. The first dimension has index type RowType, an in-

---

[7]Turbo Pascal limits the size of a data structure to 65,520 bytes.

teger subrange type that runs from 1 .. 500; the second dimension has index type ColType, defining the index range 1 .. 4.

Array F is declared as having type MultiArrayOfInt. Using our table metaphor, this array handles tables up to 500 rows and four columns; the rows are indexed over 1 .. 500, and the columns are indexed 1 .. 4. Looking at the two-dimensional array in Figure 9.8, F[2, 4] references element 45 in the 2nd row (Chicago) and 4th column (Fall).

Suppose that our data requirements specified that we will always consider just these five cities and four seasons. An alternative declaration might look something like this.

```
type
  CityType   = (LosAngeles, Chicago, Toronto, Boston, Miami);
  SeasonType = (Winter, Spring, Summer, Fall);

  TempArrayType = array [CityType, SeasonType] of integer;

var
  F : TempArrayType;
```

Again F is a two-dimensional array, but now its index type along the first dimension is the enumerated type CityType and its index type along the second dimension is the enumerated type SeasonType. Now looking at Figure 9.8, the temperature of 45 for Chicago in the Fall is referenced by F(Chicago, Fall], a considerably more readable alternative.

As in one-dimensional arrays, noninteger-subrange types (like character or enumerated types) can improve program literacy, but at the expense of flexibility. For example, RowType is a better alternative than CityType if array F needs to handle a large number of cities, or cities whose number is apt to vary from run to run.

I/O AND OTHER OPERATIONS

As in one-dimensional indexed variables, we can perform the same operations on multidimensional indexed variables as on simple variables having the same data type. As we have seen, the for-do loop is a convenient control structure for the sequential processing of one-dimensional array; as we will see, *nested* for-do loops are equally convenient for the sequential processing of multi-dimensional arrays, one for-do loop for each dimension.

EXAMPLE 9.10   INTERACTIVE I/O OF TWO-DIMENSIONAL TEMPERATURE ARRAY

Figure 9.9 shows interactive I/O for the two-dimensional temperature array shown in Figure 9.8. Figure 9.10 displays the listing for the sample program Array2F. Try roleplaying the program using the sample run, and note the following.

FIGURE 9.9   I/O for Program Array2F

```
I/O DEMO FOR 2-DIMENSIONAL ARRAY


Enter number of rows (max 255) : 5
Enter number of cols (max   4) : 5 ◄─────  Entry exceeds upper column limit
                                            for 2nd dimension
Enter number of rows (max 255) : 5
Enter number of cols (max   4) : 4

Enter array row x row, like a table...
62 72 83 74
15 73 95 45
20 65 85 55
32 56 80 62
68 85 90 75

Echo of entered array...

    62    72    83    74
    15    73    95    45
    20    65    85    55
    32    56    80    62
    68    85    90    75
```

---

1. The declarations are the same as the first set of declarations in Example 9.9 (index types as integer subranges). See Exercise 25 for the enumerated type alternative, and Exercise 27 for the three-dimensional alternative.

2. Variables Rows and Cols represent the number of rows and columns, respectively, that get filled in the array. Rows has an upper index range limit of UpperRowLimit (225); the corresponding limit for Cols is UpperColLimit (4). For *range-checking* safety, we typed Rows and Cols as type RowType and ColType, instead of type integer.[8]

3. The repeat-until loop traps input values for Rows and Cols that fall outside their upper range limits. First, however, we had to disable range checking; otherwise, the unallowable entry shown in the sample run would have terminated the run with a *range check error*. Note that this loop repeats until the entries for both Rows and Cols are permissible. Following this loop, it's a good idea to enable range checking again (as a general precaution).

4. We input the array in our accustomed row by row manner. This means that *we must place the for-do loop having the column index inside the for-do loop with the row index.* For each row (or value in Row), the inner loop sequences through all columns (all values in Col). In other words, to input the first row be-

---

[8]The row limit 255 is dictated by our use of UpperRowLimit as an element in the set constant within the repeat-until test. From our work in Chapter 7, 255 is the highest ordinal number allowed for a set element.

FIGURE 9.10   Listing of Program Array2F

```pascal
program Array2F;

   {* * * * * * * * * * * * * * * * * * * * * * * * * * * * * * * *
    *                                                             *
    *         I/O Demo for Two-Dimensional Array F                *
    *                                                             *
    *           Inputs array F interactively in table format      *
    *           Outputs array F in table format                   *
    *                                                             *
    * * * * * * * * * * * * * * * * * * * * * * * * * * * * * * *}

   {============================= Declarations =============================}

uses crt;

const
  FieldWidth    = 5;                        {Output field width}
  LowerRowLimit = 1;  UpperRowLimit = 255;  {Row index limits}
  LowerColLimit = 1;  UpperColLimit =   4;  {Col index limits}

  Title = 'I/O DEMO FOR 2-DIMENSIONAL ARRAY ';

type
  RowType = LowerRowLimit .. UpperRowLimit; {1st dim or row index type}
  ColType = LowerColLimit .. UpperColLimit; {2nd dim or col index type}

  MultiArrayOfInt = array [RowType, ColType] of integer;

var
  F          : MultiArrayOfInt; {2D array}

  Row, Rows : RowType;             {Row, Col are index variables for}
  Col, Cols : ColType;             {current row and column; Rows, Cols
                                    are number of rows and columns
                                    that are filled in array; Row runs
                                    from 1 to Rows; Col runs from 1 to Cols}

   {============================= Main Body =============================}

begin  {Array2F}

  clrscr; writeln (Title); writeln; writeln;

 {Input number of rows and cols in filled array}

    {$R-  Disable range checking on input for Rows and Cols}

    repeat
      write ('Enter number of rows (max ', UpperRowLimit :3, ') : ');
      readln (Rows);
      write ('Enter number of cols (max ', UpperColLimit :3, ') : ');
      readln (Cols);
      writeln;
    until (Rows in [LowerRowLimit .. UpperRowLimit]) and
          (Cols in [LowerColLimit .. UpperColLimit]);

    {$R+  Enable range checking}          Set constants
```

continued

FIGURE 9.10   *(continued)*

```
{Fill array row x row by interactive input}

    writeln ('Enter array row x row, like a table...');
    for Row := LowerRowLimit to Rows do              ◄──────────── Outer for-do loop
      for Col := LowerColLimit to Cols do          ◄────────────   varies rows
        read ( F[ Row, Col] );                                     Inner for-do loop
    writeln;                                                       varies columns

{Output array in table format}

    writeln ('Echo of entered array...');
    for Row := LowerRowLimit to Rows do
      begin
        writeln; ◄──────────────────────────────────────────── Clears last row to start
        for Col := LowerColLimit to Cols do                    next row on new line
          write ( F[ Row, Col] :FieldWidth);
      end; {Outer for}
    writeln;                                    Note use of field-width
end.    {Array2F}                               constant here
```

fore the second row, we must first input *all* elements in the 1st row (those indexed on columns). The sequence of index values looks like this.

Row	Col
1	1 2 3 4 ◄──╼── Completes input of 1st row
2	1 2 3 4 ◄──╼── Completes input of 2nd row
3	1 2 3 4 ◄──╼── Completes input of 3rd row
4	1 2 3 4 ◄──╼── Completes input of 4th row
5	1 2 3 4 ◄──╼── Completes input of 5th row

Note that we *must use the read statement* (not the readln statement) to input
more than one value per line; the readln statement would ignore all values on
a line to the right of the first!

5. We also output the array in the preferred (by us humans) table format. *Again,
the column loop is nested inside the row loop.* Note how the writeln statement
in the body of the outer loop serves to "clear" the previously written row by
writing blanks and moving the cursor down one line (in preparation for the
display of the next row).

NOTE

3. On indexing convention. It's customary to treat the first index in
an array as the "row" index, the second as the "column" index, and the
third as the "layer" index. This is not a restriction in Pascal; rather it's
the way many of us have been conditioned in algebraic subscript notation. We follow this convention throughout, to avoid possible confusion.

SELF-REVIEW EXERCISES

22a–b 23a 24

9.4 PROGRAMMING TIPS

. . . .

Consider the following tips to improve the design and style of your programs and to avoid some common errors.

DESIGN AND STYLE

1. Defensive Programming. Don't forget to trap the potential errors of accessing undefined array elements and, worse yet, accessing or overwriting memory locations that are referenced by out-of-range indexes. Where appropriate, write your own error-handling routines, or call utility IndexCk.

2. Think Data Structures. As in our earlier work on files (Chapter 4) and sets (Chapter 7), we need to consider the nature of data structures when working with related data. Specifically, at the design stage, we first need to conceptualize the *data structure* itself with respect to its data *relationships,* data *types, size,* and *shape.* For example, if we need to store and individually manipulate the names of months, then we can conceptualize the data structure as a column of 12 names. The data relationships given by the sequencing has meaning (February follows January, and so on), each element is a string data type with (let's say) 10 characters, the size is fixed at 12 elements, and the shape is a column of elements. At the coding stage, we can represent this data structure as a *structured variable* with a specific *structured data type.* For example, we could declare the structured data type MonthArrayType and the structured variable as the array variable Months.

```
type
  MonthNameType  = string [10];
  MonthIndexType = 1 .. 12;
  MonthArrayType = array [MonthIndexType] of MonthNameType;
                                          Structured data type
var
  Months : MonthArrayType;
                         Structured variable as array variable
```

Now, let's get a little more complicated. Suppose we need to store and manipulate the names (up to 20 characters), seasonal temperatures (whole numbers), and average hourly wages (dollars and cents) for up to 500 cities.

We can think of our *data structure* as a table that has 500 rows and the following six columns: City name, Winter temperature, Spring temperature, Summer temperature, Fall temperature, and Hourly wage. In coding this data structure, however, we can't use a single structured variable or structured data type (because of mixed typing). Instead, we can reconceptualize the data structure as the following *parallel data structure*: a column of names, a table of temperatures, and a column of hourly wages. This gives three structured variables and their data types.[9]

3. On Generalized Declarations and Generic Types. It's best to generalize the declaration of constants and types. This usually improves literacy, reduces potential maintenance, and enhances reliability. For example, IndexType in Figure 9.3 has semantic content (it's the data type for the index), and its limits are easily changed in the constant declaration section. Moreover, by typing any index in the program as type IndexType, we ensure automatic range checking of its values (if range checking is enabled). Here's an example of an undesirable declaration for DemoArray in Figure 9.3.

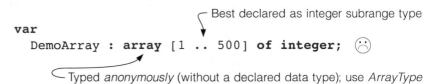

```
var
    DemoArray : array [1 .. 500] of integer;  ☹
```

⌐ Best declared as integer subrange type

⌐ Typed *anonymously* (without a declared data type); use *ArrayType*

Also, we should consider *generic typing* when developing utilities. For example, the generic types IndexType and ArrayType in procedure GetArray (Figure 9.3) allow the input of any array type whose elements can be input by the predefined read statements; otherwise, we would either need to develop a separate utility for each array type or have to modify the utility itself.

4. On Memory Management.   Arrays can take up a lot of memory, so a key data-related question we need to ask is "*Do we need to use arrays?*" If all we need to do is find the mean of *n* numbers, we don't need to store these numbers as an array. If we need to sort these numbers, as we do in Module D, an array is called for. If we have a choice of playing it either way, it's usually a matter of preference, unless the required amount of memory in using arrays is an issue.

   If we need to use arrays and we're concerned about either total available memory or Turbo Pascal's *65,520-byte* memory limitation per array, we have a *memory management* problem. In this case, we need to answer some questions. *Can we make a tradeoff between I/O costs and memory costs?* For example, if we just need to find the sum of *n* numbers and then the percent of each number, we could read in the numbers twice (presumably from a file), first to sum them, and then to find each percent. This would avoid an array

---

[9]In Chapter 11 we can implement this data structure as a single structured variable called an *array of records*.

(thereby improving memory efficiency) at the expense of additional input (which is I/O inefficient).

Can we adjust index limits? If we occasionally need to include 20,000 temperatures in an array that normally uses no more than 500 temperatures, we have to decide on the tradeoff between *storage inefficiency* and *maintenance costs.* For example, we could use an upper index limit of 20,000 and never change it, thereby incurring no program maintenance regarding this limit, but at the expense of large amount of unused storage.[10] Alternatively, we could change the array's upper index limit to 20,000 whenever we need to process that many temperatures, but keep it at 500 otherwise. This reduces storage needs but increases program maintenance. It just depends on the relative costs between storage and maintenance. By the way, in commercial environments, the focus is on lowering maintenance costs, which are labor (programmer) intensive and relatively costly.

In modular programming, we also need to think about the use of array variables as *value* or *variable parameters.* If memory is an issue, we may need to trade off safety (potential side effects) for memory efficiency by using variable parameters.

COMMON ERRORS

1. Type Mismatch Error.   If we get this compile-time error message for a program line that has arrays, then either (1) the index expression type in an indexed variable is incompatible with the declared index type or (2) corresponding arrays or indexes in formal and actual parameter lists are incompatible. An example of the first kind of error would be the reference F[Toronto] instead of F[3] if the declared index type is an integer subrange. An example of the second kind of type mismatch error would be an actual parameter typed ArrayOfInt and a corresponding formal parameter typed ArrayOfReal.

2. Range Errors.   Assuming range checking is active, the compile-time error message *Constant out of range* is displayed if the index expression is a constant that's outside the declared index range; the run-time error message *Range check error* is displayed if the index expression is evaluated at run time (if it contains a variable) and its value falls outside the declared index range. As mentioned before, we recommend active range checking at all times. If execution time is an issue, then we recommend active range checking during the debugging stage.

3. Array Variable in I/O List.   An array variable in an input or output list gives the compile-time error message *Cannot Read or Write variables of this type.* We must use an indexed variable to I/O array elements, as emphasized in Example 9.1.

---

[10]Arrays are memory hogs. For example, each real element requires 6 bytes. An array with 20,000 real elements would use up 1.2MB of primary memory. This would bust Turbo Pascal's data structure-size limitation and may exceed available primary memory on many PCs and time-sharing systems.

4. Nesting Confusion. When working with multidimensional arrays, the decision of what for-do loop to nest inside another for-do loop is confusing for many beginning programmers. Reread item 4 in Example 9.10.

REVIEW EXERCISES

EASIER	For the busy...
	1 2 4a–e 5a–b 6 7a–b 12 15 18 19 21a–b 24
NORMAL	For the thinkers...
	3 4f 5c–d 7c 8 9 10 11 13 14 16 17 20 21c–d 22 23
	25 28 29 30
TOUGHER	For the hard CORE...
	26 27 31 32

1. Write code that declares the following array types and variables.
   a. *Array type:* ArrayStock declares real elements indexed over weeks 1 to 52. *Array variables:* DJI, DJT, SP500.
   b. *Array type:* ArrayTemp declares integer elements indexed over weeks $-26..26$. *Array variables:* Lows, Highs.

2. How much memory in bytes is specified by each data structure in Exercise 1? *Hint:* See Appendix D.

3. In Example 9.1...
   a. Write code that copies the contents of ArrayB into ArrayC.
   b. Write code that displays the arrays as two side by side columns.
   c. Same as part **b**, except output the elements in reverse order.
   d. Write code that initializes the two arrays to the given elements.

4. In Example 9.2...
   a. Can we input one element per line? Explain. How must we input the data if the read statement is replaced by the readln statement?
   b. Does our code ensure that Index and UpperIndex are within their index range? Explain.
   c. What happens if we enter 0 for Elements?
   d. Suppose the index range is redeclared over -52 to 52. What's the new value in MaxElements? Would our sample I/O change?
   e. How would you apply our utility ReadLnInt? Change the code accordingly.
   *f. How would you apply our utility InputVal? Change the code accordingly.

5. In Example 9.3...
    a. Change the UpperIndexLimit to 3. How does the I/O change?
    b. How would you apply our utility ReadLnInt? Change the code accordingly.
    *c. How would you apply our utility InputVal? Change the code accordingly.
    *d. Can you think of a way to eliminate the use of Temp in the while-do approach? Any problem with this approach?

6. In Example 9.4...
    a. Suppose 50 elements had been input in Example 9.2 or 9.3. Do we need to change the code here? Explain.
    b. How else can we update the sum in Turbo Pascal?

7. In Example 9.5...
    a. Roleplay the input of −3 and 3.
    b. How can we change the example to ensure input error handling for the input of the index?
    *c. Change the code to make use of utility InputVal.

8. Indicate storage contents for arrays A, B, and C following execution of the following code. Assume each array has integer elements indexed over the integer subrange LowerIndexLimit (1) to UpperIndexLimit (5).

    ```
    for Index1 := LowerIndexLimit to UpperIndexLimit do
      begin
        A[Index1] := Index1;
        Index2    := UpperIndexLimit + 1 - Index1;
        B[Index2] := Index2;
      end;  {for}

    for Index := LowerIndexLimit to UpperIndexLimit do
        C[Index] := A[Index] * B[Index];
    ```

    Why can't we include the assignment statement for C in the first for-do loop?

9. Given the following input

        10   20
        30   40
        50   60
        70   80
        90 100

    describe output after execution of the following code segment. Assume the same array declarations as the preceding exercise.

```
   SumA := 0;  SumB := 0;  SumDiff := 0;
   for Index := LowerIndexLimit to UpperIndexLimit do
     begin
       readln ( A[Index], B[Index] );
       SumA    := SumA    + A[Index];
       SumB    := SumB    + B[Index];
       SumDiff := SumDiff + ( A[Index] - B[Index] );
     end; {for}
   writeln ('Sums..... ', SumA :5, SumB :5, SumDiff :5);
   writeln('Arrays...');
   for Index := LowerIndexLimit to UpperIndexLimit do
     writeln ('             ', A[Index] :5, B[Index] :5,
                               A[Index] - B[Index] :5);
```

*10. Procedure Exchange. A very common task in array manipulations is the exhange of two elements. For example, if A[3] stores 30 and A[5] stores 50, then an exchange between these two elements would place 50 in A[3] and 30 in A[5]. We can illustrate the steps in an exchange procedure by the following schematic.

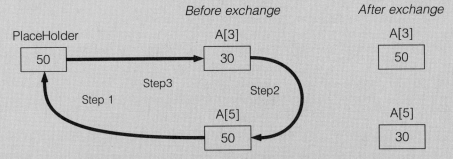

Write and test utility procedure Exchange that receives two elements and exchanges them. Use ElementType as the generic type for elements (the calling module would ensure the proper declaration for ElementType).

11. In Example 9.6...

a. What's returned for the following calls? **succ(false)**, **pred(false)**, and **ord(false)**; **succ**(Chicago), **pred**(Chicago), and **ord**(Chicago). Evaluate the maximum elements for the Boolean and uppercase letters examples using the formula that calls **ord**.

*b. Revise the for-do loop to count the number of cities.

*c. Revise the for-do loop to display the output from Miami down to Los Angeles.

*d. Write a program segment to input the average incomes and temperatures from a data file. Assume the data structure in the text file shows two columns of values, where each row is the average income and temperature for a city.

12. Write code that declares the following array types and variables.
   a. *Array types:* ArraySex declares integer elements indexed over type Gender having values Male and Female. *Array variable:* Count.
   b. *Array types:* ArrayofGrades declares real elements indexed over type Grade having values A, B, C, D, F. *Array variable:* Bounds.

*13. **Procedure IndexCk.** Revise the following code to use utility procedure IndexCk.
   a. Example 9.2.
   b. Example 9.3.
   c. Example 9.5.

(L) *14. Revise IndexCk to test the precondition that the lower index limit cannot exceed the upper index limit. If the precondition is violated, beep the speaker and write an appropriate error message. Test the utility with a driver. Add the revised utility to your personal utilities library.

(L) 15. For program ArrayIO in Figure 9.3...
   a. Run the program and reproduce our runs in Figure 9.4. What happens if we input an incorrect file specification?
   b. Develop a desk check script as GetArray gets executed for the run in Figure 9.4c. Let's get you started...

      1. Index stores 1.
      2. RangeViolation stores false.
      3. While test is true (not false and not false).
      4. A[1] stores 62.
      . . .

   c. What test condition was satisfied for terminating input in the Figure 9.4b run? Figure 9.4c run?
   d. Create and process file TEMPS2.DAT by adding the following new temperatures to the original file: 85, −10, 50, 32, 0, 60.

(L) *16. Modify ArrayIO in Figure 9.3 based on the following.
   a. **Real elements.** Revise and run the program to process the contents in TEMPS.DAT as real values.
   b. **Character subrange indexes.** Declare IndexType as the character subrange 'a'...'z'. Process file TEMPS.DAT.

(L) *17. Modify and run ArrayIO in Figure 9.3 as follows...
   a. Display the number of elements that were input just before the array is output.
   b. What would happen in GetArray if the precondition for the lower limit not exceeding the upper limit were not satisfied? This could happen, for example, if some programmer (not us, of course) mistakenly reverses these limits in the actual parameter list. Revise the procedure to trap this poten-

tial error. If the error is trapped, display an appropriate error message and terminate execution with the halt statement.

  c. Answer the same question as part **b** for procedure OutArray. In this case, display the error message, but don't halt execution.

18. Write code that declares the following array types and variables.

  a. Array type ArrayString50 defines string elements of size 50 indexed over positions $-1, 0, 1$. The array variable is Result.

  b. Array type ArrayChoice declares enumerated elements (a, b, c, d, e) typed Choice and indexed over exam questions 1 to 100. The array variables are Midterm and Final.

  c. Array type CharType declares character elements indexed over the extended ASCII character set. The array variable is Character.

  *d. Type ArrayRem defines string elements indexed over type Model (Saab99, Saab900, Saab9000). The array variables are SaabAd and SaabSpecs.

  *e. Type ArrayColor has the same index type as part **d**, but its elements are type Color (Black, Blue, Brown, Gray, Red, White). The array variable is SaabColors.

19. In Example 9.7 declare a third parallel array Population that stores the population of each city as *long* integer elements.

(L) ***20.** **String array.** Store the city names in Figure 9.5 in data file CITIES.DAT. Appropriately modify ArrayIO in Figure 9.3 to process this data file.

(L) **21.** In Example 9.8 . . .

  a. Test drive program ArrayIO2 by reproducing our sample run.

  b. Delete :20 in the output format for ArrayOne. What happens?

  c. Create file TEMPCIT2.DAT by placing data in the file as illustrated in Figure 9.5. Process this file. How are the elements in the city name array different from those in the run from part **a**?

  *d. Create and I/O file REALS.DAT for the two real arrays in Example 9.1.

22. **Multidimensional arrays.** In Figure 9.8 and Example 9.9 . . .

  a. What value is in F[1, 3]? F[5, 3]? F[3, 5]? F[10, 2]?

  b. Declare F as the illustrated 3D array, where all indexes are the given integer subranges. What value is in F[2, 3, 2]?

  *c. Declare F as the illustrated 3D array, where all indexes are the given enumerated types. What value is in F[Chicago, Summer, Y1960]?

23. **Multidimensional arrays.** Write code for the following declarations.

  a. Array GPA stores grade point averages (including the fractional part) by student and by year. Students are indexed from 1..1000 and years are indexed from 1991..1995. How would the declarations change if we also index on semester (Fall, Spring)?

  *b. Same as Exercise 18d, but also indexed over years 1985..1993.

*c. Same as part **b**, but also indexed over countries Canada, Mexico, USA.

*d. Same as part **c**, but also indexed over regions East, West, North, South.

(L) **24.** **Multidimensional arrays.** In Example 9.10...

   a. Try a sample run of Array2F. I/O the following two rows in a 2 × 3 array: 1 2 3 and 4 5 6. What happens if we forget to include the writeln statement within the outer for-do loop in the output segment of the program? Confirm your answer by trying a sample run of Array2F with braces placed around this writeln statement.

   b. What happens if we were to declare UpperRowLimit as 500? Try it and run the program. Explain. How do we need to change the code if we *had* to use 500?

   c. How must our input differ if we used a readln instead of a read statement for reading array elements?

   d. What happens if we don't deactivate/activate the range checking compiler directive, assuming range checking within the IDE is active? Try a sample with an entry for columns greater than 4 to confirm your answer.

(L) ***25.** **Multidimensional arrays.** In Example 9.10, revise Array2F to use the enumerated indexes shown in Example 9.9. Use the same test data in your sample run.

(L) ***26.** **Multidimensional arrays.** In Example 9.10, revise Array2F to calculate and output the average temperature by city and by season. In your output, try to display average city temperature at the end of a row, and average seasonal temperature at the bottom of a column.

(L) ***27.** **Multidimensional arrays.** Starting with Array2F, develop and test program Array3F to I/O the 3D temperature array seen in Figure 9.8. Use the following index ranges: 1..500 for city; (Winter, Spring, Summer, Fall) for season; (Y1990, Y1960, Y1930) for year. Use the given test data in your run, but store these data in file TEMPS3.DAT.

*28. **Identity matrix.** Write a program segment that run-time initializes every element in the (4 × 4) integer array Identity in the following manner.

```
1  0  0  0
0  1  0  0
0  0  1  0
0  0  0  1
```

Assume both rows and columns are indexed 1..Order. This is called an *identity matrix* of *order* 4 in linear algebra.

*29. Suppose a 2D real array X is already filled over rows 1..Rows and columns 1..Cols. Write code to...

   a. Interchange the corresponding elements in columns 1 and 3.

   b. Determine the smallest value in X, and its location (row and column index).

*30. Array of arrays. The element type in an array declaration need not be a simple type like real or character; it can be a structured type as well. For example, if the element type is an array type, then the declaration is called an *array of arrays*. Interestingly, an array of arrays is equivalent to a multi-dimensional array. For example, the declaration fragment

```
array [IndexType1] of array [IndexType2] of SimpleElementType
```

is structurally equivalent to the 2D declaration

```
array [IndexType1, IndexType2] of SimpleElementType
```

Moreover, the reference A[Index1][Index2] is equivalent to the reference A[Index1, Index2]. Rework the declarations in Example 9.9 using the array of arrays perspective. Which conceptualization do you think is easier to understand and implement?

*31. Array of sets. State declarations for array Colors indexed over CarType (Saturn, Tbird, Accord, and Corvette). Elements are typed ColorSetType, a set type with a base type of the enumerated colors (Black, Gray, White, Red, Blue, Green, Brown) declared under the type ColorEnumType. Are you totally confused? Give it a go. . .

*32. Revisit: HC METHSea. Let's get down to serious business with the suggestions for this exercise in Chapters 3, 4, 5, 6, and 8. Store the oil platform coordinates in arrays X and Y. Explore proposed Home Base coordinates as follows: Interactively input a range (low, high, and increment) of *x*-coordinates and a range of *y*-coordinates for proposed locations of the Home Base. Use nested loops that vary the proposed ranges. Store the resulting total distances in a two-dimensional array called D. A printout of array D is similar to a geographic contour plot. We're looking for the minimum value (the "valley floor") as the best proposed Home Base location (of those considered). High values indicate "ridges overlooking the valley floor." The selected range of coordinates should bracket the minimum value somewhere in the center of the matrix ("the valley floor should be surrounded by higher ridges"). Otherwise, the minimum may be a local minimum (the lowest "ridge" considered) instead of the global minimum (the "lowest spot on the valley floor"). Include an outer loop that asks the user if another set of ranges is desired. Typically, we start the search for the best location with wide ranges and larger increments. When we bracket a minimum, we refine the "map" with a narrower range and smaller increment. Visual search procedures of this type are fun. Enjoy. . . ! You might even win that methane gift certificate from Harvey.

ADDITIONAL EXERCISES

> **EASIER**   For the busy...
> **33 34**
>
> **NORMAL**   For the thinkers...
> **35 36 37 38**
>
> **TOUGHER**   For the hard CORE...
> **39 40**

33.   Revisit. Rework one of your earlier programs to use material from this chapter (if appropriate).

34.   Revisit: PIN confirmation. Use an array to store valid PINs in...
 a. Exercise 33, Chapter 6.
 b. Exercise 24a, Chapter 7.

35.   Statistical function suite. Develop and test one (or more) of the following utility functions for one-dimensional numeric arrays. Each function receives an array, along with lower and upper indexes.
 a.   Function Min. Returns the minimum element in the array, and its position.
 b.   Function Max. Returns the maximum element in the array, and its position.
 c.   Function Mean. Returns the mean element in the array. The *mean* is defined as the sum of elements divided by the number of elements. Do we need to make a distinction here between integer and real elements?

36.   Symmetric Matrix. A symmetric matrix is an $n \times n$ (square) matrix such that column i is identical to row i, $i = 1, \ldots, n$. For example, the following matrix is symmetric.

$$A = \begin{pmatrix} 90 & 85 & 10 & 75 & 35 \\ 85 & 80 & 20 & 70 & 40 \\ 10 & 20 & 30 & 65 & 45 \\ 75 & 70 & 65 & 60 & 50 \\ 35 & 40 & 45 & 50 & 55 \end{pmatrix}$$

Upper triangle
Lower triangle
Main diagonal

Note that the upper triangle is a "mirror image" of the lower triangle, excluding the main diagonal. Therefore, an input routine would only need to input the lower triangle and the main diagonal, and then fill in the upper triangle accordingly.

Develop an interactive program that inputs the size and lower part of a symmetric matrix, and writes the entire matrix. Use the preceding matrix as test data.

37.   **Simulation: Screen pattern.** The following procedure is a visual test of the goodness of a random number generator.

1. Initialize an $m \times n$ matrix screen to blanks, where m is the number of lines on the screen and n is the number of columns. The typical matrix is 25×80. This two-dimensional character array is a "picture" of the screen.

2. Generate a random integer number in the range 1 to m, and another in the range 1 to n (see Module C). This gives the coordinates of a position on the screen for an element in the matrix. Fill this element with the dot or period character.

3. Repeat step 2 a total of $m \times n$ times.

4. Display the matrix.

If the screen shows a random pattern of dots, without evidence of "banding," then the random number generator is doing a good job. A strong pattern would suggest a poorly performing generator. Try it on your system. Repeat screen simulations as often as desired, pausing the screen between each simulation. Any conclusions about the goodness of Turbo Pascal's random number function?

38.   **Pascal's triangle.** The French mathematician and philosopher Blaise Pascal (1623–1662) proposed the following triangular array for investigating certain mathematical properties and proving some theorems.

```
1
1  1
1  2  1
1  3  3  1
1  4  6  4  1
. . .
```

Pascal's triangle is constructed according to the following properties: Each row and column begins with 1; each succeeding number is the sum of two numbers, the one directly above it and the one to the left of the upper number. The sixth row, for example, would have the elements 1, 5, 10, 10, 5, 1.

a. Develop an interactive program that inputs the size of the triangle (number of rows or columns) and writes Pascal's triangle. Write a triangle of size 10 in your test run. Label each row with its row number followed by a separator, as in 3¦ for the third row. Allow triangles up to size 100.

b. A binomial expansion to the nth power is given by the following expression.

$$(a + b)^n$$

For example, if $n = 2$, then we have the three terms

$$a^2 + 2ab + b^2$$

Note that the third row in Pascal's triangle includes the three coefficients (1 2 1) in this binomial expansion. In general, the elements in row $(n + 1)$ in Pascal's triangle are the coefficients in a binomial expansion to the nth power.

Include an option in the program for writing coefficients in a binomial expansion. For example, if the user inputs 5 for power, then the program should display the sixth row of Pascal's triangle as follows.

Binomial Expansion to 5th power

Term	Coefficient
1	1
2	5
3	10
4	10
5	5
6	1

39. **Crime story.** The data below represent the number of arrests for felony crimes in a state over a three-year period.

Felony	Arrest Data by Year 1990	1991	1992
Homicide	1,000	1,000	1,000
Robbery	10,000	9,000	11,000
Burglary	27,000	24,000	28,000
Assault	13,000	15,000	16,000
Theft	19,000	20,000	23,000
Forgery	10,000	9,000	10,000

a. Develop a program to read the arrest data. Write out the data in a table format that includes a new row for total arrests in each year and a new column for average arrests for each crime over the past three years.

b. In the output of part **a**, label your columns 1990, 1991, 1992, and average. Label your rows according to the felony names in the above table, the last row being Totals. Store felony names in a one-dimensional array and years in another one-dimensional array.

c. Write a second table that projects arrests over the next three years. Interactively input the annual percent increases in arrests for each felony. Use the following percents for the six felonies: 2, 2, 5, 4, 8, 6. For example, we would expect 29,400 burglaries in 1993 (28,000 × 1.05). Store the percents in a one-dimensional real array and all projections in a two-dimensional integer array.

d. Instead of the 2D array in part **c**, use the following 3D array: The first layer shows projections by felony and year; the second layer shows realized actual arrests by felony and year; the third layer shows percent differences between projected and actual arrests by felony and year. The first layer is filled as described in part **c**; the second layer is interactively input; the third layer is calculated. As test data, use the following actual arrests for 1993; 1128, 11,174, 33,068, 17,352, 26,430, and 11,896.

40. **Stock portfolio.** Companies, universities, banks, pension funds, and other organizations routinely invest funds in the stock market. The set of stocks in which the organization invests its funds is called a *stock portfolio*. The accompanying table illustrates a sample stock portfolio, including the number of shares owned of each stock, the purchase price per share, and the latest price per share quoted by the stock exchange.

Stock Portfolio

Stock	Number of Shares	Purchase Price ($/share)	Current Price ($/share)
AppleC	40,000	$25\frac{7}{8}$	$39\frac{3}{4}$
Boeing	5,000	$61\frac{1}{2}$	56
EKodk	10,000	60	$54\frac{1}{2}$
HewlPk	15,000	39	50
IBM	2,500	$97\frac{1}{8}$	$120\frac{3}{4}$
Texaco	8,000	$23\frac{1}{2}$	49
TexInst	12,000	80	$45\frac{7}{8}$

a. Develop a program that calculates and displays the initial (purchase) value of the portfolio, the current value of the portfolio, and the net change in the value. *Hint:* The value of the portfolio is found by multiplying shares by corresponding prices and summing.

b. Output the portfolio before writing the items in part **a**.

c. Include a loop in the program for processing more than one portfolio. Find two copies of a newspaper that were published at least two weeks apart. Select a portfolio, make up shares owned, and use the two sets of prices for purchase and current prices. Process the given portfolio and the new portfolio in one run, and include the output of combined value of all portfolios.

SORTING AND SEARCHING

---

†Optional, more advanced material. Skip without loss of continuity, study at this point, or wait until later.

This module covers two common applications of arrays: sorting the elements in an array and searching for specific elements in an array. We also return to the table-lookup problem.

D.1   SORTING

. . . .

Sorting is the act of ordering a list of values. For example, the list of integers 40 30 50 10 20 would be sorted in *ascending* order as the list 10 20 30 40 50; the characters B A D C would be sorted in *descending* order as D C B A; and the names Tom Tani Tiny would be sorted in *ascending* order as Tani Tiny Tom.

OVERVIEW

Sorting is a popular task in computing environments. In some applications, sorting provides information for decision making. For instance, a university administrator might want student records sorted by student names, or by social security numbers, or by state of residence, or by grade-point average, depending on the objective; a hospital administrator might want patient cases sorted by diagnosis, or by attending physician, or by cost; an automotive engineer might want test track data sorted by speed or by test date; and so on. In other applications, sorting improves performance. For example, an algorithm that searches for a particular item, like social security number, often operates faster if the items are sorted to begin with. In still other applications, sorting is required as an intermediate step to finding an answer. For instance, the calculation of a median in statistics (the value such that half the items are above and the other half are below) first requires a sort of the items.

The development of sorting algorithms has been, and continues to be, a fertile area of research and experimentation for computer scientists. Depending on the particular algorithm and the nature of the data, sorting performance varies with respect to processing times, memory requirements, and other operating characteristics. The algorithms themselves vary from the intuitively obvious to the mathematically abstract.

In this module we work with algorithms that sort arrays.[1] One approach to sorting an array is to start with the *entire* array (list of values) and successively compare elements, exchanging or repositioning elements as needed.

---

[1]In Chapter 13 we show another common alternative to creating sorted lists.

This class of algorithms includes some very popular sorting algorithms: *bubble sort, selection sort,* and *insertion sort.* These algorithms are intuitive, are good for teaching sorting principles, and work well for small arrays of, say, 500 items or less. In the next section, we develop the insertion sort in detail; we leave the others to exercises.

Another approach to sorting uses a "divide and conquer" strategy that partitions the array into two or more portions, acting on each portion as a separate and simpler sorting problem.[2] These algorithms are more efficient than the above algorithms for sorting large arrays. The *quick sort* algorithm is a popular example of this approach. We explain this algorithm in Exercise 20, and let you have a go at coding it.

INSERTION SORT

Let's illustrate a reasonably fast and easily understood sorting algorithm called the **insertion sort.**

Requirements

In our sample application we work with an integer array and sort in ascending order. In the exercises, we consider descending sorts and other data types for elements. Sorts usually deal with reasonably large arrays, so let's input the array from a data file, rather than interactively. Output data include the unsorted array and the sorted array. Input data include the name of the data file and the original (unsorted) array. Constants include a lower index limit of 1 and an upper index limit of 500.

The steps in an insertion sort are illustrated in Table D.1. Note the following.

1. At the beginning of the first step, we view the first element (40) as a sorted subarray and the remaining elements as an unsorted subarray. Our task in the first step is to take the first element in the unsorted portion (30) and *insert* it into the sorted subarray. We do this by shifting the 40 one position to the right, and inserting the 30 in the first position. At the end of the first step, the sorted subarray is the first two elements.

2. The remaining steps are implemented in the same way: "Lift" the first unsorted element (the *insert element*) from its *old location,* make room (if necessary) in the sorted subarray by *shifting* elements to the right, and *insert* the lifted element into its *new location.* This algorithm is similar to having a sorted group of playing cards in our hand, lifting a new card from the deck, and inserting the new card in its proper place. If the insert element is in its proper position at the beginning of the step,

---

[2]These sorting techniques usually apply *recursion* (Module B) to the solution of each successive subproblem.

Table D.1   Sample Insertion Sort

	Array Before Step						Array After Step					
Step	*1*	*2*	*3*	*4*	*5*	...*Indexes*...	*1*	*2*	*3*	*4*	*5*	*Comment*
	Insert						Sorted subarray					
1. Insert element 30	40	30	50	10	20		30	40	50	10	20	Shift 40 to 2nd location (index 2) and insert 30 in 1st location (index 1). First two elements now sorted.
	Shift											
2. Insert element 50	30	40	50	10	20		30	40	50	10	20	No shift or insert. Element 50 is in its proper place. First three elements now sorted.
			Insert									
3. Insert element 10	30	40	50	10	20		10	30	40	50	20	Shift 50, 40, and 30 to locations 4, 3, and 2 respectively, and insert 10 in location 1. Four elements now sorted.
		Shifts										
				Insert								
4. Insert element 20	10	30	40	50	20		10	20	30	40	50	Shift 50, 40, and 30 to locations 5, 4, and 3 respectively, and insert 20 in location 2. All five elements now sorted.
			Shifts									

no moving action is undertaken. At the end of each step, we have one more element in the sorted subarray and one less in the unsorted subarray. Eventually, we have all elements in the sorted subarray and no elements in the unsorted subarray.

As visual processors, this algorithm is readily intuitive. This is because we can visually process "chunks" of unrefined tasks. To illustrate what we mean, how did we decide in step 3 that the 10 should be moved from its fourth old location to its new first location? Sure, it's visually obvious. But what individual (refined) steps are going on in our brains to make this decision? The digital processor requires more refinement. And, as we will see, the mapping of what is "intuitively obvious" for us into the eventual code that gets executed by our "dumb friend" is what algorithmic programming is all about. It's a skill and art form that few of us master in a lifetime. Let's give it a go...

Design

Let's design an ascending insertion sort on a one-dimensional array as a *utility procedure*. The program itself will be a driver that tests the sort procedure, based on the following design.

Program CkSort (Driver)

> Clear screen and write title
> Prep data file (Call utility PrepFile)
> Get array from data file (Call utility GetArray)
> Output unsorted array (Call utility OutArray)
> Sort array by insertion method (Call new utility Sort)
> Output sorted array (Call utility OutArray)

Utility PrepFile was first introduced in Chapter 6, and utilities GetArray and OutArray were developed in Chapter 9.

The user interface is nothing to brag about; it rarely is with a driver, whose purpose in life is the testing of modules. Figure D.1 shows sample I/O, to indicate where we are headed.

Now for the task at hand. We need to design (refine) procedure Sort. This procedure receives lower and upper indexes and the unsorted array, sorts the array in ascending order, and sends the sorted array. In Exercise 3a we ask you to try a descending sort. In our design, *the original (unsorted) array is replaced by the sorted array.* In Exercise 3b we work with a variation that preserves the original array.

We also assume that received lower and upper indexes are within the declared index limits, and that the lower index does not exceed the upper index. These *preconditions* must be ensured by the calling module. See Exercise 1c for consequences and fixes regarding this design element.

FIGURE D.1   I/O for Program CkSort

```
SORT DEMONSTRATION

Enter data file (like A:\GRADES\HC101.DAT)... sort.dat

Unsorted test array:  40 30 50 10 20

Sorted test array  :  10 20 30 40 50
```

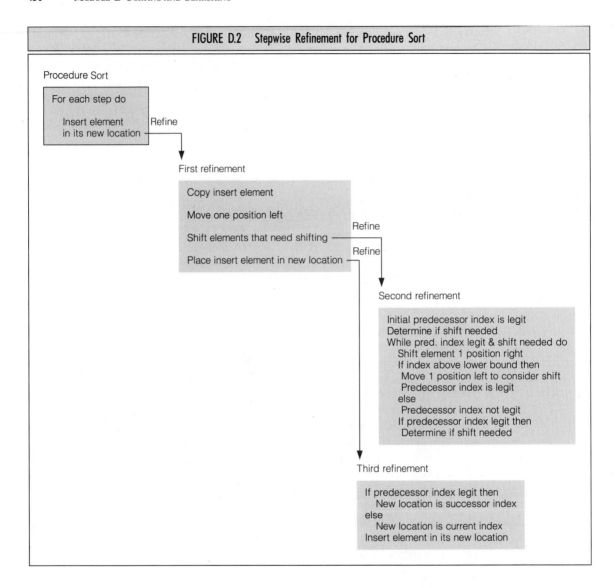

FIGURE D.2   Stepwise Refinement for Procedure Sort

Procedure Sort

For each step do

    Insert element
    in its new location — Refine

First refinement

Copy insert element

Move one position left

Shift elements that need shifting — Refine

Place insert element in new location — Refine

Second refinement

Initial predecessor index is legit
Determine if shift needed
While pred. index legit & shift needed do
    Shift element 1 position right
    If index above lower bound then
      Move 1 position left to consider shift
      Predecessor index is legit
    else
      Predecessor index not legit
    If predecessor index legit then
      Determine if shift needed

Third refinement

If predecessor index legit then
    New location is successor index
else
    New location is current index
Insert element in its new location

Figure D.2 shows a stepwise refinement for our sort procedure. Note the following.

1. Each iteration of the for-do loop is equivalent to a step in Table D.1.

2. In the first refinement, we initially need to *copy the insert element* to a placeholder, or temporary location; otherwise, assuming a shift, the insert element would be replaced (and lost) by the element to its left. The placeholder is like lifting a card in our card-playing analogy. In Table D.1, the placeholder is the same as the insert element. In step 3, for example,

the insert element is 10. Its old location is at position 4. Continuing with the pseudocode in Figure D.2, we next *move one position left to consider a shift.* Thus, we move to position 3 to consider element 50 for a possible shift. Next, we *shift all elements that need shifting.* In step 3, this means we would shift elements 50, 40, and 30 one position to the right, to positions 4, 3, and 2 respectively. We now *place the insert element in its new location.* Element 10 now gets placed in (copied to) its new location in the first position. This completes the first refinement in Figure D.2.

3. The second refinement gives details on how we *shift all elements that need shifting.* Each shift is carried out one element and one position at a time. Moreover, we only consider a shift if (a) the current position given by the index ensures a legitimate predecessor index (no lower than its lower bound, to avoid a possible range error) and (b) a shift is needed (the insert element is less than the element we're considering for a shift). In step 3, for example, we first consider shifting element 50 from position 3 to position 4. The initial index 3 has a legitimate predecessor at 2. Next in Figure D.2, we determine if a shift is needed. The insert element 10 is less than 50, meaning we should shift this element. So the while test is true, we shift element 50 one position to the right (to the fourth position), and we move one position left (the index changes from 3 to 2) after confirming that index 2 is legitimate. We now consider the next shift. This loop repeats again for elements 40 and 30, moving each one position to the right. After we move the 30, a move one position left would take us to position 0 (the 30 was at position 1), meaning that we can't consider this position (the predecessor index would not be legitimate). The resulting if test is false (we have no more elements to consider) and the while test is now false (we're through shifting).

4. The third refinement shows how we determine the new position for the insert element. In general, the new location is either one position to the right of the current index (if the predecessor index is legitimate) or at the current index (if the predecessor index is not legitimate). *The only time the predecessor index is not legitimate is when the insert element is being placed in the first position.* In these cases, the current index is at position 1. In all other cases, the insert element is placed one position above the current index.

Code

Figure D.3 shows the listing for the driver CkSort. Relate the code to the earlier pseudocode, and note the following.

1. CkSort can test any array type. We only need to make sure that the generic constants, index type, element type, and array type are compatible.

2. Utility procedures PrepFile, GetArray, IndexCk, and OutArray were developed in Chapters 6 and 9.

FIGURE D.3   Listing for Program CkSort

```pascal
program CkSort;

   {* * * * * * * * * * * * * * * * * * * * * * * * * * * * * * * *
    *                                                             *
    *        Program that tests insertion sort for various array types *
    *           ... To test different array types redeclare constant(s), *
    *              IndexType, ElementType, and ArrayType as needed *
    *                                                             *
    *        Inputs array from data file                         *
    *        Calls sort procedure                                *
    *        Outputs unsorted and sorted array                   *
    *                                                             *
    *        Initial test declares IndexType as integer subrange *
    *           1 .. 500, ElementType as integer, and ArrayType as *
    *           ArrayOfInt.                                       *
    *                                                             *
    *        Modular structure                                   *
    *           |___ GetArray         (Old utility procedure)    *
    *           |    |___ IndexCk (Old utility procedure)        *
    *           |___ OutArray        (Old utility procedure)     *
    *           |___ Sort            (New utility procedure)      *
    *                                                             *
    *        Data structure of text file                         *
    *        ----------------------------------------------------------- *
    *        Value                                               *
    *        Value                                               *
    *        ...                                                 *
    *        ----------------------------------------------------------- *
    *        Sample data files:   SORT.DAT or TEMPS.DAT          *
    *                                                             *
    * * * * * * * * * * * * * * * * * * * * * * * * * * * * * * * *}

   {============================ Declarations ============================}

uses crt, OurUnit;

const
  Title = 'SORT DEMONSTRATION';
  LowerIndexLimit = 1;  UpperIndexLimit = 500;
  SizeStr = 20;

type
  IndexType   = LowerIndexLimit .. UpperIndexLimit;
  ArrayOfChar = array [IndexType] of char;
  ArrayOfInt  = array [IndexType] of integer;
  ArrayOfReal = array [IndexType] of real;
  ArrayOfStr  = array [IndexType] of string [SizeStr];

  ElementType = integer;        {Generic element type}
  ArrayType   = ArrayOfInt;     {Generic array type}

  {ArrayType, ElementType, and IndexType needed for generic
   sort in procedure Sort}

var
  TestArray  : ArrayType;       {Needed for procedure Sort}
  TextFile   : text;            {Text file variable for data file}
  UpperIndex : IndexType;       {Index of last filled element}
```

```
┌─────────────────────────────────────────────────────────────────────┐
│                    FIGURE D.3   (continued)                          │
├─────────────────────────────────────────────────────────────────────┤
│                                                                       │
│  {====------------------- Procedure Declarations =====================}│
│                                                                       │
│        Utility procedures GetArray, IndexCk, and OutArray are not shown;│
│        these are in Figure 9.3.                                       │
│                                                                       │
│  procedure Sort (LowerIndex, UpperIndex : IndexType;                  │
│                  var A : ArrayType);                                  │
│                                                                       │
│  ...                                                        ◄──────    │
│                                                                   ╲    │
│  end;    {Sort}                                         See Figure D.4 │
│                                                                       │
│      {============================= Main Body =========================}│
│                                                                       │
│  begin  {CkSort}                                                      │
│                                                                       │
│    clrscr;                                                            │
│    writeln (Title);  writeln;                                        │
│                                                                       │
│    PrepFile (TextFile);                        {In OurUnit}          │
│                                                                       │
│    GetArray (TextFile, LowerIndexLimit, UpperIndexLimit, UpperIndex,  │
│             TestArray);                                               │
│                                                                       │
│    writeln;  write ('Unsorted test array:  ');                       │
│    OutArray (LowerIndexLimit, UpperIndex, TestArray);                │
│                                                                       │
│    Sort (LowerIndexLimit, UpperIndex, TestArray);                    │
│                                                                       │
│    writeln;  write ('Sorted test array  :  ');                       │
│    OutArray (LowerIndexLimit, UpperIndex, TestArray);                │
│  end.    {CkSort}                                                     │
│                                                                       │
└─────────────────────────────────────────────────────────────────────┘
```

3. Utility procedure Sort is listed in Figure D.4. Note the following.

a. The procedure receives a lower index, an upper index, and an array; sorts the array over the received range of index values; and sends the sorted array. Note that only the filled elements in the array are sorted. In Figure D.1, the first five elements in the temperature array were sorted (out of 500). We ensure this by using LowerIndexLimit (1) and UpperIndex (5) in the call to procedure Sort. Also note that formal parameter A is a variable parameter. This means that the original elements in real array TestArray (Figure D.3) are changed (rearranged).

b. The code and documentation in Figure D.4 is consistent with the pseudocode in Figure D.2. Take a few minutes to relate each line in the pseudocode version to each line in the Pascal version. In procedure Sort, all indexes are typed IndexType, the array is generically typed ArrayType, and the insert element is typed ElementType. The pseudocode and Pascal versions are perfectly general with respect to array types, index types, and element types; the specific types are determined by the driver. As seen in the driver (Figure D.3), IndexType

```
┌─────────────────────────────────────────────────────────────────────────┐
│                    FIGURE D.4    Listing for Procedure Sort               │
├─────────────────────────────────────────────────────────────────────────┤
│                                                                           │
│   procedure Sort (LowerIndex, UpperIndex : IndexType;                     │
│                   var A : ArrayType);                                     │
│                                                                           │
│     { Utility performs ascending insertion sort on array over received    │
│          indexes                                                          │
│       Receives LowerIndex, UpperIndex, unsorted A                         │
│       Sends sorted A }                                                    │
│                                                                           │
│     { NOTE:  The original array is changed!!!                             │
│             Preconditions assume LowerIndex and UpperIndex are within     │
│                 index limits, and LowerIndex <= UpperIndex                │
│             Assumes IndexType, ArrayType, and ElementType are declared    │
│                 in calling module }                                       │
│                                                                           │
│   var                                                                     │
│     OldLocation    : IndexType;    {Old location (index) of insert element}│
│     NewLocation    : IndexType;    {New location (index) of insert element}│
│     InsertElement  : ElementType;  {Current element being inserted}       │
│     Index          : IndexType;    {Current index}                        │
│     LegitIndex     : Boolean;      {True if Index within range; else false}│
│     Shift          : Boolean;      {True if element needs to be moved over or│
│                                     shifted one position; else false}     │
│                                                                           │
└─────────────────────────────────────────────────────────────────────────┘
```

is an integer subrange, ArrayType is identically typed as ArrayOfInt, and ElementType is **integer.** We look at other types in the exercises.

c. We increment and decrement the index by calling predeclared function **succ** and **pred,** respectively. This ensures that the sort procedure handles any ordinal index type, not just integer subranges.

d. Preconditions assume LowerIndex and UpperIndex are within the declared index range given by LowerIndexLimit and UpperIndexLimit, and that LowerIndex does not exceed UpperIndex. See Exercise 1c for the implications in violating these preconditions. The flag LegitIndex ensures that the index in the indexed variable A[Index] is not outside the received index range given by LowerIndex and UpperIndex.

e. By using LegitIndex and Shift we improve the readability of test conditions in the if and while statements. Note that we only want to evaluate Shift when the index is legitimate.

f. To really understand this algorithm, try completing the desk check in Table D.2 for our sample data. Assume the "snapshot" of memory is taken at the execution of the test condition in the while statement. We give the answer in Exercise 1d. Most of us have to do a lot of desk checking to understand algorithms that manipulate indexes. This algorithm is a good example of a problem that's easy to solve by hand/eye/mind but tricky to program.

Test
Figure D.1 shows a test run for program CkSort. Try Exercise 1 for other test runs and debugging considerations.

FIGURE D.4   (*continued*)

```
begin  {Sort}

   for OldLocation := succ(LowerIndex) to UpperIndex do

      begin  {Insert element in its new location}

        {Copy insert element}
         InsertElement := A[OldLocation];

        {Move one position left to consider shift}
         Index := pred(OldLocation);

        {Initial index is legit}
         LegitIndex := true;

        {Determine if shift needed}
         Shift := InsertElement < A[Index];

         while LegitIndex and Shift do

            begin  {Shift all elements that need shifting}

              {Shift element one position to right}
               A[succ(Index)] := A[Index];

              {Ensure predecessor index is within range}
               if Index > LowerIndex then
                 begin
                   {Move one position left to consider shift}
                   Index      := pred(Index);
                   LegitIndex := true;
                 end
               else
                 LegitIndex := false;

              {Make sure index is legit before using it in indexed variable}
               if LegitIndex then
                 {Determine if shift needed}
                 Shift := InsertElement < A[Index];

            end;  {while... We are through shifting}
        {Place insert element in its new location}
         if LegitIndex
           then NewLocation := succ(Index)
           else NewLocation := Index;
         A[NewLocation] := InsertElement;

      end;  {for... All elements have been inserted}

end;  {Sort}
{-----------------------------------------------------------------------}
```

That's it for an introduction to sorting. To deepen your understanding of sorting procedures and concepts, try solving the following exercises.

- Exercise 2, to sort other array types
- Exercise 3a, to implement descending sorts
- Exercise 3b, to preserve the original array

Table D.2   Partial Desk Check of Procedure Sort*

OldLocation	InsertElement	Index	LegitIndex	Shift	A[1]	A[2]	A[3]	A[4]	A[5]	NewLocation
2	30	1	true	true	40	30	50	10	20	Undefined
2	30	1	false	true	40	40	50	10	20	Undefined
3	50	2	true	false	30	40	50	10	20	1
4	10	3	true	true	30	40	50	10	20	3

*The memory snapshot is taken at the while line; color shows new assignments.

- Exercise 4, to explore the effects of array size on sort time
- Exercises 19 and 20, to develop procedures for the *bubble sort* and *quick sort*

SELF-REVIEW EXERCISES

1

D.2   SEARCHING

• • • • • • • • • • • • • •

Searching is the act of finding a particular element in a list. For example, we might need the computer to look up a name in a customer file, a word in a dictionary file, a social security number in a file of student numbers, and so on. In this section we introduce two kinds of computer searching algorithms: *sequential searches* and *binary searches*. We also return to the *table-lookup* problem first introduced in Chapter 6.

SEQUENTIAL SEARCH

A **sequential search**—also called **linear search** or **serial search**—searches for an element in a list by considering the first element in the list. If this element is the *search element* (the element that's the object of the search), then the search successfully terminates; otherwise, the next element in the list is considered. This process repeats while the search element is not found and more elements need to be considered. The end result is either the search element was found or it was not found. In any case, the list of elements is *sequentially* searched, starting with the first and ending with the last (if necessary).

As in sorting algorithms, we work with a filled array. The search algorithm attempts to find the search element within the list of array elements. If the search element is found, the algorithm returns the *search index,* the index that corresponds to the location of the search element. If the search is not successful, the search algorithm returns a search index that implies the search failed to find the search element. Many algorithms return a value of 0 for the search index when the search element is not found. This implies, of course, that the index type is integer and that zero is outside the declared index range for the array. In general, when the search fails, it's best if the algorithm returns a value one position less than the lower index of the array.

What we have described is a function that: receives a *search element,* a range of index values that runs from *lower index* to *upper index,* and an *array*; searches the array sequentially; and returns a *search index* that either identifies the position of the element that matches the search element (if found) or indicates that the search element was not found (by returning a value one position less than the lower index). We can describe its design as follows.

Function SearchIndex

> Assume search element not found initially
> Initialize array index to lower index
>
> While search element not found and index within upper index do
>   If array element = search element
>   then search element found
>   else increment index by one position
>
> If search element was found
>   then SearchIndex is index
>   else SearchIndex is one position less than lower index

For example, consider the following memory cells.

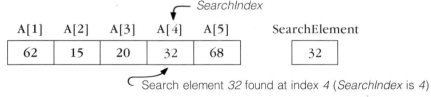

Search element *32* found at index *4* (*SearchIndex* is *4*)

Suppose we wish to search for element 32 over the range of indexes 1 to 5. In this case, SearchElement stores 32 and the search function returns 4 in SearchIndex. Suppose, however, that we try a search for the search element 5. Now the search function returns 0 for SearchIndex, or one position less than the lower index of 1.

FIGURE D.5   Listing for Utility Function SearchIndex

```
function SearchIndex (SearchElement : ElementType;
                      LowerIndex, UpperIndex : IndexType;
                      A : ArrayType ) : IndexTypeX;

  { Utility function searches for search element in array using
      sequential search algorithm
    Receives SearchElement, LowerIndex, UpperIndex, A
    Returns either index that corresponds to search element (if search
      element found) or index that is one position less than lower index
      (if not found) }

  { NOTE:  Preconditions assume LowerIndex and UpperIndex are within
             index limits, and LowerIndex <= UpperIndex
           Assumes ElementType, IndexType, ArrayType, and IndexTypeX
             are declared in calling module
           IndexTypeX is the same as IndexType, except lower limit in
             index range is eXtended one position left }

var
  Found : Boolean;          {True if search element found; false otherwise}
  Index : IndexType;        {Index of array element}

begin   {SearchIndex}

  Found := false;           {Search element not found at this point}
  Index := LowerIndex;      {Start search at lower index}

  while (not Found) and (Index <= UpperIndex) do
    if A[Index] = SearchElement
      then Found := true                {Found search element}
      else Index := succ(Index);        {Go on to next element}

  if Found
    then SearchIndex := Index
    else SearchIndex := pred(LowerIndex);

end;    {SearchIndex}
{---------------------------------------------------------------------}
```

Figure D.5 shows our Turbo Pascal version of the sequential search function SearchIndex. Note the following.

1. We made this function a utility; it resides in the Utilities Library.

2. The code closely follows our earlier pseudocode design. Make sure you relate one to the other.

3. It receives a search element typed ElementType, lower and upper indexes typed IndexType, and an array typed ArrayType. As before, these are generic data types that are declared in the calling module; they permit the handling of any array types by our utilities. The function returns a search index having type IndexTypeX, which eXtends IndexType one position below the lower index limit. Think about what could happen if we had typed the function as IndexType: We would get a *range error* whenever the search is unsuccessful (see the last if-then-else structure).

4. Our usual preconditions assume that values in LowerIndex and Upper-Index are within the declared index limits, and that the value in Lower-Index does not exceed the value in UpperIndex. In Exercise 5c we ask you to consider the implications of violating these preconditions.

Figure D.6 shows two sample runs of a driver named CkFind1. Note the following.

1. We don't show driver **CkFind1** because it's very similar to our earlier driver in Figure D.3. Check it out in Exercise 5.
2. Any module that calls the search function needs to determine whether or not the search element was found. As discussed earlier, the search function returns in **SearchIndex** the index of the array element that matches the search element (if found) or one position less than the lower index that was sent to the function. In the first run, the function returns 4; in the second run, the function returns 0. The driver stores the returned search index in variable **IndexFound** with the call

```
IndexFound := SearchIndex (SearchElement, LowerIndexLimit,
            UpperIndex, TestArray);
```

and then uses an if-then-else structure to determine whether the search element was found or not found.

```
if IndexFound >= LowerIndexLimit
  then writeln (' ', SearchElement, ' found at index ', IndexFound)
  else writeln (' ', SearchElement, ' NOT found in array');
```

FIGURE D.6   Two Test Runs of Driver CkFind1

```
SEQUENTIAL SEARCH DEMONSTRATION

Enter data file (like A:\GRADES\HC101.DAT)... temps.dat

Test array:   62 15 20 32 68

Enter search element ===> 32

  32 found at index 4


SEQUENTIAL SEARCH DEMONSTRATION

Enter data file (like A:\GRADES\HC101.DAT)... temps.dat

Test array:   62 15 20 32 68

Enter search element ===> 5

  5 NOT found in array
```

For the second run in Figure D.6, IndexFound stores 0, an index one position lower than the 1 in LowerIndexLimit. Again, this is why we typed IndexFound as IndexTypeX. In our example, IndexType defines the integer subrange 1..500, so IndexTypeX is defined over the integer subrange 0..500; otherwise, we would have a range error whenever the search element is not found.

BINARY SEARCH

In finding an item, the sequential search examines anywhere from 1 to the total number of elements in the array. For very large arrays, this "brute force" approach is time inefficient. Many search algorithms have been developed that are more efficient than sequential searches, but usually at the expense of design and coding complexity.

A search algorithm that's reasonably efficient, intuitive, and easy to code is the **binary search.** This algorithm starts with a *sorted array* (we assume ascending order), selects an element in the *middle* of the array, and checks whether the search element is at, below, or above this middle element. If the middle element equals the search element, then the search element has been found and the search is over; else if the middle element is greater than the search element, then the element sought is in the left subarray (if it's in the array at all); else the element is in the right subarray. In the latter two cases, the array is split into the *two* indicated subarrays (hence the term *binary*), and the algorithm turns its attention to the promising subarray, discarding the other from consideration. These steps are repeated until either the search element is found or the algorithm is down to a subarray with one element (which it can't further split into subarrays).

Let's illustrate a binary search by finding search element 60 within the following *sorted* array.

The index range from *left index* at 1 to *right index* at 9 defines the array under consideration. The *middle index* is the integer average of left index and right index, or 5. Thus, the middle element is A[5], or 50. The middle element 50 is less than the search element 60, so we discard the subarray from A[1] to A[5] and consider the following right subarray as the *active subarray.*

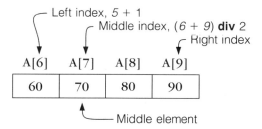

Note the change in the left index (it's one more than the previous middle index). We now recompute the middle index as 7, giving 70 as the middle element, which is greater than the search element 60. This means that the left subarray contains the matching search element (if at all). Next, we do another binary split by discarding the subarray indexed over 7..9, leaving us the following active subarray.

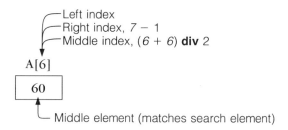

The left index stays the same at 6, the right index is recomputed as the former middle index (7) less one, giving 6, and the middle index is recalculated as 6 also. Now the middle element and search element are identical, and so the search ends with a matching search element at search index 6.

What would happen if our search element were 55? The algorithm would proceed as before, except at the last active subarray given by A[6]. Now the middle element 60 is greater than 55, so the algorithm attempts a binary split by considering an active subarray to the left of the current subarray. It recomputes the right index as 5, but we have a left index that's greater at 6! This means that we can't define an active subarray given the current subarray, so the algorithm terminates without having found a value that matches the search element. Keep in mind that as the binary search proceeds, the left index increases and the right index decreases. If they cross over each other (the right index is less than the left index), then the algorithm terminates without having found a match for the search element.

The following pseudocode design for a function describes this binary search algorithm.

Function *SearchBinIndex*

Assume desired element not found initially
Initialize *left index* to lower index
Initialize *right index* to upper index

Repeat

    Calculate *middle index*

    If *middle element = search element* then
      Search element found
    else if *middle element > search element* then {Left subarray active}
      New *right index* is 1 position less than middle index
    else {Right subarray active}
      New *left index* is 1 position more than middle index

until search element found or right/left indexes cross

If desired element was found
    then SearchBinIndex is *middle index*
    else SearchBinIndex is one position less than lower index

Figure D.7 shows the utility binary search function SearchBinIndex. Note the following.

1. The Pascal function follows readily from its design. Its array, element, and index declarations are identical to those in function SearchIndex, except IndexType is restricted to *integer subranges;* otherwise, the integer expression that calculates a value for MiddleIndex would be type incompatible. In Exercise 9 we ask you to generalize this function to other ordinal index types.

2. SearchBinIndex includes an additional precondition that the received array is sorted.

3. We developed a driver CkFind2 to test the binary search function. We ask you to test drive it in Exercise 7.

Table Lookup

So far we have implemented two different search algorithms, but we really haven't used the results in any meaningful way. This brings us to the purpose of a search. For example, the purpose in looking up a person's name in a telephone file might be to find a telephone number; the purpose in looking up a student's social security number in a student file might be to find the student's account balance, or major, or address; the purpose in looking up a city's name might be to find its corresponding temperature; and so on. In other words,

```
┌─────────────────────────────────────────────────────────────────────────┐
│         FIGURE D.7    Listing for Utility Function SearchBinIndex          │
└─────────────────────────────────────────────────────────────────────────┘

  function SearchBinIndex (SearchElement : ElementType;
                           LowerIndex, UpperIndex : IndexType;
                           A : ArrayType ) : IndexTypeX;

    { Utility function searches for search element in SORTED array using
        binary search algorithm
      Receives SearchElement, LowerIndex, UpperIndex, A
      Returns either index that corresponds to search element (if search
        element found) or index that is one position less than lower index
        (if not found) }

    { NOTE:  Preconditions assume LowerIndex and UpperIndex are within
               index limits, LowerIndex <= UpperIndex, and
               array A is SORTED in ascending order
             Assumes ElementType, IndexType, ArrayType, and IndexTypeX
               are declared in calling module
             IndexTypeX is the same as IndexType, except lower limit in
               index range is eXtended one position left
             Index types are assumed to be INTEGER subranges; otherwise
               expression with div operator not legitimate}
  var
    Found       : Boolean;       {True if search element found; else false}
    LeftIndex   : IndexType;     {Leftmost index of active subarray}
    MiddleIndex : IndexType;     {Middle index of active subarray}
    RightIndex  : IndexTypeX;    {Rightmost index of active subarray}

  begin   {SearchBinIndex}

    Found       := false;        {Search element not found at this point}
    LeftIndex   := LowerIndex;   {Initial subarray is entire array}
    RightIndex  := UpperIndex;

    repeat

      MiddleIndex := (LeftIndex + RightIndex) div 2;

      if A[MiddleIndex] = SearchElement then
        Found := true                           {Found search element}
      else if A[MiddleIndex] > SearchElement then
        RightIndex := pred(MiddleIndex)         {Left subarray is active}
      else
        LeftIndex  := succ(MiddleIndex);        {Right subarray is active}

    until (Found) or (RightIndex < LeftIndex);

    if Found
      then SearchBinIndex := MiddleIndex
      else SearchBinIndex := pred(LowerIndex);

  end;   {SearchBinIndex}
  {-----------------------------------------------------------------------}
```

the usual purpose of a search for the value of a *given attribute* (a specific person's name, student's social security number, or city's name) is to find the value of *some other related attribute* (a corresponding telephone number, address, or temperature)! This task is often called a **table lookup**, or simply **lookup.** The term *table* suggests that we can view attributes as columns in a table, where each row is the set of values for some *entity* (like a person, student, or city).

Take a look at Figure 9.5. Suppose we want to look up temperature based on city name. First, let's use our tried-and-true *visual table-lookup algorithm,* using the table in part a. For example, "What's the temperature in Boston?" It's 32. How did we look this up? We visually searched for Boston in the column for city name (which we located in the 4th row), and then looked up the temperature 32 immediately to the right in the second column. This kind of *table* arrangement is the visual approach to implementing this *lookup* task. The approach by computer is similar. Using the parallel arrays seen in Figure 9.5b, the computer searches for Boston in array CityName, giving a search index of 4; then it uses this search index to directly access the fourth element in the *parallel* array F, giving 32.

The design and coding for the lookup problem is very similar to what we have already studied. Figure D.8 shows a sample run of program Lookup, which is listed in Figure D.9. Note the following.

1. This program declares parallel arrays CityName and F, as explained earlier in Example 9.7. It also calls utilities PrepFile (Figure 6.6) and GetTwoArrays (as covered in Example 9.8).

2. The then clause in the main body shows how to directly access the parallel temperature element F[IndexFound] whenever the search city name is found at index IndexFound.

3. Our earlier sequential search function SearchIndex is used to search for the *string* elements in array CityName. Earlier we called this function to search for integer elements. The function itself is perfectly general in

---

FIGURE D.8   I/O for Program Lookup

```
LOOKUP DEMONSTRATION:  Lookup Temperature Based on City

Enter data file (like A:\GRADES\HC101.DAT)... citytemp.dat


Enter city (End with blank) ===> Boston

   Boston temperature is 32


Enter city (End with blank) ===> Windy city

***Windy city NOT found... Try again.


Enter city (End with blank) ===> Chicago

   Chicago temperature is 15


Enter city (End with blank) ===>

   End of run...
```

FIGURE D.9   Listing for Program Lookup

```
program Lookup;

  {* * * * * * * * * * * * * * * * * * * * * * * * * * * * * * * * *
   *                                                               *
   *         Table lookup for city/temperature arrays             *
   *           ... search array need not be ordered               *
   *                                                               *
   *         Inputs city and temperature arrays, search city      *
   *         Looks up temperature based on city                   *
   *         Outputs search city and its temperature (if found)   *
   *           or message (if not found)                          *
   *                                                               *
   *         Modular structure                                    *
   *           |___ GetTwoArrays     (Old utility procedure)      *
   *           |    |___ IndexCk (Old utility procedure)          *
   *           |___ SearchIndex      (Old utility function)       *
   *                                                               *
   *         Data structure of text file                          *
   *         ----------------------------------------------------- *
   *         First  city name                                     *
   *         First  city temperature                             *
   *         Second city name                                    *
   *         Second city temperature                             *
   *         ...                                                   *
   *         ----------------------------------------------------- *
   *         Sample data file:  CITYTEMP.DAT                      *
   *                                                               *
   * * * * * * * * * * * * * * * * * * * * * * * * * * * * * * * * *}

  {============================= Declarations =============================}

uses crt, OurUnit;

const
  Blank    = ' '; {Sentinel for city name}
  Title    = 'LOOKUP DEMONSTRATION:  Lookup Temperature Based on City';

  LowerIndexLimit  = 1;  UpperIndexLimit = 500;
  LowerIndexLimitX = 0;
  SizeStr = 20;

type
  IndexType   = LowerIndexLimit  .. UpperIndexLimit;
  IndexTypeX  = LowerIndexLimitX .. UpperIndexLimit;
  ArrayOfInt  = array [IndexType] of integer;
  ArrayOfStr  = array [IndexType] of string [SizeStr];

  ElementType1 = string [SizeStr];       {City name element type}
  ElementType2 = integer;                {Temperature element type}
  ArrayType1  = ArrayOfStr;              {City name array type}
  ArrayType2  = ArrayOfInt;              {Temperature array type}

  {ArrayType1, ArrayType2, and IndexType needed for generic input by
    procedure GetTwoArrays}

  ElementType = ElementType1;            {These types set to those}
  ArrayType   = ArrayType1;              {  for city name array}

  {ArrayType, ElementType, IndexType, and IndexTypeX needed for
     generic search in procedure SearchIndex}
```

continued

FIGURE D.9 (*continued*)

```
var
  CityName        : ArrayType1;       {City name array; parallel to F array}
  F               : ArrayType2;       {Fahrenheit temperature array}
  IndexFound      : IndexTypeX;       {Index found by search function}
  SearchCity      : ElementType1;     {Desired city}
  TextFile        : text;             {Text file variable for data file}
  UpperIndex      : IndexType;        {Index of last filled element}

        Function SearchIndex and procedures GetTwoArrays and IndexCk
        are not shown;  SearchIndex is in Figure D.5, GetTwoArrays is
        in Figure 9.7, and IndexCk is in Figure 9.2.

  {============================= Main Body =============================}

begin  {Lookup}

  clrscr;
  writeln (Title);  writeln;

  PrepFile (TextFile);                            {In OurUnit}

  GetTwoArrays (TextFile, LowerIndexLimit, UpperIndexLimit, UpperIndex,
             CityName, F);

  writeln;  writeln;
  write ('Enter city (End with blank) ===> ');  readln (SearchCity);

  while SearchCity <> Blank do
    begin
      IndexFound := SearchIndex (SearchCity, LowerIndexLimit,
                          UpperIndex, CityName);
                                               — Search conducted in array CityName

      if IndexFound >= LowerIndexLimit then
        begin  {City found}
          writeln;
          writeln ('  ', SearchCity, ' temperature is ', F[IndexFound]);
        end    {City found}                       — Direct access to parallel array element
      else                                          in F when SearchCity is found
        begin  {City not found}
          writeln;
          writeln (chr(7),'  ***', SearchCity,' NOT found... Try again.');
        end;   {City not found}

      writeln;  writeln;
      write ('Enter city (End with blank) ===> ');  readln (SearchCity);
    end;  {while}

  writeln;
  writeln ('  End of run...');

end.    {Lookup}
```

its treatment of array and element types; it's the calling module that determines the typing.

Rumor has it that Ms. MeteoRITE, of Example 5.6 fame, and her constant consultant, one Professor Harvey CORE, got wind of our solution to this temperature-lookup problem. They have a job for us (in Exercise 15).

For other variations on the table-lookup problem, see Exercises 13 and 16.

SELF-REVIEW EXERCISES

5a–c 7 11 12a

D.3 PROGRAMMING TIPS

• • • • • • • • • • • • • • •

Consider the following tips to improve the design and style of your programs and to avoid some common errors.

DESIGN AND STYLE

1. Generic Typing. In designing utilities, try to generalize as much as possible. When working with arrays, use generic types such as IndexType, ArrayType, and ElementType. To increment and decrement indexes, call functions **succ** and **pred**.

2. Optimization Note: Excessive Computer Time. A poorly designed algorithm is a major factor in contributing to excessive computer time. This factor is so important in certain applications that professionals in applied mathematics, statistics, and computer science have devoted extensive research efforts to improving the time efficiency of many algorithms. More often than not, this involves the development of entirely new algorithms. This is particularly true in the development of sorting and searching algorithms. For greater computer-time awareness, check out Exercises 4 and 8.

COMMON ERRORS

Many of the same common errors that apply to arrays also apply here, as described in Section 9.4. In designing utility procedures and functions, pay careful attention to *preconditions;* otherwise, we're open to logic and execution errors. You might want to review the preconditions documented in Sort, SearchIndex, and SearchBinIndex. Also, check out Exercises 1c and 5c.

REVIEW EXERCISES

> **EASIER**   For the busy...
> **1a–b 5a–b 7 11**
>
> **NORMAL**   For the thinkers...
> **1c–d 2 3 5c–d 6 9 12 13**
>
> **TOUGHER**   For the hard CORE...
> **4 8 10 14 15**

Ⓛ **1. Sorting things out.** In our sorting example...
   a. Run CkSort to sort files SORT.DAT and TEMPS.DAT.
   b. Describe what happens during the execution of Sort if the input array were already sorted.
   c. What happens if the preconditions on the indexes in Sort are violated? Describe how we might trap these errors.
   d. Complete Table D.2.

Ⓛ ***2. Sorting different array types.** Try the following using program CkSort.
   a. Run the program to duplicate our run in Figure D.1.
   b. **Character indexes.** Redeclare the index subrange as the character sub-range 'a' .. 'z'. Sort file SORT.DAT.
   c. **Real elements.** Sort the data in SORT.DAT as an array of type ArrayOfReal.
   d. **Character elements.** Create a data file named MYNAME.DAT that contains the individual characters in your last name. Sort the data in this file as an array of type ArrayOfChar.
   e. **String elements.** Our examples library has a data file named CITIES.DAT, containing the city names in Figure 9.5. Sort the data in this file as an array of type ArrayOfStr.

Ⓛ ***3. Sorting procedure variations.** Appropriately edit Sort and CkSort to develop and test the following sorting procedures.
   a. Procedure **SortD** implements a descending sort. Use file SORT.DAT in your test run.
   b. Procedure **SortS** does not alter the original array; instead it sends a separate array that's a sorted version of the original array. Use file SORT.DAT in your test run. Output both the original and sorted arrays.

Ⓛ ***4. Sorting, it's a matter of time.** Let's get an idea of how long it takes to sort large arrays using the insertion sort. Revise CkSort as follows. Declare the constant UpperIndexLimit as 5000. Don't input an integer array. Instead, create an integer array that runs from LowerIndexLimit to UpperIndex, where UpperIndex is input interactively and elements are assigned using the predefined function **random** (see Module C). Use 100 for the upper bound in the random number function's argument (this gives elements that range from 0 to 99). Don't ouput the original array. Use the predefined function **gettime** (see program Combo2) to get the time just before and just after the sort procedure is called. Display the times at these two points in the execution. Pause the screen that shows the time displays. When through noting the times, have the program clear the screen and display the sorted array (just to make a believer out of you). Try three test runs: 500, 1000, and 5000 filled elements. How long did it take to sort these arrays on your system? Try the sorts with and without range checking. Does range checking affect sort times? How long did it take others who might have used a different computer from yours? Would you say that sort time increases linearly with the number of elements sorted?

(L) **5.** **Sequential search.** In our sequential search example...

    a. Run CkFind1 to process file SORT.DAT. Find element 40. Find element 60.

    b. Suppose we were to type the function in Figure D.5 as type IndexType. What would happen whenever it can't find a search element? Try it.

    c. What happens if the preconditions on the indexes in SearchIndex are violated? Describe how you might trap these errors.

    *d. Develop desk-check scripts for the two sample runs in Figure D.6.

(L) ***6.** **Sequential, search, generalized.** In our sequential search example...

    a. What changes are needed in CkFind1 and SearchIndex for processing character elements? String elements? Real elements? Can you think of a potential problem in searching for *real* elements?

    b. Use CkFind1 to input the city name array seen in Figure 9.5 (file CITIES.DAT). Search for Toronto and NewYork.

    c. Use CkFind1 (suitably modified) to input the values in TEMPS.DAT into an array with real elements, and search for 32.0 and 70.0.

(L) **7.** **Binary search.** In our binary search example...

    a. Run CkFind2 to process file SORT.DAT. Find elements 40 and 60.

    b. What happens if the precondition for a sorted array is violated? Try it by deleting the call to Sort.

(L) ***8.** **Search-time comparisons.** Revise CkFind1 by using ideas from Exercise 4 to compare search times for the sequential and binary search algorithms. Generate 1000 random searches for elements in the range 0..999.

(L) ***9.** **Binary search, generalized index type.** Rework CkFind2 and SearchBinIndex to handle other ordinal indexes, not just integer subrange indexes. Redefine IndexType to the character subrange 'a'..'z'. Rework Exercise 7a. *Hint:* Give the **ord** function a ring.

(L) *10.   **Binary search, recursive version.** If you studied Module B, code and debug the recursive binary search function **RSearchBinIndex** by appropriately revising the algorithm in Figure D.7. *Hints:* Include LeftIndex and RightIndex as parameters; the loop exit conditions define two terminating cases in an else-if structure. Rework Exercise 7a.

(L) 11.   **Table lookup: Temperature.** Run Lookup to process file CITYTEMP.DAT. Look up the temperatures in Miami and Las Vegas.

(L) 12.   **Table lookup: Temperature.** In our Lookup example...
a. Would GetTwoArrays input values from a data file having a structure where city name and temperature appear on the same line (assuming 20 positions are allocated for city name)? If so, exactly what gets stored in City-Name[4]? Exactly what gets stored in SearchElement when we input Boston as the search city? Are these two identical? If not, do we have a problem in the test within SearchIndex when it tries to find the search element? Explain.
*b. Modify Lookup to display the two arrays. *Hint:* We have a utility for this!
*c. Consider the following parallel data structure.

Color	Quantity
Gray	1000
Silver	500
Black	5000

Adapt Lookup to look up quantity based on color. Place these data in a data file and try some test runs.

(L) *13.   **Table lookup: City name.** Revise the code in Lookup to look up city name based on temperature. Input 32, 15, and 0 in your test runs.

(L) *14.   **Revisit: Average scores.** Reread Example 4.7 and Exercise 23 in Chapter 4. Use arrays for names and scores. Display the output sorted by average score. Allow up to 200 students and 10 scores.

(L) *15.   **Menu of lookups and sorts.** Develop a program for the city/temperature problem that offers the following menu.

```
1   Look up temperature based on city
2   Look up city based on temperature
3   Display cities and temperatures sorted by city
4   Display cities and temperatures sorted by temperature
Q   Quit
```

Design a good user interface. This one is for Ms. MeteoRITE, who got spoiled by the runs in Figure 5.6. *Hint:* You might want to use utility program *MenuTemp*.

EASIER	For the busy...
NORMAL	For the thinkers...
	16 17 18
TOUGHER	For the hard CORE...
	19 20

16. **Revisit table lookup: Electra Appliances.** A common variation on the table-lookup problem searches intervals in a table, as seen in Table 6.2. In this version, the algorithm uses the order-size intervals (classes) to look up the appropriate price. The elements in the search array are the interval boundaries 100, 500, and 1000. The search is now based on the search element being *less than* (instead of equal to) the ordered elements in the search array (assume that the boundaries are always in ascending order). Revise the code in our Lookup program to handle this kind of interval table lookup, and rework Exercise 31 in Chapter 6 accordingly. You might want to redesign Lookup as a procedure that calls PrepFile, GetTwoArrays, and a modified SearchIndex. Use a text file for the lookup table with the following data, assuming orders never exceed 9999.

100	300
500	295
1000	285
9999	275

17. **Revisit: Statistical function suite.** Include Function Median in Exercise 35 of Chapter 9 to return the median element in the array, and its position. The *median* is defined as the middle element in an ordered list. The middle element is in the middle position given by

(Lower index + upper index)/2

If the middle position is fractional (true whenever we have an even number of elements), the median is the average of the two elements on each side of the middle position.

18. **Revisit: Dating service.** Rework Exercise 32 in Chapter 8 to display the output report in decreasing order of desirability. Start a business and make a million with this program...

19. **Sorting: Bubble sort.** Another simple, but rather slow, sorting procedure is the *bubble sort,* or *exchange sort.* The following describes the first two passes in an ascending sort.

```
Unsorted:   30  50  40  10  20
Pass 1:     Swap 30 and 50?  No:   30  50  40  10  20
            Swap 50 and 40?  Yes:  30  40  50  10  20
            Swap 50 and 10?  Yes:  30  40  10  50  20
            Swap 50 and 20?  Yes:  30  40  10  20  50

Pass 2:     Swap 30 and 40?  No:   30  40  10  20  50
            Swap 40 and 10?  Yes:  30  10  40  20  50
            Swap 40 and 20?  Yes:  30  10  20  40  50
            Swap 40 and 50?  No:   30  10  20  40  50
```

Get the idea? The procedure continues until an entire pass has no swaps. How did the term *bubble sort* come about? Low values rise at each pass, much like "bubbles" in a carbonated drink. No kidding...Note how the minimum 10 "rises in the glass."

a. Develop an ascending bubble sort procedure. Use the preceding array as test data, and program CkSort as your test program. *Hint:* See Exercise 10 in Chapter 9 for swaps or exchanges.

b. Use ideas from Exercise 4 to compare the performance of the bubble sort versus the insertion sort. Any conclusions?

20. **Sorting: Quick sort.** The *quick sort* algorithm is a fast sorting technique that's usually programmed as a *recursive* procedure (Module B). Consider the following sample design, where we assume the QuickSort procedure receives an array, its lower index, and its upper index; it returns the array sorted in ascending order.

Procedure QuickSort

```
If Lower index < Upper index then
    Call Split to split array into two subarrays
    Recursively call QuickSort to sort left subarray
    Recursively call QuickSort to sort right subarray
```

Procedure **Split** selects a *pivot element* as the first element in the array, and then splits the array into the following two subarrays: a subarray to the left of a repositioned pivot element with elements that are smaller than the pivot element; a right subarray whose elements are all greater than the pivot element. The following steps illustrate this procedure.

Original array is 40 30 50 10 20; Lower index is 1; Upper index is 5.

1. Select 40 as pivot element

Repeat

2. Find *left index* as position of first element from left whose value exceeds the pivot element. Left index set to 3 at 1st iteration, because 3rd element 50 exceeds 40.

3. Find *right index* as position of first element from right whose value is less than pivot element. Right index set to 5 at 1st iteration, because 5th element 20 is less than 40.

4. If *left index* < *right index* then
    Exchange elements at positions left index and right index. Exchange 50 and 20, giving revised array 40 30 20 10 50 at 1st iteration.

until left index >= right index

Revised array at last iteration is 40 30 20 10 50. Left index is 5; Right index is 4.

5. Exchange pivot element with element at right index. Exchange 40 and 10, giving split array 10 30 20 40 50.

Procedure Split receives the array and its lower and upper indexes and sends the split array along with the position of the pivot element. In our example, the split array is 10 30 20 40 50 and the pivot position is 4. We now know that the left subarray runs from lower index (1) to one position less than the pivot position (3); the right subarray runs from just above the pivot position (5) to upper index (5). The two recursive calls to QuickSort take care of sorting the left and subarrays independently. In our example, the left subarray 10 30 20 gets recursively sorted into 10 20 30; the right subarray 50 does not need sorting (the terminating condition Lower index >= upper index is immediately achieved). The entire array is now sorted, because the pivot element is already positioned in its proper place.

a. Develop procedures Split and QuickSort. Revise driver CkSort to debug these procedures. Use files SORT.DAT and TEMPS2.DAT (in Exercise 15d of Chapter 9) in your test runs. *Hint:* See Exercise 10 in Chapter 9 for exchanges.

b. Use ideas from Exercise 4 to compare the performance of the quick sort versus the insertion sort. Any conclusions?

MORE CHARACTER AND STRING PROCESSING

‡Optional material. Skip without loss of continuity, study at this point, or wait until later.

In earlier chapters, we liberally used character and string constants, variables, and expressions to store, test, search, and display nonnumeric data like names, codes, descriptions, menu selections, and replies. This chapter starts with a review and consolidation of the earlier material on character and string processing. Then it presents additional techniques, functions, and procedures in Turbo Pascal that facilitate the implementation of various tasks. These include manipulating date formats, editing text, compiling programs, inserting names and addresses in personalized and "junk" mail, transmitting secret messages, generating word counts, and analyzing writing style.

10.1 REVIEW

• • • • • • • • • • • • •

Let's start with a review of character and string processing, based on material we have covered thus far. By *character processing* we mean the manipulation of single-character data elements. This includes the declaration of character types, constants, and variables (Sections 2.2 and 2.3); the formation and evaluation of character expressions (Section 2.6); and the operations we can perform on character data, like I/O (Section 2.5), assignment (Section 2.6), and relational operations (Section 5.1). We can also use *subranges* (Section 7.1), *sets* (Sections 7.4 and 7.5), and *arrays* (Section 9.2) to process characters. *String processing* is similar to character processing, except that the basic data element is a string of characters. String processing also includes the common use of *string arrays* (Section 9.2).

CHARACTER PROCESSING

The **character** or **char type** defines a set of 256 ordered single-character values in the extended ASCII character set, as seen in Appendix I. The character type is both a *simple type* (ordered single values) and an *ordinal type* (values are listable).

A **character constant** is a character enclosed in *single quotation marks* or *apostrophes,* as in '$', 'x', or '7'. Note that 'x' is a character constant, but x is its *value*. A **declared character constant** is an identifier that's associated with a character constant. For example, the declaration

```
const
   Blank = ' ';
```

declares Blank as the character constant ' '. Elsewhere in the program we can use Blank in place of ' ' to improve readability.

A **character variable** stores a character value. It's declared in the var section by using a user-defined identifier as its name and the reserved word **char** as its data-type identifier. For example, the declaration

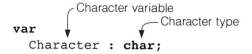

```
var
    Character : char;
```

declares Character as a character variable. This variable can store any of the 256 characters in Appendix I.

A common alternative to the character type is a **subrange character type,** a declared *subrange type* with a character *host type.* A variable so typed is a **subrange character variable.** For example, the following declares Cap as a subrange character variable whose values are restricted to the capital letters in the alphabet, as declared in the subrange character type CapLetters.

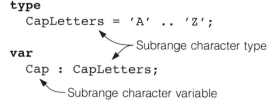

```
type
    CapLetters = 'A' .. 'Z';

var
    Cap : CapLetters;
```

An advantage of using a subrange character variable over a character variable is the automatic detection of out-of-range values when the range-checking compiler directive is active.

We can also process character data by working with *structured types*. In particular, we have worked with the *set type* (Section 7.4) and the *array type* (Chapter 9). We review *character sets* in the next section. *Character arrays* are uncommon in Turbo Pascal because the *string variable* is a character array in disguise.[1]

A **character expression** is a declared or undeclared character constant, character variable, or function call that returns a character value. The expressions ' ', Blank, Character, and **chr**(32) are all examples of character expressions. The last example is a function call that returns the blank character, which is coded ASCII 32.

Table 10.1 summarizes Turbo Pascal's predefined functions that either return or operate on character values. Note that we have used all of these functions earlier in the book, and will do so again in this chapter.

---

[1]Character arrays are needed in Standard Pascal, which does not include the string data type. They are also useful if elements in the array are subrange character types.

Table 10.1 Calls to Predefined Functions that Return or Operate on Character Values

Function Call	Description	Sample Call	Returned Value	Remark
chr(Argument)	Returns character corresponding to ASCII value of argument. (See Appendix I.)	chr(98)	b	b is coded ASCII 98
		chr(66)	B	B is coded ASCII 66
		chr(7)	☼	Rings bell
		chr(32)	☐	↖ There's a blank here
ord(Argument)	Returns the ASCII value (decimal code) that corresponds to its character argument. It's the dual or "mirror image" of **chr**.*	ord('b')	98	See **chr**(98) above
		ord(' ')	32	See **chr**(32) above
pred(Argument)	Returns the predecessor of the argument.*	pred('B')	A	Confirm this in Appendix I
		pred('A')	@	Confirm this in Appendix I
succ(Argument)	Returns the successor of the argument.*	succ('A')	B	Confirm this in Appendix I
		succ(Blank)	!	Assuming Blank is ' '
upcase(Argument)	Returns uppercase version of any character argument in range a..z.	upcase(Reply)	Y	Assuming Reply stores y
	Returns argument if argument is outside this range.	upcase('9')	9	No effect

*Functions **ord**, **pred**, and **succ** are *ordinal functions*; **ord** returns the ordinality of any ordinal argument; **pred** and **succ** return integer, Boolean, character, enumerated, or subrange values, depending on the type of argument. In our present context, the argument is a character expression.

Finally, let's summarize operations on character data using the following categories

- *Storage* using input and assignment statements
- *Retrieval* using output and assignment statements
- *Control condition* in while, repeat, if, and case statements

We can use the *read* and *readln statements* in the usual way to store character and subrange character data from either the keyboard or a data file. For example, if we type D during the execution of

```
readln (Cap);
```

the character value D is stored in the subrange character variable Cap. Similarly, the execution of

```
readln (TextFile, Cap);
```

reads one character from the assigned data file and places it in Cap. Don't forget, however, that the input value and variable must be *type compatible*. If we were to input d in the preceding example, we would get a *range-check error*. This is because the legitimate range of values for Cap is the subrange of uppercase letters.

We can also store character or subrange character data using the **character assignment statement:**

Character variable := Character expression;

Remember that the expression must be *assignment compatible* with the variable. For character data, this means that the expression and the variable just need to be *type compatible*. Examples include the following.

```
Symbol     := chr(33);           {Stores ! in Symbol}
Character  := 'd';               {Stores d in Character}
Cap        := upcase(Character); {Stores D in Cap}
```

In our last example, Cap is type subrange character and Character is type character. The given assignment is compatible because (1) one type is a subrange of the other and (2) the expression evaluates to a value that's permissible in Cap. If we were to use the following assignment, however,

```
Cap := upcase(Symbol);  ☹
```

then the assignment statement would compile, but we would get a range-check error at run time when the computer attempts to store ! in Cap.

We output character and subrange character values by calling the predefined write and writeln procedures. For example, the call

```
writeln (Cap)
```

would display a D at the current cursor position, and then move the cursor to the beginning of the next line. The call

```
write (Cap :10)
```

would display D 10 positions to the right of the current cursor position, and then hold the cursor at the next position on the same line.

We also use character expressions to control execution behavior within control structures. For instance, we often compare character expressions in *relational expressions* (such as Reply = 'y' to control execution within the *while-do structure,* the *repeat-until structure,* and the *if-then-else structure.* We commonly use a character expression as the selector in a *case statement,* especially in routing menu selections.

CHARACTER SETS

Sets are useful in character processing. If the *base type* in a set is type character or type subrange character, we have a set of characters, a **character set.** The following sample declarations show UpperVowelsSet as the *declared character set constant* ['A','E','I','O','U'] and NullSet as the *null* or *empty set.* UpperLettersType is the *character set type* having permissible values given by the capital letters (the subrange char type CapLetters), and *character set variables* UpperLetters and Codes have type UpperLettersType.

```
const
   UpperVowelsSet = ['A', 'E', 'I', 'O', 'U'];
   NullSet        = [];

type
   CapLetters = 'A' .. 'Z';
   UpperLettersType = set of CapLetters;

var
   UpperLetters, Codes : UpperLettersType;
```

We can store a *character set value* by using either a user-defined input procedure or an assignment statement, as in

```
Codes := ['S', 'M', 'L', 'X'];
```

Other common operations on character sets include set unions using the *union operator* ± to build sets and the *relational operator* **in** to test for set membership.

STRING PROCESSING

The **string type** defines a *string value* or *string* as a sequence of characters taken from the extended ASCII character set. We anonymously declare the string type by using the reserved word **string** followed by an optional size attribute enclosed in brackets:

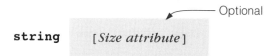

string   [*Size attribute*]   ———— Optional

A string value has a *constant* **size attribute** given by an integer in the range 1 to 255, representing the maximum number of characters allowable for that declared string type. For example, the declaration **string** [20] shows a size attribute of 20, meaning that string values up to 20 characters are permissible for that string type. If the size attribute is not declared, a *default size attribute* of *255* is used. As usual, we can declare an explicit string type in the type section, as in

type   ———— String type
    String20 = **string** [20];

The string type also includes a **length attribute** or **dynamic length**. This is the actual character count in the string value at run time. If the string value has 13 characters at run time, for example, its dynamic length is 13. The dynamic length will not exceed the size attribute. If a string type is declared with a size attribute of 20, its string values can include dynamic lengths from 0 up to 20.

A **string variable** stores a string value having a declared string type. For instance, the declarations

```
const
   SizeStr = 20;

type
   String20 = string [SizeStr];

var
   Phrase : String20;
```

state that Phrase is a string variable typed *String20,* with a size attribute of *20.* Let's say that at run time we store the string value I love Pascal in Phrase. We might show this as the memory cell in Figure 10.1.

Note the following.

1. We show character positions by the indexes 0–20.

2. The last index is *20,* the declared *size attribute.*

3. The string value I love Pascal is exactly *13* characters. This means that its dynamic length is 13. The last 7 character positions in Phrase are unused.

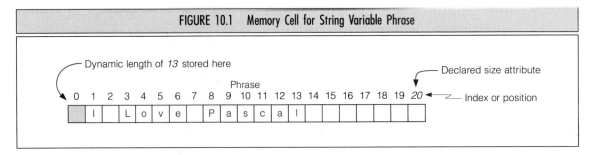

FIGURE 10.1   Memory Cell for String Variable Phrase

4. Turbo Pascal stores a character at index 0 whose ordinality is the dynamic length. Thus, **ord**(*Character in position zero*) is *13* for this example. Looking at Appendix I, the character whose ordinality is 13 (ASCII 13) is the control character *carriage return,* which is nonprintable and the reason we don't show it in position 0. We can determine the dynamic length with either of the following calls: **ord**(Phrase[0]) or **length**(Phrase).

5. In the manner of an array, the *indexed form of a string variable* given by *StringVariable[Index]* allows the access of individual characters in the stored string value. For example, Phrase[1] is I and Phrase[5] is v.

When using string variables as *parameters,* remember that the type of an *actual* parameter must be (1) identical to the type of its corresponding *variable* parameter but (2) only assignment compatible with its corresponding *value* parameter. We can relax the first condition by disabling the *Var-string checking* compiler directive. In this case, any string type variable is allowed as an actual parameter, regardless of the declared size attribute for the corresponding formal parameter. This is useful when we require multiple calls to a string function or procedure and actual parameters have varying size attributes. When using "relaxed" Var-string checking, we need to be careful about *truncation errors* that cut off characters from a string value. Try Exercise 5 to review this feature.

A **character string** is a sequence of zero or more characters enclosed within apostrophes. For example, 'I love Pascal' is a character string with a *length attribute* of 13 characters (the apostrophes don't count in the length). The predefined function call **length**('I love Pascal') would return *13*.

We represent an apostrophe within a character string with two successive apostrophes. Thus, we can include the contraction don't in our sample character string as follows: 'I don''t love Pascal'. The *value* of this string is I don't love Pascal, and its length attribute is 18.

A **string constant** is the same as a character string. A **declared string constant** is a string constant having a declared identifier. For example, the code

```
        const
           NullString = '';
```
declares NullString as the string constant ' '.

The **null string** is a character string whose length attribute is *0*. It's represented by two successive apostrophes, as in ' '. The null string is useful for initializing strings that subsequently get built up, as we will see later in this chapter.

A character string whose *length is 1* is the same as a *character constant* or a *string constant* with a length attribute of 1. Thus, a character string of length 1 is *type compatible* with type char or type string. A character string whose length is greater than 1 is type compatible with type string, but not with type char.

The null string, by the way, is type compatible with type string, but not with type char. For example, the assignment

┌─ String variable   ┌─ String constant

```
Phrase := NullString;
```
☺

is legitimate, but not the assignment

┌─ Character variable ┌─ String constant

```
Character := NullString;
```
◄── Would give *type* ☹
mismatch error

A **string expression** evaluates to a string value; it's components include one or more constants, variables, and function calls. These can be joined by the **concatenation operator** + , as in

```
chr(7) + 'Mr. ' + LastName + ',' + FirstName[1] + '.'
                              + MiddleName[1] + '.'
```

Note that type char and type string are *type compatible* in a string expression, as seen in the last example, where the chr function is included in the expression. If LastName stores CORE, FirstName stores Harvey, and MiddleName stores Abacus, then the expression evaluates to the string value

┌─ Stores the unprintable bell character

▼Mr. CORE, H.A.

If we were to assign the value of this expression to the string variable Name, execution of the output statement

```
writeln (Name);
```

would ring the bell and display Mr. CORE, H.A..

As with any other data type, the string data type includes a collection of defined operations on that data type. Again, we can summarize these in terms of *storage* (input and assignment), *retrieval* (output and assignment), and *control conditions.*

We can issue calls to the predefined procedures **read** and **readln** to input string values. When storing a string value in a string variable by calling the *read procedure,* the computer reads all characters up to an *end-of-line marker* (issued by the Enter key), or until the string variable is filled according to its size attribute, or until an *eof* function returns true. The resulting string value is then assigned to the string variable. A call to the *readln procedure* is implemented as a call to the read procedure followed by a skip to the next input line.

We can also store a string or character value in a string variable by using an *assignment statement*. As usual, the expression must be *assignment compatible* with the variable. String assignments are compatible if (1) the value of the expression is either type string or char and (2) the variable is type string. It's also permissible to assign a character value to the indexed form of a string variable, as in

```
                                     ┌── Stores!
                                     ▼
      Phrase[14]  :=  Symbol;◄──z── Dynamic length (13) of  ☹
                                     Phrase unchanged
```

This would revise the value in Phrase to I love Pascal!. Note, however, that character position 14 is beyond the dynamic length of 13 for this string variable (see Figure 10.1). Unfortunately, Turbo Pascal would not update the dynamic length in position 0 with this kind of assignment. The following assignment accomplishes the same end, and also updates the dynamic length of the string.

```
                                        Character ! added (concatenated)  ☺
   Phrase  :=  Phrase + Symbol;◄──z── to string in Phrase; dynamic
                                        length increased by 1 to 14
```

We can also make an assignment like

```
      Character  :=  Phrase[14];
```

which would place ! in the character variable Character.

When storing string values, we need to be aware of the *dynamic length* versus the *size attribute;* otherwise we might inadvertently make a *truncation error*. For example, we had no problem in our earlier assignment of the string value I love Pascal (dynamic length *13*) to the string variable Phrase (size attribute *20*). If we had declared Phrase with a size attribute of *10*, however, then Phrase could only store a maximum of 10 characters. Thus, an attempt to store I love Pascal in Phrase would truncate the stored value to the 10 characters I love Pas.

We can display string values with calls to procedures **write** and **writeln.** We can also use string expressions in *relational expressions* to express conditions in while-do, repeat-until, if-then-else, if-then, and else-if structures. For instance, the if-then structure

```
      ┌Relational expression comparing value in string variable to character value
      ▼
   if Phrase < 'M' then
      writeln (Phrase);
```

would write the value I love Pascal in Phrase because the relational expression evaluates as *true* (I is less than M).

Note that the operands on each side of a relational operator must be *type compatible*. A string operand is type compatible with either another string operand or with a character operand.

Also note that the relational operators, =, < >, <, >, < =, and > = compare string values based on the ordering of characters in the ASCII coding scheme. The comparison is carried out corresponding character by corresponding character, from left to right. In comparing a string value to a character value, the character value is treated as a string value with a length attribute of 1, as in the preceding example.

†STRING ARRAYS

A **string array** is an array whose elements are type string. To illustrate, consider the following declarations and the storage schematic in Figure 10.2 for array Day, an array that stores the names of days in a week.

```
const
    SizeStr = 9;

type
    IndexType    = 1 .. 7;
    ElementType  = string [SizeStr];
    ArrayDayType = array [IndexType] of ElementType;

var
    Day : ArrayDayType;
```

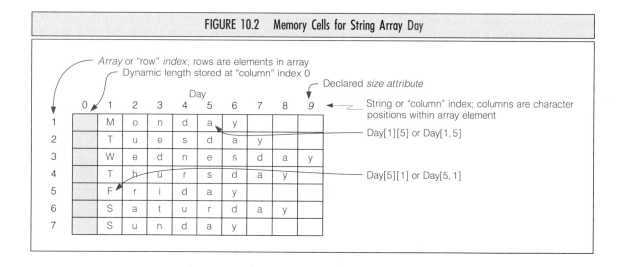

FIGURE 10.2   Memory Cells for String Array Day

---

†Optional material. Skip without loss of continuity except where indicated, study at this point, or wait until later.

Note the following.

1. Day is a string array with 7 elements indexed 1..7. Thus, the *indexed variable* Day[5] references the 5th day of the week, the string value Friday. Note that 5 is a value for the *array index*. Array index values run from 1 to 7, as seen along the left edge in Figure 10.2.

2. Each element in the array stores a string value with a size attribute of 9. This means that we can store up to 9 characters in each array element. Also, each character has an associated *string index* that runs from 0 to 9, as seen across the top edge in Figure 10.2.

3. We can view memory storage as separate memory cells for each character in the array, arranged in a row-by-column table format. In this conceptualization, each *array index* value is the "row" index and each *string index* value is the "column" index. Thus, we can reference the character at the intersection of a row and column with

    Day[*Row* or *array index*] [*Column* or *string index*]

For example, Day[5][1] is the character value F in Friday and Day[1][5] is the character value a in Monday. In this context, we view Day as an *array of an array*. Alternatively, we can treat Day as if it were a *two-dimensional* character array. We then apply the usual 2D array reference

    Day[*Row index, Column index*]

Thus, Day[5, 1] references the character F and Day[1, 5] references the character a.

Later in this chapter, we will show how we can manipulate the elements in this array at the character level.

NOTE

1. On indexes. The term *index* refers to either an array index or a string index, depending on the context. For an array variable, the *array index* identifies an element's location; for a string variable, the *string index* is the position of a character within the string. These two uses for index are conceptually the same. If we need to make a distinction between these two standard uses for this term, we use the proper qualifier, as in *array* index or *string* index. In our programs, we will use the identifier Index to mean array index and the identifier Position to mean string index.

SELF-REVIEW EXERCISES

1 2 3 4 5

10.2 Predefined String Functions and Procedures

• • • • • • • • • • • • • •

Turbo Pascal includes a collection of predefined functions and procedures that facilitate the manipulation of strings.

String Functions

Calls to Turbo Pascal's four predefined string functions are described in Table 10.2. Functions *copy* and *pos* work with subgroupings of characters within strings called **substrings**. For example, COR is a substring of three characters within the string CORE. Note that the characters in a substring appear next to each other in the string. Thus, OR is a two-character substring within CORE, but not OE. String CORE has 10 possible substrings: C, O, R, E, CO, OR, RE, COR, ORE, CORE.

Example 10.1   Loop Control with Length Function

For-do loops with termination based on the length function are handy for processing individual characters in a string. For example, if FirstName stores Harvey, the following loop displays each character on its own line.

Code: *Output:*

```
for Position := 1 to length(FirstName) do
    writeln (FirstName[Position]);
```

```
H
a
r
v
e
y
```

Example 10.2   Concatenated Date Substrings Using Functions Concat and Copy

The following code fragment extracts month, day, and year substrings within the string in Date1 having the form

2-digit month / 2-digit day / 2-digit year

Table 10.2   Calls to Predefined String Functions

Function Call*	Description†	Sample Call‡	Returned Value
concat(StringExpression list)	Returns concatenated strings in list. If concatenated length exceeds 255 characters, returned string is truncated at 255th character.	concat(SubPhrase, SubPhrase) concat(SubPhrase, ' ', SubPhrase)	lovelove love love
copy(StringExpression, Position, SubLength)	Returns *substring* of length SubLength starting at Position within string in StringExpression. **Null string returned if Position exceeds *dynamic length*. If SubLength goes beyond end of string, just remainder of string is returned.**	copy(Phrase, 3, 4) copy(Phrase, 8, 6) copy(Phrase, 15, 6) copy(Phrase, 8, 10)	love Pascal '' ← Null string Pascal
length(StringExpression)	Returns *dynamic length* of StringExpression.	length(SubPhrase) length(Phrase + SubPhrase)	4 17
pos(SubStringExpression, StringExpression)	Returns starting position of substring within string (if found) or zero (if not found).	pos(SubPhrase, Phrase) pos('hate', Phrase)	3 0

*Index and SubLength are integer expressions.
†Character expressions are also type compatible as arguments.
‡Assume Phrase stores I love Pascal and SubPhrase stores love for each example.

and displays the alternative date form

2-digit day / 2-digit month / 2-digit year

Code:

```
write ('mm/dd/yy:  ');  readln (Date1);

Month := copy(Date1, 1, 2);  {Month is in positions 1 and 2}
Day   := copy(Date1, 4, 2);  {Day is in positions 4 and 5}
Year  := copy(Date1, 7, 2);  {Year is in positions 7 and 8}

Date2 := concat(Day, '/', Month, '/', Year);

write ('dd/mm/yy:  ' + Date2);
```

Input/Output:

```
mm/dd/yy: 03/24/92
dd/mm/yy: 24/03/92
```

EXAMPLE 10.3   VALID CODES: STRING ALTERNATIVE USING FUNCTION POS VERSUS SET ALTERNATIVE

Suppose we have a list of valid codes given by S, M, L, X, Z. These codes are stored in the *string constant* ValidCodes according to the following declaration. (We threw in Beep as a bonus.)

```
const
  Beep      = chr(7);     {Beeps speaker on output}
  ValidCodes = 'SMLXZ';   {String constant}
```

Character variable Code stores a code, and we wish to communicate whether or not this code is valid. The following code segment does the trick.

```
if pos(Code, ValidCodes) <> 0 then
  writeln (Code + ' is valid...')
else
  writeln (Beep + Code + ' is INvalid...');
```

For example, if Code stores the valid code X, then **pos** returns 4 (X is found at the 4th position in ValidCodes) and the message

```
X is valid...
```

is displayed. If Code stores the invalid code B, however, then **pos** returns 0 (B is not found within ValidCodes) and the message

```
   B is INvalid...
```

is displayed.

Alternatively, we can declare the valid set of codes as a *set constant:*

```
const
   Beep      = chr(7);                    {Beeps speaker on output}
   ValidCodes = ['S','M','L','X','Z'];   {Set constant}
```

and replace the first line in the if statement with

```
if Code in ValidCodes then
```

Which approach do you like best? Compared to the second approach, the first alternative requires less storage and simplifies the declaration of the constant, but at the expense of a more complicated condition in the if statement.

---

‡EXAMPLE 10.4 DAY-OF-WEEK ABBREVIATIONS

The extraction of substrings using the **copy** function is a simple way to abbreviate strings, as the following code fragment illustrates for array Day in Figure 10.2.

Code:

```
for Index := 1 to 7 do
   writeln (copy(Day[Index], 1, 3) + ' ' + Day[Index]);
```

Output:

```
Mon   Monday
Tue   Tuesday
Wed   Wednesday
Thu   Thursday
Fri   Friday
Sat   Saturday
Sun   Sunday
```

STRING PROCEDURES

Calls to Turbo Pascal's four predefined string procedures are described in Table 10.3. Study the examples in the table before going on to the more elaborate examples that follow.

---

‡The material on string arrays on pages 485-486 is a prerequisite to this example.

Table 10.3 Calls to Predefined String Procedures

Procedure Call*	Description	Sample Call†	Result
delete (StringExpression, Position, SubLength)	Deletes *substring* of length SubLength starting at Position within string in StringExpression. Nothing is deleted if Position exceeds *length attribute*. If SubLength goes beyond end of string, remainder of string is deleted.	delete (Phrase, 3, 5) delete (Phrase, 7, 7) delete (Phrase, 15, 7) delete (Phrase, 7, 10)	I Pascal in Phrase I love in Phrase I love Pascal in Phrase I love in Phrase
insert (SubStringExpression, StringVar, Position)	Inserts *substring* into StringVar starting at Position. Inserts at end of string if Position exceeds *length attribute*. The resulting string is truncated at 255th character if its length were to exceed 255 characters. SubStringExpression is any string or character expression.	insert ('do ', Phrase, 3) insert (SubPhrase, Phrase, 20)	I do love Pascal in Phrase I love Pascallove in Phrase
str (NumExpression :FieldWidth :DecimalPlaces, StringVar)	Converts numeric value to its string representation. The string stored in StringVar is identical to the way the numeric value would be written by calling the **write** procedure.	str (RealVar :6 :2, StrVar) str (IntVar, StrVar)	■9.50 as string in StrVar if RealVar stores 9.5 as real value 100 as string in StrVar if IntVar stores 100 as integer value
val (StringExpression, NumVar, IntCode)	Converts string value to its numeric representation. The string is in the form of an integer or real constant, without trailing spaces. Its numeric version is placed in NumVar. If the form of the numeric constant is valid, then IntCode sends 0; else IntCode sends the position of the first character in error, and NumVar is set to zero.	val (StrVar, IntVar, Code) val (StrVar, RealVar, Code)	100 as integer value in IntVar and 0 in Code if StrVar stores 100 as string 9.5 as real value in RealVar and 0 in Code if StrVar stores ■9.50 as string

Optional

*Position and SubLength are integer expressions.
†Assume Phrase stores I love Pascal and SubPhrase stores love for each example that uses these.

EXAMPLE 10.5   DATE CONVERSION USING PROCEDURE VAL

In Example 10.2 we entered a date in the form mm/dd/yy and extracted the two digits for month into the substring Month. Let's revise this problem according to the following I/O.

Input/Output:

```
mm/dd/yy:  03/24/92
March 24, 1992
```

Let's further assume that we have declared and assigned array MonthName with 12 string elements indexed over the integer subrange 1..12. Thus, MonthName[1] stores January, MonthName[2] stores February, and so on. The problem now boils down to...

1. Converting the value in Month (string value 03 in our sample I/O) to its numeric representation (integer value 3 in Index) by calling procedure **val** (Table 10.3).
2. Using the resulting integer (3 in Index) as the index in MonthName.
3. Doing a fancy concatenation to get the output in the required form.

We also need to trap invalid conversions (**val** returns nonzero codes) and out-of-range array indexes, as the following code illustrates.

Code:

```
write ('mm/dd/yy:  ');  readln (Date1);  writeln;

Month := copy(Date1, 1, 2);        {Month is in positions 1 and 2}
Day   := copy(Date1, 4, 2);        {Day is in positions 4 and 5}
Year  := copy(Date1, 7, 2);        {Year is in positions 7 and 8}

val(Month, Index, Code);           {Index is array index, with legit
                                    values 1 .. 12}

if Code = 0 then   {conversion OK}

    if Index in [1 .. 12] then
      writeln (MonthName[Index] + ' ' + Day + ', 19' + Year)
    else
      writeln (Beep + 'Month digits mm outside range 1-12')

else  {Conversion NOT OK}
    writeln (Beep + 'Nonnumeric digits for month');
```

EXAMPLE 10.6   REPLACE SUBSTRING UTILITY PROCEDURE
USING DELETE AND INSERT PROCEDURES

Let's develop a utility procedure that replaces one substring with another substring. For example, suppose we have the following storage for string variable TextString.

Let's get Jack and Jill together; the string should read Jack and Jill. Thus, we wish to replace the substring or with the substring and. What we have is a substring replacement task that's commonly implemented by editors and word processors. (We're too sophisticated to brute-force retype this whole thing, right?) The usual approach is to first *delete* the unwanted substring (or) and then *insert* the replacement substring (and) in its proper place. Just after we delete or we have the following revised text string.

TextString
0 1 2 3 4 5 6 7 8 9 10 11 12 13 14 15 ···

| | J | a | c | k | | | J | i | l | l | | | | | | ··· Text string after delete step

Note that or was deleted from positions 6 and 7, and the remaining portion of the string ▮Jill in former positions 8–12 is moved up two positions to positions 6–10. Now we just need to insert the replacement substring and starting in position 6 (the original starting position of our now defunct or). This gives the following correctly revised text string.

TextString
0 1 2 3 4 5 6 7 8 9 10 11 12 13 14 15 ···

| | J | a | c | k | | a | n | d | | J | i | l | l | | | ··· Text string after insert step

Note that and now takes up positions 6–8, and the hapless ▮Jill gets moved around again (this time to positions 9–13).

Turbo Pascal makes it easy for us by providing the **delete** and **insert** procedures first described in Table 10.3. The utility string procedure Replace in Figure 10.3 shows the specifics.

Note that we need to trap the very common error of not finding the substring that's getting deleted. The **pos** function from Table 10.2 searches the string in TextString (Jack or Jill) for the substring in OldSubStr (or). If the substring is found, then StartPos is assigned the starting position of the substring (6 in our example). The else clause in the if-then-else structure then invokes the delete and insert pro-

> **FIGURE 10.3** Listing for Utility Procedure Replace

```
procedure Replace (OldSubStr, NewSubStr : TextType;
                   var TextString : TextType);

  { Utility replaces old substring with new substring in text string
    Receives OldSubStr, NewSubStr, TextString
    Sends TextString }

  { NOTE:  TextType declared in calling module }

const
  Beep = chr(7);

var
  StartPos : integer;    {Starting position of old substring in text}

begin  {Replace}

  StartPos := pos (OldSubStr, TextString);
  if StartPos = 0 then   {Old substring NOT found}
    begin
      writeln;
      writeln (Beep + '  ERROR: ' + OldSubStr + ' not found; try again...');
    end
  else   {Old substring found}
    begin
      delete (TextString, StartPos, length(OldSubStr));
      insert (NewSubStr, TextString, StartPos);
    end;  {if}

end;    {Replace}
{----------------------------------------------------------------------}
```

cedures. If the old substring is not found, then **pos** returns 0, and we trap the error in the then clause.

Finally, note that we use the generic typing TextType for the string type; the calling module would take care of declaring the proper string type for TextType (its size attribute).

We have added Replace to the *Utilities Library.*

SELF-REVIEW EXERCISES

6 7a 8a–b 9a 10 11 12a 14a–b

10.3 SELECTED APPLICATIONS

• • • • • • • • • • • • •

In this section we illustrate applications in two areas of character and string processing: (1) character subset processing for detecting desired subsets of characters within strings, and (2) cryptography, the encoding and decoding of secret messages.

Character Subsets

Here we develop an application that finds a desired character subset within a larger character set.

Requirements

Let's input any Turbo Pascal program line and find the set of Turbo Pascal symbols in that program line. The output is the labeled set of Turbo Pascal symbols that were entered as part of the program line. Let's output each symbol on the same line, with a space between each.

We don't require more than a "plain vanilla" user interface. A screen clear, title, input prompt, and output label will do.

To summarize the requirements in terms of required data...

- Output data are the Turbo Pascal symbol elements in the set of characters taken from the entered Turbo Pascal program line.
- Input data are the string of characters in the Turbo Pascal program line.
- Constant data are the title and set of allowable Turbo Pascal symbols.
- Computational data include the set of characters in the Turbo Pascal program line.

Design

The general design approach is to input the program line into a string variable, decompose the string into a set of characters, and check each ASCII character in the universal set of extended ASCII characters to determine the following: First, is the universal character a member of the set of characters in the program line? If so, then we test for membership in the Turbo Pascal set of symbols. If both tests are affirmative, then we have found a Turbo Pascal symbol in the input program line and can now write it. Let's try the following three design algorithms.

Main module

```
Clear screen
Write title
Call ReadLine: Read program line and form set of characters
Call WriteSymbols: Find and write set of symbols in program line
```

Procedure ReadLine

```
Initialize set of characters in program line to empty set
Read program line
Decompose program line into set of characters
```

Procedure WriteSymbols

```
Write output label
For each ASCII character in universal set do
    If character in set of program line characters and
        character in set of Turbo Pascal symbols then
            Write character
Issue line feed
```

Figure 10.4 shows the user interface and sample I/O. Note that the symbols output is the set of four Turbo Pascal symbols in the program line that served as sample input.

Code

Figure 10.5 shows the listing for our set find program. Note the following.

1. In the program, we declare type SetOfChars with base type **char.** Then we declare the set variable CharLineSet with type SetOfChars. Thus, the allowable elements in CharLineSet are taken from the universal set of the 256 ASCII characters seen in Appendix I. CharLineSet is used to store the set of characters in the Turbo Pascal program line. This set variable is also the parameter in the procedure calls and headings.

2. In procedure ReadLine . . .

   a. We initialize CharLineSet to the null set, since we need to build this set from the characters in the program line.

   b. The program line is input into the string variable ProgLine.

   c. The for-do loop systematically plucks each character from ProgLine and adds it to the set of characters in CharLineSet. Note that a call to **length** is the upper limit on the control variable Position. The control variable itself is used to access individual characters by position in the string. Thus, when Position stores 2, ProgLine [Position] accesses the third character in the string (u in our sample run in Figure 10.4).

FIGURE 10.4   Sample I/O Design and Run for Program SetFind

```
SET FIND APPLICATION

Please enter Pascal program line below...

  NullSet = [];

Symbols:  ; = [ ]
```

FIGURE 10.5   Listing for Program SetFind

```pascal
program SetFind;

  {* * * * * * * * * * * * * * * * * * * * * * * * * * * * * * * * * * *
   *                                                                   *
   *          Set Find Application                                     *
   *                                                                   *
   *             Inputs Pascal program line as string                 *
   *             Finds subset of Turbo Pascal symbols                 *
   *             Outputs subset of Turbo Pascal symbols               *
   *                                                                   *
   *             Modular structure                                     *
   *                 |___ ReadLine                                     *
   *                 |___ WriteSymbols                                 *
   *                                                                   *
   * * * * * * * * * * * * * * * * * * * * * * * * * * * * * * * * * * *}

  {============================ Declarations ===========================}

uses crt;

const
  NullSet = [];
  Title   = 'SET FIND APPLICATION';

type
  SetOfChars = set of char;      {Type SetOfChars includes all ASCII chars.}

var
  CharLineSet : SetOfChars;      {Set variable that stores individual
                                  characters found in program line}

  {======================= Procedure Declarations =====================}

procedure ReadLine (var CharLineSet : SetOfChars);

  { Reads program line into string variable and decomposes individual
      characters into set CharLineSet
    Receives nothing
    Sends CharLineSet }

var
  Position : integer;            {Position of character in program line}
  ProgLine : string;             {Program line as string}

begin  {ReadLine}

  CharLineSet := NullSet;        {Initialize to empty set}

  writeln ('Please enter Pascal program line below...');  writeln;
  write ('  ');  readln (ProgLine);

  {Build set of characters in program line}
    for Position := 1 to length (ProgLine) do
      CharLineSet := CharLineSet + [ ProgLine[Position] ];

end;  {ReadLine}
{----------------------------------------------------------------------}
```

continued

FIGURE 10.5   *(continued)*

```pascal
procedure WriteSymbols (CharLineSet : SetOfChars);

  { Finds and writes set of Turbo Pascal symbols in program line
    Receives CharLineSet
    Sends nothing }
const
  {Set of legitimate symbols in Turbo Pascal}
    TPsymbolsSet = [ '+', '-', '*', '/', '=', '<', '>', '[', ']', '.',
                     ',', '(', ')', ':', ';', '^', '@', '{', '}', '$',
                     '#', '_' ];

var
  Character : char;               {Control variable in for-do loop}

begin   {WriteSymbols}

  writeln;  write ('Symbols:  ');

  {Scan all 256 ASCII characters to find characters in program line set
   and symbols in TP symbols set}

     for Character := chr(0) to chr(255) do
        if (Character in CharLineSet) and (Character in TPsymbolsSet)
          then write (Character, ' ');

     writeln;

end;    {WriteSymbols}

  {============================== Main Body ==============================}

begin   {SetFind}

  clrscr;
  writeln (Title);
  writeln;
  ReadLine (CharLineSet);
  WriteSymbols (CharLineSet);

end.    {SetFind}
```

3. In procedure WriteSymbols...

   a. We use the declared set constant TPsymbolsSet to represent the legitimate symbols in Turbo Pascal.

   b. The for-do loop considers each of the 256 ASCII characters by systematically varying Character from **chr**(0) to **chr**(255).

   c. Within the loop, we write a character only by establishing that the character is a Turbo Pascal symbol in the program line. We ensure this by first confirming that the character is an element in CharLineSet (that is, it's a character in the program line) and then confirming that the character in CharLineSet is also in the set of symbols given by TPsymbolsSet (that is, it's also one of the legitimate Turbo Pascal program line symbols).

Test

The user-interface design in Figure 10.4 also shows one of our test runs. In Exercise 16a we ask you to try other test data. A common error that gives unexpected results is forgetting to initialize any set variable whose set is to be built. See Exercise 16b for the consequences in this application.

Finally, in Exercise 17 we ask you to consider a design and code that replaces the character set approach with a strictly string processing approach.

CRYPTOGRAPHY

Cryptography is the science of transforming secret messages. A message is transformed either by encoding or decoding. *Encoding* is the process of transforming a message into code; *decoding* is the translation of the code into its message form. The encoding and decoding of messages usually includes a *transformation algorithm* for transforming the messages and a *shift key* (a special number) that controls the process.

Requirements

We wish to input an actual message made up strictly of capital letters and blanks (we relax this requirement in the exercises), input a shift key, encode the message into a secret message, and write both the actual and secret messages. The user interface is simple: a screen clear, title, prompted input, and labeled output. The encoding algorithm will use the alphabet shift cipher, as explained next.

Ciphers is one of many categories of secret message encoding. In this approach the transformation algorithm either rearranges or replaces the letters of each word. *Substitution ciphers* encode messages by replacing one letter with another. The *alphabet shift cipher* is one of several substitution ciphers. It works as follows.

Alphabet Shift Cipher

> Encode each letter by replacing it with a letter that falls a given number of places after the actual letter. The *increment* or *shift key* provides the number of places that the letter is shifted. If the shift takes us beyond the end of the alphabet, then wrap around the alphabet by continuing at the beginning.

For example, if the shift key is 10, the letter A would be replaced or encoded by K, since K is 10 places beyond A in the alphabet. Similarly, *B* would be replaced by *L*, *C* would be replaced by *M*, and so on. If S is to be encoded, we realize that a shift of 10 places would take us three places beyond *Z* (see the uppercase letters in Appendix I). Thus, we would wrap around to C. The following shows the encoding of an entire message. Try confirming each encoded letter, noting that we pass through blanks untouched. Also, we use the encode character * for any character in the actual message that's not an uppercase letter.

$$Actual\ message:\quad HELP\ IS\ ON\ THE\ WAY$$
$$Secret\ message:\quad ROVZ\ SC\ YX\ DRO\ GKI$$

Design

Figure 10.6 shows our user interface and sample I/O. This figure is consistent with our description in the requirements stage.

We see two straightforward modules in our design, as described in Figure 10.7. Study this figure and note the following.

1. In the main module we initialize the secret message to the null string. We do this because we plan to build the secret message from scratch, encoded character by encoded character. The for-do loop examines each character in the actual message. If the character is blank, a blank character is added to the secret message; otherwise, a secret letter is added. The secret letter is refined as the given function.

2. This function receives the shift key and actual letter, and returns a secret letter either as an encoded character (if the actual letter is an uppercase letter) or as an * (if the actual letter is not an uppercase letter). The encoding algorithm is the alphabet shift cipher, as described in our requirements. To illustrate, consider the actual letter A. Its ASCII value is 65, which is in the range of uppercase letters given by ASCII values 65–90 (see Appendix I). If the shift key is 10, the shifted place for the encoded letter is at ASCII 75, which corresponds to the secret letter K. Now, suppose the actual letter is S. Its ASCII value is 83, which becomes ASCII 93 when shifted. Since ASCII 93 is 3 places beyond the end of the alphabet at ASCII 90, we must wrap around the alphabet to the 3rd place from the beginning (past ASCII 65 and 66) to ASCII 67. This corresponds to the encoded letter C.

Code

Figure 10.8 shows the listing for program Crypt. Note the following.

1. In the main module, the secret message string variable **SecretMsg** is initialized to the null string **NullString**. Within the for-do loop, **SecretMsg** is

---

FIGURE 10.6   Sample I/O Design and Run for Program **Crypt**

```
CRYPTOGRAPHY DEMONSTRATION

Enter actual message ===> HELP IS ON THE WAY

Enter shift key ========> 10

Actual message: HELP IS ON THE WAY
Secret message: ROVZ SC YX DRO GKI
```

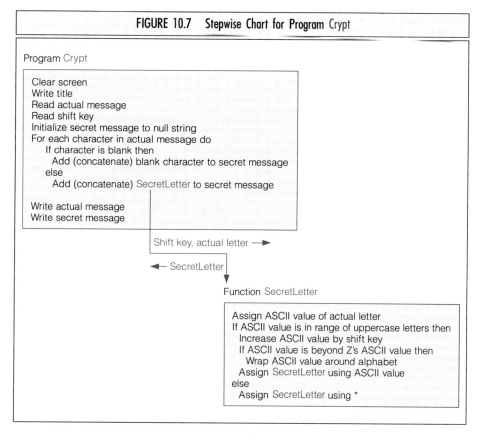

FIGURE 10.7   Stepwise Chart for Program Crypt

Program Crypt

Clear screen
Write title
Read actual message
Read shift key
Initialize secret message to null string
For each character in actual message do
   If character is blank then
      Add (concatenate) blank character to secret message
   else
      Add (concatenate) SecretLetter to secret message

Write actual message
Write secret message

Shift key, actual letter ⟶

⟵ SecretLetter

Function SecretLetter

Assign ASCII value of actual letter
If ASCII value is in range of uppercase letters then
  Increase ASCII value by shift key
  If ASCII value is beyond Z's ASCII value then
    Wrap ASCII value around alphabet
  Assign SecretLetter using ASCII value
else
  Assign SecretLetter using *

built up using the concatenation operator in a manner that looks identical to its numerical summation counterpart.

2. In function SecretLetter...

  a. Function **ord** returns the ASCII value of the actual letter. This value then serves as the basis for the range test on uppercase letters and as the value that gets revised after the shift.

  b. If the original value in ASCIIvalue is in range, ASCIIvalue is incremented by ShiftKey and tested for the possibility of an alphabet wrap. If a wrap is required, we reassign the ASCII value using

$$\text{ASCIIvalue} := \text{LoASCII} + (\text{ASCIIvalue} - \text{HiASCII}) - 1;$$

We worked this formula out from our earlier reasoning in the design stage. In that example we used the actual letter S, which has a shifted ASCII value of 93. The shift formula gives the following:

$$\text{ASCIIvalue} := 65 + (93 - 90) - 1;$$
$$:= 67$$

ASCII 67 is the encode letter C.

FIGURE 10.8   Listing for Program Crypt

```
program Crypt;

{* * * * * * * * * * * * * * * * * * * * * * * * * * * * * * * * * * *
 *                                                                   *
 *         Cryptography... Message encoding using alphabet shift cipher *
 *                                                                   *
 *            Inputs actual message and shift key                    *
 *            Encodes secret message                                 *
 *            Outputs actual and secret messages                     *
 *                                                                   *
 *            Modular structure                                      *
 *            |___   Function SecretLetter                           *
 *                                                                   *
 * * * * * * * * * * * * * * * * * * * * * * * * * * * * * * * * * * *}

{============================= Declarations ============================}

uses crt;

const
  Blank     = ' ';              {Blanks left untouched in messages}
  NullString = '';              {Used to initialize SecretMsg}

  Title = 'CRYPTOGRAPHY DEMONSTRATION';

var
  ActualMsg, SecretMsg : string;      {Actual and secret messages}
  Position,                           {Character position in string}
  ShiftKey             : integer;     {Shift key}

{====================== Function Declarations ======================}
```

To make sure you understand the program, try roleplaying the actual word WAY to its encoded counterpart GKI.

Test

Figure 10.6 shows one of our test runs. For other test runs, see Exercise 19. A common error is forgetting to initialize SecretMsg. Check out the consequences in Exercise 19d.

If you're getting into cryptography, check out Exercises 20–22.

SELF-REVIEW EXERCISES

16a–b 19

10.4   PROGRAMMING TIPS

• • • • • • • • • • • • • •

Consider the following tips to improve the design and style of your programs and to avoid some common errors.

FIGURE 10.8   (*continued*)

```pascal
function SecretLetter (ShiftKey : integer;  ActualLetter : char) : char;

  { Function uses alphabet shift cipher to encode legal actual letter as
      secret letter
    Receives shift key and actual letter
    Returns secret letter or * for illegal actual letter }

  {NOTE:  Precondition assumes that legal actual letters are in the range
          A .. Z; violations trapped and * returned as secret letter}

const
  LoASCII = 65;  HiASCII = 90;  {Decimal ASCII values for A and Z}

var
  ASCIIvalue : integer;         {Decimal ASCII value of actual letter}
  InRange    : Boolean;         {True if ASCII value in range low to
                                 high; false otherwise}

begin  {SecretLetter}

 {Determine ASCII value of actual letter}
  ASCIIvalue := ord(ActualLetter);

  InRange := ASCIIvalue in [LoASCII .. HiASCII];

 {If ASCII value in range, then encode as secret letter else use *}
  if InRange then
    begin
      ASCIIvalue := ASCIIvalue + ShiftKey;
      {If beyond last letter then wrap around alphabet}
      if ASCIIvalue > HiASCII then
        ASCIIvalue := LoASCII + (ASCIIvalue - HiASCII) - 1;
      SecretLetter := chr(ASCIIvalue);
    end {then}
  else
    SecretLetter := '*';

end;    {SecretLetter}

   {============================ Main Body ============================}

begin  {Crypt}

 {Clear screen, write title, input actual message and shift key}
  clrscr;
  writeln (Title);  writeln;
  write ('Enter actual message ===> ');  readln(ActualMsg);  writeln;
  write ('Enter shift key =======> ');  readln(ShiftKey);   writeln;

 {Initialize secret message}
  SecretMsg := NullString;

 {Encode secret message}
  for Position := 1 to length(ActualMsg) do
    if ActualMsg[Position] = Blank then
      SecretMsg := SecretMsg + Blank
    else                              ⟵── Secret message built up by concatenation
      SecretMsg := SecretMsg + SecretLetter(ShiftKey, ActualMsg[Position]);

 {Write actual and secret messages}
  writeln ('Actual message: ', ActualMsg);
  writeln ('Secret message: ', SecretMsg);

end.    {Crypt}
```

DESIGN AND STYLE

1. Defensive Programming: Use Character Choices. Use character variables as input choices in menu selections and other user-selectable options. This eliminates the possibility of run-time input errors, as in mistakenly entering a letter instead of a digit when numeric choices are given. For example, if we wish to offer four numeric-looking choices (like 1, 2, 3, or 4), then input the choice as a character and trap characters other than 1, 2, 3, and 4 using an else clause. Otherwise, the alternative of treating the choice as an integer value would require more complicated *I/O error handling*.

2. Defensive Programming: Trap Certain Call Results. Some results from calls to string functions and procedures can cause errors if not trapped. In particular, trap the possibility that a substring is not found within a string when calling function **pos**, as done in Figure 10.3. Also test the integer error code that's received from procedure **val**, as done in Example 10.5.

3. On Selecting Data Type. An early design question is the selection of data type. For the material in this chapter, we have the primary choices reviewed in Section 10.1: character or subrange character type, character set type, string type, and string array type. Sometimes the choice is obvious, as in using type character for menu selections. Often we have alternative choices, as in using either a character set or string (Example 10.3). Here are some guidelines you might consider.

> **a.** Use character type if the focus is on individual characters; use subrange character type if a subrange of characters is meaningful; consider string type if there is a need to manipulate data like names and phrases, or substrings of these data. For example, if all we need to do is count characters in text, we can read and count character type values while an eof condition is not encountered. If we need to replace one word with another, however, we have to process string type values.

> **b.** Use character sets if distinct groupings of characters have meaning, as in vowels, even digits, and so on.

> **c.** Use a string variable to process lines of text when we don't have need for the entire text at any one time; otherwise use a string array. For instance, if we just need to count the occurrences of the word the, then we can process a line and go on to the next without having to consider previous or subsequent lines. We could store each line in a string variable as needed. If we need to rearrange the text, however, then we should use a string array variable. In some applications, the array alternative simplifies coding by eliminating tedious selection structures (check out Exercise 12c).

COMMON ERRORS

1. Syntax Error. Don't forget that the concatenation operator + concatenates strings, and nothing else. This is an easy oversight when concatenating parts of an output list, as in

writeln ('Index is ' **+** Index) ☹

Use a comma

where Index is an integer variable. This would give a *type-mismatch* error.

2. Execution and Logic Errors. These errors are very common in character and string processing, possibly because they tend to be subtle and we're less accustomed to this type of processing than to numeric processing. This means we need to pay special attention to test data selection and output validation in the test stage. Also, we need to program defensively, as described in items 1 and 2 under "Design and Style."

REVIEW EXERCISES

EASIER	For the busy... **1 2 3 4 6 7 10 11**
NORMAL	For the thinkers... **5 8 9 12 13 14 15 16 17 18 19 20**
TOUGHER	For the hard CORE... **21 22**

1. Indicate output for each part given the following code fragment. Each part is independent of the others.

```
const
    Size1 = 5;   Size2 = 10;
    Blank = chr(32);

type
    StrType1 = string [Size1];
    StrType2 = string [Size2];
    SubType  = '1' .. '5';
```

```
        var
            StrVar1 : StrType1;
            StrVar2 : StrType2;
            ChrVar1 : char;
            ChrVar2 : SubType;

        begin
            StrVar1 := 'WROC';
            StrVar2 := 'Station';
            ChrVar1 := '!';
            ChrVar2 := chr(Size1*Size2);
            ...
        end;
```

a. writeln (StrVar2 + Blank + StrVar1 + ChrVar1);
b. writeln (ChrVar2 + ChrVar1);
c. writeln (succ(ChrVar1), pred(ChrVar2), ord(Blank));
d. StrVar2 := StrVar2 + Blank + StrVar1 + ChrVar1;
   writeln (StrVar2);
e. StrVar1 := StrVar1 + ChrVar1;
   writeln (StrVar1 :Size1);
f. StrVar1[4] := upcase(StrVar2[2]);
   writeln (StrVar1 :Size2);
g. ChrVar2 := ChrVar1;
   writeln (ChrVar2);
h. ChrVar1 := StrVar1[length(StrVar1)];
   writeln (ChrVar1);
i. writeln (length(StrVar2) :2, ord(StrVar2[0]) :2);

2. Given the code fragment in the preceding exercise, indicate the resulting Boolean values.
   a. StrVar1 < StrVar2
   b. ChrVar1 <= StrVar1
   c. succ(ChrVar2) = '3'
   d. StrVar1 > 'WRO'
   e. StrVar1 > 'wro'

3. Suppose Newport is stored in City, RI is stored in State, and 02840 is stored in Zip, where all values are type string. Code a **writeln** statement that displays the following.

   Newport,▮RI▮▮02840

4. Write code that replaces each blank within the value in string variable Phrase with an ∗ . Assume Blank is declared as '▮'.

5.   Consider the following declarations.

```
type
   String20 = string [20];
   String10 = string [10];

var
   BabyStrVar : String20;

procedure First (StrVar : string);
...

procedure Second (StrVar : String10);
...

procedure Third ( var StrVar : string);
```

Assuming that the *Var-string checking* compiler directive is active, indicate any problems and possible fixups for the following calls.
   a. First (BabyStrVar);
   b. Second (BabyStrVar);
   c. Third (BabyStrVar);

6.   Indicate returned values for the following, given the sample data in Table 10.2.
   a. concat(' ', upcase(SubPhrase[3]), ' ')
   b. copy(Phrase, 1, 6)
   c. length(copy(SubPhrase, 5, 1))
   d. pos(Phrase, SubPhrase)

7.   In Example 10.1 revise the loop to...
   a. Display the position of each character to the left of the character, with one space separating the character from its position.
   *b. Display the characters on the same line, in backward order, with no spaces between any of the characters.
   *c. Count the number of times the letter *e* appears.

8.   In Example 10.2...
   a. Change the code to output the form dd-mm-19yy.
   b. What happens if we enter the date 3/24/92? 12/7/41?
   *c. How might we change the code to correct the problems in the preceding part?

9.   In Example 10.3...
   a. Change the code for each alternative if we need to add the legitimate codes A, B, C.
   *b. Suppose the only legitimate codes are the two-character codes AB, BC, and CD. Do we now have a character set? If not, what's the base type of the set? Change the code for both the set and string alternatives.

10. In Example 10.4, revise the code to display just the first two characters in the abbreviation. Can you think of an alternative that would not use the copy function?

11. Indicate results for the following, given the sample data in Table 10.3.
   a. delete (SubPhrase, 3, 4)
   b. insert (Phrase, SubPhrase, 5)
   c. str (RealVar :8:3, StrVar)
   d. val(StrVar, IntVar, Code) if 1.03 is in StrVar
   e. val(StrVar, RealVar, Code) if ■■9.50■■ is in StrVar

12. In Example 10.5...
   a. Indicate output if the input is 10/19/91. How about if the input is 13/19/91? 1/19/91?
   *b. Revise the code to repeat the input until it's correct.
   *c. Rewrite the code to eliminate the use of a string array. MonthName is simply a string variable. Comment on the desirability of this approach.

*13. **Date conversion with str.** Suppose Month, Day, and Year are subrange integer variables that store correct values for month (1..12), day (1..31), and year (0..99). Write code that creates string variable Date having the form mm-dd-yy.

14. In Example 10.6, write down a call to Replace using appropriate character strings to revise...
   a. Jerk and Jill to Jack and Jill
   b. Jack and Jill to Jack and not Jill
   *c. Write a driver to test Replace using the data in parts **a** and **b**. Interactively input the text string, old substring, and new substring. Output the revised text string. In your input, try different ways of representing the old and new substrings.

*15. **Integer input error handling.** In Example 6.6 we considered one approach to trapping noninteger input values. Can you think of alternative code that calls procedure **val**? Appropriately revise and debug CkRdInt and ReadLnInt. Can we apply the same idea to the input of a real value? If so, how?

(L) **16.** **Character subsets.** For the application in Figures 10.4 and 10.5...
   a. Run program SetFind and try the sample data, but add the symbol ■ at the end of the line. What happens? Try the input end; {if}. Correct results? *Hint:* The symbol ■ is ASCII decimal 254 (see Appendix I). We can generate it by holding down the Alt key and pressing **254** on the numeric keypad.
   b. Delete the initialization for CharLineSet (or set it off in curly braces) and execute the program using the test data in Figure 10.4. What happens?
   *c. Revise the program to count and output the number of symbols.
   *d. Revise the program to display separate sets of symbols, lowercase letters, and uppercase letters. Also display a count of the members in each set.

(L) *17. **Character subsets.** Revise the program in Figure 10.5 to use the string approach rather than the set approach. Use the same test data. Which approach do you like better, and why?

(L) *18. **Character subsets.** Revise the program in Figure 10.5 to conform to Standard Pascal's omission of the string type. Instead, use a character variable for input. Use the test data in Figure 10.4 as input, and the sentinel ■ to terminate input. (See the hint in Exercise 16a.)

(L) 19. **Cryptography.** For the application in Figures 10.6 to 10.8, answer each question by desk checking, and then confirm your answer by running program Crypt.

   a. State the secret message if the shift key is 0. If the shift key is 26?

   b. State the secret message if the actual message is **Help is on the way!**

   c. What happens if we forget to trap blanks in the calling module?

   d. What happens if we forget to initialize SecretMsg?

   e. What's the secret message that corresponds to your full name?

(L) *20. **Cryptography.** Revise the cryptography program to encode messages with lowercase letters, uppercase letters, and punctuation marks. Use the following test data:

   SS Pierce: Help isn't on the way!

(L) *21. **Cryptography.** Revise the cryptography program to decode a secret message into its actual counterpart. As test data, use the same pair of messages given in Figure 10.6.

(L) *22. **Cryptography.** Revise the cryptography program to implement a *keyword coding* scheme that uses letters in a keyword to establish variable shift key values, as follows.

Keyword: I B M

— 3rd shift key value is *13* since M is 13th letter in alphabet
— 2nd shift key value is *2* since B is 2nd letter in alphabet
— 1st shift key value is *9* since I is 9th letter in alphabet

Actual Message	Shift Key	Secret Message
H	9	Q
E	2	G
L	13	Y
P	9	Y
I	2	K
S	13	F
O	9	X
N	2	P

Shift key pattern is repeated

(And so on...)

a. Develop an encoding program that inputs the keyword and an actual message, encodes the message using the keyword coding scheme, and displays both messages. In your test runs, use HELP IS ON THE WAY as the actual message and IBM as the keyword. What's the secret message if we use DEC as the keyword?

b. Develop a decoding option that decodes the secret messages from the algorithm in part **a.** This option inputs the secret message and keyword and outputs both messages.

ADDITIONAL EXERCISES

EASIER	For the busy... **23 24 25**
NORMAL	For the thinkers... **26 27 28 29 30 31**
TOUGHER	For the hard CORE... **32 33 34**

23. **Name manipulation.** Develop a program that...

a. Inputs a person's first and last name as a single string, with one blank separating the two, and outputs the name in the following format.

      `Last name,█First name`

Use the following test data: Harvey CORE, Ada Lovelace, your name. Interactively process all names in one run.

b. What happens if you enter a name like Harvey A. CORE? Revise the program to handle this format as well. The corresponding output would be CORE, Harvey A.

This file is in the Examples Library;
Use it for Exercises 24, 26, 27

File YOGI.DAT

The story goes that Yogi Berra was delivered a pizza pie, and asked whether he wanted it cut up into 6 or 8 slices. The famous catcher for the New York Yankees baseball team responded, "Make it 8, I'm hungry."

24. **Cap letters.** Develop a program that inputs a text file, counts capital letters, and displays each capital letter. Also output the count. Display letters on the same line, with two spaces between each. Use test data file YOGI.DAT.

25. **Character taxonomy I.** Develop a program that inputs a character and writes one of the following classification descriptions: Vowel, Consonant, Digit, Symbol. Input one character per line, and terminate input with the blank character. Use the following test data: **a A r 0 B 7 $. ?**.

26. **Character taxonomy II.** Develop a program that inputs a text file and displays the following report.

Character Taxonomy Report

Class	Number
Vowels	xx
Consonants	xx
Digits	xx
Symbols	xx
Blanks	xx
Total . . .	xxx

Use the test data file YOGI.DAT.

27. **Word extraction.** Develop a program that extracts words from text and displays each on a separate line. A word is defined as a substring followed by a space (this is a simplified definition). Include contractions such as *don't* in the definition of a word. Also count and display the number of words. Use file YOGI.DAT as test data.

28. **Course queries.** The course codes at a university are coded as six-character strings. The first three characters represent the department where the course is offered and the last three characters are digits that signify the academic level. For example, BIO405 is a code for a 400-level biology course. Level 100 courses are for freshmen, level 200 courses are for sophomores, and so on. Store the following test codes in a data file: BIO405 CSC201 CSC465 HIS101 HIS265 MGS105 MGS207 MGS500.

   a. Develop a program that processes the following sample queries.

```
            COURSE QUERY MENU

        1  List all courses in a department
        2  List all courses by academic level
        3  List all graduate courses (500 and above)
        Q  Quit
```

```
                    Selection? 1
                      Department? his

                                        Courses...
                                              HIS101
                                              HIS265

                      Department? eng

                                        Courses...
                                        ☼ No courses in data base

                      Department? q
                    Selection? 2
                      Enter level? 100

                                        Courses...
                                              HIS101
                                              MGS105

                      Enter level? 300

                                        Courses...
                                        ☼ No courses in data base

                      Enter level? q
                    Selection? 3

                                        Courses...
                                              MGS500

                    Selection? q
                      End of run...
```

b. Same as part **a**, except use the type of screen-oriented user interface that we illustrated in Chapter 8.

29. **Junk mail.** Write a program that prints the following personalized form letter.

```
         Ms. Jane Budwick
         10 North Road
         Kingston, RI 02881
         Dear Ms. Budwick,
              You are indeed one of the fortunate few whom
         we have selected for our Gala Prize Drawing. All you
         need to do, Jane, is fill in the enclosed handy
         magazine order form, which makes you eligible for
         one of our many Gala Prizes. Indeed, the Budwick
         residence at 10 North Road may be lucky enough
         to receive the Most Gala Prize, a free set of
         encyclopedias at a maintenance cost of only 10 cents
         per day for 30 years.
         Good luck!
         Hoodwink G. Fox, Manager
         Dill Comic Book Co., Inc.
```

In one computer run, print the letter for each of the following.

Name	Address	
Ms. Jane Budwick	10 North Road	Kingston, RI 02881
Mr. Al Bella Bitta	20 Birch St.	Cincinnati, OH 44451
Dr. H. Doolittle	10 Downing	London, UK

Store the mailing list in a data file.

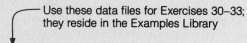

Use these data files for Exercises 30–33;
they reside in the Examples Library

Text 1 (TEXT1.DAT)

```
Jack and Jill went up the hill
  To fetch a pail of water;
Jack fell down and broke his crown,
  And Jill came tumbling after.
```

Text 2 (TEXT2.DAT)

```
    Among other duties, a regional office of the
Environmental Protection Agency (EPA) is charged with
investigating complaints regarding industrial pollution,
when "warranted." A complaint is investigated by
sending a panel of three experts, collectively called the
"proboscis patrol," to the site of the alleged offender.
By consensus, the proboscis patrol then renders one of
three opinions: low level, medium level, or high level of
pollution. (We might note that the human nose has yet
to find an electronic "equal" in detecting offending
odors.) Following an opinion, the regional director of
the EPA then has the option of issuing or not issuing a
citation to the offender. Alternatively, the EPA may
choose not to investigate the complaint and then make
a decision regarding issuance of a citation.
```

30. **Text analysis I.** Write a program that processes *any number* of separate texts and displays the following for *each* text.
   a. Number of characters
   b. Number of letters and proportion of characters that are letters
   c. Number of vowels and proportion of letters that are vowels
   d. Number of lowercase letters and proportion of letters that are lowercase
   Process each text one line at a time (maximum line length is 80 characters) and ignore trailing blanks in a line. Process the two given texts in your run.

31. Text analysis II. Write a program that processes *any number* of separate texts and displays the number and proportion of *each* letter in the alphabet for each text. Make no distinction between lowercase and uppercase letters for purposes of the count. Process each text one line at a time, where the maximum line length is 80 characters. Process the two given texts in your run.

32. Text analysis III. Write a program that processes *any number* of separate texts and displays the following for each text.
   a. Number of words
   b. Number and proportion of words specified by the user (use *the* or *The* and *and* or *And* as test input)
   c. Number and proportion of words that end in a substring specified by the user (use *ing* as test input)
   d. Number and proportion of words that begin with a letter (or more generally any substring) specified by the user (use the letters *a* or *A* and *e* or *E* as test input)

Process each text one line at a time, with the maximum line length of 80 characters. Process the two given texts in your run.

33. Text analysis IV. A typing textbook contains numerous paragraphs for students to type. These exercises vary in difficulty according to the following criteria.
   1. *Number of strokes* in the exercise. A stroke is any keyboard act, such as typing a letter, typing a space, and returning the carriage to the next line (except for the last line in the exercise), and so on.
   2. *Number of words* in the exercise. Words can include a single letter. For example, the phrase "I love computers" has three words.
   3. *Average word length* in the exercise. This is defined as the number of strokes divided by the number of words.

   The usual approach to developing these exercises is for someone to count strokes, words, and word length for each proposed exercise, to ensure that exercises with various levels of difficulty are selected. This is a tedious task, and it is where you come in. You are to computerize this task.

   Write a program that processes *any number* of separate exercises and outputs each line of the exercise followed by a count of the number of strokes and words for that line. For example, the first two lines of Text 1 might be displayed as follows:

```
                                                  Strokes  Words
                                                  ───────  ─────
        Jack and Jill went up the hill              31       7
           To fetch a pail of water;                28       6
```

At the end of each exercise write summary values for the three criteria discussed. Process each exercise one line at a time, assuming a maximum line length of 60. Use the two given texts as test data.

34. **Word game.** Remember the word game "hangman" from your early days? Let's develop a program that offers a variation of this game. The following sample I/O demonstrates one game.

```
Enter word file? wordgame
Enter difficulty level (guesses allowed)? 3
Word =>>> ------
                              Guesses thus far  = 0
                              Winnings thus far = $0

Enter letter? a
Word =>>> -a--a-
                              Guesses thus far  = 1
                              Winnings thus far = $100

Enter letter? s
Word =>>> -as-a-
                              Guesses thus far  = 2
                              Winnings thus far = $150

Enter letter? r
Word =>>> -as-a-
                              Guesses thus far  = 3
                              Winnings thus far = $150

GAME OVER... Word is Pascal
Play again (y/n)? y
...
```

Get the idea? The winning amount for a guess is $50 per letter guessed. If the word is guessed within the allowed number of guesses, there's a $500 bonus. We make no case distinction for letters. The program processes a word file indicated by the user. Our sample file is WORDGAME.DAT. Check it out in the Examples Library. The program assumes that all files have a .DAT extension. Once the words are entered in primary memory, the program selects a word by generating a random number (see Module C) in the range 1 to number of words.

RECORDS

‡Optional, more advanced material. Skip without loss of continuity, study at this point, or wait until later.

In our earlier work we defined a **field** as an attribute that describes some entity. By an *entity* we mean a person, place, or thing. For example, the entity employee might be described by the fields social security number, full name, salary, and sex code. The entity city might be described by the fields city name and temperature. The collection of fields that describes an entity is a **record.** In our two brief examples, we have described an employee record and a city record.

Up to now we have viewed records in terms of their placement in data files. We take a closer look at records and data files in both this chapter and the next. We can also hold a collection of records in primary memory by using an array. We cover arrays of records in this chapter.

The use of records and their fields is so common in computer applications that many languages pay special attention to the typing and processing of records. Turbo Pascal is especially good in this respect, as we are about to see.

11.1 RECORD TYPE

• • • • • • • • • • • • • •

Let's start with the basics by defining the record data structure, record type, and record variable.

ANOTHER DATA STRUCTURE

Consider the example in Figure 11.1. The employee record is an example of a *data structure,* a collection of related data that are arranged in a particular pattern or structure.[1] We can thus conceptualize a *record* as a data structure with adjacent *fields,* where each field is described by a particular identifier and data type. We call this a **record data structure.** In the Pascal literature, fields are often called *components* (of a record).

Records are sometimes described by a *record layout,* as seen in Table 11.1 for the employee record. The record layout is a useful tool in the requirements stage of the software development cycle, and serves as a design and documentation aid in the different stages. Relate this table to the sample record in Figure 11.1, noting the sequencing of fields and their typing. For example, SexCode is the last field, and it holds a character value.

---

[1] Earlier we covered the *set* data structure (Chapter 7) and the *array* data structure (Chapter 9). We also viewed a text file as a data structure of characters (Chapter 4).

FIGURE 11.1   Employee Record Data Structure and Sample Record

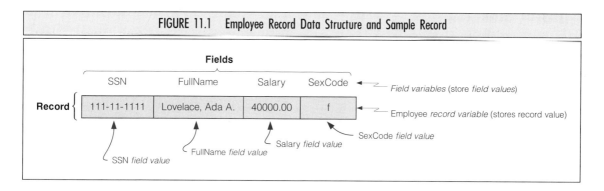

Table 11.1   Record Layout for Employee Record

Field Identifier	Field Type	Description
SSN	**string**[11]	Social security number, with dashes
FullName	**string**[25]	Last Name, First Name Initial
Salary	**real**	Salary (annual)
SexCode	**char**	Sex code (f or m)

Note that each field has an associated *field identifier* and *field type*. We can think of a field as a **field variable** that stores a *field value* according to its declared type. Thus, in Figure 11.1, the field variable Salary stores the real field value 40000.00. As we will see, however, *field variables are not declared and referenced like other simple variables*.

We can view the identifier Employee as a *record variable* that stores the collection of four values described in Figure 11.1. The **record variable** is a *structured variable* that stores multiple values based on its record data structure. The *record value* in Employee thus includes a value for each of its fields. It's a collection of field values.

A record variable must be typed by a *record type* that's declared in the type section of a program. A **record (data) type** defines a record data structure, as we will see next.

DECLARATIONS

The accompanying syntax box illustrates the declarations of record types and record variables. Note the following.

1. The record-type declaration identifies a particular record type named by an identifier. In the examples, we declared two different record types, EmployeeType and CityRecType. The declaration of each record type also includes the declaration of its fields: each field variable and its associated data type. For instance, CityRecType is defined by two fields: the

SYNTAX BOX

Record type and variable declarations for simple records*... Declare record
type in type section and record variable in var section

```
Syntax.........type
               RecordType = record
                  Field1Identifier : Field1Type;
                  Field2Identifier : Field2Type;     } Field list
                    .  }
                    .  } Other field declarations
                    .  }
               end;
           var
               RecordVariable : RecordType;

Examples......type
               EmployeeType = record
                  SSN      : string[11];      {Social security number field}
                  FullName : string[25];      {Full name field}
                  Salary   : real;            {Annual salary field}
                  SexCode  : char;            {Sex code field: f = female, m = male}
               end;   {EmployeeType}
               CityRecType = record
                  CityName : string[SizeStr]; {City name field}
                  F        : integer;         {Fahrenheit temperature field}
               end;   {CityRecType}
           var
               Employee : EmployeeType;        {Employee record}
               City     : CityRecType;         {City record}
```

Explanation... RecordType is a user-defined identifier for a *record type* that declares a record data structure
having fields given by the *field list*. Each member of the field list is a FieldIdentifier and its FieldType. The
FieldIdentifier is a user-defined identifier for the *field variable*. FieldType is any type in Turbo Pascal. The identifier **record** is a reserved word. RecordVariable is a user-defined identifier for the record variable whose type
is RecordType.

*The syntax box in Section 11.5 covers *variant records*.

field variable CityName having type string with a size attribute given by
the declared constant SizeStr and the field variable F having type integer.
Note how the declaration of EmployeeType is consistent with the record
layout in Table 11.1 and the record data structure in Figure 11.1. The record data type is another example of a *structured data type*, because it
types a data structure.[2]

    2. We use documentation to briefly describe each field.

---

[2]Other structured data types covered earlier are the array type (Section 9.1) and the set type
(Section 7.3).

3. The record variable itself is declared in the var section, with its appropriate record type. In the examples, we declared record variable Employee having type EmployeeType and record variable City having type CityRecType.

4. As usual we can type a variable *anonymously,* as in

```
                         Record variable City typed anonymously
    var
      City : record
        CityName : string[SizeStr];  ☹
        F        : integer;
      end;  {City}
```

but we don't recommend it because it's less descriptive and the record variable can't be used as a parameter in module calls and declarations.

SELF-REVIEW EXERCISES

1 2a–c 3

11.2 OPERATIONS ON RECORDS

• • • • • • • • • • • • • •

A data type is defined not only by its range of values but also by the operations permitted on those values. In this section, we take a detailed look at how to reference record variables and fields, how to store and retrieve field values, and how to use records in Boolean expressions and parameter lists.

FIELD- AND RECORD-VARIABLE REFERENCES

In referencing records and their fields, we can take two perspectives.

- *Forest* perspective: Reference entire record
- *Tree* perspective: Reference individual fields in a record

Which referencing approach we take depends on our needs and on what Turbo Pascal permits for the particular operation we have in mind. For example, we can reference an entire record simply by using the record variable, as in Employee or City.

SYNTAX BOX

Field references...Use either field variable appended to record variable or field variable within with statement

---

Syntax........*Alternative 1: Field variable appended to record variable*

    RecordVariable.FieldVariable

Examples......**writeln** (Employee.SSN);
        writeln (Employee.FullName);

        City.F := 90;
        readln (City.F);

Syntax........*Alternative 2: Field variable within with statement*

    with List of RecordVariables **do**
    Statement that directly uses FieldVariables;

Examples......**with** Employee **do**
        writeln (SSN, FullName, Salary, SexCode);

Explanation... RecordVariable and FieldVariable are user-defined identifiers for record and field names, respectively. The identifiers **with** and **do** are reserved words. List of RecordVariables is a list of record variables separated by commas. If the list contains more than one record variable and a field name is common to more than one record variable in the list, then the reference is to the rightmost record in the list.

If we work with individual field references, the entire range of operations associated with the field's data type is available to us. Just how we reference individual fields is described in the above syntax box. Note the following.

1. The with statement simplifies field references by dropping the record variable and dot that precede the field variable. This is useful when referencing multiple fields in a record, as seen in the output example. Be aware that *the direct use of field variables is allowed only within the confines of the with statement.*

2. The with statement can include references to more than one record variable. This is useful in certain applications that cross-reference records, but it can be confusing, especially if two or more records have the same field names.

The examples in the syntax box show simple I/O and assignment. Let's take a look at these operations in more detail.

I/O of Fields and Records

When working with the screen or a text data file, we can't I/O an entire record by directly using its record variable. We have to work with the individual fields by using field references, as seen in the preceding syntax box.[3]

We can use calls to the predefined procedures **read, readln, write,** and **writeln** to I/O field values whose types are among the standard types real, integer, Boolean, character, and string. For Boolean fields, we can use write and writeln statements, but not read and readln statements. For the input of Boolean fields, or the I/O of enumerated and set fields, we need to design our own procedures, as done in Chapter 7.

We input individual field values into a record variable either from a data file or interactively from the keyboard. We leave the data-file approach to Section 11.3, and illustrate the interactive approach next.

EXAMPLE 11.1   INTERACTIVE INPUT OF EMPLOYEE RECORD

The following code demonstrates how we might interactively input field values into the employee record illustrated in Figure 11.1 and declared in the syntax box on page 520.

```
with Employee do
  begin
    write ('Enter social security number......... '); readln (SSN);
    write ('Enter Last name, First name Initial... '); readln (FullName);
    write ('Enter salary........................ '); readln (Salary);
    write ('Enter sex code (f or m).............. '); readln (SexCode);
  end;  {with}
```

Note that all fields are standard types, so we can simply use readln statements. See Exercise 5c for the I/O of an enumerated type field. Also note that this with statement, unlike our example in the syntax box, includes a compound statement flanked by the usual begin/end pair.

Assignment of Fields and Records

We can use field references within expressions and assignment statements according to the same compatibility rules that operate for the data types that correspond to each field. For example, the assignment

```
Employee.Salary := (1 + InflationRate) * Employee.Salary; ☺
```

---

[3]As we will see in the next chapter, we can use a record variable to I/O entire records when working with *typed* data files.

might be used to increase an employee's salary by the inflation rate. The expression is legitimate because the field reference Employee.Salary is type real and the multiplication operation is defined for numeric operands. Moreover, the assignment is compatible because the right member is a real value and the left member is typed real. However, the assignment

```
Employee.SSN := 34449812;  ☹
```

would provoke a compile-time error because the right member is an integer constant and the left member is type string.

It's also legitimate to assign the value in one record variable to another record variable. That is, the assignment

```
RecordVariableA := RecordVariableB;
```

is permissible, provided that both record variables are *identically typed*.

EXAMPLE 11.2   RECORD-VARIABLE ASSIGNMENTS

Suppose that EmployeeDeptA and EmployeeDeptB are record variables typed EmployeeType, and we wish to copy all field values from EmployeeDeptB to EmployeeDeptA. The "brute force" approach might use the following code.

```
EmployeeDeptA.SSN      := EmployeeDeptB.SSN;
EmployeeDeptA.FullName := EmployeeDeptB.FullName;   ⎫ Field-reference approach
EmployeeDeptA.Salary   := EmployeeDeptB.Salary;     ⎬
EmployeeDeptA.SexCode  := EmployeeDeptB.SexCode;    ⎭
```

More elegantly, we could use the record variables

```
EmployeeDeptA := EmployeeDeptB;  ◄── Record-variable approach
```

Note that both record variables must be identically typed (EmployeeType in our example) and that all field values in the record are copied. If we only wish to copy selected fields, we have to use the field-reference approach.

FIELDS AND BOOLEAN EXPRESSIONS

We can use field references in Boolean expressions exactly like we use other variable references. As usual, we need to ensure that relational expressions are type compatible.

Example 11.3   Field Reference in Boolean Expression

Suppose that we wish to write the name of an employee who corresponds to a desired sex code that's entered by the user. The following code fragment does the trick

```
if Employee.SexCode = DesiredSexCode then
   writeln (Employee.FullName);
```

Note that the Boolean expression uses the field reference Employee.SexCode.

Fields and Records as Parameters

We can use field references and record variables in parameter lists just like other variables. When using record variables, we need to ensure that corresponding actual and formal record variable parameters are *identically typed*.

The use of record variables in parameter lists is particularly appealing from a *data-abstraction* point of view: We can think of a record (or record variable) as a single entity (the attributes of an employee, a city), without being concerned about the field details. Moreover, we could treat a particular record type as an *ADT* (Section 7.2) not only by declaring its type but also by developing procedures that implement operations, like input and output. For example, we might develop procedure ReadEmployee to read an employee record with the call ReadEmployee (Employee). The call to ReadEmployee also illustrates *procedural abstraction,* because at this point we don't need to be concerned about the details in reading a record. Finally, we could develop an ADT unit (Section 8.2) that's specific to that record type as an ADT. In Exercise 24 we ask you to develop an ADT unit for processing employee records.

All of our examples from this point on illustrate the use of record variables in parameter lists, along with the powerful data-abstraction concept.

NOTE

1. On terminology. Take a look at Figure 11.1 again. We use the term *record* either conceptually (as in employee record) or specifically to mean "record value." A *record variable* stores a record (value). The record value is a collection of *field values.* A *field variable* stores a field value. The field variable, however, is not a "normal" variable. Its reference is restricted to the *field-reference* syntax shown in the syntax box on page 522.

continued

2. Don't lose sight of field type. In writing code that implements operations on fields, pay attention to the type of each field. Operations on fields (like reading and writing with calls to predefined procedures) are restricted to those allowed by that data type.

3. Record-variable references. Remember that the record variable itself is directly referenced in parameter lists and in record-variable assignments. Use individual field references for screen and text file I/O.

SELF-REVIEW EXERCISES

4a 6 7 8a

*11.3   RECORDS AND DATA FILES

We have used data files throughout the book to input data. Now let's take a closer look at the record placement in and input from data files. In the next chapter we extend these ideas to the output of records onto data files.

AS DATA STRUCTURES

Check out Figure 11.2. This shows data file EMPLOYEE.DAT as a collection of three records. As mentioned in Chapter 4, we can define a *data file* as a collection of records. This approach is also consistent with the idea of a *data structure* as a collection of related values that's conceptually stored under a single name (like a set name, array name, record name, or data-file name). Thus, we can view the data file as a data structure of records that resides in an external medium like magnetic disk.

Just how we place the records in the text file itself is a matter of preference. In Figure 11.2 we placed each field value on a separate line. This reduces the likelihood of input errors when dealing with mixed-type data (as in mixing string and numeric values in a data file). Thus, in our example, a record spans four lines. Sometimes, however, it's useful to place an entire rec-

---

*This section assumes an understanding of Section 5.4.

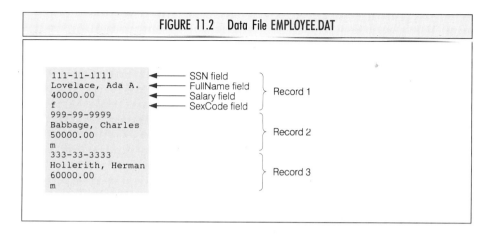

FIGURE 11.2   Data File EMPLOYEE.DAT

ord on a single line. This gives the data file the visual appearance of a table. Such data files are termed *flat files,* where each row is a record (an entity like a person) and each column is a field having a certain width. We ask you to consider this option in Exercise 9d.[4]

Reading Records from Data Files

In effect, we have been reading records from data files all along. In our earlier work, however, we used normal variables to represent field variables. This is the approach taken by languages that lack record typing. In this chapter (and the next), we read records from a data file into a record variable.

---

[4]For you history buffs, the names in Figure 11.2 are not fictitious. *Charles Babbage* was an English mathematician in the mid-1800s who designed the *Analytical Engine,* a precursor to the computer that remarkably set forth the concepts of an arithmetic unit, storage unit, I/O components, and punched card automated operation — a full century before the first working computer. *Ada Lovelace* is reputed to be the first programmer (it's controversial). She was the daughter of the poet Lord Byron and the Countess of Lovelace, Lady Annabella Milkbanke. She was also a mathematician and contemporary of Babbage and took an interest in the Analytical Engine. She wrote a key paper that explained the workings of this conceptual machine and proposed the use of binary data storage. The machine was not successfully built during their lifetimes ... the manufacturing technology for the times was not sophisticated enough to build the gears and shafts to the necessary tolerances. In the 1970s the U.S. Department of Defense began to develop a universal language for business, scientific, mathematical, and engineering applications. The language resembles Pascal and was named *Ada,* in honor of you know who. *Herman Hollerith* was an American mathematician in the late 1800s. He designed the punched card system for processing the 1890 U.S. Census. He formed a company in 1896 that, in 1924, became IBM. Incidentally, IBM ended up constructing a working model of the Analytical Engine, thus bringing us full circle. As a further and entirely suspect aside, CORE family lore has it that it was Harvey's great-great-grandfather Harvey Abacus who was commissioned to build the Analytical Engine.

EXAMPLE 11.4   INPUT AND OUTPUT OF EMPLOYEE DATA FILE

Let's develop a program that illustrates the I/O processing of the data file shown in Figure 11.2. Figure 11.3 shows the I/O design we have in mind. We might design the main body as follows.

Program Employ1

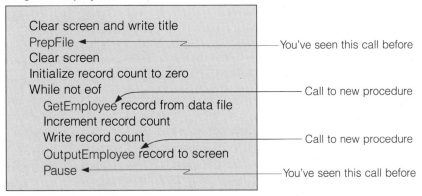

PrepFile and Pause are utility procedures we all know and love by now. GetEmployee and OutputEmployee are new procedures that specialize in reading a single employee record from a data file and writing it to the screen.

Figure 11.4. shows a listing of the program, and Figure 11.3 (as you might have guessed) is our test run. Note the following.

1. Procedures GetEmployee and OutputEmployee demonstrate the data and procedural abstraction discussed earlier. In particular, note that each parameter list simply has the record variable Employee, thereby eliminating the explicit (and messy!) use of fields as parameters.

2. The with statement improves readability by decoupling the field variables SSN, FullName, Salary, and SexCode from the record variable Employee, thereby simplifying field references. The record variable Employee simply appears to the right of *with*.

In Exercise 9 we ask you to put more "teeth" into this program by adding some new features.

FIGURE 11.3   I/O of Data File EMPLOYEE.DAT by Program Employ1

Screen 1

```
    DEMO OF PROCEDURES FOR READING AND WRITING EMPLOYEE RECORDS

    Enter data file (like A:\GRADES\HC101.DAT)... employee.dat
```

Screen 2

```
    Employee #1
       Name.................... Lovelace, Ada A.
       Social Security Number... 111-11-1111
       Sex...................... f
       Salary................... $40000.00




    Hit any key to continue...
```

Screen 3

```
    Employee #2
       Name.................... Babbage, Charles
       Social Security Number... 999-99-9999
       Sex...................... m
       Salary................... $50000.00




    Hit any key to continue...
```

Screen 4

```
    Employee #3
       Name.................... Hollerith, Herman
       Social Security Number... 333-33-3333
       Sex...................... m
       Salary................... $60000.00




    Hit any key to continue...
```

FIGURE 11.4   Listing for Program Employ1

```pascal
program Employ1;

   {* * * * * * * * * * * * * * * * * * * * * * * * * * * * * * * * * *
    *                                                                 *
    *         Demo of Procedures ReadEmployee and WriteEmployee       *
    *                                                                 *
    *            Inputs employee records from data file               *
    *                                                                 *
    *            Outputs employee records to screen                   *
    *                                                                 *
    *            Modular structure                                    *
    *                  |___ GetEmployee                               *
    *                  |___ OutputEmployee                            *
    *                                                                 *
    *            Data structure of text file EMPLOYEE.DAT             *
    *            ----------------------------------------------------- *
    *            Social Security Number                               *
    *            Last name, First name Initial                        *
    *            Salary                                               *
    *            Sex code                                            *
    *                                                                 *
    *            .                                                    *
    *            .   Repeat above four fields for each employee       *
    *            .                                                    *
    *                                                                 *
    * * * * * * * * * * * * * * * * * * * * * * * * * * * * * * * * * *}

   {============================ Declarations ===========================}

uses crt, OurUnit;

const
   Title = 'DEMO OF PROCEDURES FOR READING AND WRITING EMPLOYEE RECORDS';

type
   EmployeeType = record
      SSN      : string[11];        {Social Security Number field}
      FullName : string[25];        {Full name field}
      Salary   : real;              {Annual salary field}
      SexCode  : char;              {Sex code field: f = female, m = male}
   end;   {EmployeeType}

   FileType = text;                 {Declare text as the file type}

var
   Count    : integer;              {Record count}
   Employee : EmployeeType;         {Employee record}
   FileVar  : FileType;             {File variable for data file}

   {========================= Procedure Declarations =======================}
```

SELF-REVIEW EXERCISES

9a

FIGURE 11.4 *(continued)*

```
procedure GetEmployee (var FileVar  : FileType;           Record variable as
                       var Employee : EmployeeType);       formal parameter

   { Reads an employee record from data file into record variable Employee
     Receives nothing
     Sends Employee }

begin   {GetEmployee}

  with Employee do
    begin
      readln (FileVar, SSN);
      readln (FileVar, FullName);
      readln (FileVar, Salary);
      readln (FileVar, SexCode);
    end;   {with}

end;    {GetEmployee}
{---------------------------------------------------------------------}
procedure OutputEmployee (Employee : EmployeeType);       Record variable as
                                                          formal parameter
   { Writes a single employee record to the screen
     Receives Employee
     Sends nothing }

begin   {OutputEmployee}

  with Employee do
    begin
      writeln ('  Name.................... ', FullName);
      writeln ('  Social Security Number... ', SSN);
      writeln ('  Sex..................... ', SexCode);
      writeln ('  Salary.................. $', Salary :8:2);
    end;   {with}

end;    {OutputEmployee}

  {============================ Main Body ============================}

begin   {Employ1}

  clrscr;
  writeln;  writeln (Title);  writeln;

  PrepFile (FileVar);                                      {In OurUnit}
  clrscr;

  Count := 0;
  while not eof (FileVar) do
    begin
      GetEmployee (FileVar, Employee);
      Count := Count + 1;                      Record variable as
      writeln;  writeln ('Employee #', Count);  actual parameter
      OutputEmployee (Employee);
      Pause;                                                {In OurUnit}
    end;   {while}

end.    {Employ1}
```

11.4   RECORDS AND ARRAYS

In the previous section we processed records from a data file by temporarily storing each record within the record variable Employee. In other words, primary memory always contained a single record. The multiple records only resided in the data file. In applications like searching and sorting, however, we need to store multiple records in primary memory. The *array* is one approach to holding multiple records in RAM.[5]

AS DATA STRUCTURES

The array is a data structure whose multiple values (elements) are referenced by indexes. The record is another data structure whose multiple values (fields) are referenced by field identifiers. What do we get if we combine these two by making each element in the array a record? Another data structure called an *array of records*.

ARRAY OF RECORDS

Take a look at Figure 11.5. Earlier we declared a data structure of record type CityRecType, with fields CityName and F. If we make each record in the record

FIGURE 11.5   Array-of-Records Data Structure CityArray

Index	CityName	F	
1	Los Angeles	62	← Array element 1 is the 1st record
2	Chicago	15	← Array element 2 is the 2nd record
3	Toronto	20	← Array element 3 is the 3rd record
4	Boston	32	← Array element 4 is the 4th record
5	Miami	68	← Array element 5 is the 5th record
.	.		
.	.		
.	.		
500			← Array element 500 is the 500th record (only the first 5 elements have values)

(Fields: CityName, F)

[5]In Chapter 13, we offer an alternative approach called a *linked list*.

data structure an element in the array data structure, then we have an **array of records.** CityArray in Figure 11.5 is an array of records. Each element in the array is a record having record type CityRecType. This means that each element in the array includes values for each of the two fields CityName and F. The array itself is indexed over the elements 1 . . 500, meaning that it can store up to 500 records.

The complete declaration for this array-of-records data structure is given by the following.

```
const
    LowerIndexLimit = 1;  UpperIndexLimit = 500;
    SizeStr = 20;

type
    IndexType    = LowerIndexLimit .. UpperIndexLimit;
```

                      ┌─ Record type
```
CityRecType = record
    CityName : string[SizeStr];    {City name field}
    F        : integer;            {Fahrenheit temperature field}
end;   {CityRecType}
```
                                          ┌─ Each element in array has this record type
         ┌─ Array of records type
```
ArrayOfCityRec  = array [IndexType] of CityRecType;

var
    CityArray  : ArrayOfCityRec;   {Array of city records}
```
                                  └─ Array of records type
         └─ Array of records

Note that the array of records CityArray is typed ArrayOfCityRec, whose declared elements have type CityRecType.

An array of records can be confusing when you're seeing it for the first time, so take a moment to relate these declarations to the data structure in Figure 11.5. Also, compare this figure to the *parallel data structure* in Figure 9.5. *The array-of-records data structure is an alternative to the parallel-array data structure!*

EXAMPLE 11.5   I/O OF ARRAY OF RECORDS

In Example 9.8, we showed the input and output of city names and temperatures as two parallel arrays. In the current example seen in Figures 11.6 and 11.7, we process the *same data file CITYTEMP.DAT* using a program that implements

---

FIGURE 11.6   I/O of Data File CITYTEMP.DAT by Program ArrayIO3

```
DEMO OF PROCEDURES THAT I/O ARRAY OF RECORDS

Enter data file (like A:\GRADES\HC101.DAT)... citytemp.dat

City array...

            Los Angeles              62
                Chicago              15
                Toronto              20
                 Boston              32
                  Miami              68
```

FIGURE 11.7   Listing for Program ArrayIO3

```pascal
program ArrayIO3;

  {* * * * * * * * * * * * * * * * * * * * * * * * * * * * * * * * * * *
   *                                                                   *
   *        Demo of Procedures GetCityArray and OutCityArray           *
   *                                                                   *
   *          Inputs city records from data file into array of records *
   *            named CityArray, w/ index check                        *
   *          Outputs CityArray                                        *
   *                                                                   *
   *          Modular structure                                        *
   *               |___  GetCityArray                                  *
   *               |    |___ IndexCk                                   *
   *               |___ OutCityArray                                   *
   *                                                                   *
   *          Sample data file:  CITYTEMP.DAT                          *
   *                                                                   *
   *          See file data structure below                            *
   *                                                                   *
   * * * * * * * * * * * * * * * * * * * * * * * * * * * * * * * * * * *}

  {=========================== Declarations ===========================}

uses crt, OurUnit;

const
  LowerIndexLimit = 1;  UpperIndexLimit = 500;
  SizeStr = 20;

  Title = 'DEMO OF PROCEDURES THAT I/O ARRAY OF RECORDS';

type
  IndexType   = LowerIndexLimit .. UpperIndexLimit;

  CityRecType = record
    CityName : string[SizeStr];     {City name field}
    F        : integer;             {Fahrenheit temperature field}
  end;   {CityRecType}

  ArrayOfCityRec  = array [IndexType] of CityRecType;

var
  CityArray  : ArrayOfCityRec;    {Array of city records}
  UpperIndex : IndexType;         {Index of last element entered}
  TextFile   : text;              {Text file variable for data file}

  {======================= Procedure Declarations =======================}
```

Key changes
from Array IO2
in Figure 9.7
shown in color

FIGURE 11.7   (*continued*)

```pascal
procedure GetCityArray (var TextFile : text;
                            LowerIndexLimit, UpperIndexLimit : IndexType;
                            var UpperIndex : IndexType;
                            var CityArray  : ArrayOfCityRec);

   Documentation and declarations go here; these are similar to GetTwoArrays
   in Figure 9.7

begin   {GetCityArray}

  {$R-  Disable range checking}

   Index := LowerIndexLimit;
   IndexCk (LowerIndexLimit, UpperIndexLimit, Index, RangeViolation);
   while (not eof (TextFile)) and (not RangeViolation) do
     begin
       with CityArray[Index] do
         begin
           readln ( TextFile, CityName );
           readln ( TextFile, F );
         end;   {with}
       Index := succ(Index);
       IndexCk (LowerIndexLimit, UpperIndexLimit, Index, RangeViolation);
     end; {while}
   UpperIndex := pred(Index);

   close (TextFile);

  {$R+  Enable range checking}

end;   {GetCityArray}
{-----------------------------------------------------------------------}
procedure OutCityArray (LowerIndex, UpperIndex : IndexType;
                            CityArray : ArrayOfCityRec);

   Documentation and declarations go here; these are similar to OutTwoArrays
   in Figure 9.7

begin   {OutCityArray}

  for Index := LowerIndex to UpperIndex do
    with CityArray[Index] do
      writeln ( CityName :20, F :20);

end;    {OutCityArray}

  {============================= Main Body =============================}

begin   {ArrayIO3}

  clrscr;
  writeln;  writeln (Title);  writeln;

  PrepFile (TextFile);                        {In OurUnit}

  GetCityArray (TextFile, LowerIndexLimit, UpperIndexLimit, UpperIndex,
                CityArray);

  writeln;  writeln ('City array... ');  writeln;

  OutCityArray (LowerIndexLimit, UpperIndex, CityArray);

end.    {ArrayIO3}
```

the array-of-records data structure described in Figure 11.5. You might want to place a marker at Figure 9.7 to compare it to Figure 11.7. Note the following.

1. Program ArrayIO3 is a revision of program ArrayIO2. Key editing changes are shown in color.

2. The first set of changes relates to our declarations for CityRecType, ArrayOfCityRec, and CityArray, as explained earlier.

3. In the input procedure, we changed (a) the procedure's name to GetCityArray and (b) the array parameter to CityArray having type ArrayOfCityRec. We also used a with statement to input the fields for each record from the data file. Note that CityArray[Index] stores a specific record in the element indexed on Index. For example, CityArray[1] stores the record for Ada Lovelace and CityArray[3] stores the record for Herman Hollerith.

4. In the output procedure, we changed (a) the procedure's name to OutCityArray and (b) the array parameter to CityArray having type ArrayOfCityRec. Within the for-do loop we used a with statement and changed the output list to the field names CityName and F.

5. In the main body, we changed the I/O calls to GetCityArray and OutCityArray and used CityArray as the array parameter. Note how the procedure calls demonstrate *top-down design* and *procedural abstraction*. For example, the call to GetCityArray gets us the entire array of city records. In coding this call, we don't have to be concerned about the field input details. Moreover, the use of CityArray in the parameter lists illustrates *data abstraction*. We need not bother ourselves at this time with the field details.

---

‡SORTING AND SEARCHING

In Module D we covered sorting and searching using arrays. In this section we extend the material to the sorting and searching of arrays of records. The programs, functions, and procedures that we developed in Module D are generic—that is, they are designed to handle arrays of any declared type. Arrays of records, however, require some minor adjustments because we need to explicitly consider fields in our sorts and searches. The best way to understand these changes is by way of examples. The next two examples are counterparts of the first two sorting and searching examples in Module D.

---

‡Optional, more advanced material. Module D is a prerequisite. Skip without loss of continuity, study at this point, or wait until later.

EXAMPLE 11.6   SORTING AN ARRAY OF RECORDS

In sorting an array of records, we first need to specify the **sort key** (**field**), that is, the field on which the sort is based. For example, we could sort CityArray in Figure 11.5 by either CityName or F. In this example, let's sort the array by city names. This means that CityName is our sort key. In Exercise 11 we ask you to sort by Fahrenheit temperatures.

The I/O in Figure 11.8 shows a sort of our city array by city names. Thus, Boston is now at the top of the list, followed by Chicago, and so on. The sort is performed by program CkSort2, the array of records counterpart to program CkSort in Figure D.3. We don't show a listing of CkSort2 because the two programs are very similar. The primary differences include:

1. ArrayType is now declared as ArrayOfCityRec, and ElementType is CityRecType. These declarations are consistent with the array-of-records data structure in Figure 11.5.

2. SortRec in Figure 11.9 is a new utility sort procedure, based on a revision of the utility sort procedure Sort in Figure D.4. Editing changes are shown in color. Note how little we had to change, which is a reflection of our generic design philosophy in developing the original sorting utility. The primary changes include:

   a. The incorporation of the *sort key*. InsertElement and A[Index] are now record variables, so we append the sort key CityName, giving the field refer-

---

FIGURE 11.8   I/O for Program CkSort2

```
SORT DEMO FOR ARRAY OF RECORDS

Enter data file (like A:\GRADES\HC101.DAT)... citytemp.dat

Unsorted city array...

            Los Angeles            62
               Chicago             15
               Toronto             20
                Boston             32
                 Miami             68

Sorted city array...

                Boston             32
               Chicago             15
            Los Angeles            62
                 Miami             68
               Toronto             20
```

FIGURE 11.9   Listing for Utility Procedure SortRec

```
                                                                    Key changes from
                                                                    procedure Sort
procedure SortRec (LowerIndex, UpperIndex : IndexType;  ◄─────      in Figure D.4
                   var A : ArrayType);                              shown in color

  { Utility performs ascending insertion sort on array of records over
       received indexes
    Receives LowerIndex, UpperIndex, unsorted A
    Sends sorted A }

  { NOTE:  The original array is changed!!!
           Preconditions assume LowerIndex and UpperIndex are within
               index limits, and LowerIndex <= UpperIndex
           Assumes IndexType, ArrayType, and ElementType are declared
               in calling module
           Array is sorted based on sort key field; revise Shift
               assignments to change sort key field  }

var
  OldLocation    : IndexType;    {Old location (index) of insert element}
  NewLocation    : IndexType;    {New location (index) of insert element}
  InsertElement  : ElementType;  {Current element being inserted}
  Index          : IndexType;    {Current index}
  LegitIndex     : Boolean;      {True if Index within range; else false}
  Shift          : Boolean;      {True if element needs to be moved over or
                                   shifted one position; else false}
```

ences InsertElement.CityName and A[Index].CityName in the statements that assign a Boolean value to Shift. We must modify these statements to change the sort key.

b. The generic assignment

```
        A[NewLocation] := InsertElement;
```

is unchanged from the original procedure, but note that in our current application this implements the assignment of two field values. In other words, we have an assignment of record variables, as first described in Example 11.2.

We have added SortRec to our utilities library. In Exercise 11, we ask you to check it out by test driving program CkSort2.

EXAMPLE 11.7   SEARCHING AN ARRAY OF RECORDS

In searching an array of records, we first need to specify the **search key (field)**, that is, the field on which the search is based. For example, we could search CityArray in Figure 11.5 by looking for either a specific city name or specific temperature. In this example, let's search the array for a specific temperature. This

FIGURE 11.9   (*continued*)

```
begin   {SortRec}

   for OldLocation := succ(LowerIndex) to UpperIndex do

      begin   {Insert element in its new location}

        {Copy insert element}
         InsertElement := A[OldLocation];

        {Move one position left to consider shift}
         Index := pred(OldLocation);

        {Initial index is legit}
         LegitIndex := true;

        {Determine if shift needed}
         Shift := InsertElement.CityName < A[Index].CityName;

        {NOTE:  Change field identifier in preceding statement to change
                sort key}

         while LegitIndex and Shift do

            begin   {Shift all elements that need shifting}

              {Shift element one position to right}
               A[succ(Index)] := A[Index];

              {Ensure predecessor index is within range}
               if Index > LowerIndex then
                 begin
                   {Move one position left to consider shift}
                    Index      := pred(Index);
                    LegitIndex := true;
                   end
                 else
                   LegitIndex := false;

              {Make sure index is legit before using it in indexed variable}
               if LegitIndex then
                 {Determine if shift needed}
                  Shift := InsertElement.CityName < A[Index].CityName;

                 {NOTE:  Change field identifier in preceding statement to change
                         sort key}

            end;   {while... We are through shifting}

        {Place insert element in its new location}
         if LegitIndex
           then NewLocation := succ(Index)
           else NewLocation := Index;
         A[NewLocation] := InsertElement;

      end;   {for... All elements have been inserted}

end;   {SortRec}
{------------------------------------------------------------------------}
```

means that F is our search key. In Exercise 12 we ask you to search for specific city names.

The I/O in Figure 11.10 shows searches for temperatures of 32 and 5. Note that when a temperature is found, the name of the corresponding city is displayed. These searches were carried out by program CkFind3, the array-of-records counterpart to program CkFind1 in Module D. Key differences include the following.

1. We declared SearchKeyType as *integer*, the type for temperatures. The variable that contains the search value is SearchVal, which is typed SearchKeyType.

2. Function SearchRec in Figure 11.11 is a revision of utility function SearchIndex in Figure D.5. The primary editing changes are in color; they revolve around our need to incorporate a *search key*. Thus, in the if-test we replaced the original array element A[Index] with the search key SearchKey. We also replaced the original SearchElement with SearchVal. The comparison now is between the value in SearchKey and the value in SearchVal. Note that SearchKey is assigned A[Index].F because we are searching for Fahrenheit temperatures. In our first sample run in Figure 11.10, SearchVal stores 32. The first compari-

---

FIGURE 11.10   I/O for Program CkFind3

```
SEARCH DEMO FOR ARRAY OF RECORDS

Enter data file (like A:\GRADES\HC101.DAT)... citytemp.dat

City array...

          Los Angeles               62
             Chicago                 15
             Toronto                 20
              Boston                 32
               Miami                 68

Enter search value ===> 32

  32 found in Boston


SEARCH DEMO FOR ARRAY OF RECORDS

Enter data file (like A:\GRADES\HC101.DAT)... citytemp.dat

City array...

          Los Angeles               62
             Chicago                 15
             Toronto                 20
              Boston                 32
               Miami                 68

Enter search value ===> 5

  5 NOT found
```

FIGURE 11.11 Listing for Utility Function SearchRec

```
function SearchRec (SearchVal : SearchKeyType;
                    LowerIndex, UpperIndex : IndexType;        ◀━━  Key changes
                    A : ArrayType ) : IndexTypeX;                   from function
  { Utility function searches for search element in array using       SearchIndex
      sequential search algorithm                                     in Figure D.5
    Receives SearchVal, LowerIndex, UpperIndex, A                     shown in color
    Returns either index that corresponds to record that contains search
        value (if search value found) or index that is one position less
        than lower index (if not found) }

  { NOTE:   Preconditions assume LowerIndex and UpperIndex are within
              index limits, and LowerIndex <= UpperIndex
            Assumes SearchKeyType, IndexType, ArrayType, and IndexTypeX
              are declared in calling module
            IndexTypeX is the same as IndexType, except lower limit in
              index range is eXtended one position left
            Assign proper search key field in SearchKey assignment }

var
  Found    : Boolean;        {True if search element found; else false}
  Index    : IndexType;      {Index of array element}
  SearchKey : SearchKeyType; {Search key field}

begin  {SearchRec}

  Found := false;          {Search element not found at this point}
  Index := LowerIndex;     {Start search at lower index}

  while (not Found) and (Index <= UpperIndex) do
    begin
      SearchKey := A[Index].F;                {Assign proper search key field}
      if SearchKey = SearchVal
        then Found := true                    {Found search value}
        else Index := succ(Index);            {Go on to next element}
    end;  {while}

  if Found
    then SearchRec := Index
    else SearchRec := pred(LowerIndex);

end;    {SearchRec}
{-----------------------------------------------------------------------}
```

son is 32 against the first value in SearchKey, or 62. This gives a false Boolean value, so the next comparison is between 32 and the next value 15 in SearchKey. Again the result is false, so comparisons continue with subsequent field values in F for succeeding records. A look at the array output shows that the search value was found at the 4th index. Thus, the function returns 4 in SearchRec. In plain English, we found the temperature 32 in the 4th record, or that for Boston.

3. In the main body we now output not the index that was found, but the city name that corresponds to the array element (record) that was found. In our sample run, IndexFound stores 4, so we output Boston, or CityArray[IndexFound].CityName.

4. What we have here is a *table-lookup* problem, as described in Section D.2. In Exercise 13 we ask you to adapt this program to the table-lookup approach taken in Module D.

We have added function SearchRec to our utilities library. In Exercise 12 we ask you to try it out by running program CkFind3.

SELF-REVIEW EXERCISES

10a 11a 12a

---

‡11.5   MORE COMPLEX RECORDS

• • • • • • • • • • • • • •

In this section we consider two common record-structure variations.

- *Hierarchical records* have one or more fields that are themselves records.
- *Variant records* have different fields from one another.

HIERARCHICAL RECORDS

A **nested** or **hierarchical record** includes other records within its record data structure. Put another way, one or more fields of a hierarchical record is itself a record. For example, we could declare a home address field in an employee record as a home address record having four fields: street address, city name, state abbreviation, and postal zip code.

It's a tribute to Pascal's typing capabilities that we don't need to learn any new syntax in declaring hierarchical records. We simply extend what we already know, as we demonstrate next.

---

‡Optional, more advanced material. Skip without loss of continuity, study at this point, or wait until later.

EXAMPLE 11.8   EMPLOYEE RECORD AS A HIERARCHICAL RECORD

Let's return to our employee record example by considering a new field named HomeAddress that is itself a record of four other fields: Street, City, State, and Zip. We now revise our earlier declarations of type EmployeeType and record variable Employee on page 520 to declare the following hierarchical employee record.

```
type
  AddressType  = record
    Street    : string[25];        {Number and street name field}
    City      : string[15];        {City name field}
    State     : string[2];         {State abbreviation field}
    Zip       : string[10];        {Postal Zip code field}
  end;   {AddressType}

  EmployeeType = record
    SSN          : string[11];     {Social security number field}
    FullName     : string[25];     {Full-name field}
    Salary       : real;           {Annual salary field}
    SexCode      : char;           {Sex code field: f = female, m = male}
    HomeAddress : AddressType;     {Home address field as record}
  end;   {EmployeeType}
```

— Field *HomeAddress* is a record typed *AddressType*

```
var
  Employee : EmployeeType;         {Employee hierarchical record}
```

Note the following.

1. AddressType is a new record type with the declared fields Street, City, State, and Zip.

2. HomeAddress is a new field in record type EmployeeType. Its type is AddressType, another record type. Thus, EmployeeType is a hierarchical record type because one of its fields is typed as a record.

3. The record variable Employee is a hierarchical record variable because its type is EmployeeType, a hierarchical record type.

Figure 11.12 shows a picture of Employee's record structure in the form of a *hierarchical* or *tree diagram* having *branches* and *nodes*. Note the following.

1. Figure 11.12 is the counterpart of Figure 11.1.

2. Each field is a *node* in the tree.

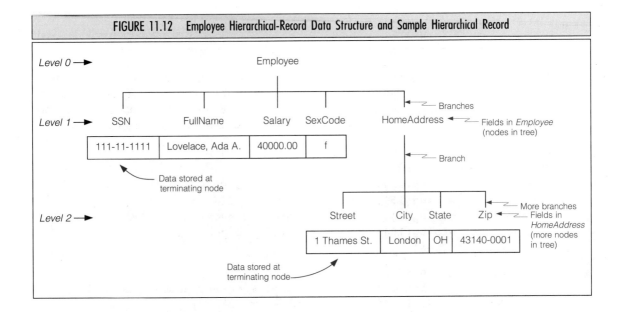

FIGURE 11.12   Employee Hierarchical-Record Data Structure and Sample Hierarchical Record

3. Each field declared in EmployeeType is at the first hierarchy level in the tree. Each field declared in AddressType is at the second hierarchy level in the tree.

4. Additional hierarchy levels are possible. For example, we could declare field Street as a record with three fields: street number, street name, and apartment number (see Exercise 16e).

5. Each *branch* terminates in a *terminating node*. Data are stored in the terminating nodes. This means that any field reference must describe a path to the terminating node, as we will see next.

As usual, we can reference fields either by appending field variables to record variables or by using a with statement. For example, to write the contents in Street we could use the statement

```
writeln (Employee.HomeAddress.Street);
```

Note how the field reference Employee.HomeAddress.Street describes a path in the tree that runs from the top of the diagram (Employee) through intermediate node HomeAddress to terminating node Street.

In applying the with statement, we could write either

```
with Employee.HomeAddress do
   writeln (Street);
```

or

```
with Employee do
  with HomeAddress do
    writeln (Street);
```

In Exercise 17 we ask you to revise program Employ1 in Figure 11.4 to process employee hierarchical records. In Exercise 16 we ask you to consider some new fields that describe other records.

Variant Records

Up to now, all records of a given type have had identical fields. In many applications it's useful to vary the number of fields and their types. For example, we might replace the salary field in the employee record with either a field that includes the salary for salaried employees or a set of fields that includes pay rate and other attributes for hourly employees.

A **variant record** is a record that's declared with a fixed part and a variant part. The *fixed part* of a variant-record type describes a list of fixed fields that are common to all records of this type. For example, the fixed part of an employee record might include the fields SSN, FullName, SexCode, and PayCode. This means that values for these fields are provided for all employees. The *variant part* of a variant record includes alternative sets of fields called *variants,* where each variant is a unique set of fields. For instance, the variant part of an employee record might include two variants, depending on whether the employee is salaried (paycode S) or hourly (paycode H). The salaried variant might just be the Salary field we used earlier; the hourly variant might include the following fields: Payrate and Scale. PayRate is a field for the hourly pay rate and Scale might be a number in the range 1..4 that's used as a basis for setting the number of regular hours in a week and the overtime-pay multiplier. For example, a scale of 1 might mean that this employee works a 40-hour week and gets paid time-and-a-half for overtime hours. An employee whose scale is 2, however, might only work 38-hour weeks and get paid for overtime hours at 1.75 times his or her regular hourly rate.

Figure 11.13 illustrates the variant-record data structure for Employee variant records. Note the following.

1. The *fixed part* of record Employee is made up of the fields SSN, FullName, SexCode, and PayCode. This means that every employee's record includes these four fields.

2. The *variant part* of record Employee is preceded by a special fixed field called the *tag field* that tags or identifies the fields in the remainder of the record. We use the identifier PayCode for the tag field in this ex-

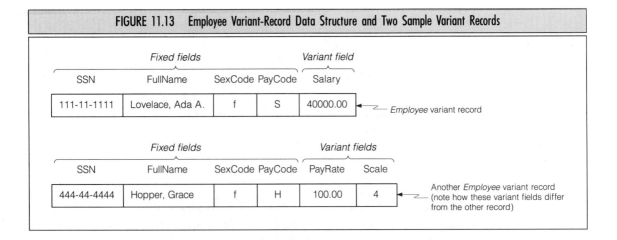

FIGURE 11.13   Employee Variant-Record Data Structure and Two Sample Variant Records

ample. If its value is the character S, then the employee is a salaried employee and the remaining field in the record is the Salary field, as seen in our first sample variant record. In our second sample variant record, a pay code of H indicates an hourly employee, giving PayRate and Scale as the concluding fields in this record.

To declare the variant-record structure described in Figure 11.13, consider the accompanying syntax box. Note the following.

1. The example in the syntax box declares the variant-record structure illustrated in Figure 11.13. Take a moment to relate the fixed-field and variant-field declarations to the sample records in the figure.
2. The *tag field* PayCode is a fixed field, although it's declared in the case line at the beginning of the variant part. Note how the documentation in the example clearly shows the fixed and variant fields.
3. The tag field necessarily precedes the variant fields, since the tag field is a fixed field. When reading a record, the value in the tag field must be read before any values in variant fields, because the tag-field value determines how the variant part of the record is to be read. We illustrate this next.

EXAMPLE 11.9   READING AN EMPLOYEE VARIANT RECORD

The following code fragment reads an Employee variant record whose structure is described in Figure 11.13 and declared in the syntax box. We assume that records are stored in a text file.

SYNTAX BOX

Record type and variable declarations for variant records... Declare record
type in type section and record variable in var section

Syntax.......**type**
       RecordType **= record**

              Field1Identifier : Field1Type;
              Field2Identifier : Field2Type;
               .
               . } Other *fixed-field* declarations
               .

→ *Fixed part*

This is a fixed-field declaration
(for the tag field)

             case TagFieldIdentifier : TagFieldType **of**
               TagFieldValue1 : (FieldList1);
               TagFieldValue2 : (FieldList2);
               .
               . } Other *variant-field* declarations
               .

→ *Variant part*

          end;

         var
            RecordVariable : RecordType;

Examples....**type**
         ScaleType = 1 .. 4;
         EmployeeType **= record**   {Fixed fields}
           SSN   : **string**[11];   {Social security number field}
           FullName : **string**[25];   {Full name field}
           SexCode : **char**;   {Sex code field: f = female, m = male}
           case PayCode : char **of**   {Pay code field: S = Salaried, H = hourly}
                                 {Variant fields}
             'S' : (Salary : real);   {Annual salary field}
             'H' : (PayRate : real;   {Hourly pay rate}
                  Scale : ScaleType); {Work scale 1 .. 4}
          end; {EmployeeType}
         var
           Employee : EmployeeType;   {Employee variant record}

Explanation... The *fixed part* is identical to that described for simple records on page 520. The *variant part* begins like a case statement, where the selector is an identifier for the tag field, TagFieldIdentifier. TagFieldType is the
type of the tag field, which must be an *ordinal type*. TagFieldValue is a unique constant that's compatible with tag-
field type. Each "case" represents a *variant-field list*. At run time, the tag-field value activates the proper variant-
field list. Each FieldList is a list of paired field identifiers and field types separated by a colon. Multiple field
declarations in the field list are separated by semicolons. Field identifiers must be unique. A single **end** reserved
word ends the declaration (a matching **end** for **case** is not used). A variant-field list that has no fields is denoted by
an empty set of parentheses.

```
with Employee do
  begin
   {Read fixed fields}
    readln (FileVar, SSN);
    readln (FileVar, FullName);
    readln (FileVar, SexCode);
    readln (FileVar, PayCode);
    PayCode := upcase (PayCode);
   {Read variant fields}
    case PayCode of
      {Salaried} 'S' : readln (FileVar, Salary);
      {Hourly}   'H' : begin
                         readln (FileVar, PayRate);
                         readln (FileVar, Scale);
                       end;   {Hourly}
    else  {Error in PayCode}
       writeln ('Error in pay code for employee ', FullName);
       halt;
    end;   {case}
  end;   {with}
```

Note that the input of the variant fields is dependent on the value in the tag field PayCode. If PayCode stores S or s, we only read in the Salary field from the remainder of the record (see the first record in Figure 11.13). If PayCode stores H or h, we read in values into fields PayRate and Scale from the remainder of the record (see the second record in Figure 11.13). If the value in the pay-code field is not legitimate, the case structure writes the indicated error message to identify the record that needs to be corrected, and halts execution.

In Exercise 19 we ask you to read in these records for real.[6]

NOTE

4. Tag-field reminders. The tag-field value needs to precede variant-field values in the record; otherwise we can't determine how to read the variant part of the record. In processing a variant record we need a selection structure to properly route input of the variant fields based on the value in the tag field. As seen in Example 11.9, the case structure is convenient and readily provides an error routine if we should process an inadmissible tag-field value. We also could have used an else-if structure in Example 11.9 (but not in the syntax box!).

---

[6]Continuing our little history lesson, *Grace Hopper* (our second record in Figure 11.13) was a captain in the U.S. Navy. She was a prime mover behind the development of the COBOL programming language from the 1950s through the 1970s. She is also credited by some with coining the term *bug* (see footnote 5 in Chapter 1).

SELF-REVIEW EXERCISES

16a–b 18

11.6 PROGRAMMING TIPS

• • • • • • • • • • • • • • •

Consider the following tips to improve the design and style of your programs and to avoid some common errors.

DESIGN AND STYLE

1. Literacy. Keep on spacing and documenting. Note how our record-type declarations indent, align, and document fields; otherwise, these declarations can be messy, especially for complex records. Picture the declaration in the syntax box on page 547 without these considerations.

2. Get Abstract. The record variable is a great variable for practicing *data abstraction.* Procedures for reading and writing records illustrate *procedural abstraction.* Putting these together in an *ADT unit* gives us the highest expression of these concepts.

3. Data-Structure Selection. Up to now we have formally treated set, array, and record data structures. Not only do we have variations within each data-structure type, but we can also embed one or more data structures within others. For example, as illustrated in this chapter, we can type elements in an array as records, giving us an array-of-records data structure. Fields within a record can be other structured types, like records (giving hierarchical records), sets (giving records of sets), or arrays (giving records of arrays). These data-structure variations illustrate the flexible and powerful typing features in Pascal. Beginning programmers, however, might think it's too much of a good thing, since it does complicate matters. The choice of a data structure very much affects the literacy, simplicity, elegance, and efficiency of a program. The final choice of the "best" data structure depends on the nature of the data, how we need to operate on the data, and "art" that comes from experience. Here are some rough guidelines for our primary material in this chapter.

  a. Generic records that include mixed data types are best processed by record variables, as opposed to simple variables that represent fields. In our first employee example, we used record variable Employee with declared fields SSN, FullName, Salary, and SexCode. This gives us the benefit of data abstraction; that is, we can conceptualize the record as a whole, an entity, which simplifies parameter passing and record assignments. We would not have these benefits if we had bypassed record typing and used the simple variables SSN, FullName, Salary, and SexCode.

b. If operations on the data require array types (like in sorting), we have some choices. If the data are homogeneous with respect to data type and attribute (as in a table of exam grades where rows represent students and columns represent exams), a two-dimensional array is best. If we include student name, ID, and other mixed-type attributes for each record, an array of records is more intuitive than parallel arrays (and gives us better data abstraction to boot). On the other hand, if we need to carry out extensive statistical manipulations on both columns (exams) and rows (students), it may be best to treat the grades as a two-dimensional array of just grades; otherwise, the manipulation of declared fields within records would be awkward.

COMMON ERRORS

1. Incorrect Field Reference.   This is probably the most common error when working with records. Remember that field variables are not referenced like other simple variables, unless they are within the influence of a with statement. For example, the employee record field reference SSN in the output statement

```
writeln (SSN);  ☹
```

would provoke an *Unknown identifier* compile-time error message. We would have to rewrite this as

```
writeln (Employee.SSN);  ☺
```

Within a with statement, however, we would use the field reference SSN.

```
with Employee do
  begin
    writeln (SSN);  ☺
    ...
  end;   {with}
```

2. Incorrect Record Variable Reference.   Remember that a record variable like Employee is referenced by itself only to the right of the reserved word *with*, as a parameter, or in a record-variable assignment. We can't simply, say, input a record from the keyboard using

```
readln (Employee);  ☹
```

The compiler would display the error message *Cannot Read or Write variables of this type.* We have to input each field individually using appropriate field references.

3. Tag-Field Mismanagement.   Forgetting the tag field in a variant record and not accounting for incorrect tag values in processing variant records have unpredictable results. Reread Note 4.

REVIEW EXERCISES

EASIER	For the busy...
	1 2a–b 3a 4a 6 7 8a 9a 10a 11a 12a 18 20b
NORMAL	For the thinkers...
	2c–e 3b 4b–c 5a–b 8b 9b–c 10b 11b 12b 16 17 19
TOUGHER	For the hard CORE...
	5c 9d 13 14 15 20c

1. State a record layout for the City record in the syntax box on page 520.

2. Alter the declarations in the syntax box on page 520 as follows.
   a. Add field Age to record Employee. Its type is the integer subrange $18 .. 72$.
   b. Add field Population to record City. Its type is long integer.
   c. Add field Region with type RegionType to record City. The legitimate regions are NorthEast, SouthEast, MidWest, SouthWest, NorthWest.
   *d. Add field Dept to record Employee. Its type DeptType is the *set* of enumerated Departments (Accounting, Advertising, Sales, Engineering, Production).
   *e. Add field Rating to record Employee. Its type RatingType is the array of integer subranges $1 .. 10$ over the index values given by the integer subrange of years $1950 .. 2000$.

3. Code the declarations for Student records having the given record layout. Use StudentType for the record type.
   a. Use the record layout in Table 11.2.
   b. Modify the record layout in Table 11.2 so that the three name fields are the fields in a NameType record. These fields are replaced by field Name in StudentType.

Table 11.2   **Record Layout for Student Record**

Field Identifier	Field Type	Description
LastName	**string**[20]	Last Name
FirstName	**string**[15]	First Name
MiddleInitial	**char**	Middle initial
SSN	**string**[11]	Social security number, with dashes
AreaCode	**integer**	Telephone area code
Phone	**string**[8]	Telephone number, with dash

4. Revise Example 11.1 to...
    a. Input the field in Exercise 2a.
    *b. Add a loop that terminates with a blank sentinel for **SSN**.
    *c. Include range-error handling for **Age** (from part **a**).

*5. Write code that interactively inputs the **City** record that's described in...
    a. The syntax box on page 520.
    b. Exercise 2b.
    c. Exercise 2c.

6. In Example 11.2, could we use a with statement in the first set of assignments? Why or why not?

7. State the problem (if any) for the following assignments, where **Employee** and **City** records are declared on page 520.
    a. `Employee := City;`
    b. `Employee.FullName := City.CityName;`

8. Revise the code in Example 11.3 to...
    a. Write the employee's full name if both a desired sex code is matched and the employee's salary exceeds the average salary (AveSalary).
    *b. Include the output of salary on a separate line from the name. Try two versions: One with a with statement and one without. Which approach do you like best?

(L) 9. Regarding Example 11.4...
    a. Run program Employ1 to duplicate our run in Figure 11.3.
    *b. Use the debugger to implement single-step tracing while you watch the value in Employee in the Watch window.
    *c. Revise the program to display a report of average salaries for males and females.
    *d. Revise the program to I/O a flat data-file structure. Place an entire record on a line in the revised data file.
    Likewise, output the records in a table format.

(L) 10. Regarding Example 11.5...
    a. Run program ArrayIO3 to duplicate our run in Figure 11.6.
    *b. Revise the program to display average temperature.

(L) 11. Regarding Example 11.6...
    a. Run program CkSort2 to duplicate our run in Figure 11.8.
    *b. Revise the program to sort the array by temperature.

(L) 12. Regarding Example 11.7...
    a. Run program CkFind3 to duplicate our run in Figure 11.10. Also search for a temperature of 68.
    *b. Revise the program to search for city names. In your test runs, search for Toronto and Montreal.

(L) *13. **Table lookup.** Revise CkFind3 by using code from Lookup in Figure D.9 to develop a program that duplicates our run in Figure D.8.

(L) *14. **Employee suite of programs.** Develop the following programs for our employee example. In all cases, use the employee data file EMPLOYEE.DAT. Edit and merge programs Employ1, ArrayIO3, CkSort2, and CkFind3 from this chapter as you see fit. Also see program Lookup in Module D.
   a. I/O the employee data file as an array of records (see Example 11.5).
   b. Sort employee records by full name (see Example 11.6).
   c. Lookup employees by social security number. When a record is found, display all fields in the record (see Example 11.7 and Figures D.8 and D.9).

(L) *15. **Binary search.** Develop a program that uses the binary-search algorithm (Figure D.7) to search the array of records in Example 11.7. Adapt and merge existing programs as you see fit. Use Figure 11.10 as the basis for your test run.

16. Revise the data-structure declarations in Example 11.8 as indicated.
   a. Include field **WorkAddress** having type **AddressType**.
   b. Include field **Telephone** as a record with fields **Home** and **Work**. Its record type is **TelType** and each field is a string of 12 characters. How does this change Figure 11.12?
   *c. Include record fields **BirthDate** and **HireDate**. These are typed **DateType**, with three declared fields: **Month** (1..12), **Day** (1..31), and **Year** (1900..1999).
   *d. Same as the preceding part, except declare the month field as the enumerated type given by the first three letters of each month. Discuss the pros and cons of this approach versus the former.
   *e. Declare **Street** as a record with three fields: integer **StreetNum**, 25-character string **StreetName**, and 5-character string **AptNum**. Also, revise the tree in Figure 11.12. How many levels are in the revised tree diagram?

(L) *17. **Hierarchical records I/O.** Revise program Employ1 and data file EMPLOYEE.DAT in Example 11.4 to I/O the hierarchical record data structure described in Example 11.8. Make up your own home addresses for the Babbage and Hollerith records.

18. Revise the variant-record data-structure declarations in the syntax box on page 547 to...
   a. Add the real field **BonusPercent** to salaried employees.
   b. Add a new variant field for temporary employees (PayCode T) with a field list having the real field **TempPayRate** and the 40-character string field **Agency**.

(L) *19. **Variant-records I/O.** Revise program Employ1 and data file EMPLOYEE.DAT in Example 11.4 to I/O the variant-record data structure described in Example 11.9. Include the Hopper record in the data file.

*20.   **Hierarchical/variant-records I/O.** Go for broke and...

   a. Construct a tree diagram that combines the record data structures in Figures 11.12 and 11.13. Assume that PayCode and the variant fields follow field HomeAddress.

   b. Come up with the punch line for a joke that goes something like "What do you get if you mate a hierarchical record and a variant record?" Communicate your punch line to Harvey CORE at the address given on page 118. If he likes it, you might win a prize...

   c. Revise data file EMPLOYEE.DAT and program Employ1 to I/O this hybrid-record data structure.

ADDITIONAL EXERCISES

EASIER	For the busy... **21**
NORMAL	For the thinkers... **22 24 25**
TOUGHER	For the hard CORE... **23 26**

21.   **Revisits.** Revise one of the following exercises by declaring an appropriate record type and reading records from a data file.
   a. Bates Motel. See end of Chapters 4 and 5.
   b. Mutual funds. See end of Chapter 5.
   c. Police car replacement. See end of Chapters 5 and 6.
   d. SAT report. See end of Chapters 6 and 7.

22.   **Revisits.** Use an array of records in...
   a. Crime story. See end of Chapter 9.
   b. Stock portfolio. See end of Chapter 9.

23.   **Revisit: Dating service.** Use records for this exercise at the end of Module D.

24.   **ADT Employee.** Incorporate an ADT Employee in a unit for processing employee records. New procedures in ADTEmployee for operations on this

record type include **GetEmployee, OutputEmployee, SortEmployeeName,** and **SortEmployeeSSN.** Two new functions include **AveSalary** (returns average salary for received sex code) and **SexCount** (returns count for received sex code). Test this ADT by writing a driver that displays a report that includes the original records, records sorted by name, records sorted by SSN, average salaries by gender, and counts by gender. Use the employee type declared on page 520. In your first test run, use the data file shown on page 527. Include another test run with seven more records (make up your own records) in addition to the original three.

25. **Alumni-file query.** The director of a graduate program wants to compute average salaries of alumni to include in a brochure of past graduates. The director collected the following data on students: name, year graduated, salary on first job after graduation, and prior work experience (Y or N).

Alumni File

Name	Year of Graduation	Salary	Work Experience
Dewey, A.	90	39000	Y
Epcot, B.	91	53000	Y
Farmer, C.	91	0	N
Garner, D.	90	34500	N
Hu, E.	91	40000	N
Jackson, F.	91	44000	Y
Kelley, G.	90	42500	Y
Moon, H.	91	33000	N
Rodriguez, I.	91	0	Y
Silver, J.	91	36000	N
Teller, K.	91	37500	Y

a. Develop an interactive query program that computes and displays the average salary for all alumni in a specified graduating year. (*Note:* Not all alumni have submitted salary data; to be part of the average salary computation the salary amount must be greater than 0.) The only interactive input variable is the specified graduating year. Use 90 and 91 as input test data. Use an appropriate record type.

b. For graduates of the specified year, also compute and display separate average salaries by work experience versus no work experience.

c. If salary data are unavailable for a given year, write a message to that effect. Use 88 as test input.

d. Offer the following main menu.

D	Display file
R	Report for given year
X	eXit program

e. Add the following main menu item.

S   display Sorted file

when S is selected, display the following Submenu

Sort by...

N   Name
S   Salary
W   Work experience
Y   Year of graduation
X   eXit to main menu

26. **Airline reservation system.** All major airlines have automated their systems for handling seat reservations. A central computer keeps a record in storage of all relevant information describing the services being sold: flight numbers, flight schedules, seats available, prices, and other data.

A reservation agent can request information on seat availability, can sell seats to passengers (provided seats are available), can cancel reservations (which increases available seats), and, if a flight is full, can put individuals on a waiting list.

Place the data in Table 11.3 in a data file and develop an interactive program that accomplishes the following.

a. Read the table of flight information into an array of records and offer the following menu options.

1. Update the flight information table. For example, if a customer requests one tourist reservation on flight number 4, the program should check

Table 11.3   Current Table of Flight Information

Flight Number	Departing Airport	Arriving Airport	Time of Departure	Time of Arrival	Available Seats First Class	Available Seats Tourist	Seats Sold First Class	Seats Sold Tourist
1	BOS	CHI	0730	0855	20	8	10	75
2	BOS	CHI	1200	1357	20	20	10	50
3	BOS	TOR	0810	1111	30	10	0	120
4	ATL	SF	1145	1604	15	1	25	129
5	CHI	BOS	0645	0948	30	25	5	90
6	CHI	NY	0945	1237	30	8	0	120
7	CHI	LA	1530	1851	20	10	30	60
8	CHI	TOR	1955	2114	5	5	25	85
9	TOR	DEN	1025	1611	10	6	60	60
10	TOR	SF	1435	1556	20	10	10	89

for available tourist seats. Since one is available, it should then adjust the available tourist seats to zero and display a message such as RESERVATION ALLOWED. If the passenger had requested two seats, however, the program should display RESERVATION DISALLOWED. SORRY, OUR HIGH ETHICAL STANDARDS DO NOT PERMIT US TO OVERBOOK.

2. Retrieve status on a particular flight by displaying the appropriate row in the flight information table.

3. Display entire flight information table.

4. Terminate the run.

Interactively process the following requests in your test run.

Option Request	Flight Number	Seat Type	Number of Tickets	Reservation Request
1	4	Tourist	1	Reserve
1	6	Tourist	4	Reserve
2	3	—	—	—
1	9	Tourist	2	Reserve
1	8	1st Class	6	Cancel
1	4	Tourist	2	Reserve
3	—	—	—	—

b. Besides the options in part **a,** give your program the capability to retrieve and display flight information on all flights between two specified airports. Test your program for flights from Boston to Chicago and Chicago to Los Angeles. In the first case, you should get a display of the first two rows; in the second case, the seventh row should be displayed.

MORE FILE PROCESSING

‡Optional, more advanced material. Skip without loss of continuity, study at this point, or wait until later.

Up to now we have used *text files* to read data from data files that reside on disk. In this chapter, we expand the treatment of files to include other file types besides text, calls to predeclared file functions and procedures, both reading from and writing to files, different methods for accessing and querying files, file-maintenance procedures for modifying files, and applications that process more than one file. These tasks are enormously important in actual computing environments.

12.1 ON FILES

A **file** is a named collection of data elements; it typically resides in an external storage medium such as a disk.[1] We can classify files in different ways, depending on their function and data type. A file whose function is to store a program is a *program file;* one whose function is to store data is a *data file.* We usually take the term *file* to mean "data file." Another important classification is by the data type of each component (data element) in the file, as we see next.

TEXT VERSUS TYPED FILES

A **text file** is a sequence of characters organized into lines, where each line ends with a hidden *end-of-line marker.* The end-of-line marker in Turbo Pascal is issued by the *Enter key* as a CarriageReturn control code (ASCII 13).

Text files are often called *ASCII files,* because their display shows recognizable text as ASCII characters. Text files are one of the standard file types. It's the only type of file we have used up to now. In fact, all of our Turbo Pascal program files (those whose names have .*PAS* extensions) and data files (.*DAT* extensions) have been text files. Any file created with the IDE's editor is a text file.

A **typed file** is a file whose data elements or *components* have a declared data type. For example, a typed file might have all integer type components, or all real type components, or all record type components, and so on.

Figure 12.1 shows the file data structures for text and typed files. Note that each component in a typed file has an associated **component number.**

---

[1]Operating systems also consider devices such as the keyboard and monitor as files. In addition, files can reside in a portion of primary memory that's set aside as a RAM "disk."

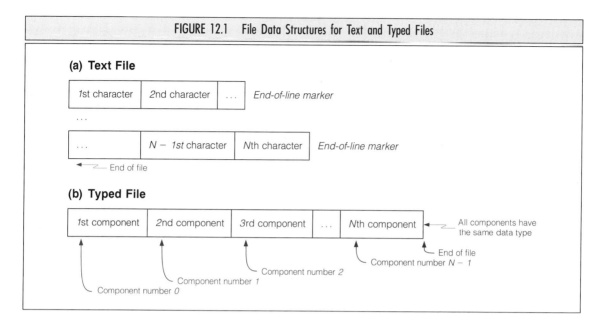

FIGURE 12.1   File Data Structures for Text and Typed Files

(a) Text File

| 1st character | 2nd character | ... | End-of-line marker |

| ... | N − 1st character | Nth character | End-of-line marker |

End of file

(b) Typed File

| 1st component | 2nd component | 3rd component | ... | Nth component | All components have the same data type |

Component number 0
Component number 1
Component number 2
Component number N − 1
End of file

Component numbers are integer values that *start at zero* and increment by one for each component in the file. The **file size** is the number of components. Thus, if the file size is N components, then component numbers run over the range *0..N − 1*. For example, a typed file with three components (N = 3) has component numbers 0, 1, and 2 (not 1, 2, and 3!). Component numbers play an important role in locating components within typed files, as we will see.

In practice, typed files are more widely used than text files. Why? Typed files usually process faster and take up less storage than equivalent text files. The storage of a noncharacter data element (for example, a real or integer value) in a text file requires a conversion from its binary representation to its character-string representation; its retrieval requires a conversion from a character-string representation to a binary-coded representation. For example, an integer component like 1942 takes up two bytes in the binary storage within a typed file, but five bytes in a text file as the character string ' 1942' (one byte for the sign and four bytes for the four digits).

Up to now, all of our data files have been text files, and we used *.DAT* extensions in their file names. In this chapter, we can create data files as either text files or typed files. To make this distinction, we will use a *.TXT* extension for text data files and a *.BIN* (for BINary) extension when naming typed data files. Our focus in this chapter is primarily on the declaration, creation, and processing of data files as typed files.

In contrast to the situation with text files, we can't enter data into a typed file using an editor or wordprocessor. Instead, we have to write a program or procedure that writes to the typed file, as we will see in Section 12.2.

SEQUENTIAL ACCESS VERSUS DIRECT ACCESS

By *processing* a file, we mean that we need to read data from or write data to the file. We can access a file for processing either *sequentially* or *directly*.

Sequential access of a file means that we process the file's components in the order of their occurrence. For example, if an employee file contains 1000 records, we can access the 900th record only after processing the first 899 records. Sequential access is analogous to the way we access musical cuts in a cassette tape. To listen to the fifth cut, we have to process past the first four cuts.

Direct access of a file means that we can directly access the component of interest without having to access any other components. For instance, if we wish to access the 900th employee record, we can go directly to that record without having to process the previous 899 records. The *component number 899* would be used to directly access the 900th record. Continuing our musical analogy, we can directly access the fifth musical cut without having to process the first four cuts if we're using a compact disc player.

The kind of file we create has implications for allowable access methods. We can access typed files either sequentially or directly. We can access text files only sequentially. *The ability to access typed files either sequentially or directly is another advantage of typed files over text files,* as we will see.

Allowable access methods depend not only on file type but also on secondary storage media. For example, a file stored on magnetic tape is accessible only by sequential methods; a file stored on magnetic disk is accessible by either sequential or direct methods.

FILE TYPES AND VARIABLES

The accompanying syntax box shows the declaration of typed files. Note the following.

1. The **file type** is a structured type that describes a file whose components are all of a single data type. The examples show two different file types: FileCharType is a file type whose components are type character; FileEmployeeType is a file type whose components are records of type EmployeeType.[2] The predeclared procedures and functions in the next section describe the operations allowed on file types.

2. The only restriction on the typing of file components is that the component type cannot include another file type. The examples show two very common component types: type *character* and type *record*. Other common component types include types *integer*, *real*, and *string*. Besides record types, another common component structured type is the *array* type.

---

[2]You might recall that we used this employee record type as a key example in Chapter 11.

SYNTAX BOX

File type and file variable declarations for typed files... Declare file type in type section and file variable in var section

Syntax ....type

```
FileType = file of ComponentType;

var

    FileVar : FileType;
```

Examples......type

```
FileCharType = file of char;          {File type with character components}

EmployeeType = record
    SSN      : string[11];            {Social security number field}
    FullName : string[25];            {Full name field}
    Salary   : real;                  {Annual salary field}
    SexCode  : char;                  {Sex code field: f = female, m = male}
    end;  {EmployeeType}

FileEmployeeType = file of EmployeeType;  {File type with employee record components}

var

    FileChar : FileCharType;          {File variable as file of characters}

    FileEmployee : FileEmployeeType;  {File variable as file of employee records}
```

Explanation... FileType is a user-defined identifier for a *file type* that declares a typed file having components of type ComponentType. ComponentType is any Turbo Pascal data type, except another file type or any structured type having a file-type component. The identifiers **file of** are reserved words.

3. The **file variable** is a structured variable whose type is a file type. The examples show two file variables: FileChar is a file variable that represents a file of characters; FileEmployee is a file variable that represents a file of employee records. We use file variables as parameters in calls to and declaration headings for functions and procedures, as we will see throughout the chapter. File variables must be *variable parameters,* not value parameters.

4. The file variable is a *structured variable* because the file type is a *structured type.* As we have mentioned before, a file is another example of a *data structure:* a collection of related data arranged in a particular pattern or structure. In this case, the **file data structure** is a collection of sequentially arranged components. Moreover, the components themselves can be another data structure (except for the file structure). Examples of these complex file data structures would be a file of arrays, a file of sets, and a file of records. In a text file, the data structure is lines of characters. Figure 12.1 describes the generic data structures for text and typed files.

5. A **file of records** is a file whose components are typed as records. In the syntax box, the file variable FileEmployee is assigned a file of employee records. In Chapter 11, we placed employee records in a text file. In this chapter, we will show how to create a typed file of employee records. Typed files of records are very common in practice and have several advantages over their text-file counterparts.

   a. Typed files of records take up less storage and process faster than equivalent text files, as mentioned earlier.

   b. Typed files of records enable direct-access processing, as in directly accessing a particular employee record without having to sequentially access all preceding records. In this sense, a file of records is like an array of records whose elements get accessed directly.

   c. Typed files of records enable the reading of an entire record from or the writing of an entire record to a typed file. With text files, we have to read and write individual fields.

6. Finally, keep in mind that the declarations in the syntax box are only for typed files, not text files. Text files are declared by using the reserved word **text** as the file variable type:

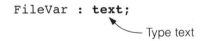

```
FileVar : text;
                  Type text
```

NOTE

1. Text file versus file of characters. Is a text file the same as a file of characters? No! True, both store data whose type is character, but the similarity ends there. We can reference characters in a file of characters by component numbers, but not the characters in a text file. The text file has end-of-line markers, and the typed file does not. Again, see Figure 12.1 to grasp the structure of these file types.

PREDECLARED FILE PROCEDURES AND FUNCTIONS

The predefined operations we can perform on file variables are restricted to certain predeclared functions and procedures in Turbo Pascal. In our work with text data files, we implemented calls to the following predeclared procedures and function.

- **assign** procedure to assign a file specification to the file variable
- **reset** procedure to open the file and reset the file position to the first component in the file
- **read** and **readln** procedures to read data from the file
- **eof** function in a while statement to detect the end of the file
- **close** procedure to close the file

In this section, we cover these and additional predeclared functions and procedures for file processing.

Tables 12.1 and 12.2 describe a common subset of procedures and functions whose calls operate on file-type variables. Take a few minutes to study these tables, before moving on (to better things!). But first note that some of these calls apply to both text and typed files, while others exclusively apply to either text or typed files. You're already familiar with those that apply to text files. In the remainder of this chapter, we focus on those that apply to typed files.

When we process files, especially typed files, we need to be aware of the file position. The **file position** is like a conceptual pointer or arrow that indicates the current location in a file where a processing action (like reading or writing) would take place next. For example, if the file position is at component number 2, then a read operation would read component number 2 and move the file position to component number 3 (or the end of the file if component number 2 is the last component, or an end-of-line marker in a text file); a write operation would write component number 2 and advance the file position by one.

Note that most calls in Table 12.1 affect the file position. For example, a call to *read, readln, write,* or *writeln* advances the file position by one; a call to *append* advances the file position to the end of the file; a call to *reset* or *rewrite* moves the file position to the beginning of the file (the first component, or component number 0 in a typed file); and a call to *seek* moves the file position to the indicated component number.

Table 12.1   Calls to Selected Predeclared File Procedures

Procedure Call Syntax and Example	Applicable File Types	Description
append (FileVar) **append** (TextFile)	Text only	Opens existing file and sets file position to end of file. Prepares TextFile for task of adding more characters at end of file. The open file is *write-only*, meaning that we can write to but not read from file that's opened by call to **append**. If file was already open, then closes and reopens file.
assign (FileVar, StringExpression) **assign** (FileEmployee, 'A:\EMPLOYEE.BIN')	Text and typed	Assigns file specification as string expression to file variable. File name EMPLOYEE.BIN in root directory of drive A: is assigned to FileEmployee. *A call to assign is a precondition to all other procedures and functions that use the file variable.*
close (FileVar) **close** (FileEmployee)	Text and typed	Updates opened file and closes it for reuse by DOS.
erase (FileVar) **erase** (FileEmployee)	Text and typed	Erases (deletes) *unopened* file assigned to file variable. In example, erases above assigned file EMPLOYEE.BIN in drive A. *Caution:* Program defensively to confirm this operation.
read (FileVar, Variable list) **read** (FileEmployee, Employee)	Text and typed	Reads current component from open typed file into current variable in list. The component type and variable type must be identical. The current file position is advanced to next component for each variable read. For open text file, reads one or more values from file into variables in list. The example reads next record in FileEmployee into record variable Employee.
readln (FileVar, Variable list) **readln** (TextFile, Price, Cost)	Text only	Executes call to read procedure and skips to next line in file.
rename (FileVar, NewName) **rename** (FileEmployee, 'EMPLOYEE.BAK')	Text and typed	Renames *unopened* existing file assigned to FileVar with new name provided by string expression NewName. In example, file assigned to employee file (EMPLOYEE.BIN above) is renamed EMPLOYEE.BAK.
reset (FileVar) **reset** (FileEmployee)	Text and typed	Opens existing file and resets file position to beginning of file. If file is *text* file, then it's opened as *read-only*, meaning that we can read from but not write to file that's been opened by call to **reset**. If file was already open, then closes and reopens file.

rewrite (FileVar) **rewrite** (FileEmployee)	Text and typed	Creates and opens new empty file and resets file position to beginning of file. If file is *text* file, then it's *write-only*. If file was already open then closes and recreates file. *Caution*: If a file by this name currently exists, it is deleted and recreated as an empty file! Program defensively to confirm this operation.
seek (FileVar, ComponentNumber) **seek** (FileEmployee, RecordNumber)	Typed only	Moves *file* position to *component number*. Each component in a typed file has an associated component number based on its location in the sequence of components. The first component has component number 0, the second component has component number 1, and so on. A file with N components has component numbers $0 .. N - 1$. ComponentNumber is an expression of type *longint*. If RecordNumber stores 899, then the file position is directly moved to record number 899 in the employee file (which is the 900th record in the file!). File must have been opened before this call.
truncate (FileVar) **truncate** (FileEmployee)	Typed only	Deletes all records past current file position of opened file. *Caution*: Program defensively to confirm this operation!
write (FileVar, Output list) **write** (FileEmployee, Employee)	Text and typed	Writes current component to open typed file as value in current variable in output list. The component type and variable type must be identical. The current file position is advanced to next component for each variable written. The file is expanded if current file position is at end of file. For open text file, writes one or more values to file from expressions in output list. The example writes record in record variable Employee as component in FileEmployee.
writeln (FileVar, Output list) **writeln** (TextFile, Price, Cost)	Text only	Executes call to write procedure and places *end-of-line marker* in file. Text file must be open for output.

Table 12.2   Calls to Selected Predeclared File Functions

Function Call Syntax and Example	Applicable File Types	Description
eof(FileVar) **eof**(FileEmployee)	Text and typed	Returns *true* if current file position is beyond last data element in file; else returns *false*.
eoln(FileVar) **eoln**(TextFile)	Text only	Returns *true* if current file position is at *end-of-line marker*; else returns *false*.
filepos(FileVar) **filepos**(FileEmployee)	Typed only	Returns current file position of opened file as longint value in range 0 (file position at beginning of file) to number of components N (file position at end of file).
filesize(FileVar) **filesize**(FileEmployee)	Typed only	Returns current size of (number of components in) opened file as longint value. Returns 0 if file is empty.
ioresult	Text and typed	Returns zero if I/O operation was successful; otherwise returns integer error code (as listed in *Turbo Pascal Programmer's Guide*). Use in defensive programming to trap I/O error like incorrect file specification. I/O checking must be off (*$I*-compiler directive).

NOTE

2. On Turbo Pascal devices. Turbo Pascal and DOS treat peripherals like the keyboard, display, and printer as *devices* that behave like *text files*. **Input** and **output** are standard text-file variables that are associated, respectively, with the PC *keyboard* and *display*. These "text files" are opened automatically when a program executes. The file variable is optional within the text-file procedure and function calls in Tables 12.1 and 12.2. If we omit the file variable, the appropriate standard text-file variable is assumed. For example, the calls for displaying output

> **write** (Output list)
> **write** (**output**, Output list)

are equivalent. The function calls for detecting an end-of-line mark at the keyboard

> **eoln**(**input**)
> **eoln**

are equivalent.

The familiar **Lst** is another standard text-file variable that's associated with the printer in the standard unit **printer**. Thus, assuming that **printer** is in our uses clause, the statement

> **write** (**Lst**, Output list)

writes to the printer.

File Processing

The remainder of this chapter is concerned with *file processing* — reading from or writing to data files for purposes of file creation, display, interrogation (queries), maintenance, or other tasks. In processing files, we need to observe the following sequential flow of executable tasks.

- *Assign* file
- *Open* file
- *Process* file
- *Close* file

Let's look at each of these tasks in more detail.

Assign File

Before we can work with a file, we need to call the *assign procedure* to assign (couple or link) a file specification to the declared file variable. In Table 12.1, we assigned the file specification A:\EMPLOYEE.BIN to the typed file variable FileEmployee. All subsequent calls that use FileEmployee as a parameter now "know" that the file of interest is EMPLOYEE.BIN in the root directory of drive A.

Open File

Next we need to "open" the file, which is analogous to our opening up a manila folder before we can "process" the contents inside. Here we have to select one of three alternative calls, all of which are described in Table 12.1.

- Call procedure *append* if we need to open a text file with the intent of appending characters at the end of the file.

- Call procedure *reset* if we need to open a file and set the file position to the beginning of the file. For a text file, the intent would be to read data from the file. For a typed file, the intent could be to either read data from or write data to the file.

- Call procedure *rewrite* if we need to create a new empty file. This also deletes any existing file with the assigned file specification. This call is DANGEROUS...a file could be unintentionally erased! From a *defensive programming* viewpoint, we should always confirm the user's intention to rewrite a file.

Process File

This is where the main action and fun take place. In processing a data file, we might undertake one or more of the following tasks, all of which require calls to procedures or functions in Tables 12.1 and 12.2.

- *Create* a new file by *writing* values (components) to the file. After opening a file with a call to *rewrite,* we would use a repetition structure to

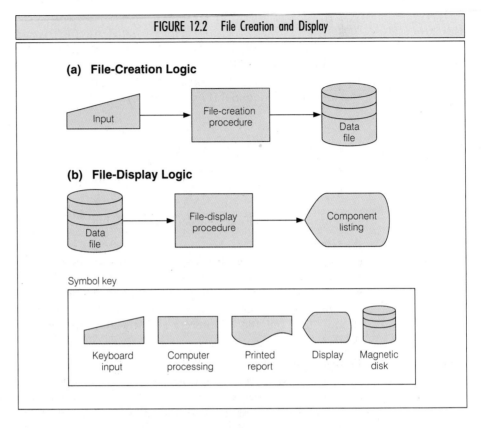

FIGURE 12.2   File Creation and Display

(a) File-Creation Logic

Input → File-creation procedure → Data file

(b) File-Display Logic

Data file → File-display procedure → Component listing

Symbol key

| Keyboard input | Computer processing | Printed report | Display | Magnetic disk |

issue calls to procedures *write* for a typed file and *write* or *writeln* for a text file. Note that the writeln procedure is inadmissible for writing to typed files, since components are not grouped into lines within typed files. Figure 12.2a illustrates the creation of a data file based on the interactive input of components. The file-creation procedure might include the following loop design.

> For each component do
>   Read value from keyboard into primary memory
>   *Write* component to file

In Section 12.2 we will show code for implementing this task.

- *Display* one or more values (components) from a file with calls to procedures *read* for a typed file and *read* or *readln* for a text file. Again, calls to line-oriented procedures like readln are inadmissible for typed files. Figure 12.2b shows file-display logic. For example, to display all components in a file we could use the following loop design (after having opened the file earlier with a call to *reset*).

> While not eof do
>   *Read* component from file into primary memory
>   Write value to screen

In Section 12.2 we will show code for this design.

- *Query* a file. Here we're interested in interrogating or querying a file and displaying the results of that query. For example, we might wish to display the record of a particular employee based on the employee's social security number. Or we might wish to display the records of all employees who earn more than $50,000. Or we might wish to display a report of male versus female average salaries. Depending on our purpose, we would either *sequentially access* all components using a *read* statement within a loop or *directly access* particular components by issuing calls to the *seek* and *read* procedures. We present file queries in Section 12.3.

- *Maintain* a file. Here we need to change an existing file by revising, deleting, or adding components. As you might imagine, these tasks are very common in practice. Many of the file procedures and functions enter the picture here, depending on the purpose and file type. Section 12.4 covers this set of tasks.

- Process *multiple files.* Multifile processing includes tasks like copying one file to another, as in backing up a file; appending one or more files to others; merging two or more files; creating sorted files from other files; and a gaggle of other important tasks. We look at these advanced tasks in Section 12.5.

Close File

Here we wrap up loose ends. A call to the *close* procedure updates an open file by moving any remaining values from the file buffer in primary memory to the file, and releasing the file for reuse by the operating system. What's a *file buffer*? It's an area in primary memory that temporarily holds file components that are in transit between primary memory and the file. Each execution of a write statement moves data to the file buffer, but not necessarily to the file itself. Periodically the operating system then moves data from the buffer to the file. Buffering I/O in primary memory is faster than actual I/O to external media. And wear and tear is reduced on the disk drive to boot! The downside? We could lose data in the buffer by not closing a file, or by having a brownout or a power outage.

SELF-REVIEW EXERCISES

1 2

12.2   FILE CREATION AND DISPLAY

•   •   •   •   •   •   •   •   •   •   •   •

Figure 12.2 showed an overview of the logic for file creation and display, and the preceding section discussed the general implementation. Now let's get specific, first by working with a file whose components are simple, and then by working with a file of records.

FILE OF STANDARD COMPONENTS

In this section, we work with a file whose components are typed as one of the Turbo Pascal standard types.

EXAMPLE 12.1   CREATION AND DISPLAY OF FILE OF STANDARD COMPONENTS

Let's develop a utility program that creates and displays a file.

Requirements
The component types of interest are real, integer, character, and string. In this example we work with integer components. In the exercises we let you make the necessary changes for the other component types. Interactive input includes the number of components to be entered and the component values. The entered component values are written to a new file, and the file is subsequently displayed on the screen.

Design
Figure 12.3 shows the desired I/O design. Note that screen 1 warns the user that any existing file by that name will be erased. Screen 2 offers the user a chance to abort the run. A yes response gives the subsequent input in screen 3, and screen 4 displays the created file.

Figure 12.4 shows the stepwise chart for our program design. Note the following.

1. The main algorithm simply calls three new utility procedures: OpenNewFile, CreateFile, and ShowFile. Calls to the predeclared file procedures and functions in Tables 12.1 and 1.2 are shown in color.

FIGURE 12.3   I/O Design and Run of Utility Program NewFile

Screen 1

```
OPEN NEW FILE

Enter data file drive:\path\name... temps.bin

Any current contents in temps.bin will be ERASED!




Hit any key to continue...
```

Screen 2

```
                         REPLY SCREEN




                    Continue? (Y/N) y
```

Screen 3

```
CREATE FILE

Enter number of values... 5

Enter one value per line... 62
Enter one value per line... 15
Enter one value per line... 20
Enter one value per line... 32
Enter one value per line... 68
```

Screen 4

```
DISPLAY FILE

62
15
20
32
68




Hit any key to continue...
```

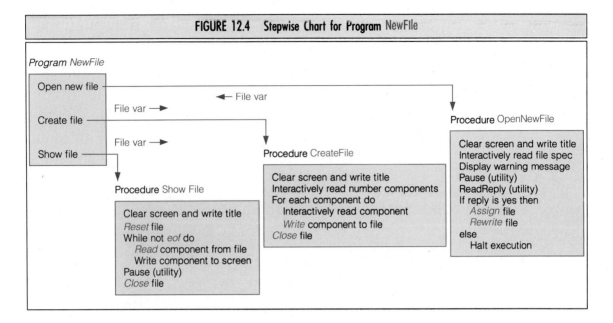

FIGURE 12.4   Stepwise Chart for Program NewFile

Program *NewFile*

Open new file

Create file ──── File var ──▶

Show file ──── File var ──▶

◀── File var

Procedure OpenNewFile

Clear screen and write title
Interactively read file spec
Display warning message
Pause (utility)
ReadReply (utility)
If reply is yes then
    Assign file
    Rewrite file
else
    Halt execution

Procedure CreateFile

Clear screen and write title
Interactively read number components
For each component do
    Interactively read component
    Write component to file
Close file

Procedure Show File

Clear screen and write title
Reset file
While not *eof* do
    Read component from file
    Write component to screen
Pause (utility)
Close file

2. OpenNewFile is a new utility procedure that opens a new file with calls to *assign* and *rewrite*. Note that the potential inadvertent erasure of an existing file is trapped by the if-then-else structure. This procedure sends the file variable to the main program. Pause and ReadReply are utility procedures from earlier chapters.

3. CreateFile is a new utility procedure that creates a file based on the interactive input of components. This procedure receives the file variable from the main program. Note the calls to the predeclared file procedures *write* and *close*.

4. ShowFile is a new utility procedure that displays components in a file. This procedure receives the file variable from the main program. Note that the file is *reset* (opened with the file position at the beginning) before it's processed. The while-do *eof* loop sequentially *reads* and displays components from the file. The while-do eof design is our method of choice for sequentially processing all records in a file. See Exercise 5 for a typed-file alternative that uses a call to *filesize* as the control in a for-do loop. Following the loop the file is *closed*.

Code

Figure 12.5 shows our code for utility program NewFile. Study the program and relate each procedure to the designs in Figures 12.3 and 12.4. Note the following.

1. NewFile itself and its procedures are generically written to handle the file types stated in the requirements. For example, ComponentType and FileType

---

FIGURE 12.5   Listing of Program NewFile

```
program NewFile;

   {* * * * * * * * * * * * * * * * * * * * * * * * * * * * * * * *
    *                                                            *
    *          Utility program that...                           *
    *            Creates and displays new file based on interactive input  *
    *                                                            *
    *            Inputs file specification and component values  *
    *            Opens new file                                  *
    *            Outputs component values to file and displays values  *
    *              stored in newly created file                  *
    *                                                            *
    *            Modular structure                               *
    *              |___ OpenNewFile          (New utility)       *
    *              |___ CreateFile           (New utility)       *
    *              |___ ShowFile             (New utility)       *
    *                                                            *
    *            Data structure of new file                      *
    *            ----------------------------------------------------------  *
    *            ComponentValueComponentValue...                 *
    *                                                            *
    * * * * * * * * * * * * * * * * * * * * * * * * * * * * * * *}

   {============================ Declarations ============================}

uses crt, OurUnit;

type
   ComponentType = integer;
   FileType      = file of ComponentType;
   {FileType      = text;}

   { NOTE:  Change these declarations to suit different component types
            and file types }

var
   FileVar : FileType;

   {======================= Procedure Declarations =======================}
```

continued

are generic types for the utility procedures. We can redeclare these types in the main program to handle different file types, as in a file of strings. No other changes are needed elsewhere in the program (check it out in Exercise 4).

2. We added NewFile as a utility program in the Utilities Library. We also added procedures OpenNewFile, CreateFile, and ShowFile to the Utilities Library. We will use these utilities in subsequent examples and in the exercises.

Test

Figure 12.3 shows our test run for this program. The created file TEMPS.BIN is the typed-file counterpart to text file TEMPS.DAT in Figure 9.4. In Exercise 4 we ask you to try test runs for other file types.

FIGURE 12.5   *(continued)*

```
procedure OpenNewFile (var FileVar : FileType);

  { Utility reads file spec, opens new file with calls to assign and rewrite
    Receives nothing
    Sends FileVar }

    { NOTE:   Requires uses clause for crt and OurUnit in host program
              Calls Pause and ReadReply in OurUnit }

        { CAUTION:   Any existing contents in file assigned to
                     FileVar will be overwritten! }
const
  Title = 'OPEN NEW FILE';

var
  FileSpec : string;      {File specification as drive:\path\file name}
  Reply    : char;        {Y/N reply}

begin   {OpenNewFile}

  clrscr;  writeln (Title);  writeln;
  write ('Enter data file drive:\path\name... ');  readln (FileSpec);
  writeln;
  writeln ('Any current contents in ', FileSpec, ' will be ERASED!');

  Pause;                          {In OurUnit}
  ReadReply (Reply);              {In OurUnit}

  if upcase(Reply) = 'Y' then
    begin {Open new file}
      assign (FileVar, FileSpec);     {Assign file spec to file variable}
      rewrite (FileVar);              {Create & open new empty file}
    end   {Open new file}
  else    {Halt execution}
    halt;

  end;    {OpenNewFile}
{-------------------------------------------------------------------}
```

FILE OF RECORDS

In the preceding chapter we worked with records and the record data type; in the first section of this chapter we discussed the advantages of working with files of records. In this section we show how to create and display a file of records.

EXAMPLE 12.2   CREATION AND DISPLAY OF FILE OF EMPLOYEE RECORDS

In Example 11.4 we created text file EMPLOYEE.DAT (Figure 11.2) using the IDE's editor. Program Employ1 then read and displayed employee records from this file.

Requirements

Let's develop a program that creates and displays a typed file of employee records. We will use the same records as those shown in Figure 11.2. We will inter-

```
                        FIGURE 12.5   (continued)

procedure CreateFile (var FileVar : FileType);

  { Utility interactively inputs values and writes to file
    Receives FileVar
    Sends nothing }

      { NOTE:  ComponentType must be declared in calling module
               Assumes file has been opened and file position is at
                  beginning of file, as in a call to utility OpenNewFile }

           { CAUTION:  Any existing contents in file assigned to
                       FileVar will be overwritten! }
  const
    Title = 'CREATE FILE';

  var
    Component : ComponentType;      {Stores current file component value}
    Item,                           {Item number, or for do control variable}
    Items     : integer;            {Number of items (components) in file}

  begin   {CreateFile}

    clrscr;  writeln (Title);  writeln;
    write ('Enter number of values... ');  readln (Items);
    writeln;
    for Item := 1 to Items do
      begin
        {Read component value from keyboard into primary memory}
        write ('Enter one value per line... ');  readln (Component);
        {Write component value from primary memory to file}
        write (FileVar, Component);
      end;   {for}
    close (FileVar);

  end;   {CreateFile}
  {-----------------------------------------------------------------------}
```

continued

actively input the fields for a record and then write this record to the file. After each record we will ask the user if another record is desired. If it is, then we interactively input the next record and write it to the file. This file-creation task continues until the user responds that no more records are desired. Finally, we process the file to display all records.

Design

Figure 12.6 shows the I/O design. Note how the designs of screens 1 and 2 are identical to those in Figure 12.3. Screens 3, 5, and 7 show the interactive input of fields for each of three records. Screens 9–11 show the file display, using the same output design as that in Figure 11.3. As you might have guessed, we're planning on reusing previously written modules. By designing *reusable modules* in the first place, we simplify subsequent programming tasks that make use of these modules. The algorithmic design for this program is similar to that described in Example 12.1, so let's move on.

FIGURE 12.5   *(continued)*

```
procedure ShowFile (var FileVar : FileType);

  { Utility reads component values from file and displays on screen
    Receives FileVar
    Sends nothing }

    { NOTE:   ComponentType must be declared in calling module
              Calls Pause in OurUnit }
const
  Title = 'DISPLAY FILE';

var
  Component : ComponentType;      {Stores current file component value}

begin    {ShowFile}

  clrscr;  writeln (Title);  writeln;

 {Open existing file and reset file position to beginning}
  reset (FileVar);

  while not eof(FileVar) do
    begin
      {Read component value from file into primary memory}
      read (FileVar, Component);
      {Write component value from primary memory to screen}
      writeln (Component);
    end;   {while}

  Pause;                                          {In OurUnit}
  close (FileVar);

end;    {ShowFile}

  {============================= Main Body ==============================}

begin    {NewFile}

 {Read file spec, assign file variable, and rewrite file}
  OpenNewFile (FileVar);

 {Interactively input component values and write to file}
  CreateFile (FileVar);

 {Read component values from file and display on screen}
  ShowFile (FileVar);

end.     {NewFile}
```

Code and Test

Figure 12.7 on pages 582–584 shows program Employ2. Relate this program to the
test run in Figure 12.6 and note the following.

1. This program borrows heavily from earlier programs. We created Employ2
   by editing Employ1 (Figure 11.4). We also used portions of NewFile in Figure 12.5.

2. The declarations of types and variables for employee records and the file are
   identical to those presented in Section 12.1.

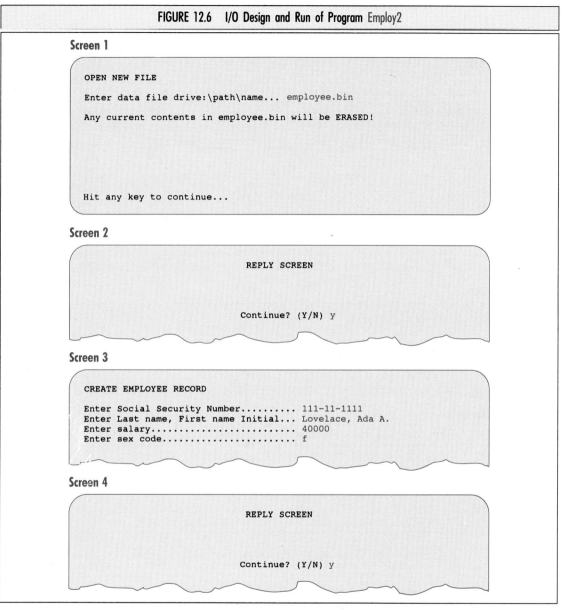

FIGURE 12.6   I/O Design and Run of Program Employ2

Screen 1

```
OPEN NEW FILE

Enter data file drive:\path\name... employee.bin

Any current contents in employee.bin will be ERASED!




Hit any key to continue...
```

Screen 2

```
                        REPLY SCREEN



                   Continue? (Y/N) y
```

Screen 3

```
CREATE EMPLOYEE RECORD

Enter Social Security Number......... 111-11-1111
Enter Last name, First name Initial... Lovelace, Ada A.
Enter salary......................... 40000
Enter sex code....................... f
```

Screen 4

```
                        REPLY SCREEN



                   Continue? (Y/N) y
```

continued

3. Utility OpenNewFile from Figure 12.5 is used without any changes.

4. Procedure CreateEmployeeFile uses the same interactive-input code as that shown earlier in Example 11.1. The interactive input of an employee record has reusable value, so we made this the new module InputEmployee. Also note that the statement

> **write** (FileEmployee, Employee);

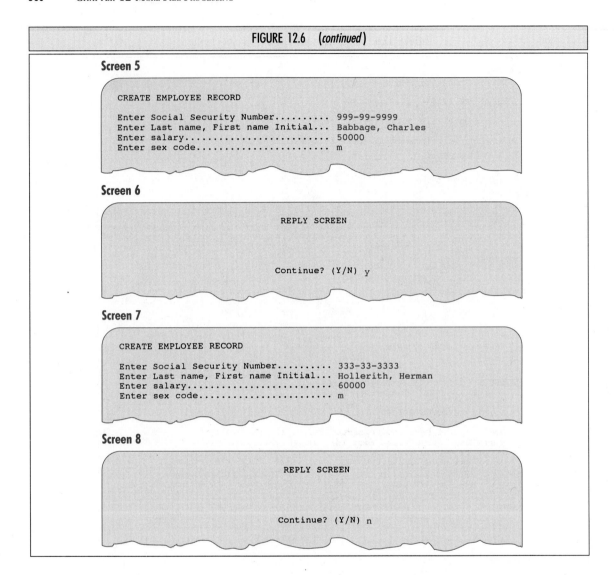

FIGURE 12.6   *(continued)*

Screen 5

```
CREATE EMPLOYEE RECORD

Enter Social Security Number......... 999-99-9999
Enter Last name, First name Initial... Babbage, Charles
Enter salary........................ 50000
Enter sex code..................... m
```

Screen 6

```
                    REPLY SCREEN



            Continue? (Y/N) y
```

Screen 7

```
CREATE EMPLOYEE RECORD

Enter Social Security Number......... 333-33-3333
Enter Last name, First name Initial... Hollerith, Herman
Enter salary........................ 60000
Enter sex code..................... m
```

Screen 8

```
                    REPLY SCREEN



            Continue? (Y/N) n
```

writes the entire record Employee in one fell swoop! This is a key advantage of working with files of records. We can read entire records from and write entire records to files. We don't need to be concerned about the field details of this record at this time. As emphasized in Chapter 11, this is *data abstraction* in action.

5. Procedure ShowEmployee incorporates the reusable module OutputEmployee from Figure 11.4. As in ShowFile from Figure 12.5, our method of choice for

FIGURE 12.6   (*continued*)

Screen 9

```
DISPLAY EMPLOYEE RECORD

Employee record #0
    Name..................... Lovelace, Ada A.
    Social Security Number... 111-11-1111
    Sex...................... f
    Salary................... $40000.00




Hit any key to continue...
```

Screen 10

```
DISPLAY EMPLOYEE RECORD

Employee record #1
    Name..................... Babbage, Charles
    Social Security Number... 999-99-9999
    Sex...................... m
    Salary................... $50000.00




Hit any key to continue...
```

Screen 11

```
DISPLAY EMPLOYEE RECORD

Employee record #2
    Name..................... Hollerith, Herman
    Social Security Number... 333-33-3333
    Sex...................... m
    Salary................... $60000.00




Hit any key to continue...
```

the loop design is an *eof*-controlled while-do structure. Note that *record numbers* are component numbers; these start at zero in Turbo Pascal, so we initialized RecNum to −1. The record displays in Figure 12.6 thus show record numbers 0..2.

FIGURE 12.7 Listing of Program Employ2

```
program Employ2;

{* * * * * * * * * * * * * * * * * * * * * * * * * * * * * * * *
 *                                                              *
 *        Creates and displays typed file of employee records   *
 *                                                              *
 *          Inputs employee records from keyboard and writes to file *
 *            of records                                        *
 *          Reads employee records from file of records and outputs *
 *            to screen                                         *
 *                                                              *
 *          Modular structure                                   *
 *            |___ OpenNewFile              (Utility)           *
 *            |___ CreateEmployeeFile                           *
 *            |    |___ InputEmployee                           *
 *            |___ ShowEmployeeFile                             *
 *                 |___ OutputEmployee      (Module in Employ1) *
 *                                                              *
 *          Data structure of typed file EMPLOYEE.BIN           *
 *          ---------------------------------------------------- *
 *          EmployeeRecord1EmployeeRecord2...                   *
 *                                                              *
 *          where each employee record has the following four fields: *
 *            Social Security Number                            *
 *            Last name, First name Initial                     *
 *            Salary                                            *
 *            Sex code                                          *
 *                                                              *
 * * * * * * * * * * * * * * * * * * * * * * * * * * * * * * * *}

 {=========================== Declarations ===========================}

uses crt, OurUnit;

type
  EmployeeType = record
    SSN      : string[11];       {Social Security Number field}
    FullName : string[25];       {Full name field}
    Salary   : real;             {Annual salary field}
    SexCode  : char;             {Sex code field: f = female, m = male}
  end;   {EmployeeType}

  FileEmployeeType = file of EmployeeType;   {File type with employee
                                              record components}

  FileType         = FileEmployeeType;       {File type needed for call to
                                              OpenNewFile}
var
  FileEmployee : FileEmployeeType;   {File var for file of employee records}

 {========================= Procedure Declarations =========================}

   Utility procedure OpenNewFile is not shown; see Figure 12.5.
```

FIGURE 12.7   *(continued)*

```pascal
procedure CreateEmployeeFile (var FileEmployee : FileEmployeeType);

  { Creates file of employee records
    Receives FileEmployee
    Sends nothing }

      { NOTE:   Assumes file has been opened and file pointer is at
                beginning of file, as in a call to utility OpenNewFile
                Calls procedure InputEmployee to input employee record
                Calls ReadReply in OurUnit to input Y/N reply }

            { CAUTION:  Any existing contents in employee file will be
                        overwritten! }
const
  Title = 'CREATE EMPLOYEE RECORD';

var
  Employee : EmployeeType;        {Employee record}
  Reply    : char;               {Y/N reply: Y = Another record}


procedure InputEmployee (var Employee : EmployeeType);

  { Reads employee record from keyboard into record variable Employee
    Receives nothing
    Sends Employee }

begin   {InputEmployee}

  with Employee do
    begin
      write ('Enter Social Security Number......... '); readln (SSN);
      write ('Enter Last name, First name Initial... '); readln (FullName);
      write ('Enter salary........................ '); readln (Salary);
      write ('Enter sex code...................... '); readln (SexCode);
    end;  {with}

end;   {InputEmployee}


begin   {CreateEmployeeFile}

  repeat
    clrscr;  writeln (Title);  writeln;
    InputEmployee (Employee);            {Input record from keyboard}
    write (FileEmployee, Employee);      {Write record to file}
    ReadReply (Reply);                   {In OurUnit}
  until upcase(Reply) = 'N';             {End input when reply is No}
  close (FileEmployee);

end;   {CreateEmployeeFile}
{------------------------------------------------------------------------}
```

continued

SELF-REVIEW EXERCISES

3 4 7

FIGURE 12.7   (*continued*)

```
procedure ShowEmployeeFile (var FileEmployee : FileEmployeeType);

   { Reads employee records from file and displays on screen
     Receives FileEmployee
     Sends nothing }

      { NOTE:  Calls procedure OutputEmployee to display employee
               record on screen
               Calls Pause in OurUnit }
const
  Title = 'DISPLAY EMPLOYEE RECORD';

var
  Employee : EmployeeType;        {Employee record}
  RecNum   : integer;             {Record number}

      Procedure OutputEmployee is declared here; it's the reusable
      module from program Employ1 in Figure 11.4.

begin   {ShowEmployeeFile}

 {Open employee file and reset file position to beginning}
  reset (FileEmployee);

  RecNum := -1;

  while not eof(FileEmployee) do
    begin
      clrscr;  writeln (Title);  writeln;
      read (FileEmployee, Employee);                {Read record from file}
      RecNum := RecNum + 1;                         {Update record number}
      writeln ('Employee record #', RecNum);
      OutputEmployee (Employee);                    {Output record to screen}
      Pause;                                        {In OurUnit}
    end;  {while}

  close (FileEmployee);

end;   {ShowEmployeeFile}

    {============================ Main Body ============================}

begin   {Employ2}

  OpenNewFile (FileEmployee);

  CreateEmployeeFile (FileEmployee);

  ShowEmployeeFile (FileEmployee);

end.    {Employ2}
```

12.3   FILE QUERIES

• • • • • • • • • • • • • • • •

A *file query* interrogates a file to extract information (if any) that satisfies the query. The displayed information can include one or more records, one or more field values within a record or across all records, or reports ranging from simple to elaborate.

Sample queries for our employee file might include the display of all female records, the display of a record having a specified record number, the display of a record that matches a specified social security number or employee name, and a report that compares average female and male salaries.

In designing algorithms that query files, we need to specifically consider the file type and access method. Text files must be processed sequentially — it's our only choice! With typed files, we have more flexibility. A query that requires the examination of all records is best processed by sequential access. A query that requires the extraction of a single record is more efficiently processed by direct access.

The direct-access alternative introduces further options. The most straightforward approach to directly accessing a record is to use the *record number* in a call to the *seek* procedure. Unfortunately, a user will not likely know the record number. More commonly, the user knows a specified field value, like a person's name or social security number. The field that's used to locate a record of interest is called the *record key*. We will describe two methods of converting a given value for the record key into a corresponding record number. Finally, we could apply one of the search function algorithms first described in Module D. We look at each of these alternatives next.

SEQUENTIAL ACCESS

Here we consider file queries that sequentially process all records in either a text or typed file.

EXAMPLE 12.3   SEQUENTIAL ACCESS FOR SEX-CODE FILE QUERY

Check out the I/O in Figure 12.8. This run queries file EMPLOYEE.BIN (the one created in Figure 12.6) to display all records that match the male sex code. Figure 12.9 shows program Query1. Note the following.

1. The new utility OpenOldFile is a slight rewrite of our earlier utility PrepFile (from Chapter 6). The revised utility uses our generic file variable *FileVar* and file type *FileType*, unlike the earlier text-file-oriented version. We also made some minor screen format changes. Note that existing typed files are always

FIGURE 12.8   I/O for Program Query1

Screen 1

```
OPEN OLD FILE

Enter data file drive:\path\name... employee.bin
```

Screen 2

```
SEX CODE SEARCH OF EMPLOYEE FILE BASED ON SEQUENTIAL ACCESS

  Enter sex code f or m... m
```

Screen 3

```
FOUND MATCHING EMPLOYEE RECORD

  Name..................... Babbage, Charles
  Social Security Number... 999-99-9999
  Sex...................... m
  Salary................... $50000.00




Hit any key to continue...
```

Screen 4

```
FOUND MATCHING EMPLOYEE RECORD

  Name..................... Hollerith, Herman
  Social Security Number... 333-33-3333
  Sex...................... m
  Salary................... $60000.00




Hit any key to continue...
```

Screen 5

```
                         REPLY SCREEN



                      Continue? (Y/N) n
```

FIGURE 12.9   Listing of Program Query1

```
program Query1;

  {* * * * * * * * * * * * * * * * * * * * * * * * * * * * * * * *
   *                                                             *
   *        Employee File Queries, Version 1:   Sequential Access for
   *                                             Sex Code        *
   *                                                             *
   *        Inputs file specification, sex code search values, and
   *          Y/N replies from keyboard                          *
   *        Sequentially searches file for sex code search value *
   *        Outputs matching records (if any) to screen          *
   *                                                             *
   *        Modular structure                                    *
   *         |___ OpenOldFile              (New utility)         *
   *         |___ QuerySex                                       *
   *                |___ OutputEmployee    (Module in Employ1)   *
   *                                                             *
   *        Data structure of typed file EMPLOYEE.BIN            *
   *        ---------------------------------------------------- *
   *        EmployeeRecord1EmployeeRecord2...                    *
   *                                                             *
   *        where each employee record has the following four fields:
   *          Social Security Number                             *
   *          Last name, First name Initial                      *
   *          Salary                                             *
   *          Sex code                                           *
   *                                                             *
   * * * * * * * * * * * * * * * * * * * * * * * * * * * * * * * *}

   {========================== Declarations ==========================}

uses crt, OurUnit;

type
  EmployeeType = record
    SSN      : string[11];      {Social Security Number field}
    FullName : string[25];      {Full name field}
    Salary   : real;            {Annual salary field}
    SexCode  : char;            {Sex code field: f = female, m = male}
  end;   {EmployeeType}

  FileEmployeeType = file of EmployeeType;  {File type with employee
                                            record components}
  FileType        = FileEmployeeType;      {File type needed for call to
                                            OpenOldFile}
var
  FileEmployee : FileEmployeeType;  {File var for file of employee records}
  Reply        : char;              {Y/N reply:  Y = another query}

   {========================= Procedure Declarations =======================}

      Procedure OutputEmployee is declared here; it's the reusable
      module from program Employ1 in Figure 11.4.
```

continued

FIGURE 12.9   (continued)

```
procedure OpenOldFile (var FileVar : FileType);

  { Utility reads file specification with line feed while handling
      input error, opens existing file with assign and reset
    Receives nothing
    Sends FileVar }

  { NOTE:  Requires uses clause for crt unit in host program
           Displays error message immediately to right of input value }

const
  Title = 'OPEN OLD FILE';

var
  FileSpec : string;      {File specification as drive:\path\file name}
  X, Y     : integer;     {Current coordinates of cursor
                                        ... at beginning of input field}

begin   {OpenOldFile}

  {$I-  Turn off automatic I/O error checking}

    clrscr;  writeln (Title);  writeln;

  {Input file spec and open file}
      write ('Enter data file drive:\path\name... ');
      X := wherex;  Y := wherey;              {Predefined functs in crt unit}
      readln (FileSpec);
      assign (FileVar, FileSpec);             {Assign file spec to file var}
      reset  (FileVar);                       {Open old file @ beginning}

                                              {Predefined function ioresult}
    while ioresult <> 0 do                    {returns zero if no I/O error}
      begin
        sound (100); delay (200); nosound;    {Beep}
        gotoxy (X,Y);  clreol;                {Clear input field}
        gotoxy (X+20,Y);                      {Cursor to right of input field}
        write ('<-- Reenter');                {Write error message}
        gotoxy (X,Y);                         {Cursor to input field}
        readln (FileSpec);                    {Reenter file spec}
        assign (FileVar, FileSpec);           {Reassign file}
        reset  (FileVar);                     {Reopen file}
        gotoxy (X+20,Y);  clreol;             {Clear error message}
        writeln;                              {Issue line feed}
      end;   {while}

  {$I+  Turn on automatic I/O error checking}

end;   {OpenOldFile}
{----------------------------------------------------------------------}
```

opened with a call to *reset* (*rewrite* would erase the file!). This also sets the file position to the first component, which we would want for a sequential processing of the entire file.

2. Procedure OutputEmployee is a reusable module used earlier in programs Employ1 (Figure 11.4) and Employ2 (Figure 12.7). We declared it within the main program's declarations (rather than within QuerySex) because we're anticipating future modules that would also use OutputEmployee.

FIGURE 12.9   *(continued)*

```
procedure QuerySex (var FileEmployee : FileEmployeeType);

    { Interactively inputs search value for sex code, sequentially accesses
        employee file, and displays employee records that match search value
      Receives FileEmployee
      Sends nothing }

      { NOTE:  Calls OutputEmployee
               Calls Pause in OurUnit }
const
  Title1 = 'SEX CODE SEARCH OF EMPLOYEE FILE BASED ON SEQUENTIAL ACCESS';
  Title2 = 'FOUND MATCHING EMPLOYEE RECORD';
  Title3 = 'MATCHING EMPLOYEE RECORD NOT FOUND';

var
  Employee  : EmployeeType;               {Employee record}
  Found     : Boolean;                    {True if record found; else false}
  SearchVal : char;                       {Object of search}

begin   {QuerySex}

  reset (FileEmployee);                   {Reset file pos to 1st component}
  Found := false;                         {No matching record found initially}
  clrscr; writeln (Title1); writeln;
  write ('  Enter sex code f or m... ');  readln (SearchVal);

  while not eof(FileEmployee) do
    begin
      read (FileEmployee, Employee);    {Read record from file}
      if upcase(SearchVal) = upcase(Employee.SexCode) then
        begin  {Matching record found:  Search value = search key}
          Found := true;
          clrscr; writeln (Title2); writeln;
          OutputEmployee (Employee);              {Output record to screen}
          Pause;                                  {In OurUnit}
        end;  {if}
    end;  {while}

  if not Found then
    begin
      clrscr;
      writeln (chr(7), Title3);
      Pause;                                      {In OurUnit}
    end;  {if}

end;    {QuerySex}

  {============================== Main Body ==============================}

begin   {Query1}

  OpenOldFile (FileEmployee);                     {New utility}
  repeat
    QuerySex (FileEmployee);
    ReadReply (Reply);                            {In OurUnit}
  until upcase(Reply) = 'N';
  close (FileEmployee);

end.    {Query1}
```

3. Procedure QuerySex is the procedure that actually queries the file. Note that sequential access of all records is achieved by an *eof while-do loop*. If the value in SearchVal matches the value in Employee.SexCode, a matching record has been found and the record is displayed by a call to OutputEmployee. This if-then structure within the loop's body also sets the logical variable Found to true. If the entire file is processed and not one matching record is found, Found retains its initialized false value and the "not found" message is displayed.

4. Finally, note that the structure of this program is deliberately designed to facilitate changes for various kinds of employee-file queries. We would only need to replace the call to QuerySex in the main algorithm and change or replace module QuerySex. Try Exercise 10 to change the nature of the query, and note how we accomplish this change in the next example.

DIRECT ACCESS USING RECORD NUMBER

The simplest approach to directly accessing a record is to move the file position to the record of interest by a call to procedure *seek*, using the *record number* as a parameter.

EXAMPLE 12.4   DIRECT ACCESS OF EMPLOYEE FILE USING RECORD NUMBER

Suppose that we wish to display a record in the employee file based on its record number. Figure 12.10 shows a sample run that displays record number 0. An attempt to display record number 3 was unsuccessful, because the employee file created in Figure 12.6 just has three records, with record numbers 0..2.

The run in Figure 12.10 is based on a program named Query2 in the Examples Library. We created Query2 by revising Query1 in Figure 12.9 as follows.

1. We made some descriptive documentation changes at the top of the program.

2. In the main algorithm, we replaced the call to QuerySex with a call to QueryRecNum.

3. We replaced module QuerySex with the new module QueryRecNum seen in Figure 12.11. Note that . . .

   a. We call function *filesize* to determine the number of components in the file, and reduce this by one in the assignment to MaxRecNum. In our sample run, the file has 3 components (the value returned by *filesize*), which means that the maximum record number is 2 (the value assigned to MaxRecNum). We then use the range 0 to MaxRecNum to trap entered record numbers outside this range.

FIGURE 12.10   I/O for Program Query2

Screen 1

```
OPEN OLD FILE

Enter data file drive:\path\name... employee.bin
```

Screen 2

```
DIRECT ACCESS OF EMPLOYEE FILE USING RECORD NUMBER

  Enter record number in range 0 to 2... 0
```

Screen 3

```
FOUND EMPLOYEE RECORD

  Name.................... Lovelace, Ada A.
  Social Security Number... 111-11-1111
  Sex..................... f
  Salary.................. $40000.00




Hit any key to continue...
```

Screen 4

```
                          REPLY SCREEN


                       Continue? (Y/N) y
```

Screen 5

```
DIRECT ACCESS OF EMPLOYEE FILE USING RECORD NUMBER

  Enter record number in range 0 to 2... 3
```

Screen 6

```
EMPLOYEE RECORD NOT FOUND
```

```
Hit any key to continue...
```

FIGURE 12.11   Listing of Procedure QueryRecNum Within Program Query2

```
procedure QueryRecNum (var FileEmployee : FileEmployeeType);

  { Interactively inputs record number and displays directly-accessed
      employee record (if any)
    Receives FileEmployee
    Sends nothing }

    { NOTE:   Calls OutputEmployee
              Calls Pause in OurUnit }
const
  Title1 = 'DIRECT ACCESS OF EMPLOYEE FILE USING RECORD NUMBER';
  Title2 = 'FOUND EMPLOYEE RECORD';
  Title3 = 'EMPLOYEE RECORD NOT FOUND';

var
  Employee  : EmployeeType;              {Employee record}
  MaxRecNum,                             {Max record number for this file}
  RecNum    : integer;                   {Record number}

begin   {QueryRecNum}

  reset (FileEmployee);                  {Reset file pos to 1st component}
  clrscr;  writeln (Title1);  writeln;
  MaxRecNum := filesize(FileEmployee) - 1;
  write ('  Enter record number in range 0 to ', MaxRecNum, '... ');
  readln (RecNum);
  clrscr;                                             Direct access of
                                                      employee record
                                                      using record number
  if (RecNum >= 0) and (RecNum <= MaxRecNum) then
    begin
      seek (FileEmployee, RecNum);       {Move file position to record #}
      read (FileEmployee, Employee);     {Read record from file}
      writeln (Title2);  writeln;
      OutputEmployee (Employee);         {Output record to screen}
    end {then}
  else {Record number out of range}
    writeln (chr(7), Title3);

  Pause;                                 {In OurUnit}

end;    {QueryRecNum}
```

b. The direct access of an employee record with an existing record number is achieved (1) by moving the file position to that record number with a call to *seek* and (2) by copying the record at the current file position from the file to primary memory with a call to *read*. Once the record of interest is stored in primary memory within record variable Employee, we can call procedure OutputEmployee to display the record.

‡Direct Access Using Record Key Transformation

The direct access of a record using its record number is relatively easy to program, as seen in Example 12.4. But what about the users who would utilize our program? They need to provide record numbers (or be provided with them), which is impractical at best and meaningless at worst. In fact, most users don't know "beans" about record numbers, but they do know of people's names, social security numbers, and account numbers. How often have you been asked for your social security number or bank account number? In a computerized query, chances are one of these numbers has been used to locate *your* record. (Records of us are everywhere!)

The field that's used to locate a record of interest is usually called the **record key.** If the record key is the social security number, then an entered social security number is used to access the matching record. We could retrieve a record with a matching social security number by the sequential-access method in Example 12.3, but it would be inefficient to do so. The preferred approach to accessing a single, unique record is by the direct access of that record. How do we do this, though, if the user has a social security number to give, but the program (more precisely the call to *seek*) requires a record number? The answer is that we first transform the entered social security number into its corresponding record number, and then that we use the record number as usual to directly access the record. How do we perform this transformation? We either use a *hash function* or an *index file*.

A **hash function** transforms a *record key value* into a *hash index,* an integer value that corresponds to the record number. Figure 12.12a shows the idea behind a hash function. In our example, the hash function receives a social security number (333-33-3333) and returns the hash index (record number 11). We will come back shortly to how it transforms the social security number into an equivalent record number. Once we have the record number that corresponds to the provided record key value, we can issue a call to *seek*, using the record number as a parameter.

An **index file** is a data file with just two fields per record: the index key and the record number. The *index key* is a field in the original file, like social security number in the employee file. The record number is the corresponding record number in the original file that contains a given index key value. In Figure 12.12b, we show an index file with social security number as the index key. This index file corresponds to the employee file created in Figure 12.6. Thus, social security number 333-33-3333 in the index file points to record number 2 in the employee file. Given an index key value, a *table-lookup* algorithm (such as the one in Module D) finds the corresponding record number

---

‡Optional, more advanced material. Skip without loss of continuity, study at this point, or wait until later.

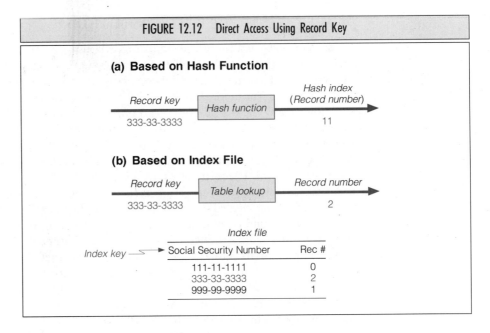

FIGURE 12.12   Direct Access Using Record Key

(a) Based on Hash Function

Record key → Hash function → Hash index (Record number)

333-33-3333 → 11

(b) Based on Index File

Record key → Table lookup → Record number

333-33-3333 → 2

Index file

Index key ⟶

Social Security Number	Rec #
111-11-1111	0
333-33-3333	2
999-99-9999	1

in the index file. Index files are always sorted by the index key, so a table lookup based on a binary search algorithm is appropriate. We could also use a modification of the query approach illustrated in Example 12.3. Once we have the record number, we use it in the call to *seek*.

The use of an index file means that the program works with two open files: the original file and the index file. In Section 12.5 we come back to index files in a multifile-processing context. Later, we ask you to program this approach in Exercises 30 and 31 (actually, you already have all the tools to do this!).

EXAMPLE 12.5   DIRECT ACCESS USING HASH FUNCTION

Let's get more specific with the hash function illustrated in Figure 12.12a. First off, *the use of a hash function to retrieve a record assumes that we created the original file using the very same hash function!* In creating the file, we call the hash function to generate a record number based on a record key value, call *seek* to move the file position based on the hash function's returned record number, and call *write* to write the record. Later, to retrieve this record, we call the hash function to return a record number based on the provided record key value, call *seek* to move the file position based on the record number returned by the hash function, and call *read* to retrieve the record.

The big question is "How does the hash function transform the record key value into a corresponding record number?" Algorithms for hash functions are a very specialized and complex topic that's been the object of much research in computer science. These are beyond the scope of this textbook, but let's sketch the approach by one popular (simplified) algorithm.

Sample hash function

> Divide a record key *integer* value by a *prime number* and use the remainder from this division as the hash index.[3]

The prime number used must be greater than or equal to the total number of desired records in the file. For example, if we wish to have a total of 90 records, we might use 97 for the prime number. If we use the numeric value 333333333 in place of the string social security number 333-33-3333 as a record key value, the hash function would return 11 as the hash index (see Figure 12.12a). This is the remainder that we would get from dividing 333333333 by 97 (check it out). The *mod operator* (see Table 2.2) is made to order for this operation: 333333333 **mod** 97 gives 11. In general, the transformation is given by

$$\text{RecordNumber := RecordKey } \textbf{mod} \text{ PrimeNumber;}$$

In practice, it's more complicated than this, because the hash index may not be unique. In other words, it's possible that a hash function would give the same hash index for two different record key values! This eventuality is called a *collision*. Algorithms for hash functions handle collisions by changing the hash index in some way. For this reason, the selected file size is generally larger than the maximum number of desired records, thereby allocating extra storage space for collided records. Otherwise, collisions may overwrite previously written records, with subsequent retrievals of missing records.

In Exercise 15 we encourage you to implement hashing by trying your hand at revising our file-creation and query routines.

DIRECT ACCESS USING SEARCH FUNCTION FOR RECORD KEY

A final alternative for direct-access queries of typed files would use one of the search algorithms (sequential or binary) that we developed in Module D and Section 11.4. The idea here is to conceptualize records in a typed file as elements in an array. The record numbers are equivalent to indexes in an array. We can then revise our array-based search algorithms to search the file directly (instead of the array) for the field value of interest, the *record key* value. We leave this approach to Exercises 16 and 17.

---

[3]A *prime number* is a positive integer that is not divisible by any positive integer except 1 and itself. For example, 2, 3, 5, 7, and 11 are the first five prime numbers.

SELF-REVIEW EXERCISES

9 13

12.4   FILE MAINTENANCE

• • • • • • • • • • • • • •

Up to now we have created, displayed, and queried files. Another important set of tasks in file processing includes the maintenance of records within files: adding, deleting, and updating records. In practice, these tasks are the "bread and butter" of file processing. For example, in an airline reservation system, file queries are very common. However, file maintenance is even more common: Passenger reservations and cancellations respectively add and delete passenger records and cause almost continuous updates to records that contain seat inventories. Just think of the daily changes that go on with bank account records, course registration records, grocery store product records, records that contian stock prices, and so on ad nauseam.

This section conceptually discusses file maintenance tasks and includes pseudocode design where appropriate. The tools for implementing these tasks are very similar to those we have already used, so we leave their programming to the exercises.

ADDING RECORDS

For *typed files*, we can append a record or component to the end of an open file as follows.

AppendRecord

> *Reset* typed file
> *Seek* new record, calling *filesize* to return new record number
> *Write* new record

Note that the new (appended) record number is returned by *filesize*. For example, if a file currently has three records, *filesize* would return 3. These records are currently numbered 0..2, so 3 would be the record number for the newly appended record in the file.

If a *record key* is used for direct access, the above *seek* and *write* calls are preceded by a call to either the *hash function* or a *table-lookup procedure* for an index file, giving the new record number.

If the file is a *text file,* we can add text as follows.

AppendText

> Open text file with call to *append*
> Call *write* or *writeln* to append more text

In Exercise 18, we ask you to try your hand at programming an append procedure.

DELETING RECORDS

One way of "deleting" a record from a *typed file* is to blank it out; that is, we *seek* the record to be deleted and then replace all numeric fields with zeros and all character and string fields with nulls using calls to *write.* In reality, of course, we don't explicitly delete the record at all. We implicitly delete it by taking a "blanked out" record to mean "deleted." This approach is especially common when direct access is based on a hash function. Check out Exercise 19 to develop a procedure that implicitly deletes records.

We can explicitly delete a record by creating a new file that includes all records from the old file, except for the record we wish to delete. The approach goes something like this.

DeleteRecord

> *Reset* old file
> *Rewrite* new file (defensively confirm)
> Input field value, record number, or record key for record to be
>   deleted.
> For each record in old file do
>   *Read* old record
>   If this is not record to be deleted then
>   *Write* old record to new file
>   else
>   Confirm that this record is to be deleted
>   If not affirmative then
>   *Write* old record to new file
> *Close* both files

See Exercise 19 to develop a procedure that explicitly deletes a record.

UPDATING RECORDS

Record updates include one of the following tasks: changing one or more fields in a single record or changing the same field across all records in the file. Let's assume that the file is a typed file. The procedure for updating one or more records in a text file is similar to that for deleting a record, as described earlier (check out Exercise 20).

The following pseudocode updates a field within a single record in an open typed file.

UpdateOneRecord

> Input record number or record key for record to be updated
> (If record key is input: Call function that returns record number based on record key, as discussed on pages 593–595)
> Call *seek* to locate record position
> Call *read* to read record from file into primary memory
> Input new field value to revise record in primary memory
> Call *seek* to bring file position back to record being updated
> Call *write* to write revised record to file

Note that the call to read moves the file position to the record that follows the record being updated. We need to call *seek* the second time in order to reposition the file back to the record of interest; otherwise we would make the *mistake of inadvertently overwriting the record just beyond the record that we thought we were updating!* See Exercise 21 to code this procedure.

To update the same field for all records, consider the following pseudocode.

UpdateAllRecords

> *Reset* file
> While not *eof* do
>   *Read* record from file into primary memory
>   Update field within record in memory
>   Call *seek* to bring file position back to record being updated
>   *Write* revised record to file

In Exercise 22 we ask you to code this procedure.

‡12.5 MULTIFILE PROCESSING

• • • • • • • • • • • • •

Most of our work in the preceding sections focused on processing one file within a single run. The exceptions were the treatment of index files in Sec-

---

‡Optional, more advanced material. Skip without loss of continuity, study at this point, or wait until later.

tion 12.3 and the explicit deletion of a record in Section 12.4. In reality, many applications and tasks require the processing of two or more files by a program. Here we consider copying one file to another, appending or joining two files, and merging or weaving files. We also return to the use of index files.

COPYING FILES

When we copy a file we create a "clone" or duplicate copy of the original file, as follows.

The duplicate copy is usually called a *backup copy* and is often named after the original file, but with the name extension .BAK.

The following design backs up a file by copying each component in the original file to the backup file.

Backup

> *Reset* original file
> *Rewrite* backup file
> While not *eof* original file do
>   *Read* component from original file
>   *Write* component to backup file
> *Close* both files

Try Exercise 23 to code this procedure.

APPENDING FILES

When we *append* or *join* two files, we create a new file whose components are all components in the first file followed by all components in the second file, as follows.

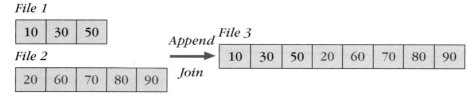

Alternatively, instead of creating a new (third) file, the components in the second file are simply appended to the existing components in the first file. The first file is thus the appended file, as follows.

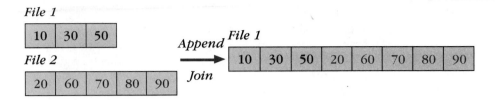

We ask you to design and code these tasks in Exercises 24–27.

MERGING FILES

Suppose two files of the same record type are each sorted by a common field, the *sort key*. For example, two employee files might be sorted by social security numbers. To *merge* or *weave* these two files, we would create a third file that contains all the records in the two original files, sorted by social security numbers.

To illustrate, consider the following file merge of two simple-component files into a third file.

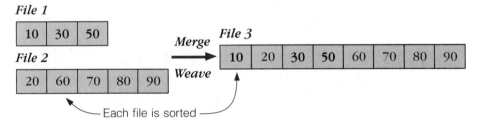

The following algorithm merges two sorted files of records.

Merge

{Open files}
  Reset Files 1 and 2
  Rewrite File 3

{Weave files while not eof for either file}
  Read File 1 record into primary memory as File 1 record variable
  Read File 2 record into primary memory as File 2 record variable
  While not *eof* File 1 and not *eof* File 2 do
    If sort key File 1 record var <= sort key File 2 record var then
      Write File 1 record variable to File 3
      Read File 1 record into primary memory as File 1 record var
    else
      Write File 2 record variable to File 3
      Read File 2 record into primary memory as File 2 record var

{Flush Files 1 and 2 record variables to File 3}
If *eof* File 1 thcn
  While not *eof* File 2 and sort keys File 2 <= File 1 do
    Write File 2 record variable to File 3
    Read File 2 record into primary memory as File 2 record var
  Write File 1 record variable to File 3
  Write File 2 record variable to File 3
else
  While not *eof* File 1 and sort keys File 1 <= File 2 do
    Write File 1 record variable to File 3
    Read File 1 record into primary memory as File 1 record var
  Write File 2 record variable to File 3
  Write File 1 record variable to File 3

{Write remaining records in longer file to File 3}
If *eof* File 1 then
  While not *eof* File 2 do
    Read File 2 record into primary memory as File 2 record var
    Write File 2 record variable to File 3
else
  While not *eof* File 1 do
    Read File 1 record into primary memory as File 1 record var
    Write File 1 record variable to File 3
Close three files

Note that we take a file-of-records perspective, but the algorithm (except for some of the wording) applies equally to files of any component type.

To understand how the algorithm works, desk check our sample merge using the algorithm. We'll get you started with the following desk-check script.

1. File 1 record variable is 10
2. File 2 record variable is 20
3. while test is true
4. if test is true (10 is less than 20)
5. 10 written to File 3
6. File 1 record variable is 30
7. while test is true
8. if test is false (30 exceeds 20)
9. 20 written to File 3
10. File 2 record variable is 60

Can you finish this script? If you do, we're sure you will understand the algorithmic logic. In Exercise 28 we ask you to complete this desk-check script. To really get this down, code the merge procedure in Exercise 29.

INDEX FILES FOR SEARCHING AND SORTING

In Figure 12.12b we showed how an *index file* is used to determine a record number based on an *index key*. In that example, the index key was social security number, and the employee file is said to be "indexed on social security number." To search for a particular social security number in the employee file, we would conduct the search not on the employee file itself but on the index file.[4] Once the desired social security number is found in the index file, we then use its corresponding record number to point to the record of interest in the employee file. To use an analogy, the index file is like an index at the back of this text: The "entries" in the index file are social security numbers; the "pages" in the index file are record numbers. It's much faster to "page" through an index file (the book's index) than it is to "page" through the employee file (the book itself). This is because read operations on an original file with many fields per record use more computer resources (memory and time) than the same number of read operations on an index file (which always has only two fields per record). Try Exercise 30 to code a search for social security number using an index file.

In Module D we introduced sorting on arrays, and in Section 11.4 we extended sorts to arrays of records. In this chapter we introduced the notion that we can conceptualize a file of records as an array of records that resides in a file rather than in primary memory. The record number is the analogue of the array index, and each component in the file is the analogue of each element in the array. Given this conceptualization, we can develop an algorithm that sorts a file based on a *sort key* by adapting the algorithm already developed in Figure 11.9. Note that we would not use an array at all! The sorting algorithm works directly on the file. We leave this to Exercise 32 by asking you to write a program that creates a new employee file sorted by name.

The sort just described on the employee file is what we would call a "brute force" sort. We take an original unsorted file and rewrite it with the same records, but sorted by a sort key like name or social security number. This approach wastes computer resources because read/write operations on multiple fields take more time and memory than read/write operations on a single field.[5] How can we avoid this inefficiency? By using an index file that's indexed on the sort key. This approach is desirable for a couple of reasons. First, it's faster to sort an index file (having two fields per record) than it is to sort the original file (having many fields per record). Second, we can avoid a sort on the original file simply by sequentially processing the index file (which is already sorted on the sort key) to point to the original file. We ask you to try this in Exercise 34.

In practice, original files like the employee file are indexed on more than one key; that is, multiple index files exist for the original file. This facilitates searches and sorts on commonly used key fields like social security numbers, account numbers, and names.

---

[4] We could search the index file in any of several ways previously discussed: by the query method in Example 12.3 or by one of the search function methods mentioned in Section 12.3.

[5] We could load all records in the file into an array in primary memory, sort the array in the usual way, and rewrite the file with the sorted array. This approach is faster than directly sorting the file, but it is memory intensive and impractical for very large commercial files. See Exercise 33 for this approach.

SELF-REVIEW EXERCISES

28

12.6 Programming Tips

• • • • • • • • • • • • • • •

Consider the following tips to improve the design and style of your programs and to avoid some common errors.

Design and Style

1. File Data Structure. An important design consideration is the file data structure that will be used. This issue is complex; it relates to factors such as speed, cost, the particular application, and the processing environment. *Typed files* have speed and storage advantages over *text files*. They also provide increased flexibility with respect to data structure (*simple* versus *structured components*) and access method (*sequential* and *direct*). One potential disadvantage of a typed file is that it may not be *transportable* from one computer system to another, as are text files. Some applications, like program editing, require text files. The data-structure flexibility of a typed file raises other design issues. For example, structured components like *records* have data-abstraction advantages over simple components.

2. Sequential Access Versus Direct Access. The access method that should be used depends on both the file medium and the particular application. A file that's stored on magnetic tape is processible only by sequential access; a file on magnetic disk is processible by either direct or sequential access. Given a choice, sequential access is best for applications with high *file activity*, in which all or most records in a file are processed. A file-backup task or a payroll application are examples that require high file activity. Direct access is best used for applications that involve low file activity and fast response, like an airline reservation system or a bank ATM system.

3. Defensive Programming. Program defensively for dangerous tasks that erase components, as in calls to *rewrite, truncate,* and *erase*. Utility OpenNewFile in Figure 12.5 illustrates this design feature, as does the pseudocode for procedure DeleteRecord in Section 12.4.

4. Reusable Modules. File processing is a great applications area for practicing the design of reusable modules. Note how program Employ2 in Figure 12.7 reused modules OpenNewFile, OutputEmployee, ReadReply, and Pause. Module OutputEmployee is used in programs Employee1, Employee2,

Query1, and Query2. Improve your programming productivity by an awareness of the utilities available to you (see inside front cover of text), and by designing reusable modules that are potentially usable by related applications.

5. Backup Files. The greatest worry in computer installations is the complete loss of a database and applications software. The loss of files through fire, theft, sabotage, *viruses*, or some other disaster is more damaging than the loss of the hardware system. Hardware is easily replaced, compared to rewriting programs and reconstructing a database. An integral part of file protection is the backup of all existing files. In large organizations, this is not a trivial task. For example, a typical airline reservation system has over 100 disk drives for its more than 1 million customer records. Half of these are a backup of the other half. Moreover, on a daily basis, these files are dumped to magnetic tape and stored off-site. Have you been backing up your own work? There are only two kinds of computer users and programmers: those who have lost files and those who *will* lose files...

6. Optimization Note: Use a Typed File Whenever Possible. This reduces processor time and file storage over text-file counterparts, as explained in Section 12.1.

COMMON ERRORS

1. What File Variable? It's easy to forget the file variable in calls to eof, eoln, read, write, and other file procedures and functions. For example, what happens in the call

> **write** (Employee); 😞

This would be a compile-time error, because record variable Employee cannot be written to the default output device (the display). Instead we meant

> **write** (FileEmployee, Employee); 😊

More subtly, what do you think would happen with the call

> **eof** 🙁

The system assumes the default input device (the keyboard) and is looking ahead to the next character that's typed, to "see" if it's the end of file *Ctrl-Z* for the keyboard input buffer. What are we doing? We're sitting there thinking the system is going to access a file on disk. We have a miscommunication standoff, and nothing happens. What to do? Press *Ctrl-Break* to break execution and revise the call to

> **eof** (FileEmployee) 😊

2. Not Closing the File. Remember to close files where appropriate; otherwise, one or more components may not be written to the file for file-creation and file-maintenance tasks.

3. Calls to readln or writeln for Typed Files. Remember that the structure of typed files does not include end-of-line markers. The readln and writeln statements are only valid for text files. Try one of these calls to a typed file and you get an *Invalid file type* compile-time error message. Keep in mind that some file procedures and functions apply to both text and typed files, but others apply to one or the other (as seen in Tables 12.1 and 12.2).

4. Component Numbers Start with Zero? Yes! It's perverse to us humans, but there are technical reasons for this. Make sure that calls to *seek* use correct component numbers, as do for-do loops that include component numbers for control.

5. Inadvertent Erasure. Program defensively to avoid logic errors regarding the unintentional deletion of records and files. See "Design and Style" tip 3 above.

REVIEW EXERCISES

EASIER	For the busy... **2a–d 3 4 5 7 9 13**
NORMAL	For the thinkers... **1 2e–f 6 8 10 12 14 18 19 20 21 22 23 24 25 26 27 28**
TOUGHER	For the hard CORE... **2g 11 15 16 17 29 30 31 32 33 34 35 36 37**

1. **Grades.** Let's consider a possible roster/grading program for an academic course.
    a. Describe possible file data structures of a student grade file for a large (say, 200 students) academic course. Data of interest include full name (up to 30 characters), social security number (without dashes), and up to eight grades per student on a 0–100 scale.
    b. Write code that declares a file-of-records variable **FileStudent** with type **FileStudentType**. The record type is **StudentType** and the record variable is **StudentRecord**. Declare a one-dimensional matrix **Grades** with type **GradesType** to hold the grades for a student.
    c. Code a statement that assigns file **HC101.BIN** in drive **C** along path **GRADES** to the file variable.

      d. Code a statement that opens a new file for this grade file.

      e. Code a statement that opens an existing file for this grade file.

      f. Code a statement that writes a record to the student file.

      g. Code a statement that reads a record from the student file.

      h. Code a statement that closes the student file.

      i. Code a statement that renames the student file **HC101.BIN** to **HC101A.BIN**.

      j. Code a statement that erases **HC101.TXT**, which has already been assigned to file variable **TextFile**.

2. Identify incorrect syntax (if any) or describe execution behavior for each of the following.

```
a. read (Employee);
b. seek (TextFile, ComponentNumber);
c. append (TextFile);
   writeln ('I LOVE file processing!');
d. reset (FileEmployee);
   truncate (FileEmployee);
e. seek (FileVar, filesize(FileVar));
   writeln(filepos(FileVar));
f. writeln (eoln);
g. while not eoln(TextFile) do
     begin
       read (TextFile, Character);
       write (Character);
     end; {while}
   writeln;
   readln (TextFile);
```

   Ⓛ **3.** **NewFile program.** With respect to Example 12.1...

      a. Test drive the program to reproduce our run in Figure 12.3. Store the data file in drive A.

      b. Load file TEMPS.BIN into the IDE editor. What do you think?

   Ⓛ **4.** **NewFile program.** Revise and run the program to create and display a...

      a. File of characters a b c d e.

      b. File of real values 1.1   1.2   1.3.

      c. File of strings HC is...Okay

          1st string —⤴   ⤴— 2nd string

      d. Text file of the same integers seen in Figure 12.3.

   Ⓛ ***5.** **NewFile program.** Revise and run the program to...

      a. Display the following at the end of the CREATE FILE screen:

        File temps.bin has been created.

        Number of components = 5

      b. Use *Include files* for utility modules OpenNewFile, CreateFile, and ShowFile.

c. Replace the while-do oof loop in procedure ShowFile with a for-do loop that uses a call to *filesize* for control. Which loop structure do you like best, and why?

(L) ***6.** **Utility DumpFile.** Write and test a new utility procedure named **DumpFile** that dumps (writes) a file to one of the following menu-selectable options.

File Dump Options...
  D   Display screen
  F   File (text)
  P   Printer
  X   eXit this menu

Test this utility as a module in program NewFile.

(L) **7.** **Employ2 program.** With respect to Example 12.2...
  a. Test drive the program to reproduce our run in Figure 12.6. Include a fourth record for **Grace Hopper** (social security number **444-44-4444**) with a salary of **$100,000**. Store the data file in drive A.
  b. Load file EMPLOYEE.BIN into the IDE editor. What do you think?

(L) ***8.** **City temperatures.** Revise or use parts of programs Employ2 and ArrayIO3 (Figure 11.7) to create and display a file of city records using the data in Figure 11.5. Name the file CITYTEMP.BIN. Don't use an array. Simply store one city record at a time in primary memory.

(L) **9.** **Query1 program.** Test drive the program in Example 12.3 by first mistyping the employee file name, then typing the correct file specification, then searching for **f**, **n** (a typo), and **m**.

(L) ***10.** **Query1 program.** Revise and run the program by adding a new module for each of the following queries.
  a. Salary greater than a user-input cutoff. Try **50000** and **100000** for the cutoffs in your test run.
  b. Name = user-input name. Try **Babbage, Charles** and **Lovelace, Ada** in your test run.
  c. SS number = user-input social security number. Try **999-99-9999** and **111111111** in your test run.

(L) ***11.** **Query1 program.** Revise and run the program by displaying a query menu that offers the f/m choice in the original program, the three choices in the preceding exercise, and a fifth choice that displays a report comparing average male and female salaries.

(L) ***12.** **City temperatures.** Revise Query1 to query the city temperatures file created in Exercise 8, as follows.
  a. Search for a specific city name to display its record. Input **Toronto**, **Boston**, and **Atlanta** in your test run.

b. Search for all cities whose temperature exceeds a cutoff. Use 50 and 70 for the cutoffs in your test run.

c. Offer a menu for the two choices in parts **a** and **b**.

(L) **13.** **Query2 program.** With respect to Example 12.4...

a. Test drive the program to access records 2, 6, and 0.

b. Will this program handle a file that contains 10,000 records? 50,000 records? 100,000 records? Explain.

(L) *14. **City temperatures.** Revise program Query2 to directly access city records in file CITYTEMP.BIN within the Examples Library. In your test run, display records 4, 0, and 5.

(L) *15. **Hash function.** With respect to Example 12.5...

a. What's the hash index for social security number 111111111? 999999999? What change would we make in the hash function if we wish the file to have 1000 records?

b. Create and display a new employee file by revising Employ2 to use the described hash function. *Hint:* You could change the typing on the social security number from *string* to *longint* (the "chicken" way out) or you could convert the string-valued social security number to its numeric longint equivalent by concatenated calls to *copy* (to strip off the dashes), followed by a call to *val* (see Chapter 10).

c. Query the file created in part **b** by revising Query2. Use 333-33-3333, 111-11-1111, and 555-55-5555 as test input. Try your own social security number!

(L) *16. **Search function for social security number record key.** Revise Query2 to implement the sequential search function in Figure 11.11. Don't use an array; rather, search the file directly based on the discussion in Section 12.3. Use 333-33-3333, 111-11-1111, and 555-55-5555 as test input. Try your own social security number!

(L) *17. **Search function for city name record key.** Revise Query2 to implement the sequential search function in Figure 11.11. Don't use an array; rather, search file CITYTEMP.BIN (in the Examples Library) directly based on the discussion in Section 12.3. Input **Toronto**, **Boston**, and **Atlanta** in your test run.

(L) *18. **AddEmployee procedure.** Write and test a procedure that adds a record to the end of the employee file. In your test run, add the Grace Hopper record in Exercise 7 to our original EMPLOYEE.BIN file.

(L) *19. **DeleteEmployee procedure.** Write and test a procedure that...

a. Implicitly deletes an employee based on social security number.

b. Explicitly deletes an employee based on social security number.

In your test run, delete Charles Babbage (333-33-3333) from our employee file.

(L) *20. **Update text-file record.** Write pseudocode to update an employee text-file record. *Hint:* It's similar to the pseudocode for deleting a record.

Ⓛ ***21.** **Update procedure I.** Write and test a procedure (**UpdateOneSal**) that updates the salary field in a specified employee-file record. Assume that the user indicates the record by entering its record number. In your test run, update Ada Lovelace's salary to $70,000.

Ⓛ ***22.** **Update procedure II.** Write and test a procedure (**UpdateAllSal**) that increases all salary fields in the employee file by a percent entered by the user. Increase salaries by 10 percent in your test run.

*23. **Backup procedure.** Write and test a utility procedure that backs up a file. In your test run, backup EMPLOYEE.BIN as file EMPLOYEE.BAK. Call utilities OpenOldFile and OpenNewFile from within this procedure.

*24. **Append procedure I for text files.** Develop a utility procedure (**Append1Text**) that appends two text files to create a third text file.
   a. Write pseudocode.
   b. Write and test code. Use the files on page 599 as test data.

*25. **Append procedure II for text files.** Develop a utility procedure (**Append2Text**) that appends text file two to text file one.
   a. Write pseudocode.
   b. Write and test code. Use the files on page 600 as test data.

*26. **Append procedure I for typed files.** Develop a utility procedure (**Append1Typed**) that appends two typed files to create a third typed file.
   a. Write pseudocode.
   b. Write and test code. Use the files on page 599 as test data.

*27. **Append procedure II for typed files.** Develop a utility procedure (**Append2Typed**) that appends typed file two to typed file one.
   a. Write pseudocode.
   b. Write and test code. Use the files on page 600 as test data.

28. **Merge desk-check script.** Complete the script on page 601.

*29. **Merge procedure.** Develop and test a procedure that merges two employee files using social security number as the sort key. In your test run, merge the following test files (which you need to create):

File 1:

```
111-11-1111   Lovelace, Ada A.    40000   f
333-33-3333   Hollerith, Herman   60000   m
999-99-9999   Babbage, Charles    50000   m
```

File 2:

```
000-00-0000   CORE, Harvey     300000   m
444-44-4444   Hopper, Grace    100000   f
```

(L) *30. **Index-file-transformation function based on social security number.** Create the index file shown in Figure 12.12b using the IDE editor. Revise Query2 by writing a function that returns the record number given the social security number. Use **333-33-3333**, **111-11-1111**, and **555-55-5555** as test input. Try your own social security number!

(L) *31. **Index-file-transformation function based on name.** Create an index file indexed on the employee's full name using the IDE editor. Revise Query2 by writing a function that returns the record number given the full name. Use **Lovelace** and **Lovelace, Ada A.** as test input. Try your own name!

(L) *32. **File sort by brute force.** Adapt the sorting algorithm in Figure 11.9 to sort file EMPLOYEE.BIN by...
a. Name
b. Social security number
Don't replace the original file; rather, create a duplicate file and sort this file directly (without using arrays).

(L) *33. **File sort by array.** Adapt the sorting algorithm in Figure 11.9 to sort file EMPLOYEE.BIN according to footnote 5 by...
a. Name
b. Social security number
Don't replace the original file; instead, create a separate sorted file.

(L) *34. **File sorts using index files.** Develop a procedure that displays the unsorted records in EMPLOYEE.BIN in ascending order by...
a. Name
b. Social security number
Use an appropriate index file to point to the appropriate records in EMPLOYEE.BIN. In this approach, the original file is not sorted; rather, the already-sorted index file is used to display records from the original file in the required order. Create the proper index files by using the IDE editor.

(L) *35. **Revisit: HC ENGINE.** Revise Exercise 20 in Chapter 6 to offer a menu for routing the output report to either the screen, printer, or a user-designated text file. Read engine data from a text file.

(L) *36. **Revisit: HC METHsea.** Revise Exercise 32 in Chapter 9 to offer a menu for routing output to either the screen, printer, or a user-designated text file. Read platform data from a text file.

(L) *37. **Employee.** Let's go the "nine yards." Develop a program for our employee example with the following features.
a. Offer the following menu system.
Main Menu...
    A   Append (join) files
    B   Backup file
    C   Create file

D   Display file
E   Erase file
M   Maintain file
Q   Query file
R   Rename file
S   Sort file
W   Weave (merge) files
X   eXit

In this part, treat the modules for options A, M, Q, S, and W as *program stubs*—modules that simply write something like "This option is not ready at this time." In your test runs, create and display the two employee files in Exercise 29, back up the original file twice, rename one of the backup files, and erase the other backup file.

b. Develop the Append module. In your test run, append your two employee files to create a third file.

c. Develop the Maintain module. This module offers the following submenu.

Maintain submenu...

A   Add record
D   Delete record
U   Update record
X   eXit

The Update choice gives the following submenu.

Update field in record...

1   Social security number
2   Full name
3   Salary
4   Sex code
X   eXit

Select your own test data to debug these menu items.

d. Develop the Query module. This module displays the following submenu.

Query by...

1   Social security
2   Full name
3   Salary cutoff
4   Sex code
X   eXit

The salary-cutoff option displays all records whose salary exceeds the salary cutoff that's entered by the user. Select your own test data to debug these menu items.

   e. Develop the Sort module. This module provides the following submenu.

   Display records sorted by...

   1   Social security number
   2   Full name
   3   Salary
   4   Sex code
   X   eXit

   See Exercises 32–34. The index-file approach is best. If you work with
   index files, the create routine should create an index file indexed on each
   field. Implement each menu item in your test run.
   f. Develop the Weave module (see Exercise 29).
   g. ADT Employee. Make use of an enhanced ADT Employee from Exercise 24 in Chapter 11.

ADDITIONAL EXERCISES

EASIER	For the busy... **38**
NORMAL	For the thinkers... **39 40**
TOUGHER	For the hard CORE... **41 42**

38. **Revisit.** Select a program that you have already written and revise it to offer
a menu for routing output to either the screen, printer, or a user-designated
text file.

39. **Revisit.** Select an additional exercise from one of the following chapters and
revise it to open, process, and close one or more data files. Use typed files
and direct access where appropriate.
   a. Chapter 9
   b. Chapter 10
   c. Chapter 11

40. Bond issue. Develop a program that offers the following main menu for managing bond issues in a state.

> Main Menu...
> A   Add records
> C   Create file
> D   Delete records
> R   Report
> S   Show file
> X   eXit

In your test runs, create and show file BOND.BIN with the following records.

County	Yes votes	No votes
Dade	300,000	400,000
Cuyahoga	100,000	75,000
Washington	50,000	30,000
Hamilton	500,000	300,000

Then add the following records and show the file again.

Orange	250,000	100,000
Broward	150,000	75,000
Orange	250,000	100,000

Then delete the duplicate record for Orange County and show the file once more. For the report option, you decide what might be interesting to show in the report.

41. Charge card. Develop a program that prints monthly bills (statements) for Muster Charge, an internationally renowned credit card company. The printout for each person should take up exactly 12 lines in order to conform to the size of the billing statement. Sample input data are described by the table below. A customer's statement should include name, address, previous balance, payments, finance charge, new purchases, new balance, and minimum payment due. Design your own statement, but make sure that it conforms to the 12-line limitation.

Account ID	Name	Address	Credit Limit	Previous Balance	Payments	New Purchases
300	Napoleon B.	19 Waterloo St. Paris, France	$ 800	$ 300.00	$ 100.00	$700.00
400	Duke Welly	1 Thames Ave. London, UK	1500	1350.70	1320.70	645.52
500	Betsy Ross	1776 Flag St. Boston, MA USA	2000	36.49	36.49	19.15

The following conditions apply to the program.

1. The finance charge is 1.5 percent of the difference between the previous month's balance and the payments made since the previous month. You should confirm the following new balances for our three sample customers: $903.00, $675.97, and $19.15.

2. The minimum payment due is determined according to one of four results.

   a. If the new balance exceeds the credit limit, then the minimum payment is the difference between the new balance and the credit limit plus 10 percent of the credit limit. Thus, for the first statement, $(903 - 800) + 10\% \cdot (800)$ gives $183.

   b. If the new balance is $100 or more and does not exceed the credit limit, then the minimum payment is 10 percent of the new balance. Thus, for the second statement, $10\% \cdot (675.97)$ gives $67.60.

   c. If the new balance is less than $100, then the minimum payment is set to the new balance, or $19.15 for the third statement.

   d. If the new balance is negative, then the minimum payment is zero.

3. A warning is printed if the credit limit is exceeded by the new balance (Muster Charge doesn't fool around). This is the case with the first statement. Use a directly accessed *master file* and a text *transaction file*. The master file contains ID, name, address, credit limit, and last billing period's ending (previous) balance for each customer. The transaction file contains ID, payments, and new purchases.

a. Run the program for the data given in the problem so that transactions are input interactively for an account, the master file is updated by direct access, the bill is printed, and the transactions for that account are written as a line in the transaction file (for a permanent record of that month's transactions).

b. Offer the following transactions menu for an account.

Transaction codes . . .

1 Payment
2 New purchases
3 Name change
4 Address change
5 Credit limit change
6 Previous balance change
7 Delete account
8 Add account
9 Statements
X eXit

These transactions directly update the master file and are written to the transaction file. Each line in the transaction file now contains the ID, transaction code, and the transaction value (name, address, and so on).

42. **Grades.** Develop a comprehensive program that maintains and processes student grades for an academic course. You might include features such as file creation, file modifications (for example, change a grade, add a grade, delete a grade, delete a record, add a record), file display, record display, calculation of final numeric grade based on weights for individual grades (including the assignment of a letter grade if applicable).... If a student is added to the file, make sure this student is placed in the correct alphabetic position. Once your program is debugged, hire yourself a marketing major and pedal your program to faculty members for an exorbitant software fee.

Dynamic Data Structures

Recall that a *data structure* is a collection of related elements that are arranged in a particular pattern. For example, the *record data structure* is a collection of fields in the order given by the record type declaration; the *array data structure* is a collection of elements in the order suggested by their indexes.

Up to now all of our data structures have been *static* in the sense that memory cells are allocated and related before program execution. In this chapter, we present methods that allow the *dynamic* creation, deletion, and relation of memory cells during program execution, with particular emphasis on a data structure called the *linked list*.

13.1 POINTERS AND DYNAMIC VARIABLES

• • • • • • • • • • • • • • •

A new data type called the *pointer type* and new variables called *pointer variables* and *dynamic variables* are central to the creation of dynamic data structures. Before defining these, let's take a closer look at what we mean by *static* and *dynamic data structures*.

STATIC VERSUS DYNAMIC DATA STRUCTURES

A **static data structure** is a data structure whose elements are allocated storage through its declaration in the var section of a program. Thus, storage is reserved in advance of program execution. A *record* (Chapter 11) and an *array of records* (Section 11.4) are common examples of static data structures.

Figure 13.1a illustrates a static data structure given by an array of city records (first seen in Figure 11.5), where each record has a city name field and a Fahrenheit temperature field. Note that the 500 elements (records) in this array are allocated before the program is executed, based on the declaration of array variable CityArray. CityArray is an example of a **static variable:** Its stored values can change during execution, but both the number of elements and their relationship to one another are *static* or fixed. Our example shows 500 fixed elements, where the *index* prescribes the relationships among elements. For example, the second element follows the first element, the third element follows the second element, and so on. As seen in the figure, the first three elements are defined (filled) during execution, and the remaining 497 elements are undefined (unused).

A **dynamic data structure** is a data structure whose elements are allocated storage during program execution. Each element is represented by a

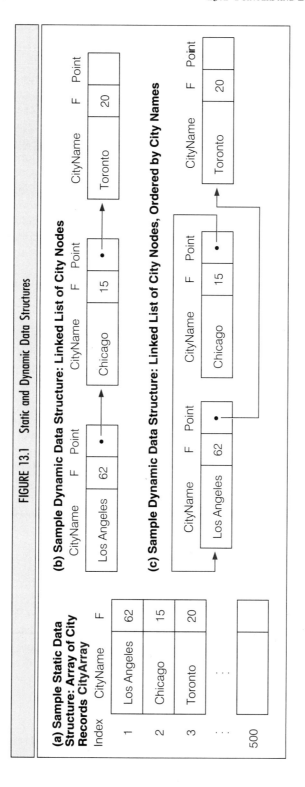

FIGURE 13.1   Static and Dynamic Data Structures

separate **dynamic variable**, and the number of elements expands and contracts based on the execution of an algorithm.

Parts b and c of Figure 13.1 show the sample city records as a dynamic data structure called a *linked list.* Note that we only create as many records as we need. Storage is not wasted, as in the array data structure in part a of the figure. If we need a fourth record, that record is created and *linked* to an existing record within the *list* of records during program execution. We can also delete a record. Moreover, by comparing parts b and c of the figure, we see that we can also dynamically redefine the relationship among elements (in part c the elements are ordered alphabetically by city name).

Each record (element) in parts b and c of Figure 13.1 is called a **node,** and its value or contents is stored within a *dynamic variable.* A node is related to another node through a special *pointer* field that points to that node. Thus, elements in dynamic data structures are related to one another by memory cells that point to other elements, as seen by the arrows in Figure 13.1. This brings us to . . .

POINTER DECLARATION AND DYNAMIC-VARIABLE CREATION

We declare and create dynamic data structures by using a new data type called the *pointer type* and two kinds of variables called *pointer variables* and *dynamic variables.* The accompanying syntax box shows the necessary syntax, together with examples. Note the following.

1. The **pointer type** is a new data type for defining values that represent addresses for memory locations of type *base type.* Put another way, a pointer-type value identifies ("points" to) another memory location; the memory location it points to stores a base-type value. In the examples, type IntPointerType is a pointer type whose values point to memory locations that store integer values, as declared by ˆ**integer**; StrPointerType is a pointer type whose values are memory addresses for other memory locations of type string, as specified by ˆ**string.** The **pointer symbol** ˆ is one of Turbo Pascal's special symbols.[1]

2. The **pointer variable,** or simply **pointer,** is a variable having type pointer type. Its purpose is to store the address of a memory location (represented by a *dynamic variable*) of type base type (as specified in its pointer type declaration). In the examples, Pointer1 and Pointer2 are declared pointers for storing the addresses of type-*integer* memory locations (integer dynamic variables). We know these point to *integer* dynamic variables because integer is specified as the base type in type IntPointerType. Similarly, Pointer3 points to a *string* dynamic variable.

---

[1] A common variation of the pointer symbol in the Pascal literature is the uparrow symbol (↑), as specified in Standard Pascal.

SYNTAX BOX

Pointer declarations and procedure new... Declare pointer type in type section, pointer variable in var section, and create dynamic variable in algorithm section

```
Syntax......type
          PointerType = ˆBaseType;    {Declares pointer type PointerType for values that point to
                                        dynamic variables of BaseType}

          var
          PointerVar : PointerType;   {Declares pointer variable PointerVar of type PointerType for
                                        pointing to dynamic variable}

          begin  {algorithm}
          ...
          new(PointerVar);            {Creates dynamic variable referenced by PointerVarˆ for storing
                                        value having type BaseType}

          ...
          end;  {algorithm}
```

```
Examples...type
          IntPointerType = ˆinteger;          {Declares pointer type IntPointerType
                                                with base type integer}
          StrPointerType = ˆstring;           {Declares pointer type StrPointerType
                                                with base type string}

          var
          Pointer1, Pointer2 : IntPointerType; {Declares pointer variables Pointer1
                                                and Pointer2 of type IntPointerType}
          Pointer3           : StrPointerType; {Declares pointer variable Pointer3 of
                                                type StrPointerType}

          begin  {algorithm}
          ...
          new (Pointer1);                     {Creates dynamic variable referenced
                                                by Pointer1ˆ for storing
                                                integer value}
          new (Pointer3);                     {Creates dynamic variable referenced
                                                by Pointer3ˆ for storing
                                                string value}

          ...
          end;  {algorithm}
```

Explanation... PointerType is a user-defined identifier for a *pointer type* that declares a set of values that points to *dynamic variables* of type BaseType. BaseType is any legitimate data type, except for a file type. The *pointer symbol* ˆ must precede BaseType. PointerVar is a user-defined identifier for the *pointer variable* whose type is PointerType. The pointer variable stores the address of a specific *dynamic variable*. The call **new** (PointerVar) to predeclared procedure **new** creates a new dynamic variable for storing a value having type BaseType. This dynamic variable is referenced by PointerVarˆ; its address or memory location is stored in the pointer variable PointerVar. Turbo Pascal includes the alternative of calling new as a function. The functional form

        PointerVar := **new** (PointerType)

is equivalent to the standard procedure call **new** (PointerVar).

To better understand the use (and debugging!) of pointers and dynamic variables, it helps to map out memory cells. At the point (pun intended) in time just following the compilation of our sample code, the three declared pointers yield the following memory scheme.

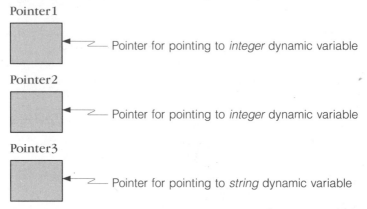

Pointer1

Pointer for pointing to *integer* dynamic variable

Pointer2

Pointer for pointing to *integer* dynamic variable

Pointer3

Pointer for pointing to *string* dynamic variable

Note that these pointers are only declared at this time. Their contents are undefined; that is, following compilation, they're not pointing to anything. Their contents are defined at run time by calling the predeclared procedure **new.**

3. We call **new** to accomplish two objectives: to create a new storage location represented by a dynamic variable, and to place the address of the dynamic variable in the pointer identified in the argument to the call. In our examples, we can represent memory at this time in the run as follows.

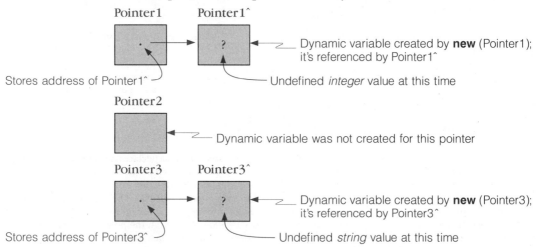

Pointer1   Pointer1^

Dynamic variable created by **new** (Pointer1); it's referenced by Pointer1^

Stores address of Pointer1^

Undefined *integer* value at this time

Pointer2

Dynamic variable was not created for this pointer

Pointer3   Pointer3^

Dynamic variable created by **new** (Pointer3); it's referenced by Pointer3^

Stores address of Pointer3^

Undefined *string* value at this time

Note that we use the dot and arrow to represent the address stored in the pointer. The arrow points to the memory cell represented by the dynamic variable. *The dynamic variable is referenced by using the name of its corresponding pointer variable, followed by an attached pointer symbol.* Thus, Pointer1ˆ is a reference to the dynamic variable pointed to by Pointer1. Finally, note that the dynamic variables (their contents) are undefined at this time, which we show by the question mark. Values are entered into dynamic variables by the usual assignment and input operations.

4. Storage locations for dynamic variables reside in a pool of storage locations called the **heap.** In Turbo Pascal, the memory available to the heap includes all free (unused) memory. Each call to procedure new allocates a previously free memory cell to the heap. For example, the call **new** (Pointer1) uses a free memory cell to allocate the contents in dynamic variable Pointer1ˆ to the heap. The second call **new** (Pointer3) uses the next free memory cell to allocate the contents in Pointer3ˆ to the heap. If insufficient free memory is available to the heap when procedure new is called, a run-time error occurs.[2]

5. We can call predeclared procedure **dispose** to eliminate dynamic variables (memory cells) from the heap. For example, the call **dispose** (Pointer1) frees the memory cell within the heap previously assigned to Pointer1ˆ and simultaneously undefines the value in pointer Pointer1.

OPERATIONS ON POINTERS AND DYNAMIC VARIABLES

In the material that follows, let's keep in mind that we're working with two new kinds of variables: the *pointer variable* or *pointer* (as in Pointer1 in our example) and the *dynamic variable* to which the pointer points.

By *operations,* we mean activities like the evaluation of expressions, the assignment of values, and I/O. In defining allowable operations on a data type, we usually need to reference variables of that data type. Pointers are referenced by name in the usual way, as in Pointer1. These variables store the addresses that point to dynamic variables. Dynamic variables are not declared, so we can't reference them by their names. In fact, they don't have names, nor do they need names! In operations, we use a variable name to access the contents of the memory cell addressed by that name. Because the memory cell address of the dynamic variable is already stored within a pointer, the dynamic variable does not need a name to access its contents. We simply reference the dynamic variable by using the name of the appropriate pointer suffixed by the pointer symbol. Thus, Pointer1ˆ references the dynamic variable pointed to by Pointer1.

The data type of a pointer variable is its declared *pointer type,* as in IntPointerType for the pointer Pointer1; the data type of a dynamic variable is the *base type* specified by the pointer type of the pointer used to create the dynamic variable. Thus, the data type for the dynamic variable referenced by Pointer1ˆ is integer, because ˆinteger was used in the declaration for IntPointerType (see the syntax box on p. 621).

---

[2]The default minimum and maximum heap sizes are, respectively, 0KB and 640KB. We can reset these heap sizes through either the IDE (Options Memory sizes) or the compiler directive {$*M*}.

Other than a quick review of terminology and concepts, what's the upshot of this discussion? Most operations require variable references, so we need to know how to reference these variables. More important, allowable operations are determined by the data type, so we need to be clear on the data type we're dealing with. The data type for pointers is a new data type for us, so we have to define its allowable operations for the first time; the data type for dynamic variables is old stuff, because the base type is any one of our earlier data types (except for the file type). To more clearly distinguish between our two kinds of variables (and their data types), let's break up the discussion of operations accordingly.[3]

Operations on Dynamic Variables

The allowable operations on a dynamic variable are identical to those allowed in our earlier discussions for the corresponding base type. For example, if the base type is integer, then all allowable operations on integer types are legitimate; if the base type is string, then all defined operations on string types are allowed.

EXAMPLE 13.1   OPERATIONS ON DYNAMIC VARIABLES

Let's continue with our earlier examples of dynamic variables. We can use assignment statements in the usual way, as in

```
Pointer1^ := 49;                  {Integer assignment}
Pointer3^ := 'I LOVE pointers!';  {String assignment}
```

Following the execution of these assignment statements, our earlier memory cells would be revised as follows.

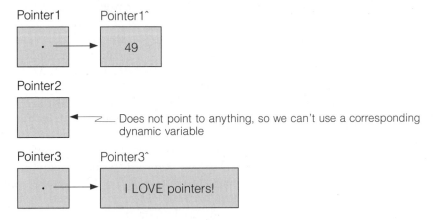

---

[3]The manipulation of pointers and dynamic variables can be weird and confusing at first. Stay with us...the more we work with these, the easier it gets.

To display the values in these dynamic variables, we would simply use write or writeln statements, as in the following.

writeln (Pointer1^, Pointer3^); {Displays 49I LOVE pointers!}

Similarly, we could use read or readln statements to store values within these dynamic variables, as in the following.

write ('Enter integer... '); **readln** (Pointer1^);
write ('Enter string.... '); **readln** (Pointer3^);

Finally, we should note that we can use a dynamic variable as an *actual parameter* (as in the above calls to writeln and readln), but not as a *formal parameter* in a module's heading.

Operations on Pointers

The pointer type defines a very restricted set of traditional operations and some new predeclared procedures and functions. First off, we can't I/O pointers. We can use assignment statements whose right-member expression is either another pointer or a predeclared *pointer constant* **nil**, which points to nothing. Moreover, the left and right members of the assignment statement have the same pointer type (**nil** is compatible with any pointer type). Relational expressions with pointers are restricted to the relational operators = and < >. Finally, pointers are legitimate parameters in module calls and headings and are therefore acted on by the algorithms within these modules. Predeclared procedures *new* and *dispose* are two such modules.

EXAMPLE 13.2   OPERATIONS ON POINTERS

Continuing with our preceding example, consider the following pointer assignment.

Pointer2 := Pointer1;

This operation assigns the value in Pointer1 to Pointer2; that is, both these pointers now point to the same dynamic variable, giving the following memory scheme.

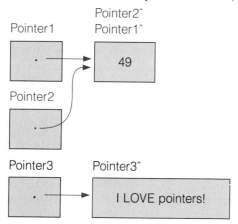

Note that Pointer2^ and Pointer1^ reference the same dynamic variable. If we follow this assignment statement with

```
Pointer1 := nil;
```

then Pointer1 is disconnected from its dynamic variable, giving the following memory configuration.

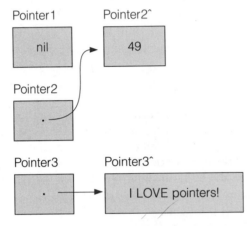

Note that we place nil within the memory cell for Pointer1 to indicate that it stores the *pointer constant* nil (it does not store the *string* nil). As we will see later, nil is useful as a means of detecting the last node in a linked list.

What would happen if we were to use the following assignment?

```
Pointer3 := nil;  ☹
```

Pointer3 would be disconnected from its dynamic variable, and we would lose the ability to reference the dynamic variable that stores the given string! The dynamic variable is still in the heap, but we've lost it because we can't reference it! This would be a logic error in our programming.

Finally, we can form relational expressions with pointers, but only by using the operators = and < >. For example, the statement

```
if Pointer1 = Pointer2 then
   ... ;
```

tests *true* in the first memory scheme above, but *false* in the second.

RECORD NODES

The implementation of a dynamic data structure requires a means by which we can relate nodes to one another. As seen in Figure 13.1, we can accomplish this by creating nodes whose base type is a record type. We then connect one node to another by including a field within the record that points to the next node. Thus, the dynamic variable that represents a node stores a record; that is, it's a *record node*.

The accompanying syntax box gives the particulars for declaring and creating record nodes. Note the following.

1. The *record pointer type* is a pointer type that uses a record type as its base type. In the example, PointerType is a record pointer type that points to the declared record type CityNodeType. Record type CityNodeType includes fields for city name and Fahrenheit temperature, as in our Chapter 11 example. Unlike the earlier example, however, we now include a *pointer field* for pointing to a record. The type of this pointer field is the very same pointer type declared just before the record type declaration. In the example, the field Point has type PointerType.

2. The following alternative declarations revise the CityNodeType declaration to a single data-field declaration that corresponds to the element's data and type.

```
type
  CityRecType = record
    CityName : string [20];      {City name field}
    F        : integer;          {Fahrenheit temperature field}
  end; {CityRecType}

  PointerType = ^CityNodeType;
  CityNodeType = record
    CityElement : CityRecType;   {City record field element}
    Point       : PointerType;   {Pointer field links city record nodes}
  end; {CityNodeType}
```

The element's data fields are now incorporated within the *record field* CityElement typed CityRecType, the same record type we used for this example in Chapter 11. In this version, we visualize a node as having a single data field and a single pointer field. The data field can be a simple type (like integer, character, string, real, or Boolean) or a structured type (like set, array, or record as above).

3. The pointer variable NodePointer has type PointerType. Its purpose is to point to a specific node. We create that node in the usual way, with a call to **new**.

Just how we create the sample dynamic data structure shown in Figure 13.1b is the topic of the next section.

SYNTAX BOX

Record pointer type and record nodes... Declare record pointer type in type section and pointer variable in var section, and create record node (dynamic variable) in algorithm section

---

Syntax......type

        PointerType = ^RecordType;   {Declares PointerType as a *record pointer type* for pointing to nodes of type RecordType}

        RecordType = **record**

           .⎫
           .⎬ Field list   — Same pointer type
           .⎭

           PointerField : PointerType;   {Declares pointer field PointerField with type PointerType as part of record}

        end;

        var
           PointerVar : PointerType;   {Declares *pointer variable* PointerVar of type PointerType for pointing to record node}

        begin {algorithm}
          ...
        new(PointerVar);   {Creates record node}
          ...
        end; {algorithm}

Examples...type
          PointerType = ^CityNodeType;
          CityNodeType = **record**
            CityName : **string** [20];   {City name field}
            F   : **integer**;   {Fahrenheit temperature field}
            Point   : PointerType;   {Pointer field links city record nodes}
          end; {CityNodeType}

        var
          NodePointer : PointerType;   {Declares pointer for pointing to city record node}

        begin {algorithm}
          ...
        new (NodePointer);   {Creates city record node pointed to by NodePointer}
          ...
        end; {algorithm}

Explanation... PointerType is a user-defined identifier for a *pointer type* that points to a node whose type is a record type. RecordType is a user-defined identifier for a record type (as defined on page 520). PointerField is a field identifier having type PointerType. Its purpose is to point to another node. Note that the declaration of PointerType references RecordType, which is used before it's declared; that is, the use of RecordType precedes its declaration. This is an exception to the rule that requires the declaration of an identifier before its first use. PointerVar is a user-defined identifier for a pointer that points to a node whose type is a record. The call to **new** creates a node whose type is a record.

NOTE

1. PointerVar versus PointerVar^. The distinction between these two is often confused by programmers just starting to work with pointers. The *pointer* PointerVar simply stores the address of another memory cell. The memory cell pointed to by the pointer is called a *dynamic variable,* or *node.* The dynamic variable stores an element of data (like a record or an integer) whose type is one of the legitimate Turbo Pascal types, except for the file type. We can fill, access, or otherwise manipulate the contents in the dynamic variable by using the reference PointerVar^. PointerVar is created by its declaration in the var section; its contents are not accessed like ordinary variables. The dynamic variable is not declared; it's created by a call to procedure new; its contents are accessed like ordinary variables, by using the reference PointerVar^.

2. Dynamic versus static structured variables. A static structured variable is used to represent a *static data structure.* For example, in Chapter 11 we used the static structured variables City to store a record data structure and CityArray to store an array-of-city-records data structure. The dynamic data structure in Figure 13.1, however, is not stored within a single variable; rather, it's stored within three separate dynamic variables...and each dynamic variable is itself a structured variable (a record)!

SELF-REVIEW EXERCISES

1 2 3

13.2 LINKED LISTS

• • • • • • • • • • • • • • • •

A **linked list,** or simply a **list,** is a sequence of nodes where each node (except the last) is linked to the next node in the sequence. The common implementation of a linked list uses record nodes, where a pointer field within each record links that node to the next node, as seen in parts b and c of Figure 13.1. The declaration of record pointer types, record node pointers, and the creation of a record node for the city list example are illustrated in our last syntax box.

The list is an important dynamic data structure with many applications that often include alternatives to and certain advantages over the array data structure. As mentioned earlier, compared to an array, the list can save memory. The list also has certain advantages over arrays in sorting applications. For example, the operations that insert a new record within a sorted list are simpler and faster than the corresponding operations that work with an array, as we will see.

The creation of lists like those in parts b and c of Figure 13.1 requires the design and implementation of algorithms. The list in Figure 13.1c is an example of an *ordered list,* where the sequence of nodes is based on the ordering of values for a *key field.* In that example, the list is ordered by city names. Thus, the node for Boston is first, followed by the node for Los Angeles, and finally the node for Toronto. We cover the creation of this ordered list in Section 13.3.

In this section, we consider the creation, display, filing, and file retrieval of an *unordered list* like that in Figure 13.1b. Note that this list is unordered in the sense that its linkages are not based on the values of a key field, like city names or temperatures. Instead, the ordering of its nodes is based on the chronological sequence with which the nodes were created.

CITY LIST APPLICATION

Let's start by describing the requirements, design, code, and test for a program that works with the city list first described in Figure 13.1. This program will serve as the basis for the remaining examples in this chapter.

Requirements

We wish a menu-driven program that manages a list of cities. The data on each city include its name (up to 20 characters) and its Fahrenheit temperature. We need to create the list in one of two ways: either in the chronological order by which city records are entered or sorted by city name. We also wish to display the list, save it to a data file, retrieve it from a data file, and search it by city name to display the data for a desired city. Finally, we wish to update the list by adding a new city at the end of the list, inserting a new city within the list, deleting a city from the list, and changing the data for a city. The initial data requirements are modest, as seen in Figure 13.1.

Design

Many of these requirements were handled by an array-of-records data structure in Chapters 11 and 12. In this application, let's work with a linked list, where each node is a city record. As seen in Figure 13.1, each record includes three fields: city name, Fahrenheit temperature, and a pointer field that points to the next city node in the list.

Figure 13.2 shows sample I/O design and an actual run. Study these screens and note the following.

1. Screen 2 shows the main menu. Selections that invoke other selections (menus) include an ellipsis (...), as in Create list....

FIGURE 13.2   I/O Design for City List Application and Run of Program List1

Screen 1

```
                            CITY LIST SYSTEM




Hit any key to continue...
```

Screen 2

```
Time is 10:49


                              MAIN MENU

              - - - - - - - - - - - - - - -
              | 1  Create list...             |
              | 2  Display list               |
              | 3  Save list                  |
              | 4  Get list                   |
              | 5  Find city                  |
              | 6  Update list...             |
              | Q  Quit                       |
              - - - - - - - - - - - - - - -

              Enter selection... 1
```

Screen 3

```
Time is 10:50


                            CREATE LIST MENU

              - - - - - - - - - - - - - - -
              | 1  Unordered list             |
              | 2  Ordered list               |
              | Q  Quit                       |

              - - - - - - - - - - - - - - -
              Enter selection... 1
```

continued

2. Screens 3–9 show the creation of an unordered city list.

3. Screens 10–13 show the display of this list.

4. Screens 14–17 show how the list is filed to a data file. Screens 15 and 16 should look familiar, assuming you studied Chapter 12.

5. Screens 18–20 show the retrieval of the list from the data file. The list is displayed once more in screens 21–24 (not shown).

FIGURE 13.2   (continued)

Screen 4

```
CREATE CITY NODE

    Enter city name................ Los Angeles
    Enter Fahrenheit temperature... 62
```

Screen 5

```
                            REPLY SCREEN


                            Continue? (Y/N) y
```

Screen 6

```
CREATE CITY NODE

    Enter city name................ Chicago
    Enter Fahrenheit temperature... 15
```

Screen 7

```
                            REPLY SCREEN


                            Continue? (Y/N) y
```

Screen 8

```
CREATE CITY NODE

    Enter city name................ Toronto
    Enter Fahrenheit temperature... 20
```

Screen 9

```
                            REPLY SCREEN


                            Continue? (Y/N) n
```

FIGURE 13.2   (*continued*)

Screen 10

```
Time is 10:52


                        MAIN MENU
                  - - - - - - - - -
                  1  Create list...
                  2  Display list
                  3  Save list
                  4  Get list
                  5  Find city
                  6  Update list...
                  Q  Quit
                  - - - - - - - - -

                  Enter selection... 2
```

Screen 11

```
DISPLAY CITY RECORD

City node #1
   City name............... Los Angeles
   Fahrenheit temperature... 62




Hit any key to continue...
```

Screen 12

```
DISPLAY CITY RECORD

City node #2
   City name............... Chicago
   Fahrenheit temperature... 15




Hit any key to continue...
```

continued

FIGURE 13.2   *(continued)*

Screen 13

```
DISPLAY CITY RECORD

City node #3
   City name................ Toronto
   Fahrenheit temperature... 20




Hit any key to continue...
```

Screen 14

```
Time is 10:54

                        MAIN MENU
          ┌ ─ ─ ─ ─ ─ ─ ─ ─ ┐
          │ 1  Create list...  │
          │ 2  Display list    │
          │ 3  Save list       │
          │ 4  Get list        │
          │ 5  Find city       │
          │ 6  Update list...  │
          │ Q  Quit            │
          └ ─ ─ ─ ─ ─ ─ ─ ─ ┘

          Enter selection... 3
```

Screen 15

```
OPEN NEW FILE

   Enter data file drive:\path\name... cities.bin

   Any current contents in cities.bin will be ERASED!




Hit any key to continue...
```

Screen 16

```
                      REPLY SCREEN



              Continue? (Y/N) y
```

FIGURE 13.2   (*continued*)

Screen 17

```
                    List file has been created...

                      Number of nodes = 3



Hit any key to continue...
```

Screen 18

```
Time is 10:60


                          MAIN MENU
                 - - - - - - - - - - -
                 1  Create list...
                 2  Display list
                 3  Save list
                 4  Get list
                 5  Find city
                 6  Update list...
                 Q  Quit
                 - - - - - - - - - - -
                 Enter selection... 4
```

Screen 19

```
OPEN OLD FILE

Enter data file drive:\path\name... cities.bin
```

Screen 20

```
                    List has been retrieved from file...

                      Number of nodes = 3



Hit any key to continue...
```

Screens 21–24 same as Screens 10–13

continued

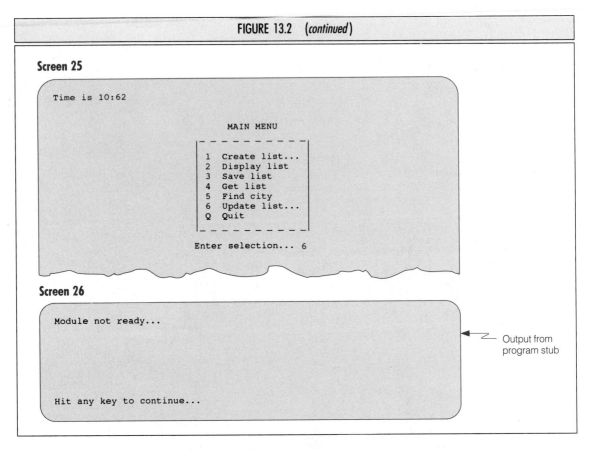

FIGURE 13.2 *(continued)*

Screen 25

```
Time is 10:62

                    MAIN MENU
              _ _ _ _ _ _ _ _ _ _
             |                    |
             | 1  Create list...  |
             | 2  Display list    |
             | 3  Save list       |
             | 4  Get list        |
             | 5  Find city       |
             | 6  Update list...  |
             | Q  Quit            |
             |_ _ _ _ _ _ _ _ _ _ |

              Enter selection... 6
```

Screen 26

```
Module not ready...




Hit any key to continue...
```

Output from program stub

6. Screens 25 and 26 show what happens when a feature of the program is not ready.

Figure 13.3 shows the structure chart and data flows for our program design. Study this figure and note the following.

1. The design assumes that we will use utility program MenuTemp. This working program offers the skeleton of a menu-based program, including modules for opening (OpeningTasks), menu (OfferMenu), and farewell (Farewell) screens. We only need to make minor changes in these modules to tailor the program to the application.

2. The design also relies on other familiar utility modules from earlier chapters: Pause, MenuError, ReadReply, OpenNewFile, and OpenOldFile.

3. We plan to immediately develop modules CreateListMenu, CreateList, NewCity, InputCity, DisplayList, OutputCity, SaveList, and GetList.

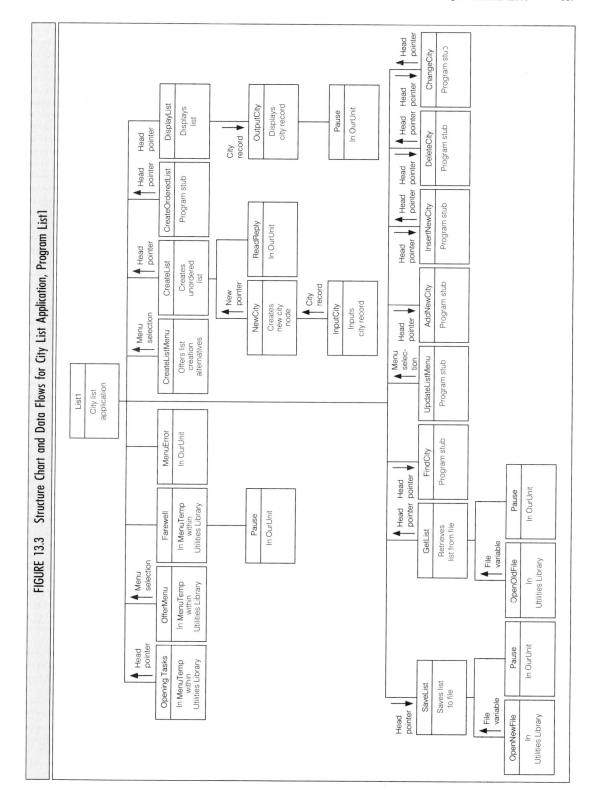

FIGURE 13.3   Structure Chart and Data Flows for City List Application, Program List1

4. Modules CreateOrderedList, FindCity, UpdateListMenu, AddNewCity, InsertNewCity, DeleteCity, and ChangeCity will be *program stubs,* or modules left unfinished for now. The use of program stubs is one way of implementing *top-down development.* We develop the first of these in the next section and leave the others for the exercises. The program stubs are working modules in the sense that they're declared and called. They just don't accomplish their intended function, yet. Screens 25 and 26 in Figure 13.2 show what happens when we attempt to access program stub UpdateListMenu.

5. Take a look at the data flows in the figure. The flows of *Menu selections, File variables,* and *City records* are straightforward. The *New pointer* points to a newly created node in the list. The *Head pointer* is a pointer that points to the first node in the list. Without a head pointer, we would have no way of knowing where the list starts. The head pointer locates the first node. Thereafter, the pointer field within each node points to the next node.

Code and Test

In the remainder of this section, we develop the modules in item 3 above. Program List1 is our working program for the city list application, and Figure 13.2 shows one of its test runs. All of the procedures in item 3 and all program stubs are included within List1. Try a test drive of List1 in Exercise 4.

NOTE

3. It's not as bad as it looks! Figure 13.3 clearly suggests that program List1 is extensive. Don't let this overwhelm you. First, focus on the big picture given by the sample run in Figure 13.2 and the structure chart in Figure 13.3. The modularity of List1 allows us to then narrow the focus to either single modules or small groups of related modules. Each discussion of the modules is like a small example. List1 is a sophisticated and realistic program. And you're ready for it by this time in your programming development.

CREATING A LIST

In this section we describe modules CreateList, NewCity, and InputCity. Menu selection 1 in screen 3 of Figure 13.2 issues a call to procedure CreateList, which creates a list of city nodes. Screens 4–9 show the creation of the linked list pictured in Figure 13.1b. Note that this option creates an *unordered list,* a list whose nodes are linked in the same sequence as their creation. Thus, the chronological input of Los Angeles, Chicago, and Toronto (see screens 4, 6, and 8) creates a list whose links flow from Los Angeles, to Chicago, to Toronto.

Figure 13.4 shows procedures NewCity, InputCity, and CreateList. NewCity creates a new node whose value is currently undefined, clears the

---

FIGURE 13.4   Listing of Procedures NewCity, InputCity, and CreateList

---

```
procedure NewCity (var NewPointer : PointerType);

  { Creates and fills new city node
    Receives nothing
    Sends NewPointer }

    { NOTE:  Calls InputCity }

const
  Title = 'CREATE CITY NODE';

procedure InputCity ( var City : CityRecType);

  { Reads city record from keyboard into city node
    Receives nothing
    Sends City }

begin   {InputCity}

  with City do
    begin
      write (' Enter city name................ '); readln (CityName);
      write (' Enter Fahrenheit temperature... '); readln (F);
    end;  {with}

end;    {InputCity}

begin   {NewCity}

  new (NewPointer);                         {Create new empty node}
  clrscr;  writeln (Title);  writeln;
  InputCity (NewPointer^.CityElement);   {Fill data record in node}

end;    {NewCity}
{-----------------------------------------------------------------------}
procedure CreateList (var HeadPointer : PointerType);

  { Creates unordered linked list
    Receives nothing
    Sends HeadPointer }

    { NOTE:  Calls NewCity, ReadReply }

var
  LastPointer,                  {Points to last (most recent) node in list}
  NewPointer  : PointerType;    {Points to new node in list}
  Reply       : char;           {Y/N reply: Y = another node}

begin   {CreateList}

  NewCity (NewPointer);                       {Create and fill first node}
  HeadPointer := NewPointer;                  {Point to new node @ head of list}
  LastPointer := NewPointer;                  {Update last pointer to new node}
  ReadReply (Reply);                          {In OurUnit}
  while upcase(Reply) = 'Y' do
    begin
      NewCity (NewPointer);                   {Create and fill another node}
      LastPointer^.Point := NewPointer;  {Point previous node to new node}
      LastPointer        := NewPointer;  {Update last pointer to new node}
      ReadReply (Reply);
    end; {while}
  LastPointer^.Point := nil;                  {Mark end of list}

end;    {CreateList}
```

screen, writes a title, and calls InputCity to fill the node, that is, input a city record from the keyboard into the node. Note that the formal parameter City is typed CityRecType, the record type described earlier in item 2 on page 627; its corresponding actual parameter is NewPointer^.CityElement.

Now let's focus on CreateList in Figure 13.4 by describing the execution of its algorithm with a desk-check script. To simplify the discussion, we restrict the script to pointer-related activities, omitting loop control actions, screen clears, and other straightforward tasks. The algorithm assumes the creation of at least one node. The first node is created before the while-do structure. Other nodes (if any) are created by iterations of the while-do loop.

1. The call

        NewCity (NewPointer)

    creates and fills a new node with NewPointer as the pointer. NewCity issues the call

        new (NewPointer)

    to create a node whose fields are currently undefined. NewPointer points to this newly created node. The call

        InputCity (NewPointer^.City Element)

    in NewCity fills the city name and F fields in the city record for the first node (Los Angeles and 62 in screen 4 of our sample run in Figure 13.2). Note that NewPointer^ is the reference to the record (node) that actually stores the city name and temperature data.

2. HeadPointer is assigned the value in NewPointer, which currently points to the first node. This ensures that we can find the beginning of the list.

3. The last or most recent pointer LastPointer is now assigned the value in NewPointer. We need to keep track of the last node in order to link it to any newly created node. At this time, we have the memory structure seen in Figure 13.5a.

4. Subsequent nodes are created and linked by iterations of the while-do structure. A second node is created at the first iteration, again with the call

        NewCity (NewPointer)

    as described in step 1 above. Note in Figure 13.5b that NewPointer is now disconnected from the first node and connected to the second node.

5. The pointer field in the last node (node 1) is assigned the pointer that currently points to node 2:

        Pointer field in last node (node 1)
                            Currently points to node 2

    LastPointer^.Point := NewPointer;

FIGURE 13.5   *Memory Diagrams for First Two Nodes Created by* CreateList

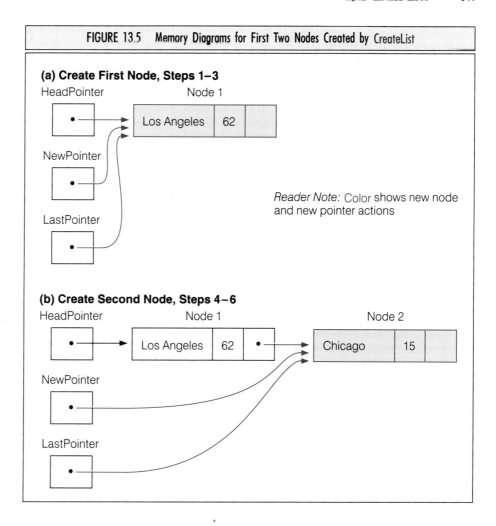

(a) Create First Node, Steps 1–3

HeadPointer   Node 1

Los Angeles | 62

NewPointer

Reader Note: Color shows new node
and new pointer actions

LastPointer

(b) Create Second Node, Steps 4–6

HeadPointer   Node 1   Node 2

Los Angeles | 62   Chicago | 15

NewPointer

LastPointer

This is the crucial operation that links the last node to the current node. In Figure 13.5b, the pointer field in node 1 now points to node 2. In other words, we have just connected node 1 to node 2.

6. LastPointer is now reset to the address in NewPointer by the assignment

```
LastPointer := NewPointer;
```

Node 2 is now our last-created node. At this time, we have the memory diagram seen in Figure 13.5b.

7. The next iteration repeats steps 4–6 for the third node. We leave this diagram to Exercise 5.

8. Execution now exits the loop (see screen 9 in Figure 13.2), and the pointer field in the last node is set to *nil* through the assignment

```
LastPointer^.Point := nil;
```

As we will see next, *nil* is a handly sentinel for detecting the ending node in a list.

DISPLAYING A LIST

Screens 10–13 in Figure 13.2 show a display of the city list just created. The selection of the display option issues a call to procedure DisplayList, as seen in the structure chart in Figure 13.3. To display any list, we have to "jump" onto the first node (via a head pointer), display its contents, "hop" to the second node (via the pointer field in the first node), display its contents, and so on while we have nodes to display. The action of processing all nodes in a list is called *traversing the list*.

Figure 13.6 shows procedures OutputCity and DisplayList. OutputCity displays the record for a node. We globally declared this procedure because the completed procedure FindCity (currently a program stub) will also call it.

Let's consider the execution of DisplayList.

1. The procedure receives HeadPointer and initializes NodePointer to HeadPointer. Thus, the node pointer now points to the first node.

2. HeadPointer does not store *nil,* so execution enters the loop.

3. The data record for the first node is now displayed with the call

    ```
    OutputCity (NodePointer^.CityElement)
    ```

    as seen in screen 11 of Figure 13.2.

4. Now the crucial step: NodePointer is reassigned the address of the next node as the value within the pointer field of the current node.

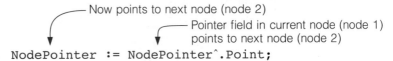

    ```
    NodePointer := NodePointer^.Point;
    ```

5. NodePointer does not store *nil* (it points to the second node), so the while-do loop repeats a second time.

6. NodePointer now points to the second node, so the call

    ```
    OutputCity (NodePointer^.CityElement)
    ```

    displays the data record in the second node.

7. NodePointer is reassigned as a pointer to node 3.

8. NodePointer does not store *nil* (it points to the third node), so the while-do loop repeats a third time.

9. The call

    ```
    OutputCity (NodePointer^.CityElement)
    ```

    displays the third node.

FIGURE 13.6   Listing of Procedures OutputCity and DisplayList

```
procedure OutputCity (City : CityRecType);

   { Writes a single city record to the screen
     Receives City
     Sends nothing }

     { NOTE:  Calls Pause }

begin  {OutputCity}

  with City do
    begin
      writeln ('  City name............... ', CityName);
      writeln ('  Fahrenheit temperature... ', F);
    end;  {with}
  Pause;                                        {In OurUnit}

end;  {OutputCity}
{-------------------------------------------------------------------}
procedure DisplayList (HeadPointer : PointerType);

   { Displays list starting at node pointed to by HeadPointer
     Receives HeadPointer
     Sends nothing }

     { NOTE:  Calls OutputCity }

const
  Title = 'DISPLAY CITY RECORD';

var
  NodeNum     : integer;                        {Node number}
  NodePointer : PointerType;                    {Points to node in list}

begin  {DisplayList}

  NodeNum     := 0;
  NodePointer := HeadPointer;                   {Point to 1st node}
  while NodePointer <> nil do
    begin
      clrscr;  writeln (Title);  writeln;
      NodeNum := NodeNum + 1;
      writeln ('City node #', NodeNum);
      OutputCity (NodePointer^.CityElement);  {Display single city record}
      NodePointer := NodePointer^.Point;       {Link next node}
    end;  {while}

end;    {DisplayList}
```

10. Now NodePointer is reassigned the value *nil* (the pointer field for the third node stores *nil*, as described in item 8 in the CreateList script).

11. Loop exit is achieved now that the sentinel *nil* is detected in the while test, and the display procedure ends.

FILING AND RETRIEVING A LIST

The tasks of filing and retrieving lists are very similar to the methods used in Chapter 12 for storing and retrieving files of records. In our descriptions within this section, we assume that you've already studied Section 12.2 and focus our attention on the pointer-related material.

Screens 14–17 show what happens at the user interface when we save the city list to data file CITIES.BIN. Procedure SaveList in Figure 13.7 implements this task. Its algorithm is very similar to the algorithm in DisplayList: It's the basic algorithm for traversing a list. The only significant difference is that we write the record to a file instead of to the screen, as seen in the call

```
write (FileCity, NodePointer^.CityElement)
```

Screens 18–20 show the I/O for retrieving the city list from file CITIES.BIN. The retrieval of a list from a file is essentially a recreation of the list. Instead of entering record values from the keyboard (as we did through CreateList earlier), we're entering these values from the data file. Procedure GetList in Figure 13.8 takes care of this task. Note the following.

1. Each iteration of the loop creates a new node through the call

```
new (NewPointer)
```

2. The read statement fills the data record within this new node in primary memory by using the dynamic-field-variable reference NewPointer^.CityElement in its input list.

3. HeadPointer is assigned the address that points to the first node.

4. As in CreateList, LastPointer^.Point points the previous node to the new node and LastPointer points to the most recent node.

NOTE

4. Sentinel nil. The pointer constant *nil* is a handy sentinel for ending the traversal of a linked list, as used in procedures DisplayList and SaveList. This means, however, that the storage of *nil* within the pointer field of the last node is a *precondition* for the while-do loop that traverses the list; otherwise we have the makings of an infinite loop.

5. Don't forget your head (pointer). Procedures that create a list (like CreateList and GetList) must ensure that the head pointer is assigned the address of the first node; otherwise we have a "lost" list (we can't locate the first node). These procedures must also ensure that head pointer is a *variable parameter;* otherwise the calling modules would not "know" where the first node is. Look at the data flows for *Head pointer* in Figure 13.3 to confirm that certain procedures send the head pointer to the calling module, while others receive the head pointer.

FIGURE 13.7 Listing of Procedure SaveList

```
procedure SaveList (HeadPointer : PointerType);

   { Saves list as file of city records
     Receives HeadPointer
     Sends nothing }

      { NOTE:  Calls OpenNewFile, Pause }

      { CAUTION:  Any contents in specified file will be overwritten! }
const
   Title = 'List file has been created...';

type
{File type with city record components}
   FileCityType = file of CityRecType;
{Generic file type needed for call to OpenNewFile}
   FileType    = FileCityType;

var
   FileCity    : FileType;      {File var for city record file}
   NodeNum     : integer;       {Number of nodes}
   NodePointer : PointerType;   {Points to node in list}


      Utility procedure OpenNewFile (Figure 12.5) is declared here.


begin   {SaveList}

   OpenNewFile (FileCity);
   NodeNum     := 0;
   NodePointer := HeadPointer;                    {Point to 1st node}
   while NodePointer <> nil do
     begin
       NodeNum := NodeNum + 1;
       write (FileCity, NodePointer^.CityElement);   {Write record to file}
       NodePointer := NodePointer^.Point;            {Link next node}
     end; {while}
   close (FileCity);
   clrscr;
   gotoxy (25, 9);   writeln (Title);
   gotoxy (30,11);   writeln ('Number of nodes = ', NodeNum);
   Pause;                                         {In OurUnit}

end;    {SaveList}
```

SELF-REVIEW EXERCISES

4 5 6 7

13.3 ORDERED LISTS

· · · · · · · · · · · · · · ·

An **ordered list** is a linked list whose nodes are positioned in ascending order based on a *key field*. For example, Figure 13.1c shows an ordered list whose

---

FIGURE 13.8   Listing of Procedure GetList

```pascal
procedure GetList (var HeadPointer : PointerType );

  { Reads city records from file and creates city list
    Receives nothing
    Sends HeadPointer }

    { NOTE:  Calls OpenOldFile, Pause }

const
  Title = 'List has been retrieved from file...';

type
 {File type with city record components}
 FileCityType = file of CityRecType;
 {Generic file type needed for call to OpenOldFile}
 FileType    = FileCityType;

var
  FileCity     : FileType;         {File var for city record file}
  LastPointer,                     {Points to last (most recent) node in list}
  NewPointer  : PointerType;       {Points to new node in list}
  NodeNum     : integer;           {Node number}


      Utility procedure OpenOldFile (Figure 12.9) is declared here.

begin   {GetList}

  OpenOldFile (FileCity);
  NodeNum := 0;
  while not eof(FileCity) do
    begin
      NodeNum := NodeNum + 1;
      {Create new node in memory}
      new (NewPointer);
      {Read record from file into new node in memory}
      read (FileCity, NewPointer^.CityElement);
      {Assign head pointer}
      if NodeNum = 1 then
        begin
          HeadPointer := NewPointer;        {Point to head of list}
          LastPointer := NewPointer;        {Update last ptr to new node}
        end
      else
        begin
          LastPointer^.Point := NewPointer; {Point previous to new node}
          LastPointer        := NewPointer; {Update last ptr to new node}
        end;  {if}
    end;  {while}

  if NodeNum <> 0 then
    LastPointer^.Point := nil;              {Mark end of list}
  else
    HeadPointer        := nil;              {Mark empty  list}
  close (FileCity);
  clrscr;
  gotoxy (22, 9);  writeln (Title);
  gotoxy (30,11);  writeln ('Number of nodes = ', NodeNum);
  Pause;                                    {In OurUnit}

end;    {GetList}
```

key field is CityName. In effect, the records are sorted alphabetically by city name. In this section, we continue with our city list problem by developing an algorithm that creates an ordered city list. Then we tie it in to the task of creating a sorted data file.

CREATING AN ORDERED LIST

We tagged procedure CreateOrderedList as a program stub in Figure 13.3. This procedure is called by selecting 1 in the Main Menu (Create list...) and 2 in the Create List Menu (Ordered list), as seen in screens 2 and 3 of Figure 13.2. We now complete this procedure by revising the first version of the city list program (List1), which we name List2.

Figure 13.9 shows the listing for CreateOrderedList. Its structure is very similar to that of CreateList (compare this figure to Figure 13.4), with the following exceptions.

1. We build the ordered list by inserting a new node in its proper slot within the existing list. In the unordered version, nodes were added at the end of the existing list.

FIGURE 13.9   Listing of Procedure CreateOrderedList

```
procedure CreateOrderedList ( var HeadPointer : PointerType);

   { Creates ordered linked list based on key field CityName
     Receives nothing
     Sends HeadPointer }

     { NOTE:  Calls NewCity, ReadReply, InsertCity }
var
   NewPointer    : PointerType;              {Points to new node in list}
   Reply         : char;                     {Y/N reply: Y = another node}

begin   {CreateOrderedList}

   NewCity (NewPointer);                     {Create and fill first node}
   HeadPointer         := NewPointer;        {Point to new node @ head of list}
   NewPointer^.Point := nil;                 {Mark 1st node as ending node}
   ReadReply (Reply);                        {In OurUnit}
   while upcase(Reply) = 'Y' do
     begin
       {Create and fill another node}
       NewCity (NewPointer);

       {Insert new city node in proper slot}
       InsertCity (NewPointer, HeadPointer);

       ReadReply (Reply);
     end; {while}

   end;    {CreateOrderedList}
```

2. The first node does not need to be inserted. It's simply created and filled with a call to NewCity (as described earlier), it gets pointed to by HeadPointer, and its pointer field is set to *nil*. Keep in mind that the pointer field of the last node in the list must contain *nil*. This ensures the proper operation of our file save and display modules, which rely on *nil* as a sentinel that terminates list traversal. At this time, we only have one node in the list, so its pointer field is set accordingly.

3. Nodes subsequent to the first are created and inserted within the while-do structure. The call to new procedure InsertCity inserts the node in its proper slot, either at the beginning, end, or middle of the list.

Before describing procedure InsertCity, let's go over our strategy for inserting and connecting nodes. Suppose we wish to enter the following records in chronological order (as done for the first three in screens 4, 6, and 8 in Figure 13.2):

Los Angeles	62
Chicago	15
Toronto	20
Boston	32
Miami	68

If we were to manually create and sketch an ordered list for these cities, we would start with the Los Angeles node, as seen in Figure 13.10a. Note that the head pointer points to Los Angeles, and Los Angeles points to nothing. Next, we create Chicago and check if it alphabetically precedes Los Angeles. It does, so we insert the Chicago node before the Los Angeles node and connect Chicago to Los Angeles. Note how the head pointer in Figure 13.10b now points to Chicago. To insert Toronto, we check if it precedes Chicago (the current first node). It doesn't, so we next test if Toronto falls in the slot between Chicago and Los Angeles (between the first and second nodes). It doesn't, so we check the next slot after Los Angeles and insert Toronto at the end of the list, as done in Figure 13.10c. Note how Los Angeles now points to Toronto (its pointer field no longer stores *nil*). Also note that Toronto's pointer field is now *nil*, because it's the new ending node in the list. Next we create and insert Boston and point it to Chicago, as seen in Figure 13.10d. Once again the head pointer is reoriented, this time to Boston. Finally, Miami is inserted in the slot between Los Angeles and Toronto in Figure 13.10e. This operation reassigns Los Angeles's pointer to Miami (thereby disconnecting Los Angeles from Toronto) and points Miami to Toronto. That's it! As is often the case, however, it's not so simple to implement as a programming algorithm.

Figure 13.11 lists procedure InsertCity. The best way to understand this algorithm is to desk check the creation of an ordered list. Let's give it a try by working with the following desk-check script for the first three cities.

1. CreateOrderedList (Figure 13.9) starts by creating the Los Angeles node, as seen in the memory diagram of Figure 13.12. Again, note that *nil* is

FIGURE 13.10   Strategy for Creating an Ordered List of Five Cities

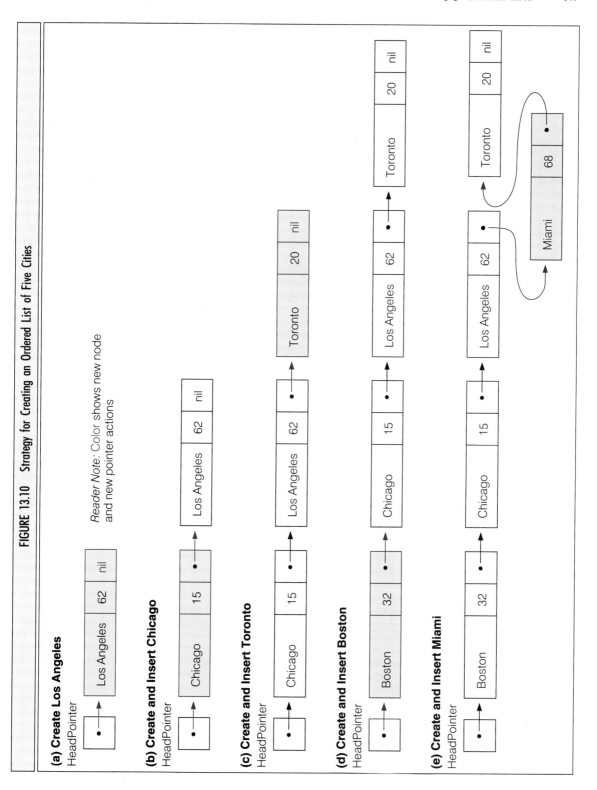

Reader Note: Color shows new node and new pointer actions

(a) Create Los Angeles
HeadPointer

(b) Create and Insert Chicago
HeadPointer

(c) Create and Insert Toronto
HeadPointer

(d) Create and Insert Boston
HeadPointer

(e) Create and Insert Miami
HeadPointer

FIGURE 13.11   Listing of Procedure InsertCity

```
procedure InsertCity (NewPointer : PointerType;
                         var HeadPointer : PointerType);

   { Inserts existing new city node into ordered city list based on
       key field CityName
     Receives NewPointer, HeadPointer
     Sends HeadPointer }

var
 {City records for new, head, and next nodes}
  CityNew, CityHead, CityNext : CityRecType;
 {These point to nodes that form slot within which new node is inserted}
  PreviousPointer, NextPointer : PointerType;

begin   {InsertCity}

  CityNew  := NewPointer^.CityElement;     {Assign new city record}
  CityHead := HeadPointer^.CityElement;    {Assign city record in head node}

  if CityNew.CityName <= CityHead.CityName then
   {Insert node at head of list}
     begin
       NewPointer^.Point  := HeadPointer;   {Point new node to previous head}
       HeadPointer         := NewPointer;   {Point head to new 1st node}
     end
  else
   {Insert node in middle or end of list}
     begin
       {Find slot between previous node and next node}
       PreviousPointer := HeadPointer;                {First two nodes form}
       NextPointer     := HeadPointer^.Point;         { 1st slot}
       CityNext        := NextPointer^.CityElement;   {Assign city record
                                                         in next node}

       while (NextPointer <> nil)
              and (CityNew.CityName > CityNext.CityName) do
         begin
          {Consider next slot}
          PreviousPointer := NextPointer;                 {Advance prev ptr}
          NextPointer     := NextPointer^.Point;          {Advance next ptr}
          CityNext        := NextPointer^.CityElement; {Assign city rec}
         end; {while}                                     { in next node}

       {Insert new node in slot}
       NewPointer^.Point       := NextPointer;  {Point new node to next node}
       PreviousPointer^.Point := NewPointer;    {Point previous node to new}
     end; {if}

end;   {InsertCity}
```

assigned to the pointer field in the Los Angeles node (Los Angeles currently defines the end of the list). Also note that HeadPointer points to the Los Angeles node (Los Angeles currently defines the beginning of the list). As mentioned earlier, it's crucial that we properly reassign HeadPointer and *nil* as we create the list.

2. The first iteration of the while-do structure creates the Chicago node and issues a call to InsertCity (Figure 13.11). The name field for the Chicago node (stored in CityNew.CityName) is compared to the name field in the

---

FIGURE 13.12   Memory Diagrams for Three Nodes Created by CreateOrderedList

---

(a) Create Los Angeles: Snapshot Taken Just Before While-Do Loop in CreateOrderedList

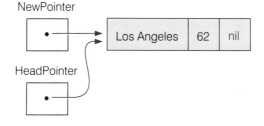

Reader Note: Color shows new node and new pointer actions

(b) Create and Insert Chicago: Snapshot Taken at End of First Iteration in CreateOrderedList, After Execution of Then Branch in InsertCity

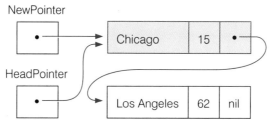

(c) Create and Insert Toronto: Snapshot Taken at End of Second Iteration in CreateOrderedList, Just Before Execution of While in InsertCity

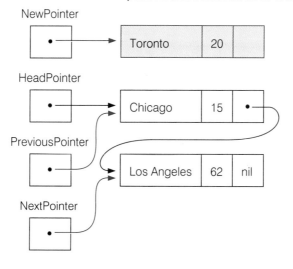

continued

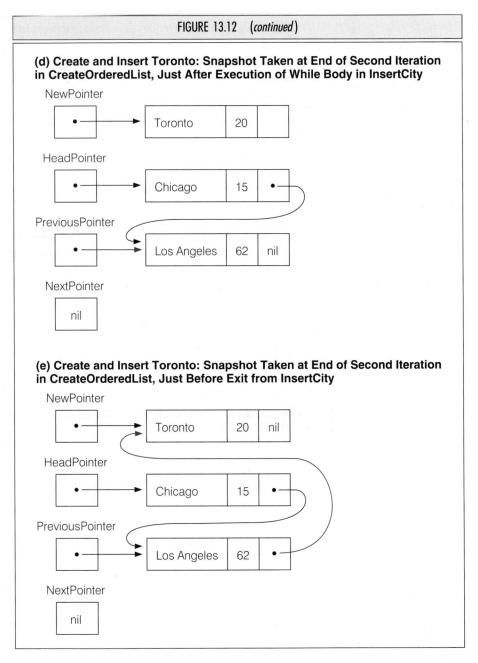

FIGURE 13.12   (*continued*)

(d) Create and Insert Toronto: Snapshot Taken at End of Second Iteration in CreateOrderedList, Just After Execution of While Body in InsertCity

NewPointer

Toronto | 20 |

HeadPointer

Chicago | 15 | •

PreviousPointer

Los Angeles | 62 | nil

NextPointer

nil

(e) Create and Insert Toronto: Snapshot Taken at End of Second Iteration in CreateOrderedList, Just Before Exit from InsertCity

NewPointer

Toronto | 20 | nil

HeadPointer

Chicago | 15 | •

PreviousPointer

Los Angeles | 62 | •

NextPointer

nil

beginning node (stored in CityHead.CityName). The string value Chicago is less than Los Angeles, so the then branch is executed. The new node (Chicago) is pointed to the previous head (Los Angeles) by executing

```
NewPointer^.Point := HeadPointer;
```

The head pointer is then pointed to the new beginning node (Chicago) by executing

```
HeadPointer := NewPointer;
```

This completes the creation and insertion of the second node and yields the memory diagram in Figure 13.12b.

3. The next iteration creates the Toronto node and again issues a call to InsertCity. The if-test asks "Is Toronto less than or equal to Chicago?", giving false. The else branch of the if-then-else structure is now executed. The idea now is to find the proper slot for the Toronto node. We accomplish this by bracketing each slot with the two existing nodes that form that slot. At this time, we have just two slots to consider: the slot between Chicago and Los Angeles and the slot between Los Angeles and *nil* (the end of the list). The pointers PreviousPointer and NextPointer will be used to point to the two nodes that define a slot.

a. Just before the while-do structure in InsertCity, PreviousPointer is pointed to the beginning node (Chicago) by the execution of

```
PreviousPointer := HeadPointer;
```

and NextPointer is pointed to the next node (Los Angeles) by the assignment

```
NextPointer := HeadPointer^.Point;
```

This gives the diagram in Figure 13.12c.

b. In the while test, it's true that the value in NextPointer (Los Angeles's address) is not equal to *nil* and it's true that the value in CityNew.CityName (Toronto) is greater than the value in CityNext.CityName (Los Angeles). So the loop body is entered, and the slot is advanced by one to that defined by Los Angeles and *nil* through the execution of

```
PreviousPointer := NextPointer;
NextPointer     := NextPointer^.Point;
```

This gives the memory diagram in Figure 13.12d.

c. The test NextPointer < > **nil** is now false, so loop exit is achieved and the Toronto node is inserted in the second slot (at the end of the list) by the execution of

```
NewPointer^.Point       := NextPointer;
PreviousPointer^.Point := NewPointer;
```

Thus Toronto is pointed to *nil* and Los Angeles is pointed to Toronto, as seen in Figure 13.12e.

That ends our three-node desk check. Like we said, this material is tricky (and challenging), so if you're lost, restudy this section and try the exercises suggested next.

In Exercise 8 we ask you to create the five-city ordered list in Figure 13.10 by running program List2. To better understand the ordered list algorithms, try Exercise 9 to complete the memory diagram in Figure 13.12; Exercise 10 to consider the issue of *short-circuit evaluation;* Exercise 11 to fix up the entry of a city name that already exists in the list; and Exercise 13 to order the city list by temperature.

SORTED FILES

An ordered list is a list already sorted by its key field. Once this list is in primary memory, we can write its elements to a file of records using procedure SaveList, giving us a sorted data file. At a later date, we can retrieve this file in the usual way (by a call to procedure GetList), which recreates the ordered list in primary memory. We ask you to try this task in Exercise 14.

Suppose we have an existing file of records that's not sorted, and we wish to create a sorted version of this file. No problem. The only difference between this task and what we accomplished earlier is that instead of entering a record into primary memory from the keyboard (by a call to InputCity), we enter a record from the data file, as done by the read statement in GetList. We could develop a new procedure, say SortFile, that combines features of CreateOrderedList and GetList to create an ordered list whose records are taken from a file. Then it would call SaveList to save the sorted city records. We ask you to try this approach in Exercise 15.

SELF-REVIEW EXERCISES

8 14

13.4 MORE LIST PROCESSING

• • • • • • • • • • • • • •

In this section, we complete the remaining requirements outlined for the city list problem in Section 13.2: finding a city within a list and displaying its fields (module FindCity in Figure 13.3), adding a city to the end of a list (AddNewCity), inserting a city in an ordered list (InsertNewCity), deleting a city from a list (DeleteCity), and changing city node fields (ChangeCity). We also describe a new requirement regarding *queries* like "What's the average temperature of the cities?". Throughout this section, we focus on describing strategies and design, leaving the programming to exercises.

SEARCHING THE LIST

Searching a list for a particular node is a common task. For example, we might wish to display the node's contents (its fields), or to change the node's contents, or both. The search is based on a *search key,* or field whose value we are searching for (the *search value* or *target*). In our city list example, we might wish to search for the city name Chicago. In this case, the search key is the field CityName and the search value or target is Chicago. Alternatively, we could search for a temperature of 32. Now the search key is field F and the target is 32.

A simple approach to searching a list sequentially tests each node for the target, starting with the first node. If the target node is found, the task at hand (node display, update, or whatever) is implemented. If the entire list is traversed without finding the target node, a message to that effect is displayed. The next example shows a design algorithm for searching a list.

EXAMPLE 13.3   DESIGN OF MODULE FINDCITY AND SEARCH FUNCTION TARGETPOINTER

Figure 13.3 shows module FindCity as a program stub. The requirements of this module are to query the user for a city name target, search for the target node, and display either the contents of the target node (if found) or a message that states the target city was not found. We might design this module as follows.

Procedure FindCity

```
Query user for target city name
If TargetPointer is nil then
    Display message that target city was not found
else
    Call OutputCity
```

TargetPointer is a search function that returns either the pointer to the target node (if the target node was found) or *nil* (if the target node was not found). OutputCity is the procedure developed earlier (in Figure 13.6).

Function TargetPointer receives the head pointer and target and returns the target pointer. The strategy is to sequentially search the list while the target node is not found and *nil* is not encountered, starting with the beginning node. If the target node is found, then the function returns its pointer; else the function returns *nil* as an indicator that the target was not found. We might design the pointer search function as follows.

Function TargetPointer

```
Initialize Found to false and Node pointer to Head pointer
While not Found and Node pointer <> nil
    If City name field = Target then
        Found is true
    else
        Advance Node pointer to next node
If Found then
    TargetPointer is Node pointer
else
    TargetPointer is nil
```

Note that if the entire list is traversed without finding the target, then Found remains false and TargetPointer is set to *nil*. In Exercise 16 we ask you to desk check and code this algorithm. In Exercises 17 and 18 we ask you to consider alternative designs for the search function.

UPDATING THE LIST

List updates include adding (appending) a node to the end of the list, inserting a node within an ordered list, deleting a node from a list, and changing one or more fields in a node. Let's briefly describe each of these tasks.

Adding a Node

To append a node at the end of a list, we need to create and fill the new node (as in calling procedure NewCity), traverse the existing list to its ending node, point the ending node to the new node, and set the pointer field of the new node to *nil*. In Exercise 19 we ask you to implement this task for the city list problem by designing and coding procedure AddNewCity.

Inserting a Node

To insert a new node within an ordered list, we need to create and fill the new node (as in calling procedure NewCity) and insert it within the list (as in calling procedure InsertCity). In Exercise 20 we ask you to implement this task for the city list problem by designing and coding procedure InsertNewCity.

Deleting a Node

To delete an existing node, we first have to find the node (as done in Example 13.3). If it's not found, we should display a message that so states; otherwise we decouple the node from the list by changing the pointer of its predecessor to its successor, and then delete the node from the heap by calling the predeclared procedure *dispose*. If this was the only node, the head pointer is set to *nil*, since the list is now empty. In Exercise 21 we ask you to implement this task for the city list problem by designing and coding procedure DeleteCity.

Changing a Node

To change one or more fields in an existing node, we first have to find the node. If the node is found, we could display its contents and offer the user a change menu for selecting the field whose value is to be changed. After each change, we could redisplay the node and reoffer the menu. This process continues until the user selects quit from the change node menu. The next example illustrates the design we have in mind.

EXAMPLE 13.4   DESIGN OF MODULE CHANGECITY

Let's show a design for procedure ChangeCity in Figure 13.3. The algorithm would be similar to FindCity in Example 13.3, except the else branch would implement a repetition structure that calls ChangeCityMenu and routes the selection to a case that changes the desired field.

Procedure ChangeCity

```
Query user for target city name
If TargetPointer is nil then
   Display message that target city was not found
else
   Call Changes
```

Procedure Changes

```
Repeat
   Call OutputCity
   Call ChangeCityMenu
   Case
      Change city name    : Enter new name into city name field of node
                            Ask user if list is ordered
                            If ordered list then
                               Move node to proper slot
      Change temperature : Enter new temperature into F field of node
      Quit                :
      else call Menu Error
   until no more changes
```

Procedure OutputCity is seen in Figure 13.6. Procedure ChangeCityMenu is similar to our menu routines. It would offer a menu with three selections: change city name, change temperature, or quit. If the name is to be changed, an added complication is whether or not the list is ordered. If it is, it's probable that a name change would affect the position of this node in the list. To move the node, we could decouple it from the list (as if we were deleting it) and then call InsertCity (Figure 13.11) to reinsert it in the proper slot.

This feature of our list processing system is rather elaborate. We ask you to give it a try in Exercise 22.

LIST QUERIES

A *list query* interrogates a list to extract information (if any) that satisfies the query. As in our work with *file queries* (Section 12.3), the displayed information can include one or more nodes (records), one or more field values within a node or across all nodes, or simple to elaborate reports. Module FindCity in Example 13.3 implements a simple query like "What's the temperature in Toronto?". Other sample queries include "What's the average temperature in the list?" and "Which cities have a temperature above 50?".

One way of implementing a query requirement in our city list system would be to add the new item "Queries..." to the main menu. Its selection would then produce a query menu that offers the available query selections and a quit option. The algorithm then routes the query selection to a procedure that implements that selection. The menuing and routing design would be similar to that for the "Update list..." selection in the current programs. How the query selection is implemented depends on the nature of the query. In some cases, we may need to search for just one node. In other cases, we may need to traverse the entire list, looking for multiple nodes that satisfy the query. In Exercise 23 we ask you to implement our posed queries for the city list problem.

13.5   OTHER DYNAMIC DATA STRUCTURES

Certain variations of the linked list data structure give rise to other commonly used dynamic data structures: *stacks, queues,* and a variety of *multiply-linked lists.* We describe each of these in turn and, where appropriate, state a design algorithm for a particular task related to that data structure. All programming is left to the exercises.

STACKS

Figure 13.13a illustrates a "physical" stack of five characters and Figure 13.13b shows its dynamic data-structure counterpart. A **stack data structure** or **stack**

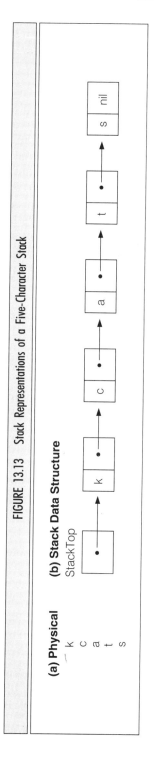

FIGURE 13.13   Stack Representations of a Five-Character Stack

is an ordered collection of identically typed elements, where each element points to the element that chronologically preceded it. A nonempty stack has a "top" element. The stack grows from the "bottom" up, and operations are performed only on the top element. Thus, the stack in Figure 13.13a was built by *pushing* (inserting on top of one another) five elements onto a previously empty stack in the order s t a c k, much like we build a pile of dirty kitchen dishes (one of our more unsavory real-world stacks). We decrease the size of the stack by removing elements from the top, a task colorfully called *popping* the stack (which is also the order in which we would clean our dirty dishes).

The stack is also called a *Last-in First-out* (*LIFO*) data structure, because the last element pushed onto the stack is the first element popped from the stack. A limited number of specialized problems in practice are LIFO problems, including reverse-order displays (k c a t s in Figure 13.13a), business inventory valuation (the cost of inventory is the cost of the last item added to inventory times the number of items in inventory), stock-market capital gains calculations (the cost basis of shares sold is the price paid for the most recent shares purchased times the number of shares), and certain specialized compiler evaluations of arithmetic expressions.

We declare the dynamic-data-structure representation of a stack (Figure 13.13b) in the usual way we declare nodes and pointers for linked lists. A pointer StackTop points to the top node in the stack, and a pointer field within each node points to the next element "below." Push and pop operations on the stack are performed strictly at the top of the list.

Certain useful procedures and functions are typically developed for stack applications, including the following.

- Procedure Push (1) receives StackTop and PushElement; (2) if the stack is not full, pushes the element onto the top of the stack by creating a new element with pointer StackTop, linking it to the stack, resetting Stack-Top, and filling its fields by a copy of PushElement; (3) sends StackTop and whether or not the operation was achieved as parameter Achieved (true if the stack was not full, false otherwise).

- Procedure Pop (1) receives StackTop; (2) if the stack is not empty, copies the top element in the stack into variable PopElement, resets StackTop to the next element in the stack, disposes the old top element; (3) sends StackTop, PopElement, and Achieved (true if the stack was not empty, false otherwise).

- Function StackEmpty receives StackTop and returns true if the stack is empty (StackTop stores *nil*) or false otherwise.

- Function StackFull receives StackTop and returns true if the stack is full or false otherwise (we assume no physical limitations on the stack other than available heap). A stack is full if the relational expression

sizeof (StackTop) > **memavail**

is true, where **sizeof** is a predeclared function that returns the number of bytes required by the dynamic variable whose pointer is StackTop and **memavail** is a predeclared function that returns the number of bytes remaining for the heap.

Stack-related declarations in the client programs that use these modules include the following.

```
type
  StackElementType = ?  ◄──── Type integer, character, string,
                                record, and so on

  StackPointer  = ^StackNodeType;
  StackNodeType = record
    StackElement : StackElementType;
    Point        : StackPointer;
  end; {StackNodeType}

var
  StackTop      : StackPointer;
  PushElement,
  PopElement    : StackElementType;
  Achieved      : Boolean;
```

Note that the declaration of the node type StackNodeType uses the alternative style offered in item 2 on page 627. StackElement contains the data for the element. In Figure 13.13, StackElement holds a character and StackElementType is **char**.

In Exercise 32 we ask you to code and implement these modules.

QUEUES

Have you been in a *waiting line* or *queue* lately? At the grocery store, the movie theater, the bank, your message in someone's telephone answering machine or electronic mailbox, your print job at the laser printer? Queues are pervasive in life and are the object of many analytic studies and algorithms in business, the social sciences, computer science, and engineering. In a simple queueing system, an arriving element joins the *back* of a single queue if service is not immediately available. An element leaves the *front* of the queue as it enters service. More complex queuing systems include multiple queues and behavioral considerations like reneging (elements leave the queue without entering service) and jockeying (elements switch from one queue to another).

A **queue data structure** or **queue** is an ordered collection of identically typed elements, where each element points to the element "behind" it. A nonempty queue has a "front" element and a "back" element. An element *departs* the queue only from the front and *joins* the queue only at the back. The queue data structure thus keeps track of a single queue whose elements behave as described earlier for a simple queuing system.

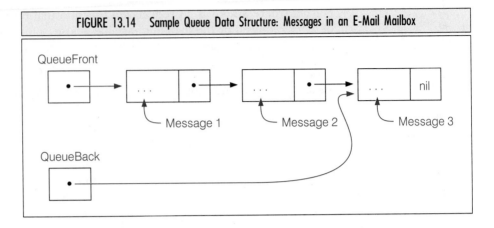

FIGURE 13.14   Sample Queue Data Structure: Messages in an E-Mail Mailbox

Figure 13.14 illustrates a three-element queue as a dynamic data structure of linked nodes. This representation looks like a linked list and is declared like a linked list, but it's not the linked list that we described in Section 13.2, for the following reasons: First, it includes two pointers, QueueFront to identify the front of the queue and QueueBack to identify the back of the queue; second, and more important, it doesn't "behave" like the linked lists we described earlier. In other words, the operations that implement changes in the size of the queue must adhere to the *First-In First-out* rule that we described for elements joining and departing the queue.[4]

This leads us to the following popular procedures in queuing applications.

- Procedure Join (1) receives QueueBack and JoinElement; (2) if the queue is not full, adds a new element to the back of the queue by creating it, linking it to the queue, resetting QueueBack, filling its fields by a copy of JoinElement, and setting its pointer field to *nil;* (3) sends QueueBack and Achieved (true if the queue was not full, false otherwise).

- Procedure Depart (1) receives QueueFront; (2) if the queue is not empty, copies the front element in the queue into variable DepartElement, resets QueueFront to the next element in the queue, disposes the old front element; (3) sends QueueFront, DepartElement, and Achieved (true if the queue was not empty, false otherwise).

- Function QueueEmpty receives QueueFront and returns true if the queue is empty (QueueFront stores *nil*) or false otherwise.

- Function QueueFull receives QueueBack and returns true if the queue is full or false otherwise, where a full queue is defined in the same manner as a full stack (using calls to functions *sizeof* and *memavail*).

---

[4]We're reminded of the political saying that goes something like "If it looks like a duck, walks like a duck, and sounds like a duck, then it must be a duck." We can model all queues as linked lists, but not all linked lists are queues.

Queue-related declarations in the client programs that use these modules include the following.

```
type
   QueueElementType = ? ◄——╮   Type integer, character, string,
                                 record, and so on

   QueuePointer  = ^QueueNodeType;
   QueueNodeType = record
      QueueElement : QueueElementType;
      Point        : QueuePointer;
   end; {QueueNodeType}

var
   QueueFront,
   QueueBack      : QueuePointer;
   JoinElement,
   DepartElement  : QueueElementType;
   Achieved       : Boolean;
```

Note that the declaration of the node type QueueNodeType uses the alternative style offered in item 2 on page 627. QueueElement contains the data for the element. In Figure 13.14 QueueElement holds a string message and QueueElementType is **string.**

In Exercise 33 we ask you to code and implement these modules.

MULTIPLY-LINKED LISTS

A **multiply-linked list** is a linked list with two or more pointer fields per node that point to other nodes in the list. This concept allows us to model a large number of linked list data structures. Here we provide an overview of some common variations, and leave any details to exercises.

Doubly-Linked Lists

A doubly-linked list is a linked list whose nodes include two pointers: PointLeft points to the preceding node and PointRight points to the suceeding node. Doubly-linked lists are convenient data structures for both forward and backward traversals. This feature is useful for displays and certain decision support algorithms in the management and computer sciences (project management, expert systems, and others). In Exercise 26 we ask you to view the unordered city list as a doubly-linked list.

Multiply-Ordered Lists

A multiply-ordered list is an ordered list whose nodes include a pointer field for each desired key field. For example, the city list in Figure 13.1c is ordered by the key field CityName. In Exercise 13 we ask you to order the list by temperature, or key field F. We could also order this list both by name and by temperature, *at the same time.* This is useful for displaying and searching lists based on different keys. It's an alternative to the use of *index files* (Section 12.5). In Exercise 27 we ask you to rework the city list problem as a multiply-ordered list.

Trees

A tree is a structure whose nodes have two pointers. In this variation, PointLeft points to a node that branches left in a memory diagram and PointRight points to a node that branches right. The resulting diagram looks like an upside-down real tree, or a genealogical (family) tree, as seen in Figure 13.15. The tree has a root at the top. Each node in the tree is a "descendant" of one or more "ancestor" nodes, except for the root node. The root node is the ancestor of all nodes. Moreover, each node is a "parent" with at most two "child" nodes. Each node spawns its own subtree, a left subtree and a right subtree. A particularly useful tree is called a *binary-search tree*. The nodes in a binary-search tree are created and ordered in a way that the key field value for the root node of the left subtree is less than the key field value for its parent node, and the key value for the root node of the right subtree is greater than the key field value for its parent node. This arrangement allows an ordered traversal of the tree and promotes computationally efficient searches of large lists in a manner similar to the binary-search algorithm that we use in Module D.

Graphs

A graph is a dynamic data structure whose multiply-linked nodes reproduce desired relationships. This dynamic data structure is the most versatile and

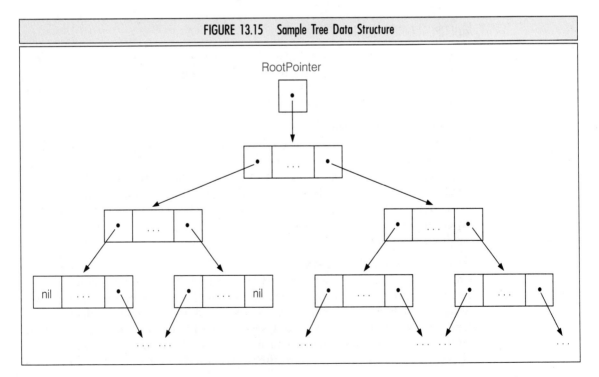

FIGURE 13.15   Sample Tree Data Structure

complex of the data structures we have mentioned. To visualize the graph data structure, picture the map of a continent, with cities as nodes. The graph might show the relationships of cities to one another as a system of interconnecting air routes. Data fields might include city names, distances, and carriers. Pointers would point to approved air routes (links). The graph data structure has important applications in modeling networks of air routes, pipeline distribution systems, land and sea transportation routes, telecommunications transmission lines, and other physical networks.

SELF-REVIEW EXERCISES

26a–b 27a–b

13.6 PROGRAMMING TIPS

• • • • • • • • • • • • • •

Consider the following tips to improve the design and style of your programs and to avoid some common errors.

DESIGN AND STYLE

1. Static Versus Dynamic Data Structures. As data needs and relationships become more demanding, we move from designs that use simple data types to designs that use structured data types. Among structured data types we have choices that include sets, arrays, records, and combinations of these like arrays of records. Each of these is a *static* data structure, requiring a fixed amount of memory at program execution.

The *dynamic* data structure is more memory efficient for applications whose number of elements is apt to vary over a wide range during execution. For example, consider elements that represent reservations in an airline reservation system. If we wish to hold all reservations at one time in primary memory (rather than external memory), and the number of reservations varies from 100 to 5000 within a day, then an array data structure would require an array with 5000 elements. For low-reservation days, many of these elements represent wasted memory. By using a dynamic data structure, the number of needed elements changes "on the fly"; that is, the number of elements expands and contracts as needed. If the number of elements used in an application is fixed or stable over a narrow range, the array alternative may be the best choice from a memory-efficiency standpoint, because the dynamic data structure requires an extra pointer field for each element, which takes up memory.

The list is more computationally efficient than the array for tasks like element traversal and insertions of sorted elements. For example, to display all elements by the array alternative, the computer needs to compute the actual memory address of each element based on its index value; the list alternative directly uses the addresses already stored within pointer fields. The ordered list also wins when inserting a new element in a sorted list. We insert a new element in a linked list by finding its slot, coupling the previous element to the new element, and coupling the new element to the next element. To insert a new element in a sorted array, we find its proper index, move all remaining elements down one position, and insert the new element. The task of moving all remaining array elements is computationally burdensome for large arrays.

On the other hand, the array is more computationally efficient for tasks that require direct access, as in directly accessing the 35th week in a group of 52 elements arranged by week. The list approach would require list traversal to the 35th element.

Finally, the dynamic data structure is more flexible in its relationships among elements. We can use pointers to reflect relationships directly, as in stacks, queues, and graphs, whereas the array alternative requires algorithmic manipulations for relationships other than linear.

2. Which Dynamic Data Structure? Given the selection of a dynamic data structure, we also need to consider which variation — an unordered or ordered list? For example, if sorted displays are useful, an ordered list is warranted. If ordered, should we have single linkages or multiple linkages? If we wish sorted displays by different field values, a multiply-ordered list is called for. What are the linkages based on? Sorts on a key field? Try an ordered list. Sorts on multiple key fields? Try a multiply-ordered list. Forward-backward double links? Try a doubly-linked list. Stacklike element behavior? Use a stack. Queuelike element behavior? Use a queue. Hierarchical relationships? Try a tree. Networklike relationships? Maybe a graph.

COMMON ERRORS

1. Inadmissible Pointer Operations. A common compile-time error is mistaking a pointer for a "normal" variable, as in assigning an integer to a pointer or writing the value in a pointer. You might want to review the defined pointer operations in Section 13.1.

2. Nil Blues. Misusing or forgetting *nil* can cause many logic errors. If we assign nil to the wrong pointer, then we lose access (forever!) to the pointer's dynamic variable, as shown in Example 13.2 for Pointer3. If we forget to assign nil to the last node in a linked list, then list traversal that relies on nil as a sentinel will have unintended results, like access to memory locations that are not part of the list, improper loop termination, and possibly an infinite loop (see Exercise 6b).

3. Head (Pointer) Blues. If we forget to assign the head pointer, we lose an entire list. If we misassign the head pointer, then we lose part of the list.

Procedures that insert and delete head nodes must ensure that the head pointer is reassigned as a variable parameter (see Note 5).

4. Heap Overflow Error. This fatal run-time error occurs when **new** attempts to allocate space on the heap and not enough free space is available. Corrective actions include resetting the heap size (see footnote 2), reducing the size of the dynamic data structure, or debugging an infinite loop.

REVIEW EXERCISES

EASIER	For the busy...
	1 2 4 6 7 8 14 26a–b 27a–b
NORMAL	For the thinkers...
	3 5 9 10 11 12 16 17 19 20 21 24 25
TOUGHER	For the hard CORE...
	13 15 18 22 23 26c 27c

1. In Example 13.1...
    a. What's wrong with the assignment

    ```
    Pointer2^ := Pointer1^
    ```
    b. Revise the memory diagram if **new** (Pointer2) and the assignment in the preceding part were executed.
    c. What's wrong with the assignment

    ```
    Pointer1^ := Pointer3^
    ```
2. In Example 13.2...
    a. What's wrong with the assignment

    ```
    Pointer2 := Pointer3
    ```
    b. What's wrong with the assignment

    ```
    Pointer1 := 49
    ```
    c. What's wrong with

    ```
    writeln (Pointer3)
    ```
    d. How does the second memory diagram change if the following assignment is executed?

    ```
    Pointer2 := nil
    ```
    Can we access the "49"? Explain.
    e. State code that writes the value pointed to by Pointer3, but only if Pointer3 is unequal to nil.

3. Suppose P1 and P2 are type pointer with base type character.
   a. Sketch a memory diagram after the execution of the following statements.

   ```
   new (P1);    new (P2);
   P1^ := 'H';   P2^ := 'C';
   ```

   b. State output after execution of the following statement.

   ```
   writeln (P1^, P2^)
   ```

   c. Revise the memory diagram after execution of the following assignment.

   ```
   P1 := P2
   ```

   d. Restate the output in part **b**, given the memory diagram in part **c**.
   e. Go back to the diagram in part **a**. Write down code that exchanges the nodes pointed to by P1 and P2. How does the diagram change? *Hint:* Use a temporary pointer TempP that points to P1^, assuming TempP is the same type as P1 and P2.

(L) 4. **Program List1 test.** Test drive program List1 by recreating our run in Figure 13.2.

5. **Procedure CreateList.** Complete the diagram in Figure 13.5 for the third node.

(L) 6. **Procedure DisplayList.** With respect to the procedures in Figure 13.6 . . .
   a. What would be implied if HeadPointer stores nil? What would happen when DisplayList is called?
   b. What do you think would happen if the pointer field for the third node did not store nil (its contents were undefined)? Confirm your answer by enclosing the statement that assigns nil in CreateList in braces and running List1 to recreate and display the list.

7. **Procedure GetList.** What would happen during a call to GetList in Figure 13.8 if . . .
   a. The file is empty?
   b. We replace the if-then-else structure with the two statements that assign LastPointer^. Point and LastPointer?

(L) 8. **Program List2 test.** Test drive program List2 by creating the ordered list in Figure 13.10. Display, file, retrieve, and redisplay the list.

*9. **Procedures CreateOrderedList, NewCity, and InsertCity.** Complete the diagram in Figure 13.12 for nodes Boston and Miami.

*10. **Procedure InsertCity.** Do you see a problem with a compiler that uses complete evaluation (unlike Turbo Pascal's *short-circuit evaluation*) when evaluating the following Boolean expression?

   ```
   (NextPointer <> nil)
   and (NewPointer^.CityName > NextPointer^.CityName)
   ```

   How might we rewrite this logic?

(L) *11.   **Procedures CreateOrderedList and InsertCity.** With respect to creating an ordered list . . .

   a. Indicate what would happen in Figure 13.12 if some user (not us!) spaced out and were to input the Toronto node twice in succession?

   b. Modify InsertCity to detect this possibility. If an identically named node is found, InsertCity does not insert the new city and sends false for parameter Achieved; else InsertCity inserts the city and sends true for Achieved.

   c. Revise CreateOrderedList to account for Achieved. If city insertion is not achieved, then display an error message to that effect.

   d. Test these changes by entering the following cities in succession: Los Angeles, Chicago, Toronto, Toronto.

(L) *12.   **Procedure DeleteList.** Revise List2 as List3 to include the main menu option of deleting the entire list. Confirm this selection by a Y/N reply. *Hint:* Traverse the list calling **dispose.**

(L) *13.   **Ordered city list by temperature.** Revise List2 as List3 to include the option of ordering the list by temperature. The create list menu now offers the following options.

   1 Unordered list
   2 Ordered list by name
   3 Ordered list by temperature
   Q Quit

Repeat Exercise 8 as your test run.

(L) 14.   **Creating sorted city file.** Run List2 to create an ordered list of Los Angeles, Chicago, Toronto, Boston, and Miami by city name. The respective temperatures are 62, 15, 20, 32, and 68. Display the list. File the city records to file CITIES2.BIN. Is this data file sorted? Retrieve the records from the file and redisplay the list. Sketch the memory diagram of the list that's created from the file retrieval.

(L) *15.   **Sorting: City list.** Revise List2 as List3 to include a seventh main menu option "Sort city file." This option inputs an unsorted file of city records (like those in Chapter 12) and creates an ordered list by city name. It then files the city records in the list as a sorted file. Develop procedure **SortFile** as described in Section 13.3. For your test run, use the file of city records created in Exercise 8 from Chapter 12. (We made it easy for you by including file CITYTEMP.BIN in the Examples Library.) Name your sorted file CITIES3.BIN. Get this file and display the resulting list of cities. Are they sorted?

(L) *16.   **Procedure FindCity.** For Example 13.3 . . .

   a. Develop desk-check scripts to find cities Boston, Los Angeles, Toronto, and London, given the list in Figure 13.10e.

   b. Code and test procedure **FindCity** within program List2. Name the new program List3. In your test run, find the cities mentioned in part **a.**

*17.   Function TargetPointer short-circuit version. Revise the pseudocode for function TargetPointer in Example 13.3 to eliminate Boolean variable Found by directly incorporating the name field test within the while test. Compare the pros and cons of the two approaches.

*18.   Function TargetPointer recursive version. Revise the pseudocode for function TargetPointer in Example 13.3 to use recursive calls (as covered in Module B).

(L) ***19.   Procedure AddNewCity.** Develop and test procedure AddNewCity, as seen in Figure 13.3. Start with program List2 and name the revised program List3. In your test run, create the unordered list in Figure 13.1b, then add cities Boston with temperature 32 and Miami with temperature 68. Redisplay the list after each addition.

(L) ***20.   Procedure InsertNewCity.** Develop and test procedure InsertNewCity, as seen in Figure 13.3. Start with program List2 and name the revised program List3. In your test run, create the ordered list in Figure 13.1c, then insert cities Boston with temperature 32 and Miami with temperature 62. Redisplay the list after each insertion.

(L) ***21.   Procedure DeleteCity.** Develop and test procedure DeleteCity, as seen in Figure 13.3. Start with program List2 and name the revised program List3. In your test run, create the ordered list in Figure 10.10e, then delete cities Boston, Miami, and Toronto. Redisplay the list after each deletion.

(L) ***22.   Procedure ChangeCity.** Develop and test procedure ChangeCity in Example 13.4. Start with program List2 and name the revised program List3. In your test run, create the ordered list in Figure 13.10e, except mistakenly enter Boston as Voston, then make the following changes: (a) Change Miami's temperature to 72; (b) change Los Angeles to San Francisco; (c) change Voston to Boston. Redisplay the list following all changes.

(L) ***23.   City list queries.** Implement the query menu option discussed in Section 13.4 by revising List2 as List3. In your test run, answer the queries posed. Add any other query options you think might be appropriate.

(L) ***24.   City list prints.** Revise DisplayList within List2 to ask if the displayed cities should be printed (Y/N). Send the reply to OutputCity and accordingly modify that routine. Name the revised program List3. In your test run, print the list displayed in Figure 13.2.

(L) ***25.   City list unit.** Develop unit CityUnit to house the type and procedure declarations in List2. Revise List2 as List4 to use CityUnit. In your test runs, reproduce the run in Figure 13.2 and create/display the ordered list in Figure 10.10e.

(L) **26.   Doubly-linked city list.** For our city list problem . . .
   a. Rework the diagram in Figure 13.1b as a doubly-linked list. Use PointLeft and PointRight as the pointer fields; use HeadPointer and FootPointer to point accordingly.

b. Appropriately change the declarations on page 628.

*c. Revise List2 as List5 to include a doubly-linked option for the unordered list. Add the item "Doubly-linked unordered" to the Create List Menu. When the display main menu option is selected, ask the user if the list is to be displayed forward or backward.

(L) **27.** **Multiply-ordered city list.** For our city list problem...

a. Rework the diagram in Figure 13.1c as a multiply-ordered list. Use PointName and PointF as the pointer fields; use HeadPointerName and HeadPointerF accordingly.

b. Appropriately change the declarations on page 628.

*c. Revise List2 as List6 to multiply order all ordered lists by city name and temperature. When the display main menu option is selected, ask the user if the list is to be displayed by name or temperature.

ADDITIONAL EXERCISES

EASIER	For the busy... **28**	
NORMAL	For the thinkers... **29 30 31 32 33**	
TOUGHER	For the hard CORE... **34 35 36 37**	

28. **Revisit.** Rework an application you developed earlier to use a dynamic data structure of your choice, if appropriate. Compare the pros and cons of the two versions.

29. **Revisit: Mirror, mirror...** Rework the exercise in Module B by using the stack data structure.

30. **Revisit: Bond issue.** Rework the exercise in Chapter 12 by using a bond list ordered by county.

31. **Employee list.** Consider the employee records that we worked with in Chapters 11 and 12.

a. Revise List1 to manage a list of employees.

b. Revise List2 to manage a list of employees. The ordered list option orders the list by social security number.

    c. Incorporate one or more of the features in Exercises 15, 16, and 19–24.

    d. Develop and use an employee unit that houses all employee type and procedure declarations.

Use the test data in Figure 12.6 for a three-employee test list. Reproduce an equivalent run to that in Figure 13.2, both for an unordered and ordered list. *Hint:* Start with List1 or List2, and revise accordingly. Use the **Search Replace** command options in the IDE to replace CITY with EMPLOYEE, city with **employee**, and City with Employee.

32. **Stack.** Develop a program that creates, displays, and breaks down the stack in Figure 13.13. Include the four modules described in Section 13.5.

33. **Queue.** Develop a program that...

    a. Builds, displays, and eliminates the queue in Figure 13.14. Include the four modules described in Section 13.5. Use the strings Message 1..., Message 2..., and Message 3... for the messages.

    b. Suppose we wish to keep track of the queue length with the integer variable QueueLength. Appropriately modify the code in part **a.**

    c. Suppose the client program also declares record variable Queue with the following record type.

```
QueueType = record
    Front, Back : QueuePointer;   {Pointers}
    Length      : word;           {Queue length}
end; {QueueType}
```

    Queue is used as a parameter for passing a record variable that holds queue-related pointers and operating characteristics like queue length, average queue length, and so on. Appropriately modify the code in part **a.**

34. **Revisit: Dating service.** Rework the exercise in Chapter 8 by using a client list ordered by...

    a. Last name

    b. Age

    c. Education

    d. Income

    e. Multiply ordered by the fields in parts **a–d.**

Include options for filing and getting the client list. In your test runs, include ordered displays of the clients.

35. **Revisit: Alumni-file query.** Rework the exercise in Chapter 11 by using an alumni list ordered by...

    a. Last name

    b. Year of graduation

    c. Salary

    d. Multiply ordered by the fields in parts **a–c.**

Include options for filing and getting the alumni list. In your test runs, include ordered displays of the alumni.

36. **Revisit: Airline reservation system.** Rework the exercise in Chapter 11 by using a flight list ordered by...

a. Flight number

b. Departing airport

c. Arriving airport

d. Multiply ordered by the fields in parts **a–c.**

Include options for filing and getting the flight list. In your test runs, include ordered displays of the flights.

37. **Simulation: Queue.** Let's simulate events in an E-mail queue, as seen in Figure 13.14. An *event* is either an arrival or a departure. Suppose that the probability that the next event is an arrival is 0.7; the probability that the next event is a departure is 0.3. Use function **random** (Module C) to simulate events. Perform 20 simulations, starting with an empty queue. Use the four modules described in Section 13.5. Each element is a string message. Store the string messages as **Message 1 ...**, **Message 2 ...**, and so on in order of arrivals. Display the contents of the queue and its size after each event.

OBJECT-ORIENTED PROGRAMMING

It's promising a software development revolution. Its philosophy and implementation affect the entire spectrum of the software development cycle. It views the programming world in a manner similar to the way we humans view the physical and conceptual objects we deal with. Its approach turns top-down programming upside down, requires an unlearning of certain approaches to programming, and undoubtedly engenders resistance among programming professionals (as did top-down principles in the 1970s and 1980s). It's been a long time coming, it's arrived in fine form in Turbo Pascal (since Version 5.5), we've been using one of its implementations all along in the IDE (since Version 6.0), and it's called *object-oriented programming (OOP)*.[1]

14.1 PRINCIPLES

· · · · · · · · · · · ·

Look around you. What do you see? Objects! Objects everywhere! We deal with objects all the time. They are fundamental to the way we perceive and relate to our physical world. How might we define objects? How about this book? We might say this book is an object with such and such dimensions, such and such colors, so many pages, and so on. These are attributes of the book. Suppose we said this is an object that teaches Turbo Pascal, serves as a reference, and looks good on my desk. Now we're talking about the functions of the book.

Similarly, we could say that a portable computer is an object with attributes like size, weight, memory, disk capacity, speed, and so on. Moreover, it takes actions (has functions or manifests behavior) like display data, beep the speaker, store a file, and so on. In short, objects have both *attributes* and *functions*. Attributes and functions together describe the essence of an object. One without the other doesn't tell the whole story.

---

[1]*Simula-67* was the first object-oriented (OO) language (in 1967). Its purpose was the simulation of real phenomena by conceptually reproducing the attributes and behavior of objects in our physical environment. In the early 1970s, Xerox Corporation's famous Palo Alto Research Center (PARC) developed the second OO language, *Smalltalk*. In the mid-1980s, Smalltalk's OO philosophy served as the genesis of Apple's *Macintosh* graphic user interface and Microsoft's DOS counterpart *Windows*. AT&T's Bell Laboratory exposed the professional programming community to OOP with the *C++* language in the early 1980s. Borland International extended this benefit to the Pascal masses starting with Version 5.5 of *Turbo Pascal* in 1989.

From a software standpoint, attributes are described by *data* and functionality or behavior is described by algorithmic actions in *procedures and functions.* In effect, we have been implicitly working with the nature of objects all along, but we have conceptually torn apart objects by decoupling their attributes and functions as separate constituents in software development. Each only tells part of the story, and sometimes we lose sight of these parts (as in mismatching a procedure and its data-type requirements). The object-oriented (*OO*) philosophy makes the object whole again by forcing us to consider both its attributes and its functions. In other words, we treat it as a unified entity called an *object.*

OOP SCOOP

Object-oriented programming (**OOP**) is a form of *modular programming* whose modules are objects. An **object** is a software entity with two parts: its data and the routines that act on its data. By routines we mean *procedures* and *functions,* which are called the object's **methods** in OOP. The data describe the attributes of the object and the methods describe its behavior, actions, or functions. This concept of bundling together the data and methods that act on the data is called **encapsulation.** The methods in an object only operate on the encapsulated data within that object.

Each object belongs to a **class** of objects having the same data types and methods. The declaration of a class of objects is equivalent to the declaration of an **object type.** In the OO literature, the terms *class, object class,* and *object type* are synonymous. An object has an object type, just as a variable has a data type. In fact, objects are declared like variables in Turbo Pascal, as we will see. To say that an object like OurPerson has a particular object type like Person is to say that the object OurPerson belongs to the class Person.

Let's get more specific. Consider the representation for two object types in Figure 14.1. As we can see, the **object chart** identifies object types (classes, not objects!), the relationships among them, and the data and methods that define each object type. The top figure shows an object type named Person. Its real-world counterpart might be the class of persons within a college. As with the real McCoy, our software object type Person includes attributes (data) and actions (methods). ID and FullName are data fields in the manner of *records* (Chapter 11). Methods Init, Display, and Update are procedures that act on the data fields ID and FullName. Init initializes the fields, Display writes their values to the screen, and Update revises and displays fields. By declaring the data structure and its operations within one neatly wrapped bundle, we have defined the ultimate *ADT.*

Note that Person *is not the object itself;* it's the class or data type of the object. An **object** is an *instance* (realization) of its data type; it's a member of its class. We *instantiate* (how's that for a verb?) an object by declaring it like a variable, as follows.

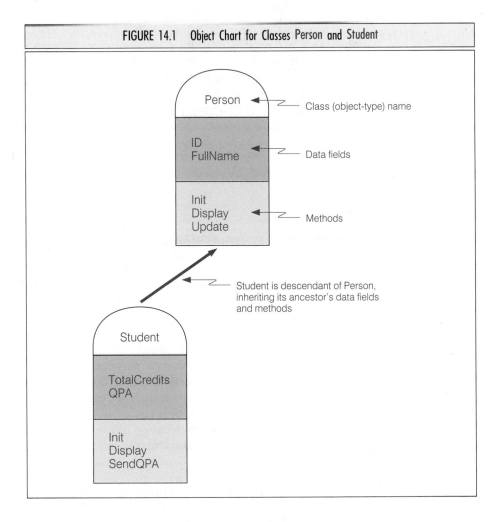

FIGURE 14.1   Object Chart for Classes Person and Student

var
      OurPerson, ThatPerson, APerson : Person;

Thus OurPerson, ThatPerson, and APerson are object instances of class Person, or simply *Person objects*. Each of these objects has the same data structure and methods that operate on that data structure. The only differences among them will be the precise data values that get set at run time, that is, the ID and full name of each. We can also take different actions on each object. For example, we might choose to display just one and not the other two, although all three objects have the same display capabilities. Think of an object as a specific set of data (according to its data structure) and the methods that operate on that data. *An object is an instance of a structured ADT,* an ADT with one or more structured data types along with all its defined operations on those data types.

In the real world, we are instances of people. All of us (people) belong to a class called person by the very fact that each member of this class has the same attributes and functions as any other member. Thus, any person has attributes like name, height, weight, gender, eye color, and so on. Moreover, people take common actions like walk, talk, sleep, run, eat, and so forth. In our college software example, each member of class Person has the same attributes (name and identification) and performs the same actions (initializes, displays, and updates). The only difference between OurPerson and ThatPerson is that each has a different name and different ID (presumably). They are each capable of the same actions (Init, Display, and Update), which is the OOP equivalent of equality in the real world!

By the way, OOP talk is replete with anthropomorphic references to objects. For example, we might describe an output action on a document object as "Output yourself." While some computer scientists decry our tendency to anthropomorphize,[2] others believe it enhances understanding when used properly. In the present context, an object's data (attributes) and methods (behavior) constitute the object, so it makes as much sense to tell an object to output itself (show its attributes) as it does to tell a person "explain yourself." The traditional software approach would say "Send data to a called output routine," a less colorful descriptive action that fails to capture the notion of a document as an object that's relatable to humans. Additionally, it doesn't convey the concept that a document is an object with two interrelated properties: attributes (data) and behavior (output). In the same humanlike vein, a request like "Output yourself" is called a *message.* We invoke actions in OOP by sending messages! (We show you how in Section 14.2.)

Now let's consider our favorite people, students. We know that a student is a person as well because the fields and methods for class Person also characterize class Student. In OOP talk we say that Student is an immediate **descendant** of Person. As you might guess, we also say that Person is the immediate **ancestor** of Student. We also realize that a student is more than a person (in the OOP sense), in that we can also describe a student by total credits, quality-point average, and other attributes.

In Figure 14.1, we describe object type Student with two new fields (TotalCredits and QPA) and three methods (Init, Display, and SendQPA). The upward arrow that connects Student to Person identifies Student as a descendant of Person. This means that Student automatically inherits the data fields and methods in Person, an OOP property called **inheritance.** Inheritance is a powerful property of OOP and has important implications in software *re-*

---

[2]Remember that to *anthropomorphize* is to assign human attributes to objects, animals, gods, and so on. You might want to review footnote 5 in Chapter 1.

usability. For example, once we debug a method within a particular object class, any of its descendants can use that method without further modification. Moreover, we don't need to redeclare the inherited data fields.

The Student class shows two additional fields that distinguish a student's data from a person's data: TotalCredits and QPA. Thus, a student object like OurStudent would have four descriptive data fields: the two inherited fields (ID and FullName) and the two new fields (TotalCredits and QPA). The methods Init and Display in Student have the same names as those in Person, but they *override* their ancestral counterparts as methods whose algorithms differ from those in their earlier namesakes. Within Student, Init and Display have to initialize and display two additional fields. The new method SendQPA is a function that returns the value stored in the QPA field of the object. This new method *extends* the inherited methods. In other words, Student includes a method not found in its ancestor.

Inheritance thus includes *extensibility,* the ability to create descendant objects that add data fields and methods to those they have inherited. The added methods can be new (as in including the new function SendQPA) or they can override inherited methods (as in Init and Display above). With reusability and extensibility we "can have our cake and eat it too"; we can *reuse* the fields and methods that we already have (without any code modifications at all!) and *extend* what we don't have (by writing new code for new fields and methods).

OOP also permits the declaration of a single method that describes a common behavior among descendant classes but that operates differently depending on the descendant object type that applies. For example, we show a method named Update in the Person class of Figure 14.1; its purpose is to display an object, fill an object with new data, and redisplay that object. Student inherits this method and does not override it with its own update method. To update a person object, we would send it a *message* to update itself; to update a student object, we would also send it the same update message. The student object would use the very same method to update itself as does the person object. How is this possible, given that the fields in the student object are different from the fields in the person object? It's the ability of OOP to adapt the same method to objects from different classes, depending on where the message gets sent at run time. This property is called **polymorphism** (Greek for "*many shapes*") and, as we demonstrate in Section 14.3, it also promotes extensibility.

The concepts of classes, objects, encapsulation, inheritance, and polymorphism, together with the attendant benefits of modularity, reusability, and extensibility, put OOP in a very different (and higher) orbit from other approaches to programming.

OOP AND EVENT-DRIVEN PROGRAMMING

An *event* is an occurrence to which a program should respond. Kinds of events include the following.

- *Keyboard events,* like pressing the F2 key or Esc key
- *Mouse events,* like clicking a button or moving the mouse pointer
- *Message events,* like responding to a selected menu command
- *Null event,* a nonevent or nonexistent event that's useful in assessing the event state of the system

In traditional programming, events are handled by a loop that inputs the event, routes the event using a selection structure, and calls the proper procedure to implement the required response. The OOP approach works much the same way, except the event is a messge that gets sent to the proper object. What makes OOP an attractive alternative to traditional programming is that many of the objects that respond to events are visible on the screen.

To illustrate, consider Turbo Pascal's now familiar IDE. The IDE implementation operates as an OOP program, where objects include the menu bar at the top, the desktop in the middle, and the status line at the bottom. We're also capable of littering the desktop with other objects, like file windows, a dialog box, an output window, a pull-down menu, and other paraphernalia. Obviously, a lot can happen on the screen!

From our user perspective, the screen makes sense because we view its components as distinct objects whose behavior we have control over. Thus, its straightforward (once we know how) to remove, shrink, or drag a file window. From the IDE's applications program viewpoint, these events are handled as messages to objects. The implementation of these tasks is more natural in an OOP environment than in a traditional programming environment.

The notion of elements on the screen as objects on a desktop follows the *desktop metaphor.* The idea is that non-computer users will feel more comfortable with computers if the screen gives the illusion of manipulable "objects" on a "desktop," a practice that's familiar to almost everyone. As it turns out, computer veterans have also taken to this idea. In a well-designed user interface, we can implement commands and tasks much faster by manipulating objects than by typing command sequences.

OOP and the Software Development Cycle

OOP necessarily revises the software development cycle first presented in Chapter 1 and summarized inside the front cover of the text.[3] In traditional programming, often called *procedural programming,* software development uses an approach that's usually identified by terms like *waterfall model, waterfall paradigm,* or *procedural model.* This is the model we have been

---

[3]More generally, OOP changes the systems life cycle mentioned in Chapter 1. OO development is an advanced and evolving topic within the systems life cycle literature. For a good read on this topic, see the special issue titled *"Object Oriented Design," Communications of the ACM,* vol. 33, no. 9, September 1990.

using all along. Its basis is the application of *top-down design* to functionally decompose a problem into *modules* characterized by procedures and functions. The procedural model primarily focuses on the application's actions (the needed procedures and functions) and relegates the data structures to the secondary role of satisfying the data requirements and "feeding" the procedures and functions. The process flows from the top to the bottom, as described in Chapter 3. Like a waterfall, the model doesn't really have built-in provisions for *conceptually* reintegrating previously passed points (stages) along the "waterfall" whenever changes require revisits to previous stages. From a practical standpoint, the model does allow recycling, but its philosophy is more comfortable with the notion that "What's past is past."

OOP offers a *fountain model, fountain paradigm,* or simply *OO model.* Its approach combines elements of *bottom-up design* and *top-down design.* It's bottom up in the sense that it turns the focus upside down—from functional decomposition of actions into modules to the composition of modules as objects that contain data. The focus starts with the data structure of an object and then defines the needed actions (methods) based on the object's data. As software development proceeds, the flow is upward (we're building object classes from the ground up) and then downward as methods are developed (in a top-down fashion). Each stage interacts more naturally with the preceding stage, much like the behavior of water in a fountain. As we will see, *OOP views a program as a cooperating society of (happy) objects.* So much for concepts. Let's get specific with . . .

EXAMPLE 14.1   OOP COLLEGE APPLICATION REQUIREMENTS AND DESIGN

Figure 14.2 shows a memo from Harvey CORE, our by-now familiar and intrepid computational sciences hero. As you can see, it describes the *requirements* for a college application that reflects the OO model. The I/O design mentioned in the memo is pictured in Figure 14.3.

Now let's consider how we might go about *designing* this application. To start, we might identify the object classes and their relationships. Figure 14.4 shows several ways of sketching this design element, variously called the **inheritance graph, object hierarchy tree,** and **taxonomy chart.** The primary objective here is to identify a complete set of object types, together with their inheritance relationships. For example, Person is the *root class* that spawns all other classes in the hierarchy. Student, Faculty, and Staff are all immediate *descendants* of Person. This means that all student, faculty, and staff objects *inherit* the data fields and methods in class Person; objects in any one of these three classes, however, can include *extensions* of the data fields and methods in any person object. Moreover, it would be to their advantage to *reuse* any inherited fields and methods. The student class spawns two other classes mentioned in the memo: National and International. Similarly, PartTime and FullTime classes descend from the faculty

---

FIGURE 14.2   Requirements Memo from Harvey for OOP College Application

---

M E M O R A N D U M

To ....   OOP Aspirant and newly hired CAD analyst
From .....   Harvey CORE, Professor and CEO of CAD
Date ......   April 1, 1993
Subject ...   OOP in college

I read OOP here, OOP there, OOP everywhere. It sounds like it's to programming in the 1990s what oatbran was to health in the 1980s. I don't think oatbran was a fad, a "flash in the pan," and I feel the same way about OOP.

I want you to put together a little OO demonstration program that initializes and displays some data for different types of people in a college. For now consider just two kinds of people: students and faculty. Both have names and IDs. Further, students have current values for total credits and quality-point average; faculty have rank (like instructor, professor, and so on) and a salary in dollars and cents.

Enclosed is sample I/O for what I have in mind. Later we will expand the actions to include updates that display the current data for a student or faculty member, fill new data, and redisplay the data. We might also consider other useful methods, like returning data field values. Still later we can include staff people, national and international students, and part-time and full-time faculty.

In the meantime, I'm off to my villa in Varadero Beach. If you do a first-rate job, maybe I'll have you down for some R&R . . . the weather is great, the surf is up, the drinks soothe the brow, the food is sassy, and . . .

Let's see if you're worth the $70,000 starting salary I'm paying you! Adios . . .

HC

FIGURE 14.3   I/O Design for OOP College Application, Version 1

```
Student...
    Name....................
    Identification.......... 000-00-0000
    Total credits.......... 0
    Quality point average... 0.00


Faculty...
    Name....................
    Identification.......... 000-00-0000
    Rank...................
    Salary................. $0.00
```

---

class. These classes would be needed if we wished to keep track of different fields peculiar to these subclasses. For example, we might wish to keep track of country of origin, visa number, and "green" card number for international students. *Note how data requirements are driving this design,* rather than the actions we will eventually take on the data. This is what we mean by *bottom-up design.*

Next we might specify the data fields and methods for each class. The *object chart* described earlier serves the purpose here, as seen in Figure 14.5. The specific data fields and methods for the primary three classes of interest (Person,

---

FIGURE 14.4 Alternative Design Diagrams That Show Object-Class Inheritance Relationships

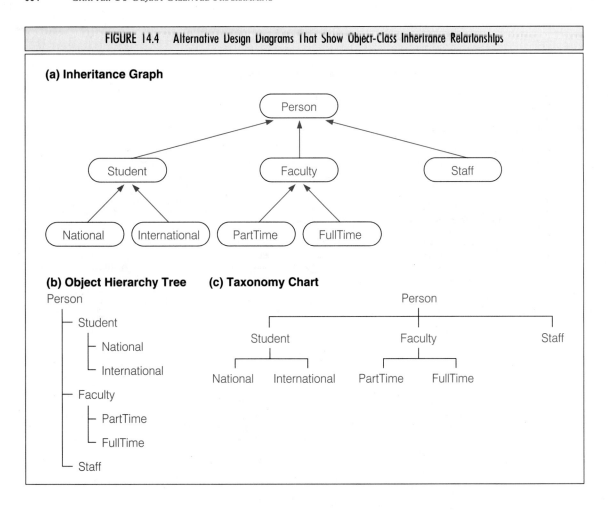

(a) Inheritance Graph

(b) Object Hierarchy Tree **(c) Taxonomy Chart**

Student, and Faculty) follow readily from the requirements and our earlier discussions. In later examples and exercises, we consider additional methods for these classes and include the other classes in Figure 14.4.

At this point in our design we can start applying top-down principles for each method. For example, what tasks need to be accomplished by method Display within the Person class? (Display ID and FullName.) Should we use a procedure or function? How many of each? (One procedure.) Should we develop pseudocode and specify control structures? (Usually yes, but this application is simple.)

Did you notice the new object class Session? This class is used in the design to declare OurSession as the *session object* or *applications program object*. Its purpose is to invoke or run the college application by sending appropriate messages to the other objects. Its methods perform three fundamental tasks that initialize (method Init), run (method Run), and terminate (method Done) the application.

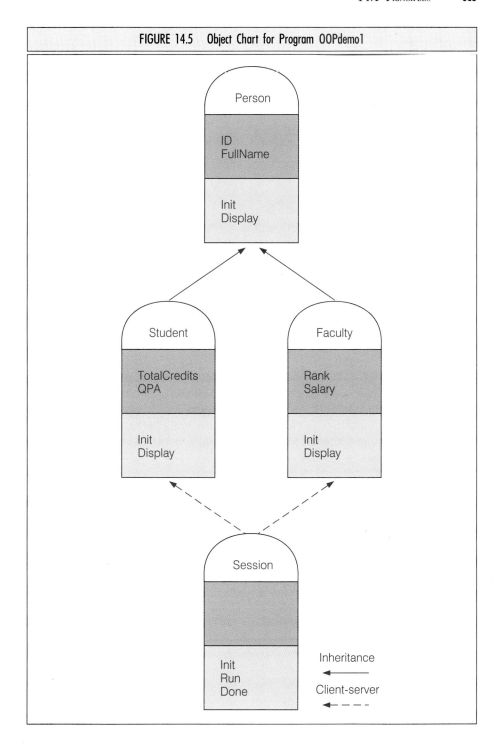

FIGURE 14.5 Object Chart for Program OOPdemo1

Class Session is not a descendant class; rather its object OurSession controls the application by sending messages to other objects. In this sense, OurSession is a *client* that requests *services* from other objects. This **client-server** relationship is shown by the broken arrows in Figure 14.5. In our example, a session object requests services from a student object and a faculty object. The services rendered are initialization and display, as seen by the I/O in Figure 14.3.

Think of a session object as the "boss" that controls the application. As we will see, our program's main algorithm will send messages to the session object to initialize, run, and terminate the application. In other words, our main algorithm's design looks like this:

Main algorithm

Send initialization message to OurSession
Send run message to OurSession
Send done message to OurSession

All of our OO programs will have this main algorithm. Note that *we specified the main algorithm last in this design process, which further illustrates the bottom-up approach in OO design.*

Our entire program is now made up entirely of modules represented by objects (or object classes if you prefer). By conceptualizing our entire program as a collection of objects, we accomplish complete modularity. In fact, the object chart is to the OO model as the structure chart is to the procedural model! (Good T/F question on an exam...) Finally, we're ready to move on to *Coding* and *Testing*.

SELF-REVIEW EXERCISES

1 2 3 4a 5a

14.2   IMPLEMENTATION

• • • • • • • • • • • • • •

This section describes the construction of a complete OO program, its debugging, and the use of units.

OBJECT TYPE AND OBJECT DECLARATIONS

An *object class* or *object type* is declared by declaring its data fields in the manner of *records* and its methods in the manner of procedure and function declarations in the interface section of a unit, as seen in the accompanying syntax box. Note the following.

1. In the Person declaration, ID and FullName are data fields and the method declarations Init and Display are like forward declarations (the actual methods are declared elsewhere, as we will see). This declaration essentially says that objects of type Person have ID and FullName data fields that are acted on by procedures Init and Display. Because formal parameters and local variables share the same scope, the formal parameter identifiers *Name* and *SSN* must be different from their field counterpart identifiers FullName and ID.

2. Object type Student is a descendant of object type Person because its declaration includes the clause (Person) following the reserved word **object.** This means that Student inherits Person's fields and methods. Student, though, can *override* (replace) Person's methods, but not its data fields. Thus, Student (and any other descendant of Person) must have field identifiers that are different from its inherited field identifiers. The two method identifiers Init and Display in Student are identical to those in Person. This means that Person's Init and Display methods are overridden in Student. We did this because these methods in Student must work with four fields, instead of the two in Person. This will be more obvious when we show the implementations of these methods.

3. OurPerson and OurStudent are respective instances of object types Person and Student. In other words, OurPerson is a person object and OurStudent is a student object. *Objects are declared just like variables.* And just like variables, they take up memory and have memory addresses. Unlike a variable, *the structure of an object includes addresses to the methods that are encapsulated within.*

4. Inheritance complicates *assignment-compatibility* rules. A descendant type inherits type compatibility with its ancestor types, but this compatibility extends only from descendant to ancestor. In other words, an *ancestor type is compatible with a descendant type, but not vice versa.* To illustrate, the *object assignment*

      OurPerson := OurStudent; ☺

is permissible, but not the assignment

      OurStudent := OurPerson; ☹

This makes sense when we realize, first, that object assignments only assign fields that the two object types have in common and, second, that

SYNTAX BOX

Object type and object declarations (Static methods version)*... Declare object type in type section and object in var section

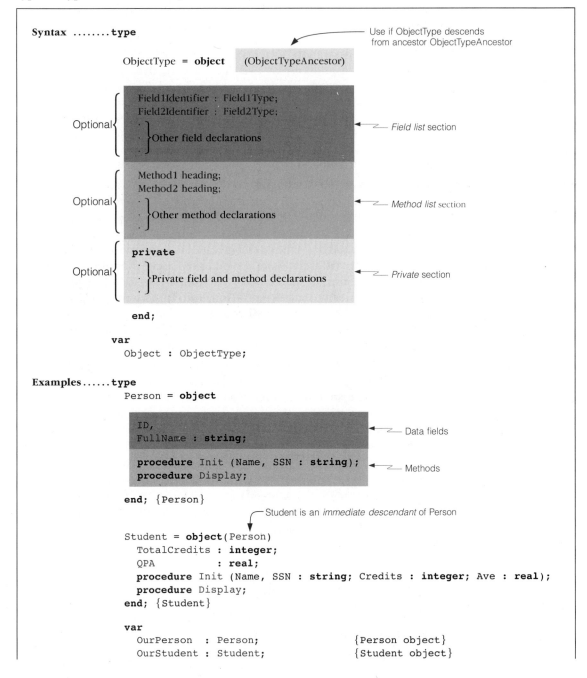

Syntax .... **type**

Use if ObjectType descends from ancestor ObjectTypeAncestor

ObjectType = **object** (ObjectTypeAncestor)

Optional {
```
Field1Identifier : Field1Type;
Field2Identifier : Field2Type;
  .
  .  } Other field declarations
  .
```
Field list section

Optional {
```
Method1 heading;
Method2 heading;
  .
  .  } Other method declarations
  .
```
Method list section

Optional {
```
private
  .
  .  } Private field and method declarations
  .
```
Private section

```
        end;

    var
        Object : ObjectType;
```

Examples ...... **type**
```
        Person = object
```
```
            ID,
            FullName : string;
```
Data fields
```
            procedure Init (Name, SSN : string);
            procedure Display;
```
Methods
```
        end; {Person}
```

Student is an *immediate descendant* of Person
```
        Student = object(Person)
            TotalCredits : integer;
            QPA          : real;
            procedure Init (Name, SSN : string; Credits : integer; Ave : real);
            procedure Display;
        end; {Student}

        var
            OurPerson  : Person;              {Person object}
            OurStudent : Student;             {Student object}
```

Explanation....ObjectType is a user-defined identifier for an *object type*. The identifiers **type, object, private, end,** and **var** are reserved words. ObjectTypeAncestor is an optional object-type identifier for a previously declared object type. ObjectTypeAncestor is the immediate ancestor of ObjectType. By the *inheritance property,* ObjectType inherits all data fields and methods associated with ObjectTypeAncestor and its ancestral lineage. The field declarations are in the manner of a record data structure with data fields given by the *field list.* Each member of the field list is a FieldIdentifier and its FieldType. The FieldIdentifier is a user-defined identifier for the *field variable.* FieldType is any allowable type in Turbo Pascal. All data-field declarations must precede method declarations. The *method list* section is a list of method headings separated by semicolons. A Method heading for *static methods* has the same syntax as *forward declarations* or *procedure* and *function* declarations in the *interface* section of a *unit.* A *static method* is any method that's not *virtual.* A method heading includes one of the reserved words **procedure, function, constructor,** or **destructor.** We describe the latter two under virtual methods in the next section. The reserved word **private** identifies a section whose field and method declarations are accessible only to other objects whose types are declared within the unit. In other words, private fields and methods enforce encapsulation by preventing their export to other programs and units. The *scope* of field and method identifiers extends over the *domain* given by the object type declaration, its descendants, and the implementation of that object type's methods. The *implementation* of a method is similar to the declaration of a procedure or function (see next subsection). Because they share the same scope, data fields and methods are freely available to an object type's methods. Object is a user-defined identifier for the object whose type is ObjectType.

*The syntax box on page 700 covers *virtual methods.*

the fields in the ancestor object (OurPerson) are a subset of the fields in the descendant object (OurStudent). Thus, the first assignment is legal because all of the fields in OurPerson (ID and FullName) would be filled with the corresponding field values in OurStudent; the two other fields in OurStudent (TotalCredits and QPA) are simply ignored. The second assignment is illegal because two (TotalCredits and QPA) of the four fields in OurStudent would be undefined!

5. The assignment-compatibility rule also has its counterpart in the type compatibility of *object parameters* in method calls. A method with a formal parameter (either value or **var**) typed Person can be called with a corresponding actual parameter whose type is Person, Student, or any descendant of Person. If the formal parameter is Student, however, the actual parameter cannot be Person; it must be Student or one of Student's descendants. The object as actual parameter is called a **polymorphic object** because it illustrates a form of *polymorphism* that expands the ability of a procedure or function to accept calls whose actual parameters have different types from the formal parameters. In other words, *polymorphic objects permit the processing of objects whose types are not known at compile time.*

METHOD DECLARATIONS AND CALLS

Method declarations and calls are very similar to what we know already. The best way to describe these is by example.

EXAMPLE 14.2   OOP COLLEGE APPLICATION CODE AND TEST

Figure 14.6 shows the complete program for our sample OOP application. Note the following.

1. The object type declarations are those we have already discussed, except for Faculty and Session, which follow readily from our object chart and discussion in Example 14.1. Note that *ancestors are declared before descendants*. The object declarations in the var section also follow readily. Many programmers place the var declarations just before the main body; we like placing these just after the type declarations, which makes it easier to locate the object type declaration that corresponds to an object (they're in the same vicinity).

2. The implementations (complete declarations) of methods follow next. A method's implementation syntax is identical to the syntax of a procedure or function, except for the following.

   a. We can substitute the reserved word **constructor** or **destructor** for **procedure** or **function.** Constructor and destructor methods are best explained when we describe virtual methods in the next section.

   b. The method's identifier has the form

      ObjectType.MethodName

      where ObjectType is the user-defined object type identifier and MethodName is the user-defined method name identifier. Thus, Person.Init is the method identifier in the implementation of Person's Init method and Student.Init is the method identifier in the implementation of Student's Init method. This syntax is identical to the *dot form* that we used in referencing record fields. In its present version, it identifies a particular object type's method.

   c. The formal parameter list is optional; we like to include it because it makes it easier to relate the formal parameter identifiers and their types to the code.

   d. A method's block is within the same scope as its object type declaration. This means that it directly accesses its type's fields. For example, ID and FullName are directly accessed in procedures Person.Init and Person.Display.

   e. A method could also directly access its inherited fields, but it would not be good form to do so because it exposes an ancestor object's fields to manipulation by descendant objects, thereby violating the principle of encapsulation and degrading the reliability of maintenance. To illustrate, take a look at the code in Student.Init. This method not only needs to initialize its extended fields TotalCredits and QPA, but also its inherited

---

FIGURE 14.6   Listing for Program OOPdemo1

```pascal
program OOPdemo1;

   {* * * * * * * * * * * * * * * * * * * * * * * * * * * * * * * * *
    *                                                               *
    *           OOP Demonstration, Version 1                        *
    *                                                               *
    *           Session is a class whose object OurSession is manipulated  *
    *           to initialize, run, and terminate this application program  *
    *           Its methods are used to...                          *
    *             Initialize and display Student and Faculty objects  *
    *                                                               *
    *           Object hierarchy tree                               *
    *             Session                                           *
    *             Person                                            *
    *                |___ Student                                   *
    *                |___ Faculty                                   *
    *                                                               *
    * * * * * * * * * * * * * * * * * * * * * * * * * * * * * * * * *}

   {=========================== Declarations ===========================}

uses crt, OurUnit;

type
  Person = object
    ID,                          {Identification}
    FullName : string;           {Last name, First name  Initial}
    procedure Init (Name, SSN : string);
    procedure Display;
  end; {Person}

  Student = object(Person)
    TotalCredits : integer;      {Total credits to date}
    QPA          : real;         {Quality Point Average}
    procedure Init (Name, SSN : string;  Credits : integer;  Ave : real);
    procedure Display;
  end; {Student}

  Faculty = object(Person)
    Rank   : string;             {Professor, Instructor, etc}
    Salary : real;               {Annual salary}
    procedure Init (Name, SSN, Position : string;  Pay : real);
    procedure Display;
  end; {Faculty}

  Session = object
    procedure Init;
    procedure Run;
    procedure Done;
  end; {Session}

var
  OurStudent : Student;          {Student object}
  OurFaculty : Faculty;          {Faculty object}
  OurSession : Session;          {Session object}
```

continued

FIGURE 14.6   *(continued)*

```pascal
{============================ Person Methods ============================}
procedure Person.Init (Name, SSN : string);

  { Initializes fields in Person object }

begin

  FullName := Name;
  ID       := SSN;

end; {Person.Init}


procedure Person.Display;

  { Displays fields in Person object }

begin

  writeln ('   Name....................   ', FullName);
  writeln ('   Identification..........   ', ID );

end; {Person.Display}

  {=========================== Student Methods ===========================}
procedure Student.Init (Name, SSN : string;
                        Credits   : integer;
                        Ave       : real);

  { Initializes fields in Student object }

begin

 {Call to Person's Init initializes inherited fields}
  Person.Init (Name, SSN) ;

 {Initialize uninherited fields}
  TotalCredits := Credits;
  QPA          := Ave;

end; {Student.Init}


procedure Student.Display;

  { Displays fields in Student object }

begin

  writeln;  writeln ('Student...');

 {Call to Person's Display writes inherited fields}
  Person.Display ;

 {Write uninherited fields}
  writeln ('   Total credits...........   ', TotalCredits );
  writeln ('   Quality point average...   ', QPA :3:2);
  writeln;

end; {Student.Display}
```

FIGURE 14.6   (*continued*)

```
{============================ Faculty Methods ==========================}

procedure Faculty.Init (Name, SSN, Position : string;
                        Pay                  : real);

  { Initializes fields in Faculty object }

begin

 {Call to Person's Init initializes inherited fields}
  Person.Init (Name, SSN);

 {Initialize uninherited fields}
  Rank   := Position;
  Salary := Pay;

end; {Faculty.Init}


procedure Faculty.Display;

  { Displays fields in Faculty object }

begin

  writeln;  writeln ('Faculty...');

 {Call to Person's Display writes inherited fields}
  Person.Display;

 {Write uninherited fields}
  writeln ('  Rank.................. ', Rank);
  writeln ('  Salary................ $', Salary :4:2);
  writeln;

end; {Faculty.Display}

   {=========================== Session Methods =========================}

procedure Session.Init;

  { Initializes objects }

begin

 {Initialization call to Student object (server) from Session (client) }
  OurStudent.Init (' ', '000-00-0000', 0, 0.0);

 {Initialization call to Faculty object (server) from Session (client) }
  OurFaculty.Init (' ', '000-00-0000', ' ', 0.0);

  clrscr;

end; {Session.Init}
```

Note that call is to student object's (OurStudent's) Init method, not to Student class's (Student's)

Same idea here

continued

FIGURE 14.6   *(continued)*

```
procedure Session.Run;

  { Displays objects Student and Faculty}

begin

 {Display call to Student object (server) from Session (client) }
   OurStudent.Display;                                        ◄   And here

 {Display call to Faculty object (server) from Session (client) }
   OurFaculty.Display;                                        ◄   And here

end; {Session.Run}


procedure Session.Done;

  { Displays farewell message }

begin

   writeln;  writeln ('<<<<<<<<<<<<  Easy, yes?  >>>>>>>>>>>>');

end; {Session.Done}

   {============================= Main Body =============================}

begin   {OOPdemo1}

   OurSession.Init;
   OurSession.Run;
   OurSession.Done;         ◄   Note references to object OurSession,
                                not to class Session
   end.    {OOPdemo1}
```

---

fields ID and FullName. Rather than directly initializing its inherited fields, it makes a service call to Person.Init, letting the person class handle its own declared fields. In effect, it sends a message to person saying "Initialize my ID and FullName for me." Note that the syntax for a *hierarchical method call* to an ancestor is

> ObjectTypeAncestor.MethodName **(Actual parameter list)**

as in

> Person.Init **(Name, SSN).**

f. A descendant can override its ancestor's methods. For example, method Student.Init overrides method Person.Init. This would not be necessary if the code in Student's Init were identical to the code in Person's Init. In the next section we show a situation where a method can inherit and use an ancestral method as is.

3. As explained in Example 14.1, object type Session simply includes methods for initializing, running, and terminating the application. Its methods make service method calls to appropriate methods in other objects. For example,

Session.Init sends the following identical message to objects OurStudent and OurFaculty: "Initialize thyself." The syntax for a *client-server method call* is

```
Object.MethodName (Actual parameter list)
```

as in

```
OurStudent.Display.
```

Note that this service call is to (a) an object and not an object type and (b) a client object that's not part of Session's hierarchy, unlike the service call in item 2e above.

4. The main algorithm simply makes service calls to object OurSession. In effect it sends the messages "Initialize this session," "Run this session," and "Finish this session." The syntax for these calls is the same as that for client-server method calls. Alternatively, as with records, we can use the *with statement* (Section 11.2) to issue client-server method calls as follows.

```
with OurSession do
    begin
        Init;
        Run;
        Done;
    end; {OurSession}
```

> ## NOTE
>
> **1. Abstract object types.** Did you notice that we never created an object instance (like OurPerson) for object type Person in OOPdemo1? Person is an example of an *abstract object type*. Its purpose is to bequeath inheritable features and provide services to its descendants, not to have instances. In Exercise 6 we ask you to consider an instance of Person.

OO Debugging

The principle of encapsulation reduces the likelihood of bugs because of the tight coupling of data and their methods and because of the object's isolation from other objects. Methodologically, we debug OO programs as we do procedural programs.

Debugging an OO program with the IDE's debugger (Module A) is really no different from debugging any other modular program. Method calls are treated like ordinary procedure and function calls. Their names in the Call Stack window include the dot form identifier, as in Student.Init. The display of objects in the Watch, Evaluate and Modify windows is similar to that of records. Check it out by working Exercise 7.

OBJECT UNITS AND LIBRARIES

An *object unit* is a unit that declares one or more object types. Units for objects are a natural, as are units for ADTs. It's an excellent way to consolidate the idea of an application as a "cooperating society of objects." For example, we could declare our Person, Student, and Faculty classes (and any other future classes) within one unit. Or we could declare separate units for each class, where the Student and Faculty units use the Person unit to declare their own descendant class. Any program that requires these classes would then import them from the proper object units.

The structure of an object unit is the same as that of any other unit. The *interface* section includes public object type declarations and the *implementation* section includes the implemented methods and any privately declared object types and their methods. A declared class in the interface section can have descendants in the implementation section. If a unit uses another object unit, it can declare descendants of its imported classes. In our next example, we will work with a unit for the college application.

Object units are also convenient as "toolboxes" or "toolkits" in *object libraries.* For example, an applications environment that processes people in many of its applications would benefit from a unit that declares a person class; an environment that frequently uses graphics figures like lines, circles, bars, and so on could import these figures from a unit as object classes.[4]

SELF-REVIEW EXERCISES

4b–c 6

14.3   VIRTUAL METHODS

• • • • • • • • • • • • •

Up to now we have strictly used *static methods.* To define these and motivate the need for *virtual methods,* we need to consider...

---

[4]Check out the unit FIGURES.PAS on Borland's Turbo Pascal Utilities Disk. It's the basis of their examples of geometric figures as objects in the *Turbo Pascal User's Guide.* In Module E we introduce Turbo Pascal's object libraries.

Binding

The compilation of a source file (program or unit) creates an object file that includes a code segment and a data segment. The *code segment* includes the module's routines, like procedures and functions, and their addresses. Similarly, the *data segment* includes variables and their addresses, and constants. A call to a procedure or function provides the calling module the *address* of that procedure or function, not the routine itself. Thus a "call" to a routine connects or *binds* the "caller" and "callee" by providing the routine's address, a process called **binding**. The usual binding is *early binding* or *static binding*. In this form of binding, the address is provided at compile time, the earliest opportunity. In *late binding* or *dynamic binding,* the address is provided at run time.

It turns out that **static methods** are bound early and **virtual methods** are bound late. Up to now we have strictly used static methods. Why would we want to implement late binding? Let's explain by example.

Example 14.3   OOP College Application: Static Versus Virtual Methods

Suppose we redefine class Person to include two new methods, Fill and Update, as follows.

```
Person = object
  ID,
  FullName : string;
  procedure Init (Name, SSN : string);
  procedure Display;
  procedure Fill;
  procedure Update;
end; {Person}
```

Procedure Fill fills data fields by interactively entering ID and FullName. Procedure Update updates data fields with the following implementation.

```
procedure Person.Update
begin
  Display;
  Fill;
  Display;
end; {Person.Update}
```

If we were to have an instance of Person, say OurPerson, then the calls

```
OurPerson.Init;
OurPerson.Update;
```

would initialize and then update (display, fill, and redisplay) object OurPerson. So far, so good . . .

Now let's revise the declaration for Student by adding its own Fill procedure.

```
Student = object(Person)
  TotalCredits : integer;
  QPA          : real;
  procedure Init (Name, SSN : string; Credits : integer; Ave : real);
  procedure Display;
  procedure Fill;
end; {Student}
```

Student's Fill procedure overrides Person's, as did Init and Display. In this case, the implementation of Student.Fill would call Person.Fill to fill the ID and FullName fields, and then would interactively input its own new fields TotalCredits and QPA. No problem.

But what about updating a student object? Note that we did not declare Update in Student. We simply decided to *inherit* Person's Update without redefining it, because the implementation of Student's Update would look identical to that of Person, except for the object type identifier in the heading's method name (it would change from Person.Update to Student.Update). Now, what would happen if the following calls are executed?

```
OurStudent.Init;
OurStudent.Update;
```

The student object would get initialized all right, but only its person fields (ID and FullName) would get filled and displayed! The problem here is early binding. When the call to Update is implemented, the system looks for the Update method's address in object OurStudent. Not finding it, it moves up the hierarchy to Person and finds it. Now look at the code in Update's implementation: It calls Display, then Fill, then Display again. But which Display and Fill? *Person's* Display and Fill! It was the addresses to Person's Display and Fill that were statically bound to Person's Update at compile time.

It's now clear that we want Update in this case to call *Student's* Display and Fill methods. But Update is already bound to Person's Display and Fill methods. If you're on top of it today, you might say "Let's override Person's Update by also declaring it within Student." And you would be right. We could solve our little dilemma by declaring Update within Student and then implementing it in Student's methods. It's a *kludgy* solution, though, isn't it?[5] As stated earlier, the code in Student.Update would be identical to that in Person.Update above. This would be wasteful and contrary to OO's reusability philosophy.

The best solution is to make methods Display and Fill *virtual methods*. This means the system would use late binding for calls to Display and Fill, and would

---

[5]Computer cognoscenti use kludgy to mean a solution that works inelegantly, usually due to hardware or software patches that could have been avoided by a more elegant design in the first place.

employ *Student's* Display and Fill within the inherited Upate whenever the call to Update is made within the student object.

This is *polymorphism* in action. At compile time, we may not know what object will be updated. In effect, we're telling the system at compile time "Don't make a decision yet about which object type will be updated; wait for the object itself to request this service at run time." Polymorphism also supports *extensibility,* as mentioned in Section 14.1. For example, a newly added object in the hierarchy (like Staff) could also use Update.

And as it turns out, it's very straightforward to "virtualize" methods, as we see next.

DECLARATIONS AND IMPLEMENTATION

The accompanying syntax box illustrates the declaration of *virtual methods* and describes the use of *constructors* and *destructors* as special methods. Note the following.

1. Based on our conclusions in Example 14.3, we made Display and Fill virtual methods by using the reserved word **virtual** in their headings. This further means that we must . . .

    a. Make Display and Fill virtual methods in all related object types that declare these, as done in Person and Student.

    b. Use identical *headings* for virtual methods that have the same name in different objects along the hierarchy, as done for Display and Fill in Person and Student. Note that parameter lists also have to be identical for corresponding virtual methods in the hierarchy.

    c. Each object type that has a virtual method must include a *constructor* whose call initializes the object, as done with constructor Init in both Person and Student. As suggested by Turbo Pascal, we used the identifier *Init* for constructors.[6]

2. Student inherits Update, per our discussion in Example 14.3.

3. As a matter of good form and efficient memory usage, we also declared a *destructor* as the last method in Person. Typically, a method like Done concludes terminating tasks in a run, like closing files, clearing the screen, or disposing of a dynamic object. Turbo Pascal suggests the identifier *Done* for methods that clean up after an object. In our example,

---

[6]The constructor initializes the object by, among other things, establishing a link between the object calling the constructor and the object type's *virtual method table (VMT)*. The VMT is a data segment inhabitant that includes the size of an object type and pointers to the implementations of its virtual methods.

SYNTAX BOX

Object type declarations with virtual methods, constructors, and destructors... Declare an object type's virtual methods, constructors, and destructors in type section

Syntax .... Same method as syntax box on page 688, except place **virtual** following method heading to make the method virtual. **constructor** is used in method heading for a constructor, and **destructor** is used in method heading for a destructor.

Examples......type

```
Person = object
    ID,
    FullName : string;

    constructor  Init (Name, SSN : string);

    procedure Display;    virtual;
    procedure Fill;       virtual;
    procedure Update;     virtual;
    destructor Done;      virtual;
end; {Person}
Student = object(Person)
    TotalCredits : integer;
    QPA          : real;

    constructor  Init (Name, SSN : string; Credits : integer; Ave : real);

    procedure Display;    virtual;
    procedure Fill;       virtual;
end; {Student}
```

Explanation... The reserved word **virtual** makes the method a *virtual method*. Calls to virtual methods use late binding. If an object type contains virtual methods, then instances of that object type must be initialized by a call to that object's constructor, before any one of the object's virtual methods is called. A method is a *constructor* if the reserved word **constructor** is used in place of **procedure** or **function** in the method's heading. Constructors cannot be virtual, because the mechanism that sets up a virtual method depends on a call to the constructor itself. Turbo Pascal suggests *Init* for constructor names. The headings for a virtual method must remain identical down the object hierarchy. A *static method* is any method that's not virtual. A static method cannot override a virtual method. This means that all descendant types that declare a method having the same name as one of it's ancestor's virtual methods must also tag the method virtual. A method is a *destructor* if the reserved word **destructor** is used in the method's heading. Destructors clean up what constructors created. Destructors are primarily used to dispose of dynamic objects (Section 14.4). They are not needed for static objects, even if such objects have virtual methods; however, they do improve memory management for static objects. A destructor can be static or virtual. Turbo Pascal suggests Done for destructor names.

Student inherits Done because we don't plan any different terminating tasks in Student from those in Person.

NOTE

2. Static versus virtual methods. Constructor methods must be static by law; otherwise, it's a good idea to make all methods virtual. Static methods are a bit faster and more memory efficient, but virtual methods allow *polymorphism's* reusability benefits. If there's any chance that a method might be overridden by future software updates, then make it virtual. This ensures that we need not change previously written source code within a class to convert from static to virtual methods. This especially makes compiled library units more robust, since their source code is often unavailable to users. Did you notice that we made Update and Done virtual methods in our example? This is the reason why.

3. Call Init first! Don't forget that any object that has virtual methods must be initialized by a call to its constructor before any other of its virtual methods is called; otherwise we might get the bane of all users: a *system lockup*. Turbo Pascal suggests using active range checking as a safety net beneath virtual method calls while shaking out the program.

EXAMPLE 14.4   OOP COLLEGE APPLICATION WITH OBJECT UNIT, VIRTUAL METHODS, CONSTRUCTORS, AND DESTRUCTORS

Now let's put it all together with a second version of our OOP demo program. Figure 14.7 shows revised I/O for our college application. Note that the student and faculty objects are now updated, including displays just before and just after new values are entered, as suggested in Example 14.3.

Figure 14.8 shows the listing for OOPdemo2. Note the following.

1. OOPdemo2 imports object types Person, Student, and Staff from object unit College1. Instances of these object types are still declared in the var section.

2. The program itself must declare the session object. This is because its methods use client-server calls to objects OurStudent and OurFaculty, and these objects are necessarily instantiated in the program itself.

3. We made methods Run and Done virtual, as suggested in Note 2. And as discussed earlier, we made Init a constructor and Done a destructor.

FIGURE 14.7   I/O for OOP College Application, Version 2

Screen 1

```
Student...
   Name.................
   Identification.........  000-00-0000
   Total credits..........  0
   Quality point average...  0.00

Enter full name, last first > CORE, Harvey Jr.
Enter identification >>>>>>> 222-22-2222
Enter credits this term >>>>> 25
Enter QPA this term >>>>>>>>> 4.0

Student...
   Name.................  CORE, Harvey Jr.
   Identification.........  222-22-2222
   Total credits..........  25
   Quality point average...  4.00




Hit any key to continue...
```

Screen 2

```
Faculty...
   Name.................
   Identification.........  000-00-0000
   Rank.................
   Salary................  $0.00

Enter full name, last first > CORE, Harvey Sr.
Enter identification >>>>>>> 111-11-1111
Enter rank >>>>>>>>>>>>>>>>> Professor
Enter salary >>>>>>>>>>>>>>> 300000

Faculty...
   Name.................  CORE, Harvey Sr.
   Identification.........  111-11-1111
   Rank.................  Professor
   Salary................  $300000.00




Hit any key to continue...
```

---

4. As stated in the syntax box and in Note 3, an object with virtual methods must be initialized by a call to its constructor before any other call to one of its virtual methods. This is accomplished for object OurSession by the call OurSession.Init in the main body, and for objects OurStudent and OurFaculty with the calls OurStudent.Init and OurFaculty.Init in Session.Init.

5. The implementation of method Run invokes the Update calls to objects OurStudent and OurFaculty.

FIGURE 14.8   Listing for Program OOPdemo2

```
program OOPdemo2;

  {* * * * * * * * * * * * * * * * * * * * * * * * * * * * * * * * * *
   *                                                                 *
   *            OOP Demonstration, Version 2                         *
   *                                                                 *
   *            As in Version 1...                                   *
   *              Session is a class whose object OurSession is manipulated  *
   *              to initialize, run, and terminate this application program  *
   *              Its methods are used to...                         *
   *                                                                 *
   *            Version 2...                                         *
   *              Initialize, update, and display Student and Faculty objects *
   *              This version also demonstrates...                  *
   *                Virtual methods, constructors, and destructors   *
   *                Use of object unit College1                      *
   *                                                                 *
   * * * * * * * * * * * * * * * * * * * * * * * * * * * * * * * * * *}

  {=========================== Declarations ===========================}
uses crt, College1;              {College1 unit declares Person, Student,
                                    and Faculty classes}
type
  Session = object
    constructor Init;                        Session declared here,
    procedure Run;        virtual;           not in College1
    destructor Done;      virtual;
  end; {Session}                             Note use of constructor,
                                             destructor, virtual

  var
  OurStudent : Student;            {Student object}
  OurFaculty : Faculty;            {Faculty object}     Student and faculty
  OurSession : Session;            {Session object}     objects declared here

  {=========================== Session Methods ===========================}

constructor Session.Init;                                Now a constructor

  { Initializes objects }

begin

  {Initialization call to Student (server) from Session (client) }
  OurStudent.Init (' ', '000-00-0000', 0, 0.0);

  {Initialization call to Faculty (server) from Session (client) }
  OurFaculty.Init (' ', '000-00-0000', ' ', 0.0);

  clrscr;

end; {Session.Init}
```

Note: Key changes from declarations in OOPdemo1 are in color

continued

6. The call OurSession.Done implements OurSession's destructor, which in turn tidies up memory by calling the Done destructors in objects OurStudent and OurFaculty.

Figure 14.9 shows the listing for object unit College1. Note the following.

1. The structure of this unit is like that of any other unit.

FIGURE 14.8   *(continued)*

```
procedure Session.Run;

  { Updates objects by displaying, filling, and redisplaying }

begin

 {Update call to Student (server) from Session (client) }
  OurStudent.Update;                                           ◄──────── We now call Update
                                                                          instead of Display
 {Update call to Faculty (server) from Session (client) }
  OurFaculty.Update;                                           ◄────────

end; {Session.Run}


destructor Session.Done;                                       ◄──────── Now a destructor

  { Cleans up objects and displays farewell message }

begin

  OurStudent.Done;              {Clean up OurStudent} ◄────────
  OurFaculty.Done;              {Clean up OurFaculty} ◄────────  Client-server calls
                                                                 to object destructors
   writeln;  writeln ('<<<<<<<<<<<<  Easy, yes?  >>>>>>>>>>>');

end; {Session.Done}

  {============================ Main Body ============================}

begin  {OOPdemo2}

  OurSession.Init;
  OurSession.Run;
  OurSession.Done;

end.   {OOPdemo2}
```

2. Virtual methods, constructors, and destructors are handled as previously discussed.

3. The fill methods are new in this version. Note how Person's Fill is overridden in Student's and Faculty's Fill, and how it's also called within its descendants. This treatment is like that of Display.

4. Method Update is described in Example 14.3. Note how it's inherited and not declared in Student and Faculty. This is the method that demonstrates polymorphism, and the reason why we needed to make Display and Fill virtual.

5. Destructor Done is declared in Person and inherited by Student and Faculty. It doesn't accomplish any explicit tasks in this application (at this time), but it's included to tidy up memory.

FIGURE 14.9   Listing for Object Unit College1

```
unit College1;

  {* * * * * * * * * * * * * * * * * * * * * * * * * * * * * * * *
   *                                                              *
   *        Unit for OOP College Application, Version 1           *
   *                                                              *
   *        Source file name:   COLLEGE1.PAS                      *
   *                                                              *
   *        Object hierarchy tree                                 *
   *          Person                                              *
   *            |___ Student                                      *
   *            |___ Faculty                                      *
   *                                                              *
   *        Class      Fields          Methods                    *
   *        ---------------------------------------------         *
   *        Person     ID              Init                       *
   *                   FullName        Display                    *
   *                                   Fill                       *
   *                                   Update                     *
   *                                   Done                       *
   *                                                              *
   *        Student    TotalCredits    Init                       *
   *                   QPA             Display                    *
   *                                   Fill                       *
   *                                                              *
   *        Faculty    Rank            Init                       *
   *                   Salary          Display                    *
   *                                   Fill                       *
   *                                                              *
   * * * * * * * * * * * * * * * * * * * * * * * * * * * * * * * *}

{--------}
interface
{--------}

uses crt, OurUnit;

type
  Person = object
    ID,
    FullName : string;              {Identification}
    constructor Init (Name, SSN : string);   {Last name, First name  Initial}
    procedure Display;  virtual;
    procedure Fill;     virtual;
    procedure Update;   virtual;
    destructor Done;    virtual;
  end; {Person}

  Student = object(Person)
    TotalCredits : integer;      {Total credits to date}
    QPA          : real;         {Quality Point Average}
    constructor Init (Name, SSN : string;  Credits : integer;  Ave : real);
    procedure Display;  virtual;
    procedure Fill;     virtual;
  end; {Student}                    ⟵  Update and Done inherited

  Faculty = object(Person)
    Rank   : string;             {Professor, Instructor, etc}
    Salary : real;               {Annual salary}
    constructor Init (Name, SSN, Position : string;  Pay : real);
    procedure Display;  virtual;
    procedure Fill;     virtual;
  end; {Faculty}                    ⟵  Update and Done inherited
```

Note: Key changes from the declarations in OOPdemo1 are in color or screened

continued

FIGURE 14.9   *(continued)*

```
{------------}
implementation
{------------}

{=========================== Person Methods ===========================}

constructor Person.Init (Name, SSN : string);

   { Initializes fields in Person object }

begin

  FullName := Name;
  ID       := SSN;

end; {Person.Init}


procedure Person.Display;

   { Displays fields in Person object }

begin

    writeln ('  Name...................  ', FullName);
    writeln ('  Identification..........  ', ID);

end; {Person.Display}
```

```
procedure Person.Fill;

   { Fills fields in Person object }

begin

    write ('Enter full name, last first > ');  readln (FullName);
    write ('Enter identification >>>>>>> ');  readln (ID);

end; {Person.Fill}
```
◄ ⸱⸱— New method

```
procedure Person.Update;

   { Updates fields in Person object: displays, fills, and redisplays }

begin

  Display;
  Fill;
  Display;
  Pause;                        {Call serviced by OurUnit}

end; {Person.Update}
```
◄ ⸱⸱— New method

```
destructor Person.Done;

   { System cleans up memory when this destructor is executed}

begin

   { No other tasks required by this particular destructor }

end; {Person.Done}
```
◄ ⸱⸱— New method

FIGURE 14.9   *(continued)*

```
{========================= Student Methods =========================}

constructor Student.Init (Name, SSN : string;
                          Credits   : integer;
                          Ave       : real);

   { Initializes fields in Student object }

begin

 {Call to Person's Init initializes inherited fields}
  Person.Init (Name, SSN);

 {Initialize uninherited fields}
  TotalCredits := Credits;
  QPA          := Ave;

end; {Student.Init}


procedure Student.Display;

   { Displays fields in Student object }

begin

  writeln;  writeln ('Student...');

 {Call to Person's Display writes inherited fields}
  Person.Display;

 {Write uninherited fields}
  writeln ('  Total credits.......... ', TotalCredits);
  writeln ('  Quality point average... ', QPA :3:2);
  writeln;

end; {Student.Display}
```

```
procedure Student.Fill;

   { Fills fields in Student object }

var
  TermAve     : real;          {QPA this term}
  TermCredits : integer;       {Credits this term}
  TotalPoints : real;          {Total points after this term}

begin

 {Call to Person's Fill fills inherited fields}
  Person.Fill;

  write ('Enter credits this term >>>>> ');  readln (TermCredits);
  write ('Enter QPA this term >>>>>>>>> ');  readln (TermAve);
  TotalPoints  := (QPA * TotalCredits) + (TermAve * TermCredits);

 {Fill uninherited fields}
  TotalCredits := TotalCredits + TermCredits;
  if TotalCredits = 0 then QPA := 0.0
                      else QPA := TotalPoints / TotalCredits;

end; {Student.Fill}
```

← New method

continued

FIGURE 14.9 *(continued)*

```
{============================ Faculty Methods =========================}

constructor Faculty.Init (Name, SSN, Position : string;
                          Pay                  : real);

  { Initializes fields in Faculty object }

begin

 {Call to Person's Init initializes inherited fields}
  Person.Init (Name, SSN);

 {Initialize uninherited fields}
  Rank   := Position;
  Salary := Pay;

end; {Faculty.Init}


procedure Faculty.Display;

  { Displays fields in Faculty object }

begin

  writeln;  writeln ('Faculty...');

 {Call to Person's Display writes inherited fields}
  Person.Display;

 {Write uninherited fields}
  writeln ('  Rank.................... ', Rank);
  writeln ('  Salary................. $', Salary :4:2);
  writeln;

end; {Faculty.Display}


procedure Faculty.Fill;

  { Fills fields in Faculty object }

begin

 {Call to Person's Fill fills inherited fields}
  Person.Fill;

 {Fill uninherited fields}
  write ('Enter rank >>>>>>>>>>>>>>>>> ');  readln (Rank);
  write ('Enter salary >>>>>>>>>>>>>>> ');  readln (Salary);

end; {Faculty.Fill}

{------------------------------------------------------------------------}

end.  {College1}
```

← ∼ New method

> ## NOTE
>
> **4. Max abstraction.** Method calls illustrate the extremely high level of data and procedural abstraction that OOP offers. The call OurStudent.Update in OOPdemo2 sends the following message to object OurStudent: "Update yourself." The call has no parameter list, and the object itself implements three separate tasks with calls to procedures Display, Fill, and Display, again with no parameter lists.
>
> **5. On pure OO programs.** We could have chosen not to declare Session and OurSession in OOPdemo2, thereby directly incorporating the method calls in OurSession as the main algorithm (see Exercise 9c). Moreover, we can include nonmethod procedure and function declarations in the program, as well as non-OO code in the main algorithm. To do so, however, is not good form in an OO program. The modules in a "pure" OO program are strictly objects, and the main algorithm simply implements calls to its session or applications object.

SELF-REVIEW EXERCISES

9

14.4 DYNAMIC OBJECTS

• • • • • • • • • • • • • • •

In Chapter 13 we covered *dynamic* data structures as alternatives to *static* data structures. The OO counterparts are static objects and dynamic objects.

STATIC VERSUS DYNAMIC OBJECTS

Each object we have created up to now is a **static object,** an instance of an object type created by its *var declaration* and allocated in the data segment and on the stack at compile time. Static objects are static in the sense that their presence (allocation) is fixed at compile time and throughout program execution. As we did with dynamic variables, we can create a **dynamic object** as an instance of an object type allocated at run time on the heap by the *new procedure,* manipulated with pointer references, and disposed with a call to the *dispose procedure.*

Declarations, Creation, and Disposition

As before, we declare a *pointer type* in the type section and a *pointer variable* in the var section, except now *the base type is an object type.* Then we create the dynamic object with the usual call to procedure *new*, again with the pointer variable as the argument. If the dynamic object includes virtual methods, then its *constructor* must be called before any of its other virtual methods is called. Method calls are made as before, except now the object is referenced by its pointer variable and its attached caret (^) symbol. Finally, the dynamic object is deallocated by calls to its *destructor* and the predefined procedure *dispose*. Note that the destructor *must* be called for dynamic objects, since it guarantees that the correct number of heap bytes is released when dispose does its cleanup.

Turbo Pascal has enhanced the new and dispose procedures from the standard syntax given in Chapter 13 to the following OO syntax.

> **new** (ObjectPointerVar, Constructor call)
> **dispose** (ObjectPointerVar, Destructor call)

We can also use the functional form when calling new, as follows.

> ObjectPointerVariable := **new**(ObjectPointerType, Constructor call)

Let's get specific with...

Example 14.5   OOP College Application with Dynamic Objects

Let's describe how we might go about changing our earlier student object from a static to a dynamic object. Recall that object unit College1 (Figure 14.9) declares object type Student as follows.

```
Student = object(Person)
   TotalCredits : integer;
   QPA          : real;
   constructor Init (Name, SSN : string; Credits : integer; Ave : real);
   procedure Display;  virtual;
   procedure Fill;     virtual;
end; {Student}
```

In the type section of College1, we can make Student the base type for pointer type StudentPointer.

```
StudentPointer = ^ Student;
```

In the var section of OOPdemo2 (Figure 14.8), we now replace

OurStudent : Student

— *Static* student object

with

```
OurStudentPointer : StudentPointer
```

— Pointer to *dynamic* student object

Note that OurStudentPointer is a pointer variable to the dynamic student object, not the dynamic student itself. In fact, the dynamic student object is yet to be created. We create it by replacing OurStudent.Init within Session.Init with the following alternative calls to the enhanced *new* procedure

```
new(OurStudentPointer, Init (' ', '000-00-0000', 0, 0.0) );
```

or

```
OurStudentPointer := new(StudentPointer, Init (' ', '000-00-0000', 0, 0.0) );
```

Note that either approach accomplishes the following in one convenient step: points the pointer OurStudentPointer to the newly created dynamic student object referenced by OurStudentPointer^ and initializes the object with a call to its constructor. Alternatively, we could have used the standard version of new to create the dynamic object and followed it with a call to its constructor.

```
new (OurStudentPointer);
OurStudentPointer^.Init (' ', '000-00-0000', 0, 0.0) );
```

Note that method calls use the name form

```
ObjectPointerVar^.MethodName
```

as in

```
OurStudentPointer^.Init
```

Within the new procedure, however, just Init is used, because there's no ambiguity as to which pointer is referenced (OurStudentPointer is the first parameter in the first new call).

The dynamic student object is now allocated and initialized in the heap, and referenced with OurStudentPointer^. Note that the static object counterpart to this dynamic object reference is OurStudent. In other words, our earlier examples referenced the *static* student object with OurStudent and our current example references the *dynamic* student object with OurStudentPointer^. Figure 14.10 diagrams this distinction.

FIGURE 14.10   Student Objects

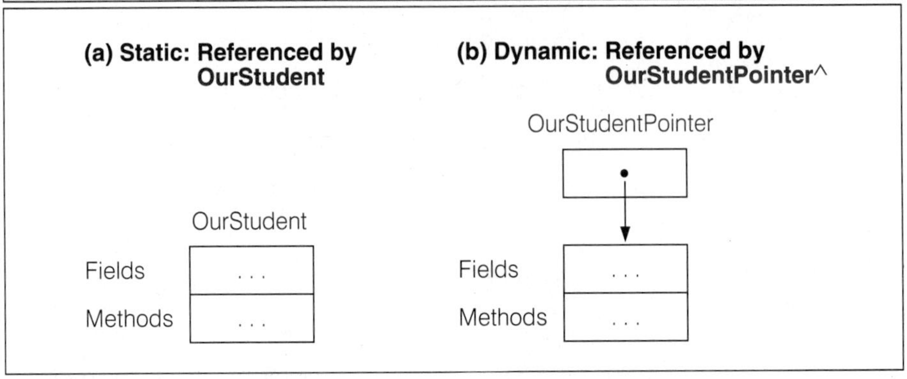

(a) Static: Referenced by
OurStudent

(b) Dynamic: Referenced by
OurStudentPointer^

OurStudentPointer

OurStudent

Fields	. . .
Methods	. . .

Fields	. . .
Methods	. . .

Back to our dynamic treatment of the student object in OOPdemo2, we now change the call to Update from

```
OurStudent.Update
```

to

```
OurStudentPointer^.Update
```

Finally, we clean up the dynamic student object by replacing the call

```
OurStudent.Done
```

with the call

```
dispose (OurStudentPointer, Done)
```

This call first calls the student object's destructor Done and then disposes the dynamic object pointed to by OurStudentPointer.

In Exercise 15 we ask you to revise OOPdemo2 to use dynamic student and faculty objects.

SELF-REVIEW EXERCISES

4d

14.5 PROGRAMMING TIPS

Consider the following tips to improve the design and style of your programs and to avoid some common errors.

DESIGN AND STYLE

1. OO Design Philosophy. Note from our discussion in Section 14.1 that OO design reverses the emphasis from a top-down task orientation to a bottom-up data orientation. Moreover, tasks and data are not viewed as two separate issues; rather, they get *encapsulated* into a single entity, an *object,* that exhibits both attributes and behavior that are characteristic of its *object type* or *class.* Thus, we need to specify both fields and methods for each object class at the design stage. We also need to consider how objects are related to one another. These *inheritance* relationshps and their *polymorphic* properties have important implications regarding *reusability* and *extensibility.*

2. OO Diagrams. A key design tool is a *tree, graph,* or *chart* that shows the inheritance structure (Figure 14.4). Another important tool is an *object chart* (Figure 14.5), to specify not only the inheritance relationships among classes, but also the fields and methods for each class and any *client-server* relationships among objects that are not part of the same hierarchy.

3. Object Units. Object types that are to be exported to multiple applications are good candidates for organization into a unit, as illustrated by unit College1 in Figure 14.9. Generally, it's a good idea to bulk up an object's methods by being comprehensive, even if current applications may have no need for some of these methods. By defining a complete set of behavior for the class, we reduce future maintenance of object-class code. Moreover, there's no downside to the performance or size of the object program (.EXE file): Turbo Pascal's *smart linker* strips out unused methods within each client object file.

4. Object Libraries. The design also needs to consider any available object libraries. These can significantly affect the developmental productivity and maintainability of an application. They can also give all applications that use a library a "common look and feel," with important productivity gains when training users across a suite of applications. Also, the importation of object classes into an application has an obvious influence on the inheritance and client-server relationships for an application. Unlike traditional approaches that often adapt existing library code, OO libraries allow us to descend and extend. In Module E we introduce Turbo Pascal's *TurboVision* object library.

5. Short Main Block. Another key design goal is a short main block. By using a *session (application) object,* our OO programs have a simple main algorithm of three calls (to the application's *Init, Run,* and *Done* methods). It's also best, but not always practical, to design pure OO programs (see Note 5).

6. OO Documentation. The hierarchy diagrams and object charts serve as both design and documentation tools. Within programs and units, it's a good idea to document class names and hierarchical relationships, pointers (if any), fields, and methods (see Figure 14.9).

COMMON ERRORS

1. System Lockup. Remember to use a constructor and to call it first if an object includes virtual methods; otherwise, we might get a system lockup (see Note 3).

2. Scope Violation. Scope rules require that formal parameters and local variables share the same scope. Thus, any formal parameters within methods must be identified differently from fields names. For example, if we were to use ID in place of SSN in Person's Init method (see Figure 14.9), then we would get the compile-time error message *Duplicate identifier (ID)*.

REVIEW EXERCISES

EASIER	For the busy... **1 2 3 6 7**	
NORMAL	For the thinkers... **4 5 8 9 10 11 12**	
TOUGHER	For the hard CORE... **13 14 15**	

1. Do all objects in OO programs have physical counterparts in the real world? Put another way, can you think of any conceptual objects, including fields and their methods?

2. Describe some objects, including attributes and behavior, for an application that simulates the design of a kitchen. Why would it make sense to define *Location* as an object type? What would be its fields? Methods? Would it be high or low in the hierarchy?

3. **Virtual (artificial) reality.** Virtual or artificial reality is an evolving field of study that projects a person into a world that's artificially constructed and manipulated by computer hardware, software, and peripherals like *data gloves* (for implementing movement of the person through the artificial world) and *goggles* (for controlling the view that we see of the artificial world). Early appli-

cations of this technology include aircraft training simulations, architectural designs that can be "entered" and "manipulated" by clients, and "voyages" within the human body by physicians. How does this field relate to OOP? How might virtual reality apply to the kitchen simulation in the preceding exercise?

4. Consider classes National and International as object types that descend from Student. National students have string fields for city and state; international students have string fields for country and visa number. Each class has two methods, one for initializing the fields and another for displaying the fields.
   a. Appropriately revise Figure 14.5.
   b. Write code that declares each class, given the Student declaration in the syntax box on page 688.
   c. Write code that declares a static instance of each class.
   d. Write code that declares a dynamic instance of each class.

5. Suppose staff people are either union or nonunion. Union members belong to one of three unions: American Federation of Labor, Teamsters, or Harvey CORE Laborers. Nonunion staff are classified as either salaried or hourly.
   a. Appropriately modify Figure 14.4.
   *b. Suppose staff people include two fields: a three-character department code and a four-digit department telephone extension. We wish to keep track of retirement plan code (a single character) for nonunion staff, annual salary in dollars and cents for nonunion salaried staff, and hourly pay in dollars and cents for nonunion hourly staff. We also wish to record union office telephone (eight characters) and contract expiration year (four characters) for union staff. Finally, AFL and Teamsters members are on hourly pay, but HCL members are salaried. Appropriately modify Figure 14.5. For each new class, assume an initialization method and appropriate get and set methods for each field.
   *c. Write code that declares each class in the preceding part.

(L) 6. In Example 14.2...
   a. Test drive OOPdemo1.
   b. Change the code to initialize and display a person object.
   c. Is Person an abstract object type in the preceding part? Can you think of a reason why we might wish to "deabstract" Person?

(L) *7. OO debugging. Use the IDE's debugger to set a breakpoint at OurSession.Run in OOPdemo1. Try some stepping over and tracing while you watch objects OurStudent and OurFaculty.

*8. Make changes in the code for Example 14.3 to illustrate a kludgy, nonvirtual solution to the problem.

(L) 9. In Example 14.4...
   a. Test drive OOPdemo2.
   b. Make the fields private in unit College1 and rerun the application. Why is this a good idea?

c. Revise the program to entirely eliminate class Session. Is this a good idea? Why or why not?

(L) ***10.** In Example 14.4...

a. Revise and test the code to include sex code and home telephone for each person.

b. Revise and test the code to include student class (a string like Freshman, Graduate, Special, and so on). How would an enumerated student class change the application?

c. Create separate units for Person, Student, and Faculty. Rerun a revised OOPdemo2. Can you think of any advantages to this approach? Disadvantages?

(L) ***11.** In Example 14.4...

a. Write and test code to incorporate the national and international students described in Exercise 4.

b. Write and test code to incorporate the staff class and its descendants, as described in Exercise 5.

(L) ***12.** Change the code in Example 14.4 to...

a. Include a loop to update a student object from one semester to another. Use the test data for Harvey Jr. in Figure 14.7 as the first iteration. Jr. took 20 credits and got a 2.0 in the next term.

b. Run data for yourself to answer "What if...?" questions like "What's the effect on my QPA if I get a 3.5 this term?" Enter your cumulative credits and QPA as your first iteration.

(L) ***13.** Change the code in Example 14.4 to...

a. Initialize a faculty member by interactive input. Use the data for Harvey Sr. in Figure 14.7 as test data.

b. Include a loop that initializes faculty and stores their records in a file. Use Harvey Sr. for the first faculty member, and make up three other faculty in your test run.

c. Read the faculty file from part **b,** update faculty salary with a prompted percent salary increase, and refile the faculty. Use a 10 percent increase in faculty pay for your test run.

d. Try using an array of faculty objects to satisfy the requirements.

(L) ***14.** Change the code in Example 14.4 to offer a menu with three selections: Student, Faculty, and eXit. The first selection implements the features in Exercise 12; the second implements the features in Exercise 13.

(L) ***15.** Use Example 14.5 as a basis to revise OOPdemo2 and College1 so that the student and faculty objects are dynamic. Use the same test data as that in Figure 14.7.

ADDITIONAL EXERCISES

EASIER	For the busy...
	16
NORMAL	For the thinkers...
	17 18 19
TOUGHER	For the hard CORE...
	20

(L) **16. Graphics figures.** Test drive and tinker with program *FIGDEMO.PAS* in Turbo Pascal's Utilities Library.

17. Revisit: City temperatures. In Chapters 9, 11, and 12 we worked with a city temperature problem. Adapt this problem as an OO application with classes City, Foreign, and Domestic. At a minimum, include display and data entry for city names and temperatures, both foreign and domestic.

18. Revisit: Employee record. In Figure 11.13 we show employee variant records. Adapt this problem in an OO application with classes Employee, Salaried, and Hourly. At a minimum, include display and data entry for salaried and hourly employees.

19. Revisit. Select an earlier programming assignment and convert it to an OO program, if appropriate.

20. Linked object lists. Create and display a linked object list for one of the following.[7]
    a. Revisit: OOP college. Link three student objects from our sample application in this chapter. Use your own test data.
    b. Revisit: City temperatures. Link five city objects based on our sample application in the last chapter. Use the test data on page 648.

---

[7]This exercise requires knowledge of Chapter 13. Instead of creating an object node with a pointer field to another object node, a *record* (not object) *node* is created that points both to its corresponding dynamic object and to the next record node in the list. A separate static *list object* is created whose field points to the first node and whose methods include procedures that add nodes and display the list. The program ListDemo on the Turbo Pascal Utilities Disk illustrates a linked object list; it's also (briefly) described in the *Turbo Pascal User's Guide*.

TURBO VISION

Turbo Vision (TV) is Turbo Pascal's event-driven OO applications framework for DOS. It's an object library that includes object classes for pull-down menus, multiple windows, dialog boxes, and many other objects that are common to event-driven interfaces. And it includes built-in support for special keystrokes (like *Esc* and *function key* presses) and mouse actions (like menu option selection and window manipulations).

E.1 OVERVIEW

. . . .

Let's start with an overview of TV and a return to our college application from the last chapter.

OUR KIND OF TV!

Actually, we're already quite familiar with the use and behavior of a TV-developed program: the IDE! Borland International developed the IDE using TV. The OO programs we write with TV's tools and design discipline will "look and feel" exactly like the IDE's interface. It gives our Turbo Pascal programs a sophisticated, event-driven interface designed by a world-class team of programmers. As suggested by Borland, programs that use TV *inherit the wheel,* instead of reinventing it. They provide the skeletal framework for our TV application, and we flesh it out. Unlike a traditional (non-OO) library, we get the benefits of encapsulation, inheritance, and polymorphism. Instead of adapting and rewriting, we reuse and extend library code.

Sounds great, doesn't it? And it is. As with just about everything, however, there's a downside: It ain't easy to learn. First, we have to be reasonably knowledgeable in OOP; second, TV liberally uses dynamic objects, so we have to be on top of our pointers as well; finally, the object library is comprehensive and complex, including an object hierarchy tree of more than 40 classes with hundreds of new predefined types, fields, and methods.[1]

As you might imagine, a thorough explanation of TV would require a textbook in itself. Our intent here is to introduce TV by developing a working TV program. Although elementary by TV standards, our program offers a very sophisticated user interface by conventional standards. By the end of this section, we will be writing TV applications. In the exercises, we encourage you to extend your TV knowledge to other features that we mention but don't develop.

---

[1]Borland's *Turbo Vision Guide* explains all of this in a 400-plus-page manual.

TV College Application

Before we explain how to get there, let's see where we're going. Figure E.1 shows a sample run of TVdemo, our TV college program. Note the following.

1. Screen 1 shows the fundamental objects that make up the screen: the **menu bar** at the top, the **desktop** in the middle, and the **status line** at the bottom. These are implemented as objects and are identical in look and behavior to those in the IDE. At this time, the main menu simply shows one selection, Student; the status line displays two hot-key shortcuts, Alt-X and F10; and the desktop is empty.

2. Screen 2 shows the **pull-down menu** that we get by selecting Student from the menu bar. This submenu is the standard pull-down menu we've come to know and love in the IDE. This pull-down menu is also an object, with encapsulated fields and methods, that responds to user events like mouse clicks and key presses.

3. Screens 3 and 6 show the familiar **dialog boxes.** These are used to interactively communicate (have a *dialog*) with the user. They can display

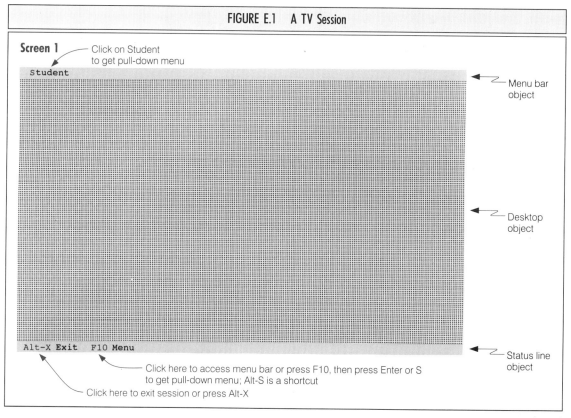

FIGURE E.1   A TV Session

Screen 1 — Click on Student to get pull-down menu

Student

Menu bar object

Desktop object

Alt-X Exit   F10 Menu

Status line object

Click here to access menu bar or press F10, then press Enter or S to get pull-down menu; Alt-S is a shortcut

Click here to exit session or press Alt-X

continued

FIGURE E.1   (*continued*)

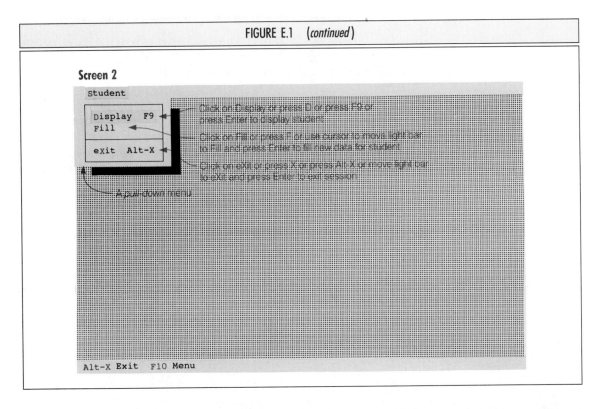

Screen 2

information (as in screen 6), prompt the user for responses to questions, and serve as data entry forms (as in screen 3). Dialog boxes include titles, labels, data fields, the usual *close box icon, buttons* like *Ok* and *Cancel,* and other elements that we discuss later. As you might guess, the dialog box is also an object, with attributes and behavior specific to itself. For example, we can manipulate it in certain ways, as in dragging it to another location on the desktop and, of course, making it disappear. In addition, it's a special kind of *window* on the desktop, and elements within it are also objects. Note how the use of "shadows" promotes the illusion that these are objects on a surface.

4. The dialogs in Figure E.1 are called *modal dialogs,* because they force a modal state, or limited mode of operation. For example, in screen 6 we (or the program) can't do anything else (enter some other mode) until we click the close box icon [■], press the Esc key, click Ok, press the O key, or press the Enter key. *Modeless dialogs* don't limit operations because they don't require actions. The Watch window in the IDE is an example of a modeless dialog.

5. Compare this interface to that in Figure 14.7. No contest, eh!? In particular, note how we handle input in each case. The approach in Figure 14.7 is traditional. The approach in screen 3 of Figure E.1 uses a *forms metaphor,* where the dialog box is like a paper form with labels and empty

FIGURE E.1   (*continued*)

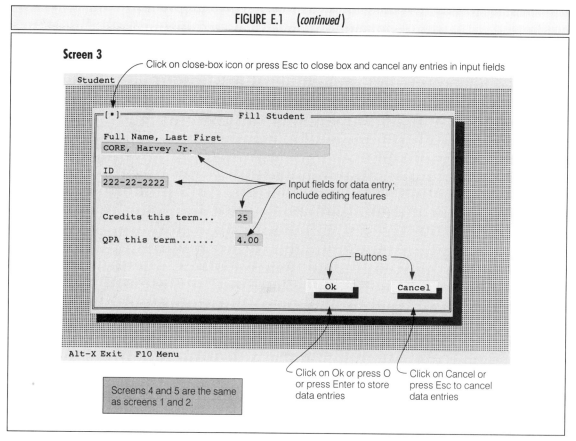

Screen 3

Click on close-box icon or press Esc to close box and cancel any entries in input fields

Student

┌─[■]──────────────── Fill Student ────────────┐

Full Name, Last First
CORE, Harvey Jr.

ID
222-22-2222 ◀───

Input fields for data entry;
include editing features

Credits this term...   25

QPA this term.......   4.00

Buttons

Ok   Cancel

Alt-X Exit   F10 Menu

Screens 4 and 5 are the same as screens 1 and 2.

Click on Ok or press O
or press Enter to store
data entries

Click on Cancel or
press Esc to cancel
data entries

continued

spaces for handwritten or typewritten input. In this approach, we can move at will among the input fields (with the mouse or the *tab* key), inserting, deleting, or editing input fields.

In the exercises, we get you to add faculty to the application.

NOTE

1. User-interface golden rules. The screens in Figure E.1 illustrate some important rules in designing user interfaces:
a. Always indicate what the user can do next.
b. Always give the user a way forward and a way back.
c. Always give the user a clear exit from the session.

2. If you got it, use it! TV is pointer-device-aware. This means if you have a mouse, trackball, or other pointing device that's mouse-compatible, then use it. These pointing devices considerably simplify actions

continued

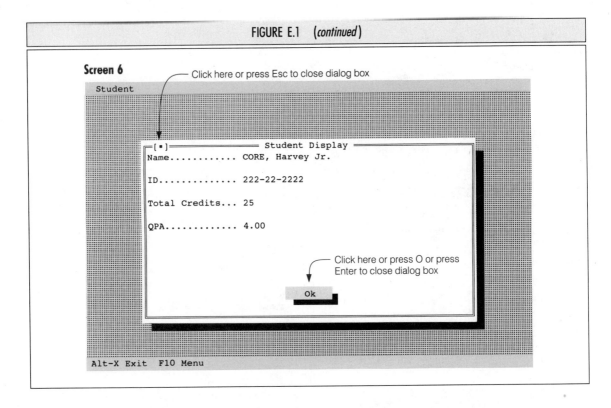

FIGURE E.1   (*continued*)

Screen 6

— Click here or press Esc to close dialog box

Student

```
=[■]=============== Student Display ====
Name............ CORE, Harvey Jr.

ID............. 222-22-2222

Total Credits... 25

QPA............ 4.00
```

— Click here or press O or press
  Enter to close dialog box

```
                     Ok
```

Alt-X Exit   F10 Menu

like menu selections and object manipulations. Moreover, their use re-inforces the illusion that we're manipulating "objects on a desktop," a key design goal in the desktop metaphor discussed in Section 14.1.

SELF-REVIEW EXERCISES

1

E.2 IMPLEMENTATION

• • • • • • • • • • •

Let's describe the implementation of a TV program by example.

SYNTAX BOX

Suggested TV program structure... Use this structure to write TV-compliant applications programs

Syntax.........**program** Heading;

    uses TVunits list,
        OurUnits list;

    const
      Declarations;

    type
      Declare Session class as descendant of **TApplication;**

    var
      Declare pointers to dynamic objects specific to application;
      Declare Session object;

    Method declarations for Session class

    begin {Main body}
      Call Session object's Init constructor
      Call Session object's Run method
      Call Session object's Done destructor
    end. {Main body}

Examples......See Figure E.2.

Explanation ... TVunits list is a list of new units that export TV's classes, fields, methods, constants, types, and variables: **app** for all event-driven applications; **dialogs** for dialog boxes; **drivers** for handling mouse events, keyboard events, and other devices and events; **histlist** for input line history lists; **memory** for memory management routines that improve heap management for safer programming; **menus** for the menuing system; **objects** for the basic object definitions, both visible and nonvisible; **textview** for specialized text-scrolling applications; and **views** for the basic visible elements, like windows, their frames, scrollbars, and so on. OurUnits list is a list of units that are specific to the application. Session class defines an object type for the application's run-time session, and Session object is its instance. **TApplication** is the ancestor of Session; it's a TV abstract object type that provides the classes, fields, and methods that are needed by all TV applications programs. The main body is a sequence of calls to the Session object's Init, Run, and Done methods.

FIGURE E.2   Listing for Program TVdemo

```pascal
program TVdemo;

{* * * * * * * * * * * * * * * * * * * * * * * * * * * * * * * *
 *                                                              *
 *          Turbo Vision Demonstration                          *
 *                                                              *
 *          Imports Person, Student, Faculty classes and their pointers *
 *          from unit College2.                                 *
 *                                                              *
 * * * * * * * * * * * * * * * * * * * * * * * * * * * * * * * *}

{============================ Declarations ============================}

uses app, dialogs, drivers, menus, objects, views,      {TV units}
     College2;                                           {College unit, ver 2}

const
  cmStudentDisplay = 101;          {Student Display menu command}
  cmStudentFill    = 102;          {Student Fill menu command}

type
  Session = object(TApplication)
    constructor Init;
    procedure InitMenuBar;                            virtual;
    procedure InitStatusLine;                         virtual;
    procedure HandleEvent (var Event: TEvent);        virtual;
    procedure DisplayStudent;                         virtual;
    procedure FillStudent;                            virtual;
    destructor Done;                                  virtual;
  end; {Session}

  var
    OurStudentPointer : StudentPointer;
    OurSession        : Session;

  {=========================== Session Methods ===========================}

constructor Session.Init;

  { Application Initialization }

begin

  {Call ancestor's Init}
  TApplication.Init;

  {Create and initialize dynamic student object}
  OurStudentPointer := new (StudentPointer, Init);

end;   {Session.Init}
```

TV PROGRAM STRUCTURE

The accompanying syntax box on page 725 shows our suggested structure for
a TV program, and Figure E.2 shows our sample TV program, TVdemo. This
program is long for a text example, but short for a TV application. It also imports and inherits an army of ancestor fields and methods. A conventional program that does what this program does would be unbelievably long (for our
application). For now, take a "forest" view of this figure; we will explain the
"trees" in the remainder of this section. Before going on, note the following.

```
procedure Session.InitMenuBar;

  { Menu Bar Initializations }

var
  R : TRect;                       {Rectangle object}

begin

 {Set coordinates}
  GetExtent(R);                    {Get full screen coordinates}
  R.B.Y := R.A.Y + 1;              {Set bottom 1 line below top}

 {Create and initialize menu bar object}
  MenuBar := new (PMenuBar, Init(R, NewMenu(
    NewSubMenu('~S~tudent', hcNoContext, NewMenu(
      NewItem('~D~isplay', 'F9', kbF9,      cmStudentDisplay, hcNoContext,
      NewItem('~F~ill',    '',   kbNoKey, cmStudentFill,    hcNoContext,
      NewLine(
      NewItem('e~X~it', 'Alt-X', kbAltX, cmQuit, hcNoContext,

      nil))))),                    {No more items}
    nil))                          {No more submenus}
  ));                              {End of bar}

end; {Session.InitMenuBar}
```

Student menu entry and its submenu with items Display, Fill, and eXit

```
procedure Session.InitStatusLine;

  { Status Line Initializations }

var
  R : TRect;                       {Rectangle object}

begin

 {Set coordinates}
  GetExtent(R);                    {Get full screen coordinates}
  R.A.Y := R.B.Y - 1;              {Set top one line above bottom}

 {Create and initialize status line object}
  StatusLine := new (PStatusLine, Init(R,
    NewStatusDef(0, $FFFF,
      NewStatusKey('~Alt-X~ Exit', kbAltX, cmQuit,
      NewStatusKey('~F10~ Menu', kbF10, cmMenu,

      nil)),                       {No more keys}
    nil)                           {No more defs}
  ));                              {End of line}

end; {Session.InitStatusLine}
```

Entries in status line for hot keys Alt-X and F10

continued

1. We recommend using the following predefined TV units for most TV applications: **app, dialogs, drivers, menus, objects,** and **views.**

2. Unit College2 is our revised college unit for TV applications, as seen in Figure E.3 on pages 732–734. Note how we use pointers like StudentPointer. We also redefined methods as functions that *get* (return)

FIGURE E.2 *(continued)*

```
procedure Session.HandleEvent (var Event: TEvent);

  { Event Handler }

begin

 {Call ancestor event handler}
  TApplication.HandleEvent (Event);

 {Handle current events}
  if Event.What = evCommand then
    begin
      case Event.Command of
        cmStudentDisplay : DisplayStudent;
        cmStudentFill    : FillStudent;
      else
        exit;
      end; {case}
      ClearEvent (Event);
    end; {if}

end; {Session.HandleEvent}
```

— Cases for implementing submenu
commands Display and Fill

```
procedure Session.DisplayStudent;

  { Student Data Display as Dialog Box }

const
  Title = 'Student Display';

var
  R           : TRect;          {Placeholder for various rectangle objects}
  DialogPtr : PDialog;          {Pointer to dialog box object}
  Control   : word;             {Control variable}
  TCString,                     {Total credits as string}
  QPAString : string;           {QPA as string}

begin

 {Set corners of dialog box and create box}
  R.Assign(10, 4, 70, 20);
  DialogPtr := new (PDialog, Init(R, Title));

 {Create and insert controls into dialog}
  with DialogPtr^ do
    begin

    {Insert data fields...}
      {Name}
      R.Assign( 1, 1, 45, 2);
      Insert(new (PStaticText, Init (R, 'Name............ ' +
                                      OurStudentPointer^.GetFullName)));

      {ID}
      R.Assign( 1, 3, 45, 4);
      Insert(new (PStaticText, Init (R, 'ID.............. ' +
                                      OurStudentPointer^.GetID)));

      {Credits}
      R.Assign( 1, 5, 45, 6);
      str (OurStudentPointer^.GetTotalCredits, TCString);
      Insert(new (PStaticText, Init (R, 'Total Credits... ' + TCString)));
```

```
    {QPA}
     R.Assign( 1,  7, 45,  8);
     str (OurStudentPointer^.GetQPA :4:2, QPAString);
     Insert(new (PStaticText, Init (R, 'QPA............. ' + QPAString)));

    {Set corners of Ok button within dialog box and create button}
     R.Assign(25, 13, 35, 15);
     Insert (new (PButton, Init (R, '~O~k', cmOK, bfDefault)));

   end; {with}

 {Display/use modal dialog and set control variable to dialog result}
  Control := DeskTop^.ExecView(DialogPtr);

 {Clean up dialog box object}
  dispose (DialogPtr, Done);

end;  {Session.DisplayStudent}


procedure Session.FillStudent;

  { Student Data Entry Form as Dialog Box }

const
  Title = 'Fill Student';
  NameLength    = 40;             {Forms record string lengths...}
  IDLength      = 11;
  CreditsLength = 2;
  AveLength     = 4;

type
  FormRecType = record
    FullName          : string[NameLength];    {Full name field}
    ID                : string[IDLength];       {ID field}
    TermCreditsString : string[CreditsLength];  {Term credits as string field}
    TermAveString     : string[AveLength];      {Term QPA as string field}
  end; {FormRecType}

var
  Code            : integer;      {=0 if val sends valid numeric value}
  Control         : word;         {Control variable}
  Cptr            : PView;        {Placeholder for various control pointers}
  DialogPtr       : PDialog;      {Pointer to dialog box object}
  FormRec         : FormRecType;  {Record variable w/ form's data fields}
  NewTotalPoints,                 {New total points}
  TermAve         : real;         {QPA this term}
  NewTotalCredits,
  TermCredits     : integer;      {Credits this term}
  R               : TRect;        {Placeholder for various rectangle objects}

begin

 {Set corners of dialog box and create box}
  R.Assign(5, 2, 70, 20);
  DialogPtr := new (PDialog, Init(R, Title));
```

continued

FIGURE E.2   (continued)

```
{Create and insert controls into dialog}
with DialogPtr^ do
  begin

    {NOTE:   Insert input lines in same order as fields in form record.
             Make sure input line lengths correspond to lengths of
             fields in form record.}

    {Insert Name label and input line}
     R.Assign( 1, 3, 45, 4);
     CPtr := new (PInputLine, Init (R, NameLength));
     Insert (CPtr);
     R.Assign( 1, 2, 45, 3);
     Insert (new (PLabel, Init (R, 'Full Name, Last First', CPtr)));

    {Insert ID label and input line}
     R.Assign( 1, 6, 14, 7);
     CPtr := new (PInputLine, Init (R, IDLength));
     Insert (CPtr);
     R.Assign( 1, 5, 20, 6);
     Insert (new (PLabel, Init (R, 'ID', CPtr)));

    {Insert Credits label and input line}
     R.Assign( 25, 9, 29, 10);
     CPtr := new (PInputLine, Init (R, CreditsLength));
     Insert (CPtr);
     R.Assign( 1, 9, 23, 10);
     Insert (new (PLabel, Init (R, 'Credits this term... ', CPtr)));

    {Insert QPA label and input line}
     R.Assign( 25, 11, 31, 12);
     CPtr := new (PInputLine, Init (R, AveLength));
     Insert (CPtr);
     R.Assign( 1, 11, 23, 12);
     Insert (new (PLabel, Init (R, 'QPA this term....... ', CPtr)));

    {Set corners of buttons within dialog box and create buttons}
     R.Assign(38, 15, 48, 17);
     Insert (new (PButton, Init (R, '~O~k', cmOK, bfDefault)));
     R.Assign(53, 15, 63, 17);
     Insert (new (PButton, Init (R, 'Cancel', cmCancel, bfNormal)));

    {Assign current input line values to FormRec fields}
     with FormRec do
       begin
         FullName          := OurStudentPointer^.GetFullName;
         ID                := OurStudentPointer^.GetID;
         TermCreditsString := ' ';
         TermAveString     := ' ';
       end; {FormRec with}

    {Copy data from form record to dialog object}
     SetData (FormRec);

  end; { DialogPtr^ with}
```

```
{Display/use modal dialog and set control variable to dialog result}
  Control := DeskTop^.ExecView(DialogPtr);

{Copy data to student object if dialog box not cancelled}
  if Control <> cmCancel then
    begin

      {Copy data from dialog object to form record}
        DialogPtr^.GetData(FormRec);

      {Copy data from form record to student object}
        OurStudentPointer^.SetFullName(FormRec.FullName);
        OurStudentPointer^.SetID(FormRec.ID);
        val (FormRec.TermAveString, TermAve, Code);
        val (FormRec.TermCreditsString, TermCredits, Code);
        NewTotalPoints  := (OurStudentPointer^.GetQPA
                            * OurStudentPointer^.GetTotalCredits)
                           + (TermAve * TermCredits);
        NewTotalCredits := OurStudentPointer^.GetTotalCredits + TermCredits;
        OurStudentPointer^.SetTotalCredits(NewTotalCredits);
        if NewTotalCredits = 0
          then OurStudentPointer^.SetQPA(0.0)
          else OurStudentPointer^.SetQPA(NewTotalPoints/NewTotalCredits);

    end;  {if}

{Clean up dialog box object}
  dispose (DialogPtr, Done);

end;  {Session.FillStudent}


destructor Session.Done;

  { Object Cleanups }

begin

  TApplication.Done;                       {Call inherited Done}
  dispose (OurStudentPointer, Done);       {Clean up student object}

end; {Session.Done}


  {============================= Main Body =============================}

begin  {TVdemo}

  OurSession.Init;
  OurSession.Run;
  OurSession.Done;

end.    {TVdemo}
```

FIGURE E.3   Listing for Unit College2

```
unit College2;

{* * * * * * * * * * * * * * * * * * * * * * * * * * * * * * * *
 *                                                             *
 *         Unit for OOP College Application, Version 2         *
 *                                                             *
 *         Source file name:   COLLEGE2.PAS                    *
 *                                                             *
 *         Object hierarchy tree                               *
 *          Person                                             *
 *            |___  Student                                    *
 *            |___  Faculty                                    *
 *                                                             *
 *         Class      Pointer         Fields       Methods     *
 *         ---------------------------------------------       *
 *         Person     PersonPointer   ID           Init        *
 *                                    FullName      GetID      *
 *                                    (All private) GetFullName*
 *                                                  SetID      *
 *                                                  SetFullName*
 *                                                  Done       *
 *                                                             *
 *         Student    StudentPointer  TotalCredits  Init       *
 *                                    QPA           GetTotalCredits*
 *                                    (All private) GetQPA     *
 *                                                  SetTotalCredits*
 *                                                  SetQPA     *
 *                                                             *
 *         Faculty    FacultyPointer  Rank          Init       *
 *                                    Salary        GetRank    *
 *                                    (All private) GetSalary  *
 *                                                  SetRank    *
 *                                                  SetSalary  *
 *                                                             *
 * * * * * * * * * * * * * * * * * * * * * * * * * * * * * * *}

{-------}
interface
{-------}

type
  PersonPointer = ^Person;
  Person = object
    constructor Init;
    function GetID       : string;
    function GetFullName : string;
    procedure SetID (SSN : string);
    procedure SetFullName (Name : string);
    destructor Done;                         virtual;
  private
    ID,                        {Identification}
    FullName : string;         {Last name, First name  Initial}
  end; {Person}

  StudentPointer = ^Student;
  Student = object(Person)
    constructor Init;
    function GetTotalCredits : integer;
    function GetQPA          : real;
    procedure SetTotalCredits (Credits : integer);
    procedure SetQPA (Ave : real);

  private
    TotalCredits : integer;    {Total credits to date}
    QPA          : real;       {Quality Point Average}
  end; {Student}
```

FIGURE E.3   (*continued*)

```pascal
      FacultyPointer = ^Faculty;
      Faculty = object(Person)
        constructor Init;
        function GetRank    : string;
        function GetSalary : real;
        procedure SetRank (Position : string);
        procedure SetSalary (Pay : real);
      private
        Rank   : string;              {Professor, Instructor, etc}
        Salary : real;                {Annual salary}
      end; {Faculty}

{------------}
implementation
{------------}

  {=========================== Person Methods ===========================}

constructor Person.Init;
begin
  FullName := ' ';
  ID       := '000-00-0000';
end;

function Person.GetID : string;
begin
  GetID := ID;
end;

function Person.GetFullName : string;
begin
  GetFullName := FullName;
end;

procedure Person.SetID (SSN : string);
begin
  ID := SSN;
end;

procedure Person.SetFullName (Name : string);
begin
  FullName := Name;
end;

destructor Person.Done;
begin
  { No other tasks required by this particular destructor }
end;
  {=========================== Student Methods ===========================}

constructor Student.Init;
begin
  Person.Init;
  TotalCredits := 0;
  QPA          := 0.0;
end;

function Student.GetTotalCredits : integer;
begin
  GetTotalCredits := TotalCredits;
end;
```

continued

```
function Student.GetQPA : real;
begin
  GetQPA := QPA;
end;

procedure Student.SetTotalCredits (Credits : integer);
begin
  TotalCredits := Credits;
end;

procedure Student.SetQPA (Ave : real);
begin
  QPA := Ave;
end;

    {=========================== Faculty Methods ===========================}

constructor Faculty.Init;
begin
  Person.Init;
  Rank    := ' ';
  Salary := 0.0;
end;

function Faculty.GetRank : string;
begin
  GetRank := Rank;
end;

function Faculty.GetSalary : real;
begin
  GetSalary := Salary;
end;

procedure Faculty.SetRank (Position : string);
begin
  Rank := Position;
end;

procedure Faculty.SetSalary (Pay : real);
begin
  Salary := Pay;
end;

  {-----------------------------------------------------------------------}

end.   {College2}
```

---

and procedures that *set* (assign) data-field values. This allows the privatization of an object's data fields within the **private** section, to prevent their direct access by programs and units that import these definitions. *Get* and *Set* methods are very common in OOP, and TV uses them liberally.

3. As usual we declare class Session, except now it's a descendant of TV's class **TApplication**. Think of it this way: **TApplication** provides the "bones" and Session provides the "meat." *All TV programs declare a session object type that descends from the TApplication object type.* Don't worry about Session's methods (yet).

4. The var section declares OurStudentPointer with the imported type StudentPointer from unit College2. As usual, we also declare an instance OurSession of our session class.

5. The main body is our typical main OO body: calls to OurSession's Init, Run, and Done methods. Let's take a closer look at the implementation of these methods.

   a. Session.Init first calls its immediate ancestor's initialization constructor, **TApplication.Init**. This is our usual practice to ensure the proper initialization of inherited fields. Note how TV uses **Init** as the name for its constructors, a suggested convention that we have been following. In this case, TApplication's Init constructor brings the interface to life: It clears the screen; constructs the menu bar, desktop, and status line; and performs many other initialization services. Session.Init also creates and initializes a dynamic student object (we leave the faculty object to an exercise).

   b. Where's Session's Run method? We did not declare it as a method in Session's declaration. It's entirely inherited from TApplication! This is TV's big black box for handling event-driven programming run sessions. Conceptually, **TApplication.Run** (and its call in OurSession.Run) is a procedure that implements a repetition structure that gets and handles *events* until the user issues a quit event. We need not be concerned how it works; we just need to know that its call handles the events in our run-time session. This is *procedural abstraction* in action!

   c. Session.Done first calls the inherited destructor **TApplication.Done** to dispose of objects like the menu bar, desktop, and status line, among other things; then it disposes objects specific to the application, or the student object in our case.

A TV program is basically a collection of view objects and mute objects. A *view* or *view object* is any element that's visible on the screen. If it's visible, it's a view. Field values, labels, menu bars, and windows are all examples of views; they are always displayed as rectangles. For example, a character is displayed within a rectangle that's one column wide and one row high. Views respond to *events,* as described earlier in Section 14.1. The ancestral view class is **TView.** All view classes descend from this class, including **TApplication.**

Mute objects are any other objects that are not views. They're "mute" because they don't "speak" to the screen. Instead, they handle internal tasks like device handling, calculations, and other grunt work.

That's pretty much the big picture! Now let's get down to specifics for creating and handling the menu bar, desktop, status line, and dialog boxes.

MENU BAR, STATUS LINE, AND EVENT HANDLER

The call to **TApplication.Init** within Session.Init sets up the menu bar, desktop, and status line. **TApplication.Init** includes calls to two virtual methods in TApplication that create the menu bar and status line: **InitMenuBar** and **InitStatusLine**. To customize the menu bar and status line, our program needs to override these methods with its own declarations and implementations by the same names: InitMenuBar and InitStatusLine, as seen in the declaration of Session in Figure E.2. Because these methods are virtual, the hierarchical method call **TApplication.Init** within Session.Init calls the versions of Init-MenuBar and InitStatusLine that are declared in Session.

As mentioned earlier, the call OurSession.Run executes TApplication's inherited Run method. Among other things, **TApplication.Run** handles events. It includes a virtual method by the name **HandleEvent** that responds to user inputs. Because we are customizing the menu bar, we need to teach the application how to respond to menu selections and their hot keys (if any). We do this by overriding TApplication's HandleEvent with Session's own HandleEvent, as seen in Figure E.2.

Each TV application we write will include overrides for methods **Init-MenuBar, InitStatusLine,** and **HandleEvent.** Let's take a look at the specific implementations for each of these methods in Figure E.2. (Keep the page open to the proper place in Figure E.2 to follow this discussion.)

InitMenuBar

This method starts by calling its inherited method **GetExtent**(R) to get the coordinates for the full-screen rectangle object R, with inherited object type **TRect.** Class **TRect** includes two fields — **A** for the upper-left corner and **B** for the lower-right corner, each of type **TPoint,** yet another object class with two fields of its own: **X** for the screen column of the point and **Y** for the screen row of the point. Thus, the reference R.**A.Y** stores the rectangle's upper-left y-coordinate and R.**B.Y** its lower-right y-coordinate. The strange-looking assignment

```
R.B.Y := R.A.Y + 1
```

thus sets the bottom of the menu bar one line below the top.

Next, we create and initialize a dynamic menu bar object. The convoluted assignment with the inherited pointer **MenuBar** of pointer type **PMenuBar** as the left member cleverly does the trick of creating a dynamic menu bar object, complete with main menu selections and corresponding submenu items. This creates an entire menu tree in one statement! The call **new** creates the dynamic menu bar object, **Init** initializes the menu bar rectangle, **NewMenu** creates a new menu, **NewSubMenu** a new submenu, and **NewItem** a new item within the submenu.[2]

To simplify menu maintenance and break through the nested calls' complexity, we use the conventional indentation seen in the program. Relate this syntax to screen 2 in Figure E.1 and note that each new entry in the menu bar starts with a **NewSubMenu** call at the left that defines the menu bar selection (Student). We then indent **NewItem** calls for each submenu item (Display, Fill, and eXit). The call **NewLine** inserts a line that visually separates eXit from its command predecessors (see screen 2). By following this convention for each new menu bar selection, we simplify the construction and interpretation of menus.

To add another item (command) to a submenu, we add another **NewItem** call and insert an additional closing parenthesis in the line labeled {No more items}. To add another menu bar selection (like Faculty), we add another **NewSubMenu** call, another **nil** with a closing parenthesis, plus one more closing parenthesis for each **NewSubMenu.** The last line simply ends with two closing parentheses. The best way to understand this is to try it (check out Exercise 4).

NewSubMenu requires three parameters. The first is the menu selection string, as in '~S~tudent'. The tildes that surround the S mean that we can select this command by pressing the hot key S when the menu is active. We can also activate this menu and implement this command with the shortcut Alt S key combination. Make these hot keys unique within the submenu. The second parameter is **hcNoContext**, a predefined TV constant that indicates online help is not available for this command. The last parameter is a call to **NewMenu,** whose arguments include nested calls to **NewItem** for each new item.

NewItem takes four parameters. The command's name is first, using the same syntax as that described above. The second parameter defines an alternative hot key as a string. We used 'F9' for the Display command and the null string ' ' for the Fill command. Note how these show up in screen 2 of Figure E.1. The third parameter begins with **kb.** These are predefined "keyboard" constants for implementing new item hot keys. Thus, we use **kbF9** to implement command Display with key F9, **kbNoKey** to implement no hot key for command Fill, and **kbAltX** to implement the key combination Alt X for command eXit. The fourth parameter begins with **cm** and identifies a **command** integer constant that's used by the event handler to route the menu selection

---

[2]You might have noticed by now that TV's standard identifiers for types begin with the letter T and for pointer types with the letter P. T-types are usually objects, and P-types are usually pointers to objects.

to the appropriate object. **cm**StudentDisplay and **cm**StudentFill are constants in the const section of our program; **cmQuit** is a TV predefined constant to quit the application. TV reserves the integer constants 0–99 and 256–999 for its predefined constants. In our program, we selected 101 and 102 for our two command constants. We will see exactly how these cm-constants are used to handle menu selections shortly. The last argument specifies the help context.

InitStatusLine

This method defines our customized status line. Its syntax is very similar to that of InitMenuBar. Relate its syntax to our preceding discussion and to the displayed status line in Figure E.1, noting how the method binds hot keys to commands.

HandleEvent

Now that we have defined customized menu commands, we need to teach our session object how to respond to menu selections. Parameter **Event** is a predefined record variable of type **TEvent,** which includes field **What** of integer type word to store the next event processed. First, we issue a hierarchical call to **TApplication.HandleEvent** to implement standard event-handling behavior, as defined in ancestor **TApplication.** Then we code a nested selection structure to handle our menuing behavior. The outer if-then structure tests data field **Event.What** against the predefined **event** constant **evCommand.** If the event is a command event (as in selecting a menu command), the then clause is executed; otherwise, we exit this event handler. The then clause includes a case structure for routing menu commands. Note that the case constant **cm**StudentDisplay corresponds to the menu selection sequence Student and Display. The command constant **cm**StudentDisplay is defined in the const section, and it's linked to the Student Display command sequence in method InitMenuBar, as described earlier. The same goes for case **cm**StudentFill. If neither command is issued, the call to **exit** exits the if-block. The call to TV's method **ClearEvent(Event)** signals that the event has been handled successfully, thereby clearing the event from the event handler's queue.

DIALOGS

Screens 3 and 6 in Figure E.1 show dialog boxes for filling and displaying student data fields. In Figure E.2, the case structure in Session.HandleEvent routes the student display and fill menu events to OurSession's methods DisplayStudent and FillStudent. These methods define the dialog boxes seen in Figure E.1.

DisplayStudent

The first task is to set the corners of the dialog box. The call

```
R.Assign (10, 4, 70, 20)
```

assigns a rectangle object that covers the screen from point $(10, 4)$ at the upper-left corner to point $(70, 20)$ at the lower-right corner. As usual, the first entry in the coordinate pair is the column position and the second is the row position. Thus, $(10, 4)$ is a point at column 10 and row 4. In effect, screen 6 shows a rectangle (dialog box) that spans 60 columns (70–10) and 16 rows $(20–4)$.[3]

The dialog box (object) itself is created by the call to procedure new. Note that the dialog box is a dynamic object pointed to by DialogPtr with predefined type **PDialog**. The nested **Init** call passes the assigned rectangle coordinates and the dialog box title 'Student Display'. As usual, we can "grab" the title with the mouse and move it around the screen (all dialog boxes include "drag" behavior that's implemented by an inherited method).

Next, we insert the four data fields with labels as static text objects within the dialog box. For example, the labeled data field

$(1,5)$

```
    Total Credits... 25
```

$(45,6)$

in screen 6 is actually a view rectangle that runs from point $(1,5)$ to point $(45,6)$ within the dialog box. Note that *the grid coordinates (1, 5) and (45, 6) are coordinates of the grid within the dialog box itself, not the coordinates for the entire screen.* The grid dimensions within this dialog box cover 60 columns and 16 rows.

We assign and create this rectangle object just about like we assigned and created the dialog box object: by calls to R.**Assign, new,** and **Init.** The latter two calls are implemented as parameters in a call to the inherited method **Insert. PStaticText** is a pointer type for a pointer that points to a view (rectangle object R) that contains a fixed (static) string. If you're sharp today (and studied Chapter 10), you might have noticed that the returned integer total credits field value in the student object (OurStudentPointer^.GetTotalCredits) is converted to its string representation (TCString) by a call to the string function **str** (see Table 10.3). We then used TCString in **Init,** because static text is required within rectangles whose pointers are type **PStaticText.** We need a similar manipulation for QPA, but not for FullName and ID, since these are already strings.

The Ok buttom is a fifth object within this dialog box. It's pointed to by a pointer with type **PButton,** as seen in its creation with the call to procedure

---

[3]TV coordinates are *grid points,* where each tiny rectangle in the grid contains a potential screen character. The coordinate $(10, 4)$ actually specifies a grid point that's in the upper-left corner of a little rectangle that covers the single-character position in column 10 and row 4. As you might recall from our earlier discussion on views, we can show a single character in a view as the content of a rectangle object. The size of this single-character rectangle object would be identical to one of these grid rectangles. The *home coordinate* is $(0, 0)$.

new. Its **Init** method includes the following parameters: the assigned rectangle object R; the label '˜O˜k', which species key O as a hot key; the predefined command constant **cmOK;** and the predefined button flag constant **bfDefault,** to indicate that this button is the default button (the button that gets "pressed" when the *Enter* key is pressed). If more than one button is in a dialog box, then only one default button is permissible; we would make the others normal buttons by specifying **bfNormal.**

Finally, note that each of our data-field boxes and the button are dynamic objects that "belong" to or are inserted within the dialog box, which is why we use a surrounding with statement for the dialog object reference DialogPrt˜.

The function call

DeskTop˜.ExecView(DialogPtr)

executes the inherited desktop object's view function to execute the dialog; that is, the dialog box gets displayed, the user's action is processed, and the box is closed (providing the user took any of the legitimate actions described in screen 6). The **ExecView** function's returned value is stored in variable Control as an integer that designates the action taken by the user. Control is normally used to route the results of an action. In DisplayStudent we don't have this need, so we could eliminate it altogether by using Turbo Pascal's extended syntax option for treating function calls like procedure calls (see Exercise 3).

Finally, we clean up the dialog object by a call to **dispose,** which includes a call to the object's **Done** destructor. Dialog objects are heap memory hogs, so it's a good idea to dispatch a dialog into oblivion once we're through with it.

FillStudent

This method implements the dialog seen in screen 3 of Figure E.1. As before, we start with setting the dimensions and creating the dialog box. Unlike the display dialog box, however, this dialog includes movement within the box as input fields are filled, deleted, or edited. This means we have to create and insert "controls" into the dialog in the form of *input lines* and their labels, unlike the static text we inserted before.

Let's look at the big picture first. On the one hand we have a student object with data fields for FullName, ID, TotalCredits, and QPA. The total credits and QPA fields reflect all credits and the resulting average up to this point in the student's college life. Changes to these data fields are our ultimate objective. On the other hand, we have a screen form (a dialog object) with data fields for the student's full name, ID, credits this term, and QPA this term. Somehow, we have to move the entered data on the screen to the student object, with appropriate calculations that update the total credits and QPA fields. The TV approach is to create a student *form record* that serves as an intermediary between the dialog object seen on the screen and the student object squirreled away in the heap.[4] This record has the same fields as those in the dialog object (not those in the student object). Our tasks might be summarized as follows.

> Insert labels and input lines in the dialog object
> Insert buttons
> Initialize student form record
> Copy student form record to dialog object
> Execute (display and use) dialog object
> If dialog not canceled then
>   Copy data from dialog object to student form record
>   Copy data from student form record to student object, including any
>   needed calculations

Now (we think) the code in FillStudent should make more sense. First off, note that the student form record is record variable FormRec. Its type is FormRecType, which includes the data fields mentioned earlier. *All data fields are strings because all input lines in dialog objects are strings.*

The specification and creation of this dialog box are similar to our display dialog box, except now we insert a *label object* whose pointer is type **PLabel** and an *input line* object whose pointer is type **PInputLine** in place of static text objects. We also assign control pointers CPtr that relate a label and its corresponding input line. Unless you like to deal with inscrutable logic bugs, observe the following two rules.

- *Insert input lines within the dialog box in the same order as fields in the forms record.*
- *Make sure input line lengths in the dialog box correspond to field lengths in the forms record.*

In the program, note how the sequence of inserts corresponds to the sequence of fields in the form record type. Also note that our use of the string length constants NameLength, IDLength, CreditsLength, and AveLength ensures compliance with the second rule.

In this dialog box we insert two buttons: the usual default Ok button and a Cancel button. Note that the command for the cancel button is **cmCancel**. As we will see, the student object is updated only if the Ok button is pressed. Actions like closing the box or pressing the Esc key or Cancel button will not update the student object.

---

[4]The reasons for this seemingly circuitous route have to do with more efficient code and memory management.

The form record is initialized next by a sequence of assignments. Form record fields are referenced as field variables inside the with statement and student object records are referenced using the *dot form* for field references. Alternatively, we could eliminate the with statement and use the dot form for the form record as well.

The form record is copied to the dialog object by calling the predefined and inherited method **SetData.** Then the dialog is executed, the user enters data, and a concluding action is taken (like Ok button press or Cancel button press). Note that the result of the dialog is stored in Control, and this variable is used in the if-test that follows.

If the user were to cancel the dialog (by pressing the Esc key, the Cancel button, or closing the box), Control would store **cmCancel** (a predefined integer constant) and the then clause would be skipped (the student object would not be updated). If the Ok button is pressed, data are copied from the dialog object to the form record with a call to the dialog's **GetData** procedure and the student object is updated by a series of assignments based on data in the form record. Note that the term average and credits fields have to be converted from string to numeric counterparts using the **val** procedure described in Table 10.3.

We don't show these, but we can also include radio buttons and check boxes in dialog boxes. *Radio buttons* form a cluster of buttons that require the user to press one and only one radio button from the cluster. The appropriate metaphor, of course, is our car radio buttons. *Check boxes* form a cluster of boxes that allow the user to check as many boxes as desired. Radio buttons are commonly used to specify mutually exclusive options, and check boxes are used to specify multiple options. You're already familiar with these through the IDE. Check out the Options command to see a number of dialog boxes that include radio buttons and check boxes.

Windows, Gadgets, and Other Goodies

We've really only scratched the (deep) surface of TV's capabilities. As you know from the IDE, TV also includes **windows** as view objects that we can scroll horizontally or vertically, resize, overlap, or tile. We can both display and edit a window's content. The Edit window in the IDE is a good example of this capability. We can also colorize windows and their contents. A dialog box is a special kind of window.

TV has retired our tried-and-true **write** and **writeln** procedure calls. These are calls *non grata* in the TV environment and have been replaced by calls to the TV output procedures **writestr, writechar, writeline,** and **writebuf.**

TV also includes **streams,** objects that store the data contents of a collection of other objects for I/O processing to devices like disk files. Streams and their methods offer powerful facilities for the movement of data that are encapsulated within objects, similar to the way we I/O records in standard Pascal programming.

Collection objects are supported by TV as objects that store collections of pointers. The standard counterparts to these objects are arrays. Unlike arrays, collections are dynamic and polymorphic and include inheritable methods for their manipulation. In effect, collections fold data structures like arrays and linked lists into inheritable objects that we can reuse and extend.

Resource files are TV objects that save and retrieve other objects by name. These are primarily used to store object initializations for later retrieval. This allows the separation of initializations like dialog box titles, menu commands, and colors from program code that manipulates these objects. The use of resources both simplifies the application's code (we could eliminate all those cluttering view Inits) and separates the look of the application (within a resource) from what it does (in the application program).

TV also offers *gadgets* like a clock, calendar, calculator, and Rolodex-type file. As we might expect, these are objects that we can place and manipulate on our desktop.

NOTE

3. Go for the TV! We think you're going to like Turbo Pascal's version of TV. It will take some effort to learn, but the results are impressive. As we mentioned earlier, our TV space is limited, so we encourage you to try some of the exercises that extend our material. Learn on your own by experimenting, using the help system, checking out Borland's *Turbo Vision Guide,* and adapting both our TVdemo program and the collection of TV programs on Turbo Pascal's utility disk. Enjoy!

SELF-REVIEW EXERCISES

3

E.3 PROGRAMMING TIPS

. . . .

Consider the following tips to improve the design and style of your programs and to avoid some common errors.

DESIGN AND STYLE

The same OOP "Design and Style" tips discussed in Section 14.5 apply to TV programs as well. When working with *object units,* it's also a good idea to make fields *private,* so renegade client programs and objects don't directly access an object's fields (see unit College2 in Figure E.3). This enforces encapsulation. Typical public methods for objects that have private fields include *Get* and *Send* methods for each field, as seen in our College2 unit. Moreover, some methods (sort routines come to mind) might perform very specific services for other methods within the object and may not be appropriate for clients. These methods also should be private.

COMMON ERRORS

Inserting new status-line keys and new submenus and items can give us headaches. The most common problem is the compile-time error *")" expected.* Look over our suggestions on page 737 when you work with menu bars and status lines.

In dialog boxes, the most vexing errors are inconsistencies between corresponding dialog input lines and form record fields. Again, check out the two rules on page 741.

The sheer scope of Turbo Vision presents problems of its own. It takes time to get oriented to the hundreds of new standard identifiers. The list inside the back cover organizes the standard identifiers described in this module. Use this list to get your bearings.

REVIEW EXERCISES

EASIER	For the busy. . .
	1
NORMAL	For the thinkers . . .
	2 3
TOUGHER	For the hard CORE . . .
	4 5

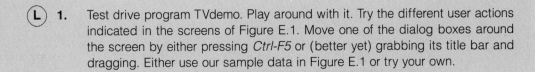

(L) **1.** Test drive program TVdemo. Play around with it. Try the different user actions indicated in the screens of Figure E.1. Move one of the dialog boxes around the screen by either pressing *Ctrl-F5* or (better yet) grabbing its title bar and dragging. Either use our sample data in Figure E.1 or try your own.

(L) *2. Fool around with changes in the size and position of the Student Display box in TVdemo. For example, change the horizontal box size to run from column 5 to column 75. Make some changes in the size and position of the Ok button. For instance, shift it to the bottom-right corner of the dialog box.

(L) 3. Do we do anything with Control in method DisplayStudent in Figure E.2? Try eliminating this variable altogether by implementing Turbo Pascal's extended syntax option to treat a function call like a procedure call. Did you get a compile-time error? If so, activate the extended syntax directive (see Appendix G).

(L) *4. Incorporate a Faculty menu option in TVdemo. Its submenu commands are the same as those for Student. Fill and display Harvey Sr.'s data in Figure 14.7.

NOTE

4. On your own. Take Note 3 to heart. Exercise 5 does not have counterpart TV material in this module. Take the plunge . . . only for the hard CORE . . .

(L) *5. Revise TVdemo to . . .
  a. Use color for desktop objects.
  b. Add a DOS shell option to the submenu (like the IDE's in the File submenu).
  c. Pop an error-message dialog box if nonnumeric entries are made in the term credits and QPA input fields.
  d. Add a Help button to the Fill Student box. Make up your own help message.
  e. Add a clock to the menu bar.
  f. Add a surprise main menu item. Its selection randomly displays multiple, overlapping windows. You might want to include a greeting in the window that's written in color using **writestr.**

ADDITIONAL EXERCISES

EASIER	For the busy . . .
NORMAL	For the thinkers . . .
TOUGHER	For the hard CORE . . .
	6 7 8

6. **Revisit: City temperatures.** Rework Exercise 17 in Chapter 14 as a TV application.

7. **Revisit: Employee record.** Rework Exercise 18 in Chapter 14 as a TV application.

8. **Revisit.** Select an earlier programming assignment and convert it to a TV application.

POSTSCRIPT

At the beginning of the course we expressed a desire to translate your programming curiosity into a productive, rewarding, and continuing experience. Hopefully, you're well on your way toward accomplishing this goal.

You now have a "license" to extend your knowledge and skills, by further instruction or on your own. Keep computing. Consult reference manuals and other works, experiment by trying out new ideas, push your computing bounds...and enjoy!

DOS Reference

• • • • • • • • • • • • • • • • • • •

Our primary work in this course is within Turbo Pascal's *Integrated Development Environment (IDE)*, as described in Chapter 1 and Appendix B. The IDE implements its tasks within the larger context of Microsoft's **Disk Operating System (DOS)**. When using the IDE and writing Turbo Pascal programs, we need a basic knowledge of DOS directory and file conventions. Occasionally, we may also wish to directly work within DOS itself by issuing certain commands, pressing special keys, and undertaking other useful operations. This appendix briefly reviews and summarizes selected elements of DOS.

Directories and Files

• • • • • • • • • • • • • •

A **file** is a *named* collection of data that we usually store on a disk medium. In this course, our most common file contains a Turbo Pascal program. The DOS file-naming convention specifies a two-part *file name*.

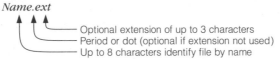

Name.ext

— Optional extension of up to 3 characters
— Period or dot (optional if extension not used)
— Up to 8 characters identify file by name

We can use certain special symbols in file names and extensions, but generally we simply use any of the alphabetic characters *A* through *Z* and any of the digits 0 through 9, without any intervening spaces. Case is immaterial. For example, the file named ENGINE1.PAS is the same as the file named engine1.pas. We can type more than eight characters in the name part, but only the first eight are retained.

DOS allows us to organize a set of files within a *named* **directory.** We can think of our disk as a filing cabinet drawer with folders. Each folder is a directory, with an associated name. And each directory (folder) contains a group of files (documents). The DOS directory structure is called a *directory tree,* because it looks like a family tree when sketched. At the top is the *root directory.* Branches off of the root directory define other directories called *subdirectories.* Branches off of subdirectories define other subdirectories, and so on. A *path* identifies a specific directory within the directory tree; it's a route from the root directory to a specified directory.

We name directories as we name files: a name up to eight characters and an optional dot and three-character extension. The root directory is referenced by the backslash symbol (\). The current directory is referenced by name or by a period (.). The parent directory of the current directory is referenced by its name or by a double period (..).

We use names to specify directories and paths. For example, a path that leads from the root directory (\) to directories parent and daughter, where daughter is a subdirectory of parent, would be specified as \parent\daughter. The first backslash specifies the root directory, and the next separates the other two directories in the hierarchy.

A *file specification* locates a particular file within a disk drive and directory, as follows.

Drive:Path\FileName

For example, the file specification A:\exlib\engine3.dat locates file engine3.dat within directory exlib in floppy drive A.

DOS commands are used to display the directory tree, make directories, change directories, and remove directories, among other tasks.

Selected Commands

DOS (or a shell such as MS-DOS Shell or Windows) is accessible from within the IDE with the command sequence File DOS Shell. DOS commands are typed at the *command line,* which starts with a *command prompt* that includes a drive designation and path. For example, the command prompt C:\> awaits a DOS command and indicates that the current drive is C and the current directory is the root directory (\). The command prompt C:\EXLIB> shows drive C as the current drive and exlib as the current directory.

We can change the current drive at the command prompt by typing the drive letter followed by a colon. For instance, typing a: changes the current drive to drive A.

At the command prompt we can type a DOS command to carry out a desired task, as follows.

CommandName parameters(s) switch(es)   Enter key

CommandName states the desired action, the optional *parameter(s)* define the objects that are acted on, and the optional *switch(es)* (which start with a forward slash /) indicate modifications to or options in the desired action. For example, the command

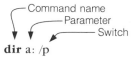

displays a list of the subdirectories and file names within the current directory in drive A, and pauses the listing (/p) if more than one screenful is required. To implement the command, press the Enter key.

The *wildcard* character * is often used in file names to specify or match groups of files. For instance,

dir *.pas

lists all file names in the current drive and directory whose extension is pas.

The accompanying table summarizes some common DOS commands. We omit syntactic detail, focusing instead on examples. Check out your local *DOS User's Guide and Reference* for the gory details.

SPECIAL DOS KEYS

• • • • • • • • • • • • • •

Certain keys and key combinations invoke special operations in DOS. The table on page 753 summarizes these special DOS keys.

REDIRECTING OUTPUT

• • • • • • • • • • • • • •

By default, DOS accepts input from the keyboard and sends output to the screen. *Redirection* is the act of redirecting this I/O to devices other than the keyboard and monitor, such as the printer or a disk file.

Our interest here is on output redirection, which is accomplished with the *redirection character* >. For example, to print the directory listing of the current directory, we would type

dir > **prn**

where **prn** is the DOS name for the line printer. If instead we wish to store this directory listing in the file dirlist.txt within the root directory in drive A, we would redirect the output from the **dir** command as follows.

dir > A:\dirlist.txt

Now we can print this file with the **print** command, list it to the screen with the **type** command, or edit it with the **edit** command, or a wordprocessor, or the IDE's editor. A doubling up of the redirection character (>>) appends output to the specified file.[1]

---

[1]When executing noninteractive Turbo Pascal programs with more than one screen of output, it may be useful to redirect output from the screen to either the printer or a file. When you get there, check out Exercise 26 in Chapter 4.

Quick Reference to Sample DOS Commands*

Command Name	Examples	Remarks
Disk		
diskcopy	**diskcopy** a: b: /v	Copy contents of floppy disk in drive A to floppy disk in drive B and verify that the copy is error free. Use to back up an entire diskette with an exact copy, including any hidden or system files. Both disks must have identical formats. *Caution:* The contents of the destination disk are destroyed.
format	**format** a:	Format the disk in drive A based on the drive type (1.44MB, or 2.88MB, or whatever). Use to prepare an unformatted or previously formatted disk. *Caution:* Any previous files on this disk are "lost"; use **unformat** command to recover if a format was unintended.
unformat	**unformat** a:	Restore disk erased by format command.
Directory		
chdir or **cd**	**cd**	Display name of current directory.
	cd	Change directory to root directory.
	cd..	Change directory to parent of current directory.
	cd \exlib	Change to subdirectory exlib off of root directory.
	cd exlib	Change to subdirectory exlib off of current directory.
	cd \pascal\progs	Change to subdirectory progs, which descends from pascal, which descends from root directory.
dir	**dir** /o/p	Display list of current directory's subdirectories and files, ordered alphabetically, pausing multiple-screen listings.
	dir a:\	Display list of root directory's subdirectories and files in drive A.
mkdir or **md**	**md** exlib	Create (make) subdirectory exlib from current directory.
	md a:\pascal\progs	Create subdirectory progs from directory pascal in drive A.
rmdir or **rd**	**rd** exlib	Remove (delete) exlib, a subdirectory of the current directory. The subdirectory must be empty.
	rd a:\pascal\progs	Remove progs, a subdirectory of directory pascal in drive A. The subdirectory must be empty.
tree	**tree**	Display graph of directory tree starting at current directory.
	tree a:\	Display graph of entire directory tree in drive A.

Quick Reference to Sample DOS Commands* continued

Command Name	Examples	Remarks
File		
copy	**copy** `a:project1.pas b:`	Copy file project1.pas from current directory in drive A to current directory in drive B. Use to back up a file.
	copy `*.pas *.bak`	Copy all files in the current directory with a pas extension to files having the same names in the current directory, but with a bak extension. Use to back up a group of files within the same directory.
del or **erase**	**del** `a:\exlib\*.*`	Delete all files in directory exlib on drive A.
	del `buggy.pas`	Delete file buggy.pas in the current directory.[†]
print	**print** `project1.pas`	Print file project1.pas on the line printer.[†]
rename or **ren**	**ren** `project1.pas prog1.pas`	Rename file project1.pas to prog1.pas.
type	**type** `prog1.pas`	Display file prog1.pas (on the screen).
undelete	**undelete** `buggy.pas`	Restore previously deleted file buggy.pas.
Miscellaneous		
doskey	**doskey**	Load and start a *terminate-and-stay-resident* (*TSR*) program that simplifies command-line editing. Issue this command to edit the command line with cursor keys, Home key, End key, Insert key, Delete key, and so on — and to select previously issued commands from a history list.[†]
edit	**edit**	Start the DOS editor, to edit text files.
exit	**exit**	Quit command interpreter and return to program that started command interpreter.
graphics	**graphics**	Load and start a TSR program to enable the printing of a graphics screen. Issue this command before pressing Shift-Print Screen.[†]
help	**help**	Display every DOS command along with a brief description.
	help `format`	Display an explanation of the format command.

*Commands in color are new to DOS Version 5.0.
[†]This command is best avoided when the IDE is active.

Quick Reference to Special DOS Keys

Key(s)*	Effect
Alt-Ctrl-Del	Reboot (restart) the computer. Hold down the **Alt** and **Ctrl** keys and press the **Del** key. Use this if your keyboard locks up. This sometimes happens within a running application (like the IDE). *Caution:* This action wipes out the contents in RAM. Before invoking, try pressing the Esc key or Ctrl-Break one or more times.
Alt-Key pad numbers	Generates a character from the extended ASCII characters in Appendix I. For example, Alt-254 displays ■.
Backspace	Use this key for crude editing of the current command line. *Hint:* The editing offered by the **doskey** command is superior.
Ctrl-Break	Cancels execution of a command or program. For example, press to terminate an ongoing listing to the screen (issued by the **type** command).
Ctrl-C	This is the same as Ctrl-Break.
Ctrl-S	Temporarily stops output from a command. Press any key except Pause to continue. For example, press to pause a long listing to the screen; press again to resume the listing.
F1	Displays the previous command one character at a time.
F3	Displays all of the previous command. Use this to reissue the previous command without retyping. *Hint:* The **doskey** command allows the redisplay and management of a command history.
Pause	This is the same as Ctrl-S.
Shift-Print Screen	Use to dump the screen to the printer. If the screen includes graphics (like the IDE screen), issue the **graphics** command first.

*A key combination like **Ctrl-S** means hold down the **Ctrl** key and press the **S** key.

IDE R*eference*

This appendix offers a quick reference to commands (menu selections) within Turbo Pascal's **Integrated Development Environment** (**IDE**). See Chapter 1 of this book for an introduction to the IDE and Turbo Pascal's *User's Guide* for a detailed reference. And don't forget that context-sensitive interactive help is just a keystroke away with the **F1** key.

NOTE

1. IDE introduction. The best way to learn the IDE is by using it. Work out Exercises 1–5 in Chapter 1, and use the table that follows as a reference. Also, check out the *Editor Reference* in Appendix C next, which is part of the IDE.

2. On your own. Explore the IDE on your own. Experiment! The IDE usually works as you might expect it to work. It's a superb piece of software that's been developed by a world-class team of programmers at Borland International.

Quick Reference to IDE Menus and Their Command Selections*

Menu	Commands	Hot Key	Action
☰	About		Open dialog box with copyright and version number.
	Refresh Display		Restore IDE screen.
	Clear Desktop		Clear desktop objects.
File	Open	F3	Open dialog box with file names. Select a file and *Open* to load file in new Edit window or *Replace* to replace existing file in Edit window with selected file.
	New		Open new Edit window with default file name.
	Save	F2	Save file in active Edit window to disk.
	Save As		Save file in active Edit window under a different file specification.
	Save All		Save all modified files in multiple Edit windows.
	Change Dir		Open dialog box to change the current drive and path.
	Print		Print file in active Edit window.
	Get Info		Display box containing information on the current file and memory.
	DOS Shell		Exit IDE to enter a DOS command or execute a program; return to IDE with DOS **exit** command.
	Exit	Alt-X	Exit IDE and remove IDE from memory.
Edit	Restore Line		Restore last edited or deleted line as it was.
	Cut	**Shift-Delete**	Delete marked text and place in Clipboard. Use to move blocks of text in combination with **Paste**.
	Copy	**Ctrl-Insert**	Copy marked text to Clipboard. Use to duplicate identical sections of code.
	Paste	**Shift-Insert**	Insert marked text from Clipboard to current cursor position in Edit window.
	Copy Example		Copy sample text in Help window to Clipboard.
	Show Clipboard		Open Clipboard window. Use to edit and mark text for pasting.
	Clear	**Ctrl-Delete**	Delete marked text. *Caution:* This text is gone forever!
Search	Find	**Alt-S F**	Open dialog box to find desired text in current file.
	Replace	**Alt-S R**	Open dialog box to find desired text and replace it with new text.
	Search Again	**Ctrl-L**	Repeat last find or find/search command.
	Go to Line Number		Open dialog box to find a specific line number in the file.
	Find Procedure		Open dialog box to find a specific function or procedure in the file. This command is available only during a debugging session. (See Module A following Chapter 4.)
	Find Error	**Alt-F8**	Find location of run-time error.

Quick Reference to IDE Menus and Their Command Selections* continued

Menu	Commands	Hot Key	Action
Run	Run	Ctrl-F9	Execute program in active Edit window.
	Program Reset	Ctrl-F2	Stop current debugging session. (See Module A following Chapter 4.)
	Go to Cursor	F4	Execute program from run bar to line having cursor. (See Module A following Chapter 4.)
	Trace Into	F7	Execute program line by line. (See Module A following Chapter 4.)
	Step Over	F8	Execute next line in current procedure. (See Module A following Chapter 4.)
	Parameters		Provide running program DOS command-line parameters and switches.
Compile	Compile	Alt-F9	Compile program in active Edit window.
	Make	F9	Make an .EXE (object) file by compiling program and any other source files (such as units) that are used by the program, provided their source files have been changed since the program was last compiled.
	Build		This is the same as Make, except all object files are rebuilt unconditionally, whether or not they are out of date.
	Destination		Toggle destination to *Memory* or *Disk*. If *Memory*, the object program resides in RAM and is lost on IDE exit; if *Disk*, the object program is stored as an .EXE file on disk.
	Primary File		Select file that gets compiled with Make or Build. If not specified, these compilation commands compile the file in the active Edit window. Use when editing an Include file or unit (Chapter 8) in the active Edit window.
Debug	Evaluate/Modify	Ctrl-F4	Open dialog box to evaluate an expression by viewing its value and to assign a new value to a variable. (See Module A following Chapter 4.)
	Watches		Display pop-up menu to control watchpoints. (See Module A following Chapter 4.)
	Toggle Breakpoint	Ctrl-F8	Set or clear a breakpoint at line given by current cursor position. (See Module A following Chapter 4.)
	Breakpoints		Open dialog box to manage breakpoints. (See Module A following Chapter 4.)
Options	Compiler		Open dialog box to manage compiler directives (Appendix G), code-generation options, and debugging options.
	Memory Sizes		Set default memory requirements.
	Linker		Open dialog box to set options used by the *linker* to link any required object files to the current object program.

Command	Shortcut	Description
Debugger		Open dialog box to set debugger options. (See Module A following Chapter 4.)
Directories		Open dialog box to set default directories for object (.EXE and .TPU) files, Include files, units, and assembly-language routines (.OBJ files).
Environment		Display pop-up menu that offers these selections: Open a *Preferences* dialog box to set options like screen size and auto save preferences; open an *Editor Options* dialog box to set editing characteristics like auto-indenting, insert mode, and the creation of backup files; open a *Mouse* dialog box to specify mouse settings regarding the function of the right button, the double-click speed, and button reversal; open a *Startup Options* dialog box to set the use of expanded memory, video characteristics, and other options at IDE startup; open a *Colors* dialog box to customize the IDE's colors.
Save Options		Open a dialog box that provides for saving certain settings in the Search menu, Compile menu, and Options menu. These options are saved in a user-named file.
Retrieve Options		Open a dialog box to retrieve the settings saved by Save Options command. Use to facilitate the implementation of various IDE configurations.
Window		
Size/Move	Ctrl-F5	Change size (*Shift* key and *cursor* key) or position (*cursor* key) of active window. *Mouse bint:* Size the window by *dragging* (hold down left button while moving mouse) the *resize corner* at the bottom right and move the window by dragging its *title bar*.
Zoom	F5	Toggle active window between its maximum size and its previous size. *Mouse bint:* Click the *zoom box* in the upper-right corner, or double-click on the top line.
Tile		Tile (nonoverlap) all open windows.
Cascade		Cascade (overlap) all open windows.
Next	F6	Make the next window active.
Previous	Shift-F6	Make the previous window active.
Close	Alt-F3	Close the active window. *Mouse bint:* Click the *close box* in the upper-left corner.
Watch		Open the Watch window and make it active. (See Module A following Chapter 4.)
Register		Open the Register window and make it active. This is used to debug assembly code.
Output		Open the Output window and make it active. Use to view the source program and its I/O at the same time.

Quick Reference to IDE Menus and Their Command Selections* continued

Menu	Commands	Hot Key	Action
	Call Stack	Ctrl-F3	Open the Call stack window to show the sequence of function and procedure calls. (See Module A following Chapter 4.)
	User Screen	Alt-F5	View I/O in a screen by itself. Any key press or click brings back the IDE.
	List	Alt-0	Display list of all open windows and select window to activate. To directly open a specific window, type Alt followed by the window's number.
Help	Contents		Open the Help window to display table of contents for the help system. Use to select a help topic.
	Index		Open a dialog box to display and select a list of help keywords.
	Topic Search	Ctrl-F1	Display help on the item touched by the cursor in the Edit window.
	Previous Topic	Alt-F1	Open the Help window and redisplay the previously viewed text.
	Help on Help	F1	Open a text screen that explains how to use the help system.

*With a mouse or other pointing device, select menus and their commands by pointing and clicking the left button. With the keyboard, select a menu by holding down Alt and pressing the key that corresponds to the highlighted menu letter, as in Alt-F for the file menu. Or press key F10 to make the menu bar active. Select menus and commands by pressing the indicated hot keys, or using cursor keys and the Enter key, or pressing the highlighted letter within the menu or command name. A hot-key combination like Shift-Insert means hold down the Shift key and press the Insert key. Press the Esc key to back out of an error condition, menu, or help screen.

EDITOR REFERENCE

This book uses Turbo Pascal's editor to enter, edit, and save programs. The editor is active whenever the cursor is within an *Edit window*. A good part of our relationship with the editor, as with a wordprocessor, is straight-out typing. To effectively use an editor, however, we need to know how to efficiently navigate the document, make deletions and insertions, copy and move blocks of text, find or replace selected text, and carry out various other operations.

This appendix is a quick reference to the editor that's part of Turbo Pascal's Integrated Development Environment (IDE). Chapter 1 introduces the IDE and Appendix B gives a quick reference. This appendix does not show all of the variations or features of the editor. Rather, it's a somewhat minimalist treatment that focuses on the simplest key (or mouse) strokes that accomplish the given operation and bypasses some little-used and exotic operations altogether. See Turbo Pascal's *User's Guide* for a detailed reference of the editor's full complement of keystrokes and operations.

NOTE

1. Marking blocks of text. Many editing actions work with a marked *block* of text, which is shown as a highlighted continuous segment within the Edit window. For example, to delete, copy, or move a block of text, we first have to mark it, as follows.

   To mark a *line*...
      Mouse ......Double-click anywhere on line.
      Keyboard...Press **Ctrl-K L** anywhere on line.
   To mark any other *block* of text...
      Mouse ......Drag pointer over desired text, while holding down left
                  button.
      Keyboard...Press **Shift** key while pressing an appropriate arrow
                  (cursor) key over desired text.
   To unmark a line or block...
      Mouse ......Click anywhere.
      Keyboard...Move cursor above block and press **Ctrl-K K**.

Note that the Cut, Copy, Paste, and Clear commands in the IDE's *Edit menu* (Appendix B) work with marked blocks of text.

2. The Clipboard. The editor includes a *Clipboard* that facilitates block cutting and pasting. For example, to copy a block of code from one part of the document to another part of the same document (or to another document in

continued

---

its Edit window), we first copy the block to the Clipboard and then insert it into the document at the cursor by pasting it from the Clipboard. We can even view and edit the Clipboard in its own window by selecting the IDE command Edit Show Clipboard.

3. Autoindentation. Throughout the book we indent blocks of code to improve readability. The editor includes an autoindent mode that positions the cursor under the first nonblank character in the preceding line. To enable this feature at the IDE's startup, check Autoindent Mode in the dialog box accessed by Options Environment Editor, or press Ctrl-O I from within the Edit window. Do it! It's very handy.

4. Editor introduction. The best way to learn the IDE's editor is by using it. Work out Exercises 3 and 5 in Chapter 1 and use the accompanying table as a reference. Explore on your own as well. Review Appendix B and access the editor by opening an Edit window with the command File Open or File New. Extend the editing portions of the exercises on your own by trying out the actions described in the following quick reference table. Write and print a love letter!

Quick Reference to Actions Within the IDE's Editor*

Desired Action	Keyboard Implementation	Mouse Implementation†
Navigate		
Character left	Press ←.	Click left character.
Character right	Press →.	Click right character.
Word left	Press Ctrl-←.	Click beginning of left word.
Word right	Press Ctrl-→.	Click beginning of right word.
Line up	Press ↑.	Click one line up.
Line down	Press →.	Click one line down.
Line start	Press Home.	Click beginning of line.
Line end	Press End.	Click end of line.
Page up	Press Page Up.	Click above *scroll box* in vertical *scroll bar*.
Page down	Press Page Down.	Click below *scroll box* in vertical *scroll bar*.
Window top	Press Ctrl-Home.	Click top of window.
Window bottom	Press Ctrl-End.	Click bottom of window.
File top	Press Ctrl-Page Up.	Drag *scroll box* (■) in vertical *scroll bar* to top of bar.
File bottom	Press Ctrl-Page Down.	Drag *scroll box* (■) in vertical *scroll bar* to bottom of bar.
File relative position	...	Drag *scroll box* (■) in vertical *scroll bar* to relative spot on bar.
Scroll up one line	Press Ctrl-W.	Click up arrow (▲) at top of vertical *scroll bar*.
Scroll down one line	Press Ctrl-Z.	Click down arrow (▼) at top of vertical *scroll bar*.
Scroll up continuously	Hold down Ctrl-W.	Hold down button on up arrow (▲) at top of vertical *scroll bar*.
Scroll down continuously	Hold down Ctrl-Z.	Hold down button on down arrow (▼) at top of vertical *scroll bar*.
Insert		
Character	Position cursor, type character. (Toggle Insert to insert or overstrike.)	...
Line	Position cursor at beginning of line, press Enter, type line (or nothing for blank line).	...

Quick Reference to Actions Within the IDE's Editor* continued

Desired Action	Keyboard Implementation	Mouse Implementation†
Block from Clipboard	Position cursor, press **Shift-Insert**.	Position cursor, click Edit Paste.
Block from Disk	Position cursor, press **Ctrl-K R**, type or select file name, press **Enter**.	…
Delete		
Character at cursor	Press **Delete**.	
Character at left	Press **Backspace**.	
Line	Position cursor on line, press **Ctrl-Y**.	Mark line, click Edit Clear.
Block	Mark block, press **Ctrl-Delete**.	Mark block, click Edit Clear.
Block to Clipboard	Mark block, press **Shift-Delete**.	Mark block, click Edit Cut.
Copy		
Block to Clipboard	Mark block, press **Ctrl-Insert**.	Mark block, click Edit Copy.
Block to File	Mark block, press **Ctrl-K W**, type or select file name, press **Enter**.	…
Move		
Line	Mark line, press **Shift-Delete**, reposition cursor, press **Shift-Insert**.	Mark line, click Edit Cut, reposition cursor, click Edit Paste.
Block	Mark block, press **Shift-Delete**, reposition cursor, press **Shift-Insert**.	Mark block, click Edit Cut, reposition cursor, click Edit Paste.

Search

	Press	Click
Find text	Press **Alt-S F**, type text, set options and buttons, press **Enter**.	Click Search **Find**, type text, click options and buttons, click OK.
Replace text	Press **Alt-S R**, type old and new text, set options and buttons, press **Enter**.	Click Search **Replace**, type old and new text, click options and buttons, click OK.

Miscellaneous

	Press	Click
Block indent	Mark block, press **Ctrl-K I**.	...
Block unindent	Mark block, press **Ctrl-K U**.	...
Edit window close	Press **Alt-F3**.	Click close box (■) in upper-left corner.
Edit window open	Press **Alt-*Window number***.	Click in window if it shows; otherwise, click Window List, double-click desired window.
File save!	Press **F2**.	Click **F2 Save** in *status line*.
File open	Press **F3**, type or select file name, press **Enter**.	Click **F3 Open** in *status line*, double-click file name.
Print block	Mark block, press **Ctrl-K P**.	...
Print file	Press **Alt-F P**.	Click File Print.

*A key combination connected by a hyphen means hold down the first key and then press the second. For example, Ctrl-O I means hold down the Ctrl key, press the O key, release these two keys, and then press the I key. Use the Esc key to abort an action in progress. *Drag* means move the pointer while holding down the left mouse button.

†*Click* means locate the pointer where desired and press the left mouse button.

DATA TYPES

The following tables classify Turbo Pascal's data types. Types shown in color are not supported by Standard Pascal.

Integer Data Types

Standard Identifier	. . . . Range			
	Smallest	*to*	*Largest*	*Bytes*
integer	−32768	to	32767	2
shortint	−128	to	127	1
longint	−2147483648	to	2147483647	4
byte	0	to	255	1
word	0	to	65535	2

Real Data Types

Standard Identifier	. . . . Range			Significant Digits	Bytes
	Smallest	*to*	*Largest*	*Digits*	*Bytes*
real	2.9×10^{-39}	to	1.7×10^{38}	11–12	6
single	1.5×10^{-45}	to	3.4×10^{38}	7–8	4
double	5.0×10^{-324}	to	1.7×10^{308}	15–16	8
extended	3.4×10^{-4932}	to	1.1×10^{4932}	19–20	10
comp	-9.2×10^{18}	to	9.2×10^{18}	19–20	8

All Data Types

Class	Description	Associated Identifiers	Introduced in...
1. *Simple types*	Ordered single values		
a. *Real types*	Floating-point values	`real`	Chapter 2
		`single`	Chapter 2
		`double`	Chapter 2
		`extended`	Chapter 2
		`comp`	Chapter 2
b. *Ordinal types*	Listed values		
i. *Integer types*		`integer`	Chapter 2
		`shortint`	Chapter 2
		`longint`	Chapter 2
		`byte`	Chapter 2
		`word`	Chapter 2
ii. *Boolean type*		`Boolean`	Chapter 5
iii. *Character type*		`char`	Chapter 2
iv. *Enumerated type*			Chapter 7
v. *Subrange type*			Chapter 7
2. *String type*	Sequence of characters	`string`	Chapter 2
3. *Structured Types*	Groupings of related values		
a. *Set type*		`set of`	Chapter 7
b. *Array types*		`array of`	Chapter 9
		`packed array of`	Not covered
c. *Record type*		`record`	Chapter 11
d. *File types*		`file of`	Chapter 12
		`text`	Chapter 4
e. *Object type*		`object`	Chapter 14
4. *Pointer Type*	Sets of values that point to dynamic variables		Chapter 13
5. *Procedural Types*	Procedures and functions as data objects		Not covered

SELECTED PREDECLARED PROCEDURES

This appendix summarizes the predeclared procedures that are used in this book. See Turbo Pascal's *Library Reference* for a comprehensive list and more detailed descriptions.

NOTE

1. Interactive help. When you're online, don't forget that help on procedures is just a few keystrokes or mouseclicks away. With a mouse, click Help Contents, double-click Procedures, and double-click the desired procedure from the list. With the keyboard, press **Alt-H C**, navigate to Procedures, press **Enter**, navigate to the desired procedure, and press **Enter**.

2. Parameter compatibility. The **accompanying table** shows procedure declarations rather than calls, to better assess how we need to type actual parameters. Don't forget that an actual parameter in the call must be *assignment compatible* with its corresponding formal parameter if the latter is a value parameter. If the formal parameter is a variable (**var**) parameter, the actual parameter must be *identically typed*.

Predeclared Procedures Used in This Book

Declaration*	Unit†	Also See Page(s)‡	Description
append (**var** FileVar : **text**)		566	Opens existing file assigned to FileVar and sets file position to end of file for appending.
assign (**var** FileVar : AnyFileType; FileSpec : **string**)		147, 566	Assigns FileSpec to FileVar.
circle (X, Y : **integer**; Radius : **word**)	**graph**	373	Draws circle of given Radius at pixel coordinate (X,Y).
close (**var** FileVar : AnyFileType)		148, 566	Closes open file assigned to FileVar.
closegraph	**graph**	371	Puts the graphics system to bed.
clreol	**crt**	217	Clears characters from cursor to end of line, without moving cursor.
clrscr	**crt**	211	Clears window and places cursor in home position.
dec (**var** X : AnyOrdinalType; Step : **longint**)		?	Decrements X by Step, or by one ordinal position if Step is omitted.
delay (Duration : **word**)	**crt**	298, 360	Delays execution by Delay milliseconds.
delete (**var** StrVar : AnyStrType; Position, Sublength : **integer**)		491, 494	Deletes substring of length Sublength starting at given Position within StrVar.
dispose (**var** PointerVar : AnyPointerType)		710	Disposes dynamic variable pointed to by PointerVar. In OOP, Turbo Pascal optionally includes a call to a destructor as a second parameter.
erase (**var** FileVar : AnyFileType)		566	Deletes unopened file assigned to FileVar. *Caution*: Program defensively to confirm this operation.
exit		738	Exits current block. Halts execution from main block; returns from procedure or function block.
getdate (**var** Year, Month, Day, DayOfWeek : **word**)	**dos**	361	Gets current date set by DOS.
gettime (**var** Hour, Minute, Second, Second100 : **word**)	**dos**	361	Gets current time set by DOS.

Predeclared Procedures Used in This Book continued

Declaration*	Unit†	Also See Page(s)‡	Description
gotoxy (X, Y : byte)	crt	211	Positions cursor at column X and line Y. The *home position* is (1, 1). The call is ignored if X and Y are outside the window's coordinates.
halt		576	Halts execution and returns to state of system before run (IDE or DOS).
highvideo	crt	359	Selects high-intensity characters for any subsequent display.
inc (var X : AnyOrdinalType; Step : longint)		212	Increments X by Step, or by one ordinal position if Step is omitted.
initgraph (var Driver, Mode : integer; DriverPath : string)	graph	371	Initializes graphics system based on given graphics Driver and Mode, where Driver is located in directory given by DriverPath. *Note:* Assign Driver to predeclared graphics constant **Detect** for autodetection of installed video hardware. Call this procedure before calling any other graphics procedures.
insert (SubString : string; var StrVar : AnyStrType; Position : integer)		491, 494	Inserts SubString into StrVar starting at given Position. Inserts at end of string if Position exceeds dynamic length.
line (X1, Y1, X2, Y2 : integer)	graph	372	Draws line from pixel coordinates (X1,Y1) to (X2,Y2).
lowvideo	crt	?	Selects low-intensity characters for any subsequent display.
moveto (X, Y : integer)	graph	373	Moves the current pointer to pixel coordinate (X,Y).
new (var PointerVar : AnyPointerType)		621, 710	Creates new dynamic variable pointed to by PointerVar. In OOP, creates new dynamic object; Turbo Pascal optionally allows a call to a constructor as a second parameter. *Note:* This procedure has a functional form in Appendix F.

Procedure	Unit	Page	Description
`normvideo`	`crt`	359	Selects screen attributes at program startup for any subsequent display.
`nosound`	`crt`	360	Turns off sound coming through speaker.
`outtext (StrVar : string)`	`graph`	373	Outputs StrVar at current pointer.
`outtextxy (X, Y : integer; StrVar : string)`	`graph`	373	Outputs StrVar at pixel coordinate (X,Y).
`putpixel (X, Y : integer; Color : word)`	`graph`	372	Plots pixel at pixel coordinate (X,Y) using given Color. (Table 8.2 shows range of colors.)
`randomize`		386	Initializes the random number generator's seed.
`read (FileVar : AnyFileType; var Variable list)`		135, 566	Reads values from file assigned to FileVar and assigns to variables in variable list. If FileVar is omitted, file **input** (the keyboard) is assumed.
`readln (FileVar : text; var Variable list)`		45, 566	Executes read procedure and advances to next line in file.
`rectangle (X1, Y1, X2, Y2 : integer)`	`graph`	372	Draws rectangle from pixel coordinates (X1,Y1) to (X2,Y2).
`rename (var FileVar : AnyFileType; NewName : string)`		566	Renames unopened existing file assigned to FileVar as NewName.
`reset (var FileVar : AnyFileType)`		147, 566	Opens existing file assigned to FileVar and resets file position to beginning of file.
`rewrite (var FileVar : AnyFileType)`		567	Creates and opens new file assigned to FileVar and resets file position to beginning of file. *Caution:* Any existing file with the same file specification is deleted and recreated as an empty file.
`seek (var FileVar : AnyTypedFileType; ComponentNumber : longint)`		567	Moves file position to ComponentNumber in file assigned to FileVar.
`setbkcolor (ColorNum : word)`	`graph`	?	Sets current background color based on ColorNum, which ranges from 0 to 15, as seen in Table 8.2.
`setcolor (ColorNum : word)`	`graph`	?	Sets current foreground color based on ColorNum, which ranges from 0 to 15, as seen in Table 8.2.

Predeclared Procedures Used in This Book continued

Declaration*	Unit†	Also See Page(s)‡	Description
sound (Cps : **word**)	**crt**	360	Emits sound through speaker at frequency Cps (hertz).
str (X : AnyNumericType; **var** StrVar : AnyStringType)		491	Converts numeric X to its string representation in StrVar. X optionally includes the format specification :*FieldWidth* :*DecimalPlaces*.
textbackground (ColorBackground : **byte**)	**crt**	358	Selects background color for any subsequent display based on ColorBackground, which ranges from 0 to 7 in Table 8.2.
textcolor (ColorForeground : **byte**)	**crt**	358	Selects foreground color for any subsequent display based on ColorForeground, which ranges from 0 to 15 in Table 8.2.
truncate (**var** FileVar : AnyTypedFileType)		567	Deletes all records past current position in opened file assigned to FileVar. *Caution:* Program defensively to confirm this operation.
val (StrVar : **string**; **var** NumVar : AnyNumericType; **var** Code : **integer**)		491, 492	Converts string value in StrVar to its numeric representation in NumVar and assigns 0 to Code, provided string value represents a proper numeric constant; otherwise Code is set to the position of the first character in error and NumVar is assigned 0.
write (FileVar : AnyFileType; Output list)		45, 567	Writes values in Output list to file assigned to FileVar. If FileVar is omitted, file **output** (the screen) is assumed.
writeln (FileVar : **text**; Output list)		45, 567	Executes write procedure and writes an end-of-line marker.

*Procedures in color are not part of Standard Pascal.
†A blank entry means that this procedure is in Turbo Pascal's run-time library, the *system unit*, and is available to all programs and units; all other units require a uses clause in the client program or unit. Calls to any procedure in unit **graph** must follow a call to **initgraph**, to ensure graphics mode.
‡A question mark (?) means that this procedure's call may be useful in an exercise.

Selected Predeclared Functions

This appendix summarizes the predeclared functions that are used in this book. See Turbo Pascal's *Library Reference* for a comprehensive list and more detailed descriptions.

NOTE

1. Interactive help. When you're online, don't forget that help on functions is just a few keystrokes or mouseclicks away. With a mouse, click Help Contents, double-click Functions, and double-click the desired function from the list. With the keyboard, press **Alt-H C**, navigate to Functions, press **Enter**, navigate to the desired function, and press **Enter**.

2. Parameter compatibility. The **accompanying table** shows function declarations rather than calls, to better assess how we need to type not only actual parameters but also the variable assigned to the value returned by the function. If a formal parameter is a value parameter, its corresponding actual parameter (argument) must be *assignment compatible*. If a formal parameter is a variable (**var**) parameter, its corresponding actual argument must be *typed identically*. Any variable assigned the value returned by the function must also be *assignment compatible* with the function's type.

Predeclared Functions Used in This Book

Declaration*	Unit†	Also See Page(s)‡	Description
`abs (X : AnyNumericType) : SameTypeAsArgument`		131	Returns absolute value of X.
`chr (X : byte) : char`		127, 478	Returns character whose ASCII value is X.
`concat (StrVar list : AnyStringTypes) : string`		488, 489	Returns concatenated strings in list.
`copy (StrVar : AnyStringType; Position, SubLength : integer) : string`		488, 489	Returns substring of length SubLength starting at given Position within StrVar. Null string returned if Position exceeds dynamic length in StrVar. Remainder of string in StrVar returned if SubLength goes beyond end of string in StrVar.
`eof (var FileVar : AnyFileType) : Boolean`		221, 568	Returns true if current file position in file assigned to FileVar is beyond last data element in file; else returns false. *Caution:* If FileVar is omitted, file **input** (the keyboard) is assumed, which if unintended may seem like a system "hang" when the function call is used as a control in a while-do structure.
`eoln (var FileVar : text) : Boolean`		568	Returns true if current file position in file assigned to FileVar is at end-of-line marker; else returns false.
`exp (X : AnyRealType) : RealType`		96	Returns exponential of X, or e^X, where e is the base of natural logarithms.
`filepos (var FileVar : AnyTypedFileType) : longint`		568	Returns current file position of opened file assigned to FileVar, in range 0 to number of components in file.
`filesize (var FileVar : AnyTypedFileType) : longint`		568	Returns number of components in opened file assigned to FileVar, or 0 if file is empty.
`getmaxx : integer`	**graph**	372	Returns rightmost pixel column or x-resolution of current graphics driver and mode.

Unit	Function	Page	Description
graph	getmaxy : integer	372	Returns bottommost pixel row or y-resolution of current graphics driver and mode.
	int (X : AnyRealType) : RealType	?	Returns integer part of X.
	ioresult : word	272, 568	Returns 0 if I/O operation was successful; otherwise returns integer error code.
crt	keypressed : Boolean	231	Returns true if key was pressed; else returns false.
	length (StrVar : AnyStringType) : integer	487, 488	Returns dynamic length in StrVar.
	ln (X : AnyRealType) : RealType	96	Returns natural (base e) logarithm of positive value in X; fatal run-time error if X stores either 0 or negative value.
	memavail : longint	660	Returns bytes of free memory in the heap.
	new (AnyPointerType) : SameTypeAsArgument	710	Creates new dynamic variable of base type in AnyPointerType and returns its address. In OOP, creates new dynamic object; Turbo Pascal optionally allows a call to a constructor as a second parameter. *Note:* This is the functional form of procedure new in Appendix E.
	ord (X : AnyOrdinalType) : longint	337, 478	Returns ordinal number of value in X.
	pi : RealType	?	Returns the value of pi, or 3.1415926536....
	pos (SubStr, StrVar : AnyStringType) : byte	488, 489	Returns starting position of SubStr within StrVar, if found; else returns 0.
	pred (X : AnyOrdinalType) : SameTypeAsArgument	409, 478	Returns predecessor of X.
	random : real	385	Returns real random number in range 0 or more but less than 1.
	random (X : word) : word	385	Returns integer random number in range 0 or more but less than X.
crt	readkey : char	211	Reads character from keyboard, without echoing to screen.
	round (X : AnyRealType) : longint	?	Returns long integer value as value in X rounded to nearest whole number.
	sizeof (X) : word	660	Returns number of bytes of memory occupied by X, where X is either a variable or a type identifier.

Predeclared Functions Used in This Book continued

Declaration*	Unit†	Also See Page(s)‡	Description
`sqr (X : AnyNumericType) : SameTypeAsArgument`		93	Returns square of X, or X*X.
`sqrt (X : AnyRealType) : RealType`		91	Returns positive square root of nonnegative value in X; fatal run-time error if X stores negative value.
`succ (X : AnyOrdinalType) : SameTypeAsArgument`		409, 478	Returns successor of X.
`trunc (X : AnyRealType) : longint`		?	Returns long integer value as truncated value in (integer part of) X.
`upcase (CharVar : char) : char`		198, 478	Returns uppercase of character in CharVar if CharVar stores value in range a..z; else returns value in CharVar.
`wherex : byte`	crt	270	Returns column position or x-coordinate of cursor's location in window.
`wherey : byte`	crt	270	Returns line position or y-coordinate of cursor's location in window.

*Functions in color are not part of Standard Pascal.
†A blank entry means that this function is in Turbo Pascal's run-time library, the *system unit*, and is available to all programs and units; all other units require a uses clause in the client program or unit. Calls to any function in unit **graph** must follow a call to procedure **initgraph**, to ensure graphics mode.
‡A question mark (?) means that this function's call may be useful in an exercise.

Selected Compiler Directives

A **compiler directive** sets an optional feature offered by the compiler. For example, we can tell the compiler whether or not to generate range-checking code that detects out-of-range values for a variable. There are two ways to specify a compiler directive: (1) Specify the directive through the IDE's Options menu; (2) specify the directive within the source code as a special comment, according to the syntax box below.

SYNTAX BOX

Compiler directive... Insert in source code as shown to set or change compiler option.

Syntax......... *Switch directive:*
      { **$** NameSwitch }
    Parameter directive:
      { **$** Name parameters }

Examples...... `{$R+ Enable range checking}`
      `{$R- Disable range checking}`
      `{$I A:\UTILIB\PAUSE.PRO Include utility procedure Pause}`
      `{$N+,E+ Enable both numeric processing and emulation}`

Explanation... The comment braces { and } are used to enclose the compiler directive. The symbol $ and the directive's **Name** immediately follow the opening brace, without any intervening spaces. For switch directives, the **Switch** + (to enable the directive) or − (to disable the directive) immediately follows the name, again with no intervening space. For parameter directives, one or more parameters follow the name, with at least one blank following the name. Directives can be grouped in a list, as seen in the last example; only the first directive includes the dollar symbol, and a space is not used following a comma. Directives are assigned default values by Turbo Pascal; these are resetable within the IDE's Options menu. Directives in the source code always override default values. Switch directives are either global or local. A *global* directive affects the entire compilation and must appear between a program or unit heading and the first declaration section. A *local* directive can appear anywhere in the source code and affects that part of the compilation from the directive to the next occurrence of the same directive. *Note:* Recompile the source code whenever a compiler directive is changed within the IDE; otherwise, the object program will not reflect this directive's setting.

The accompanying table summarizes the compiler directives used in this book. For a complete list, see Turbo Pascal's *Programmer's Guide*.

Compiler Directives Used in This Book

Directive/Comment Form	Default	Scope	IDE Menu Command	Purpose
Boolean evaluation `{$B+}` or `{$B-}`	`{$B-}`	Local	Options Compiler Complete Boolean Eval	Generates code when enabled that completely evaluates Boolean expressions having the operators **and** and **or**; otherwise uses *short-circuit evaluation* to terminate the evaluation as soon as the result is known. See Section 5.1.
Debug information `{$D+}` or `{$D-}`	`{$D+}`	Global	Options Compiler Debug Information	Generates code when enabled that allows single-step traces, breakpoints, and error location with the IDE's debugger. Use `{$D+}` and `{$L+}` for interactive debugging. See Module A.
Emulation `{$E+}` or `{$E-}`	`{$E+}`	Global	Options Compiler Emulation	Generates code when enabled that emulates a numeric coprocessor if one is not onboard. Enable this directive along with `{$N+}` if the computer lacks a numeric coprocessor and support for *single, double, extended*, and *comp* real types is desired. See Example 4.4.
Include file `{$I FileSpec}`			Options Directories Include Directories	Instructs the compiler to compile the named file at this point in the compilation If the file specification does not include a path, Turbo Pascal searches for the file in the current directory and in the Include directories specified in the Directories dialog box. See Example 8.1.
I/O checking `{$I+}` or `{$I-}`	`{$I+}`	Local	Options Compiler I/O Checking	Generates code when enabled that terminates program execution when a run-time error occurs during a call to an I/O procedure. Disable this directive to handle I/O errors with a call to function **ioresult**. See Section 6.4.

Directive		Default	Options Compiler	Description
Local symbols information {$L+} or {$L-}	{$L+}	Global	Local Symbols	Generates code when enabled to watch and modify local variables with the IDE's debugger, as well as to follow the sequence of calls in the *Call stack window*. This directive is ignored if {$D−} is used. See Module A.
Memory allocation sizes {$M StackSize,HeapMin,HeapMax}			Memory Sizes	Specifies the size of the *stack* in bytes as an integer number in the range 1024 to 65520; the minimum *heap* size in bytes as an integer number in the range 0 to 655360; and the maximum *heap* size as an integer number in the range HeapMin to 655360. See Sections B.3 and 13.6.
Numeric processing {$N+} or {$N-}	{$N-}	Global	8087/80287	Generates code when enabled to perform all real type calculations using a numeric coprocessor; otherwise floating-point code is generated to carry out the calculations in software. Enable this directive to support *single, double, extended,* and *comp* real types. Combine with {$E+} if that expensive numeric coprocessor is missing. See Example 4.4.
Range checking {$R+} or {$R-}	{$R-}	Local	Range Checking	Generates code when enabled to detect out-of-range values for real variables, subrange variables, and indexed expressions for strings and arrays. In OOP, enabling this directive checks virtual method calls to ensure that the object instance making the call has been initialized by its constructor. A fatal run-time error occurs if a range check fails, unless range checking is disabled. Use enabled range checking, except when error handling range errors. See Example 7.3.

Compiler Directives Used in This Book continued

Directive/Comment Form	Default	Scope	IDE Menu Command	Purpose
Stack-overflow checking {$s+} or {$s-}	{$s+}	Local	Options Compiler Stack Checking	Generates code when enabled to check for sufficient stack space. A call to a procedure or function when stack space is insufficient may cause a fatal run-time error. Enable this directive to avoid potential system crashes or invalid results. Also see the $M compiler directive and Section B.3.
Var-string checking {$v+} or {$v-}	{$v+}	Local	Options Compiler Strict Var-Strings	Generates code when enabled that enforces identical string types between an actual string parameter and its corresponding variable (var) parameter. If disabled, string types with different size attributes are permitted as actual parameters.
eXtended syntax {$x+} or {$x-}	{$x-}	Global	Options Compiler Extended Syntax	Generates code when enabled that allows the form of a function call to be that of a procedure call. This is handy when a function performs one or more tasks and the returned value is not needed by the calling module. Does not apply to functions in system unit. See Exercise 11b in Chapter 5 and Exercise 3 in Module E.

Turbo Versus Standard Pascal

Standard Pascal is a term for a standardized version of the Pascal language that was jointly developed by the *American National Standards Institute* and the *Institute of Electrical and Electronics Engineers.*[1] As stated in the foreword of their joint publication, the purpose of Standard Pascal is "to facilitate portability of Pascal programs for use on a wide variety of data processing systems."

Language standards not only encourage portability but also promote the spread of the language. *"Real" or actually used programs, however, are not written in Standard Pascal.* This is because a language standard essentially defines a "least-common denominator," a vehicle that's "all things to all people." Realistic programs are necessarily more specialized to the local environment, to take advantage of OS features or specialized hardware like graphics boards and monitors. And commercially distributed compilers offer "enhancements" that reflect additions to and more flexible variations than the offerings in Standard Pascal.

Turbo Pascal is a de facto standard in the DOS-dominated PC world, simply because it is so prevalent. Still, interest remains in the differences between Turbo and Standard Pascal. This interest is primarily academic, but it does take on practical significance when portions of a Turbo Pascal program need to be ported to non-DOS machines.

This appendix summarizes chapter-by-chapter differences between the elements of Turbo Pascal (**TP**) covered in this book and Standard Pascal (**SP**). TP includes not only the language elements in its standard run-time library (the *system unit*) but also the enhancements that are available through its other units (*printer, crt, graph,* and others).

Chapter 1

Operating system commands like those in DOS, development environments like the IDE, and editors are not addressed by SP.

---

[1]Standard Pascal is officially named *American National Standard Pascal Computer Programming Language.* This standard is set forth in the publication *American National Standard Pascal Computer Programming Language,* IEEE Pascal Standards Committee of the IEEE Computer Society and ANSI/X3J9 of American National Standards Committee X3 (New York: Institute of Electrical and Electronics Engineers, 1983).

CHAPTER 2

• • • • • • • • • • • • • •

Identifiers. All characters are significant in SP, but only the first 63 are significant in TP. TP—but not SP—allows an underscore character after the first character.

Data Types. SP does not recognize the following data types in Appendix D: single, double, extended, comp, shortint, longint, byte, word, string, and object.

Program Composition. As the program composition inside the back cover indicates, SP does not include a uses clause, and it requires the various declarations in the order shown. Also, SP allows just one section for each kind of declaration, whereas TP allows multiple sections, in any order. For example, a TP program can include two var sections within its declarations section.

Program Heading. SP requires all I/O files as part of the program heading, as in

> **program** ProgramName (**input, output**);

where **input** and **output** are standard identifiers for the system's standard input (the keyboard in DOS) and output (the monitor in DOS) devices.

Constant Declarations. SP only allows a constant value or previously declared constant in a constant expression. Constant expressions like RealConstant1 * RealConstant2 or **trunc**(−99.99) are not permitted in SP, as they are in TP.

Comments. Each comment in TP must begin and end with a matching comment delimiter, as in { Comment } or (* Comment *). SP allows mismatched pairs, as in { Comment *). TP allows nested comments, but SP doesn't. A comment in TP that begins with the symbol $ defines a *compiler directive* (Appendix G); SP treats this as a normal comment, because compiler directives are not part of the standard.

I/O Statements. In SP any character that's not part of a signed number terminates input into an integer or real variable; in TP only a space, tab (from the Tab key), or end-of-line marker (from the Enter key) terminates the input of a numeric variable. SP makes no provision for output to a printer.

Strings. SP does not support data type string. In SP strings are processed as character arrays (Chapter 9). SP does define a *text constant* (*string constant* in this chapter)—as in 'Enter value: '—for output lists and declared constants.

CHAPTER 3

• • • • • • • • • • • • • •

Standard Procedures and Functions. Appendixes E and F show the predeclared procedures and functions used in this book; those in color are not defined by SP.

Functions. SP requires the assignment of the function identifier in the body of the function; TP does not detect this omission. By enabling its extended syntax compiler directive with **{$X+}**, TP allows a function call to have the same form as a procedure call. Exercise 11b in Chapter 5 and Exercise 3 in Module E show why this is useful in some applications.

Chapter 4

• • • • • • • • • • • • •

For Statement. SP does not permit reassignment of the control variable within the for-do loop; TP does (but we don't suggest it).

Text-File Processing. SP does not support predeclared procedures **assign** and **close.** (The procedures in color in Appendix E are not defined by SP.) No distinction is made between the text-file variable and the text-file name—they are one and the same. The text-file variable is included in the device list within the program heading and its type is **text.** For example, to input from file EngineDat we would specify the file as a parameter in the program heading

```
program Engine3 (EngineDat, output);
```

declare it in the var section,

```
var
   EngineDat : text;
```

and use the following in the main body.

```
reset (EngineDat);
readln (EngineDat, NumberEngines);
readln (EngineDat, Name, SizeCC, Price, Units);
```

The termination of numeric input is handled according to the discussion under *"I/O Statements"* in Chapter 2.

Module A

• • • • • • • • • • • • •

SP does not address the use of a debugger.

Chapter 5

• • • • • • • • • • • • •

Boolean Operators. SP does not define operator **xor** in Table 5.3.

Short-Circuit Evaluation. SP does not define short-circuit evaluation; Boolean expressions are evaluated to completion. TP includes the compiler directive **{$B+}** (see Appendix G) to enforce complete evaluation.

PC-Style Programming. This is a good example of where standard-conforming programs fall far short of accepted user interfaces. *Crt unit* routines like the predeclared procedures **clrscr, clreol,** and **gotoxy** and the predeclared function **readkey** are not defined in SP. How do we clear a 25-line screen in Standard Pascal? By writing 25 blank lines!

Chapter 6

• • • • • • • • • • • • • •

Case Statement.   SP does not include an else clause in the definition of its case statement. If a selector is outside the list of case constant values, a run-time error occurs.
The standard method of handling this error condition is to enclose the case statement
within a protective if-then-else structure. See Exercise 11b.

Error Handling.   Error-handling facilities are nonexistent in SP because run-time
error detection is so specific to hardware, operating systems, and compilers. For example, compiler directives that switch off compiler options, like {$I−}, are not ad-
dressed by SP. As in PC-style programming, no self-respecting real interactive program
would omit this feature.

Module B

• • • • • • • • • • • • • •

There are no differences between TP and SP in our treatment of recursion. Note, however, that our sample programs would not fly in a pure SP environment: Function FacR
uses extended type; procedures ReadRep and RepErr call predeclared procedures
clrscr, clreol, delay, and **gotoxy** in the crt unit.

Chapter 7

• • • • • • • • • • • • • •

Type Section.   The type section in SP is placed between the const and var sections.
TP allows multiple type sections, placed anywhere within the declarations section.

Range Checking.   Range checking is active by default in SP, with no provision for
its disablement. This means that SP does not address range-error handling, which requires at least the temporary suspension of fatal run-time range errors (as seen in
Example 7.3).

Chapter 8

• • • • • • • • • • • • • •

SP draws a goose egg on Include files, units, crt effects, OS access, and graphics; the
standard makes no provision for these hardware- and OS-specific facilities.

MODULE C

· · · · · · · · · · · · · · ·

Predeclared function **random,** procedure **randomize,** and variable **RandSeed** are undefined in SP. Standard-conforming code for simulations would have to use a generic library function that codes a random number generator based on one of the established mathematical algorithms.

CHAPTER 9

· · · · · · · · · · · · · · ·

There are no differences between TP and SP in our treatment of arrays. As mentioned above under Chapter 7, however, SP does not make provisions for disabling *range checking,* as done in Examples 9.3 and 9.5 and as required by utility IndexCk in Figure 9.2.

MODULE D

· · · · · · · · · · · · · · ·

There are no differences between TP and SP in our treatment of sorting and searching with arrays.

CHAPTER 10

· · · · · · · · · · · · · · ·

Character Processing.   Predeclared function **upcase** is not supported in SP.

String Processing.   As stated under Chapter 1 above, SP does not define type **string.** Consequently, predeclared functions and procedures that process strings and the *concatenation operator* (+) are also undefined in SP. String processing in SP is treated as a form of character processing, where a "string value" is stored in a character array. Turbo Pascal's approach is superior for two reasons: Working with string variables is simpler than working with arrays; calls to the predeclared string functions and procedures in Tables 10.2 and 10.3 considerably reduce the complexity and length of string processing code.

Chapter 11

· · · · · · · · · · · · ·

There are no differences between TP and SP in our treatment of the record type. Remember, however, that input into a record's fields from a text file differs according to the discussion under *"Text-File Processing"* in Chapter 4 above.

Chapter 12

· · · · · · · · · · · · ·

Text Files. SP handles text-file input as described under *"Text-File Processing"* in Chapter 4 above; it similarly handles text-file output, except that a call to **rewrite** is used to create the new file. As in TP, the file variable is placed first in the output list of a write or writeln statement.

Predeclared Procedures and Functions. In Tables 12.1 and 12.2, SP only defines **read, readln, reset, rewrite, write, writeln, eof,** and **eoln.** However, the I/O statements read, readln, write, and writeln are reserved exclusively for reading and writing *text* files. TP extends these to include input from and output to *typed* files. Typed-file I/O in SP is handled by calls to predeclared procedures **get** and **put,** which TP does not define.

Direct Access. SP does not define a procedure like **seek;** hence, it makes no provisions for directly accessing a typed file.

Chapter 13

· · · · · · · · · · · · ·

Pointer Symbol. In addition to ^, SP includes @ as an alternative pointer symbol. In TP @ is used as an operator that returns a pointer to its operand.

Functional Form of New. SP does not include the functional form of predeclared procedure new, as described in the syntax box for pointer declarations and procedure new.

Errors. SP defines some error conditions not defined by TP: If a pointer variable PtrVar is *nil* or undefined, it's an error to reference its nonexistent dynamic variable with PtrVar^; it's also an error to reassign the value in a pointer while the dynamic variable it points to has not been disposed of.

CHAPTER 14

• • • • • • • • • • • • • • • •

Objects are undefined in SP.

MODULE E

• • • • • • • • • • • • • • • •

TV is definitely undefined in SP!

Extended *ASCII* Character Set

The **American Standard Code for Information Interchange** (**ASCII,** pronounced *ask-ee*) codes a set of characters and control instructions using a seven-bit binary coding scheme. The inclusion of an eighth bit in the coding scheme allows an additional 128 characters, called *extended* characters, for a total of 256 characters. Extended characters include some non-English-language symbols, graphics symbols, mathematical symbols, and other special symbols. Turbo Pascal, DOS, and PCs in general use the *extended ASCII character set*.

Part 1 of the accompanying ASCII table gives the original 128 ASCII characters according to their decimal position or *ASCII value*. Note that the original ASCII values run from 0 to 127 (not 1 to 128). Part 2 shows the extended characters based on the ASCII values 128 to 255.

The "characters" with ASCII values 0 to 31 are reserved as *control characters* or *control codes*. Control characters include special instructions to I/O devices. For instance, ASCII 7 rings the bell (beeps the speaker), ASCII 10 issues a line feed, and ASCII 26 marks the end of a file. Some control characters are printable, like the gender symbols given by ASCII 11 and 12, which actually represent the instructions "Cursor home" and "Form feed," and the symbols for ASCII 28–31, which specify cursor movements. Other control characters, such as the bell and the backspace, are not printable.

Predeclared functions **chr** and **ord** (see Appendix F) are "mirror image" functions that return ASCII characters and values, respectively. For example, **chr**(57) returns character 9 and **chr**(82) returns character *R*; **ord**('*9*') returns ASCII value 57 as an integer and **ord**('*R*') returns integer 82.

To write control characters, we can use either **chr**(ASCIIvalue) in the list of an output statement or output #ASCIIvalue as part of a character string. For instance, to write 'Ring', ring the bell, issue a line feed and carriage return, and write 'Hi there!', all in a single output statement, we can write either

    writeln ('Ring', **chr**(7), **chr**(10), **chr**(13), 'Hi there!')

or

    writeln ('Ring'#7#10#13'Hi there!')

In either case, the output would look like this.

    Ring ☼
    Hi there!

ASCII Table, Part 1: Original Characters

ASCII Value	Char	ASCII Value	Char	ASCII Value	Char	ASCII Value	Char
0	Null	32	Blank	64	@	96	'
1	☺	33	!	65	A	97	a
2	☻	34	"	66	B	98	b
3	♥	35	#	67	C	99	c
4	♦	36	$	68	D	100	d
5	♣	37	%	69	E	101	e
6	♠	38	&	70	F	102	f
7	Bell	39	'	71	G	103	g
8	Backspace	40	(	72	H	104	h
9	Tab	41	)	73	I	105	i
10	LineFeed	42	*	74	J	106	j
11	♂	43	+	75	K	107	k
12	♀	44	,	76	L	108	l
13	CarriageRet	45	–	77	M	109	m
14	♪	46	.	78	N	110	n
15	☼	47	/	79	O	111	o
16	►	48	0	80	P	112	p
17	◄	49	1	81	Q	113	q
18	↕	50	2	82	R	114	r
19	‼	51	3	83	S	115	s
20	¶	52	4	84	T	116	t
21	§	53	5	85	U	117	u
22	■	54	6	86	V	118	v
23	↨	55	7	87	W	119	w
24	↑	56	8	88	X	120	x
25	↓	57	9	89	Y	121	y
26	Eof	58	:	90	Z	122	z
27	Esc	59	;	91	[	123	{
28	∟	60	<	92	\	124	|
29	↔	61	=	93	]	125	}
30	▲	62	>	94	^	126	~
31	▼	63	?	95	_	127	⌂

ASCII Table, Part 2: Extended Characters

ASCII Value	Char	ASCII Value	Char	ASCII Value	Char	ASCII Value	Char
128	ç	160	á	192	└	224	α
129	ü	161	í	193	┴	225	β
130	é	162	ó	194	┬	226	Γ
131	â	163	ú	195	├	227	π
132	ä	164	ñ	196	─	228	Σ
133	à	165	Ñ	197	┼	229	σ
134	å	166	ª	198	╞	230	μ
135	ç	167	º	199	╟	231	τ
136	ê	168	¿	200	╚	232	Φ
137	ë	169	⌐	201	╔	233	Θ
138	è	170	¬	202	╩	234	Ω
139	ï	171	½	203	╦	235	δ
140	î	172	¼	204	╠	236	∞
141	ì	173	¡	205	═	237	ϕ
142	Ä	174	«	206	╬	238	ϵ
143	Å	175	»	207	╧	239	$\cap$
144	É	176	░	208	╨	240	$\equiv$
145	æ	177	▒	209	╤	241	$\pm$
146	Æ	178	▓	210	╥	242	$\geq$
147	ô	179	│	211	╙	243	$\leq$
148	ö	180	┤	212	╘	244	$\lceil$
149	ò	181	╡	213	╒	245	$\rfloor$
150	û	182	╢	214	╓	246	$\div$
151	ù	183	╖	215	╫	247	$\approx$
152	ÿ	184	╕	216	╪	248	°
153	Ö	185	╣	217	┘	249	·
154	Ü	186	║	218	┌	250	·
155	¢	187	╗	219	█	251	$\sqrt{}$
156	£	188	╝	220	▄	252	^{n}
157	¥	189	╜	221	▌	253	^{2}
158	₧	190	╛	222	▐	254	■
159	ƒ	191	┐	223	▀	255	

ANSWERS TO UNSTARRED REVIEW EXERCISES

CHAPTER 1

Answers not required for these exercises.

CHAPTER 2

1. **(a)** Acceptable, but not very descriptive.   **(b)** Acceptable, but conventional usage capitalizes first letter.   **(c)** Unacceptable; can't start with numeric character.   **(d)** Acceptable.   **(e)** Unacceptable; underscore only permitted symbol.   **(f)** Unacceptable; user-defined identifier can't be reserved word.   **(g)** Unacceptable; embedded blanks not permitted.   **(h)** Unacceptable; underscore only permitted symbol.   **(i)** Acceptable.   **(j)** Acceptable, and usually preferred over version in part **i** because it conforms to Standard Pascal usage.

2. **(a)** Unacceptable; comma not permitted. Correct as in part **b**.   **(b)** Acceptable integer constant.   **(c)** Acceptable real constant.   **(d)** Acceptable integer constant.   **(e)** Acceptable real constant.   **(f)** Acceptable character constant.   **(g)** Acceptable character constant.   **(h)** Unacceptable character constant; double up on inner single quotes: 'You' 're Ok, I' 'm Ok'.   **(i)** Unacceptable character constant; add missing closing quote.   **(j)** Unacceptable character constant; add missing surrounding quotes: '$'.

3. **(a)** The integer expression Price * Units evaluates "on paper" to 4,500,000. This exceeds 32767, the upper range on integer values (as seen in Appendix D). We have *integer overflow,* which is not detected in Turbo Pascal.   **(b)** You should have gotten a compile-time error in the statements that write Price and Sales. Delete the formatting :0 in both cases. Run 1 gives the correct output 4500 for Sales; run 2 gives the junk value −21984 for Sales, because the expression Price * Units had integer overflow.   **(c)** Run 1 proceeds correctly as before; run 2 evaluates the expression Price * Units as the long integer 45000000, because Price is typed longint. This value is properly stored within longint Sales.

4. In all parts, 70 is placed in Grade1, 80 is placed in Grade2, and 90 is placed in Grade3.
    (a) `Enter three grades...` 70 80 90 ◄──── Could also enter on separate lines
    (b) `Enter three grades...`
       70 80 90 ◄──────────────── Could also enter on separate lines
    (c) Same as part **a.**
    (d) `Enter three grades...` 70
       80 ◄──────────────── Now must enter on separate lines
       90

8. Insert

    `uses printer;`

    just before the **const** section. Replace the two writeln statements that don't have parenthetic output lists with

    `writeln (Lst);`

    Insert **Lst,** at the beginning of each output list in the other nine writeln statements. Try it using Engine1. (Make sure the printer is online!)

9.   **(a)** Use variable as left member. RealVar := 5.65.   **(b)** Not assignment compatible; *Type mismatch* compile-time error message.   **(c)** Missing colon; "*:=*" *expected* compile-time error message.   **(d)** Shortcut not permissible; use = operator, not := . Rewrite as

```
const
    Constant1 = 10;  Constant2 = Constant1;
```

which also shows better style by using a separate line for **const** and the single constant 10.   **(e)** OK. Unary arithmetic performed on IntVar2 and the result is multiplied by 4. A more readable version would either place the minus sign in front of 4 or use the parenthetic expression (−IntVar2).   **(f)** Not assignment compatible; *Type mismatch* compile-time error message.   **(g)** OK.

10.   **(a)** X * X * X   **(b)** (X − A) * (X − A)/(S + 4)   **(c)–(d)** We're not ready for these yet; they require functions that are discussed in the next chapter.   **(e)** One alternative: most readable

```
((X - Y)/100) * (1/(A + B)) + Y - 5/(X * T)
```

Another alternative: less readable

```
(X - Y) / 100 * 1 / (A + B) + Y - 5 / X / T
```

11.   IntVar stores 40.
IntVar stores 14. (Expression is 13 + 1)
RealVar stores 1.333...

12.   **(a) var**
```
        City  : string[10];
        State : string[2];
        Zip   : string[5];
```
   (b)   City := 'Incline Village';
```
        State := 'NV';
        Zip   := '89450';
```
   Incline Village gets truncated in City to the 10 characters Incline Vi. Replace the 10 with 15 or greater. It's best to use a size attribute that is just large enough to handle the longest anticipated city name.
   (c) write ('Enter city............. '); **readln** (City);
```
        writeln;
        write ('Enter state initials... '); readln (State);
        writeln;
        write ('Enter zip code......... '); readln (Zip);
        writeln;  writeln;  writeln;
```
   (d) writeln (City + ',■' + State + '■■■' + Zip);
   (e) writeln ('Code: ' + State + Zip[4] + Zip[5]);

Chapter 3

1.   Move the bodies of procedures WriteIntro and Calculate to the main body, and delete the declarations of these procedures. The main body now has the following look.

```
    writeln;
    writeln ('Start of program Engine, Version 2.0');
    writeln;
```
← Former body of WriteIntro

```
ReadInput    (Name, Price, Size_cc, Units);
```

```
Size_ci := MetricConversion * Size_cc;        ◄─── Former body
Sales    := Price * Units;                          of Calculate
```

```
WriteReport (Name, Units, Size_cc, Size_ci, Price, Sales);
```

This simplifies the modular structure, but at the expense of a more elaborate main body. Try it. You should get the same output as before.

4.

	Var1	Var2	SumScaled	One	Two	AdjSum	Scale
(a)	5	15	200.0	5.0	15.0	. . .	10.0

SumScaled address

(b)	5	15	200.0	5.0	15.0	. . .	10.0

AdjSum now both receives (precondition) and sends (postcondition) values. Note that in the part **b** version, we don't have a need for data flows regarding Var1 and Var2. We could rewrite the procedure heading as

```
procedure Adjust (var AdjSum : real);
```

and the call as

```
Adjust (SumScaled);
```

(c) `function SumScaled (One, Two : real) : real;`

```
var
  Scale : real;
begin {SumScaled}
  Scale := 10.0;
  SumScaled := (One + Two) * Scale;
end;  {SumScaled}
```

In Test, we would delete SumScaled from the **var** declarations, delete the call to Adjust, and replace the writeln statement with

```
writeln ('Scaled sum = ', SumScaled (Var1, Var2):10:1);
```

Preference? The procedure is more convenient and efficient if SumScaled were needed at different points in the program; otherwise it's "Six of one or a half dozen of the other."

5.

	A	B	C	D	E	F
(a)	5	10	25	5	20	. . . ◄── Address of C
(b)	35	10	15	15	20	. . . ◄── Address of A
(c)	5	10	15	5	20	25
(d)	5	20	25	. . .	. . .	. . . ◄── Address of A, B, and C

6. **(a)** Yes; procedure I is declared within the main block of TestScope. **(b)** Yes; procedure I is declared before procedure III, and both are declared in the main block. **(c)** Yes; procedure II is declared within procedure I's block. **(d)** No; procedure II is local to procedure I. **(e)** No; procedure II is local to procedure I. **(f)** Yes; procedure III is declared within TestScope's main block. **(g)** No; both are declared in the main block, but procedure III is declared after procedure I.

9. **(a)** You should get the fatal run-time error *Invalid floating point operation;* the base must be a positive value because it's the argument for function **ln**. **(b)** No problem with negative powers; the answer is 0.50. **(c)** No problem with a power of zero; the answer is 1.00. **(d)** You should get the fatal run-time error *Floating point overflow;* the value in Power1 is too large for its real type. **(e)** Now you should get the correct answer 1.07374182400000002E+0039. *Note:* If you get the compile-time error *Must be in 8087 mode to compile this,* make sure that the **O**ptions **C**ompiler **8**087/80287 box in the IDE is checked and recompile. If you then get the run-time error *Numeric coprocessor required,* check the box **O**ptions **C**ompiler **E**mulation and recompile. Appendix G describes these *numeric processing* and *emulation* compiler directives.

10. In the last three written statements, replace X with 1 + X and P with P − 1. The correct answers for the two sample runs are 9.00 when X stores 2.0 and P stores 3.0 and 5.67 when X stores 2.1 and P stores 3.2.

11. **(a)** Yes; integer actual parameters are assignment compatible with real-value parameters.   **(b)** Did you get a syntax error by forgetting to eliminate :2 in the output formats? As in the original run, you should get an answer of 8.00. An entry of 2.1 for X should have given you the fatal run-time error *Invalid numeric format*.

16. The distances 21.59, 26.63, and 20.62 from the platforms to the home base are all wrong; zeros used in Xhome and Yhome.

17. The distances 10.30, 22.20, and 21.19 from the platforms to the home base are all wrong; zero used in Yhome.

18. The distances 8.60 and 8.60 from platforms A and B to the home base are wrong; the coordinates of platform C were used for all platforms.

CHAPTER 4

1. **(a)** 10　　　　　　**(b)** 0 iterations　　　　**(c)** 20
　　　　11　　　　　　　　　　　　　　　　　　　　　19
　　　　　.　　　　　　　　　　　　　　　　　　　　18
　　　　　.　　　　　　　　　　　　　　　　　　　　17
　　　　　.　　　　　　　　　　　　　　　　　　　　16
　　　　30　　　　　　　　　　　　　　　　　　　　15
　　　　21 iterations　　　　　　　　　　　　　　6 iterations

2. **(a)** `for UpLetter := 'A' to 'Z' do`
　　　　　　`write (UpLetter);`
　　(b) `for UpLetter := 'Z' downto 'A' do`
　　　　　　`writeln (UpLetter);`

3. `for BoolVar := false to true do`
　　`writeln (BoolVar);`

4. T
　　U
　　R
　　B
　　O

6. **(a)**　　　Iterations? 2　　　――― The loop body is now the single write statement that gets executed twice

　　　　Enter number Enter number　　5
　　　　　　　Square = 25　　　　―― The readln and writeln statements now follow the loop

7. Note that ASCII 7 rings the bell (beeps the speaker), 8 is a backspace, 9 is a tab, 10 is a line feed, 13 is a carriage return, 27 is the Escape character (key), and 32 is the space character. To dump output to the printer as it gets written to the screen, try pressing Ctrl-Print Screen during interactive input (while the program is running). Press this key combination again to disable printed ouput.

8. Add the declared constant

　　　`Beep = chr(7);`

and insert Beep in the statements that output Intro and Foot:

　　　　`writeln (Beep, Intro);`
　　　　`writeln (Foot, Beep);`

11. **(a)**

NumberScores	ScoreNumber	Score	SumScores
5			0
	1	70	70
	2	60	130
	3	90	220
	4	100	320
	5	90	410

(b) `inc (SumScores, Score);`

12. **(a)** For 0! . . .
    3 entered in Number
    0 entered in X
    0 passed in call to Fac
        Factorial set to 1.0
        Loop bypassed
        Fac set to 1.0
    Output: 0! is . . . 1.00000000000000E+0000
    1 entered in X
    1 passed in call to Fac
        Factorial set to 1.0
        Loop bypassed
        Fac set to 1.0
    Output: 1! is . . . 1.00000000000000E+0000
    3 entered in X
    3 passed in call to Fac
        Factorial set to 1.0
        Loop iterations:
            For 2 in K, Factorial set to 2.0
            For 3 in K, Factorial set to 6.0
        Fac set to 6.0
    Ouput: 3! is . . . 6.00000000000000E+0000

(b) 1755. Try 1754 and then 1755. **(c)** If numeric processing is disabled, you should get the compile-time error *Must be in 8087 mode to compile this.* If you don't have a numeric processor on board and emulation is disabled, you should get the fatal run-time error *Numeric coprocessor required.* To ensure proper execution with respect to these compiler directives, you could insert {**$N+,E+**}just before the var section in CkFac. Try disabling these compiler directives within the IDE, inserting them within the program, recompiling, and rerunning. The program now works regardless of the IDE's settings for these compiler directives.

14. **(a)** Iterations evaluates to 8. The output is
        -15 -10   -5   0   5   10   15   20
(b) Iterations evaluates to −3. The loop is bypassed, so there's no output.
(c) Iterations evaluates to 5. The output is
        40   35   30   25   20
(d) Increment must not equal zero to avoid the fatal run-time error *Division by zero.* An entry of zero for the increment implies an infinite loop.

16.

(a)				**(b)**				**(c)**		
1	1	1		2	3	5		1	1	2
1	1	2						1	2	3
1	2	1						1	3	4
1	2	2						2	1	3
1	3	1						2	2	4
1	3	2						2	3	5
2	1	1								
2	1	2								
2	2	1								
2	2	2								
2	3	1								
2	3	2								

(d) 1   3   4   **(o)** 1   2   3   1   2   3
    2   3   5

17.   **(a)** For Joshua Clay, the sum varies from 95 to 185 to 285, giving the correct average 95.0; for J. K. Dunn, the sum varies from 335 to 425 to 493, giving the incorrect average 164.3 (albeit lucky indeed for Dunn). *Hint:* To "watch" the actual sums, place a writeln statement that outputs SumScores within the ScoreNumber loop; in Module A following this chapter, we have a better way to watch variables.   **(b)** The prompt for name is written, but it is immediately followed on the same line with the prompt for three scores. If we now enter the three scores for J. K. Dunn, the output shows a blank for name and the correct average. Execution of the readln statement for the second name reads beyond the end of the input line that shows Joshua Clay's scores, giving no (a null) value in Name. We need the readln statement without the input list to "clear" the previous input line, before we read the next name.

18.   **(a)** A "phantom" fourth engine is processed with a null value in Name and zeros in the numeric input variables, as described in item 5b under "Common Errors."   **(b)** If the size attribute is 9, the first 9 characters in Momma Four are stored in Name at the second iteration. This leaves an unread ʳ in the text file for Momma Four's record. The next variable in the readln input list is the real variable Size_cc. Its attempted input gives the fatal run-time error *Invalid numeric format,* as Turbo Pascal attempts to convert the ʳ into a numeric value for storage in Size_cc. If the size attribute is 15, names and sizes are incorrectly stored. For example, input of the third record gives the 15 characters Poppa Six■■■100 in Name, and zero in Size_cc.   **(c)** In ClosingTasks . . .

> Add NumberEngines as a value parameter typed integer.
> Declare the following constant:

```
Foot2 = 'Average sales......... $';
```

> Insert the following third writeln statement:

```
writeln (Foot2, TotalSales/NumberEngines :W:D+2);
```

In the main body. . .

> Add NumberEngines as an actual parameter in the call to ClosingTasks.

19.   No changes are needed in the program. The advantage of this text-file data structure is that it's less dependent on the size attribute for Name. The original data file assumes a size attribute of 10, as declared in Engine3. Try changing the size attribute to 15 and reprocess this file. Unlike the result in Exercise 18b, the file is processed without a hitch. As in Exercise 18b, however, we have the same problem with size attributes less than 10. The disadvantage of this approach? We humans like our records on one visual line (if possible); it's what we grew up with in our manual record-keeping systems.

MODULE A

1.   Follow each example step by step to get the same results as the book. Did you find the help facility useful?

2.   **(a)** The slick way to add this expression to the Watch window: Place the cursor on F in the expression Factorial * K and press **Crtl-F7,** giving Factorial as the watch expression in the Add Watch box; extend the expression by moving the cursor right, past Factorial, and watch the remaining part of the expression *K appear as it gets copied from the Edit window. This excercise shows how we can also include general expression (not just variables) in the Watch window.   **(b)** We can place this expression in the Evaluate and Modify box by extending the selection in the Edit window, as we did in part **a** (except that we press **Crtl-F4** to start the process). The Result box should show 0.0 after pressing the Enter key. In step 15 place 2 (instead of 1) in the New value box and press the Enter key. The Result box should state that the expression "Cannot be modified." The New value box applies to variables, not general expressions.

3.   You should have viewed a warning that the breakpoint in AveScore is invalid. Respond yes to include it anyway. After pressing **Crtl-F9,** Debug executes, not AveScore, and we get an additional warning regarding invalid breakpoints. The moral: Explicitly end the previous debugging session.

CHAPTER 5

1.   **(a)** False. **(b)** True. **(c)** False. **(d)** False. **(e)** True. **(f)** False. **(g)** True. **(h)** True. **(i)** True. **(j)** True. **(k)** The right operands in parts **h** and **i** don't get evaluated.

2. **(a)** True. **(b)** True. **(c)** Operands not type compatible, giving type-mismatch compile-time error: Left operand for **and** is real (2.5 * Original) and right operand is Boolean (Name1 > Name2).

3.
```
WrongReply := (Reply <> 'Y') and (Reply <> 'y') and
              (Reply <> 'N') and (Reply <> 'n');
```
Or we can code
```
        WrongReply := not CorrectReply;
```
if CorrectReply is already coded.

4. **(a)** Loop output: 15 16 17 18 19 20; Iterations: 6. **(b)** No loop output; zero iterations.

5. **(a)** Loop output: 15 15 . . . (infinite loop); Iterations: indefinite (until we "pull the plug" or press Ctrl-Break). **(b)** Another infinite loop with output: 15 14 13 . . . **(c)** No loop output; zero iterations. **(d)** The increment must be a positive integer whenever Initial ≤ Final. If Initial > Final, then the increment is irrelevant.

6. **(a)** Simple solution: **upcase**(Code) <> 'X'; Other solution: (Code <> 'X') **and** (Code <> 'x'). **(b)** Note that Code is not explicitly initialized at the first loop test. Turbo Pascal stores null for the code, so the while test is true and the loop body is executed. The I/O for A, B, and C proceed as before, but not the I/O for X. When the sentinel is input, it is also output, followed by loop termination. Thus, the sentinel gets processed as a legitimate code, which is undesirable.

8. **(a)** Right. **(b)** **not** (Fahrenheit = −999); the original approach seems a bit more straightforward. **(c)** Type MoreTemperatures Boolean in the var section of Temp1. Just before the while statement and just after the call to ReadTempt insert
```
        MoreTemperatures := Fahrenheit <> -999;
```
Replace the while line with
```
        while MoreTemperatures do
```
This approach includes more code but is more readable than the former approach.

10. **(a)** HC likes it. **(b)** Type Stop Boolean in the var section of Temp2. Just before the until line insert
```
        Stop := upcase(Reply) = 'N';
```
Replace the until line with
```
        until Stop;
```
This approach includes more code but is more readable than the former approach.

12. **(a)** No answer required. **(b)** Units is not input from the file for the Poppa Six record, giving zero in Units and incorrect calculations for sales and total sales.

CHAPTER 6

1. **(a)** `if LastName <> 'CORE' then writeln ('Where''s Harvey?');`
        Alternative Boolean expression: **not** (LastName = 'CORE')
  (b)
```
if LastName = 'CORE'
    then writeln ('Harvey is my kind of guy')
    else inc (Counter);
```
  (c)
```
if Credits >= 12 then   {Full-timers}
    begin
      Tuition := 1200;
      inc (FullTimeTuitionSum, Tuition);
      inc (FullTimeStudentCount);
    end
  else   {Part-timers}
    begin
      Tuition := 100 * Credits;
      inc (PartTimeTuitionSum, Tuition);
      inc (PartTimeStudentCount);
    end;   {if Credits}
```

2. **(a)** When Age stores 18
      AgeOk is false
      If-test is false
      Bell rings and 'Entry denied!' is written
      Count is incremented to 51

      When Age stores 21 . . .
      AgeOk is true
      If-test is true
      'Entry permitted' is written

3.
```
if (OrderSize >= BreakPoint) and ((Code = 'D') or (Code = 'P')) then
    OrderCost := Price2 * OrderSize
else
    OrderCost := Price1 * OrderSize;
```
Note that it's now possible for a customer to have a large order (at least 100) but still pay the higher price (Price1) if the code is not D or P.

4. **(a)**
```
if OrderSize < MinOrderSize then
    begin
        MinOrderSize        := OrderSize;
        MinCustomerAccount := CustomerAccount;
    end; {if OrderSize}
```
   (b) First, insert the code in Example 6.1 just after the order size is input. This if-then-else structure is also at the top of the loop body. Its appearance in two places suggests that a function for order cost may be desirable. Next, insert the following initialization between the order-cost assignment and the beginning of the loop.
```
MinOrderCost := OrderCost;
```
Within the loop, just before or after the if-then structure for the minimum order size, insert the following.
```
if OrderCost < MinOrderCost then
    MinOrderCost := OrderCost;
```

7. **(a)**
```
if Age >= 65 then
    if SexCode = 'F' then {Female}
        begin
            writeln ('Female senior citizen');
            inc (CountFemale);
        end
    else {Male}
        begin
            writeln ('Male senior citizen');
            inc (CountMale);
        end; {Age and SexCode nested if}
```
   (b)
```
if Age >= 65 then
    begin
        inc (CountAtLeast65);
        if SexCode = 'F' then {Female}
            begin
                writeln ('Female senior citizen');
                inc (CountFemale);
            end
        else {Male}
            begin
                writeln ('Male senior citizen');
                inc (CountMale);
            end; {if SexCode}
    end; {if Age}
```

8. **(a)** `if sqr(B) - 4 * A * C > 0.0 then`
    `    writeln ('Two real roots exist')`
    `else if sqr(B) - 4 * A * C = 0.0 then`
    `    writeln ('One repeated real root exists')`
    `else`
    `    writeln ('No real roots exist');`

    Note: The error in approximating real values may cause a false second if-test when the expression is mathematically zero. This issue is addressed under "Common Errors" at the end of the chapter.

    (b) `case ClassCode of`
    `    {Freshman}    1 : inc (FreshmanCount);`
    `    {Sophomore}   2 : inc (SophomoreCount);`
    `    {Junior}      3 : inc (JuniorCount);`
    `    {Senior}      4 : inc (SeniorCount);`
    `else {error in ClassCode}`
    `    writeln (chr(7), 'Class code ', ClassCode, ' is incorrect);`
    `end; {case}`

11. **(a)** No. Color would be a nonordinal selector. We would have to code colors using an integer or character selector, as we did in Exercise 8b.

12. **(a)** Try out some of your own "combos" and factorials too. Now you're ready for that first "stats" course!

17. **(a)** Beats the readln statement for entering a single integer value, doesn't it?   **(b)** You should get the fatal run-time error *Range check error.* If you disable range checking through the IDE (and recompile!), the same input echoes the incorrect value −13391.

Module B

1. Did you get a stack-overflow run-time error when evaluating the factorial of 1000? Take a peek at what's said about this in item 1 under "Common Errors." You should get stack overflow with the stack size at the default value of 16,384 bytes. If you raise the stack size (say, to 30KB out of the allowable maximum 65,520 bytes), you should get a solution. It took about 10 seconds to evaluate the factorial of 1000 by recursion on a 16-MHz 386 machine, but less than one second by iteration using program CkFac.

2. The algorithm would recurse infinitely, giving stack overflow, as mentioned in item 2 under "Common Errors." If X starts with a negative value, it never hits the terminating case at a zero value (the recursion keeps decrementing X). Just before the recursive if-then-else structure, insert the following fix.

    `if X < 0 then`
    `    begin`
    `        writeln (chr(7), 'Factorials of negative values are`
    `            undefined...  Factorial set to 1.');`
    `        X := 0;`
    `    end; {if}`

4. **(a)** Piece of cake.   **(b)** Replace the forward declaration for RepErr with one for ReadRep (actually, just replace RepErr with ReadRep, since their formal parameter lists are the same); move the ReadRep block to a position just below the block for RepErr; move the formal parameter list from ReadRep to RepErr. Try it and rerun the program.

Chapter 7

1. **(a)** `type`
    `    LowLetter = 'a' .. 'z';     {Subrange type}`
    `var`
    `    Code : LowLetter;           {Subrange variable}`

    (b) `type`
    `    DayName = (Sun, Mon, Tue, Wed, Thu, Fri, Sat);  {Enumerated type}`
    `var`
    `    Day : DayName;                                  {Enumerated var}`

2.   **(a)** No. 'E' is between 'D' and 'F' in the subrange 'A' . . 'F'; use enumerated type Grade in Example 7.2.   **(b)** Input of 3 gives output: 1 2 3; input of 9 gives a range-check error (9 is outside the range 1 . . 7), assuming the range-checking compiler directive is enabled.

3.   **(a)** `Grade = (A, B, C, D, F, I, S, U);`   **(b)** `ItemCode = (F, X, Y);` F is an enumerated value in two enumerated type declarations within the same block, giving a compile-time error.   **(c)** No; the compiler gives an *Unknown identifier* compile-time error because G is not one of the enumerated values in type Grade.

4.   **(a)** `type`

```
     Seasons = (Winter, Spring, Summer, Fall);

  var
     Season: Seasons;
     Month : 1..12;

  case Month of
     1, 2, 12   :  Season := Winter;
     3 ..    5  :  Season := Spring;
     6 ..    8  :  Season := Summer;
     9 ..   11  :  Season := Fall;
```

The else-if structure is another (cumbersome) alternative.

No. The writeln statement does not write enumerated variables. We would have to code our own write routine, as illustrated in Section 7.2.

6.   **(a)** The inputs 9 and 0 are out-of-range values. The program simply handles these range errors by repeating the input prompt. The input q is a potential I/O error (character instead of integer input). The program handles this I/O error by beeping the speaker, issuing a reenter message, and repositioning the cursor at the input field. The input 1 is OK.   **(b)** We get a range-check error when 9 is input. Check it out by deleting ,R− in procedure ReadLnVal. Make sure range checking is enabled in the IDE, recompile, and rerun the program.

9.   **(a)** Enter an A for yourself.

10.   **(a)** OK; the base type is enumerated.   **(b)** Can't have the string constant 'XL' as an enumerated value; it's not an ordinal type.   **(c)** Can't mix ordinal types; this shows an integer subrange and a character subrange; okay if we surround the 1 and 7 with single quotation marks, giving character types for both subranges.   **(d)** Can't repeat the 9; the ordinal values for −10 and 1000 to 10000 exceed the required range 0 . . 255 for set elements.   **(e)** Rewrite as

```
     not (Letter in ['a' .. 'z', 'A' .. 'Z']).
```

11.   **(a)** `SexCodes = ['F', 'f', 'M', 'm'];`   **(b)** `DaySet = [1 .. 7];`   **(c)** `DaySet = [Sun .. Sat];` *Note:* `Sun .. Sat` is a subrange of the enumerated type DayName in Exercise **1b**; declare DayName before declaring DaySet.   **(d)** `CoinSet = [Penny, Nickel, Dime, Quarter, Fifty, Dollar];` *Note:* Declare enumerated type Coin before we declare Coinset.

12.   **(a)** `type DayType = set of 1 .. 7;`
       (b) `type DayName = (Sun, Mon, Tue, Wed, Thu, Fri, Sat); DayType = set of DayName;`
       `var WeekDay, WeekEnd : DayType;`

13.   **(a)** `['a', 'e', 'i', 'o', 'u'].`   **(b)** `['a' .. 'z'].`   **(c)** The set of lowercase consonants.
       (d) The empty set [ ].   **(e)** Same as part **c**.   **(f)** The empty set [ ].

14.   **(a)** False.   **(b)** True.   **(c)** False.   **(d)** True.   **(e)** True.   **(f)** True.

15.   **(a)** `SexCode in SexCodes;` *Note:* SexCodes is the set constant declared in Exercise **11a**.   **(b)** `Age in [0 .. 18, 65 .. 75];` *Note:* Assume Age cannot store negative values.   **(c)** `Coin in CoinSet;` *Note:* CoinSet is the set constant declared in Exercise **11d**.

16.   **(a)** Reply stores S, giving false for the until test, and another loop repetition; Reply stores o, giving false for the until test, and another loop repetition; Reply stores y, giving true for the until test, and loop exit.
       (b) `until Reply in ['Y', 'y', 'N', 'n'];` we believe the former approach is more literate and simplifies maintenance if the declared constant CorrectReply appears in more than one place in the program.

17.   **(a)** `repeat`
```
     write ('Enter menu choice: ');   readln (MenuSelection);
  until MenuSelection in [1 .. 5, 9];
```

(b) `repeat`
```
     write ('Enter menu choice: ');
     MenuSelection := upcase (readkey);
  until MenuSelection in ['A' .. 'F', 'X'];
```
Or simply replace the approach in part **a** with the revised set constant. The call to predeclared procedure readkey means that the user can input the menu selection without pressing the Enter key, a common feature in commercial applications.

20.   **(a)** The input SSMLX. is followed by the output L M S X. The union operator does not add the second S to the set because it's already a member of the set. No output (an empty set) follows the input smlx.   **(b)** It's a logic error; the resulting set not only includes the added codes L M S X but also includes other "junk" codes.   **(c)** Delete the line in the type section that declares CapLetters and replace CapLetters in the SetOfCaps declaration with 'A' .. 'Z'. We like the former approach, although it is a matter of preference. CapLetters would be more useful if the program were to include variables having this subrange type. **(d)** Insert

```
     Code := upcase(Code);
```

just after the read statement for Code. Now the input sSMLX. converts the s to S, and the algorithm adds this S to the set. In the former version, the algorithm assigned true to CodeErr after the input of s. The second S is now ignored, and the remaining characters are added to the set, giving the output L M S X.

22.   The string type wears two hats as a simple type and a structured type (see its placement in Table 2.4). It's a simple type in the sense that it defines single-valued character strings, with order based on the sequence of individual characters in the string; it's a structured type in the sense that it defines a collection of characters arranged in a linear (sequential) structure. Individual elements in this string structure are accessible using the indexed form of a string variable, as in FirstName[1].

CHAPTER 8

1.   Remember that the include directory is where the include file READLNIN.PRO is located. Within the {$I} directive in CkRdInt2 use the path that leads to your local utilities library or diskette. For example, if you have file READLNIN.PRO in the root directory of a diskette in drive A, then the include directory is A:\ and the include file compiler directive in the program should read {$I A:\READLNIN.PRO}. You might also want to check the include directory specified within your IDE. Try the command sequence **O**ptions **D**irectories **I**nclude directories. This is Turbo Pascal's last resort for finding your include file if you don't specify its directory within the program and it can't find it in the current directory. While you're at it, check the setting for your current directory with the menu sequence **F**ile **C**hange Dir. Are ya cookin'?

3.   Do you know where source file OURUNIT.PAS and its object-file counterpart OURUNIT.TPU are located on your system? They should be in the directory that contains the Examples Library from this book. Typically, source (.PAS) program or unit files compiled to disk as object files are placed in the same directory as their counterpart source files and are given either .EXE extensions for program files or .TPU extensions for unit files. Turbo Pascal will look for OURUNIT.TPU in your current directory first, and, if it doesn't find it, in the .EXE & TPU directory next. The *.EXE & TPU directory* is specified within the IDE in the Directories dialog box accessed with the command sequence **O**ptions **D**irectories. Check this setting in your IDE. It should show the directory path for the Examples Library. For example, if you carry the Examples Library within the root directory of a diskette that you always place in drive A, the .EXE & TPU directory should be A:\; if the Examples Library is in directory EXLIB in the drive A diskette, the .EXE & TPU directory should be A:\EXLIB

4.   You might want to call your own unit MyUnit. Harvey calls his HarveyUnit.

5.   Review the comments in the answer to Exercise 3.

10.   Unit ADTGrade is files ADTGRADE.PAS and ADTGRADE.TPU in the Examples Library. Review the comments in the answer to Exercise 3.

13.   **(a)** Insert a call to **clrscr** just before the writeln statement.
(b) Insert the statements

```
        textbackground (LightGray);  textcolor (Black);
```

14.   **(a)** Switch the color constants **Red** and **Blue**.   **(b)** Delete the call to **highvideo**.

18.   **(a)** Beats Combo1, doesn't it? What do you think of our Main Menu colors?!   **(b)** Only the portions of the menu screen that get written are painted with the cyan background color, giving two background colors: cyan and the startup background color. It's unattractive, isn't it?   **(c)** The User screen (and Output window) inherit the colors (yellow over blue) of the Farewell screen. This is an example of an ill-behaved program: Like its litterbug counterpart in the human world, it litters the environment.   **(d)** The prompt "Enter selection..." is also in reverse video.   **(e)** Replace the calls to readln for the input of N and K with calls to our utility ReadLnInt.

20.   Remember that file MENUTEMP.PAS is in the Utilities Library, which may be different on your system from the Examples Library. Do you know where the utilities are located in your system? The colors for the Main Menu here are a bit more conservative than those in Combo2's main menu! Change colors to your liking. This program is a good vehicle for experimenting with color combinations. And this template can save you a chunk of time if you have a menuing program in your future.

21.   The quality of the graphics will differ according to the resolution of your graphics board and monitor. This is a good program to experiment with graphics. Have fun...

MODULE C

1.   A sample 50-throw simulation gave no 2s and four 7s, or estimated probabilities of 0 percent for rolling a 2 and 8 percent (or 4/50) for rolling a 7. A sample 100-throw simulation showed four 2s and nineteen 7s, or probabilities of 4 percent and 19 percent for rolling a 2 and a 7, respectively. The theoretical probabilities are 2.8 percent (or 1/36) for rolling a 2 and 17 percent (or 6/36) for rolling a 7. The results of the 100-throw simulation are closer to these theoretical probabilities than those of the 50-throw simulation. You might want to explore this issue further by working Exercise 3.

2.   **(a)** The same seed is used in each simulation, giving identical tables in the two runs.   **(b)** Sample runs with the same seed (2001) gave identical tables that showed scores of 9, 5, 7, 5, and 4.

CHAPTER 9

1.   **(a)** `type ArrayStock = array [1 .. 52] of real;`
     `var DJI, DJT, SP500 : ArrayStock;`
   (b) `type ArrayTemp = array [-26 .. 26] of integer;`
     `var Lows, Highs : ArrayTemp;`

2.   ArrayStock declares 52 real elements, where each real element requires 6 bytes of storage. Each of the three arrays declared with type ArrayStock thus are allocated 312 bytes of storage. Type ArrayTemp specifies 53 integer elements, or 106 bytes at 2 bytes per element. Arrays Lows and Highs thus take up 106 bytes each. Note that the type declaration specifies storage but does not allocate it; it's the var declarations that allocate storage.

3.   **(a)** Provided that the two arrays are identically typed: `ArrayC := ArrayB;`
   (b) `for Index := LowerIndexBound to UpperIndexBound do`
       `writeln (ArrayA[Index] :5:1, ArrayB[Index] :5:1);`
   (c) `for Index := UpperIndexBound downto LowerIndexBound do`
       `writeln (ArrayA[Index] :5:1, ArrayB[Index] :5:1);`
   (d) `Step := 0.1; ArrayA[-5] := 0.1; ArrayB[-5] := 1.1;`
     `for Index := LowerIndexBound + 1 to UpperIndexBound do`
       `begin`
         `ArrayA[Index] := ArrayA[Index - 1] + Step;`
         `ArrayB[Index] := ArrayB[Index - 1] - Step;`
       `end; {for}`
     Sample desk check for ArrayA when Index is 2:
             ArrayA[2] := ArrayA[2−1] + Step;
             ArrayA[2] := ArrayA[1]   + Step;
             ArrayA[2] :=   0.7   + 0.1;
             ArrayA[2] := 0.8

4. **(a)** Yes; the read procedure encounters a line feed and seeks the next value at the next line. We must input one value per line if the readln statement is used. **(b)** Yes; Elements is a positive integer with a maximum value in MaxElements. The declaration of MaxElements and the expression that evaluates UpperIndex ensure that UpperIndex is within the index range LowerIndexLimit to UpperIndexLimit. The for statement controls the value in Index over the range LowerIndexLimit to UpperIndex. **(c)** UpperIndex is assigned one less than LowerIndexLimit (zero in our example). This means that the initial expression (LowerIndexLimit) exceeds the final expression (UpperIndex) in the for statement, correctly giving a loop bypass. **(d)** MaxElements evaluates as 105. The only change in the sample I/O is in the input prompt: 500 changes to 105. Internally, it's a different story. Now UpperIndex stores -48 and the for-do loop fills elements that run over the indexes -52 to -48. As usual, the for-do loop fills the leftmost elements in the array data structure. **(e)** Remember that ReadLnInt reads a single integer value with a line feed while handling I/O errors. We can use it to input Elements and elements in array F by replacing **readln** and **read** with ReadLnInt. In the latter case, we would have to input each element on a separate line.

5. **(a)** Let's roleplay this one. At the first iteraton, F[1] stores 62, Index gets incremented to 2, 15 is read into Temp, and the while test gives a green light for the second iteration. At the second iteration, F[2] stores 15, Index is updated to 3, 20 is placed in Temp, and the while test is true. At the third iteration, F[3] stores 20, Index gets bumped to 4, and 32 is placed in Temp. Now the while test evaluates the second operand as false (4 is not less than 3), the loop is history, and UpperIndex is set to 3. The I/O looks the same, but only the first three elements are placed in F. The input values 68 and -999 are not processed by the loop. Any subsequent code that implements interactive input should first include a readln statement without an input list, to "flush" the unused portion of this input line. **(b)** Replace **read** with ReadLnInt, but now we must input one temperature per line.

6. **(a)** Elements is directly input in Example 9.2, but it's not assigned in Example 9.3. In the latter case, we need to insert the following assignment somewhere between the two code segments in Examples 9.3 and 9.4: Elements := UpperIndex $-$ LowerIndexLimit $+$ 1. **(b)** Replace the assignment statement for Sum with the call **inc** (Sum, F[Index]).

7. **(a)** For -3: Index stores -3, while test is true, first operand in if-test is false (-3 is less than 1), the bell rings, and the message "Enter 1 to 5" is displayed. For 3: Index stores 3, while test is true, if-test is true, F[3] is output in the display "Temperature is 20". **(b)** Replace the call **readln** (Index) with the call ReadLnInt (Index), where ReadLnInt resides in OurUnit.

8.

A[1]	A[2]	A[3]	A[4]	A[5]
1	2	3	4	5

B[1]	B[2]	B[3]	B[4]	B[5]
1	2	3	4	5

C[1]	C[2]	C[3]	C[4]	C[5]
1	4	9	16	25

The elements in C are determined from corresponding elements (those elements with the same index) in A and B. The first loop fills elements from the left in A and from the right in B. Thus, all elements in A and B must be defined to properly assign elements in C. This means the first loop must finish its tasks before elements in C are assigned.

9.

Sums.....	250	300	-50
Arrays....			
	10	20	-10
	30	40	-10
	50	60	-10
	70	80	-10
	90	100	-10

11. **(a)** TRUE, TRUE, 0; Toronto, LosAngeles, 1. MaxElements for the Boolean index example is 2 (or $1 - 0 + 1$); for the uppercase letters index example it's 26 ($90 - 65 + 1$). *Note:* Did the second TRUE

surprise you? We can view ordinal values as if arranged in a circle. For example, the ordinal values for Boolean false and true are 0 and 1, respectively, giving the following circle.

That's why **pred(false)** returns TRUE. The predecessor of 0 is 1, as we see by moving counterclockwise on the circle from 0 (false) to 1 (true)! In the city example, what is returned by the call **pred**(LosAngeles)? Miami! **succ**(Miami)? LosAngeles!

12. **(a)** `type`
```
    Gender    = (Male, Female);
    ArraySex = array [Gender] of integer;
```
`var`
```
    Count : ArraySex;
```
(b) `type`
```
    Grade = (A, B, C, D, F);
    ArrayOfGrades  = array [Grade] of real;
```
`var`
```
    Bounds : ArrayOfGrades;
```

15. **(a)** We get razzed and have to reenter the file specification. Try it.
(b)   5. Index stores 2.
        6. RangeViolation stores false.
        7. While test is true (not false and not false).
        8. A[2] stores 15.
        9. Index stores 3.
        10. RangeViolation stores false.
        11. While test is true (not false and not false).
        12. A[3] stores 20.
        13. Index stores 4.
        14. RangeViolation stores true (the index 4 is now greater than the upper limit 3) and IndexCk executes error routine.
        15. While test is false (not false and not true).
        16. UpperIndex is assigned 3.
        17. Text file is closed.
   Note: The values in the text file are actually entered into the global array ArrayDemo, because array A is a variable parameter. We use array A in the desk-check script out of convenience.
   (c) In the Figure 9.4b run, **eof**(TextFile) returned true after the fifth element, giving false for the first operand in the while test. In the Figure 9.4c run, IndexCk returned true for RangeViolation after the third element, giving false for the second operand in the while test.
   (d) You should get a "clean" run that I/Os 11 temperatures. Did you take the "express" approach of loading file TEMPS.DAT, adding 6 new temperatures, and saving as TEMPS2.DAT? Or did you start from scratch by opening a new file, typing 11 temperatures, and saving?

18. **(a)** `type`
```
    String50       = string[50];
    ArrayString50 = array [-1 .. 1] of String50;
```
`var`
```
    Result : ArrayString50;
```
(b) `type`
```
    Choice       = (a, b, c, d, e);
    Questions  = 1 .. 100;
    ArrayChoice = array [Questions] of Choice;
```
`var`
```
    Midterm, Final : ArrayChoice;
```

(c) `type`

      `CharType = array [char] of char;`

    `var`

      `Character : CharType;`

19.   Add the following declaration to the type section.

        `ArrayOfLongInt = array [IndexType] of longint;`

    Add the following declaration to the var section.

        `Population : ArrayOfLongInt;`

21.   **(a)** No sweat. **(b)** In the original approach, each output field for city name is 20 characters wide. On output, blanks are padded at the front of each field to account for the different number of characters in each city name. If we eliminate the output format specification :20, the width of each output field is determined by the number of characters in the city name. In this case, on output, city names are left-justified in their field, and the temperature column is ragged. This would not happen if we were to use the data-file version in the next part. **(c)** Allow 20 characters in the field width for city name within file TEMPCIT2.DAT. In other words, start the city temperature column at position 21 or greater. The elements in the city name array now include padded blanks between the end of the city name and the 20th character position in the memory cell. In part **a,** the end-of-line marker after each city name terminates input at the last character in the actual city name. For example, in part **a,** Array1[5] stores Miami; in this part, it stores Miami▮▮▮▮▮▮▮▮▮▮▮▮▮▮▮, or Miami followed by 15 blanks. On output, the city names would appear left-justified in their column, a more customary convention.

22.   **(a)** 83. 90. Index is out of range. Element is undefined.

    (b) Add the following declaration to the const section.

        `LowerLayerLimit = 1;   UpperLayerLimit = 3;`

    Add the following declaration to the type section.

        `LayerType = LowerLayerLimit .. UpperLayerLimit;`

    Revise the array type declaration as follows.

        `MultiArrayOfInt = array[RowType, ColType, LayerType] of integer;`

    F[2, 3, 2] stores 82.

23.   **(a)** `type`

      `Students     = 1 .. 1000;`

      `Years        = 1991 .. 1995;`

      `ArrayGPAType = array [Students, Years] of real;`

    `var`

      `GPA : ArrayGPAType;`

    Indexing on semester as well gives a 3D array. Add the enumerated type declaration

        `Semesters    = (Fall, Spring);`

    and revise the array type declaration to

        `ArrayGPAType = array [Students, Years, Semesters] of real;`

24.   **(a)** The output rows run together. **(b)** Compilation fails because no element in a set can have an ordinal value greater than 255; an upper row limit of 500 violates this limitation. To avoid this problem we would have to rephrase the Boolean expression in the until test.

      `until (Rows >= LowerRowLimit) and (Rows <= UpperRowLimit) and`

      `(Cols in [LowerColLimit .. UpperColLimit])`

    (c) We would have to enter each element on a separate line, thereby giving up the more familiar table metaphor. **(d)** An entry greater than 255 for number of rows or greater than 4 for number of columns causes a fatal range-check error.

Module D

1. **(a)** It doesn't get any easier than this.   **(b)** Each insert element is considered, but no shifts or inserts are implemented. In procedure Sort, Shift evaluates to false for each iteration of the for-do loop, the while-do loop is never entered, NewLocation is always set to OldLocation, and the array element A[NewLocation] is replaced by itself.   **(c)** If LowerIndex and/or UpperIndex are outside the index limits, a fatal range-check error is committed, provided the range-check compiler directive is enabled. If it's not enabled, the sort will be incorrect and code damage may result as the algorithm accesses and overwrites memory cells outside the proper index range. As we stressed in Chapter 9, this is a dangerous defensive programming oversight. Any client program or module that calls Sort should ensure that indexes are within their limits, either through program declarations and logic or through range error handling in the case of input, as we have done all along. A violation of the second precondition means that the lower index exceeds the upper index. In this event, the for-do loop is not entered and the sort is not performed. This brings no harm, but it's best if the client module is alerted to the problem. The solution is to surround the current body of Sort with the following if-then-else structure.

```
If lower index does not exceed upper index then

    .⎤
    . ⎬Current sort body
    .⎦
else
    Write error message
```

(d) Table D.2   Desk Check of Procedure Sort*

OldLocation	InsertElement	Index	LegitIndex	Shift	A[1]	A[2]	A[3]	A[4]	A[5]	NewLocation
2	30	1	true	true	40	30	50	10	20	Undefined
2	30	1	false	true	40	40	50	10	20	Undefined
3	50	2	true	false	30	40	50	10	20	1
4	10	3	true	true	30	40	50	10	20	3
4	10	2	true	true	30	40	50	50	20	3
4	10	1	true	true	30	40	40	50	20	3
4	10	1	false	true	30	30	40	50	20	3
5	20	4	true	true	10	30	40	50	20	1
5	20	3	true	true	10	30	40	50	50	1
5	20	2	true	true	10	30	40	40	50	1
5	20	1	true	false	10	30	30	40	50	1
At exit from sort...										
5	20	1	true	false	10	20	30	40	50	2

*Memory snapshot is taken at while line; color shows new assignments.

5. **(a)** 40 is found at index 1 and 60 is not found.   **(b)** Assuming enabled range checking, the result is a fatal run-time range-check error at the if-then-else structure in SearchIndex. To implement this, you just have to delete X from IndexTypeX in two places: in the function heading and in the declaration of variable Index-Found in SearchCk. Then rework part **a.**   **(c)** See the answer to **1c,** with the following differences: With disabled range checking and a violation of the first precondition, memory cells would not be overwritten, because SearchIndex does not reassign array cells; with a violation of the second precondition, the while test is false, the loop body is bypassed, and Found remains false.

7. **(a)** 40 is found at index 4, and 60 is not found. Note that the search index value differs from that in Exercise 5a. The array is now sorted, so element 40 is in position 4 (not position 1, as in the unsorted array).   **(b)** It properly finds 40 and 50, but not 10, 20, and 30. Here's why. Consider the search for 10. The algorithm compares the middle element 50 to 10, and assumes 10 is in the left subarray (and it's not). It discards the right subarray (50 10 20) and searches for 10 in the left subarray (40 30). Thus, 10 is not found. Similarly, 20 and 30 would not be found. It finds the 50 because it happens to be the middle element in the unsorted array; it finds 40 because it turns out to be the middle element of the left subarray.

11. Miami is a balmy 68 (for winter) and LasVegas is nowhere to be found.

12.   **(a)** Yes. CityName[4] stores Boston followed by 14 blanks; SearchElement stores Boston with no trailing blanks. Boston would not be found by SearchIndex because the Boolean expression for the if-test within the while loop evaluates to false, as follows.

```
A[Index] = SearchElement
A[  4  ] = SearchElement
Boston■■■■■■■■■■■■■■ = Boston
            false
```

CHAPTER 10

1.   **(a)** Station WROC!.   **(b)** 2!.   **(c)** "132.   **(d)** Station WR.   **(e)** WROC!.   **(f)** ■■■■■■WROT
      (g) Range-check error; '!' is outside the range '1'..'5'.   **(h)** C.   **(i)** 7 7.

2.   **(a)** False.   **(b)** True.   **(c)** True.   **(d)** True.   **(e)** False.

3.    ```
writeln (City + ',■' + State + '■■' + ZIP);
```

4.    ```
for Index := 1 to length(Phrase) do
   if Phrase[Index] = Blank then
      Phrase[Index] := '*';
```

5.   **(a)** No problem.   **(b)** No problem as far as the compiler is concerned: The actual parameter is assignment compatible with the formal value parameter. A logic error is possible if the dynamic length of BabyStrVar is greater than 10; the assigned value to StrVar would get truncated.   **(c)** *Type mismatch* compile-time error; StrVar is now a variable parameter and its type is not identical to that of BabyStrVar. We could relax strict string parameter checking with the {$V−} compiler directive, but that opens the door to a potential trunca-tion error if the procedure "sends" more than 20 characters.

6.   **(a)** ■V■.   **(b)** I love.   **(c)** 0.   **(d)** 0.

7.   **(a)** ```
writeln (Position, '■', FirstName[Position]);
```

8.    **(a)** ```
Date2 := concat(Day, '-', Month, '-19', Year);
write ('dd-mm-19yy: ' + Date2)
```
      (b) The output is

```
dd/mm/yy:    4//3//2
```

because Month stores 3/, Day stores 4/, and Year stores 2. In the second case, Month, Day, and Year store 12, 7/, and 1, respectively, giving the output:

```
dd/mm/yy:    7//12/1
```

9.   **(a)** Revise the string constant to 'SMLXZABC' for the first alternative. Revise the set constant to ['S', 'M', 'L', 'X', 'Z', 'A', 'B', 'C'] for the second alternative.

10.   Replace the 3 with 2 in the argument list of the copy function. Replace the original writeln statement with either

```
writeln (Day[Index][1] + Day[Index][2] + '  ' + Day[Index]);
```

or

```
writeln (Day[Index, 1] + Day[Index, 2] + '  ' + Day[Index]);
```

11.   **(a)** SubPhrase stores lo.   **(b)** SubPhrase stores lovel love Pascal.   **(c)** StrVar stores ■■■9.500.   **(d)** IntVar stores 0 and Code stores 2.   **(e)** RealVar stores 0 and Code stores 7.

12.   **(a)** For input 10/19/91 the output is October 19, 1991. For input 13/19/91 the output is a speaker beep and the message Month digits mm outside range 1–12. For input 1/19/91 the output is a speaker beep and the message Nonnumeric digits for month.

14.   **(a)** ```
Replace ('er', 'ac', TextString).
```
```

(b) Replace ('Ji', 'not Ji', TextString). Note that we would not want to use something like 'J' for the first parameter and 'not J' for the second parameter. This would give the revised text string not Jack and Jill. The caller needs to be careful that the old substring (the one being replaced) is unique. In an editor, the old and new substrings would be input variables.

16.   **(a)** The symbol ▮ is an ASCII symbol, but it's not in the set of Turbo Pascal symbols. You should get the same output as in Figure 10.4. The input end;　{if} results in the output ; 　{ }. **(b)** As we stressed in Chapter 7, to build a set we first have to initialize it. Your run should show "junk" output that also includes the symbols that were input.

19.   **(a)** HELP IS ON THE WAY. HELP IS ON THE WAY. **(b)** R*** ** ** *** ****. **(c)** The blank character is ASCII 32, so InRange is assigned false and SecretLetter is assigned *. The actual message in Figure 10.6 would get encoded as ROVZ*SC*YX*DRO*GKI. How we treat the blank is a requirements preference. **(d)** "Junk" characters are included in the secret message. **(e)** Yours truly's secret name is BSMRKBN WYTOXK (wouldn't care for the possible nickname here).

CHAPTER 11

1.   Record Layout for City Record

Field Identifier	Field Type	Description
CityName	**string[20]**	City name
F	**integer**	Fahrenheit temperature

2.   **(a)** Within the employee record type declaration insert Age : 18 .. 72;. **(b)** Within the city record type declaration insert Population : **longint**;. **(c)** Before the city record type declaration insert RegionType = (NorthEast, SouthEast, MidWest, SouthWest, NorthWest);. Within the city record type declaration insert Region : RegionType;

3.   **(a) type**

```
    StudentType = record
        LastName      : string[20];    {Last name}
        FirstName     : string[15];    {First name}
        MiddleInitial : char;          {Middle initial}
        SSN           : string[11];    {Social security number}
        AreaCode      : integer;       {Telephone area code}
        Phone         : string[8];     {Telephone number}
    end; {StudentType}
```

(b) type

```
    NameType     = record
        LastName      : string[20];    {Last name}
        FirstName     : string[15];    {First name}
        MiddleInitial : char;          {Middle initial}
    end; {NameType}

    StudentType = record
        Name          : NameType;      {Record type with 3 name parts}
        SSN           : string[11];    {Social security number}
        AreaCode      : integer;       {Telephone area code}
        Phone         : string[8];     {Telephone number}
    end; {StudentType}

    var
        Student : StudentType;
```

Note that the field Name in the StudentType record declaration is like a record variable — it's a structured field. We identify this record structure as a *hierarchical record* in Section 11.5.

4.   **(a)** Insert the following statements within the with statement.

> **write** ('Enter age (in range 18 .. 72)......... '); **readln** (Age);

> *Note:* This input is vulnerable to a range-check error. Try part **c** for the fixup.

6.   No. The compiler would associate field names with the second record in the code

> **with** EmployeeDeptA, EmployeeDeptB **do**

but we would have no way to assign the fields because the field names are identical in both records.

7.   **(a)** A compile-time error is generated because the two record variables must be identically typed.   **(b)** OK syntactically (both fields are string types), but it probably doesn't make sense in practice, unless parents were into naming their kids after cities.

8.   **(a)** **if** (Employee.SexCode = DesiredSexCode) **and**
            (Employee.Salary > AveSalary) **then**
                writeln (Employee.FullName);

> Or

> **with** Employee **do**
>   **if** (SexCode = DesiredSexCode) **and** (Salary > AveSalary) **then**
>   **writeln** (FullName);

Which approach do you like better? The more fields that need referencing, the more "clean" the with-statement approach.

9.   **(a)** No problem.

10.   **(a)** Also no problem.

11.   **(a)** Still no problem?

12.   **(a)** A bit cool for Miami, unless it's winter.

16.   **(a)** In the declaration for EmployeeType insert WorkAddress : AddressType;.   **(b)** Before the declaration for EmployeeType insert the following.

>   TelType = **record**
>   Home : **string**[12];   {Home telephone number}
>   Work : **string**[12];   {Work telephone number}
>   **end**; {TelType}

In the declaration for EmployeeType insert Telephone : TelType;. We now have another nested record within the employee record. In Figure 11.12 we would add Telephone at level 1 to the right of HomeAddress. The branch from Telephone would reach level 2, with fields Home and Work

18.   **(a)** Revise case 'S' as follows.

>   'S' : (Salary   : **real**;   {Annual salary field}
>   BonusPercent : **real**);   {Bonus percent field}

(b) Insert case 'T' as follows.

>   'T' : (TempPayRate : **real**;   {Hourly pay rate for temps}
>   Agency   : **string**[40]; {Referring agency}

Chapter 12

1.   **(a)** A file of student records makes sense. Each component in the file is a student record that includes a string field for full name (FullName), a long integer field for social security number (SSN), and an array field for grades (Grades). The grade array is one dimensional (it holds the grades for a single student) and has eight byte (integer) elements.

(b) type

```
    GradesType = array [1..8] of byte;

    StudentType = record
      FullName : string[30];
      SSN      : longint;
      Grades   : GradesType;
    end; {StudentType}

    FileStudentType = file of StudentType;

  var
    StudentRecord : StudentType;
    FileStudent   : FileStudentType;
```

(c) assign (FileStudent, 'C:\GRADES\HC101.BIN').
(d) rewrite (FileStudent).
(e) reset (FileStudent).
(f) write (FileStudent, StudentRecord).
(g) read (FileStudent, StudentRecord).
(h) close (FileStudent).
(i) rename (FileStudent, 'C:\GRADES\HC101A.BIN').
(j) erase (TextFile).

2.   **(a)** Missing file variable. Should be **read** (FileEmployee, Employee).   **(b)** The call to *seek* requires a typed-file variable as the first parameter.   **(c)** *Appends* I LOVE file processing! and an end-of-line marker to the end of an existing text file.   **(d)** All records in the file are deleted: The call to *reset* opens an existing file and sets the file position to the beginning of the file; the call to *truncate* deletes all records past the file position.   **(e)** The call to *filesize* returns the number of components (*N*) in the file. Let's assume the file has five components, that is, *N* is 5. The call to *seek* moves the file position to component number *N*, or 5. But the last component in the file is component number 4 (remember that components are numbered $0 .. N - 1$). Thus, the file position is moved to the end of the file. The call to *filepos* returns the current file position 5. The write statement writes 5.   **(f)** The file variable is not specified in the call to *eoln*, so the keyboard is assumed. Execution pauses until the Enter key is pressed. TRUE is displayed.   **(g)** Displays a single line from a text file because the loop repeats the tasks of reading a character from the file and displaying it on the screen, while an end-of-line marker is not encountered. The writeln statement terminates the display line and the readln statement gets past the end-of-line marker in the file (to the next line). Check it out! Create a text file with, say, your name and address and display its lines by writing a little test program that codes this routine within an outer eof loop.

3.   **(a)** Don't forget to specify drive A: (or a file specification that doesn't overwrite our version of TEMPS.BIN).   **(b)** Not too readable! Remember that it's a typed file, not a text file.

4.   **(a)** Don't forget to replace **integer** with **char** in declaring the global ComponentType. It's that simple.   **(b)** Replace **char** in part **a** with **real**.   **(c)** Replace **real** in part **b** with **string**.   **(d)** We made it easy for you in the type section. Don't forget to change the component type back to integer. Note that the resulting text file just has one line. Why? A write (not write*ln*) statement was used.

7.   **(a)** Don't forget to specify drive A: (or a file specification that doesn't overwrite our version of EM-PLOYEE.BIN).   **(b)** A display only a computer could love!

9.   Do you like the "beep" in OpenOldFile better than the one in PrepFile? Input n does not find a matching employee record.

13.   **(a)** Input 6 does not find an employee record.   **(b)** Yes. No. No. MaxRecNum is typed *integer* in procedure QueryRecNum. From Appendix D, type integer has an upper-range value of 32767. Thus, this program can handle up to 32,767 records, without encountering integer overflow. By using type *word,* the program handles up to 65,535 records; type *longint* handles about a third of the world's population, or 2,147,483,647 records. Of course, birth control isn't our only problem here; file capacity could be a concern. Each employee record takes up 45 bytes (11 for SSN plus 1 for its dynamic-length byte, 25 for Full-Name + 1 for its dynamic-length byte, 6 for Salary, and 1 for SexCode). For the longint case, we get about 9.66×10^{10} bytes, or a corresponding file size of about 92.160MB (90GB)!

28.   11. while test is true
12. if-test is true (30 is less than 60)
13. 30 written to File 3
14. File 1 record variable is 50
15. while test is false (eof at File 1)
16. "Eof" if test is true
17. while test is false (60 is not less than 50)
18. 50 written to File 3
19. 60 written to File 3
20. "Eof" if-test is true
21. while test is true
22. File 2 record variable is 70
23. 70 written to File 3
24. while test is true
25. File 2 record variable is 80
26. 80 written to File 3
27. while test is true
28. File 2 record variable is 90
29. 90 written to File 3
30. while test is false (eof at file 2)
31. three files closed

CHAPTER 13

1. **(a)** The dynamic variable Pointer2^ has not been created with a call to *new.*
(b) Pointer2   Pointer2^

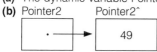

(c) The base types are not assignment compatible: Pointer3^ stores type string values and Pointer1^ stores integer values.

2. **(a)** The pointer types are not assignment compatible: Pointer3 points to a type string dynamic variable and Pointer2 points to a type integer dynamic variable.   **(b)** It's not assignment compatible: The right member is an integer value and the left member is a pointer type. If the left member is a pointer type, the right member must be another compatible pointer type or the pointer constant **nil.** If the right member is an integer value that is to be assigned to a dynamic variable, the left member must be a dynamic variable with an integer base type, such as Pointer1^ or Pointer2^.   **(c)** I/O operations for pointer variables are not defined.
(d) Place nil in the memory cell for Pointer2 and erase the arrow; Pointer2 now points to oblivion. The 49 is "lost"— its memory cell in the heap is not pointed to by any pointer variable.   **(e) if** Pointer3 < > **nil then writeln** (Pointer3^).

3.   **(a)** P1   P1^

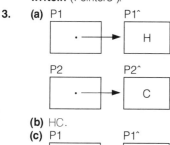

(b) HC.
(c) P1   P1^

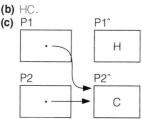

(d) CC

(e) `TempP := P1;  P1 := P2;  P2 := TempP;`

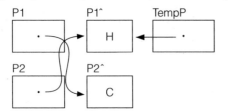

4.   It's as easy as 1 1 2 3 4 2 6 Q.

5.   Create third node, steps 7–8.

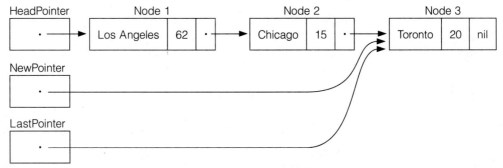

6.   **(a)** An empty list is implied. The loop is bypassed and nothing is displayed.   **(b)** The loop iterates beyond the end of the list at node 3. With an absent sentinel *nil* to terminate iterations, the loop iterates indefinitely, displaying "junk" nodes as it approaches a losing encounter with the heap's capacity.

7.   **(a)** The while loop is not entered, the if-test is false, the file is closed, and `Number of nodes = 0` is output following the title.   **(b)** HeadPointer would be undefined for this list — the list would be inaccessible because an algorithm would not know the location of the first node.

8.   You could follow our Figure 13.2 run, except create an ordered list. It's as easy as 1 2 2 3 4 2 6 Q.

14.   Yes. See the diagram in Figure 13.10e.

26.   **(a)**

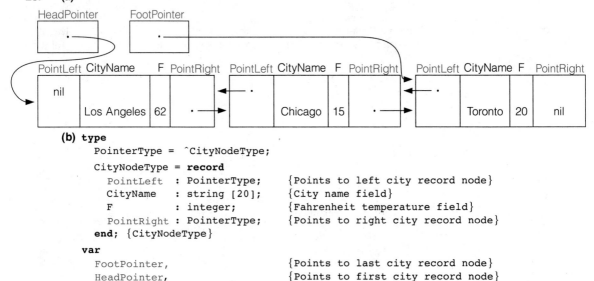

(b) `type`

```
    PointerType = ^CityNodeType;

    CityNodeType = record
       PointLeft  : PointerType;     {Points to left city record node}
       CityName   : string [20];     {City name field}
       F          : integer;         {Fahrenheit temperature field}
       PointRight : PointerType;     {Points to right city record node}
    end; {CityNodeType}

 var
    FootPointer,                      {Points to last city record node}
    HeadPointer,                      {Points to first city record node}
    NodePointer  : PointerType;       {Points to city record node}
```

27.   (a)

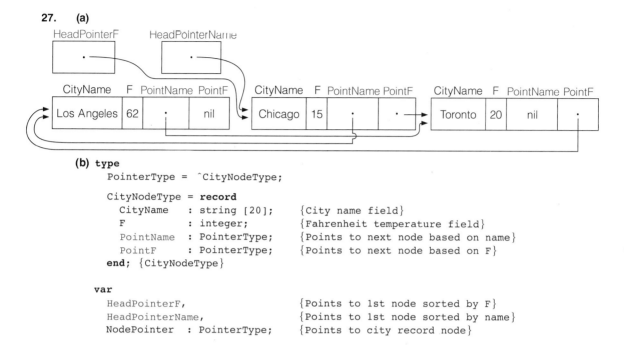

(b) type
```
        PointerType  =  ^CityNodeType;

        CityNodeType = record
          CityName    : string [20];     {City name field}
          F           : integer;         {Fahrenheit temperature field}
          PointName   : PointerType;     {Points to next node based on name}
          PointF      : PointerType;     {Points to next node based on F}
        end; {CityNodeType}

     var
        HeadPointerF,                    {Points to 1st node sorted by F}
        HeadPointerName,                 {Points to 1st node sorted by name}
        NodePointer  : PointerType;      {Points to city record node}
```

CHAPTER 14

1.   Object OurSession in our programs is conceptual. An object such as Flight 101 in an airline reservation system is conceptual. Its fields might include number and costs of available tourist-class seats. Methods might include a make-reservation procedure and functions for getting data. An instance of Location in the next exercise is also a conceptual object.

2.   This OOP application would not be short of objects. For example, an object like Oven would have fields for cooking options (bake or broil), temperature setting, clock time, size, color, and so on. Its methods might include procedures and functions for setting the cooking option, the temperature, and the clock. Location makes sense as an object class because its fields (x-, y-, and z-coordinates) and methods (initialize coordinate, get x, and so on) are characteristics of all other object classes in the hierarchy. For example, in a kitchen-design simulation, we would need to specify and access the location of the oven object, the countertop object, and so forth. The location object type would be very high in the object hierarchy, because we would want its fields and methods to be inherited by the physical kitchen objects.

3.   We can think of OOP applications as simulations of object-based phenomena. The projection of a person into an artificial world of objects is equivalent to the addition of a person object. To be sure, the artificial reality application is considerably more complicated than its static counterpart, because the person object interacts with and affects other objects in the application. In the kitchen application, the person (client or designer) can "enter" the "kitchen," move around to "view" different perspectives, shift objects, and so on. Keep an eye on this field of study. Its impact will grow considerably in the 1990s as computers get faster, smaller, and more graphically sophisticated. The next time you're in a video store, check out the ultimate artificial reality vacation in the movie *Total Recall*. It's coming . . .

4.   **(a)** Add two new figures under the Student figure: The National object type has fields City and State, with methods Init and Display; the International object type has fields Country and Visa, with methods Init and Display. Connect each to Student with an inheritance arrow. Draw additional client-server arrows from Session to these new figures.
(b) Insert the following after the declaration for Student type.

```
National - object(Student)
   City  : string;
   State : string;
   procedure Init (Name, SSN, ACity, AState : string;
                   Credits : integer;  Ave : real);
   procedure Display;
end; {National}

InterNational = object(Student)
   Country : string;
   Visa    : string;
   procedure Init (Name, SSN, ACountry, AVisa : string;
                   Credits : integer;  Ave : real);
   procedure Display;
end; {InterNational}
```

(c) var

```
   NationalStudent      : National;
   InternationalStudent : International;
```

(d) Eliminate the var declarations in part **c** and insert the following in the type section after the declarations for the National and International types.

```
   NationalPointer      : ^National;
   InternationalPointer : ^International;
```

By now, we would also want to update the declarations for National and International to include Display as a virtual method and Init as a constructor.

5. **(a)** In each figure, under Staff, include branches for Union and NonUnion. Off of Union, draw branches for AFL, Teamsters, and HCL. Off of NonUnion draw branches for Salaried and Hourly.

6. **(a)** This is as easy as it gets. **(b)** Add the person object to the var section with the declaration OurPerson : Person;. Add the call

```
   OurPerson.Init (' ', '000-00-0000');
```

to the beginning of Session.Init and the call

```
   OurPerson.Display;
```

to the beginning of Session.Run. **(c)** No. Probably not. A person at the college would have to be unclassified. Person is useful as an abstract object type, as discussed in Note 1.

9. **(a)** This one takes a bit more work than the OOPdemo1 run. **(b)** In College1, insert **private** just after the method declarations in the Person, Student, and Faculty declarations. Move the fields for each into the private section. Recompile the unit to *disk* and rerun OOPdemo2. By making the fields private we enforce encapsulation—client programs and objects can't directly access an object's fields except through calls to its methods. **(c)** Delete the declaration for Session, which is to say, delete the type section altogether. Delete the declaration for OurSession in the var section. In the main body, delete the calls to OurSession's Init, Run, and Done methods. Move the calls to OurStudent's and OurFaculty's methods in Session.Init, Session.Run, and Session.Done to the main body. You could also move the writeln statement to the main body. Delete everything that's left in Session's methods declarations. The main body now directly follows the var section. Rerun OOPdemo2. This version works, but at the expense of complicating the main block. See item 5 under "Design and Style" in Section 14.5.

Module E

1. Not a bad user interface, eh?

3. No. It's there to satisfy the syntactic needs for a function call. Check the **E**xtended syntax option in the Compiler Options dialog box. Delete the declaration for Control in the var section and delete Control := in the procedure's body. Rerun the program as before.

INDEX

Program Composition

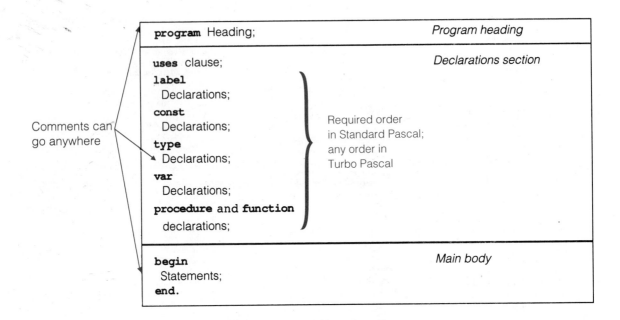

program Heading;	*Program heading*
uses clause;	*Declarations section*
label Declarations;	
const Declarations;	Required order in Standard Pascal; any order in Turbo Pascal
type Declarations;	
var Declarations;	
procedure and **function** declarations;	
begin Statements; **end.**	*Main body*

Comments can go anywhere

Reserved Words

The following are reserved words in Turbo Pascal. You can't use these for your own identifiers. Those in color are not reserved words in Standard Pascal.

and	end	nil	shr
asm	file	not	string
array	for	object	then
begin	function	of	to
case	goto	or	type
const	if	packed	unit
constuctor	implementation	procedure	until
destructor	in	program	uses
div	inline	record	var
do	interface	repeat	while
downto	label	set	with
else	mod	shl	xor

Turbo Pascal also includes *standard directives* that are similar to reserved words; these are redefinable, but it's not recommended. Those in color are not standard identifiers in Standard Pascal.

absolute	external	**forward**	near
assembler	far	interrupt	private
			virtual

SELECTED STANDARD IDENTIFIERS

• • • • • • • • • • •

The following standard identifiers are used in the book. You can redefine these, but it's not a good idea because you lose the intended functionality. Those in color are not standard identifiers in Standard Pascal.

Constants...

Black	Cyan	Green	LightGreen	Red
Blink	DarkGray	LightBlue	LightMagenta	**true**
Blue	Detect	LightCyan	LightRed	White
Brown	**false**	LightGray	Magenta	Yellow

Files...

input	**output**

Functions...

abs	filepos	length	**pred**	**succ**
chr	filesize	**ln**	random	**trunc**
concat	getmaxx	memavail	readkey	upcase
copy	getmaxy	new	**round**	wherex
eof	int	**ord**	sizeof	wherey
eoln	ioresult	pi	**sqr**	
exp	keypressed	pos	**sqrt**	

Procedures...

append	**dispose**	insert	randomize	sound
assign	erase	line	**read**	str
circle	exit	lowvideo	**readln**	textbackground
close	getdate	moveto	rectangle	textcolor
closegraph	gettime	**new**	rename	truncate
clreol	gotoxy	normvideo	**reset**	val
clrscr	halt	nosound	**rewrite**	**write**
dec	highvideo	outtext	seek	**writeln**
delay	inc	outtextxy	setbkcolor	
delete	initgraph	putpixel	setcolor	

Types...

Boolean	comp	**integer**	shortint	word
byte	double	longint	single	
char	extended	**real**	**text**	

Units...

crt	graph	overlay	printer	system
dos				

Variables...

Lst	RandSeed	TextAttr

Turbo Vision Constants...

bfDefault	cmMenu	evCommand	kbAltX	kbF10
bfNormal	cmOK	hcNoContext	kbF9	kbNoKey
cmCancel	cmQuit			

Turbo Vision Fields...

A	Command	What	X	Y
B				

Turbo Vision Methods...

Assign	GetExtent	Insert	NewStatusKey	writechar
ClearEvent	HandleEvent	NewItem	NewSubMenu	writeline
Done	Init	NewLine	Run	writestr
ExecView	InitMenuBar	NewMenu	SetData	
GetData	InitStatusLine	NewStatusDef	writebuf	

Turbo Vision Object Pointers...

DeskTop	MenuBar	StatusLine

Turbo Vision Object Types...

TApplication	TEvent	TPoint	TRect	TView

Turbo Vison Pointer Types...

PButton	PInputLine	PMenuBar	PStaticText	PStatusLine
PDialog	PLabel			

Turbo Vision Units...

app	drivers	memory	objects	views
dialogs	histlist	menus	textview	

Turbo Vision Variables...

Event